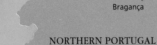

Bragança

NORTHERN PORTUGAL

aga

Guimarães

Vila Real

0 kilometers   50

0 miles   25

**DOURO AND
TRÁS-OS-MONTES**
Pages 232–261

Viseu

Guarda

**CENTRAL
PORTUGAL**

oimbra

Castelo Branco

**ESTREMADURA
AND RIBATEJO**
Pages 170–193

THE BEIRAS
Pages 194–221

Portalegre

Évora

Beja

**SOUTHERN
PORTUGAL**

ALENTEJO
Pages 290–313

ALGARVE
Pages 314–331

Faro

DK TRAVEL GUIDES

PORTUGAL

WITH MADEIRA & THE AZORES

DORLING KINDERSLEY *TRAVEL GUIDES*

PORTUGAL

WITH MADEIRA & THE AZORES

Main Consultant: MARTIN SYMINGTON

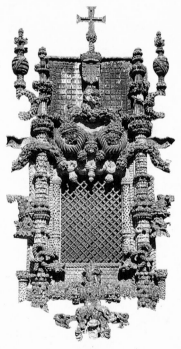

DORLING KINDERSLEY, INC.

LONDON • NEW YORK • SYDNEY • MOSCOW • DELHI

www.dk.com

DORLING KINDERSLEY, INC.

www.dk.com

PROJECT EDITOR Ferdie Mc Donald
ART EDITOR Vanessa Hamilton
EDITORS Caroline Ball, Francesca Machiavelli
US EDITORS Mary Sutherland, Michael Wise
DESIGNERS Anthea Forlee, Carolyn Hewitson,
Nicola Rodway, Dutjapun Williams

MAIN CONTRIBUTORS
Susie Boulton, Christopher Catling, Clive Gilbert, Marion Kaplan,
Sarah McAlister, Alice Peebles, Carol Rankin, Norman Renouf,
Joe Staines, Robert Strauss, Nigel Tisdall, Edite Vieira

PHOTOGRAPHERS
Joe Cornish, Paul Harris, Robert Reichenfeld,
Linda Whitwam, Peter Wilson, Francesca Yorke

ILLUSTRATORS
Richard Draper, Paul Guest, Stephen Gyapay,
Claire Littlejohn, Maltings Partnership, Isidoro González-Adalid
Cabezas/Acanto Arquitectura y Urbanismo S.L., Paul Weston,
John Woodcock, Martin Woodward

Reproduced by Colourscan (Singapore)
Printed and bound by Dai Nippon Printing Co., (Hong Kong) Ltd

First American Edition, 1997
4 6 8 10 9 7 5 3

Published in the United States
Dorling Kindersley, Inc.,
95 Madison Avenue, New York, NY 10016
Reprinted with revisions 1999, 2000

Copyright © 1997, 2000 Dorling Kindersley Limited, London

Library of Congress Cataloging-in-Publication Data

Portugal
        p. cm. -- (Eyewitness travel guides)
        Includes index
        ISBN 0-7894-1948-3
        1. Portugal -- Guidebooks. I. Series.
DP516.P582 1997   97–12455
914.6904'44--dc21   CIP
THROUGHOUT THIS BOOK, FLOORS ARE REFERRED TO IN ACCORDANCE WITH EUROPEAN
USAGE, I.E. THE "FIRST FLOOR" IS ONE FLOOR UP.

The information in every
Dorling Kindersley Travel Guide is checked annually.
Every effort has been made to ensure that this book is as up-to-
date as possible at the time of going to press. Some details,
however, such as telephone numbers, opening hours, prices,
gallery hanging arrangements and travel information are liable to
change. The publishers cannot accept responsibility for any
consequences arising from the use of this book. We value the
views and suggestions of our readers very highly. Please write to:
Editorial Director, Dorling Kindersley Travel Guides,
Dorling Kindersley, 9 Henrietta Street, London WC2E 8PS.

◁ **Palácio da Pena rising above the wooded Parque da Pena, Sintra**

CONTENTS

**Equestrian statue of José I
in Praça do Comércio, Lisbon**

INTRODUCING
PORTUGAL

LISBON

**Everyday scene in the Alfama,
the oldest quarter in Lisbon**

CENTRAL PORTUGAL

Typical blue-trim house near Beja in the Alentejo

Entrance to the chapterhouse at
Alcobaça monastery, Estremadura

NORTHERN PORTUGAL

SOUTHERN PORTUGAL

PORTUGAL'S ISLANDS

TRAVELERS' NEEDS

SURVIVAL GUIDE

17th-century tile decoration
on Palácio Fronteira, Lisbon

The great Gothic
monastery of Batalha

HOW TO USE THIS GUIDE

THIS GUIDE helps you get the most from a visit to Portugal, providing expert recommendations as well as detailed practical information. The opening chapter *Introducing Portugal* maps the country and sets it in its historical and cultural context. Each of the nine regional chapters, plus *Lisbon*, describe important sights, using maps, pictures, and illustrations. Features cover topics from architecture and festivals to beaches and food. Hotel and restaurant recommendations can be found in *Travelers' Needs*. The *Survival Guide* contains practical information on everything from transportation to personal safety.

LISBON

Lisbon has been divided into five main sightseeing areas. Each of these areas has its own chapter, which opens with a list of the major sights described. All sights are numbered and plotted on an *Area Map*. Information on the sights is easy to locate as the order in which they appear in the chapter follows the numerical order used on the map.

Sights at a Glance lists the chapter's sights by category: Churches, Museums and Galleries, Historic Buildings, Parks and Gardens.

1 **Area Map**
For easy reference, the sights covered in the chapter are numbered and located on a map. The sights are also marked on the Street Finder *maps on pages 126–39.*

A locator map shows clearly where the area is in relation to other parts of the city.

All the pages relating to Lisbon have red thumb tabs.

2 **Street-by-Street Map**
This gives a bird's-eye view of the heart of each of the sightseeing areas.

A suggested route for a walk is shown in red.

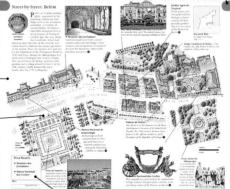

Stars indicate the sights that no visitor should miss.

3 **Detailed Information**
All the sights in Lisbon are described individually. Addresses and practical information are provided. The key to the symbols used in the information block is shown on the back flap.

1 Introduction
A general account of the landscape, history, and character of each region is given here, explaining both how the area has developed over the centuries and what attractions it has to offer the visitor today.

PORTUGAL REGION BY REGION
Outside Lisbon, the rest of Portugal has been divided into nine regions, each of which has a separate chapter. The most interesting cities, towns, and sights to visit are located and numbered on a *Pictorial Map*.

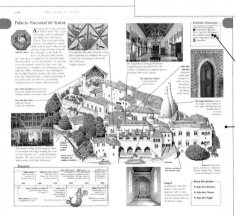

2 Pictorial Map
This shows the main road network and gives an illustrated overview of the region. All entries are numbered, and there are also useful tips on getting around the region.

Each area of Portugal can be identified quickly by its color coding, shown on the inside front cover.

3 Detailed Information
All the important towns and other places to visit are described individually. They are listed in order, following the numbering given on the Pictorial Map. Within each entry, there is further detailed information on important buildings and other sights.

Story boxes explore specific subjects further.

For all the top sights, a Visitors' Checklist provides the practical information you need to plan your visit.

4 The Top Sights
These are given two or more full pages. Historic buildings are dissected to reveal their interiors; museums and galleries have color-coded floor plans to help you locate the most interesting exhibits.

INTRODUCING
PORTUGAL

Putting Portugal on the Map

SITUATED IN THE EXTREME southwest corner of Europe, Portugal occupies roughly one-sixth of the Iberian Peninsula and has a population of just over 10 million. To the north and east, a border measuring approximately 1,300 km (800 miles) separates Portugal from its only neighboring country: Spain. To the south and west, 830 km (500 miles) of coastline meets the Atlantic Ocean. The Atlantic archipelagos of Madeira and the Azores are included in Portugal's territory.

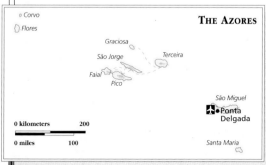

THE AZORES

Corvo
Flores
Graciosa
São Jorge
Faial
Pico
Terceira
São Miguel
Ponta Delgada
Santa Maria

| 0 kilometers | 200 |
| 0 miles | 100 |

The Azores
The Azores lie 1,300 km (800 miles) to the west of Lisbon in the Atlantic Ocean. Of volcanic origin, the islands are scattered over a distance of 650 km (400 miles).

MADEIRA

Porto Santo
Ilha do Porto Santo
Madeira
R101
Funchal

| 0 kilometers | 20 |
| 0 miles | 10 |

Madeira
Lying 965 km (600 miles) southwest of Lisbon in the Atlantic Ocean, the Madeiran archipelago has two inhabited islands, Madeira and Porto Santo.

KEY

✈	International airport
⚓	Ferry port
▬▬	Highway
▬▬	Major road
═══	Minor road
────	Main railroad line
─ ∙ ─	International boundary

Pontevedra
Ourense
Vigo
N120
Braga
Guimarãe
Oporto (Porto)
Douro
IP5
Viseu
Figueira da Foz
Coimbra
POR
Santarém
LISBON (Lisboa)
Évor
Setúbal
Sado
Bej
Sines
ATLANTIC
OCEAN
Portimão N125
IP1

| 0 **kilometers** | 100 |
| 0 miles | 50 |

◁ **Landscape near Lagos in the Algarve by Sir Cedric Morris (1889–1982)**

EUROPE

SPAIN

GREATER LISBON

Greater Lisbon
*The capital of Portugal is a hilly city on the Tagus
estuary. The country's main port and business center,
Greater Lisbon has a population of just over a million.*

A PORTRAIT OF PORTUGAL

MOST VISITORS TO PORTUGAL *head for the sandy coves, pretty fishing villages, and manicured golf links of the Algarve. But beyond the south coast resorts lies the least explored corner of Western Europe: a country of rugged landscapes, sophisticated cities, rural backwaters, and sharply contrasting traditions.*

Portugal appears to have no obvious geographical claim to nationhood, yet this western extremity of the Iberian Peninsula has existed within borders virtually unchanged for nearly 800 years. Its ten million people speak their own language, follow their own unique cultural traditions, and have a centuries-old history of proud independence from, and deep distrust of, neighboring Spain.

For a small country, the regions of Portugal are immensely varied. The rural Minho and Trás-os-Montes in the north are the most traditional – some might say backward. Over the last few decades many inhabitants of these neglected regions have been forced to emigrate in search of work.

Horseman at festival in Vila Franca de Xira, Ribatejo

The south of the country could not be more different. The Algarve, blessed with beautiful sandy beaches and a wonderful, warm Mediterranean climate all year round, has been transformed into a vacation playground for North Europeans.

Two great rivers, the Tagus and the Douro, rise in Spain and then flow westward across Portugal to the Atlantic Ocean. From the wild upper reaches of the Douro valley comes Portugal's most famous product – port wine, from steeply terraced vineyards hewn out of the mountainsides. The Tagus, by contrast, is wide and languid, often spilling out over the flat, fertile, Ribatejo flood plain where fine horses and fighting bulls graze.

Crowded beach in tourist season at Albufeira in the Algarve

◁ **Traditional agriculture on smallholdings near Ponte de Lima in the Minho**

Rolling grassland of the Alentejo with village and medieval castle of Terena

At the mouths of the Tagus and Douro stand Portugal's two major cities, Lisbon and Oporto respectively. Lisbon, the capital, is a cosmopolitan metropolis with a rich cultural life and many national museums and art galleries. Oporto is a serious rival to Lisbon, especially in terms of commerce and industry. Most centers of population, however, are very much smaller, from the fishing communities on the Atlantic coast to the tiny medieval villages in the vast sun-baked plains of the Alentejo and the mountainous interior of the Beiras.

Woman stripping osiers for wickerwork in Madeira

Far out in the Atlantic Ocean lie two remote archipelagos that are self-governing regions of the Portuguese state: warm, luxuriant Madeira off the coast of Morocco, and the nine rainy green volcano tips that make up the Azores, about one third of the way across the Atlantic between Lisbon and New York.

POLITICS AND ECONOMICS

In the final quarter of the 20th century, a new era of Portuguese history has begun. From the late 1920s, under the dictatorship of António Salazar, the country was a virtual recluse in the world community. The principal concern of foreign policy was the ultimately futile defense of Portugal's African and Asian colonies. Domestic industry and commerce were dominated by a few wealthy families, in an economic framework of extreme fiscal tightness.

The Carnation Revolution of 1974 brought this era to an end. At first the reestablishment of democracy was a painful process, but since the 1980s Portugal has assumed an increasingly confident Western European demeanor. Entry into the European Community in 1986 was welcomed at all levels of society and led to an explosion of new construction,

Barredo quarter of Oporto, Portugal's second city

the like of which Portugal had never seen. Traditional exports such as cork, resin, textiles, canned sardines, and wine have been joined by new, heavier industries such as vehicle construction and cement manufacturing.

Grants and loans from the EU have funded the building of new roads, bridges, and hospitals, and brought significant improvements in agriculture. Even though Portugal still has the second lowest GDP in the European Union, for huge sections of the population, standards of living have risen enormously.

Luxury yachts in the harbor at Vilamoura in the Algarve

THE PORTUGUESE WAY OF LIFE

Travelers in Portugal will find a mild-mannered, easy-going people. At the same time they have an innate sense of politeness, a quality they respect in others. The Portuguese also tend to dress well, if rather conservatively, and to use formal modes of address: for example, only the young will call new acquaintances by their first names.

Collecting seaweed for fertilizer in the Ria de Aveiro lagoon

In spite of this, they are gregarious people, often seen eating, drinking, and making merry in large groups at a *festa* or in a restaurant celebrating a birthday or a first communion. There is a special weakness for children, who are cherished, indulged, and welcomed everywhere. Visitors to the country who bring their youngsters with them will discover an immediate point of contact with their hosts. Nevertheless, behind the smiles and the good humor, there is a deep-rooted aspect of the national psyche that the Portuguese themselves call *saudade*,

View from the mountaintop village of Monsanto near the border with Spain

Farmworkers breaking for a picnic lunch in the fields of the Alentejo

The family is the bosom of Portuguese daily life. Although old customs are gradually changing, especially in the cities, it is quite common for three generations to live under one roof, and it is normal for both men and women to remain living in the family home until they marry. One thing that has changed dramatically is family size. A generation ago, families of ten or more children were common, especially in remote, rural areas. Nowadays, one or two children constitute an average-size family, often looked after by a grandmother while both parents go out to work.

a sort of ethereal, aching melancholy that seems to yearn for something lost or unattainable.

Insofar as these generalizations hold true, so do a couple of Portuguese characteristics that can prove irritating. The first is a relaxed attitude to time: no visitor should interpret lack of punctuality as a personal slight. The second is the fact that many Portuguese tend to discard their native courtesy completely when they are behind the wheel of a car. Reckless driving, particularly high-speed tailgating, is a national pastime.

Catholicism is at the heart of Portuguese life, especially in the north, where you will see a crucifix or the image of a saint watching over most homes, cafés, and

Tiled housefront in Alcochete, a small town on the Tagus estuary

barbershops. Weddings and first communion services are deeply religious occasions. Although church attendance is in decline, particularly in the cities, national devotion to Our Lady of Fátima remains steadfast, as does delight in festivals *(romarias)* honoring local saints, another tradition that is strongest in the north.

Town gate of Óbidos with shrine of Nossa Senhora da Piedade, lined with 18th-century tiles

LANGUAGE AND CULTURE

There are few *faux pas* more injurious to national esteem than to suggest that Portuguese is a mere dialect of Spanish. Great pride is taken in the language and literature. *Os Lusíadas*, the national epic by 16th-century poet Camões, is studied reverentially, while many Portuguese also delight in the

Religious procession in the village of Vidigueira in the Alentejo

detached, ironic portrait of themselves in the 19th-century novels of Eça de Queirós. Pride too, is taken in *fado*, the native musical tradition that expresses the notion of *saudade*. In rural areas, especially the Minho, there is still an enthusiastic following for folk dancing.

There are several excellent newspapers, but the country's best-selling daily is *A Bola*, which is devoted exclusively to sports, soccer being a national obsession. Bullfighting too has its adherents, although with nothing like the passion found in Spain.

Donkey rider in remote Beira Alta

The Portuguese have long been avid television watchers and are now producing many homegrown soap operas, films, and documentaries. Up until just a few years ago, virtually all of these were imported from abroad.

The country has become more forward-looking in recent years, but most aspects of heritage hark back to the Discoveries. The best-loved monuments are those built in the one uniquely Portuguese style of architecture, the Manueline, which dates from this period. Many *azulejo* tile paintings, another cherished tradition, also glory in Portugal's great maritime past.

When the Portuguese joined the European Community in 1986, Commission President Jacques Delors solemnly warned them that they should think of themselves as "Portuguese first, and European second." Typically, the Portuguese were too polite to laugh out loud. How could anyone have imagined that this little country was in danger of suddenly throwing overboard centuries of culture nurtured in staunch independence?

Open-air café in Praça da Figueira in Lisbon's Baixa

Vernacular Architecture

Window in Marvão (see p294)

PORTUGAL'S RURAL ARCHITECTURE differs greatly according to climatic conditions and locally available building materials. In the north, thick-walled granite houses are built to give protection from cold winters and rain. The Beiras have a milder climate, but their houses, made of brick or limestone, usually face south to avoid the north wind. In the Alentejo and the Ribatejo, clay houses are long and low, hiding from the hot summer sun and chilly winters. Hills protect the Algarve from these extremes, and houses of clay or stone are built to enjoy the Mediterranean climate.

Yellow-trimmed houses below walls of Óbidos (see pp174–5)

Chimneys are small or non-existent. Instead, smoke escapes through openings in the roof.

Roofs are constructed of slate or schist tiles, or occasionally thatch.

Village houses in the Minho (see p263) and Trás-os-Montes regions (see p233) are two-storied and usually built with the staircase on the outside. The veranda is used for extra living space.

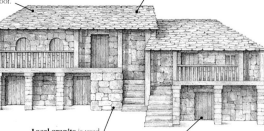

Local granite is used for rustic stonework.

The ground floor is used to keep animals and for storage.

Fishermen's houses found in the Costa Nova region south of Aveiro (see p201) are painted in brightly colored stripes. Forests planted to prevent the sand dunes from encroaching on the land provide the raw material.

Raised platforms guard against flooding.

Modern examples use tiles or painted façades to continue the tradition of striped houses.

Different colored stripes painted onto the wood allowed the fishermen to identify their houses through the region's frequent mists.

TILED ROOFS

Throughout Portugal, red clay roof tiles give towns and villages a memorable skyline. The most traditional and widely used type of roof tile is the *telha de canudo*, or tubu-

Telhados de quatro águas , the distinctive tiled roofs found in Tavira, the Algarve (see p330)

Rooftops of Castelo de Vide in the Alentejo (see p295)

lar tile. Originating from the Moors, these half-cylindrical tiles are placed in two layers: the first is placed with the concave side facing up, and the second with the concave side facing down, covering the joints of the first

Telbas de canudo are used to cover the roof.

Verandas are glassed in and can be used all year round.

Limestone used for the walls is usually stuccoed and whitewashed.

Wooden beams

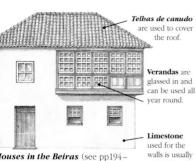

...ouses in the Beiras (see pp194–21) *often have verandas, usually on ...e first floor. These are built to face ...e sun, at the same time affording ...rotection from the cold north winds.*

...batched houses in the Sado *...stuary* (see p169) *are now ...are. Surviving examples ...ave walls that consist ...f a wooden frame ...upporting woven ...ections made of ...raw and reed. The ...mple houses use ...nly local materials.*

PORTUGAL'S WINDMILLS

Windmills are thought to have been used in Portugal since the 11th century. Many still dot the hillsides of the country, particularly in coastal regions.

Most windmills have a cylindrical brick or stone base. The upper section revolves to catch the wind in its canvas sails. Estremadura (see pp170–93) *has good examples.*

Azorean windmills, such as this one on Faial (see pp370–71), *are fairly similar to the Portuguese model, but show the clear influence of early Dutch and Flemish settlers in their sail design.*

Some roof tiles can be removed in summer for more light.

Wooden windows have a painted frame.

Huge chimneys provide spaces for smoking hams and sausages.

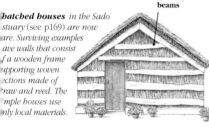

Color-trimmed bouses of the Alentejo and Ribatejo *regions are mainly constructed of clay. Long and oblong in shape, they have few openings to ensure that the heat is trapped in winter and kept out in summer.*

Whitewashing protects the walls, deflects the hot summer sun, and acts as a deterrent for pests and vermin. Many householders consider it a point of honor ro renew their whitewash each year.

...HIMNEYS OF THE ALGARVE

...hese are an important decorative ...ature of houses in the Algarve ...ee pp314–31). The Moorish ...fluence can be seen in their ...lindrical or prismatic shapes ...d the geometric designs per-...rating the clay. The chimneys ...e whitewashed, and many ...ve details picked out in color to ...ccentuate their ornamentation.

Manueline Architecture

THE STYLE OF ARCHITECTURE that flourished in the reign of Manuel I *(see pp46–9)* and continued after his death is essentially a Portuguese variant of Late Gothic. It is typified by maritime motifs inspired by Portugal's Age of Discovery, and by elaborate "all-over" decoration. The artists behind it include João de Castilho and Diogo Boitac, renowned for the cloister of the Mosteiro dos Jerónimos *(see pp106–7)*, and Francisco and Diogo de Arruda, designers of the Torre de Belém *(see p110)*.

Twisted Manueline pillory in Chaves *(see pp256–7)*

Cross of the Order of Christ *(see p185)*

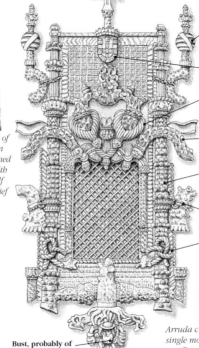

Armillary sphere

Coat of Arms of Manuel I

Cables

Swathes of seaweed

Coral-encrusted masts

Anchor chains

Twisted ropes

The portal of the church of Conceição Velha in Lisbon (see p87) *was commissioned by Manuel in the early 16th century. The king himself appears in the carved relief in the tympanum.*

Bust, probably of the designer Diogo de Arruda

The ornate window in the Convento de Cristo at Tomar (see pp186–7) *was commissioned by Manuel and designed by Diogo de Arruda c.1510. It is the best known single motif of Manueline architecture, illustrating its exotic naturalism and complex use of maritime detail.*

Gil Vicente created the Belém Monstrance (1506) from the first gold brought back from India. Made for Santa Maria de Belém (see p107), its superstructure echoes the south portal.

DECORATIVE DETAILS

The most important motifs in Manueline architecture are the armillary sphere, the Cross of the Order of Christ, and twisted rope. Naturalistic and fantastic forms are often used, as well as flatter, finely crafted designs similar to those found on contemporary Spanish silverware. Later Manueline designs sometimes incorporate Italian Renaissance ornamentation.

The armillary sphere was a navigational device that became the emblem of Manuel I himself.

The Cross of the Order of Christ was the emblem of a military order that helped to finance early voyages. It also emblazoned sails and flags.

REBUILDING THE MANUELINE PORTAL OF MADRE DE DEUS

The Manueline portal of the church of Madre de Deus in Lisbon *(see p123)* was destroyed in the 1755 earthquake, but it was not until 1872 that João Maria Nepomuceno was commissioned to rebuild it. For accuracy, he referred to an early 16th-century painting by an unknown artist, *The Arrival of the Relics of Santa Auta at the Church of Madre de Deus*, now in the Museu Nacional de Arte Antiga *(see pp96–9)*. The splendid procession in the picture is shown heading toward the Manueline portal of the church, which is clearly depicted. Like others of that period, it projects out from the building and dominates the façade. The Manueline style favored rounded rather than pointed arches, and this one has an interesting trefoil shape.

Portal of Madre de Deus church today

The painting of *The Arrival of the Relics* showing the original 16th-century portal

---

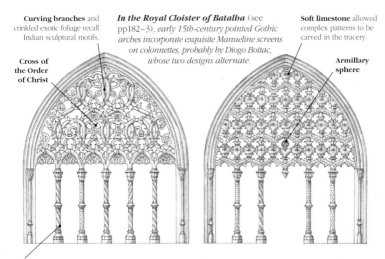

Curving branches and crinkled exotic foliage recall Indian sculptural motifs.

Cross of the Order of Christ

In the Royal Cloister of Batalha (see pp182–3), *early 15th-century pointed Gothic arches incorporate exquisite Manueline screens on colonnettes, probably by Diogo Boitac, whose two designs alternate.*

Soft limestone allowed complex patterns to be carved in the tracery.

Armillary sphere

The colonnettes have all-over ornamentation, with repeated patterns of pearls, shells, and coil motifs.

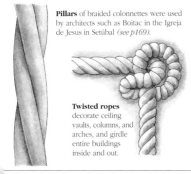

Pillars of braided colonnettes were used by architects such as Boitac in the Igreja de Jesus in Setúbal *(see p169)*.

Twisted ropes decorate ceiling vaults, columns, and arches, and girdle entire buildings inside and out.

The Buçaco Palace, *today a luxury hotel* (see p210), *was originally built as a royal hunting lodge near the end of the 19th century. An extraordinary building, the palace incorporates every conceivable element of Manueline architecture and decoration, illustrating the persistence of the style in Portuguese design that continues to this day.*

Azulejos – Painted Ceramic Tiles

T HE IDEA OF COVERING walls, floors, and even ceilings with tiles was introduced to Spain and Portugal by the Moors. From the 16th century onward, Portugal started producing its own decorative tiles. By the 18th century, no other European country was producing as many tiles, for such a variety of purposes and in so many different designs; the blue and white tiles of the Baroque era are considered by many to be the finest. *Azulejos* became and still remain a very important addition to the interior and exterior architecture of Portuguese buildings.

1716 *Detail from Panel of Christ Teaching in the Temple* Around 1690 blue and white storytelling tiles began to be produced. These figures are from a typical design by António de Oliveira Bernardes (c.1660–1732), the greatest master of the genre. The central panels are surrounded by a complex architectural border *(Misericórdia church, Évora, see p303)*.

c.1520 *Frieze of Spanish made Tiles* These Moorish-style tiles were produced by compartmental techniques using raised and depressed areas to prevent the tin-glaze colors from running *(Palácio Nacional de Sintra, see pp158–9)*.

c.1680 *Hunting Cat* Naturalistic panels of this period were often naively drawn but used a wide range of colors *(Museu Nacional do Azulejo, see pp122–3)*.

1500	1600	1700
RENAISSANCE	**MANNERIST**	**BAROQUE**
1500	1600	1700

1565 *Susannah and the Elders* The mid-16th century saw the introduction of the majolica technique. This allowed artists to paint directly onto prepared flat tiles using several colors, as these did not run in the firing process. This panel of a biblical episode is one of the earliest produced in Portugal. The decorative details are typical of the Renaissance *(Quinta da Bacalhoa, see p167)*.

c.1650 *Carpet Tiles* So called because they imitated the patterns of Moorish rugs, these were produced mainly in blue, yellow, and white. They often covered whole walls *(Museu Nacional do Azulejo, see pp122–3)*.

1736 *Capela de São Filipe* The small chapel inside Setúbal's castle is a fine example of a complete decorative design using blue and white tiles. The panels, illustrating the life of St. Philip, are signed by Policarpo de Oliveira Bernardes, son of the great António *(Castelo de São Filipe, see p168)*.

c.1670 *Tiled Altar Frontal* The exuberant scheme incorporates Hindu motifs and other exotic themes inspired by the printed calicoes and chintzes brought back from India *(Museu Nacional do Azulejo, see pp122–3)*.

1865 *Viúva Lamego Tile Factory, Lisbon*
For the first half of the 19th century, relatively few tiles were produced. The fashion then returned for covering whole surfaces with tiles, and simple stylized designs were used to decorate store fronts and residential areas. This naive, chinoiserie figure is part of a design dating from 1865 that covers the entire façade of the factory.

c.1970 *Tile Pattern*
The original design for this strikingly modern design by architect Raúl Lino dates from about 1910. Many of Portugal's leading modern artists have worked with *azulejos* (*Museu Nacional do Azulejo, see pp122–3).*

c.1770–84 *Corredor das Mangas*
The Rococo period saw the reintroduction of polychromatic *azulejos*. This antechamber in the royal palace at Queluz has tiled panels showing hunting scenes, the seasons, and the continents (*Palácio de Queluz, see pp164–5).*

1927 *Battle of Ourique*
The early years of the 20th century saw a revival of large-scale historical scenes in traditional blue and white. This panel is by Jorge Colaço (*Carlos Lopes Pavilion, Parque Eduardo VII, Lisbon, see p115).*

1800	1900

NEO-CLASSICAL ART NOUVEAU MODERN

1800	1900

c.1800 *The Story of António Joaquim Carneiro, Hatmaker*
Delicate Neo-Classical ornamentation surrounds the blue and white central subject matter in this charming tale of a shepherd boy who makes his fortune as a hatmaker in the big city. Sophisticated designs of this kind disappeared during the upheavals of the Peninsular War (*see p54*) at the beginning of the 19th century (*Museu Nacional do Azulejo, see pp122–3).*

TILES IN DOMESTIC ARCHITECTURE

Art Nouveau friezes and decorations in deep colors enliven the façade of this early 20th-century house in Aveiro. To this day, tiles are used to cover façades of houses. They are relatively cheap to produce, long-lasting, and need little maintenance. Tiled houses brighten up many Portuguese towns and villages. The town of Ovar (*see pp198–9*) is particularly striking.

Vila Africana, Aveiro (*see p200*)

c.1770 *Gatekeeper*
"Cut out" figures like this musketeer are an amusing feature of tile designs in many palaces and mansions from the 18th century onward. They stand guard at the entrance, on landings, or on staircases (*Museu Nacional do Azulejo, see pp122–3).*

Decorated Ceramics

SMALL, TRADITIONAL local potteries *(olarias)*, many of them family concerns, are found in most parts of Portugal. Different regions have their own distinct styles, and attractive pottery can be bought from factories and local markets throughout the country. Choose from a variety of wares that include the excellent, practical brown earthenware, brightly colored figurines *(bonecos)*, intricate hand-painted designs, and fine porcelain.

MINHO

Barcelos (see p273) *is the northern center for pottery. Terra-cotta jars, vases, flowerpots, and lanterns, and figurines in primary colors, are made in country workshops.*

The finest porcelain in *Portugal, famous for its delicacy, is made at Vista Alegre (see p201). The factory is well worth visiting for its museum that charts the evolution of the art.*

The faïence tradition *of Coimbra (see pp202–5) and its environs continues today in numerous factories, such as Estrela de Conimbriga, south of the city, where this candlestick was made. Detailed Moorish, 17th- and 18th-century designs are painted by hand onto all kinds of domestic objects and artifacts.*

ESTREMADURA AND RIBATEJ

Caldas da Rainha (see *p175) prides itself on its cabbageware and other lookalike vegetable, fish, and fruit ceramics, such as these "gourds." The factory also makes dinner sets with reliefs of flowers and foliage.*

LISBON

THE LISBON COAST

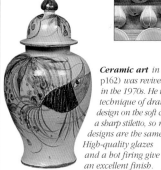

Ceramic art *in Cascais (see p162) was revived by Luís Soares in the 1970s. He used the ancient technique of drawing a free design on the soft clay with a sharp stiletto, so no two designs are the same. High-quality glazes and a hot firing give an excellent finish.*

| 0 kilometers | 50 |
| 0 miles | 25 |

Porches Pottery *was founded in 1968 to revive a local craft and preserve ancient Iberian and Moorish patterns. Each piece is hand glazed and painted in a free-flowing style in blue, green, and turquoise.*

BROWN EARTHENWARE

Matte and glazed earthenware, plain or painted with simple patterns, is widely used and sold at country fairs and markets throughout Portugal. The dishes make attractive and resilient cookware. They range from tall, lidded storage pots and sturdy, oven-proof casserole dishes to portable alcohol stoves that are used for grilling *chouriço* sausages at the table.

DOURO AND TRÁS-OS-MONTES

THE BEIRAS

Bisalhães and other villages near Vila Real (see p255) make an unusual black or dark gray pottery, colored by wood smoke during slow firing. These tough pots are used for storing oil and olives, carrying water, and cooking.

White floral patterning on plain terra-cotta is the hallmark of pottery from Nisa in the Alentejo. Shiny quartz or marble chips are painstakingly applied in lacy floral patterns reminiscent of embroidery.

The red clay of Estremoz (see pp300–1) is valued for its malleable qualities. Typical products are patterned in relief with bold decorative flourishes. Estremoz is also famous for its eccentric bonecos.

The hand-painted pottery of Redondo (see p300) has a distinctive homey style. Plates may be decorated with fresh floral designs or, as here, charming scenes of pastoral life.

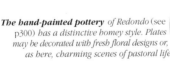

ALENTEJO

ALGARVE

A potter in São Pedro do Corval throws a jar "off the hump." This means she can produce, by eye, a number of equal sized jars from one large lump of clay. She is using a rib tool to shape and finish off the pot. Many small cooperative potteries can be found in the villages around Reguengos de Monsaraz (see p307).

Harvesting the Ocean

Terra-cotta octopus pots

A VITAL INDUSTRY IN PORTUGAL, fishing employs about 34,000 men, trawling treacherous coastal waters for a huge variety of fish destined for local consumption or export. Among the best places to see fishermen at work are Viana do Castelo, Peniche, Nazaré, Sesimbra, and Ericeira in the west, and Sagres, Lagos, and Olhão in the south.

- Viana do Castelo
  MINHO
- Póvoa de Varzim
  Oporto
  DOURO AND
  TRÁS-OS-MONTE
- Aveiro
  THE BEIRAS
- Figueira da Foz
- Nazaré
  ESTREMADURA
  AND RIBATEJO
- Peniche
- Ericeira
  LISBON THE LISBON
  COAST
  Cascais Setúbal
  Sesimbra ALENTEJO
- Sines
  ALGARVE
  Portimão Tavira
  Lagos Olhão
  Sagres

Fishermen mend *nets at Peniche (see p174), an important center for sardines, which are at their best in the summer. About 275,000 tons are caught annually around the coast – for freezing, canning, or eating fresh in seaside restaurants.*

A dockside stall *at Sesimbra (see p166) displays the local catch. In the foreground are several types of bream and bass. Traditionally, fishwives, or varinas, would sort the fish as it came in, ready for sale.*

Ferragudo *is a typical small Algarvian fishing community on the Arade estuary. Its tiny boats fish close to the coast mainly for local needs, leaving the heavy fishing to nearby Portimão, the most important sardine center on the Algarve.*

FISHING BOATS

Of Portugal's 10,000 registered boats, many are ancient and weather beaten. The largest, 24-m (80-ft) trawlers, have diesel engines and radios. Smaller trawlers are used for inshore fishing. At the other end of the scale is the oar-powered 5-m (16-ft) meia-lua. In some places this is hauled back up the beach by oxen.

A typical Algarve *fishing boat, a small trawler (traineira), is less than 12 m (40 ft) long. This means that fishermen cannot go far out to sea or gather very large hauls.*

The frail **meia-lua** *(half-moon) with its flat bottom and high prow, is still used on the west coast. It may be painted with a good luck symbol such as the Cross of the Order of Christ (see p185).*

The festival of Nossa Senhora da Agonia at Viano do Castelo (see pp274–5) is one of several celebrations to honor the supreme guardian of fishermen. A statue of the Virgin is paraded through the streets, then carried out to sea in a flower-decked boat to bless the fleet.

At Cascais on the Lisbon coast, an auction is held each evening at the fish market to sell the day's catch. It is a noisy, bustling affair and a major attraction for locals and visitors alike.

Clamdiggers return from the shellfish beds at Cabanas, east of Tavira in the Algarve. Clams, cockles, whelks, and razor clams all flourish here in the warm, shallow waters of the lagoon and are gathered at low tide.

The trawler (traineira) fishes farthest offshore, mainly for sardines. In a tradition dating back to the Phoenicians, trawlers are usually painted in bright colors, making them easily recognizable out at sea.

TYPES OF FISH

The choice of fish in Portugal seems almost endless, from the ubiquitous, delicious sardine through bream, bass, mullet, and tuna, to members of the eel and octopus families. Strangely, the national favorite is neither Portuguese nor eaten fresh: dried, salted cod *(bacalhau)* is known as *o fiel amigo*, the faithful friend, and has inspired countless recipes.

Sardines *(sardinhas)* or young pilchards are the leading fresh fish catch. Trawlers catch them with purse-seine nets as they swim in schools 25–40 m (80–130 ft) below the surface.

Horse mackerel *(carapau)*, favored for its low cost and abundance, is baked, grilled, or fried. It can also be marinated after cooking to improve flavor.

Tuna *(atum)* can reach 4 m (13 ft) and are found in schools near the Azores and the Algarve – the smaller the fish, the larger the school. Tuna is sold fresh, or canned for export.

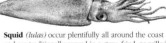

Squid *(lulas)* occur plentifully all around the coast and are traditionally served in a stew, fried, or grilled. The related cuttlefish *(chocos)* and octopus *(polvos)* are equally popular.

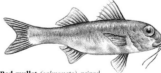

Red mullet *(salmonete)*, prized for its delicate flavor, frequents the coast around Setúbal, where the most famous recipes come from.

Scabbard fish *(peixe espada)* is a tasty, long, thin fish particular to Sesimbra and Madeira. It should not be confused with the similar-sounding but chunkier *peixe espadarte* or swordfish, which tastes quite different.

The Wines of Portugal

Sᴉɴᴄᴇ ᴊᴏɪɴɪɴɢ ᴛʜᴇ ᴇᴜ in 1986, Portugal has been improving its range of wines. Long-established port *(see pp228–9)*, Madeira *(see p349)*, and *vinhos verdes* or "green wines," so called because they are drunk when young and fresh, are unique to the country. The classic fruity reds of Bairrada and Dão regions are now gaining much wider recognition, while the Alentejo and Ribatejo regions are starting to produce high-quality reds that are growing in popularity.

Rosés such as *Mateus are Portugal's great export success. To obtain the pink color, the skins of the red grapes remain in contact with the must (juice) for a short time after crushing.*

WINE REGIONS

Each *região demarcada* (demarcated wine region) is designated by law and guarantees wine of high quality. The first region to be demarcated was the Douro, in the reign of King José (1750–77).

KEY

☐	Vinhos Verdes
☐	Douro
☐	Dão
☐	Bairrada
☐	Bucelas
☐	Colares
☐	Moscatel de Setúbal
☐	Ribatejo
☐	Alentejo
☐	Lagoa

OPORTO

LISBON

0 kilometers 50
0 miles 25

Vinho verde vineyards in the village of Lapela, near Monção in the Minho

Cellar of the Buçaco Palace Hotel *(see pp210–11)*, **famous for its red wine**

HOW TO READ A WINE LABEL

Apart from *branco, tinto,* and *rosado* (white, red, and rosé), terms to note on a wine label are *adamado* or *doce* (sweet), *seco* (dry), *bruto* (dry, sparkling), *licoroso* (fortified), and *maduro* (aged in a vat). *Generoso* indicates an apéritif or dessert wine, *clarete* a Bordeaux-style wine, and *claro* is used for a new or *nouveau* wine. *Reserva* is used for wines from an outstanding vintage year. The phrase *engarrafado na origem* indicates that the wine is estate-bottled, while the words *adega* (cellar) and *quinta* (estate) often appear on wine labels as part of the producer's name.

Vinhos Sogrape is the name of the producer responsible for bottling and distributing this wine.

This wine is *a vinho verde,* a light and slightly sparkling white. *Vinho verde* may also be red.

Denominação de origem controlada is the Portuguese equivalent of the French *appellation contrôlée.*

The alcohol content at 9.5 percent is fairly high for *vinho verde.*

The style of wine shows it to be a dry white.

VINHOS V SOGRAPE

Chello
VINHO VERDE
DENOMINAÇÃO DE ORIGEM CONTROLADA
BRANCO SECO

Vinhos verdes *from the Minho are usually white but can be red. They are made from grapes grown high above the soil on fences or trees. The grapes are picked before fully ripe and the wine is fermented in the bottle, which ensures its delicacy and slight sparkle.*

White Bucelas *is produced just northwest of Lisbon, mainly from the* Arinto *grape, which grows especially well in the soil of this small district. Dry and exquisite, the wine has often been compared with Chablis and goes well with fish dishes.*

Moscatel de Setúbal *is a world-famous dessert wine produced in the Arrábida hills around Palmela, mainly by the long-established firm of José Maria da Fonseca. Their cellars, where the wine is kept in oak casks for up to 50 years before bottling, are open to the public.*

The Douro *has about 80,000 vine-yards along its valley, and although the region is more widely known for its port, just as many grapes are grown for making table wines. Portugal's most expensive table wine, the long-matured Barca Velha, comes from this region.*

The Ribatejo *is becoming a successful region for wine pro-duction, with red and white grapes growing abundantly on the sandy flood plain of the Tagus. The region of Coruche is becoming highly regarded for its soft and fruity reds.*

Full-bodied red Dão *is the most abundant of Portugal's vinhos maduros. Containing at least 20 percent of the* Touriga Nacional *grape, it is aged in wood for several years to ensure quality. Crisp white Dão, which accounts for ten percent of the region's production, should be drunk relatively young.*

Picking grapes for *vinho verde* near Amarante (*see pp248–9*)

The Alentejo region *is now making many of Portugal's best new wines. Single estates produce limited quantities of superlative reds, and labels such as Borba, Redondo, Moura and Reguengos are all worth looking out for. Both reds and whites are high in alcohol content.*

Bairrada *wines from the Beiras have been famous for over 1,000 years. The predominant red grape variety is the* Baga, *yielding the fruity and intense red that rivals Dão and also requires years of aging. White wines are fewer and not so successful, with the exception of a sparkling version.*

Colares *is a small, historic wine region near Sintra. Vines are planted in trenches dug in sand dunes in order to protect the grapes from the Atlantic winds. The resulting reds are full-bodied and high in tannin, but soften with age; the rarer whites are dry maduro wines.*

Lagoa *produces the best wine from the recently de-marcated region of the Algarve. It is a straightforward wine that does not travel well, but when bought by the garrafão (flagon), it is very inexpensive and makes a suitable accompani-ment for the local fish dishes.*

PORTUGAL THROUGH THE YEAR

W HILE JULY and August are the most popular months for visiting, spring and autumn can be more rewarding if you want to tour and experience local culture. Free of excessive heat and crowds, the country is more relaxed. There is deep-rooted respect throughout the country for ancient traditions, which

Monção's Festa da Coca (June)

are most often reflected in religious festivals. *Festas* are held throughout the year, most frequently celebrating saints' days, but also marking the end of the harvest, or gastronomic and even sporting events. *Festas* call for prayers, processions, fireworks, eating and drinking, traditional folk dances, and general merrymaking.

SPRING

F ROM THE ALGARVE to Trás-os-Montes, the country erupts in wildflowers as warmer days set in. This is the time to see the countryside at its most beautiful, although rain can be expected until the end of May.

Easter is a time of great religious celebration, with Holy Week processions taking place all over the country.

MARCH

Open Golf Championship *(mid-Mar).* Venue changes from year to year.
Festival Intercéltico do Porto *(end Mar or early Apr),* Oporto. A festival of music from Portugal and Spain.

Funchal Flower Festival (April)

APRIL

Holy Week *(week before Easter),* Braga. Events in the country's religious capital are particularly traditional and solemn. Torchlit processions are led by church authorities.

Fátima on May 13, when 100,000 pilgrims gather every year

Easter Sunday is also the beginning of the bullfighting season throughout Portugal.
Mãe Soberana *(second Sun after Easter),* Loulé, Algarve. Pilgrimage to Nossa Senhora da Piedade *(see p324).*
FIAPE *(mid-Apr)* Estremoz. An international agricultural, cattle, and handicrafts fair.
Flower Festival *(Apr/May),* Funchal, Madeira. Shops and houses are decorated with flowers. Ends with a parade of flower-covered floats.

MAY

Festas das Cruzes *(early May),* Barcelos. The Festival of the Crosses celebrates the day the shape of a cross appeared in the earth in 1504.
Pilgrimage to Fátima *(May 12–13).* Huge crowds travel to the place where the Virgin appeared to three children in 1917 *(see p184).*
Queima das Fitas *(mid-May),* Coimbra. Lively celebrations mark end of the university's academic year *(see p207).*

Festa do Senhor Santo Cristo dos Milagres *(fifth Sun after Easter),* Ponta Delgada, São Miguel, Azores. The largest religious festival in the Azores.
Festa do Espírito Santo *(Pentecost),* Azores. High point of the festival of the Holy Spirit *(see p367).*
Pilgrimage to Bom Jesus *(Pentecost),* Braga. Penitents climb the spectacular staircase on their knees *(see pp278–9).*
Algarve Music Festival *(May and Jun),* throughout region. Concerts and performances by the Gulbenkian Ballet.

Children carrying a cross at the Festas das Cruzes, Barcelos (May)

SUMMER

MOST VISITORS choose the summer months to visit Portugal. Since many businesses shut down in August, it is vacation time for locals too. Many families spend the entire summer at the shore.

Summer is a good time to visit the cooler Minho, when the north is busy with saints' day festivals (*see pp226–7*).

The famed horsemen of the Ribatejo, Vila Franca de Xira (July)

JUNE

Festa de São Gonçalo (*first weekend*), Amarante. Young, unmarried men and women in the town swap phallus-shaped cakes as tokens of love.
Feira Nacional da Agricultura (*early Jun*), Santarém. A combination of agricultural fairs, bullfighting, and displays of folk dancing.
Santo António (*Jun 12–13*), Lisbon. Celebrated in the Alfama district with singing and dancing, food and drink. Locals put up lanterns and streamers and bring out chairs for the thousands who arrive.
Festa da Coca (*Thu after Trinity Sun*), Monção. Part of the Corpus Christi Day celebrations, the festival features scenes of St. George in comic battle with the dragon.
São João (*Jun 23–24*), Oporto. Midsummer festivities include making wishes while jumping over small fires, and the *barcos rabelos* boat race (*see pp226–7*).
São Pedro (*Jun 29*), Lisbon. More street celebrations with eating, dancing and singing.
Festival de Música de Sintra (*Jun 15–Jul 16*), Sintra. Classical music concerts and ballet.

JULY

Festa do Colete Encarnado (*first weekend*), Vila Franca de Xira. Named after the traditional costume of the Ribatejo horsemen, the "Red Waistcoat Festival" consists of bullfights and the running of bulls through the streets.
Festa dos Tabuleiros (*mid–Jul, every two or three years*), Tomar. The main event is a parade of 400 young women carrying trays with 30 decorated loaves on their heads. There is also music, dancing, fireworks, and a bullfight (*see pp184–5*).
Festa da Ria (*all month*) Aveiro. Folk dances, boat races, and a best-decorated boat competition (see *p201*).

AUGUST

Festas Gualterianas (*first weekend*), Guimarães. Three-day festival dating back to 1452. Torchlight procession, dancing, and medieval parade.
Festa da Nossa Senhora da Boa Viagem (*first weekend*), Peniche. A crowd gathers at the harbor with lighted candles to greet a statue of the Virgin that arrives by boat. Fireworks and dancing continue into the night.
Festival Internacional da Cerveja (*early Aug*), Castelo de Silves. Lively beer festival with folk dancing.

Festa dos Tabuleiros, Tomar

Madeira Wine Rally (*early Aug*), Funchal, Madeira. Car enthusiasts flock to this challenging car rally, one of the stages of the European championships.
Semana do Mar (*1 week in Aug*), Horta, Faial, Azores. Food, music, crafts, water sports, and lively competitions in this sea festival.
Festival do Marisco (*mid-Aug*), Olhão. A seafood festival, hosted by the largest fishing port in the Algarve.
Romaria de Nossa Senhora da Agonia (*weekend closest to Aug 20*), Viana do Castelo. Religious procession, followed by display of floats, drinking, folk dancing, fireworks, and bands. There is also a Saturday afternoon bullfight and a ceremonial blessing of the town's fishing boats.

Girl in traditional dress, Viana do Castelo

The sun-drenched Algarve, a major attraction for summer visitors

Procession at the Romaria de Nossa Senhora da Nazaré

AUTUMN

IN MANY WAYS, this is the best season for touring and sightseeing. From mid-September temperatures cool sharply, and autumn is usually drier than spring. This is a mellow, fruitful time of year with the countryside a collage of brown, gold, and red.

September is also the start of the *vindima* (the vintage) season. Grapes are harvested and crushed to wine in a spirit of festivity, especially in the port-growing Douro region.

SEPTEMBER

Romaria de Nossa Senhora dos Remédios *(Sep 8)*, Lamego. The annual pilgrimage to this famous Baroque shrine is the main feature of three days of celebration. Activities include a torchlit procession and live bands.
Romaria de Nossa Senhora da Nazaré *(Sep 8 and following weekend)*, Nazaré. Includes processions, folk dancing, and bullfights.
Feiras Novas *(mid-Sep)*, Ponte de Lima. A huge market with fairground, fireworks, carnival costumes, and a brass band competition.
Portuguese Grand Prix *(date varies)*, Estoril. Huge crowds come for the Formula One racing competion, which is held in the Autodromo on the Sintra Road.

National Folklore Festival *(mid-Sep)*, the Algarve. Colorful music and dance groups converge from all over Portugal to various towns and resorts in the Algarve.
Wine Festival *(all month)*, Funchal and Estreito de Câmara de Lobos, Madeira. The Funchal wine festival is a lively, popular event, but for a more authentic celebration, visit the one held in Estreito de Câmara de Lobos, the vineyard capital of the island.
Festa de São Mateus *(last week)*, Elvas. Festival offering a mixture of religious, cultural, and agricultural events.

Musicians in regional costume at the National Folklore Festival in September

Damon Hill winning the Grand Prix at Estoril in 1995

OCTOBER

Feira de Outubro *(first week)*, Vila Franca de Xira. Bulls are run through the streets and bullfights staged.

Pilgrimage to Fátima *(Oct 12–13)*. Final pilgrimage of the year, on the date of the Virgin's last appearance.
Festival de Gastronomia *(last two weeks)*, Santarém. Sample the best of regional cooking at this food festival.
International Algarve Car Rally *(Oct–Nov)*, Algarve.

NOVEMBER

All Saints' Day *(Nov 1)*. Candles are lit and flowers placed on graves to honor the dead.
Feira Nacional do Cavalo *(first 2 weeks)*, Golegã. Horse enthusiasts and bullfighters come to see horse parades and races. Included are celebrations for St. Martin's Day *(Nov 11)* with a grand parade and running of bulls.
Encontros de Fotografia *(mid-Nov)*, Coimbra. An exhibition including the work of new photographers.
Feira de Artesanato do Porto *(Dec)*, Oporto. Popular handicraft fair with a stand displaying examples of each region's particular specialty.

Horsemen at the Feira Nacional do Cavalo, Golegã

Wintry snow scene in the Serra de Montemuro, south of Cinfães *(see p249)*

WINTER

Seekers of mild, sunny climes fly south to the Algarve, where many of the resorts remain alive in winter. For golfers too, the coolest months of the year are the most appealing. January and February also see the spectacular blossoming of almond trees all across southern Portugal.

Other visitors migrate even farther south to subtropical Madeira where winter, in particular Christmas and the New Year, is tourist season.

Bolo rei, a cake enjoyed over the Christmas period

PUBLIC HOLIDAYS

New Year's Day (Jan 1)
Carnaval (Feb)
Good Friday
(Mar or Apr)
Dia 25 de Abril,
commemorating 1974 Revolution (Apr 25)
Dia do Trabalhador,
Labor Day (May 1)
Corpus Christi (Jun 6)
Camões Day (Jun 10)
Assumption Day
(Aug 15)
Republic Day (Oct 5)
All Saints' Day (Nov 1)
Dia da Restauração,
commemorating independence from Spain, 1640 (Dec 1)
Immaculate Conception (Dec 8)
Christmas Day (Dec 25)

DECEMBER

Christmas *(Dec 25)*. Everywhere churches and shops display cribs. On Christmas Eve *bacalhau* (salted dried cod) is eaten. Presents are opened, and people go to midnight mass. In Madeira traditional *bolo de mel* (honey cake) is made, and children plant wheat, corn, or barley in pots. The pots are placed around the crib to symbolize renewal and plenty.

JANUARY

New Year. Celebrations all over Portugal with spectacular firework displays welcoming in the New Year.
Festa dos Rapazes *(Dec 25 – Jan 6)*, around Bragança. Boys dress up in masks and rampage through their villages in an ancient pagan rite of passage. *(see p227)*.
Epiphany *(Jan 6)*. The traditional crown-shaped cake

Men in Carnaval costume, Ovar

for Epiphany, *bolo rei* (king's cake), is made with a lucky charm and a bean inside. The person who gets the bean must buy the next cake. *Bolo rei* is also made at Christmas.
Festa de São Gonçalinho *(2nd week)*, Aveiro. Festival in which loaves of bread are thrown to the crowds from the top of a chapel in thanks for the safe return of a fisherman, or for finding a husband.

Almond trees in blossom in February, the Algarve

FEBRUARY

Fantasporto *(Feb 1–15)*, Oporto. An important international film festival, showing many films by new directors, including science fiction films.
Carnaval *(varies according to Easter)*. Celebrated all over Portugal with spectacular costumes and floats; particularly colorful parades take place in Ovar, Sesimbra, Torres Vedras, Funchal and Loulé. Loulé's festivities are connected with the annual Almond Gatherers' Fair.

The Climate of Portugal

MAINLAND PORTUGAL has a pleasant climate with long, hot summers and mild winters. In the north winters are cool and wet; heading farther south temperatures increase and rainfall decreases all the way down to the Algarve, where it rarely falls below freezing. Farther inland a more Continental climate prevails with summers hotter and winters colder than coastal regions. Madeira is rainy in the north, warmer and drier in the south, and the Azores are mild with year-round rainfall and strong winds.

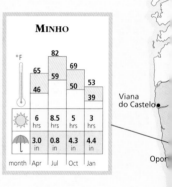

MINHO

°F			
65	82	69	
46	59	50	53
			39

☀			
6 hrs	8.5 hrs	5 hrs	3 hrs

☂			
3.0 in	0.8 in	4.3 in	4.4 in

| month | Apr | Jul | Oct | Jan |

Viana do Castelo

Opor

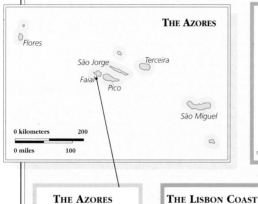

THE AZORES

Flores

São Jorge

Terceira

Faial

Pico

São Miguel

0 kilometers 200

0 miles 100

ESTREMADURA AND RIBATEJO

°F			
63	69	67	
53	61	58	57
			48

☀			
8 hrs	11 hrs	6.5 hrs	4.5 hrs

☂			
2.2 in	0.1 in	2.4 in	3.6 in

| month | Apr | Jul | Oct | Jan |

Aveir

BEIRA LITORA

Leiri

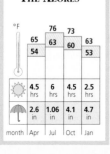

THE AZORES

°F			
65	76	73	
54	63	60	63
			53

☀			
4.5 hrs	6 hrs	4.5 hrs	2.5 hrs

☂			
2.6 in	1.06 in	4.1 in	4.7 in

| month | Apr | Jul | Oct | Jan |

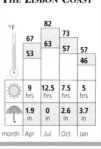

THE LISBON COAST

°F			
67	82	73	
53	63	57	57
			46

☀			
9 hrs	12.5 hrs	7.5 hrs	5 hrs

☂			
1.9 in	0 in	2.6 in	3.7 in

| month | Apr | Jul | Oct | Jan |

Santarém

LISBON

Setúbal

Sin

MADEIRA

Porto Santo

Madeira

Funchal

0 kilometers 20

0 miles 10

MADEIRA

°F			
67	76	75	
56	64	63	66
			55

☀			
6 hrs	7.5 hrs	6 hrs	4.5 hrs

☂			
1.5 in	0.1 in	2.9 in	4.1 in

| month | Apr | Jul | Oct | Jan |

Lag

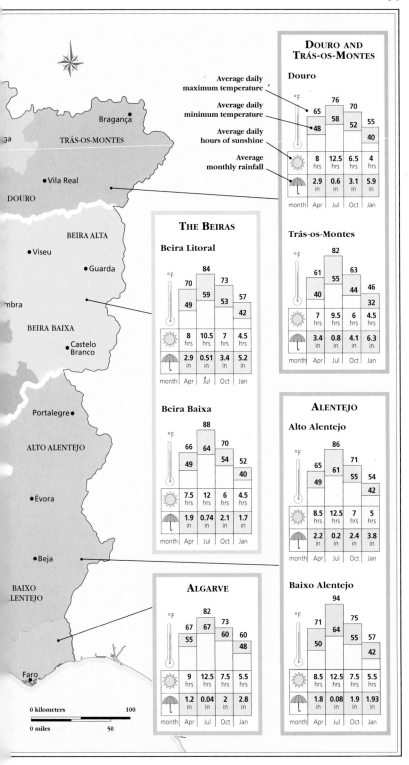

DOURO AND TRÁS-OS-MONTES

Average daily maximum temperature
Average daily minimum temperature
Average daily hours of sunshine
Average monthly rainfall

Douro

°F				
	65	76	70	55
	48	58	52	40
☀	8 hrs	12.5 hrs	6.5 hrs	4 hrs
☂	2.9 in	0.6 in	3.1 in	5.9 in
month	Apr	Jul	Oct	Jan

THE BEIRAS

Beira Litoral

°F				
	70	84	73	57
	49	59	53	42
☀	8 hrs	10.5 hrs	7 hrs	4.5 hrs
☂	2.9 in	0.51 in	3.4 in	5.2 in
month	Apr	Jul	Oct	Jan

Trás-os-Montes

°F				
	61	82	63	46
	40	55	44	32
☀	7 hrs	9.5 hrs	6 hrs	4.5 hrs
☂	3.4 in	0.8 in	4.1 in	6.3 in
month	Apr	Jul	Oct	Jan

Beira Baixa

°F				
	66	88	70	52
	49	64	54	40
☀	7.5 hrs	12 hrs	6 hrs	4.5 hrs
☂	1.9 in	0.74 in	2.1 in	1.7 in
month	Apr	Jul	Oct	Jan

ALENTEJO

Alto Alentejo

°F				
	65	86	71	54
	49	61	55	42
☀	8.5 hrs	12.5 hrs	7 hrs	5 hrs
☂	2.2 in	0.2 in	2.4 in	3.8 in
month	Apr	Jul	Oct	Jan

ALGARVE

°F				
	67	82	73	60
	55	67	60	48
☀	9 hrs	12.5 hrs	7.5 hrs	5.5 hrs
☂	1.2 in	0.04 in	2 in	2.8 in
month	Apr	Jul	Oct	Jan

Baixo Alentejo

°F				
	71	94	75	57
	50	64	55	42
☀	8.5 hrs	12.5 hrs	7.5 hrs	5.5 hrs
☂	1.8 in	0.08 in	1.9 in	1.93 in
month	Apr	Jul	Oct	Jan

Bragança
TRÁS-OS-MONTES
Vila Real
DOURO
BEIRA ALTA
Viseu
Guarda
BEIRA BAIXA
Castelo Branco
Portalegre
ALTO ALENTEJO
Évora
Beja
BAIXO ALENTEJO
Faro

0 kilometers 100
0 miles 50

OM MANVEL

per gr̃aca de dõ Rey de portugall
τ dõ algaruee. Daquem τ dalẽ m̃
em africa. senor de guinee τ da conquista nauegacaṃ τ c̃
merco dethiopia arabia persia. τ da jndia τ c̃. S̃
quantoe. esto a perpetua memoria ferto buen fazen
saber que assi como o propo τ pñçpall cuydado dos
tem algũi cargo deue ser trabalhar como as cousae
lhes sam encarregadae sciam postas. no mais. prosp̃
τ mellorado estado que ser possa. assy tanto mais a
sto nos Reis. τ pñçepes fazello. quanto com mais. e
cellente preminençia sam per dõ postos na terra po̅
bem della τ de sene vassallos. τ pa toda execuçaṃ τ ẽ
plo de virtude. C por que esta obrigaçaṃ tam deui

THE HISTORY OF PORTUGAL

PORTUGAL IS ONE of the oldest nation states in Europe: its foundation in 1139 predates that of its neighbor, Spain, by nearly 350 years. The Romans, who arrived in 216 BC, called the whole peninsula Hispania, but the region between the Douro and Tagus Rivers was named Lusitania after the Celtiberian tribe that lived there. When the Roman Empire collapsed in the 5th century, Hispania was overrun first by Germanic tribes, then by Moors from North Africa in 711. Military reconquest by the Christian kingdoms of the north began in earnest in the 11th century, and it was during this long process that Portucale, a small county of the kingdom of León and Castile, was declared independent by its first king, Afonso Henriques.

The new kingdom expanded southward to the Algarve, and Portuguese sailors began to explore the African coast and the Atlantic. Portugal's golden age reached its zenith in the reign of Manuel I with Vasco da Gama's voyage to India in 1498 and the discovery of Brazil in 1500. Eastern trade brought incredible wealth, but

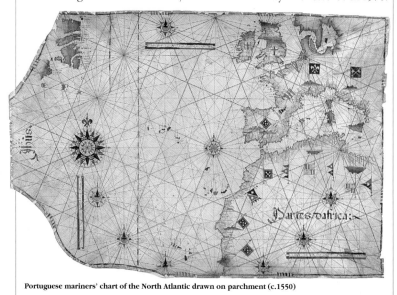

Portuguese ship (c.1500)

military defeat in Morocco meant that the prosperity was short-lived. Spain invaded in 1580 and Spanish kings ruled Portugal for the next 60 years.

After Portugal regained independence, her fortunes were restored by the discovery of gold in Brazil. In the second half of the 18th century, the chief minister, the Marquês de Pombal, began to modernize the country and to limit the reactionary influence of the church. However, Napoleon's invasion in 1807 and the loss of Brazil in 1825 left Portugal impoverished and divided. Power struggles between Absolutists and Constitutionalists further weakened the country, and despite a period of stability from the 1850s, the debt crisis worsened. In 1910, a republican revolution overthrew the monarchy.

The economy deteriorated until a military coup in 1926 led to a long period of dictatorship. António Salazar, who held power from 1928 to 1968, rid the country of its debts, but poverty was widespread and all opposition banned. The Carnation Revolution ended the dictatorship in 1974, and full democracy was restored in 1976.

Portuguese mariners' chart of the North Atlantic drawn on parchment (c.1550)

◁ Illuminated frontispiece of the *Leitura Nova*, showing Portugal's coat of arms and portrait of Manuel I (c.1520)

The Rulers of Portugal

AFONSO HENRIQUES declared himself Portugal's first king in 1139, but his descendants' ties of marriage to various Spanish kingdoms led to dynastic disputes. João I's defeat of the Castilians in 1385 established the House of Avis, which presided over the golden age of Portuguese imperialism. Then in 1580, in the absence of a direct heir, Portugal was ruled by Spanish kings for 60 years before the Duke of Bragança became João IV. A republican uprising ended the monarchy in 1910. However, in the first 16 years of the republic there were 40 different governments, and in 1926 Portugal became a dictatorship under the eventual leadership of Salazar. Democracy was restored by the "Carnation" Revolution of 1974.

1481–95
João II

1438–81
Afonso V

1211–23 Afonso II

1185–1211
Sancho I

1248–79
Afonso III

1279–1325 Dinis

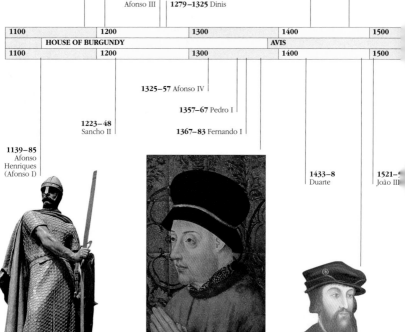

1100	1200	1300	1400	1500
HOUSE OF BURGUNDY			AVIS	
1100	1200	1300	1400	1500

1325–57 Afonso IV

1357–67 Pedro I

1367–83 Fernando I

1223–48
Sancho II

1139–85
Afonso
Henriques
(Afonso I)

1433–8
Duarte

1521–
João III

1385–1433 João I

1495–1521 Manuel I

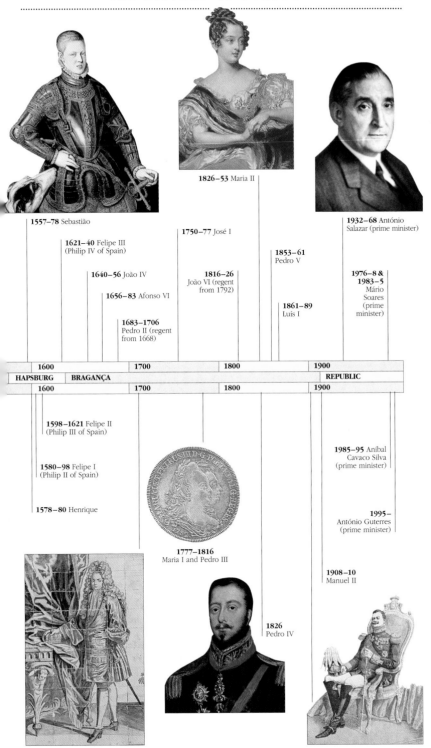

1826–53 Maria II

1557–78 Sebastião

1932–68 António Salazar (prime minister)

1750–77 José I

1621–40 Felipe III (Philip IV of Spain)

1853–61 Pedro V

1640–56 João IV

1816–26 João VI (regent from 1792)

1976–8 & 1983–5 Mário Soares (prime minister)

1656–83 Afonso VI

1861–89 Luís I

1683–1706 Pedro II (regent from 1668)

1600	1700	1800	1900
HAPSBURG	BRAGANÇA		REPUBLIC
1600	1700	1800	1900

1598–1621 Felipe II (Philip III of Spain)

1985–95 Aníbal Cavaco Silva (prime minister)

1580–98 Felipe I (Philip II of Spain)

1578–80 Henrique

1995– António Guterres (prime minister)

1777–1816 Maria I and Pedro III

1908–10 Manuel II

1826 Pedro IV

1706–50 João V

1889–1908 Carlos I

Prehistoric and Roman Portugal

FROM ABOUT 2000 BC Portugal's Stone Age communities were supplanted by foreign invaders, most notably the Iberians and the Celts. When Rome defeated the Carthaginians in 216 BC and took over all their territories in eastern Spain, she still had to subdue Celtiberian tribes living in the west. One of these, the Lusitani, put up fierce resistance. After their defeat in 139 BC, their name was preserved in Lusitania, a province of Roman Iberia, corresponding roughly to present-day Portugal. Romanization led to four centuries of stability and prosperity, but as the Roman Empire collapsed, Lusitania was overrun by Germanic tribes, first the Suevi and then the Visigoths.

Gold solidus
(c.400 AD)

IBERIAN PENINSULA IN 27 BC

☐ *Roman provinces*

HISPANIA
TARRACONENSIS

LUSITANIA

BAETICA

The amphitheater probably dated from the building boom of the 1st century AD.

The forum and principal temple

Dolmen of Comenda
Dolmens such as this one near Évora were communal burial chambers. Many were built by the Neolithic peoples who lived in the Iberian Peninsula in the third millennium BC.

The main·road led north to Aeminium (Coimbra).

Porca of Murça
Trás-os-Montes has preserved 16 statues of animals like this granite pig (see p257), probably used in Celtic fertility rituals.

Palestra (exercise area of the baths)

The Baths of Trajan had a spectacular view of the ravine below the city walls.

TIMELINE

c.2000 BC Iberian tribes arrive in the peninsula, probably from Africa

Iberian gold gorget

139 BC Celtiberian resistance to Roman rule ends with the death of Viriatus, leader of the Lusitani tribe

3000 BC	2000 BC	1000 BC

2500 BC Portugal inhabited by late Stone Age people. Many megalithic tombs date from this time

Celtic stone warrior, 1st millennium BC

1000 BC Phoenicians set up trading stations and settlements along the southern coast

c.700 BC Celtic invaders settle in Portugal

218 BC The Romans invade the Iberian Peninsula

Floor Mosaic
Under Roman rule the wealthy built lavishly decorated villas. This mosaic of a triton (1st century AD) comes from the House of the Fountains just outside the walls of Conimbriga.

WHERE TO SEE PREHISTORIC AND ROMAN PORTUGAL

The Alentejo is rich in Stone Age megaliths *(see p306),* while the north has the two best examples of Celtiberian settlements at Sanfins *(p248)* and Briteiros. Many traces of the Roman period, including roads and bridges, are found throughout Portugal. Apart from Conimbriga, major sites, such as the villas at Pisões *(p311)* and Milreu *(p325),* are mainly in the south. Faro's Museu Municipal *(p327)* has a good collection of local finds.

Roman Amphora
Garum, a popular, spiced sauce made of fermented fish, was manufactured at Tróia (see p169) and exported in 27-liter (7-gallon) amphorae like this one.

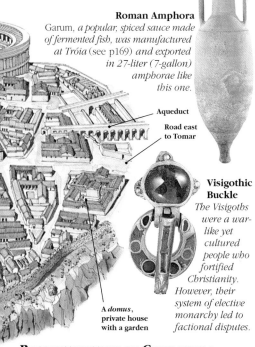

Aqueduct

Road east to Tomar

Visigothic Buckle
The Visigoths were a war-like yet cultured people who fortified Christianity. However, their system of elective monarchy led to factional disputes.

A *domus*, private house with a garden

***Citânia de Briteiros**, a hilltop settlement founded around the 5th century AD, survived until well into the Roman period. It was discovered in 1874 (p281).*

RECONSTRUCTION OF CONIMBRIGA

The extensive remains of Conimbriga *(see p208)* give a vivid picture of how thoroughly Romanized Portugal became under the empire. The town expanded rapidly in the 1st century AD, when it achieved the self-governing status of a *municipium*. It fell to the Suevi in AD 468.

***Évora's temple** dates from the 2nd century AD (see p302). It is almost all that remains of an important Roman city.*

AD 73 Emperor Vespasian grants towns in the Iberian Peninsula same rights as Latin towns in Italy	**415** Visigoths invade the peninsula and drive out the Vandals and the Alani	**585** Visigoths take over the Suevian kingdom, fixing their capital at Toledo in Spain	
	AD 200 Christianity becomes established in the peninsula		
AD 1	**AD 200**	**AD 400**	**AD 600**
27 BC During the rule of Augustus the Iberian Peninsula is divided into three; Lusitania is the name given to the central province south of the River Douro	**409** Invasion by "barbarian" tribes from central Europe: the Vandals, the Alani, and the Suevi	*Visigothic chapel at São Frutuoso (see p277)*	
	411 Suevian kingdom established in Galicia and northern Portugal		

Moorish Domination and Christian Reconquest

IBERIAN PENINSULA IN 1100

☐ *County of Portucale*

☐ *Kingdom of León and Castile*

☐ *Moorish kingdoms*

Bronze Moorish oil lamp in the shape of a bird

W̶HEN MUSLIMS from North Africa defeated the Visigoths in 711, the Iberian Peninsula became a province of the Caliphate of Damascus. Then, in 756, Abd al Rahman established the independent kingdom of Al Andalus, his capital Córdoba becoming one of the world's great centers of culture. Moorish control of the peninsula remained virtually undisputed for the next 300 years until the small Christian kingdoms in the north began the Reconquest. In the 11th century, as Moorish power waned, "Portucale" was just a small county of the Kingdom of León and Castile, centered on the Douro. It became independent after Afonso Henriques defeated the Moors at Ourique in 1139.

Without the Virgin to watch over them, the Faro fishermen's nets are empty.

Moorish Plate
Vivid depictions of a hunting dog, a falcon, and a gazelle decorate this 11th-century plate found at Mértola, a river port on the Guadiana used by eastern traders.

The fishermen set off with new hope.

Coexistence
Under Moorish rule, cooperation between the faiths was common. This miniature from the 13th century shows the friendly meeting of two knights, one a Christian, the other a Moor.

TIMELINE

711 Large Muslim army of Berbers and Arabs (the Moors) conquers Iberian Peninsula following dispute over Visigothic succession

722 Christian victory at Covadonga in Asturias marks start of gradual reconquest

868 Vímara Peres takes Oporto from the Moors

878 Christian forces recapture Coimbra

10th-century Hispano-Moorish ivory casket

AD 700	AD 800	AD 900	AD 1000

756 Battle of Al Musara; Abd al Rahman defeats governor of Córdoba and founds kingdom of Al Andalus

Nora, a bucket wheel for raising water introduced by the Moors

955 Moorish leader Al Mansur retakes Coimbra, then forces Christian frontier back to the River Douro

1008–31 Civil war; Al Andalus divided into small kingdoms known as *taifas*

Stone Relief of São Tiago
In wars against the Moors, the apostle St. James (São Tiago) assumed a special role. At Ourique in 1139, soldiers claimed to have seen him leading Christian forces into battle.

WHERE TO SEE MOORISH PORTUGAL

The influence of the Moors is strongest in the south, in towns like Lagos (see p320), Faro (p326), and Silves, where they ruled for longer and the architecture (p19) retains many Arab features. In Mértola (p313), the church preserves much of the old mosque. Farther north, the Castelo dos Mouros, in Sintra (p157), and many other fortresses were taken over and rebuilt by the Christians.

12th-century Silver Dirham
This coin was minted at Beja by the Almohads, a Muslim sect even stricter than their forerunners, the Almoravids.

A cistern well has been uncovered in the red sandstone castle at Silves, a major Moorish citadel in the Algarve (p322).

The lost statue of the Virgin is recovered from the sea and restored to its rightful place on the walls.

Out at sea the fishermen's nets are full once more.

Capture of Lisbon
The Reconquest was given the status of a crusade by the pope. Lisbon was taken in 1147 with the aid of English troops bound for the Holy Land.

FARO UNDER MOORISH RULE

Christians who lived under Moorish rule were called Mozarabs. At Faro they placed a statue of the Virgin on the walls of the city, but resentful Muslims took the statue down. These four scenes from the *Cantigas de Santa Maria* tell the story of the miracle that followed.

1097 Alfonso VI of León and Castile entrusts Portucale to his son-in-law Henry of Burgundy

1086 Invasion of the Almoravids

1139 Battle of Ourique; Afonso Henriques declares himself King of Portugal

1143 Treaty of Zamora establishes Portugal's independence

1165–9 Geraldo sem Pavor captures a number of cities from the Almohads, including Évora and Badajoz

1050	1100	1150

1064 Christians regain Coimbra

Henry of Burgundy

1128 Battle of São Mamede; Afonso Henriques defeats his mother, Teresa, to win control of county of Portucale

1153 Founding of Cistercian Abbey at Alcobaça

1147 Fall of Lisbon to Crusader army; Almoravid empire falls to the Almohads

The New Kingdom

14th-century statue of armed knight

THE PORTUGUESE RECONQUEST was completed in 1249 when Afonso III captured Faro in the Algarve. His successor, King Dinis, encouraged agriculture and commerce, earning the nickname of the "farmer king." He also built castles to defend the border from Castilian attack and expanded the navy. Territorial disputes with Castile came to a head in 1383 when King Fernando died and his son-in-law, Juan I of Castile, claimed the Portuguese throne for his wife, Beatriz. Juan's opponents favored Pedro I's illegitimate son, João of Avis, elected king by the *cortes* (parliament) in Coimbra in 1385.

IBERIAN PENINSULA IN 1200

☐ *Kingdom of Portugal*

☐ *Spanish kingdoms*

☐ *Territory under Moorish rule*

The faithful dog at the feet of the deceased was a common feature of Gothic tombs.

Coat of arms of Portugal

The frieze shows scenes from the life of Pedro and Inês.

The aedicules contain finely carved scenes from the life of St. Bartholomew, Dom Pedro's patron saint.

Cancioneiro da Ajuda
King Dinis was a fine musician and poet. This illumination is from a collection of troubador songs, many by the king himself.

Fortifications of Serpa
King Dinis had a chain of fortified towns and castles built along the borders with Castile and Moorish Spain. This 16th-century drawing shows the medieval walls and towers of Serpa (see p310).

TIMELINE

1185 Sancho I becomes king; his victories in the Algarve are reversed by Al-Mansur, the Almohad caliph

1211 First *cortes* (parliament) held at Coimbra

Leiria Castle

1254 The *cortes* held at Leiria includes representatives of the towns

1200

1250

1173 Remains of St. Vincent brought from Cabo de São Vicente to Lisbon

1179 Portugal recognized as kingdom by the pope

Afonso III

1248 Anarchic reign of Sancho II ends in his deposition by his brother Afonso III

1249 Afonso III completes reconquest of the Algarve, but his claim to sovereignty is challenged by Castile

1256 Lisbon becomes capital of Portugal in place of Coimbra

St. Isabel (1271–1336)
King Dinis did not approve of his wife's acts of charity. A legend tells how the bread Queen Isabel was about to distribute to the poor turned into roses when she was challenged by her husband.

Six angels support the recumbent king.

St. Bartholomew is martyred by being skinned alive.

Cross of Sancho I
Sancho's reign (1185–1211) saw royal power and wealth increase despite disputes between the king and his bishops over papal authority.

TOMB OF PEDRO I
The Gothic carvings on the royal tomb at Alcobaça *(see pp178–9)* are the finest of their kind in Portugal. The forthright Pedro, who ruled from 1357–67, is remembered chiefly for the tragic tale of his murdered mistress, Inês de Castro, whose matching tomb stands facing Pedro's.

WHERE TO SEE MEDIEVAL PORTUGAL

Of the many castles built or rebuilt in this period, the most picturesque are at Almourol *(see p189)* and Óbidos. In the citadel of Bragança *(p258–9)* stands the Domus Municipalis, a medieval meeting hall. Most surviving Romanesque buildings, however, are religious: the cathedrals in Oporto, Lisbon *(p74)* and Coimbra *(p204)* and many smaller churches in the north, such as those at Rates *(p272)*, Roriz *(p248)*, and Bravães *(p267)*.

Óbidos Castle, *now a pousada, was rebuilt by King Dinis when he gave this fairy-tale town to his wife Isabel as a wedding present in 1282* (p172).

Oporto's Sé (p240) *has been much altered, but the twin-towered west front retains its original 13th-century character.*

The House of Avis

AFTER JOÃO OF AVIS had defeated the Castilians in 1385 to become João I of Portugal, he strengthened his position through an important alliance with England. His long reign saw the start of Portuguese imperialism and the beginning of maritime expeditions promoted by his son, Henry the Navigator *(see pp48–9)*. Further voyages of discovery in the reign of Manuel I "the Fortunate" led to trade with India and the East and, following Afonso de Albuquerque's capture of Goa, initially brought great wealth. So, too, did the colonization of Brazil. However, the lure of overseas adventure weakened mainland Portugal, which suffered serious depopulation. The age of expansion ended when a foolhardy military expedition to Morocco, led by King Sebastião, was soundly defeated in 1578.

IBERIAN PENINSULA IN 1500

▨ *Portugal*

☐ *Spain (Castile and Aragon)*

16th-century Porcelain Plate
In 1557 the Portuguese were granted Macão as a trading post in China. This Chinese plate bears the arms of Matias de Albuquerque, a descendant of the great Afonso, conqueror of Goa.

Arms of English royal family

John of Gaunt used the alliance with Portugal to pursue his own claim to the throne of Castile.

Troops Landing at Arzila
The kings of the Avis dynasty constantly sought to extend their domains to Morocco, where they established a small colony around Tangier. This Flemish tapestry celebrates Afonso V's capture of Arzila in 1471.

Luís de Camões
After serving in India and Morocco, where he lost an eye, the poet wrote Os Lusíadas (see p188), an epic on the Discoveries.

TIMELINE

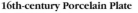

1385 João I defeats Castilian army at Battle of Aljubarrota	**c.1425** *Leal Conselheiro*, a treatise on courtly behavior written by King Duarte	**1496** Jews expelled from the country or forcibly converted
1415 Capture of Ceuta in Morocco	**1441** Lagos is site of first slave market in modern Europe	**1495–1521** Reign of Manuel I and great period of discoveries

1400	**1425**	**1450**	**1475**

1386 Alliance with England formalized by Treaty of Windsor	**1418** Henry the Navigator made governor of the Algarve	**1471** Conquest of Moroccan fortresses of Arzila and Tangier	**1494** Spain and Portugal divide the Atlantic region by Treaty of Tordesillas
		King Duarte **1482–3** João II successfully resists the Conspiracy of the Nobles	

Wedding of Manuel I
Manuel's reign marked the highest point in Portugal's golden age of discovery and conquest. His marriages were made to reinforce ties with Spain. Shown here is his third: to Leonor, sister of Carlos I of Spain, in 1518.

João I drew support from the merchants of Lisbon and Oporto rather than the nobles, many of whom sided with Castile.

Archbishop of Braga

Portugal's bishops took João's side after the pope had refused to legitimize the children of Inês de Castro *(see pp44–5).*

JOÃO I AND THE ENGLISH
João's alliance with England against Castile led to his marriage in 1387 to Philippa of Lancaster, daughter of John of Gaunt, son of Edward III. This illustration from the chronicle of Jean de Wavrin shows the new king entertaining his father-in-law.

WHERE TO SEE GOTHIC PORTUGAL
Many churches include Gothic elements, such as the cloister of the Sé in Oporto *(see p240)* and the richly sculpted portal of the Sé in Évora *(p304)*. Tomar's Convento de Cristo *(pp186–7)* is predominantly Gothic, as is the church at Alcobaça *(pp178–9)*. The finest church, however, is at Batalha, built in thanks for João I's victory at the Battle of Aljubarrota. It also contains major examples of Manueline architecture *(see pp20–21)*.

Batalha (pp182–3) incorporates a wide range of Gothic styles. The plain, lofty nave contrasts with the ornamented exterior.

Battle of Alcácer-Quibir (1578)
King Sebastião saw his African expedition as a crusade against Islam. After Alcácer-Quibir, he and 8,000 of his troops lay dead, 15,000 captives were sold into slavery, and the House of Avis dynasty was doomed.

Belém Monstrance (see p20) | **1531** Inquisition introduced into Portugal

1510 Beginning of Portuguese empire in Asia; Goa conquered by Afonso de Albuquerque

1536 Death of Gil Vicente, Portugal's greatest dramatist

1572 Publication of *Os Lusíadas*, a verse epic celebrating Portugal's history by Luís de Camões

1500 | **1525** | **1550** | **1575**

c.1502 Work starts on the Jerónimos monastery in Belém *(see pp106–7)*

Gil Vicente

1559 Jesuit University established at Évora *(see p304)*

1578 King Sebastião's expedition to Morocco ends in his death and total defeat at the Battle of Alcácer-Quibir

1498 Vasco da Gama reaches India

1521–57 Reign of João III, known as "the Pious"

The Age of Discovery

Portuguese
padrão

PORTUGAL'S ASTONISHING PERIOD of conquest and exploration began in 1415 with the capture of the North African city of Ceuta. Maritime expeditions into the Atlantic and along the West African coast followed, motivated by traditional Christian hostility toward Islam and desire for commercial gain. Great riches were made from the gold and slaves taken from the Guinea coast, but the real breakthrough for Portuguese imperialism occurred in 1498 when Vasco da Gama (see p108) reached India. Portugal soon controlled the Indian Ocean and the spice trade, and established an eastern capital at Goa. With Pedro Álvares Cabral's "discovery" of Brazil, Portugal became a mercantile super-power rivaled only by Spain.

Armillary Sphere
This celestial globe with the earth in its center was used by navigators for measuring the positions of the stars. It became the personal emblem of Manuel I.

Magellan (c.1480–1521)
With Spanish funding, Portuguese sailor Fernão de Magalhães, known as Magellan, led the first circumnavigation of the globe (1519–22). He was killed in the Philippines before the voyage's end.

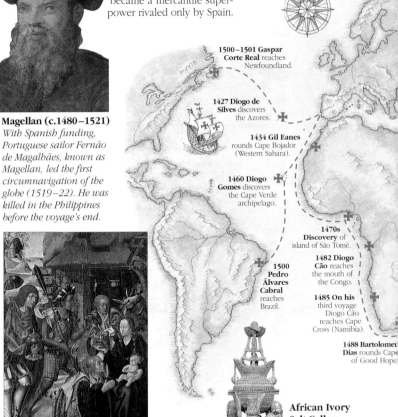

1500–1501 Gaspar Corte Real reaches Newfoundland.

1427 Diogo de Silves discovers the Azores.

1434 Gil Eanes rounds Cape Bojador (Western Sahara).

1460 Diogo Gomes discovers the Cape Verde archipelago.

1470s Discovery of island of São Tomé.

1500 Pedro Álvares Cabral reaches Brazil.

1482 Diogo Cão reaches the mouth of the Congo.

1485 On his third voyage Diogo Cão reaches Cape Cross (Namibia).

1488 Bartolomeu Dias rounds Cape of Good Hope.

The Adoration of the Magi
Painted for Viseu Cathedral shortly after Cabral returned from Brazil in 1500, this panel is attributed to Grão Vasco (see p213). The second king, Baltazar, is depicted as a Tupi Indian.

African Ivory Salt Cellar
This 16th-century ivory carving shows Portuguese warriors supporting a globe and a ship. A sailor peers out from the crow's nest at the top.

apanese Screen (c.1600)
his screen shows traders unloading a nau, *r great ship. Between 1575 and their expul-ion in 1638, the Portuguese monopolized be trade route between China and Japan.*

HENRY THE NAVIGATOR

Although he did not sail himself, Henry (1394–1460), the third son of João I, laid the foundations for Portugal's maritime expansion that were later built upon by João II and consolidated by Manuel I. As Master of the wealthy Order of Christ and Governor of the Algarve, Henry was able to finance expeditions along the African coast. By the time he died he had a monopoly on all trade south of Cape Bojador. Legend tells that he founded a great school of navigation either at Sagres *(see p320)* or Lagos.

1543 Portuguese arrive in Japan.

1513 Trading posts set up in China at Macao and Canton.

1510 Capture of Goa.

1498 Vasco da Gama reaches Calicut in India.

1518 Fortress built in Colombo (Sri Lanka).

1512 Portuguese reach Ternate in the Moluccas (Spice Islands).

KEY

– – – Discoverers' routes

Cloves

Pepper

Nutmeg

Cinnamon

The Spice Trade
Exotic spices were a great source of wealth for Portugal. The much-disputed Moluccas, or Spice Islands, were pur-chased from Spain in 1528.

PORTUGUESE DISCOVERIES
.he systematic attempt to find a sea route to .ndia, which led to a monopoly of the spice .rade, began in 1482 with the first voyage of)iogo Cão, who planted a *padrão* (stone .ross) on the shores where he landed.

Lateen-rigged Caravel
These ships with three triangular sails were favored by the first Portuguese explorers who sailed close to the African coast. For later journeys across the open ocean, square sails were found more effective.

Crow's nest

Square sail on foremast

Cross of the Order of Christ *(see p185)*

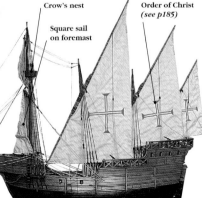

Spanish Rule

**Philip II
of Spain**

W HEN HENRIQUE, the Cardinal-King, died without an heir in 1580, Philip II of Spain successfully claimed the Portuguese throne through his mother, a daughter of Manuel I. Under Spanish rule influential positions were held by Portuguese nobles, but a common foreign policy led to a steady loss of colonies to the Dutch. In 1640 a Portuguese revolt took place in Lisbon, and the Duke of Bragança was chosen to become King João IV. Spain retaliated and the ensuing war continued until 1668. Meanwhile Portugal was forced to rely economically on her overseas territories.

Restoration of João IV
Two weeks after his supporters had ousted the Spanish in 1640, João was crowned on a platform outside the Royal Palace in Lisbon.

Spanish Armada
In 1588 Philip II of Spain hoped to invade England with his great fleet. It sailed from Lisbon where it had been equipped and provisioned.

**The Graça
fort** was held by the Spanish.

António Vieira
Vieira (1606–97) was a Jesuit priest, writer, and orator. He was sent on many diplomatic missions and clashed with the Inquisition over his support for Christianized Jews.

WAR OF INDEPENDENCE

Portugal's long war against Spain (1640–68) was fought mostly in the Alentejo. This *azulejo* panel from Palácio Fronteira in Lisbon *(see p125)* shows the Battle of Linhas de Elvas (1658). A Portuguese army besieged in Elvas *(see pp296–7)* was relieved by fresh troops from Estremoz, who soundly defeated the Spanish.

TIMELINE

1580 Battle of Alcântara; Spanish invade, and Philip II of Spain becomes King of Portugal

1588 Spanish Armada sets sail from Lisbon to invade England

1614 Publication of the *Peregrinação* by Fernão Mendes Pinto, an account of his travels in Asia in the mid-16th century

1624 Dutch capture Portuguese colony of Bahia in Brazil

1631 Birth of painter Josefa de Óbidos

1580 — **1600** — **1620**

1583 Philip returns to Spain leaving his nephew, Cardinal-Archduke Albert of Austria, as viceroy

1581 The king invites Italian architect Filippo Terzi to Lisbon to remodel the Royal Palace and to build many churches

Church of São Vicente de Fora (see p72) by Filippo Terzi and Baltasar Álvares, completed in 1627

1626 Jesuit missionary António de Andrade crosses the Himalayas into Tibet

Indo-Portuguese Contador
Luxury cabinets, known as contadores, *were made from teak and ebony in Portugal's overseas colonies. Many came from Goa. This fine 17th-century example is from the Museu Nacional de Arte Antiga (see pp96–9).*

The besieged Portuguese army at Elvas was retreating from a previous unsuccessful campaign in Spain.

Stout bastions deflected the attackers' cannon fire.

The relieving army from Estremoz surprised and routed the Spanish.

Josefa de Óbidos
Born in Spain, Josefa (1631–84) came to Óbidos (see p172) when young. Trained by her father, she painted religious subjects and realistic still lifes.

WHERE TO SEE 17TH-CENTURY PORTUGAL

Under Spanish rule an austere style of architecture prevailed, typified by São Vicente de Fora *(see p72)* in Lisbon, the Sé Nova in Coimbra *(p204)*, and Santarém's Jesuit church *(p191)*. At Vila Viçosa the style is evident in the long, plain façade of the palace of the Dukes of Bragança *(pp298–9)*. Colorful *azulejos* from the period can be seen at Palácio Fronteira *(p125)* and the Museu Nacional do Azulejo *(pp122–3)*.

Palácio dos Biscainhos *in Braga (p277) was built by rich emigrants returning from Brazil. Enlarged in later centuries, it retains its 17th-century core.*

The Inquisition
In the 16th and 17th centuries the Inquisition, set up by the Catholic church, burned heretics in Lisbon's Terreiro do Paço to ensure religious conformity.

---

639 Portuguese vessels barred from Japanese ports

1654 Fall of Pernambuco; Dutch driven from Brazil

1656 Death of João IV; his widow, Luisa de Guzmán, is regent for young King Afonso VI

1665 Spanish defeated at Battle of Montes Claros

1668 Spain recognizes Portuguese independence

1683 Pedro II becomes King

Pedro II

1640

Catherine of Bragança

1640 The Restoration: 4th Duke of Bragança crowned King João IV after uprising against Spanish rule

1660

1667 Degenerate Afonso VI is deposed by his brother Pedro, who marries Afonso's French wife and becomes regent

1662 Catherine of Bragança marries Charles II of England

1680

1697 Gold discovered in Minas Gerais region of Brazil

1698 Last meeting of Portuguese *cortes*

The Age of Absolutism

THE 18TH CENTURY was a period of mixed fortune for Portugal. Despite vast revenues from Brazilian gold and diamonds, João V almost bankrupted the country with his extravagance. In contrast, Pombal, chief minister of João's successor José I, applied the ideas of the Enlightenment, reforming government, commerce, and education. When Maria I succeeded in 1777, she reversed many of Pombal's decrees. The French invasion of 1807 forced Maria, by then mad, and the royal family into exile in Brazil.

Gold coin of João V

Tightrope Walker
This device, used at Coimbra University in the later 18th century, shows the center of gravity when an object is in balance.

The library contains richly carved Baroque bookcases and more than 40,000 volumes.

Marquês de Pombal (1699–1782)
Pombal insisted that Lisbon be rebuilt on strictly rational lines after the 1755 earthquake (see pp62–3). Here he proudly presents the new city.

Queen's apartments

João V
This miniature (1720) by Castriotto shows João V drinking chocolate, a fashionable drink of the nobility, served to him by the Infante Miguel.

The basilica contains many marble statues made by Italian masters set amid a stunning scheme of yellow, pink, red, and blue marble.

TIMELINE

Bom Jesus do Monte

1703 Methuen Treaty with Britain secures market for Portuguese wines in Britain and for British woolen goods in Portugal	**1723** Building of Baroque staircase of Bom Jesus near Braga (see pp278–9)	**1755** Earthquake devastates Lisbon and much of southern Portugal
	1730 Consecration of basilica at monastery-palace at Mafra	
1700	**1720**	**1740**
1706–50 Reign of João V "the Magnanimous," a period of great artistic extravagance	**1733** First Portuguese opera, *The Patience of Socrates* by António de Almeida, performed at Royal Palace in Lisbon	**1748** First water flows along Águas Livres aqueduct in Lisbon
		1750 José I succeeds João V

Águas Livres Aqueduct
Opened in 1748, the aqueduct was paid for by the citizens of Lisbon. João V had it built across the Alcântara valley against the advice of his engineers.

Where to See 18th-Century Portugal

Baroque churches are found throughout Portugal, many with ornate interiors of gilded wood *(talha dourada)* such as São Francisco *(see p241)* and Santa Clara *(p239)* in Oporto. Tiled interiors are also very common *(pp22–3)*. Coimbra University houses the glittering Capela de São Miguel and a fine Baroque library. As well as the palaces at Mafra and Queluz, many elegant country houses, notably the Casa de Mateus, date from this era *(pp254–5)*.

Monks' refectory

18th-Century Dressing Chair
This richly gilded walnut chair has sturdy cabriole legs, showing the influence of the English Queen Anne style.

Queluz Palace *(pp164–5), residence of Maria I, was begun in 1747. It is the finest example of Rococo architecture in Portugal.*

The bell towers contain a carillon of 114 bells.

Monastery at Mafra
Begun in 1717, this vast monument to João V incorporates a royal palace, a church and a monastery *(see p152)*. It took 38 years to complete and contains some 880 rooms and 300 monks' cells.

The King's apartments are separated from the Queen's by a long gallery.

The Capela de São Miguel *at Coimbra University (pp206–7) was redecorated in Baroque style in the reign of João V.*

1756 Douro valley becomes world's first demarcated wine region

1759 Pombal expels Jesuits from Portugal

1772 Pombal reorganizes Coimbra University, adding mathematics and natural sciences to the syllabus

1777 Accession of Maria I, who dismisses Pombal

Maria I

1808 French forced to retreat by Anglo-Portuguese force under Sir Arthur Wellesley; Treaty of Sintra

1760

1780

1800

1762 Spain declares war on Portugal

Statue of José I

1775 Machado de Castro's statue of José I unveiled as centerpiece of reconstructed Lisbon

1789 Portuguese suppress Brazilian independence movement in Minas Gerais

1799 Maria I's son João named Regent

1807 The French, under Junot, invade Portugal; royal family flees to Brazil

Reform and Revolution

Portugal suffered many depredations during the upheavals of the Peninsular War, and after the loss of Brazil. A period of chaos culminated, in 1832, in civil war between the Liberal Pedro IV and the Absolutist Miguel: the War of the Two Brothers. Though the Liberals won, later governments were often reactionary. The second half of the century saw a period of stability and industrial growth, but attempts at expansion in Africa failed. By 1910, discontent with the constitutional monarchy was such that a Republican uprising forced King Manuel II into exile.

1820 Revolution
The revolution led to the royal family's return from Brazil and a new Liberal constitution. This proved unworkable and was revoked following an army coup in 1823.

Zé Povinho
This long-suffering, Everyman figure first appeared in 1875, created by artist and potter Rafael Bordalo Pinheiro. He expressed the concerns of the average Portuguese working man.

Republican ships shell the king's palace in Lisbon.

Personification of Portuguese Republic

Priests are led away by Republican soldiers.

Peninsular War (1808–14)
Napoleon tried twice to invade Portugal but was repulsed by an Anglo-Portuguese force led by Wellington. A key victory for the allies came at Buçaco (see pp210–11) in 1810.

THE BIRTH OF THE REPUBLIC

Republicanism spread among the middle classes and the army via a secret society called the Carbonária. The revolution took place in Lisbon in October 1910 and lasted less than five days. This contemporary poster celebrates the main events.

TIMELINE

1809–20 Regency dominated by Viscount Beresford, English commander of Portuguese army

1822 Radical new constitution. Brazil becomes independent under João VI's son Pedro

Teatro Nacional Dona Maria II

1853 First Portuguese postage stamps issued

1856 Opening of first railroad from Lisbon to Carregado

1810

1830

1850

1826 Moderate charter introduced by Pedro IV, who then abdicates in favor of his young daughter Maria

1810 Battle of Buçaco

1828 Miguel, who is betrothed to his niece Maria, is crowned king

1842 Founding of National Theater

1834 Monasteries dissolved

1832–4 War of the Two Brothers; defeat of Absolutist Miguel

1851–80 The Regeneration: period of industrial development

5 Reis stamp

The Drunkards by José Malhôa *Malhôa (1855– 1933) created a virtual social history of the period in genre paintings like this one, showing a group of peasants sampling new wine.*

King Manuel II flees to England from Ericeira aboard the royal yacht.

Portugal and Africa *Captain Serpa Pinto's crossing of southern Africa in 1879 led to a plan to form a Portuguese colony from coast to coast.*

Republican troops set up barricades at key points in Lisbon. They meet with little opposition.

Leading figures of the Republican party

Eça de Queirós *The great novelist (1845– 1900) painted a scathing picture of the Portuguese bourgeoisie. He spent many years abroad as a diplomat.*

WHERE TO SEE 19TH-CENTURY PORTUGAL

Neo-Classicism, which dominated the early part of the century, can be seen in Lisbon's Palácio da Ajuda *(see p111)*. More Romantic historical styles emerged later in the century, ranging from the fantastical Neo-Gothic of the Palácio da Pena *(pp160–61)* in Sintra to the subtle Orientalism of Monserrate *(p155)*. Notable stations associated with the spread of Portugal's railroads include Lisbon's Rossio and São Bento in Oporto *(p239)*.

***Rossio station** (p82) in Lisbon has a striking façade in Neo-Manueline style by José Luís Monteiro. Completed in 1887, the station contains one of the first iron vaults in Portugal.*

***Ponte de Dom Luís I** (p242) in Oporto dates from 1886. Its two-tier design by Teófilo Seyrig was inspired by the nearby railroad bridge built by Gustave Eiffel.*

1865–8 Coalition of two main parties	**1888** Publication of *Os Maias* by Eça de Queirós, a satirical examination of Portuguese lethargy	*Manuel II*	**1910** Revolution: Manuel II abdicates and flees into exile
1869 Slave trade abolished in all Portuguese territories			
1870		**1890**	**1910**
1861–89 Reign of moderate Luís I	**1886** Building of Ponte de Dom Luís I in Oporto	**1908** Carlos I and his heir, Luís, assassinated by Republicans	
1877 Serpa Pinto sets out from Benguela in Angola to cross southern Africa		**1890** Plan to link African colonies of Mozambique and Angola is thwarted by ultimatum from the British	

Modern Portugal

Modern tiles decorating a Lisbon metro station

THE EARLY YEARS of the new Republic were marked by political and economic crisis, until a military coup in 1926 paved the way for the New State of 1933. Under the oppressive regime of Prime Minister António Salazar, the country was freed of its debts, but suffered poverty and unemployment. Portugal's reliance on its African colonies led to costly wars, unrest in the army, and the overthrow of the government in 1974. The painful return to democracy was rewarded by admission to the European Community in 1986.

1935 Death of poet Fernando Pessoa, who wrote under four different names in four distinct styles. This portrait by José de Almada Negreiros is in Lisbon's Centro de Arte Moderna *(see p120)*

1922 First flight across the South Atlantic by Gago Coutinho and Sacadura Cabral

1949 Portugal signs the North Atlantic Treaty and becomes a founder member of NATO

1933 Founding of the *Estado Novo* (New State), harsh dictatorship led by Salazar. Government bans all strikes and censors the press, crushing opposition through brutal secret police force, the PIDE

1911 Women given the vote

1910	1920	1930	1940	1950

1910	1920	1930	1940	1950

1916 Portugal enters World War I on side of the British and French

1918 Assassination of President Sidónio Pais; postwar years are period of social unrest with frequent strikes and changes of government

1928 António Salazar made finance minister; he imposes austerity measures, balancing the budget by 1929. In 1932 he becomes prime minister

1949 Neurosurgeon António Egas Moniz wins Nobel Prize for Medicine for his work developing the prefrontal lobotomy

1917 Three peasant children in Fátima claim to see Virgin Mary; site of vision becomes focus of major pilgrimage

1926 Coup puts military in charge of Republic; General Carmona is new president, holding office until his death in 1951

1942 Salazar meets Spanish dictator Franco to confirm mutual policy of nonaggression

1939–45 In World War II Portugal is theoretically neutral but, after threats to her shipping, is forced to sell minerals to Germany. From 1943 Portugal permits British and American bases in the Azores. Here Salazar *(center)* talks to troops stationed there

1966 Opening of Ponte Salazar (now Ponte 25 de Abril) across the Tagus (see p114)

1986 Portugal joins European Community. Soares becomes the first civilian president of Portugal in 60 years

1997 Lisbon prepares for Expo '98; the mascot Gil embodies the theme of water and the oceans

1966 National soccer team with brilliant Eusébio (center, kneeling) reach quarterfinals of World Cup

1985 Social Democrats under Aníbal Cavaco Silva come to power

1955 Armenian oil magnate Calouste Gulbenkian dies leaving 2,355 million escudos ($275 million) to set up a foundation for the arts and education

1974 Carnation Revolution: in a near bloodless coup, Marcelo Caetano's regime is overthrown by the MFA (Armed Forces Movement), a group of discontented left-wing army officers

1995 António Guterres of the Socialist Party elected prime minister

1960	1970	1980	1990

1960	1970	1980	1990

1961 India annexes Portuguese colonies of Goa, Damão, and Diu

1968 Salazar retires after stroke and is succeeded by the more moderate Caetano

1976 In the first free elections for nearly 50 years, the Socialist Mário Soares becomes prime minister

1988 Rosa Mota (center) wins women's marathon at the Olympic Games in Seoul

1958 In the presidential elections, the opposition candidate General Delgado wins so much support that the result is rigged against him. He is later assassinated

1975 All of Portugal's remaining colonies except Macau are granted independence, putting an end to long, unwinnable wars in Africa. Troops, such as these on patrol in the Angolan bush, are hastily brought home

THE CARNATION REVOLUTION

The revolution of April 25, 1974 gained its popular name when people began placing red carnations in the barrels of soldiers' guns. Led by army officers disaffected by the colonial wars in Africa, the revolution heralded a period of great celebration, as Portugal emerged from decades of insularity. The political situation, however, was chaotic: the new government pushed through a controversial program of nationalization and land reform in favor of the peasants, but in November 1975 the left-wing radicals were ousted by a short-lived countercoup.

GOLPE MILITAR
"MOVIMENTO DAS FORÇAS ARMADAS" DESENCADEIA ACÇÃO DE MADRUGADA

Newspaper headline announcing revolution

LISBON

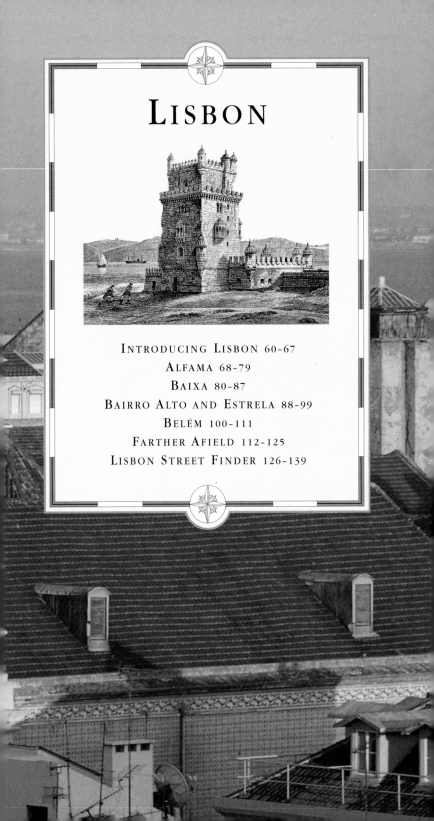

Lisbon at a Glance

Pᴏʀᴛᴜɢᴀʟ's ᴄᴀᴘɪᴛᴀʟ sits on the north bank of the Tagus estuary, 17 km (10 miles) from the Atlantic. The city has a population of about 700,000, but the conurbation of "Grande Lisboa," which has engulfed many surrounding villages, has over one million people. Razed to the ground by the earthquake of 1755 *(see pp62–3)*, the city center is essentially 18th century, with carefully planned, elegant streets in the Baixa. On the hills on either side of the center, the narrow streets of the Alfama and Bairro Alto make it a personal, approachable city. Since its days of glory during the Age of Discovery, when the city was at the forefront of world trade, Lisbon has been an important port. Although the docks have been moved, the great monuments in Belém still bear witness to the city's maritime past.

The Museu Nacional de Arte Antiga *houses paintings, decorative art, and sculpture. Of particular interest are the Flemish-influenced Portuguese paintings such as this* Apparition of Christ to the Virgin *by Jorge Afonso (see pp96–7).*

The Mosteiro dos Jerónimos *is a magnificent 16th-century monastery. Commissioned by Manuel I, much of it is built in the peculiarly Portuguese style of architecture known as Manueline. The extravagantly sculpted south portal of the church, designed by João de Castilho in 1516, is one of the finest expressions of the style (see pp106–7).*

BELÉM
(See pp100–111)

The Torre de Belém *was a beacon for navigators returning from the Indies and the New World, and a symbol of Portuguese naval power (see p110).*

◁ **Twin Romanesque towers of the Sé rising over the rooftops of the Baixa**

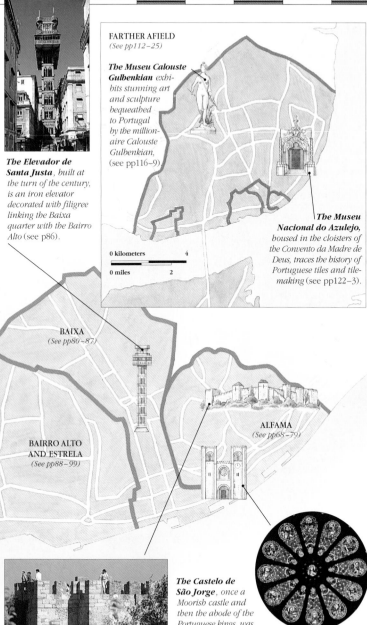

The Elevador de Santa Justa, built at the turn of the century, is an iron elevator decorated with filigree linking the Baixa quarter with the Bairro Alto (see p86).

FARTHER AFIELD
(See pp112–25)

The Museu Calouste Gulbenkian exhibits stunning art and sculpture bequeathed to Portugal by the millionaire Calouste Gulbenkian, (see pp116–9).

The Museu Nacional do Azulejo, housed in the cloisters of the Convento da Madre de Deus, traces the history of Portuguese tiles and tilemaking (see pp122–3).

0 kilometers 4
0 miles 2

BAIXA
(See pp80–87)

BAIRRO ALTO AND ESTRELA
(See pp88–99)

ALFAMA
(See pp68–79)

The Castelo de São Jorge, once a Moorish castle and then the abode of the Portuguese kings, was transformed in the 1930s into tranquil public gardens. The battlements offer spectacular views of the city (see pp78–9).

The Sé, Lisbon's greatly restored cathedral, is a sturdy Romanesque building lit by a beautiful rose window. The relics of St. Vincent, the city's patron saint, are among the religious objects on display in the treasury (see p74).

0 meters 500
0 yards 500

The 1755 Lisbon Earthquake

Votive tile panel offered by survivors

T HE FIRST TREMOR of the devastating earthquake was felt at 9:30am on November 1. A few minutes later there was a second, far more violent shock, reducing over half the city to rubble. Although the epicenter was close to the Algarve, Lisbon, as the most populated area, bore the worst. Over 20 churches collapsed, crushing the crowds who had assembled for All Saints' Day. A third shock was followed by fires that quickly spread. An hour later, huge waves came rolling in from the Tagus and flooded the lower part of the city. Most of Portugal suffered damage, and the shock was felt as far away as Italy. As many as 15,000 people lost their lives in Lisbon alone.

This anonymous painting of the arrival of a papal ambassador at court in 1693 shows how Terreiro do Paço looked before the earthquake.

Some buildings that might have survived an earthquake alone were destroyed by the fire that followed.

The old royal palace, the 16th-century Paço da Ribeira, was utterly ruined by the earthquake and ensuing flood.

The royal family was staying at the palace in Belém, a place far less affected than Lisbon, and survived the disaster unscathed. Here the king surveys the city's devastation.

Ships crammed full of people fleeing the fire were wrecked and anchors thrown up to water level.

This detail is from a votive painting dedicated to Nossa Senhora da Estrela, given by a grateful father in thanks for the sparing of his daughter's life in the earthquake. The girl was found miraculously alive after being buried under rubble for seven hours.

THE RECONSTRUCTION OF LISBON

Marquês de Pombal (1699–1782)

No sooner had the tremors abated than Sebastião José de Carvalho e Melo, chief minister to José I and later to become Marquês de Pombal, was outlining ideas for rebuilding the city. While philosophers moralized, Pombal reacted with practicality. "Bury the dead and feed the living" was his initial response. He restored order, then began a progressive city-planning program. His efficient handling of the crisis gained him almost total political control.

REACTIONS TO THE DISASTER

French author Voltaire

The earthquake had a profound effect on European thought. Eyewitness accounts appeared in the papers, many written by foreigners living in Lisbon. A heated debate developed over whether the earthquake was a natural phenomenon or divine wrath. Pre-earthquake Lisbon had been a flourishing city, famed for its wealth – also for its Inquisition and idolatry. Interpreting the quake as punishment, preachers prophesied further catastrophes. Famous literary figures debated the significance of the event, among them the French writer Voltaire, who wrote a poem about the disaster, propounding his views that evil exists and man is weak and powerless, doomed to an unhappy fate on earth.

The ancient castle walls succumbed to the reverberating shock waves.

Flames erupted as the candles lit for All Saints' Day ignited the city's churches. The fire raged for seven days.

Some of Lisbon's finest buildings were destroyed, along with gold, jewelry, priceless furniture, archives, books, and paintings.

At 11am, tidal waves rolled into Terreiro do Paço. The Alcântara docks, to the west, bore the brunt of the impact.

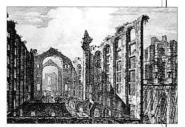

Churches, homes, and public buildings all suffered in the disaster. The Royal Opera House, here shown in ruins, had been completed in March the same year.

A CONTEMPORARY VIEW OF THE EARTHQUAKE

This anonymous German engraving of 1775 gives a vivid picture of the scale of the disaster. Many who fled the flames made for the Tagus but were washed away in the huge waves that struck the Terreiro do Paço. The human and material losses were incalculable.

The reconstruction of the center of Lisbon took place rapidly. By the end of November the Marquês de Pombal had devised a strikingly modern plan for a grid of parallel streets running from the waterfront to Rossio. The new buildings are shown in yellow.

Modern-day Lisbon holds many reminders of the earthquake. Pombal's innovative grid system is clearly visible in this aerial view of the Baixa (see pp80 – 87). The plan took many years to complete, and the triumphal arch spanning Rua Augusta was not finished until over a century later, in 1873.

ENTERTAINMENT IN LISBON

THOUGH QUITE SMALL compared to other European capitals, Lisbon boasts an outstanding cultural calendar. Chosen as Cultural Capital of Europe 1994, the city hosts both modern and traditional events from classical music, ballet, and opera to street festivals, fairs, and bullfights. Pop and rock concerts are held all year round and traditional *fado (see pp66–7)* is widely performed. Soccer fans can spend an afternoon watching Benfica or Sporting. The city also offers excellent late-night entertainment, focused on lively, fashionable clubs and bars along the waterfront and in the Bairro Alto.

BOOKING TICKETS

TICKETS CAN BE reserved by phoning the Agência de Bilhetes para Espectáculos Públicos (**ABEP**). Pay in cash when you pick them up from the kiosk. Movies and theaters will not take phone or credit card bookings – only the major cultural centers do.

ABEP kiosk selling tickets on Praça dos Restauradores

LISTINGS MAGAZINES

PREVIEWS of forthcoming events and listings of bars and clubs appear in several magazines in Lisbon. English-language publications offered include the monthly *What's On* and *LISBOAem*, which are available free from tourist offices. Also available free, but in Portuguese, is the monthly *Agenda Cultural.*

FILM AND THEATER

MOVIE-GOERS are extremely well served in Lisbon. Movies are shown in their original language with subtitles in Portuguese, and tickets are inexpensive. There are plenty of movies to choose from, and the futuristic **Amoreiras Shopping Center** *(see p114)* has a multiplex center with ten screens showing all the latest Hollywood releases. Cult movies and international art-house films can be seen at the Cinemateca Portuguesa, which has a comprehensive monthly film calendar. Copies are available at the box office or tourist office. Most theaters offer reductions on Mondays.

Theater lovers can enjoy performances of Portuguese and foreign language plays at the **Teatro Nacional Dona Maria II**. For a slightly less formal but most entertaining show try **Chapitô** in the Alfama quarter, an arts center with splendid river views, which stages open-air performances.

CLASSICAL MUSIC, OPERA, AND DANCE

LISBON'S TOP CULTURAL centers are the modern **Centro Cultural de Belém** *(see p108)* and the **Fundação Calouste Gulbenkian** *(see pp116–19)*. They host a variety of national and international events including concerts, ballet, and opera. A calendar of events for each venue is available from the box office or the tourist office. Operas and classical concerts also take place at the **Teatro Nacional de São Carlos** *(see p93)* and the **Coliseu dos Recreios**.

Clowns performing at Chapitô, Alfama's informal arts center

WORLD MUSIC, JAZZ, FOLK, AND ROCK

THOUGH LISBON'S musical soul is *fado*, the city also swings to a variety of sounds from the rhythms of Africa and South America through contemporary jazz to heavy rock. For Brazilian music, try **Bar Pintaí** or **Pé Sujo**, and **B. Leza** and **Ritz Clube** are popular for African music.

Every summer the Fundação Calouste Gulbenkian puts on the International Jazz Festival. The **Hot Clube** is a favorite

The house orchestra playing at the Fundação Calouste Gulbenkian

Brazilian musician at Pé Sujo

jazz spot on a smaller scale, and it also plays host to a variety of popular folk singers and bands, such as Fausto and Sérgio Godinho.

Top pop and rock bands mostly play stadium concerts but some international bands appear at the Coliseu dos Recreios. Live rock is offered at bars such as **Johnny Guitar** and **Anos Sessenta**.

BARS AND CLUBS

FOR NIGHT-TIME DRINKING the most fashionable bars and clubs are concentrated in two areas: the traditional night-spot of Bairro Alto and the riverside Avenida 24 de Julho. Bairro Alto has a range of popular and fashionable bars and discotheques, including **Portas Largas**, **Três Pastorinhos**, and the hip boogie club **Frágil**. For a quieter, more restrained atmosphere, try the eccentrically decorated **Pavilhão Chinês**.

Avenida 24 de Julho is Lisbon's fastest-growing after-hours destination, with larger bars and nightclubs in converted warehouses and other attractive riverside buildings. The young and chic frequent fashionable **Kapital**, a night-club on three floors with a rooftop veranda. Next door, **Kremlin** is a lively haunt for fans of techno music.

Below Ponte 25 de Abril lies an array of terraced river-side cafés, known as the Docas (docks), which provide an ideal spot for an early-evening drink.

SPORTS

MOST SPORTS take place outside the city, but Lisbon has two soccer teams, Benfica and Sporting. One or the other plays at home almost every Sunday, Benfica at **Estádio da Luz** and Sporting at **Estádio José Alvalade**.

Bullfights are held from April to October in Lisbon's Campo Pequeno *(see p120)*. Ticket prices vary depending on whether you sit in *sol* or *sombra* (sun or shade).

DIRECTORY

BOOKING TICKETS

ABEP
Praça dos Restauradores.
Map 7 A2.
21-347 58 24.

FILM AND THEATER

Amoreiras Shopping Center
Avenida Engenheiro Duarte Pacheco.
Map 5 A5.
21-381 02 00.

Chapitô
Costa do Castelo 1–7.
Map 7 C3.
21-886 14 10.

Cinemateca Portuguesa
Rua Barata Salgueiro 39.
Map 5 C5.
21-354 62 79.

Teatro Nacional Dona Maria II
Praça Dom Pedro IV.
Map 7 B3.
21-342 84 49.

CLASSICAL MUSIC, OPERA, AND DANCE

Centro Cultural de Belém
Praça do Império.
Map 1 C5.
21-361 24 44.

Coliseu dos Recreios
Rua das Portas de Santo Antão 96.
Map 7 A2.
21-324 05 80.

Fundação Calouste Gulbenkian
Avenida de Berna 45.
Map 5 B2.
21-796 63 06 (tickets).

Teatro Nacional de São Carlos
Rua Serpa Pinto 9.
Map 7 A4.
21-346 59 14.

WORLD MUSIC, JAZZ, FOLK, AND ROCK

Anos Sessenta
Largo do Terreirinho 21.
Map 7 C2.
21-887 34 44.

B. Leza
Largo do Conde Barão 50.
Map 4 E3.
21-396 37 35.

Bar Pintaí
Largo da Trindade 22–3.
Map 7 A3.
21-342 48 02.

Hot Clube
Praça da Alegria 39.
Map 4 F1.
21-346 73 69.

Johnny Guitar
Calçada Marquês de Abrantes 72.
Map 4 E3.
21-396 04 15.

Pé Sujo
Largo de S. Martinho 6–7.
Map 8 D4.
21-797 89 24.

Ritz Clube
Rua da Glória 57.
Map 4 F1.
21-342 51 40.

BARS AND CLUBS

Frágil
Rua da Atalaia 128.
Map 4 F2.
21-346 95 78.

Kapital
Avenida 24 de Julho 68.
Map 4 E3.
21-395 59 63.

Kremlin
Escadinhas da Praia 5.
Map 4 D3.
21-390 87 68.

Pavilhão Chinês
Rua Dom Pedro V 89.
Map 4 F2.
21-342 47 29.

Portas Largas
Rua da Atalaia 105.
Map 4 F2.
21-346 63 79.

Três Pastorinhos
Rua da Barroca 111.
Map 4 F2.
21-346 43 01.

SPORTS

Estádio José Alvalade
Alameda das Linhas de Torres.
21-759 94 59.

Estádio da Luz
Avenida General Norton Matos.
21-726 61 29.

Fado: the Music of Lisbon

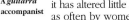

L IKE THE BLUES, *fado* is an expression of
longing and sorrow. Literally meaning
"fate," the term may be applied to an
individual song as well as the genre
itself. The music owes much to the
concept known as *saudade*, meaning
a longing both for what has been lost
and for what has never been attained,
which perhaps accounts for its emotional
power. The people of Lisbon have nurtured
this poignant music in back-street cafés
and restaurants for over 150 years, and
it has altered little in that time. It is sung
as often by women as men,
always accompanied by the *guitarra*
and *viola* (acoustic guitar). *Fado* from
Coimbra has developed its own
distinctive, light-hearted style.

A *guitarra*
accompanist

**A graphic depiction of the music's
low-life associations from the 1920s**

Argentina Santos is perhaps the
leading traditional singer of today.
All female *fadistas* wear a black
shawl in memory of Maria Severa.

The *guitarrista* plays
the melody and will
occasionally perform a
solo instrumental piece.

*Maria Severa (1810–36) was the
first great* fadista *and the subject
of the first Portuguese sound movie
in 1931. Her scandalous life and
early death are pivotal to* fado *history, and her spiritual influence
has been enormous, inspiring*
fados, *poems, novels, and plays.*

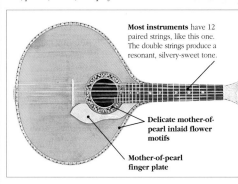

Most instruments have 12
paired strings, like this one.
The double strings produce a
resonant, silvery-sweet tone.

**Delicate mother-of-
pearl inlaid flower
motifs**

**Mother-of-pearl
finger plate**

THE GUITARRA

Unique to Portuguese culture, the
guitarra is a flat-backed instrument shaped like a mandolin, with
eight, ten, or twelve strings,
arranged in pairs. It has
evolved from a simple
19th-century design into
a finely decorated piece,
sometimes inlaid with mother-of-
pearl. The sound of the *guitarra*
is an essential ingredient of a good
fado, echoing and enhancing the
singer's melody line.

Alfredo Duarte (1891–1982) was a renowned writer of fado *lyrics dealing with love, death, longing, tragedy, and triumph. Affectionately known as O Marceneiro (the master carpenter) because of his skill as a joiner, he is still revered and his work widely performed.*

All kinds of themes may occur in fado. *This song of 1910, for example, celebrates the dawning of the liberal republic. Such songsheets remained a favored means of dissemination, even after the first records were made in 1904.*

A cultural icon for the Portuguese, Amália Rodrigues (born 1921) has been the leading exponent of fado *for over 50 years. She crystalized the music's style in the postwar years and made it known around the world.*

The *viola* provides rhythm accompaniment, but the player will never perform a solo.

The music has long inspired great writers and painters. O Fado *(1910) by José Malhôa (see p55) shows it in an intimate setting with the* fadista *captivating his listener. The air of abandonment underlines the earthiness of many of the songs.*

THE FADO HOUSE

Lisbon's best *fado* houses, such as the famous Parreirinha de Alfama, which belongs to Argentina Santos *(shown above)*, are run by the *fadistas* themselves for love of the music, not as a tourist attraction. They continue the tradition that began originally in the Alfama, whereby cafés and restaurants gave the music of the people a home. Such authentic venues still provide a good meal and a sense of history as well as entertainment. The oldest is Luso, which has been in existence since the 1930s.

WHERE TO ENJOY FADO IN LISBON

Any of these establishments will offer you the essential ingredients of Lisbon's nightlife: good food, wine, and music to stir the emotions.

Adega Machado
Rua do Norte 91.
Map 7 A3. (*21-342 87 13.*

Lisboa à Noite
Rua das Gáveas 69.
Map 7 A3. (*21-346 26 03.*

Luso
Travessa da Queimada 10.
Map 7 A3. (*21-342 22 81.*

Parreirinha de Alfama
Beco do Espírito Santo 1.
Map 7 E4. (*21-886 82 09.*

Senhor Vinho
Rua do Meio à Lapa 18.
Map 4 D3. (*21-397 26 81.*

A Severa
Rua das Gáveas 51.
Map 7 A4. (*21-342 83 14.*

ALFAMA

IT IS DIFFICULT TO BELIEVE that this humble neighborhood was once the most desirable quarter of Lisbon. For the Moors, the tightly packed alleyways around the fortified castle comprised the whole city. The seeds of decline were sown in the Middle Ages when wealthy residents moved west for fear of earthquakes, leaving the quarter to fishermen and paupers. The buildings survived the 1755 earthquake *(see pp62–3)*, and, although there are no Moorish houses still standing, the quarter retains its Casbah-like layout. Compact houses line steep streets and stairways, their façades strung with washing.

Portugal's coat of arms in the treasury of the Sé

Long overdue restoration is under way in the most dilapidated areas, but daily life still revolves around local grocery stores and small, cellarlike tavernas.

Above the Alfama, the imposing Castelo de São Jorge crowns Lisbon's eastern hill. This natural vantage point, a defensive stronghold and royal palace until the 16th century, is today a popular promenade, with spectacular views from its greatly restored ramparts.

West of the Alfama stand the proud twin towers of the Sé. To the northeast, the domed church of Santa Engrácia and the white façade of São Vicente de Fora dominate the skyline.

SIGHTS AT A GLANCE

Museums and Galleries
Museu de Artes
  Decorativas **2**
Museu Nacional da
  Marioneta **11**
Museu Militar **6**

Historic Buildings
Casa dos Bicos **7**
Castelo de São Jorge pp78–9 **10**

Churches
Santo António à Sé **9**
Santa Engrácia **5**
São Vicente de Fora **3**
Sé **8**

Belvederes
Miradouro da Graça **12**
Miradouro de Santa Luzia **1**

Markets
Feira da Ladra **4**

GETTING THERE

The 12 and 28 trolleys rattle up the narrow streets of the Alfama from the Baixa. Bus 37 does a circuit from the Castle to Rossio. Many buses run east along Avenida Dom Infante Henrique to Santa Apolónia station and west to Belém.

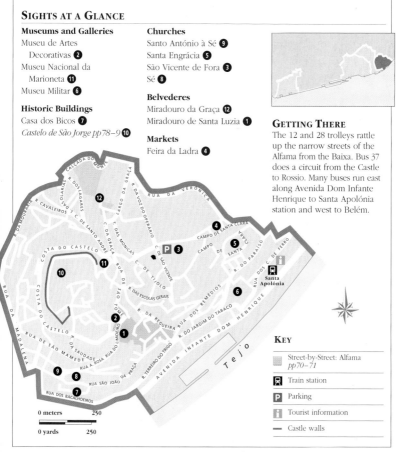

KEY

Street-by-Street: Alfama *pp70–71*

Train station

Parking

Tourist information

Castle walls

0 meters   250
0 yards   250

◁ **Ironwork balconies on a house in Rua dos Bacalhoeiros, beside the Casa dos Bicos**

Street-by-Street: Alfama

A FASCINATING QUARTER at any time of day, the Alfama comes to life in the late afternoon and early evening when the locals emerge from their doorways, and the small tavernas start to fill. Many African immigrants live here, and several places play music from Mozambique and the Cape Verde Islands. Given the steep streets of the quarter, the least strenuous approach is to start at the top and work your way down. A walk around the maze of alleyways will reveal picturesque corners and crumbling churches as well as panoramic views from the shady terraces, such as the Miradouro de Santa Luzia.

On Largo das Portas do Sol, café tables look out over the Alfama toward the Tagus estuary. Portas do Sol was one of the entrance gates to the old city.

The church of Santa Luzia has 18th-century blue and white *azulejo* panels on its south wall.

A modern statue of St. Vincent holding the emblem of Lisbon, a boat with two ravens *(see p74)*, stands in Largo das Portas do Sol.

L. DAS PORTAS DO SOL

BECO DE SANTA HELENA

R. DO C

Castelo de São Jorge

R U A N. DE ARAÚJO

★ Museu de Artes Decorativas
Set up as a museum by the banker Ricardo do Espírito Santo Silva, the 17th-century Palácio Azurara houses fine 17th- and 18th-century Portuguese furniture and decorative arts ❷

KEY
− − − Suggested route

0 meters   25

0 yards   25

★ Miradouro de Santa Luzia
The view from this bougainvillea-clad terrace spans the tiled roofs of the Alfama toward the Tagus. This is a pleasant place to rest after a walk around the area's steep streets ❶

STAR SIGHTS

★ Miradouro de
 Santa Luzia

★ Museu de Artes
 Decorativas

Beco dos Cruzes, like most of the alleyways *(becos)* that snake their way through the Alfama, is a steep cobbled street. Locals often hang washing between the tightly packed houses.

LOCATOR MAP
See Lisbon Street Finder map 8

Rua de São Pedro is the scene of a lively early-morning fish market where the *varinas* sell the catch of the day. *Peixe espada* (scabbard fish) is one of the fish sold here.

Largo do Chafariz de Dentro is named after the 17th-century fountain *(chafariz)* that was originally placed within *(dentro)* rather than outside the 14th-century walls.

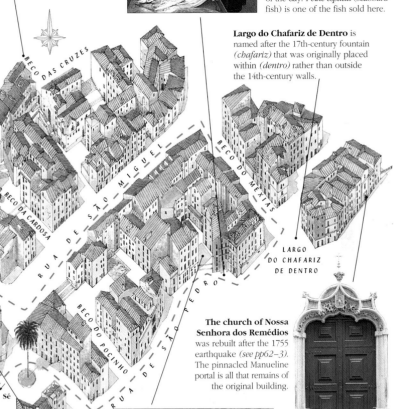

The church of Nossa Senhora dos Remédios was rebuilt after the 1755 earthquake (*see pp62–3*). The pinnacled Manueline portal is all that remains of the original building.

São Miguel was rebuilt after it was damaged in the 1755 earthquake. It retains a few earlier features, including a fine ceiling of Brazilian jacaranda wood.

Popular restaurants hidden in the labyrinth of alleyways spill out onto open-air patios. The *Lautasco* (*see p404*), in Beco do Azinhal, serves excellent Portuguese food.

Tile panel showing pre-earthquake Praça do Comércio, Santa Luzia

Miradouro de Santa Luzia ❶

Rua do Limoeiro. **Map** 8 D4. 🚌 28.

THE TERRACE by the church of Santa Luzia provides a sweeping view over the Alfama and the River Tagus. Distinctive landmarks, from left to right, are the cupola of Santa Engrácia, the church of Santo Estêvão, and the two startling white towers of São Miguel. While tourists admire the views, old men play cards under the bougainvillea-clad pergola. The south wall of Santa Luzia has two modern tiled panels, one of Praça do Comércio before it was flattened by the earthquake, the other showing the Christians attacking the Castelo de São Jorge *(see pp78–9)* in 1147.

Museu de Artes Decorativas ❷

Largo das Portas do Sol 2. **Map** 8 D3. 🛈 21-886 21 83. 🚃 37. 🚌 12, 28. 🕙 10am–5pm Tue–Sun. 🌑 Jan 1, Easter, May 1, Dec 25. 🎟️ 👍

ALSO KNOWN AS the Ricardo do Espírito Santo Silva Foundation, the museum was set up in 1953 to preserve the traditions and increase public awareness of the Portuguese decorative arts. The foundation was named after a banker who bought the 17th-century Palácio Azurara in 1947 to house his fine collection of furniture, textiles, silver, and ceramics. Among the 17th- and 18th-century antiques displayed in this handsome four-story mansion are many fine pieces in exotic woods, including an 18th-century rosewood back-gammon and chess table. Also of note are the collections of 18th-century silver and Chinese porcelain, and the Arraiolos carpets *(see p301)*. The spacious rooms still retain some original ceilings and *azulejo* panels.

18th-century china cutlery case, Museu de Artes Decorativas

Workshops are housed in the adjoining building, where visitors can watch artisans preserving the techniques of cabinet-making, gilding, book-binding, and other traditional crafts. Temporary exhibitions, lectures, and concerts are also held in the palace.

Stone figure of a woman praying by the tomb of Carlos I in São Vicente de Fora

São Vicente de Fora ❸

Largo de São Vicente. **Map** 8 E3. 🛈 21-882 44 00. 🚃 28. 🕙 9am–12:30pm, 3–6pm Tue–Fri, 9am–12:30pm, 3–7pm Sat, 9am–12:30pm, 3–5pm Sun. 🎟️ 📷 🎥 to cloisters.

ST. VINCENT was proclaimed Lisbon's patron saint in 1173, when his relics, now in the Sé *(see p74)*, were transferred from the Algarve *(see p319)* to a church on this site outside *(fora)* the city walls. Designed by Italian architect Filippo Terzi, and completed in 1627, the off-white Italianate façade is sober and symmetrical, with towers on either side and statues of saints Vincent, Augustine, and Sebastian over the entrance. Inside, one is drawn immediately to Machado de Castro's Baroque canopy over the altar, flanked by life-size wooden statues.

The adjoining former Augustinian monastery, reached via the nave, retains its 16th-century cistern and vestiges of the former cloister but is visited for its 18th-century *azulejos*. Among the panels in the entrance hall off the first cloister there are lively, but historically inaccurate, tile scenes of Afonso Henriques attacking Lisbon and Santarém. Around the cloisters the tiled rural scenes, surrounded by floral designs and cherubs, illustrate the fables of La Fontaine. A passageway leads behind the church to the old refectory, transformed into the Bragança Pantheon in 1885. The stone sarcophagi of almost every king and queen are here, from the first of that dynasty, João IV, who died in 1656, to Manuel II, last king of Portugal. Only Maria I and Pedro IV are not buried here. A stone mourner kneels at the tomb of Carlos I and his son Luís Felipe, assassinated in Praça do Comércio in 1908.

Feira da Ladra ❹

Campo de Santa Clara. **Map** 8 F2.
🚻 7:30am–1pm Tue & Sat. 🚌 28.

THE STALLS of the so-called "Thieves' Market" have occupied this site on the edge of the Alfama for over a century, laid out under the shade of trees or canopies. As the fame of this flea market has grown, bargains are increasingly hard to find among the mass of bric-a-brac, but a few of the vendors have interesting wrought-iron work, prints, and tiles, as well as second-hand clothes. The influence of the African colonies can be seen in some of the stalls selling statuary, masks, and jewelry. Fish, vegetables, and herbs are sold in the nearby wrought-iron marketplace.

Bric-a-brac for sale in the Feira da Ladra

Santa Engrácia ❺

Campo de Santa Clara. **Map** 8 F2.
📞 21-888 15 29. 🚌 28. 🚻 10am–5pm Tue–Sun. ⊘ Jan 1, Easter, May 1, Dec 25. 🎟 📷 ♿

ONE OF LISBON'S most striking landmarks, the soaring dome of Santa Engrácia punctuates the skyline in the east of the city. The original church collapsed in a storm in 1681. The first stone of the new Baroque monument, laid in 1682, marked the beginning of a 284-year saga, which led to the invention of a saying that a Santa Engrácia job was never done. The church was not completed until 1966.

The interior, paved with colored marble and crowned by a giant cupola, emanates a feeling of space. As the National Pantheon, it houses cenotaphs of heroes of Portuguese history, such as Vasco da Gama (see p108) and Afonso de Albuquerque, Viceroy of India (1502–15) on the left, and on the right Henry the Navigator (see p49) and Luís Vaz de Camões (see p188). You can ask to take the elevator up to the dome and enjoy a 360-degree panorama of the city.

Museu Militar ❻

Largo do Museu da Artilharia. **Map** 8 F3. 📞 21-888 21 31. 🚌 12, 46, 107. 🚌 28. 🚻 10am–5pm Tue–Sun. ⊘ public hols. 🎟

APTLY LOCATED on the site of a 16th-century cannon foundry and arms depot, the military museum contains an extensive display of arms, uniforms, and historical military documents. Visits begin in the Vasco da Gama Room with a collection of old cannons and modern murals depicting the discovery of the sea route to India. The Salas da Grande Guerra, on the first floor, display World War I related exhibits. Other rooms are devoted to the evolution of weapons in Portugal, from primitive flints through spears to rifles. The large courtyard, flanked by cannons, tells the story of Portugal in tiled panels, from the Christian Reconquest to World War I. The Portuguese artillery section in the oldest part of the museum displays the wagon used to transport the triumphal arch to Rua Augusta (see p87).

The multicolored marble interior beneath Santa Engrácia's dome

Casa dos Bicos ❼

Rua dos Bacalhoeiros. **Map** 8 D4. 📞 21-881 09 00. 🚌 1, 13, 46, 91. 🚻 for temporary exhibitions only.

THIS CONSPICUOUS house, faced with diamond-shaped stones (bicos), was built in 1523 for Brás de Albuquerque, illegitimate son of Afonso, Viceroy of India and conqueror of Goa and Malacca. The strange façade is an adaptation of a style popular in Mediterranean Europe during the 16th century. The two top stories, ruined in the earthquake of 1755, were only restored in the 1980s, recreating the original from old views of Lisbon in tile panels and engravings. In the interim the building was used for salting fish (Rua dos Bacalhoeiros means street of the cod fishermen). The modern interior of the lower floors is used as a site for temporary exhibitions.

The curiously faceted Casa dos Bicos and surrounding buildings

The façade of the Sé, the city's cathedral

Sé ●

Largo da Sé. **Map** 8 D4. **▸** *21-886 67 52.* **▬** *37.* **🚊** *28.* **◯** *9am–5pm daily.* **🚪** **📷** **Cloister & treasury** *10am–5pm Sat–Mon.* **📷**

I N 1150, THREE YEARS after Afonso Henriques recaptured Lisbon from the Moors, he built a cathedral for the first bishop of Lisbon, the English crusader Gilbert of Hastings, on the site of the old mosque. Sé is short for Sedes Episcopalis, the seat (or see) of a bishop. Devasted by three earth tremors in the 14th century, as well as the earthquake of 1755, and renovated over the centuries, the cathedral of today blends a variety of architectural styles. The façade, with two castellated bell towers and a splendid rose window, retains its solid Romanesque aspect. The gloomy interior, for the most part, is simple and austere, and hardly anything remains of the embellishment lavished upon it by King João V in the first half of the 18th century. Beyond the renovated Romanesque nave are the nine Gothic chapels of the ambulatory. The Capela de Santo Ildefonso contains the 14th-century sarcophagi of Lopo Fernandes Pacheco, companion in arms to King Afonso IV, and his wife, Maria Vilalobos. The bearded nobleman, sword in hand, and his wife, clutching a prayer book, are carved onto the tombs with their dogs sitting faithfully at their

Detail of the Baroque nativity scene by Joaquim Machado de Castro

feet. In the adjacent chancel are the tombs of Afonso IV and his wife, Dona Beatriz.

The Gothic **cloister**, reached via the third chapel in the ambulatory, has elegant double arches with some finely carved capitals. One of the chapels is still fitted with its 13th-century wrought-iron gate. Archaeological excavations in the cloister have unearthed various Roman and other remains.

To the left of the cathedral entrance the Franciscan chapel contains the font where the saint was baptized in 1195 and is decorated with a charming tiled scene of St. Antony preaching to the fishes. The adjacent chapel contains a Baroque nativity scene made of cork, wood, and terracotta by Machado de Castro (1766).

The **treasury** is at the top of the staircase on the

Carved tomb of the 14th-century nobleman Lopo Fernandes Pacheco in chapel in the ambulatory

right as you enter. It houses a varied collection of silver, statuary, ecclesiastical robes, illustrated manuscripts, and a selection of relics associated with St. Vincent. The cathedral's most prized possession is the casket containing the remains of the saint which were transferred to Lisbon from Cape St. Vincent in 1173 *(see p319)*. Legend has it that two sacred ravens kept a permanent vigil over the boat that transported the relics, and the raven, seen on the city's coat of arms, became the symbol of Lisbon's liberation from Muslim rule. The descendants of the two ravens used to live in the cloisters of the cathedral, but the last one died in 1978.

SANTO ANTÓNIO (c.1195–1231)

To the chagrin of the Lisboetas, their best-loved saint is known as St. Antony of Padua. Although born and brought up in Lisbon, he spent the last months of his life in Padua, Italy.

St. Antony joined the Franciscan Order in 1220, impressed by some crusading friars he had met at Coimbra where he was studying. The Franciscan friar was a learned and passionate preacher, renowned for his devotion to the poor and his ability to convert heretics. Many statues and paintings of St. Antony depict him carrying the Infant Jesus on a book, while others show him preaching to the fishes, as St. Francis preached to the birds. He is also often called upon to help find lost objects.

In 1934 Pope Pius XI declared St. Antony a patron saint of Portugal. The year 1995 saw the 800th anniversary of his birth – a cause for major celebrations throughout the city.

Santo António à Sé ⑨

Largo Santo António da Sé. **Map** 7 C4.
📞 21-886 91 45. 🚌 37. 🚋 28.
🕐 8am–7:30pm daily. 🔔 **Museu Antoniano** 📞 21-886 04 47.
🕐 10am–1pm, 2–6pm Tue–Sun. 🚫

THE POPULAR LITTLE church of Santo António allegedly stands on the site of the house in which St. Antony was born. The crypt, reached via the tiled sacristy on the left of the church, is all that remains of the original church destroyed by the earthquake of 1755. Work began on the new church in 1757 headed by Mateus Vicente, architect of the Basílica da Estrela (see p95) and was partially funded by donations collected by local children with the cry "a small coin for St. Antony." Even today the floor of the tiny chapel in the crypt is strewn with escudos, and the walls are scrawled with devotional messages from worshipers.

The church's façade blends the undulating curves of the Baroque style with Neo-Classical Ionic columns on either side of the main portal. Inside, on the way down to the crypt, a modern *azulejo* panel commemorates the visit of Pope John Paul II in 1982. In 1995 the church was given a facelift for the saint's eighth centenary. It is traditional for couples to visit the church on their wedding day and leave flowers for St. Antony, who is believed to bring good luck to new marriages.

Next door the small **Museu Antoniano** houses ex-votos, images, and manuscripts, all relating to St. Antony, as well

The Miradouro and Igreja da Graça seen from the Castelo de São Jorge

as gold and silverware, which used to decorate the church. The most charming exhibit is a 17th-century tiled panel of St. Antony preaching to the fishes.

Castelo de São Jorge ⑩

See pp78–9.

Museu Nacional da Marioneta ⑪

Largo Rodrigues de Freitas 19.
Map 8 D3. 📞 21-888 57 94. 🚌 37. 🚋 28.
🕐 10am–1pm, 2–7pm Tue–Sun. 🚫

A SCARY ENTRANCE takes you up to this small, eccentric puppet museum. The collection includes characters from 17th- and 18th-century opera and theater, among them knights, jesters, princesses, devils, and satirical figures. The puppets are finely crafted, but their gruesome, contorted features are unlikely to appeal to small children. The museum runs videos of puppet shows, and there are occasionally live performances on the small stage set.

Puppet, Museu Nacional da Marioneta

Miradouro da Graça ⑫

Map 8 D2. 🚌 37. 🚋 12, 28.

THE WORKING-CLASS quarter of Graça developed at the end of the 19th century. Today, it is visited chiefly for the views from its *miradouro* (belvedere). The panorama of rooftops and skyscrapers is less spectacular than the view from the castle, but it is a popular spot, particularly in the early evenings when couples sit at café tables under the pines. Behind the *miradouro* stands an Augustinian monastery, founded in 1271 and rebuilt after the earthquake. Once a flourishing complex, the huge building is now used as barracks but the church, the **Igreja da Graça**, can still be visited. Inside, in the right transept, is the *Senhor dos Passos*, a representation of Christ carrying the cross on the way to Calvary. This figure, clad in brilliant purple clothes, is carried on a procession through Graça on the second Sunday in Lent. The *azulejos* on the altar front, dating from the 17th century, imitate the brocaded textiles usually draped over the altar.

20th-century tiled panel recording Pope John Paul II's visit to Santo António à Sé

Castelo de São Jorge ⑩

Stone head of Martim Moniz

FOLLOWING THE RECAPTURE of Lisbon from the Moors in 1147, King Afonso Henriques transformed their hilltop citadel into the residence of the Portuguese kings. In 1511 Manuel I built a more lavish palace in what is now the Praça do Comércio and the castle was used variously as a theater, prison, and arms depot. After the 1755 earthquake the ramparts remained in ruins until 1938 when Salazar (see pp56–7) began a complete renovation, rebuilding the "medieval" walls and adding gardens and wildfowl. The castle may not be authentic but the gardens and the narrow streets of the Santa Cruz district within the walls make a pleasant stroll, and the views are the finest in Lisbon.

A steep stairway leads down to the outlying Torre de São Lourenço.

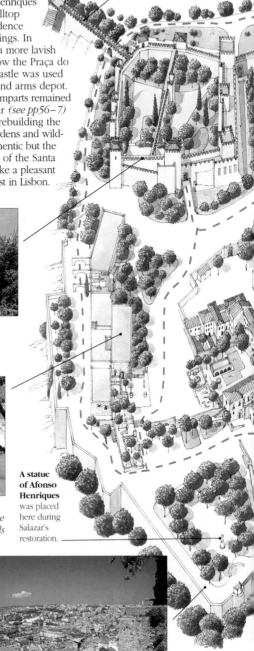

★ Battlements
Visitors can climb the towers and walk along the reconstructed ramparts of the castle walls.

Casa do Leão Restaurant
Part of the former royal residence can be reserved for evening meals and parties (see p404).

A statue of Afonso Henriques was placed here during Salazar's restoration.

★ Observation Terrace
This large shaded square affords spectacular views over Lisbon and the Tagus. Local men play backgammon and cards under the trees.

KEY

– – – Suggested route

◁ **Delightful hidden courtyard among the run-down houses in Santa Cruz, within the castle walls**

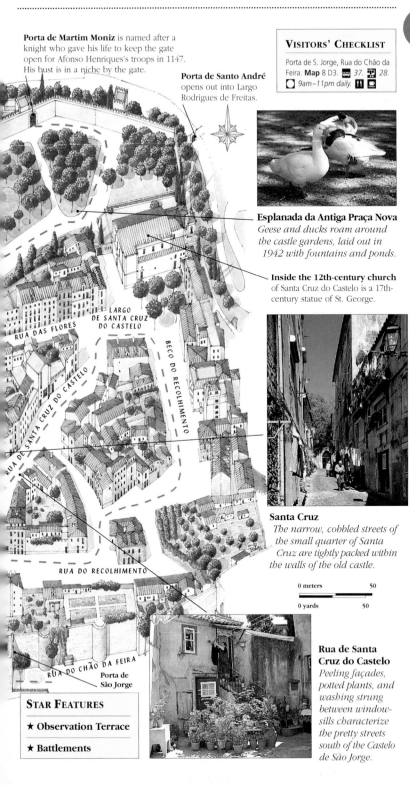

Porta de Martim Moniz is named after a knight who gave his life to keep the gate open for Afonso Henriques's troops in 1147. His bust is in a niche by the gate.

Porta de Santo André opens out into Largo Rodrigues de Freitas.

VISITORS' CHECKLIST

Porta de S. Jorge, Rua do Chão da Feira. **Map** 8 D3. 🚌 *37*. 🚃 *28*. ⬛ 9am–11pm daily. 🚻 ⬛

Esplanada da Antiga Praça Nova
Geese and ducks roam around the castle gardens, laid out in 1942 with fountains and ponds.

Inside the 12th-century church of Santa Cruz do Castelo is a 17th-century statue of St. George.

LARGO DE SANTA CRUZ DO CASTELO

RUA DAS FLORES

RUA DE SANTA CRUZ DO CASTELO

BECO DO RECOLHIMENTO

RUA DO RECOLHIMENTO

Santa Cruz
The narrow, cobbled streets of the small quarter of Santa Cruz are tightly packed within the walls of the old castle.

0 meters   50
0 yards   50

RUA DO CHÃO DA FEIRA

Porta de São Jorge

Rua de Santa Cruz do Castelo
Peeling façades, potted plants, and washing strung between window-sills characterize the pretty streets south of the Castelo de São Jorge.

STAR FEATURES

★ **Observation Terrace**

★ **Battlements**

BAIXA

FROM THE RUINS of Lisbon, devastated by the earthquake of 1755 *(see pp62–3)*, the Marquês de Pombal created an entirely new center. Using a grid layout of streets, he linked the stately arcaded Praça do Comércio beside the Tagus with the busy central square of Rossio. The streets were flanked by uniform, Neo-Classical buildings and named according to the shopkeepers and craftsmen who traded there.

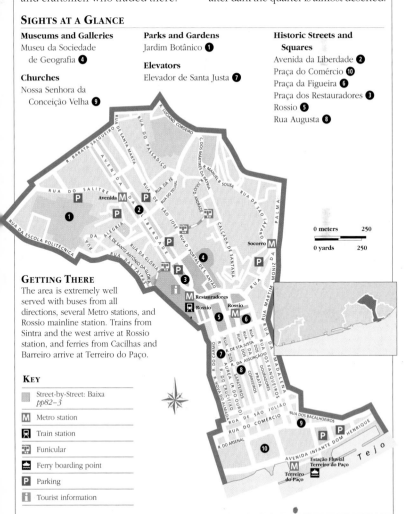

**Detail on statue of José I
in Praça do Comércio**

The Baixa (lower town) is still the commercial hub of the capital, housing banks, offices, and stores. At its center, Rossio is a popular meeting point with cafés, theaters, and restaurants. The geometric layout of the area has been retained, but most of the buildings constructed since the mid-18th century have not adhered to Pombaline formality. The streets are crowded by day, particularly the lively Rua Augusta, but after dark the quarter is almost deserted.

SIGHTS AT A GLANCE

Museums and Galleries
Museu da Sociedade
de Geografia **4**

Churches
Nossa Senhora da
Conceição Velha **9**

Parks and Gardens
Jardim Botânico **1**

Elevators
Elevador de Santa Justa **7**

**Historic Streets and
Squares**
Avenida da Liberdade **2**
Praça do Comércio **10**
Praça da Figueira **6**
Praça dos Restauradores **3**
Rossio **5**
Rua Augusta **8**

GETTING THERE
The area is extremely well served with buses from all directions, several Metro stations, and Rossio mainline station. Trains from Sintra and the west arrive at Rossio station, and ferries from Cacilhas and Barreiro arrive at Terreiro do Paço.

KEY

	Street-by-Street: Baixa *pp82–3*
M	Metro station
R	Train station
	Funicular
	Ferry boarding point
P	Parking
i	Tourist information

◁ **The triumphal arch in Praça do Comércio leading into Rua Augusta and the Baixa**

Street-by-Street: Baixa

THIS IS THE BUSIEST PART of the city, especially the central squares of Rossio and Praça da Figueira. Totally rebuilt after the earthquake of 1755 *(see pp62–3)*, the area was one of Europe's first examples of town planning. Today, the large Neo-Classical buildings on the wide streets and squares house business offices. The atmosphere and surroundings are best absorbed from one of the busy sidewalk cafés. Rua das Portas de Santo Antão, a pedestrian street where restaurants display tanks of live lobsters, is more relaxing for a stroll.

Tiled panel on façade of the Tabacaria Monaco

Palácio Foz, once a magnificent 18th-century palace built by the Italian architect Francesco Fabri, now houses the city's tourist office.

The Elevador da Glória is a bright yellow funicular that rattles up the hill to the Bairro Alto as far as the Miradouro de São Pedro de Alcântara *(see p94).*

Praça dos Restauradores
This large tree-lined square, named after the men who gave their lives during the War of Restoration, is a busy through street with café terraces on the patterned pavement ❸

Restauradores

KEY

— — — Suggested route

STAR SIGHT

★ **Rossio**

Rossio station, designed by José Luís Monteiro, is an eye-catching late 19th-century Neo-Manueline building with a pair of Moorish horseshoe arches

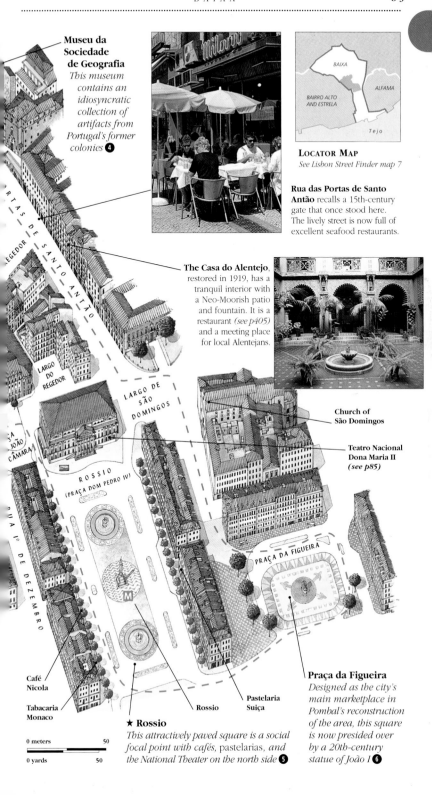

Museu da Sociedade de Geografia
This museum contains an idiosyncratic collection of artifacts from Portugal's former colonies **4**

LOCATOR MAP
See Lisbon Street Finder map 7

Rua das Portas de Santo Antão recalls a 15th-century gate that once stood here. The lively street is now full of excellent seafood restaurants.

The Casa do Alentejo, restored in 1919, has a tranquil interior with a Neo-Moorish patio and fountain. It is a restaurant *(see p405)* and a meeting place for local Alentejans.

Church of São Domingos

Teatro Nacional Dona Maria II *(see p85)*

LARGO DE SÃO DOMINGOS

ROSSIO (PRAÇA DOM PEDRO IV)

PRAÇA DA FIGUEIRA

Café Nicola

Tabacaria Monaco

Rossio

Pastelaria Suiça

★ Rossio
This attractively paved square is a social focal point with cafés, pastelarias, and the National Theater on the north side **5**

Praça da Figueira
Designed as the city's main marketplace in Pombal's reconstruction of the area, this square is now presided over by a 20th-century statue of João I **6**

0 meters   50
0 yards   50

Bridge and pond shaded by trees in the Jardim Botânico

Jardim Botânico ❶

Rua da Escola Politécnica 56. **Map** 4 F1.
📞 21-396 15 21. 🚌 15, 58, 100.
Ⓜ *Avenida.* **Gardens** ◻ 9am–6pm
(Apr–Sep: 8pm) Mon–Fri, 10am–6pm
(Apr–Sep: 8pm) Sat & Sun. ● Jan 1,
Dec 25. 🎟 ♿ **Museu de História**
Natural ◻ for exhibitions only. 🎟
Museu da Ciência ◻ 10am–1pm,
2–5pm Mon–Fri, 3–6pm Sat.
● public hols. 🎟

THE COMPLEX, owned by the
university, comprises two
museums and 10 acres (4 ha)
of gardens. The botanical
gardens, which slope down
from the upper level by the
main entrance toward Rua da
Alegria, have a distinct air of
neglect. However, it is worth
paying the entrance fee to
wander among the exotic trees
and dense shady paths of the
gardens as they descend to the
second entrance. A magnificent
avenue of lofty palms connects
the two different levels.

The **Museu de História**
Natural (Natural History
Museum) opens only for temporary exhibitions and these
are well advertised throughout
the city. The **Museu da**
Ciência (Science Museum),
whose exhibits demonstrate
basic scientific principles, is
popular with school children.

Avenida da Liberdade ❷

Map 7 A2. 🚌 2, 9, 36 & many other
routes. Ⓜ *Restauradores, Avenida.*

FOLLOWING THE earthquake
of 1755 *(see pp62–3)*, the
Marquês de Pombal created
the Passeio Público (public
promenade) in the area now
occupied by the lower part of
Avenida da Liberdade and
Praça dos Restauradores.

Despite its name,
enjoyment of the
park was restricted to
Lisbon's high society,
and walls and gates
ensured the exclu-
sion of the lower
classes. In 1821,
when the Liberals
came to power, the
barriers were pulled
down and the
Avenida and square
became open to all.

The boulevard
you see today was
built in 1879–82 in
the style of the
Champs-Elysées
in Paris. The wide
tree-lined avenue
became a focus for
pageants, festivities,
and demonstrations.
A war memorial
stands as a tribute to
those who died in
World War I. The
avenue still retains
a certain elegance
with fountains and
café tables shaded by trees;
however, it no longer makes
for a peaceful stroll. The once
majestic thoroughfare, 90 m
(295 ft) wide and decorated
with abstract pavement patterns, is now divided by seven
lanes of traffic linking Praça
dos Restauradores and Praça
Marquês de Pombal to the
north. Some of the original
mansions have been preserved,
including the Neo-Classical
Tivoli theater at No. 188, with
an original 1920s kiosk outside,
and Casa Lambertini with its
colorful mosaic decoration at
No. 166. However, many of
the Art Nouveau façades have
unfortunately given way to
newer ones occupied by
offices, hotels, or shopping
complexes.

Detail from the memorial to the dead of
World War I in Avenida da Liberdade

19th-century monument in honor of the
Restoration in Praça dos Restauradores

Praça dos Restauradores ❸

Map 7 A2. 🚌 2, 9, 36, 46 & many
other routes. Ⓜ *Restauradores.*

THE SQUARE, distinguished by
its soaring obelisk, erected
in 1886, commemorates the
country's liberation from the
Spanish yoke in 1640 *(see
pp50–51)*. The bronze figures
on the pedestal depict Victory,
holding a palm and a crown,
and Freedom. The names and
dates inscribed on the obelisk
are those of the battles of the
War of Restoration.

On the west side the Palácio
Foz, housing the main tourist
office, was built by Francesco
Savario Fabri in 1755–
77 for the Marquês
de Castelo-Melhor.
It was renamed
after the Marquês
de Foz, who lived
here in the 19th century.
The smart Avenida Palace
Hotel *(see p381)* stands on
the southwest side of the
square. This building was
designed by José Luís
Monteiro (1849–1942),
who also built Rossio
train station *(see p82)*.

Museu da Sociedade de Geografia ❶

Rua das Portas de Santo Antão 100.
Map 7 A2. ☎ *21-342 54 01.* 🚌 *9, 80, 90.* Ⓜ *Restauradores.* ⭘ *11am & 3pm Mon, Wed & Fri.* 📷 *compulsory.*

LOCATED in the Geographical Society building, the museum houses an idiosyncratic ethnographical collection brought back from Portugal's former colonies. On display are circumcision masks from Guinea Bissau, musical instruments, and snake spears. From Angola there are neckrests to sustain coiffures and the original *padrão* – the stone pillar erected by the Portuguese in 1482 to mark their sovereignty over the colony. Most of the exhibits are arranged along the splendid Sala Portugal, a large hall used also for conferences.

Rossio ❺

Map 6 B3. 🚌 *2, 36, 44, 45 & many other routes.* Ⓜ *Rossio.*

FORMALLY CALLED Praça de Dom Pedro IV, this large square has been the nerve center of Lisbon for six centuries. During its history it has been the stage of bullfights, festivals, military parades, and gruesome *autos da fé (see p51).* However, today there is little more than an occasional political rally, and the sober

Teatro Nacional Dona Maria II in Rossio illuminated by night

Pombaline buildings, disfigured on the upper level by rusting neon advertisements, are occupied at street level by small souvenir shops, jewelers, and cafés. Center stage stands a statue of Dom Pedro IV, the first emperor of independent Brazil *(see p54).* At the foot of the statue, the four female figures are allegories of Justice, Wisdom, Strength, and Moderation – qualities dubiously attributed to Dom Pedro.

In the mid-19th century the square was paved with wave-patterned mosaics, which gave it the nickname of "Rolling Motion Square." The hand-cut gray and white stone cubes were the first such designs to decorate the city's pavements. Today, only a small central section of the design survives.

On the north side of the square is the Teatro Nacional Dona Maria II, named after Dom Pedro's daughter. The Neo-Classical structure was built in the 1840s by the Italian architect Fortunato Lodi. On top of the pediment is Gil Vicente (1465–1536), the founder of Portuguese theater.

Café Nicola on the west side of the square was a favourite meeting place among writers. A regular of the original café (the present one dates from 1929) was the poet Manuel du Bocage (1765–1805), notorious for his satires.

Praça da Figueira ❻

Map 6 B3. 🚌 *14, 43, 59, 60 & many other routes.* 🚋 *15.* Ⓜ *Rossio.*

BEFORE THE 1755 earthquake *(see pp62–3)* the square next to Rossio was the site of the Hospital de Todos-os-Santos (All Saints). In Pombal's new design for the Baixa, the square took on the role of the city's central marketplace. In 1885 a covered market was introduced, but this was pulled down in the 1950s. Today, the four-story buildings are home to hotels, shops, and cafés, and the square is no longer a marketplace. Perhaps its most eye-catching feature is the multitude of pigeons that perch on the pedestal supporting Leopoldo de Almeida's bronze equestrian statue of João I, erected in 1971.

Bronze statue of King João I in Praça da Figueira

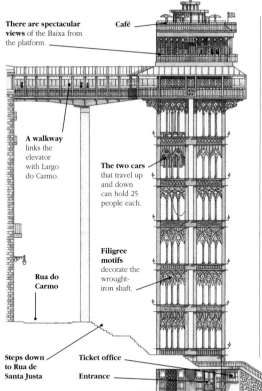

There are spectacular **views** of the Baixa from the platform.

Café

A walkway links the elevator with Largo do Carmo.

The two cars that travel up and down can hold 25 people each.

Filigree motifs decorate the wrought-iron shaft.

Rua do Carmo

Steps down to Rua de Santa Justa

Ticket office

Entrance

Elevador de Santa Justa ●

Rua de Santa Justa & Largo do Carmo.
Map 7 B3. 🗋 21-363 20 21.
⏰ 7am–11pm Mon–Sat, 9am–11pm
Sun & public hols. 💳

Aʟsᴏ ᴋɴᴏᴡɴ as the Elevador do Carmo, this Neo-Gothic elevator, built at the turn of the century by the French

Café on the top platform of the Elevador de Santa Justa

architect Raoul Mesnier du Ponsard, an apprentice of Alexandre Gustave Eiffel, is one of the more eccentric features of the Baixa. Made of iron, and embellished with filigree, the elevator within a tower provides regular service between the Baixa and the Bairro Alto, 32 m (105 ft) above, and is the most convenient way to reach the upper part of town. Two wood-paneled cabins with brass fittings travel up and down within the tower depositing passengers on a walkway leading to the nearby Largo do Carmo and the ruined Igreja do Carmo *(see p92)*.

The very top of the tower, reached by a tight spiral stairway, is filled with café tables. This high vantage point commands splendid views of Rossio, the grid pattern of the Baixa, the castle on the opposite hill, the river, and the nearby ruins of the Carmo church. The fire that gutted the Chiado district in 1988 *(see p92)* was extinguished very close to the elevator.

Rua Augusta ●

Map 7 B4. M *Rossio.* 🚋 *2, 14, 36, 40 & many other routes.*

A ʟɪᴠᴇʟʏ ᴘᴇᴅᴇsᴛʀɪᴀɴ street decorated with mosaic sidewalks and lined with boutiques and open-air cafés, Rua Augusta is the main tourist thoroughfare and the most stylish in the Baixa. Street performers provide entertainment, and vendors sell lottery tickets, books, and souvenirs. The eye is drawn to the triumphal Arco da Rua Augusta framing the equestrian statue of José I in Praça do Comércio. Designed by the architect Santos de Carvalho to commemorate the city's recovery from the earthquake *(see pp62–3)*, the arch was completed in 1873.

The other main thoroughfares of the Baixa are Rua da Prata (silversmiths' street) and Rua do Ouro or Rua Aurea (goldsmiths' street). Cutting across these main streets full of shops and banks are smaller streets that give glimpses up to the Bairro Alto to the west and the Castelo de São Jorge *(see pp78–9)* to the east. Many of the streets retain shops that gave them their name: there are jewelers in Rua da Prata and Rua do Ouro, shoemakers in Rua dos Sapateiros, and banks in Rua do Comércio.

The most incongruous sight in the heart of the Baixa is a small section of the Roman baths, located within the Banco Comercial Português in Rua dos Correeiros. The ruins and mosaics can be seen from the street window at the rear side of the bank; alternatively you can go on a Thursday when the "museum" is open.

Shoppers and strollers in the bustling Rua Augusta

Nossa Senhora da Conceição Velha ⑨

Rua da Alfândega. **Map** 7 C4.
☎ 21-887 02 02. 🚌 9, 46, 90.
🚊 18. 🕐 8am–1pm, 4–7pm daily.
⬤ Aug. 🚹 📷 ♿

Tʜᴇ ᴇʟᴀʙᴏʀᴀᴛᴇ Manueline doorway of the church is the only feature that survived from the original 16th-century Nossa Senhora da Misericórdia, which stood here until the 1755 earthquake. The portal is decorated with a profusion of Manueline detail including angels, beasts, flowers, armillary spheres, and the cross of the Order of Christ (see pp18–19). In the tympanum, the Virgin Mary spreads her protective mantle over various contemporary figures. These include Pope Leo X, Manuel I (see pp46–7) and his sister, Queen Leonor, widow of João II. It was Leonor who founded the original Misericórdia (poor house) on the site of a former synagogue.

Detail from portal of Conceição Velha

Unfortunately, enjoyment of the portal is hampered by the stream of traffic hurtling along Rua da Alfândega and the cars that park right in front of the church. The gloomy interior has an unusual stucco ceiling; in the second chapel on the right is a statue of Our Lady of Restelo. This came from the Belém chapel where navigators prayed before embarking on their historic voyages east.

Praça do Comércio ⑩

Map 7 C5. 🚌 2, 14, 40, 46 & many other routes. 🚊 15, 18.

Mᴏʀᴇ ᴄᴏᴍᴍᴏɴʟʏ known by the locals as Terreiro do Paço (Palace Square), this huge open space was the site of the royal palace for 400 years. Manuel I transferred the royal residence from Castelo de São Jorge to this more convenient location by the river in 1511. The first palace, along with its library and 70,000 books, was destroyed in the earthquake of 1755. In the rebuilding of the city, the square became the pièce de résistance of Pombal's Baixa design. The new palace occupied spacious arcaded buildings that extended around three sides of the square. After the revolution of 1910 (see pp54–5) these were converted into government administrative offices and painted Republican pink. However, they have since been repainted royal yellow.

The south side, graced by two square towers, looks across the wide expanse of the Tagus. This has always been the finest gateway to Lisbon, where royalty and ambassadors would alight and take the marble steps up from the river. You can still experience the dramatic approach by taking a ferry across from Cacilhas on the southern bank. However, today the spectacle is spoiled by the busy Avenida Infante Dom Henrique, which runs along the waterfront.

In the center of Praça do Comércio is the equestrian statue of King José I erected in 1775 by Machado de Castro, the leading Portuguese sculptor of the 18th century. The bronze horse, depicted trampling on serpents, earned the square its third name of "Black Horse Square," used by English travelers and merchants. Over the years, however, the horse has acquired a green patina.

Shaded arcades along the north side of Praça do Comércio

The impressive triumphal arch on the north side of the square leads into Rua Augusta and is the gateway to the Baixa. The arch is decorated with statues of historical figures, including Vasco da Gama (see p108) and the Marquês de Pombal (see pp52–3). Nearby, in the northeast corner of the square, stands Lisbon's oldest café, the Martinho da Arcada, formerly a haunt of the city's literati.

On February 1, 1908, King Carlos and his son, Luís Felipe, were assassinated as they were passing through the square (see p55). In 1974 the square saw the first uprising of the Armed Forces Movement, which overthrew the Caetano regime in a bloodless revolution (see p57). For many years the area was used as a parking lot, but today it has been reclaimed for the use of open-air cafés and stalls.

Marble steps leading up to Praça do Comércio from the Tagus

BAIRRO ALTO AND ESTRELA

L AID OUT IN A GRID pattern
in the late 16th century, the
hilltop Bairro Alto is one
of the most picturesque districts
of the city. First settled by rich
citizens who moved out of the
disreputable Alfama, by the
19th century it had become a
run-down area frequented by
prostitutes. Today, it retains a
traditional way of life, with
small workshops and family-
run *tascas* (cheap restaurants).

Tile panel in Largo
Rafael Bordalo
Pinheiro, Bairro Alto

Very different in character to
the heart of the Bairro Alto is
the elegant commercial district known as the Chiado,
where affluent Lisboetas do
their shopping. To the northwest, the Estrela quarter is
centered on the huge domed
basilica and popular gardens.
The mid-18th century district
of Lapa, to the southwest, is
home to foreign embassies
and large, stylish residences.

SIGHTS AT A GLANCE

Museums and Galleries
Museu do Chiado **5**
*Museu Nacional de Arte
Antiga pp96–9* **11**

Churches
Basílica da Estrela **13**
Igreja do Carmo **2**
São Roque **1**

**Historic Buildings
and Districts**
Chiado **3**
Palácio de São Bento **10**
Solar do Vinho do Porto **7**
Teatro Nacional
de São Carlos **4**

Markets
Mercado
24 de
Julho **6**

Gardens and Belvederes
Jardim da Estrela **12**
Miradouro de São Pedro
de Alcântara **8**
Praça do Príncipe Real **9**

GETTING THERE

This area is reached effortlessly
with the Elevador da Glória from
Praça dos Restauradores or the
Elevador de Santa Justa from the
Baixa. Otherwise it is a steep
but pleasant walk. There is
also a metro station on Largo do
Chiado. From Bairro Alto, trolleys
24 and 28 go to Estrela and Lapa.

KEY

Street-by-Street: Bairro Alto
pp90–91

M Metro station

Train station

Funicular

Ferry boarding point

P Parking

Railroad line

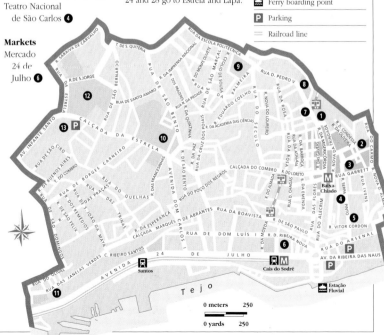

◁ **Art Nouveau decoration in the Chiado's Café Brasileira, once popular with writers and intellectuals**

Street-by-Street: Bairro Alto

Baroque cherub,
Igreja do Carmo

THE BAIRRO ALTO (high quarter) is a fascinating area of cobbled streets, peeling houses, and tiny grocery stores selling fruit and flasks of local wine. Traditionally a bohemian quarter, notorious for prostitution and gambling, today the Bairro Alto is a residential area, with the spirit of a close-knit community. In recent years it has become fashionable at night for its bars and *casas de fado (see pp66–7).* In contrast, the Chiado is an area of elegant shops and old-style cafés that extends down from Praça Luís de Camões towards Rua do Carmo and the Baixa. Major renovation work has taken place since a fire in 1988 *(see p92)* destroyed many of the buildings.

Rua do Norte and Rua das Gáveas are at the heart of the traditional Bairro Alto where nighttime revelers crowd the bars after dark.

Chiado
*Once a haunt of writers
and intellectuals, this area
is now an elegant shop-
ping district. The 1920s
Brasileira café, on Largo
do Chiado, is adorned
with gilded
mirrors* ❸

**Praça Luís
de Camões**

**Largo do
Chiado** is flanked
by the churches
of Loreto and Nossa
Senhora da Encarnação.

Baixa/Chiado

**The statue of Eça de
Queirós** (1845–1900), by
Teixeira Lopes, was erected
in 1903. The great novelist
takes inspiration from a
scantily veiled muse.

Rua Garrett
is the main shopping
street of the Chiado.

0 meters   50

0 yards   50

KEY

– – – Suggested route

Tavares, at No. 37
Rua da Misericórdia,
first opened as a
café in 1784. Today
it is an elegant res-
taurant *(see p405)*
decorated at the turn
of the century with
mirrors and elabo-
rate stucco designs.

Elevador da Glória

The Museu de Arte Sacra has an interesting exhibition of religious artifacts and explains the history of the treasures in the church of São Roque next door.

BAIXA

BAIRRO ALTO AND ESTRELA

Tejo

LOCATOR MAP
See Lisbon Street Finder map 7

Cervejaria Trindade is a popular beer hall and restaurant decorated with *azulejo* panels.

Teatro da Trindade

★ São Roque
Opulent mosaics and semiprecious stones adorn the Baroque Capela de São João inside the 16th-century church of São Roque ❶

The tile decoration on the façade of this house, erected in 1864 on Largo Rafael Bordalo Pinheiro, features allegorical figures of Science, Agriculture, Industry, and Commerce.

★ Igreja do Carmo
The graceful skeletal arches of this Carmelite church, once the largest in Lisbon, stand as a reminder of the earthquake of 1755. The chancel, the only part that remains intact, holds an archaeological museum ❷

Elevador de Santa Justa *(see p86)*

The shops in Rua do Carmo are gradually being restored after the devastating fire in 1988 *(see p92)*.

STAR SIGHTS

★ São Roque

★ Igreja do Carmo

Ruins of the 14th-century Igreja do Carmo seen from the Baixa

São Roque ❶

Largo Trindade Coelho. **Map** 7 A3.
📞 21-323 50 00. 🚌 58, 100. 🚋 28.
🕐 9am–5pm (public hols: 1pm)
daily. ✚ **Museu de Arte Sacra**
🕐 10am–5pm Tue–Sun. ● public
hols. 📷 📷

Sᴀᴏ ʀᴏǫᴜᴇ'ѕ plain façade belies a remarkably rich interior. The church was founded at the end of the 16th century by the Jesuit Order, then at the peak of its power. In 1742 the Chapel of St. John the Baptist (last on the left) was commissioned by the prodigal João V from the Italian architects Luigi Vanvitelli and Nicola Salvi. Constructed in Rome and embellished with lapis lazuli, agate, alabaster, amethyst, precious marbles, gold, silver, and mosaics, the chapel was given the Pope's blessing in the church of Sant'Antonio dei Portoghesi in Rome, dismantled, and sent to Lisbon in three ships.

Among the many tiles in the church, the oldest and most interesting are those in the third chapel on the right, dating from the mid-16th century and dedicated to São Roque (St. Roch), protector against the plague. Other noteworthy features of the church are the painted *trompe l'oeil* ceiling, showing a dome and scenes of the Apocalypse, and the sacristy, with its coffered ceiling and painted panels of the life of St. Francis Xavier, the 16th-century Jesuit missionary.

Treasures from the Chapel of St. John, including the silver and lapis lazuli altar front, can be seen in the adjoining **Museu de Arte Sacra**.

Igreja do Carmo ❷

Largo do Carmo. **Map** 7 B3.
📞 21-346 04 73. 🚋 28 & Santa
Justa elevator. ● until further notice.

Tile detail in the Chapel of St. Roch

Tʜᴇ ɢᴏᴛʜɪᴄ ʀᴜɪɴѕ of this Carmelite church, built on a slope overlooking the Baixa, are evocative reminders of the devastation left by the earthquake of 1755. Founded in the late 14th century by Nuno Álvares Pereira (*see p183*), the commander who became a member of the Carmelite Order, the church was at one time the biggest in Lisbon. At present day, the roofless nave, open to the sky, is all that remains of the arches and rubble that caved in on the congregation as they were attending mass. Roses wind their way around its ancient pillars, pigeons perch on the ruined arches, and cats wander among the scattered statuary and capitals.

The chancel, whose roof withstood the shock, is now an **archaeological museum** with a small, heterogeneous collection of sarcophagi, statuary, ceramics, and mosaics. Among the more ancient finds from Europe are a remnant from a Visigothic pillar and a Roman tomb carved with reliefs depicting the Muses. There are also finds from Mexico and South America, including ancient mummies.

Outside the ruins, in the Largo do Carmo, stands the Chafariz do Carmo, an 18th-century fountain designed by Ângelo Belasco, elaborately but tastefully decorated with four dolphins.

Chiado ❸

Map 7 A4. 🚌 58. 🚋 28. Ⓜ Chiado.

Hʏᴘᴏᴛʜᴇѕᴇѕ abound for the origin of the word Chiado, in use since 1567. One of the most interesting recalls the creak (*chiar*) of the wheels of the carts as they negotiated the area's steep slopes. A second theory refers to the nickname given to the 16th-century poet António Ribeiro, "O Chiado."

THE CHIADO FIRE

On August 25, 1988 a disastrous fire began in a store in Rua do Carmo, the street that links the Baixa with the Bairro Alto. Fire engines were unable to enter this pedestrian street, and the fire spread into Rua Garrett. Along with shops and offices, many important 18th-century buildings were destroyed, the worst damage being in Rua do Carmo. The renovation project, which will preserve where possible the original façades, is headed by the leading Portuguese architect, Álvaro Siza Vieira.

Firemen attending the raging fire in Rua do Carmo

Stalls and circle of the 18th-century Teatro Nacional de São Carlos

An area traditionally known for its intellectual associations, statues of literary figures can be found here. A statue of Fernando Pessoa, Portugal's most famous 20th-century poet, is seated at a table outside the Café Brasileira. This was a favorite rendezvous of intellectuals in the 1920s.

The name Chiado is often used to mean just Rua Garrett, the main shopping street of the area, named after the author and poet João Almeida Garrett (1799–1854). This street, which descends from Largo do Chiado toward the Baixa, is known for its chic stores. Devastated by fire in 1988, the former elegance of this quarter is gradually being restored.

On Largo do Chiado stand two Baroque churches: the Italian church, Igreja do Loreto, on the north side and opposite, Nossa Senhora da Encarnação, whose exterior walls are partly decorated with *azulejos*.

Teatro Nacional de São Carlos ●

Rua Serpa Pinto 9. **Map** 7 A4. 21-346 84 08. 58. 28. Chiado. for performances only.

REPLACING a former opera house ruined by the earthquake of 1755, the Teatro de São Carlos was built in 1792–5 by José da Costa e Silva. Designed on the lines of La Scala in Milan and the San Carlo in Naples, the building has a beautifully proportioned façade and an enchanting Rococo interior. Views of the exterior, however, are spoiled by the parking lot, invariably crammed, which occupies the square in front. The opera season lasts from September to June, but concerts and ballets are also staged here at other times of the year.

Museu do Chiado ●

Rua Serpa Pinto 4–6. **Map** 7 A5. 21-343 21 48. 58. 24, 28. Chiado. 10am–6pm Wed–Sun, 2–6pm Tue. Jan 1, Easter, May 1, Dec 25.

THE NATIONAL MUSEUM of Contemporary Art, whose collection of 1850–1950 paintings could no longer be termed contemporary, changed its name in 1994 and moved to a stylishly restored warehouse. The paintings and sculpture, arranged in 12 rooms, each with a different theme, illustrate the development from Romanticism to Modernism. The majority are works by Portuguese, often showing the marked influence from other European countries. This is particularly noticeable in the 19th-century landscape painters who had contact with artists from the French Barbizon School. The few international works of art include drawings by Rodin (1840–1917) and French sculpture from the late 19th century. Temporary exhibitions are held for "very new artists, preferably inspired by the permanent collection."

A vegetable stall holder in the daily Mercado 24 de Julho

Mercado 24 de Julho ●

Avenida 24 de Julho. **Map** 4 F3. Cais do Sodré. 14, 32, 40. 15, 28. 3am–noon Mon–Sat.

FROM EARLY MORNING to noon this conspicuous, domed building is the scene of the food and flower market. The hall is packed with boxes of seasonal vegetables, fruit, and bags of beans and nuts. Surrounding stalls sell cheese, meat, fresh fish, and dried cod. Today most of the produce arrives in the early morning by cart, truck, or van, but you can still spot a few vendors disembarking from ferries, with crates of vegetables on their heads. A modern tiled scene in a fishmonger's is another reminder of bygone days when fresh fish was sold from the dock by the barefooted *varinas* or fishwives *(see p198)*.

The café inside the market is popular with both traders and late-night revelers who come here to sober up in the early hours of the morning.

Art Nouveau façade of the popular Café Brasileira in the Chiado

The wide selection of port at the Solar do Vinho do Porto

Solar do Vinho do Porto ⑦

Rua de São Pedro de Alcântara 45.
Map 4 F2. 🔲 *21-347 57 07.*
🚌 *58.* 🚋 *28, Elevador da Glória.*
🕐 *10am–11:30pm Mon–Fri,*
11am–10:30pm Sat. ⚫ *public hols.*

THE PORTUGUESE WORD *solar*
means mansion or manor
house, and the Solar do Vinho
do Porto occupies the ground
floor of an 18th-century mansion. The building was once
owned by the German architect, Johann Friedrich Ludwig
(Ludovice), who built the
monastery at Mafra *(see p152)*.
Similar to the Solar do Vinho
do Porto in Oporto *(see p243)*,
this bar has up to 6,000 varieties of port, including rare
vintages dating back as far as
1937. You can try about 300 of
these rich fortified wines, from
the younger red-colored ruby
port, through the lighter
tawny, to the aristocratic vintages from the great shippers
of Oporto *(see pp228–9)*.
Although rather expensive,
these can be tasted at the bar
or in the comfort of armchairs
in the clublike sitting room.

Miradouro de São Pedro de Alcântara ⑧

Rua de São Pedro de Alcântara. **Map** 7
A2. 🚌 *58.* 🚋 *28, Elevador da Glória.*

THE BELVEDERE (*miradouro*)
commands a sweeping
view of eastern Lisbon, seen
across the Baixa. A tiled map,
conveniently placed against
the balustrade, helps you
locate the landmarks in the
city below. The panorama
extends from the battlements
of the Castelo de São
Jorge *(see pp78–9)*,
clearly seen surrounded
by trees on the hill to
the southeast, to the
18th-century church of
Penha da França in the
northwest. The large
monastery complex of
the Igreja da Graça *(see
p75)* is also visible on
the hill, and in the dis-
tance São Vicente de
Fora *(see p73)* is recognizable
by the symmetrical towers
that flank its white façade.

Benches and ample shade
from the trees make this
terrace a pleasant stop after
the steep walk up Calçada da
Glória from the Baixa. Alternatively, the yellow funicular,
Elevador da Glória, will drop
you off nearby.

The memorial in the garden,
erected in 1904, depicts
Eduardo Coelho (1835–89),
founder of the newspaper
Diário de Notícias, and below
him a ragged paper boy running with copies of the famous

daily. This area was once the
center of the newspaper industry; the modern printing
presses have now moved to
more spacious premises west
of the city.

The view is most attractive at
sunset and by night when the
castle is floodlit and the terrace
becomes a popular meeting
point for young Lisboetas.

Praça do Príncipe Real ⑨

Map 4 F1. 🚌 *58, 100.*

Playing cards in Praça do Príncipe Real

LAID OUT IN 1860 as a prime
residential quarter, the
square still retains an air of
affluence. Stylishly painted
mansions surround a particularly pleasant park with an
open-air café, statuary, and
some splendid robinia, magnolia, and Judas trees. The
branches of a huge cedar tree
have been trained on a trellis,
creating a shady spot for the
locals who play cards there.
On the square, at No. 26, the
eye-catching pink and white
Neo-Moorish building with
domes and pinnacles is part
of Lisbon university.

View across the city to Castelo de São Jorge from Miradouro de São Pedro de Alcântara

Attractive wrought-iron music pavilion in Jardim da Estrela

Palácio de São Bento ⑩

Rua de São Bento. **Map** 4 E2.
📞 21-396 01 41. 🚌 6, 49.
🕐 by appt only.

ALSO KNOWN as the Palácio da Assembleia Nacional, this enormous white Neo-Classical building is the seat of the Portuguese Parliament. It started life at the end of the 16th century as the Benedictine monastery of São Bento. After the dissolution of the religious orders in 1834, the building became the seat of Parliament, known as the Palácio das Cortes. The interior is suitably grandiose with marble pillars and Neo-Classical statues.

Museu Nacional de Arte Antiga ⑪

See pp96–9.

Jardim da Estrela ⑫

Praça da Estrela. **Map** 4 D2. 🚌 9, 20, 22, 38. 🚋 25, 28.

LAID OUT IN the middle of the 19th century, opposite the Basílica da Estrela, the popular gardens are a focal part of the Estrela quarter. Local families congregate here on weekends to feed the ducks and the large carp in the lake, sit at the waterside café, or wander among the pleasant flower beds, plants, and trees. The formal gardens are planted with neat herbaceous borders and shrubs surrounding plane trees and elms. The central feature of the park is a green wrought-iron bandstand, decorated with elegant filigree, where musicians strike up in the summer months. This was built in 1884 and originally stood on the Passeio Público, before the creation of Avenida da Liberdade *(see p84)*.

The English Cemetery to the north of the gardens is best known as the burial place of Henry Fielding (1707–54), the English novelist and playwright who died in Lisbon at the age of 47. The *Journal of a Voyage to Lisbon*, published posthumously in 1775, recounts his last voyage to Portugal made in a fruitless attempt to recover his failing health.

Basílica da Estrela ⑬

Praça da Estrela. **Map** 4 D2. 📞 21-396 09 15. 🚌 9, 20, 22, 38. 🚋 25, 28. 🕐 7:30am–1pm, 3–8pm daily.
🔼 📷

The tomb of the pious Maria I in the Basílica da Estrela

IN THE SECOND half of the 18th century Maria I *(see p165)*, daughter of José I, vowed she would build a church if she bore a son and heir to the throne. Her wish was granted and construction of the basilica began in 1779. However, her son José died of smallpox two years before the completion of the church in 1790. The huge domed basilica, set on a hill in the west of the city, is one of Lisbon's great landmarks. A simpler version of the basilica at Mafra *(see p152)*, the church was built by architects from the Mafra School in late Baroque and Neo-Classical style. The façade is flanked by twin bell towers and decorated with an array of statues of saints and allegorical figures.

The spacious, somewhat awe-inspiring interior, where light streams down from the pierced dome, is clad in gray, pink, and yellow marble. The elaborate Empire-style tomb of Queen Maria I, who died in Brazil, lies in the right transept. Locked in a room nearby is Machado de Castro's extraordinary Nativity scene, composed of more than 500 cork and terra-cotta figures. (To see it, ask the sacristan.)

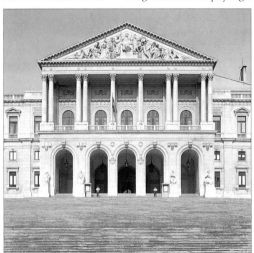

Neo-Classical façade and stairway of Palácio de São Bento

Museu Nacional de Arte Antiga ⓫

15th-century wood carving of St. George

ORTUGAL'S NATIONAL ART COLLECTION is housed in a 17th-century palace that was built for the counts of Alvor. In 1770 it was acquired by the Marquês de Pombal and remained in the possession of his family for over a century. Inaugurated in 1884, the museum is familiarly known to locals as the Casa das Janelas Verdes, referring to the former green windows of the palace. In 1940 a modern annex (including the main façade) was added. This was built on the site of the St. Albert Carmelite monastery, destroyed in the 1755 earthquake *(see pp62–3)*. The only surviving feature was the chapel, which has been integrated into the museum.

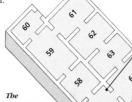

★ **St. Jerome**
This masterly portrayal of old age by Albrecht Dürer expresses one of the central dilemmas of Renaissance humanism: the ephemeral nature of man (1521).

GALLERY GUIDE

The ground floor contains 14th–19th-century European paintings, as well as some decorative arts and furniture. Oriental and African art, Chinese and Portuguese ceramics and silver, gold, and jewelry are on display on the first floor. The top floor is dedicated to Portuguese art and sculpture.

Stairs down to 🅿 🚻 ♿

The Temptations of St. Antony by Hieronymus Bosch

St. Augustine by Piero della Francesca

The Virgin and Child and Saints
Hans Holbein the Elder's balanced composition of a Sacra Conversazione (1519) is set among majestic Renaissance architecture with saints in detailed contemporary costumes sewing or reading.

Ecce Homo
Painted in the late 15th century by an artist of the Portuguese school, the unusual depiction of the accused Jesus, with the shroud lowered over his eyes, retains an air of dignified calm, despite the crown of thorns, the rope, and the specks of blood.

KEY TO FLOOR PLAN

- ☐ European art
- ☐ Portuguese painting and sculpture
- ☐ Portuguese and Chinese ceramics
- ☐ Oriental and African art
- ☐ Silver, gold, and jewelry
- ☐ Decorative arts
- ☐ Chapel of St. Albert
- ☐ Temporary exhibitions
- ☐ Nonexhibition space

STAR EXHIBITS

- ★ **St. Jerome** by Dürer
- ★ **Namban Screens**
- ★ **Adoration of St. Vincent** by Gonçalves

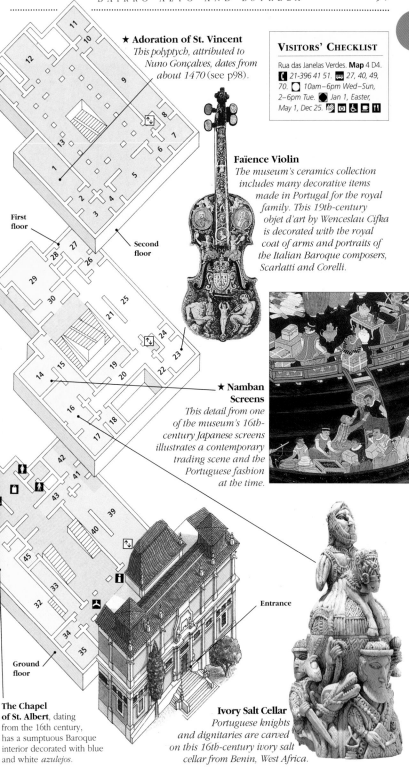

★ Adoration of St. Vincent
This polyptych, attributed to
Nuno Gonçalves, dates from
about 1470 (see p98).

VISITORS' CHECKLIST

Rua das Janelas Verdes. **Map** 4 D4.
☎ 21-396 41 51. 🚍 27, 40, 49,
70. ◯ 10am–6pm Wed–Sun,
2–6pm Tue. ● Jan 1, Easter,
May 1, Dec 25. 🌀 🄯 🛗 🖴 🛉

Faïence Violin
The museum's ceramics collection
includes many decorative items
made in Portugal for the royal
family. This 19th-century
objet d'art by Wenceslau Cifka
is decorated with the royal
coat of arms and portraits of
the Italian Baroque composers,
Scarlatti and Corelli.

First
floor

Second
floor

**★ Namban
Screens**
This detail from one
of the museum's 16th-
century Japanese screens
illustrates a contemporary
trading scene and the
Portuguese fashion
at the time.

Entrance

**The Chapel
of St. Albert**, dating
from the 16th century,
has a sumptuous Baroque
interior decorated with blue
and white *azulejos*.

Ground
floor

Ivory Salt Cellar
Portuguese knights
and dignitaries are carved
on this 16th-century ivory salt
cellar from Benin, West Africa.

Exploring the Collections of the Museu Nacional de Arte Antiga

T HE MUSEUM has the largest collection of paintings in Portugal and is particularly strong on early religious works by Portuguese artists. The majority of exhibits came from convents and monasteries following the suppression of religious orders in 1834. There are also extensive displays of sculpture, silverware, porcelain and applied arts giving an overview of Portuguese art from the Middle Ages to the 19th century, complemented by many fine European and Oriental pieces. The theme of the discoveries is ever-present, illustrating Portugal's links with Brazil, Africa, India, China, and Japan.

EUROPEAN ART

P AINTINGS by European artists, dating from the 14th to the 19th century, are arranged chronologically on the ground floor. Unlike the Portuguese art, most of the works were donated from private collections, contributing to the great diversity of works on display. The first rooms, dedicated to the 14th and 15th centuries, trace the transition from medieval Gothic taste to the aesthetic of the Renaissance.

The painters best represented in the European Art section are 16th-century German and Flemish artists. Notable works are *St. Jerome* by Albrecht Dürer (1471–1528), *Salomé* by Lucas Cranach the Elder (1472–1553), *Virgin and Child* by Hans Memling (c.1430–94), and *The Temptations of St. Antony* by the great Flemish master of fantasy, Hieronymus Bosch (1450–1516). Of the small number of Italian works, the finest are *St. Augustine* by

the Renaissance painter Piero della Francesca (c.1420–92) and a graceful early altar panel representing the Resurrection by Raphael (1483–1520).

Some Portuguese painters, including Josefa de Óbidos (*see p51*) and Gregório Lopes (1490–1550), are also displayed in the galleries of European art.

PORTUGUESE PAINTING AND SCULPTURE

M ANY OF THE EARLIEST works of art are by the Portuguese primitive painters who were influenced by the realistic detail of Flemish artists. There had always been strong trading links between Portugal and Flanders, and in the 15th and 16th centuries several painters of Flemish origin, like Frey Carlos of Évora, set up workshops in Portugal.

Prominently featured is the São Vicente de Fora polyptych, the most important painting of 15th-century Portuguese art and one that has become a

Central panel of *The Temptations of St. Antony* by Hieronymus Bosch

ADORATION OF ST. VINCENT

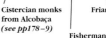

Cistercian monks from Alcobaça (*see pp178–9*)   **Friar**

Fisherman

symbol of national pride in the Age of Discovery. Painted in about 1467–70, and generally believed to be by Nuno Gonçalves, the altarpiece portrays the *Adoration of St. Vincent*, patron saint of Portugal, surrounded by dignitaries, knights, and monks as well as fishermen and beggars. The accurate portrayal of contemporary figures makes the painting an invaluable historical and social document.

Later works include a 16th-century portrait of the young Dom Sebastião (*see pp46–7*) by Cristóvão de Morais and paintings by Neo-Classical artist Domingos António de Sequeira.

The museum's sculpture collection has many Gothic polychrome stone and wood statues of Christ, the Virgin, and saints. There are also statues from the 17th century and an 18th-century nativity scene by Machado de Castro in the Chapel of St. Albert.

PORTUGUESE AND CHINESE CERAMICS

T HE EXTENSIVE collection of ceramics enables visitors to trace the evolution of Chinese porcelain and Portuguese faïence and to see the influence of oriental designs on

Nuno Gonçalves, self-portrait of the artist

Queen Eleonor of Aragon, the Queen mother

Henry the Navigator *(see p49)*

Archbishop of Lisbon, Jorge da Costa

Moorish knight

Jewish scholar

Beggar

Queen Isabel

Infante João (King João II)

King Afonso V

Infante Fernão, the king's brother

Knight

St. Vincent

Duke of Bragança

Priest holding a fragment of St. Vincent's skull

Portuguese pieces, and vice versa. From the 16th century Portuguese ceramics show a marked Ming influence and conversely the Chinese pieces bear Portuguese motifs, such as coats of arms. By the mid-18th century indi-vidual potters had begun to develop an increasingly personalized, European form, with popular, rustic designs. The collection also includes ceramics from Italy, Spain, and the Netherlands.

Chinese porcelain vase, 16th century

ORIENTAL AND AFRICAN ART

THE COLLECTION of ivories and furniture, with their Euro-pean motifs, further illustrates the reciprocal influences of Portugal and her colonies. The 16th-century predilection for the exotic gave rise to a huge demand for items, such as carved ivory hunting horns from Africa. The fascinating 16th-century Japanese Namban screens show the Portuguese trading in Japan. *Namban-jin* (barbarians from the south) is the name the Japanese gave to the Portuguese.

SILVER, GOLD AND JEWELRY

AMONG THE MUSEUM'S fine collection of ecclesiastical treasures are King Sancho I's gold cross (1214) and the Belém monstrance (1506) *(see p20)*. Also on display is the 16th-century Madre de Deus reliquary, which allegedly holds a thorn from the crown of Christ. Highlight of the for-eign collection is a sumptuous set of rare 18th-century silver tableware. Commissioned by José I from the Paris workshop of Thomas Germain, the 1,200 pieces include intricately de-corated tureens, sauce boats and salt cellars. The rich col-lection of jewels came from the convents, originally donated by members of the nobility and wealthy bourgeoisie on entering the religious orders.

APPLIED ARTS

FURNITURE, tapestries, and textiles, liturgical vestments and bishops' miters are among the wide range of objects on display. The furniture collection

has many examples from the reigns of King João V, King José, and Queen Maria I, tracing the progress from Baroque to Neo-Classical styles. Of the foreign furniture, French pieces from the 18th century are the most prominent.

The textiles include 17th-century bedspreads, tapestries, many of Flemish origin, such as the *Baptism of Christ* (16th century), embroidered rugs, and Arraiolos carpets *(see p301)*.

Gold Madre de Deus reliquary inlaid with precious stones (c.1502)

Belém

At the mouth of the Tagus River, where the caravels set sail on their voyages of discovery, Belém is inextricably linked with Portugal's Golden Age *(see pp46–9)*. When Manuel I came to power in 1495 he reaped the profits of those heady days of expansion, building grandiose monuments and churches that mirrored the spirit of the time. Two of the finest examples of the exuberant and exotic Manueline style of architecture *(see pp20–21)* are the Mosteiro dos Jerónimos and the Torre de Belém.

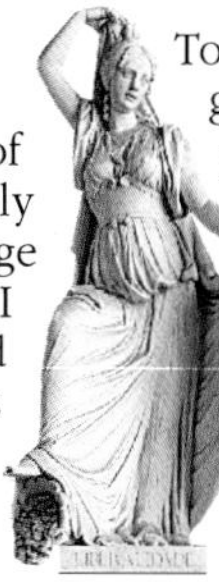

***Generosity*, statue at entrance to Palácio da Ajuda**

Today Belém is a spacious, relatively green suburb with many museums, parks, and gardens, as well as an attractive riverside setting with cafés and a promenade. On sunny days there is a distinct seaside feel to the embankment.

Before the Tagus receded, the monks in the monastery used to look out onto the river and watch the boats set forth. In contrast today several lanes of traffic along the busy Avenida da Índia cut central Belém off from the picturesque waterfront, and silver and yellow trains rattle regularly past.

Sights at a Glance

Museums and Galleries
Museu de Arte Popular 10
Museu da Marinha 7
Museu Nacional de Arqueologia 5
Museu Nacional dos Coches 2
Planetário Calouste Gulbenkian 6

Parks and Gardens
Jardim Agrícola Tropical 3
Jardim Botânico da Ajuda 14

Churches and Monasteries
Ermida de São Jerónimo 12
Igreja da Memória 13
Mosteiro dos Jerónimos pp106–7 4

Historic Buildings
Palácio de Belém 1
Palácio Nacional da Ajuda 15
Torre de Belém p110 11

Monuments
Monument to the Discoveries 9

Cultural Centers
Centro Cultural de Belém 8

Key
Street-by-Street: Belém *pp102–3*
Train station
Ferry boarding point
Parking
Railroad line

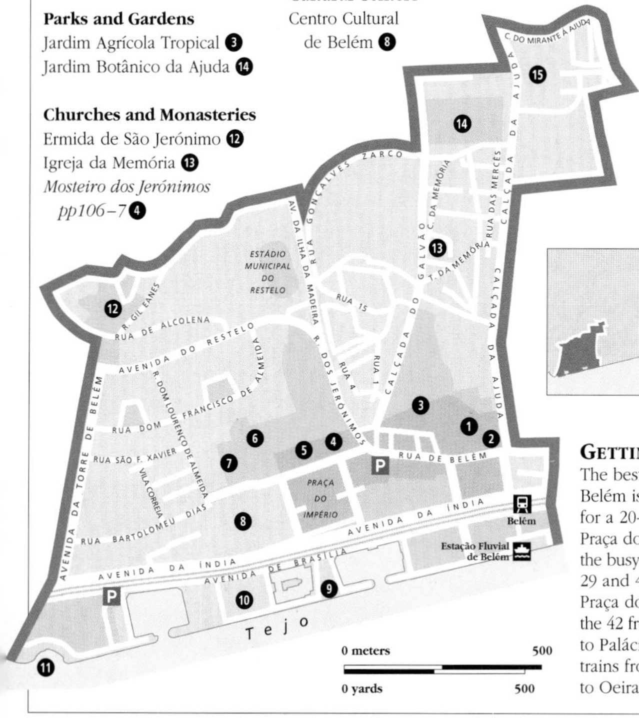

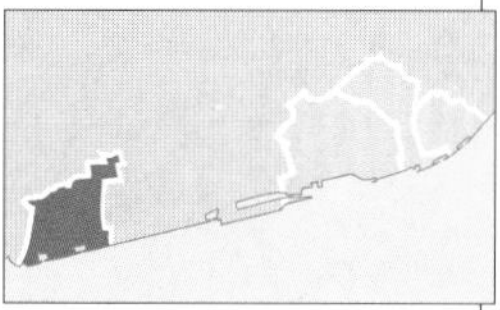

Getting There

The best way to reach Belém is to take tram 15 for a 20-minute ride from Praça do Comércio along the busy waterfront. Buses 29 and 43 also leave from Praça do Comércio, and the 42 from Saldanha goes to Palácio da Ajuda. Slow trains from Cais do Sodré to Oeiras stop at Belém.

◁ **Nave of Santa Maria de Belém, the church of the Jerónimos monastery**

Street-by-Street: Belém

PORTUGAL'S FORMER maritime glory, expressed in the imposing, exuberant buildings such as the Jerónimos monastery, is evident all around Belém. In Salazar's *(see p56)* attempted revival of awareness of Portugal's Golden Age, the area along the waterfront, which had silted up since the days of the caravels, was restructured to celebrate the former greatness of the nation. Praça do Império was laid out for the Exhibition of the Portuguese World in 1940, and Praça Afonso de Albuquerque was dedicated to Portugal's first viceroy of India. The royal Palácio de Belém, restored with gardens and a riding school by João V in the 18th century, briefly housed the royal family after the 1755 earthquake.

Stone caravel, Jerónimos monastery

★ **Mosteiro dos Jerónimos**
Vaulted arcades and richly carved columns adorned with foliage, exotic animals, and navigational instruments decorate the Manueline cloister of the Jerónimos monastery ❹

L A R G O

D O S

J E R Ó N I M O S

P R A Ç A   D O   I M P É R I O

Museu Nacional de Arqueologia
Archaeological finds ranging from an Iron Age gold bracelet to Moorish artifacts are among the interesting exhibits on display ❺

Torre de Belém
(see p110)

STAR SIGHTS

★ **Mosteiro dos Jerónimos**

★ **Museu Nacional dos Coches**

KEY

— — — Suggested route

Praça do Império, an impressive square that opens out in front of the monastery, is lit up on special occasions with a colorful light display in the central fountain.

Rua Vieira Portuense runs along a small park. Its colorful 16th- and 17th-century houses contrast with the typically imposing buildings in Belém.

Jardim Agrícola Tropical
Exotic plants and trees gathered from Portugal's former colonies fill these peaceful gardens, which were once part of the Palácio de Belém ❸

Antiga Confeitaria de Belém, a 19th-century café, sells *pastéis de Belém*, rich custard in a flaky pastry cup.

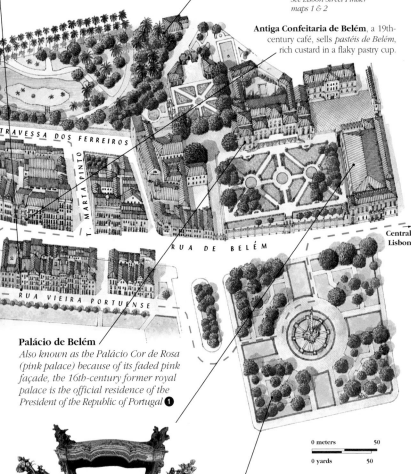

TRAVESSA DOS FERREIROS

T. MARTA PINTO

RUA DE BELÉM

Central Lisbon

RUA VIEIRA PORTUENSE

Palácio de Belém
Also known as the Palácio Cor de Rosa (pink palace) because of its faded pink façade, the 16th-century former royal palace is the official residence of the President of the Republic of Portugal ❶

| 0 meters | 50 |
| 0 yards | 50 |

★ Museu Nacional dos Coches
This 18th-century coach used by the ambassador to Pope Clement XI is part of the collection in the old riding school of the Palácio de Belém ❷

Praça Afonso de Albuquerque is named after the first Portuguese viceroy of India. A Neo-Manueline column in the center bears his statue, with scenes of his life carved on the base.

Palácio de Belém ➊

Praça Afonso de Albuquerque.
Map 1 C4. 🚇 21-361 46 00. 🚌 14, 28, 43, 49. 🚊 15. 🚉 Belém.
🕐 3rd Sun (am) of month. 🅿️ ♿

BUILT BY the Conde de Aveiras in 1559 before the Tagus had receded, this summer palace once had gardens bordering the river. In the 18th century it was bought by João V, who had acquired vast wealth through gold from Brazil *(see pp52–3)*. He radically altered the palace, added a riding school and rendered the interior suitably lavish for his amorous liaisons.

When the great earthquake struck in 1755 *(see pp62–3)*, the king, José I, and his family were staying here and thus survived the devastation of central Lisbon. Fearing another earth tremor, the royal family temporarily set up camp in tents in the palace grounds, and the palace interior was used as a hospital. Today the elegant pink building, which resembles a country estate, is the residence of the President of Portugal.

Pink façade of the Palácio de Belém, home of the President of Portugal

Museu Nacional dos Coches ➋

Praça Afonso de Albuquerque.
Map 2 D4. 🚇 21-361 08 50. 🚌 14, 28, 43, 49. 🚊 15. 🚉 Belém.
🕐 10am–5.30pm Tue–Sun. ⬤ Jan 1, Easter, May 1, Dec 25. 🎫 🅿️

THE MUSEUM's collection of coaches is arguably the finest in Europe. Occupying the east wing of the Palácio de Belém, this was formerly the riding school built by the Italian architect Giacomo Azzolini in 1726. Seated in the upper gallery, the royal family used to watch their beautiful Lusitanian horses *(see p296)* performing in the arena. In 1905 the riding school was turned into a museum by King Carlos's wife, Dona Amélia, whose pink riding cloak is on display.

Made in Portugal, Italy, France, Austria, and Spain, the coaches span three centuries and range from the plain to the preposterous. The main gallery, in Louis XVI style with splendid painted ceiling, is the setting for two straight, regimented rows of coaches created for Portuguese royalty.

The collection starts with the comparatively plain 17th-century red leather and wood coach of Philip II of Spain *(see pp50–51)*. The coaches become increasingly sumptuous, interiors lined with red velvet and gold, exteriors profusely carved and decorated with allegories and royal coats of arms. The rows end with three huge Baroque coaches made in Rome for the Portuguese ambassador to the Vatican, Dom Rodrigo Almeida e Menezes, the Marquês de Abrantes. The epitome of pomp and extravagance, but not necessarily of comfort, these 5-ton carriages are embellished with a plush interior and life-size gilded statues.

The neighboring gallery has more examples of royal carriages, including two-wheeled cabriolets, landaus, and pony-drawn chaises used by young members of the royal family. There is also a 19th-century Lisbon cab, painted black and green, the colors of

Rear view of a coach built in 1716 for the Marquês de Abrantes, the Portuguese ambassador to Pope Clement XI

taxis right up to the 1990s. The 18th-century Eyeglass Chaise, whose black leather hood is pierced by sinister eyelike windows, was made during the era of Pombal *(see pp52–3)* when lavish decoration was discouraged. The upper gallery has a collection of harnesses, court costumes, and portraits of members of the royal family.

Jardim Agrícola Tropical ❸

Calçada do Galvão. **Map** 1 C4.
(21-362 02 10. **▦** 27, 28, 43, 51.
▦ 15. **◯** call to check.
◉ public hols. **Ⓐ &** **Museu Tropical ◯** by appt only.

ALSO KNOWN AS the Jardim do Ultramar, this peaceful park with ponds, waterfowl, and peacocks, attracts surprisingly few visitors. Laid out at the beginning of the 20th century as the research center of the Institute for Tropical Sciences, it is more of an arboretum than a flower garden. The emphasis is on rare tropical and subtropical trees and plants, many of them endangered species. Among the most striking are dragon trees, native to the Canary Islands and Madeira, monkey puzzle trees from South America, and a handsome avenue of lofty Washington palms. The oriental garden with its streams, bridges, and hibiscus is heralded by a large Chinese-style gateway, which represented Macão in the Exhibition of the Portuguese World in 1940 *(see p102)*.

The research buildings and **Museu Tropical** are housed in the Palácio dos Condes da Calheta, an 18th-century mansion whose interior walls are covered with *azulejos* spanning three centuries. The museum has 50,000 dried plant specimens and 2,414 samples of wood.

Mosteiro dos Jerónimos ❹

See pp106–7.

Washington palms in the Jardim Agrícola Tropical

Museu Nacional de Arqueologia ❺

Praça do Império. **Map** 1 B4. **(** 21-362 00 00. **▦** 28, 43, 49, 51. **▦** 15.
◯ 10am–6pm Wed–Sun, 2pm–6pm Tue. **◉** Jan 1, Easter, May 1, Dec 25.
Ⓐ ◙ &

THE LONG west wing of the Mosteiro dos Jerónimos *(see pp106–7)*, formerly the monks' dormitory, has been a museum since 1893. Reconstructed in the middle of the 19th century, the building is a poor imitation of the Manueline original. The museum houses Portugal's main archaeological research center and the exhibits, from sites all over the country, include a gold Iron Age bracelet found at Grândola in the Alentejo, Visigothic jewelry from Beja *(see p311)*, Roman ornaments and early 8th-century Moorish artefacts. The main Egyptian and Greco-Roman section is strong on funerary art, featuring figurines, tombstones, masks, terra-cotta amulets, and funeral cones inscribed with hieroglyphics alluding to the solar system. The dimly lit Room of Treasures has an exquisite collection of coins, necklaces, bracelets, and other jewelry dating from 1800–500 BC but a frustrating

Visigothic gold buckle, Museu de Arqueologia

lack of information. Some of the space is devoted to long-running temporary exhibits, and part of the permanent collection is not on display.

Planetário Calouste Gulbenkian ❻

Praça do Império. **Map** 1 B4. **(** 21-362 00 02. **▦** 28, 43, 49, 51. **▦** 15.
◯ for shows: 4pm & 5pm Sat & Sun (also school hols: 11am, 3pm & 4:15pm Wed & Thu). Special shows for children 11am Sun. **◉** public hols. **Ⓐ ◙ &**

FINANCED BY the Gulbenkian Foundation *(see p119)* and built in 1965, this modern building sits incongruously beside the Jerónimos monastery. Inside, the Planetarium recreates the sky at night and reveals the mysteries of the cosmos. There are shows in Portuguese, English, and French explaining the movement of the stars and our solar system, as well as presentations on more specific themes, such as the constellations or the Star of Bethlehem (Belém).

The dome of the Planetário Calouste Gulbenkian

Mosteiro dos Jerónimos

Armillary sphere in the cloister

A MONUMENT TO THE WEALTH of the Age of Discovery *(see pp48–9)*, the monastery is the culmination of Manueline architecture *(see pp20–21)*. Commissioned by Manuel I in 1501, soon after Vasco da Gama's return from his historic voyage, it was financed largely by "pepper money," the profits made from the spice trade. Various masterbuilders worked on the building, the most notable of whom was Diogo Boitac, replaced by João de Castilho in 1516. The monastery was entrusted to the Order of St. Jerome (Hieronymites) until 1834, when all religious orders were disbanded.

Tomb of Vasco da Gama
The 19th-century tomb of the explorer (see p108) *is carved with ropes, armillary spheres, and other seafaring symbols.*

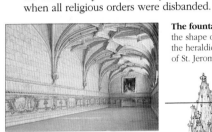

Refectory
The walls of the refectory are tiled with 18th-century azulejos. The panel at the northern end depicts the Feeding of the Five Thousand.

The fountain is in the shape of a lion, the heraldic animal of St. Jerome.

The modern wing, built in 1850 in Neo-Manueline style, houses the Museu Nacional de Arqueologia *(see p105)*.

The west portal was designed by the French sculptor Nicolau Chanterène.

Entrance to church and cloister

Gallery

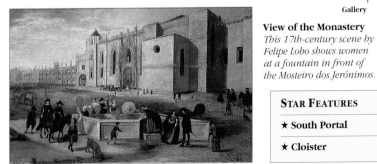

View of the Monastery
This 17th-century scene by Felipe Lobo shows women at a fountain in front of the Mosteiro dos Jerónimos.

STAR FEATURES
★ **South Portal**
★ **Cloister**

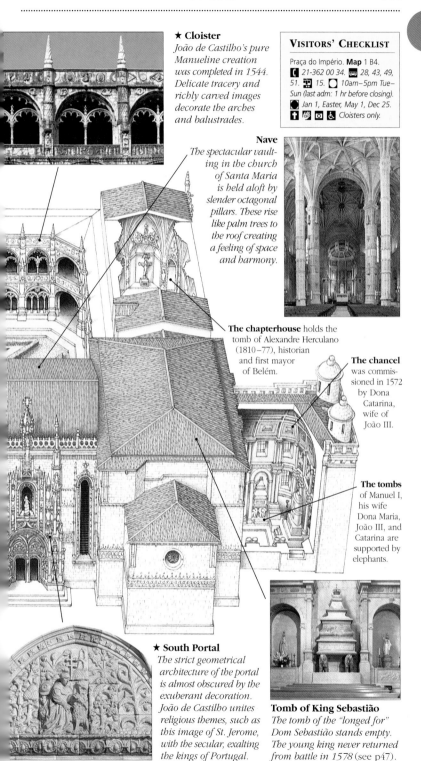

★ **Cloister**
João de Castilho's pure Manueline creation was completed in 1544. Delicate tracery and richly carved images decorate the arches and balustrades.

Nave
The spectacular vaulting in the church of Santa Maria is held aloft by slender octagonal pillars. These rise like palm trees to the roof creating a feeling of space and harmony.

The chapterhouse holds the tomb of Alexandre Herculano (1810–77), historian and first mayor of Belém.

The chancel was commissioned in 1572 by Dona Catarina, wife of João III.

The tombs of Manuel I, his wife Dona Maria, João III, and Catarina are supported by elephants.

★ **South Portal**
The strict geometrical architecture of the portal is almost obscured by the exuberant decoration. João de Castilho unites religious themes, such as this image of St. Jerome, with the secular, exalting the kings of Portugal.

Tomb of King Sebastião
The tomb of the "longed for" Dom Sebastião stands empty. The young king never returned from battle in 1578 (see p47).

Façade of the Museu da Marinha

Museu da Marinha ➐

Praça do Império. **Map** 1 B4. **C** 21-362 00 19. **🚌** 28, 43, 49, 51. **🚊** 15. **◻** 10am–6pm (Oct–May: 5pm) Tue–Sun. **◯** public hols. **🖼️ 📷 ♿**

T HE MARITIME MUSEUM was inaugurated in 1962 in the west wing of the Jerónimos monastery (see pp106–7). The site was significant since it was here, in the chapel built by Henry the Navigator (see p49), that mariners took mass before embarking on their historic voyages. A hall devoted to the Discoveries illustrates the rapid progress in shipbuilding from the mid-15th century, capitalizing on the experience of the long-distance explorers. Small replicas show the transition from the bark to the lateen-rigged caravel, through the faster square-rigged caravel, to the Portuguese *nau*. Also relating to the Discoveries are navigational instruments, astrolabes, and replicas of 16th-century maps showing the world as it was then known. The stone pillars, carved with the Cross of the Knights of Christ, are replicas of the types of *padrão* set up as monuments to Portuguese sovereignty on the lands discovered. Beyond the Hall of Discoveries a series of rooms displaying models of modern Portuguese ships leads on to the Royal Quarters where you can see the exquisitely furnished wood-paneled cabin of King Carlos and Queen Amélia from the royal yacht *Amélia*, built in Scotland in 1900.

The modern, incongruous pavilion opposite houses original royal barges, the most extravagant of which is the royal brig built in 1780 for Maria I. The collection ends with a display of seaplanes, including the *Santa Clara*, which made the first crossing of the South Atlantic in 1922.

Centro Cultural de Belém ➑

Praça do Império. **Map** 1 B5. **C** 21-361 24 00. **🚌** 28, 43, 49, 51. **🚊** 15. **◻** 8am–10pm Mon–Fri, 10am–7pm Sat–Sun. **♿ Exhibition Center** **◻** 11am–8pm. **🖼️ ♿**

T HE CONSTRUCTION of a stark modern building directly between the Jerónimos monastery and the Tagus was clearly controversial. Built in 1990 as the headquarters of the Portuguese presidency of the European Community, it opened as a cultural center in 1993. It stresses music, performing arts, and photography, with a large **Exhibition Center** used for temporary displays. Lecture halls are named after places in Asia visited by the author Fernão Mendes Pinto (1510–83).

The centre is somewhat soulless, but on weekends it is enlivened by street performers, actors, and rollerbladers.

The modern complex of the Centro Cultural de Belém

Monument to the Discoveries ➒

Padrão dos Descobrimentos, Avenida de Brasília. **Map** 1 C5. **C** 21-301 62 28. **🚌** 28, 29, 43, 51. **🚊** 15. **◻** 9:30am–6:30pm Tue–Sun. **●** public hols. **🖼️** for elevator. **📷**

S TANDING PROMINENTLY on the Belém waterfront, this massive angular monument, the Padrão dos Descobrimentos, was built in 1960 to mark the 500th anniversary of the death of Henry the Navigator (see p49). The 52-m (170-ft) high monument, commissioned by the Salazar regime, commemorates the mariners, royal patrons, and all those who participated in the rapid development of the Portuguese Age

VASCO DA GAMA (c.1460–1524)

In 1498 Vasco da Gama sailed around the Cape of Good Hope and opened the sea route to India (see pp48–9). Although the Hindu ruler of Calicut, who received him wearing diamond and ruby rings, was not impressed by his humble offerings of cloth and wash basins, da Gama returned to Portugal with a cargo of spices. In 1502 he sailed again to India, establishing Portuguese trade routes in the Indian Ocean. João III nominated him Viceroy of India in 1524, but he died of a fever soon after.

16th-century painting of Vasco da Gama in Goa

The huge sidewalk compass in front of the Monument to the Discoveries

Museu de Arte Popular ⑩

Avenida de Brasília. **Map** 1 B5. 21-301 12 82. 28, 29, 43, 51. 15. 10am–12:30pm, 2–5pm Tue–Sun. Jan 1, Easter, May 1, Dec 25.

THE DRAB BUILDING on the waterfront, between the Monument to the Discoveries and the Torre de Belém *(see p110)*, houses the museum of Portuguese folk art and traditional handicrafts, opened in 1948. The exhibits, which are arranged by province, include local pottery, agricultural tools, costumes, musical instruments, jewelry, and brightly colored saddles. The display gives a vivid indication of the diversity between the different regions.

Each area has its specialty such as the colorful ox yokes and ceramic cocks from the Minho, basketware from Trás-os-Montes, cowbells and terra-cotta casseroles from the Alentejo, and fishing equipment from the Algarve. The labeling is sparse, and the visitor is given little information when it comes to the more obscure or extinct handicrafts. However, if you are planning to travel around the country the museum offers an excellent preview to the traditional handicrafts of the provinces that you will visit.

of Discovery. The monument is designed in the shape of a caravel, with Portugal's coat of arms on the sides and the sword of the Royal House of Avis rising above the entrance. Henry the Navigator stands at the prow with a caravel in hand. In two sloping lines either side of the monument are stone statues of Portuguese heroes linked with the Age of Discovery. On the western face these include Dom Manuel I holding an armillary sphere, the poet Camões with a copy of *Os Lusíadas*, the painter Nuno Gonçalves with a paint pallet, as well as famous navigators, cartographers, and kings.

On the monument's north side, the huge mariner's compass cut into the paving stone was a present from the Republic of South Africa

in 1960. The central map, dotted with galleons and mermaids, shows the routes of the discoverers in the 15th and 16th centuries. Inside an elevator whisks you up to the sixth floor where steps then lead to the top for a splendid panorama of the river and Belém. The basement level is used for temporary exhibitions but not necessarily related to the Discoveries.

The rather ostentatious Padrão is not to everyone's taste, but the setting is undeniably splendid and the caravel design is imaginative. The monument looks particularly dramatic when viewed from the west in the light of the late afternoon sun.

Traditional costume from Trás-os-Montes

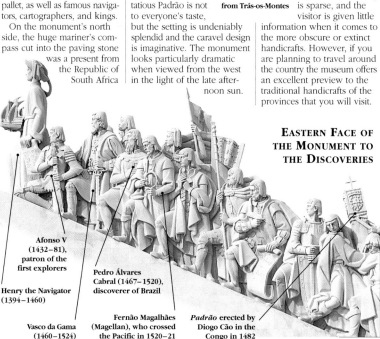

EASTERN FACE OF THE MONUMENT TO THE DISCOVERIES

Afonso V (1432–81), patron of the first explorers

Henry the Navigator (1394–1460)

Pedro Álvares Cabral (1467–1520), discoverer of Brazil

Vasco da Gama (1460–1524)

Fernão Magalhães (Magellan), who crossed the Pacific in 1520–21

Padrão erected by Diogo Cão in the Congo in 1482

Torre de Belém

Arms of Manuel I

COMMISSIONED BY Manuel I, the tower was built as a fortress in the middle of the Tagus in 1515–21. Starting point for the navigators who set out to discover the trade routes, this Manueline gem became a symbol of Portugal's great era of expansion. The real beauty of the tower lies in the decoration of the exterior. Adorned with rope carved in stone, it has openwork balconies, Moorish-style watchtowers, and distinctive battlements in the shape of shields. The Gothic interior below the terrace, which served as a storeroom for arms and a prison, is very austere, but the private quarters in the tower are worth visiting for the loggia and the panorama.

VISITORS' CHECKLIST

Avenida da India. **Map** 1 A5.
☎ 21-362 00 34. 🚌 14, 28, 43, 51. 🚋 15. 🚉 Belém.
⏰ 10am–5pm Tue–Sun.
⬤ Jan 1, Easter, May 1, Dec 25.
📷 👍 ground floor only.

Armillary spheres and nautical rope are symbols of Portugal's seafaring prowess.

Renaissance Loggia
The elegant arcaded loggia, inspired by Italian architecture, gives a light touch to the defensive battlements of the tower.

Royal coat of arms of Manuel I

Chapel

Battlements are decorated with the cross of the Order of Christ (*see pp20–21*).

Virgin and Child
A statue of Our Lady of Safe Homecoming faces the sea, a symbol of protection for sailors on their voyages of discovery.

Governor's room

Gangway to shore

Entrance

Sentry posts

The vaulted dungeon was used as a prison until the 19th century.

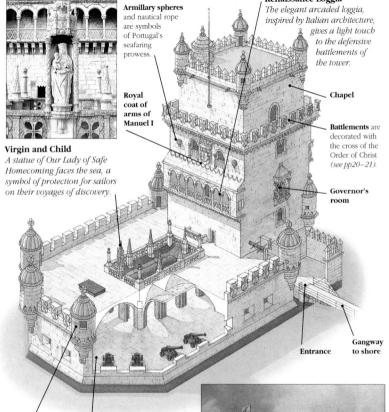

The Torre de Belém in 1811
This painting of a British ship navigating the Tagus, by JT Serres, shows the tower much farther from the shore than it is today. In the 19th century land on the north bank was reclaimed, making the river narrower.

The simple Manueline chapel, Ermida de São Jerónimo

Ermida de São Jerónimo ⑫

Rua Pedro de Covilhã. **Map** 1 A3. 🕿 21-301 86 48. 🚍 27, 28, 41. ⏱ by appt only.

Also known as the Capela de São Jerónimo, this elegant little chapel was constructed in 1514 when Diogo Boitac was working on the Jerónimos monastery *(see pp106–7)*. Although a far simpler building, it is also Manueline in style and may have been built to a design by Boitac. The only decorative elements on the monolithic chapel are the four pinnacles, corner gargoyles, and Manueline portal. Perched on a quiet hill above Belém, the chapel has fine views down to the River Tagus, and a path from the terrace winds down the hill toward the Torre de Belém.

Igreja da Memória ⑬

Calçada do Galvão, Ajuda. **Map** 1 C3. 🕿 21-363 52 95. 🚍 14, 29, 73. ⏱ 4–6pm Mon–Sat. 🚹 🚻

Built in 1760, the church was founded by King José I in gratitude for his escape from an assassination plot on this site in 1758. The king was returning from a secret liaison with a lady of the noble Távora family when his carriage was attacked, and a bullet hit him in the arm. Pombal *(see pp52–3)*, whose power had now become absolute, used this as an excuse to get rid of his enemies in the Távora family, accusing them of conspiracy. In 1759 they were tortured and executed. Their deaths are commemorated by a pillar in Beco do Chão Salgado, off Rua de Belém.

The Neo-Classical domed church has a marble-clad interior and a small chapel, on the right, containing the tomb of Pombal. He died at the age of 83, a year after he had been banished from Lisbon.

Jardim Botânico da Ajuda ⑭

Calçada da Ajuda. **Map** 1 C2. 🚍 14, 29, 73. 🚋 18. ⏱ 8am–5pm Mon–Fri. ⬤ public hols. 🎟 🚻

Laid out on two levels by Pombal *(see pp52–3)* in 1768, these Italian-style gardens provide a pleasant respite from the noisy suburbs of Belém. The entrance, through green wrought-iron gates in a pink wall, is easy to miss. The park holds tropical trees and geometrical boxwood hedge gardens surrounding neat flower beds. Notable features are the 400-year-old dragon tree, native of Madeira, and the large and flamboyant 18th-century fountain decorated with writhing serpents, winged fish, sea horses, and mythical creatures. A broad, majestic terrace looks out over the lower level of the gardens.

Palácio Nacional da Ajuda ⑮

Largo da Ajuda. **Map** 2 D2. 🕿 21-363 70 95. 🚍 42, 60. 🚋 18. ⏱ 10am–5pm Thu–Tue. ⬤ Jan 1, Easter, May 1, Dec 25. 🎟 🚻

The royal palace, destroyed by fire in 1795, was replaced in the early 19th century by the Neo-Classical building you see today. This was left incomplete when the royal family was forced into exile in Brazil in 1807 *(see pp52–3)*.

The palace only became a permanent residence of the royal family when Luís I became king in 1861 and married an Italian Princess, Maria Pia di Savoia. No expense was spared in furnishing the apartments. The ostentatious rooms are decorated with silk wallpaper, Sèvres porcelain, and crystal chandeliers.

A prime example of regal excess is the extraordinary Saxe Room, a wedding present to Maria Pia from the King of Saxony, where every piece of furniture is decorated with Meissen porcelain. On the first floor the huge Banqueting Hall, with crystal chandeliers, silk-covered chairs, and an allegory of the birth of João VI on the frescoed ceiling, is truly impressive. At the other end of the palace, Luís I's Neo-Gothic painting studio is a more intimate display of intricately carved furniture.

19th-century throne from the Palácio Nacional da Ajuda

Manicured formal gardens of the Jardim Botânico da Ajuda

FARTHER AFIELD

THE MAJORITY of the outlying sights, which include some of Lisbon's finest museums, are easily accessible by bus or metro from the city center. A ten-minute walk north from the gardens of the Parque Eduardo VII brings you to Portugal's great cultural complex, the Calouste Gulbenkian Foundation, set in a pleasant park. Few tourists go farther north than the Gulbenkian, but the Museu da Cidade on Campo Grande is worth a detour for its fascinating overview of Lisbon's history.

Azulejo **panel from Palácio Fronteira**

The charming Palácio Fronteira, decorated with splendid tiles, is one of the many villas built for the aristocracy that now overlook the city suburbs. Those interested in tiles will also enjoy the Museu Nacional do Azulejo in the cloisters of the Madre de Deus convent. Visitors with half a day to spare can cross the Tagus to the Cristo Rei monument. Northeast of the city center, the vast Oceanarium is part of Expo '98, a project that has regenerated the area into a residential and commercial center.

SIGHTS AT A GLANCE

Museums and Galleries
Centro de Arte Moderna **7**
Museu da Água **9**
Museu Calouste Gulbenkian pp116–19 **6**
Museu da Cidade **12**
Museu Nacional do Azulejo pp122–3 **10**

Modern Architecture
Amoreiras Shopping Center **3**
Cristo Rei **1**
Ponte 25 de Abril **2**

Historic Architecture
Aqueduto das Águas Livres **14**
Campo Pequeno **8**
Palácio Fronteira **15**
Praça Marquês de Pombal **4**

Parks and Gardens
Parque Eduardo VII **5**
Parque do Monteiro-Mor **16**

Zoos
Jardim Zoológico **13**
Pavilhão dos Oceanos **11**

KEY

  Main sightseeing areas

 ✈ Airport

 ⛴ Ferry boarding point

 ═ Highway

 ═ Major road

 ═ Minor road

0 kilometers 4

0 miles 2

SIGHTS BEYOND THE CITY CENTER

◁ **Nymph fountain among tropical vegetation inside the Estufa Fria, Parque Eduardo VII**

Cristo Rei

Santuário Nacional do Cristo Rei, Alto do Pragal, Almada. *21-275 10 00.* *from Praça do Comércio & Cais do Sodré to Cacilhas then 101.* **Elevator** *9:30am–6pm daily.*

MODELED ON the more famous Cristo Redentor in Rio de Janeiro, this giant-sized statue stands, with arms outstretched, on the south bank of the Tagus. The 28 m (92 ft) tall figure of Christ, mounted on a huge pedestal, was built by Francisco Franco in 1949–59 at the instigation of Prime Minister Salazar.

You can see the monument from various viewpoints in the city, but it is fun to take a ferry to the Outra Banda (the other bank), then a bus or taxi to the monument. (Rush hour is best avoided.) An elevator, plus some steps, takes you 82 m (269 ft) to the pedestal top, giving fine views of the city and river.

The towering monument of Cristo Rei overlooking the Tagus

Ponte 25 de Abril ➋

Map 3 A5. *52, 53.*

ORIGINALLY CALLED the Ponte Salazar after the dictator who had it built in 1966, Lisbon's suspension bridge was renamed (like many other monuments) to commemorate the revolution of April 25, 1974 that restored democracy to Portugal *(see p57).*

Inspired by San Francisco's Golden Gate in the United States, this steel construction stretches for 2 km (1 mile). Work currently being done will add a new tier under the bridge for a much-needed railroad across the Tagus. The bridge is notorious for traffic congestion, particularly on weekends, but the problem has at least been partly re-solved by the construction of the 12-km (7-mile) Vasco da Gama bridge. Spanning the river from Montijo to Sacavém, north of the Expo site, this bridge was completed in 1998.

Amoreiras Shopping Center ➌

Avenida Engenheiro Duarte Pacheco. **Map** 5 A5. *21-381 02 00.* **M** *Rotunda.* *11, 23, 53.* *10am–11pm daily.* *Dec 25.*

IN THE 18TH CENTURY, the Marquês de Pombal *(see pp52–3)* planted mulberry trees *(amoreiras)* on the western edge of the city to create food for silk worms. Hence the name of the futuristic shopping center that was built here in 1985. This massive complex, with pink and blue towers, houses 370 shops, ten movie theaters, and cafés. An incon-gruous feature of Lisbon, it nevertheless manages to draw the crowds, particularly the young, and has taken many shoppers away from the more traditional quarters of the city.

Ponte 25 de Abril linking central Lisbon with the Outra Banda, the south bank of the Tagus

Tropical plants in the Estufa Quente glasshouse, Parque Eduardo VII

Praça Marquês de Pombal ●

Map 5 C5. **M** Rotunda. 🚌 11, 23, 36, 101 & many other routes.

AT THE TOP of the Avenida da Liberdade *(see p84)*, traffic thunders around the "Rotunda" (traffic circle), as the praça is also known. At the center rises the lofty monument to Pombal, unveiled in 1934. The despotic statesman, who virtually ruled Portugal from 1750–77, stands on the top of the column, his hand on a lion (symbol of power) and his eyes directed down to the Baixa, whose creation he masterminded *(see pp62–3).*

Detail representing agricultural toil on the base of the monument in Praça Marquês de Pombal

Allegorical images depicting Pombal's political, educational, and agricultural reforms decorate the base of the monument. Standing figures represent Coimbra University where he introduced a new Faculty of Science. Although greatly feared, this dynamic politician propelled the country into the Age of Enlightenment. Broken blocks of stone at the foot of the monument and tidal waves flooding the city are an allegory of the destruction caused by the 1755 earthquake.

The sculptures on the pedestal and the inscriptions relating to Pombal's achievements can be seen by taking the underpass into the center of the square. This also leads to the Rotunda metro station and the well-tended Parque Eduardo VII that extends northward behind the square. The paving stones around the Rotunda are decorated with a mosaic of Lisbon's coat of arms. Similar patterns in small black and white cobbles decorate many of the city's streets and squares.

Parque Eduardo VII ●

Praça Marquês de Pombal. **Map** 5 B4. **C** 21-388 22 78. **M** Rotunda. 🚌 2, 11, 22, 36. **Estufa Fria** 🕐 May–Sep: 9am–5:30pm daily; Oct–Apr: 9am–4:30pm daily. ● Jan 1, Apr 25, May 1, Dec 25. 🎫

THE LARGEST PARK in central Lisbon was named in honor of King Edward VII of England who came to Lisbon in 1902 to reaffirm the Anglo-Portuguese alliance. The wide grassy slope, extending for 62 acres (25 ha), was created as a continuation of Avenida da Liberdade *(see p84)* at the beginning of the 20th century. Neatly clipped box hedging, flanked by mosaic patterned walkways, stretches uphill from the Praça Marquês de Pombal to a belvedere at the top that gives fine views of the city and the distant hills on the far side of the Tagus. On clear days it is possible to see as far as the Serra da Arrábida *(see p167).*

Located at the northwest corner, the most inspiring feature of this rather monotonous park is the junglelike **Estufa Fria**, or greenhouse, where exotic plants, streams, and waterfalls provide an oasis from the city streets. There are in fact two greenhouses: in the Estufa Fria (cold greenhouse), palms push through the slatted bamboo roof, and paths wind through a forest of ferns, fuchsias, flowering shrubs, and banana trees. The warmer Estufa Quente, or hothouse, is a glassed-over garden with lush plants, waterlily ponds, and cacti, as well as tropical birds in cages.

Near the estufas a shallow pond with large carp and a play area in the shape of a galleon are popular with children. On the east side the **Pavilhão Carlos Lopes**, named after the winner of the 1984 Olympic marathon, is now a spot for concerts and conferences. The dazzling white and ocher façade is decorated with a series of modern tiled scenes by Jorge Colaço *(see p23)*, mainly of Portuguese battles. A pleasant waterside café lies to the north of the pavilion.

Museu Calouste Gulbenkian ◐

T HANKS TO A WEALTHY Armenian oil magnate, Calouste
Gulbenkian *(see p119)*, with wide-ranging tastes and
an eye for a masterpiece, the museum has one of the
finest collections of art in Europe. Inaugurated in 1969,
the built-to-order museum was created as part of the
charitable institution bequeathed to Portugal by the
multimillionaire. The design of the building, set in a
spacious park allowing natural light to fill some
of the rooms, was devised to create
the best layout for the founder's
varied collection.

Mustard Barrel
*This 18th-century
silver mustard barrel
was made in France by
Antoine Sébastien
Durand.*

Lalique Corsage Ornament
*The sinuous curves of the
gold and enamel snakes are
typical of René Lalique's
Art Nouveau jewelry.*

★ Diana
*This fine marble statue
(1780) by the French
sculptor Jean-Antoine
Houdon, was once owned
by Catherine the Great of
Russia but was considered
too obscene to exhibit. The
graceful Diana, goddess
of the hunt, stands
with a bow and
arrow in hand.*

Entrance

Stairs to

★ St. Catherine
*This serene bust
of St. Catherine
was painted by
the Flemish artist
Roger Van der
Weyden (1400–64).
The thin strip of
landscape on the
left of the wooden
panel brings light
and depth to the
still portrait.*

STAR EXHIBITS

★ **Portrait of an Old Man by Rembrandt**

★ **Diana by Houdon**

★ **St. Catherine by Van der Weyden**

★ Portrait of an Old Man
Rembrandt was a master of light and shade. In this expressive portrait, dated 1645, the fragile countenance of the old man is contrasted with the strong and dramatic lighting.

Vase of a Hundred Birds
The enamel decoration that adorns this Chinese porcelain vase is known as Famille Verte. *This type of elaborate design is characteristic of the Ch'ing dynasty during the reign of the Emperor K'ang Hsi (1662–1722).*

Renaissance art

GALLERY GUIDE
The galleries are laid out both chronologically and geographically, the first section (rooms 1–6) dedicated to Classical and Oriental art, the second section (rooms 7–17) housing the European collection of paintings, sculpture, furniture, silverware, and jewelry.

Armenian art

Egyptian Bronze Cat
This bronze of a cat feeding her kittens dates from the Saite Period (8th century BC). Other stunning Egyptian pieces include a gilded mask of a mummy.

Persian faïence

Turkish Faïence Plate
The factories at Iznik in Turkey produced some of the most beautiful jugs, plates, and vases of the Islamic world, including this 17th-century deep plate decorated with stylized animal forms.

KEY TO FLOOR PLAN

- ☐ Egyptian, Classical, and Mesopotamian art
- ☐ Oriental Islamic art
- ☐ Far Eastern art
- ☐ European art (14th–17th centuries)
- ☐ French 18th-century decorative arts
- ☐ European art (18th–19th centuries)
- ☐ Lalique collection
- ☐ Nonexhibition space

Exploring the Gulbenkian Collection

Housing CALOUSTE GULBENKIAN's unique collection of art, the museum ranks with the Museu de Arte Antiga (*see pp96–9*) as the finest in Lisbon. The exhibits, which span over 4,000 years from ancient Egyptian statuettes, through translucent Islamic glassware, to Art Nouveau brooches, are displayed in spacious and well-lit galleries, many overlooking the gardens or courtyards. The museum is quite small, but each individual work of art, from the magnificent pieces that make up the rich display of Oriental and Islamic art to the selection of European paintings and furniture, is worthy of attention.

Late 16th-century Persian faïence tile from the School of Isfahan

EGYPTIAN, CLASSICAL, AND MESOPOTAMIAN ART

Priceless treasures chart the evolution of Egyptian art from the Old Kingdom (c.2700 BC) to the Roman Period (1st century BC). The exhibits range from an alabaster bowl of the 3rd Dynasty to a surprisingly modern-looking blue terra-cotta torso of a statuette of *Venus Anadyomene* from the Roman period.

Outstanding pieces in the Classical art section are a magnificent red-figure Greek vase and 11 Roman medallions found in Egypt. These are believed to have been struck on the occasion of the commemorative games held in Macedonia in AD 242 in honor of Alexander the Great. In the Mesopotamian art section the large Assyrian alabaster bas-relief represents the winged genius of Spring, carrying a container of sacred water (9th century BC).

5th-century BC Greek vase

ORIENTAL ISLAMIC ART

Being ARMENIAN, Calouste Gulbenkian had a great interest in art from the Near and Middle East. The Oriental Islamic gallery has a fine collection of Persian and Turkish carpets, textiles, costumes, and ceramics. In the section overlooking the courtyard, the Syrian mosque lamps and bottles, commissioned by princes and sultans, are decorated with colored enamel on glass. The Armenian section has some illustrated manuscripts from the 16th to 18th centuries, produced by Armenian refugees in Istanbul, Persia, and the Crimea.

French ivory triptych of
***Scenes from the Life of the Virgin* (14th century)**

FAR EASTERN ART

Calouste Gulbenkian acquired a large collection of Chinese porcelain between 1910 and 1930. One of the rarest pieces is the small blue-glazed bowl from the Yüan Dynasty (1279–1368), on the right as you go into the gallery. The majority of exhibits, however, are the later, more exuberantly decorated *famille verte* porcelain and the K'ang Hsi biscuitware of the 17th and 18th centuries. Other exhibits from the Far East are translucent Chinese jades and other semiprecious stones, brocaded silk hangings, Japanese prints and bound books, and lacquerware.

EUROPEAN ART (14TH–17TH CENTURIES)

Illuminated MANUSCRIPTS, rare printed books, and medieval ivories introduce the section on Western art. The delicately sculpted 14th-century ivory diptychs and triptychs, made in France, show scenes from the lives of Christ and the Virgin.

The collection of early European paintings starts with panels of *St. Joseph* and *St. Catherine* by Roger van der Weyden, leading painter of the mid-15th century in Flanders. Italian Renaissance painting is represented by Cima da Conegliano's *Sacra Conversazione* from the late 15th century and Domenico Ghirlandaio's *Portrait of a Young Woman* (1485).

The collection progresses to Flemish and Dutch works of the 17th century, including two works by Rembrandt: *Portrait of an Old Man* (1645), a masterpiece of psychological insight, and *Alexander the Great* (1660), said to have been modeled on Rembrandt's son, Titus, and previously thought to have portrayed the Greek goddess Pallas Athena. Rubens is represented by three paintings, the most remarkable of which is the *Portrait of Hélène Fourment* (1630), the artist's second wife.

The gallery beyond the Dutch and Flemish paintings has tapestries and textiles from Italy and Flanders, Italian ceramics, rare 15th-century medallions, and sculpture.

FRENCH 18TH-CENTURY DECORATIVE ARTS

SOME REMARKABLY elaborate Louis XV and Louis XVI pieces, many commissioned by royalty, feature in the collection of French 18th-century furniture. The exhibits, many of them embellished with laquer panels, ebony, and bronze, are grouped together according to historical style with Beauvais and "chinoiserie" Aubusson tapestries decorating the walls.

The French silverware from the same period, much of which once adorned the dining tables of Russian palaces, includes lavishly decorated soup tureens, saltcellars, and platters.

Louis XV chest of drawers inlaid with ebony and bronze

EUROPEAN ART (18TH–19TH CENTURIES)

THE ART of the 18th century is dominated by French painters, including Watteau (1684–1721), Fragonard (1732–1806), and Boucher (1703–70). The most celebrated piece of sculpture is a statue of *Diana* by Jean-Antoine Houdon. Commissioned in 1780 by the Duke of Saxe-Gotha for his

View of the Molo with the Ducal Palace (1790) by Francesco Guardi

gardens, it became one of the principal exhibits in the Hermitage in Russia during the 19th and early 20th centuries.

One whole room is devoted to views of Venice by the 18th-century Venetian painter Francesco Guardi, and a small collection of British art includes works by leading 18th-century portraitists, such as Gainsborough's *Portrait of Mrs Lowndes-Stone* (c.1775) and Romney's *Portrait of Mrs Constable* (1787). There are also two stormy seascapes by JMW Turner (1775–1851). French 19th-century landscape painting is well represented here, reflecting Gulbenkian's preference for naturalism, with works by the Barbizon school, the Realists, and the Impressionists. The best-known paintings in the section, however, are probably Manet's *Boy with Cherries*, painted in about 1858 at the beginning of the artist's career, and *Boy Blowing Bubbles*, painted about 1867. Renoir's *Portrait of Madame Claude Monet* was painted in about 1872 when the artist was staying with Monet at his country home in Argenteuil, on the outskirts of Paris.

LALIQUE COLLECTION

THE TOUR of the museum ends with an entire room filled with the flamboyant creations of French Art Nouveau jeweler, René Lalique (1860–1945). Gulbenkian was a close friend of Lalique's, and he acquired many of the pieces of jewelry, glassware, and ivory on display here directly from the artist. Inlaid with semiprecious stones and covered with gold leaf or enamel, the brooches, necklaces, vases, and combs are decorated with the dragonfly, peacock, or sensual female nude motifs characteristic of Art Nouveau.

CALOUSTE GULBENKIAN

Born in Scutari (Turkey) in 1869, Gulbenkian started his art collection at the age of 14 when he bought some ancient coins in a bazaar. In 1928 he was granted a 5 percent stake in four major oil companies, including BP and Shell, in thanks for his part in the transfer of the assets of the Iraq Petroleum Company to those four companies. He thereby earned himself the nickname of "Mr. Five Percent." With the wealth he accumulated, Gulbenkian was able to indulge his passion for fine works of art. During World War II, he went to live in neutral Portugal and, on his death in 1955, bequeathed his estate to the Portuguese in the form of a charitable trust. The Foundation supports numerous cultural activities and has its own orchestra, libraries, ballet company, and concert halls.

Henry Moore sculpture in garden of the Centro de Arte Moderna

Centro de Arte Moderna ➐

Rua Dr Nicolau de Bettencourt.
Map 5 B3. █ 21-795 02 41. Ⓜ São Sebastião. 🚌 41, 46. ⭘ Jun–Sep: 10am–5pm Tue, Thu, Fri & Sun, 2–7pm Wed & Sat; Oct–May: 10am–5pm Tue–Sun. ⬤ public hols. 🖼 ♿

THE MODERN ART MUSEUM lies across the gardens from the Calouste Gulbenkian museum and is part of the same cultural foundation *(see p119)*. The permanent collection housed in the center features paintings and sculpture by Portuguese artists from the turn of the 20th century to the present day. The most famous painting is the striking portrait of poet Fernando Pessoa in the Café Irmãos Unidos (1964) by José de Almada Negreiros (1893–1970), a main exponent of Portuguese Modernism. Also of interest are paintings by Eduardo Viana (1881–1967), Amadeo de Sousa Cardoso (1887–1910), as well as contemporary artists such as Paula Rego, Rui Sanches, Graça Morais, and Teresa Magalhães.

The museum is light and spacious with pleasant gardens and a cafeteria, which attracts very long lines on weekends.

Campo Pequeno ➑

Map 5 C1. Ⓜ Campo Pequeno. 🚌 22, 45. **Bullring** █ 21-793 24 42. ⭘ Easter–Oct: for bullfights. 🖼 ♿

THIS SQUARE is dominated by the red-brick Neo-Moorish bullring built in the late 19th century. A large building, accommodating up to 9,000 spectators, its keyhole-shaped windows and double cupolas decorated with a crescent moon evoke Moorish-style architecture. Bullfights *(see pp144–5)* take place once or twice a week in season. During the rest of the year, the bullring is occasionally used for concerts and other shows, such as the annual circus at Christmas.

Renovated 19th-century steam pump in the Museu da Água

Museu da Água ➒

Rua do Alviela 12. █ 21-813 55 22. 🚌 35, 104, 105, 107. ⭘ 10am–6pm Mon–Sat. ⬤ public hols. 🖼 📷

DEDICATED TO the history of Lisbon's water supply, this small but informative museum was imaginatively created around the city's first steam pumping station. It commemorates Manuel da Maia, the 18th-century engineer who masterminded the Águas Livres aqueduct *(see p124)*. The excellent layout of the museum earned it the Council of Europe Museum Prize in 1990.

Featured prominently are four lovingly preserved steam engines, one of which still functions (by electricity) and can be switched on for visitors. The development of technology relating to the city's water supply is documented with photographs. Particularly interesting are the sections on the Águas Livres aqueduct and the Alfama's 17th-century Chafariz d'El Rei, one of Lisbon's first fountains. Locals used to line up at one of six founts, depending on their social status.

Museu Nacional do Azulejo ➓

Neo-Moorish façade of the bullring in Campo Pequeno

See pp122–3.

Pavilhão dos Oceanos ⓫

Doca das Olivais. ☎ 21-891 70 02.
Ⓜ Oriente. 🚌 18, 28, 50, 82.
🚊 Gare do Oriente. 🕐 10am–
6pm daily. 📷 ♿

O N THE BANKS of the Tagus,
centrally located within
the Expo complex, this huge
and innovative Ocean Pavilion
is the largest in Europe and
the second biggest in the
world. Built for Expo '98, the
pavilion illustrates the environmental theme of "The Oceans:
A Heritage for the Future." It
was conceived by an American
architect, Peter Chermayeff,
to enhance public awareness
of the diversity of the oceans'
vast natural resources and
to encourage mankind's responsibility to preserve the
seas for future generations.

The central feature is the
gigantic aquarium, the
"Open Tank," with
a volume of water
equivalent to that of four
Olympic swimming pools.
Representing the open
ocean, this features
the fauna of the
high seas, from
shoals of sardines
to sharks. Around
the main tank four
smaller aquariums
reconstruct the
eco-systems of the
Atlantic, Antarctic,
Pacific, and Indian
oceans. Each one
features fauna and flora specific to the ocean, from seals
in the Antarctic to the coral
reefs of the Indian Ocean.

Museu da Cidade ⓬

Campo Grande 245. ☎ 21-759 16 17.
Ⓜ Campo Grande. 🚌 1, 7, 36, 101.
🕐 10am–1pm, 2–6pm Tue–Sun.
● public hols. 📷 ♿

P ALÁCIO PIMENTA was allegedly
commissioned by João V
(see pp52–3) for his mistress
Madre Paula, a nun from the
nearby convent at Odivelas.
When the mansion was built,
in the middle of the 18th century, it occupied a peaceful
rural site outside the capital.
Today it has to contend with

Original 18th-century tiled kitchen in the Museu da Cidade

the teeming traffic of Campo
Grande and the city's main
east-west overpass nearby.
The house itself, however,
still retains its period
charm, and the
city museum,
established here
in 1979, is one
of the most in-
teresting in Lisbon.

The displays
follow the devel-
opment of the city,
from prehistoric
times, through the
Romans, Visigoths,
and Moors, traced
by means of tiles,
drawings, paintings,
models, and his-
torical documents.
Another tour will take you
through the former living
quarters of the mansion,
including the kitchen, decorated with blue and white tile
panels of fish, flowers,
and hanging game.
Other rooms contain
period furniture,
paintings, and toys.
A collection of 18th-
century ceramics
includes intricately
modeled statuettes,
tureens, and plates
made at the royal
china factory in Rato.

Some of the most
fascinating exhibits are
those depicting the city
before the earthquake
of 1755, including a
highly detailed model

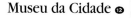
**18th-century Indian
toy, Museu da Cidade**

made in the 1950s, and an
impressive 17th-century
oil painting by Dirk Stoop
(1610–86) of *Terreiro do Paço*,
as Praça do Comércio was
known then *(see p87)*. One
room is devoted to the Águas
Livres aqueduct *(see p124)* with
detailed architectural plans for
its construction as well as prints
and watercolors of the completed aqueduct by foreign
and Portuguese artists.

The earthquake theme is
resumed with pictures of the
devastated city and plans for
its reconstruction. The museum
introduces the 20th century
with a poster celebrating the
Revolution of 1910 and the
proclamation of the new
republic *(see pp54–5)*. Several
other exhibits depict life and
customs in 20th-century
Lisbon, including an evocative
painting of *O Fado* (1910) by
José Malhôa *(see p67)*.

**Detail of Dirk Stoop's 17th-century view of
the Terreiro do Paço, Museu da Cidade**

Museu Nacional do Azulejo ⑩

Pelican on the Manueline portal

DONA LEONOR, widow of King João II, founded the Convento da Madre de Deus in 1509. Originally built in Manueline style, the church was restored under João III using simple Renaissance designs. The striking Baroque decoration was added by João V.

The convent cloisters provide a stunning setting for the National Tile Museum. Decorative panels, individual tiles, and photographs trace the evolution of tile-making from its introduction by the Moors, through Spanish influence and the development of Portugal's own style *(see pp22–3)*, up to the present day.

First floor

Panorama of Lisbon
A striking 18th-century panel, along one wall of the cloister, depicts Lisbon before the 1755 earthquake (see pp62–3). *This detail shows the royal palace on Terreiro do Paço.*

Hunting Scene
Artisans rather than artists began to decorate tiles in the 17th century. This detail shows a naïve representation of a hunt.

Ground floor

KEY TO FLOOR PLAN

- Moorish tiles
- 16th-century tiles
- 17th-century tiles
- 18th-century tiles
- 19th-century tiles
- 20th-century tiles
- Temporary exhibition space
- Nonexhibition space

STAR FEATURES

★ **Madre de Deus**

★ **Manueline Cloister**

★ **Nossa Senhora da Vida**

★ **Nossa Senhora da Vida**
This detail showing St. John is part of a fine 16th-century maiolica altarpiece. The central panel of the huge work depicts The Adoration of the Shepherds.

Tiles from the 17th century with oriental influences are displayed here.

Café Tiles
The walls of the restaurant are lined with 20th-century tiles showing hanging game (including boar and pheasant) and sausages.

VISITORS' CHECKLIST

Rua da Madre de Deus 4. ☎ 21-814 77 47. 🚌 18, 42, 104, 105.
⏰ 2–6pm Tue, 10am–6pm Wed–Sun (last adm: 30 mins before closing). ● Jan 1, Easter, May 1, Dec 25. 🎟 🅾 🛍 🍴

Moorish Tiles
Bold geometric designs were characteristic of Moorish azulejo patterns. These 15th-century tiles, decorated with stylized animal motifs, were probably made by Moorish artisans in Seville.

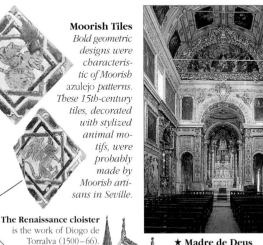

Entrance

The Renaissance cloister
is the work of Diogo de Torralva (1500–66).

★ Madre de Deus
Completed in the mid-16th century, it was not until two centuries later, under João V, that the church of Madre de Deus acquired its ornate decoration. The sumptuous Rococo altarpiece was added after the earthquake of 1755.

The carved Manueline portal *(see p21)* was recreated from a 16th-century painting.

GALLERY GUIDE
The rooms around the central cloister are arranged chronologically, from the Moorish tiles near the entrance to the 20th-century tiles upstairs. A room on the ground floor explains the history of the museum and tile-making techniques.

Exhibition on museum's history

★ Manueline Cloister
An important surviving feature of the original convent is the graceful Manueline cloister. Fine geometrical patterned tiles were added to the cloister walls in the 17th century.

Jardim Zoológico

Estrada de Benfica 158–60. **C** *21-723 29 00.* **M** *Sete-Rios.* **52** *16, 34, 54, 68.* **O** *9am–6pm (Apr–Sep: 8pm) daily.*

THE GARDENS of the Jardim Zoológico are as much a feature as the actual zoo, and some of the plants look a great deal happier than the animals. Opened in 1905, some cages and aviaries still date from this time, although plans are afoot to revamp the park and improve the conditions for the inmates. The most bizarre feature is the dogs' cemetery, complete with tombstones and flowers. Current attractions of the zoo include a cable car, which tours the park, a reptile house, and dolphin shows. The area is divided into four zones, and the admission charge is based on how many you visit.

Dolphins performing in the aquarium of the Jardim Zoológico

Aqueduto das Águas Livres

Calçada da Quintinha. **C** *21-813 55 22.* **52** *2, 58, 74.* **O** *for guided tours by appt only (Museu da Água, 21-813 55 22).* **Mãe d'Água das Amoreiras**, Praça das Amoreiras. **O** *for exhibitions.*

CONSIDERED THE most beautiful sight in Lisbon at the turn of the century, the impressive structure of the Aqueduto das Águas Livres looms over the Alcântara valley to the northwest of the city. The construction of an aqueduct to bring fresh water to the city gave João V *(see pp52–3)* an ideal opportunity to indulge his passion for grandiose build-ing plans, since the only area of Lisbon with fresh drinking water was the Alfama. A tax on meat, wine, olive oil, and other foodstuffs funded the project, and although not complete until the 19th century, it was already supplying the city with water by 1748. The main pipeline measures 19 km (12 miles), but the total length, including all the secondary channels, is 58 km (36 miles). The most visible part of this imposing structure are the 14 arches that stride across the Alcântara valley, the tallest of which rise to a spectacular 65 m (213 ft) above the city.

The public walkway along the aqueduct, once a pleasant promenade, has been closed since 1853. This is partly due to Diogo Alves, the infamous robber who threw his victims over the edge. Today, it is possible to take a lively, infor-mative guided tour, organized by the Museu da Água *(see p120)*, over the Alcântara arches. There are also tours of the Mãe d'Água reservoir and to the Mãe d'Água springs, but these tours can be irregular, so it is advisable to contact the museum in advance.

At the end of the aqueduct, the **Mãe d'Água das Amoreiras** is a castlelike building that once served as a reservoir for the water supplied from the aqueduct. The original design of 1745 was by the Hungarian architect Carlos Mardel, who worked under Pombal *(see pp62–3)* in the rebuilding of the Baixa. Completed in 1834, it became a popular meeting place and acquired a reputation as the rendezvous for kings and their mistresses. Today the 5-m (16-ft) thick walls, surrounding the water-filled basin, are used to display temporary exhibi-tions of art by local artists.

Imposing arches of the Aqueduto das Águas Livres spanning the Alcântara valley

Palácio Fronteira ⓯

Largo São Domingos de Benfica 1.
📞 21-778 20 23. 🅼 Sete-Rios.
🚍 72. 🚉 Benfica. ⏱ for guided tours only, at 11am and noon Mon–Sat. 🎫 ⏺ public hols. ♿ 📷

Tiled terrace leading to the chapel of the Palácio Fronteira

T HIS DELIGHTFUL country manor house was built as a hunting pavilion for João de Mascarenhas, the first Marquês de Fronteira, in 1640. Although skyscrapers are visible in the distance, it still occupies a quiet rural spot, bordering the wooded Parque Florestal de Monsanto. Both house and garden have striking *azulejo* decorations whose subjects range from battle scenes to trumpet-blowing monkeys.

Although the palace is still occupied by the 12th Marquis, some of the living rooms and the library, as well as the formal gardens, are included in the tour. The Battles Room has lively tiled panels depicting scenes of the War of Restoration *(see pp50–51)*, with a detail showing João de Fronteira fighting a Spanish general. It was his loyalty to Pedro II during this war that earned him the title of Marquis. Interesting comparisons can be made between these naive 17th-century Portuguese tiles and the Delft ones from the same period in the dining room, depicting naturalistic scenes. The dining room is also decorated with frescoed panels and portraits of Portuguese nobility by artists such as Domingos António de Sequeira (1768–1837).

The late 16th-century chapel is the oldest part of the house. The façade is adorned with stones, shells, broken glass, and bits of china. These fragments of crockery are believed to have been used at the feast inaugurating the palace and then smashed to make sure no one else could eat off the same set. Visits to the **garden** start at the chapel terrace, where tiled niches are decorated with figures personifying the arts and mythological creatures.

Bust of João I in gardens of Palácio Fronteira

In the formal Italian garden the immaculate boxwood hedges are cut into shapes representing the seasons of the year. At one end, tiled scenes of dashing knights on horseback, representing ancestors of the Fronteira family, are reflected in the waters of a large tank. On either side of the water a grand staircase leads to a terrace above. Here, decorative niches contain the busts of Portuguese kings, and colorful majolica reliefs adorn the arcades. More blue and white tiled scenes, realistic and allegorical, decorate the wall at the far end of the garden.

Entrance to the theater museum in Parque do Monteiro-Mor

Parque do Monteiro-Mor ⓰

Largo Júlio Castilho. 📞 21-759 03 18.
🅼 Campo Grande. 🚍 3, 7, 36.
Park ⏺ 10am–6pm Tue–Sun.
⏺ Jan 1, Easter, May 1, Dec 25.
Museu Nacional do Traje ⏺ 10am–6pm Tue–Sun. **Museu Nacional do Teatro** ⏺ 10am–6pm Wed–Sun, 2–6pm Tue. 🎫 combined ticket for park & museums. 📷 ♿

M ONTEIRO-MOR PARK was sold to the state in 1975, and the 18th-century palace buildings were converted to museums. Relatively few visitors come here because of the distance from the city center, but the gardens are attractive and more romantic than the manicured boxwood hedge gardens so typical of Lisbon. Much of the land is wooded, but the area around the museums has gardens with flowering shrubs, duck ponds, and tropical trees.

The rather old-fashioned **Museu Nacional do Traje** (costume museum) has a varied collection of costumes worn by musicians, politicians, poets, aristocrats, and soldiers.

The **Museu Nacional do Teatro** has two buildings, one devoted to temporary exhibitions, the other containing a very small permanent collection. Photographs, posters, and cartoons feature famous 20th-century Portuguese actors, and one section is devoted to Amália Rodrigues, the famous *fado* singer *(see pp66 – 7)*.

LISBON STREET FINDER

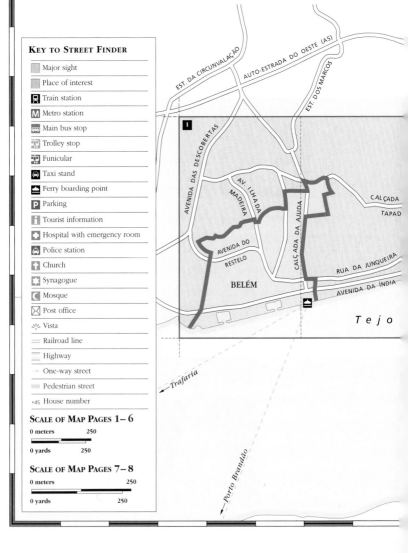

MAP REFERENCES given in this guide for sights and entertainment spots in Lisbon refer to the Street Finder maps on the following pages. Map references are also given for Lisbon's hotels *(see pp380–83)* and restaurants *(see pp404–7)*. The first figure in the map reference indicates which Street Finder map to turn to, and the letter and number that follow refer to the grid reference on that map. The map below shows the area of Lisbon covered by the eight Street Finder maps. Symbols used for sights and useful information are displayed in the key below. Lisbon's Metro network *(see pp448–9)* is being extended, and those stations marked on the map include those scheduled to open by 2001.

KEY TO STREET FINDER

	Major sight
	Place of interest
🚉	Train station
Ⓜ	Metro station
🚌	Main bus stop
🚋	Trolley stop
🚡	Funicular
🚕	Taxi stand
⛴	Ferry boarding point
P	Parking
ℹ	Tourist information
✚	Hospital with emergency room
🚓	Police station
✝	Church
✡	Synagogue
☪	Mosque
⊠	Post office
⚜	Vista
—	Railroad line
—	Highway
–	One-way street
	Pedestrian street
◦45	House number

SCALE OF MAP PAGES 1–6

0 meters   250

0 yards   250

SCALE OF MAP PAGES 7–8

0 meters   250

0 yards   250

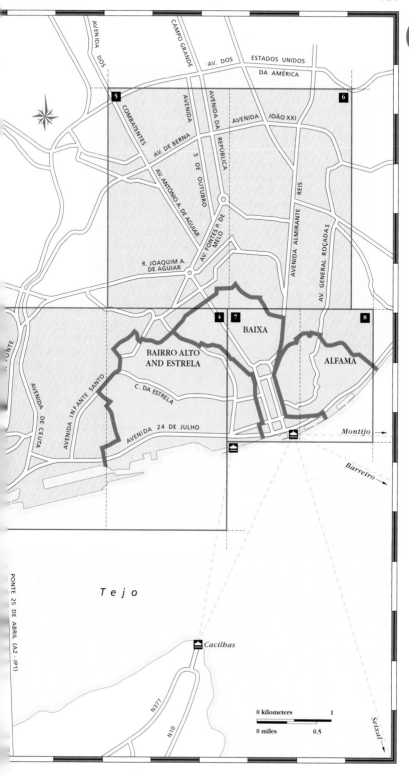

Street Finder Index

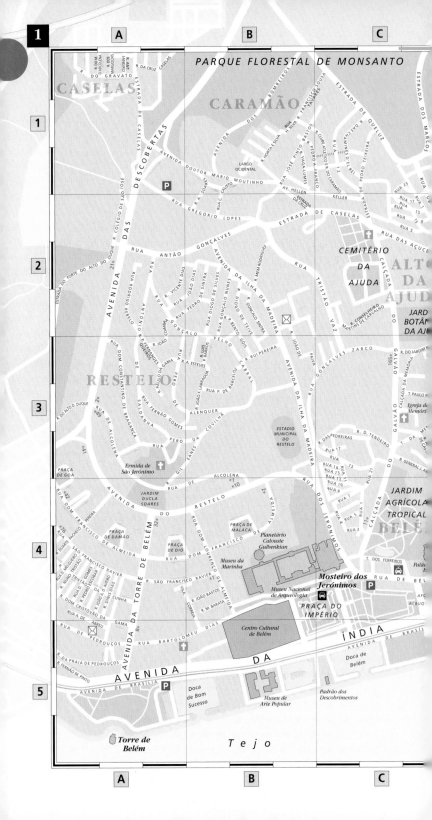

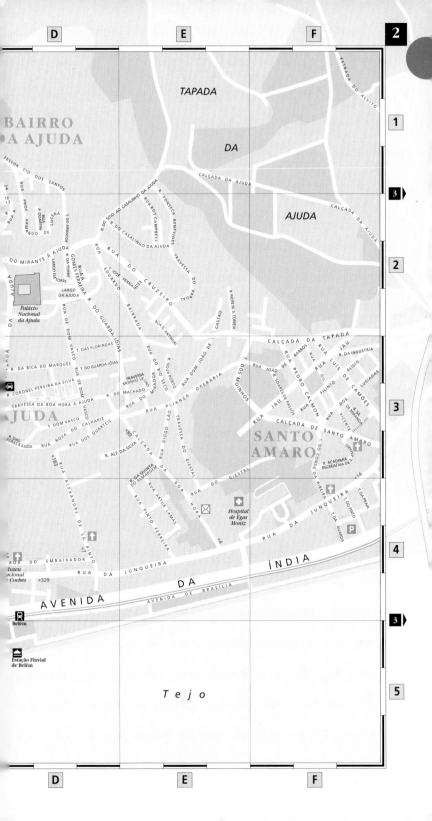

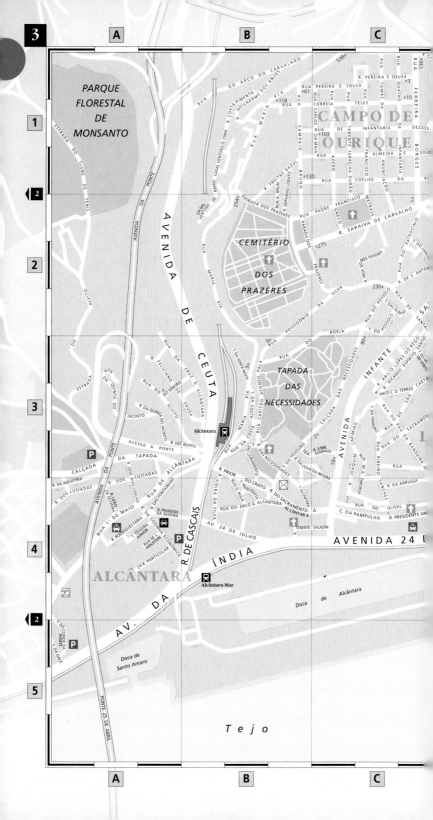

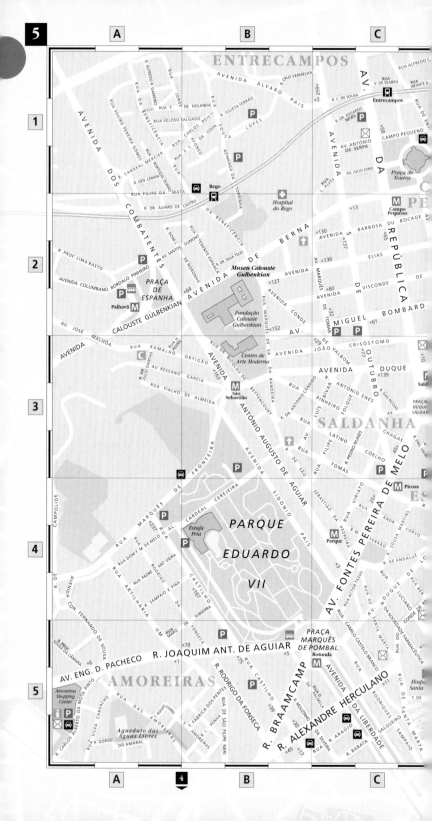

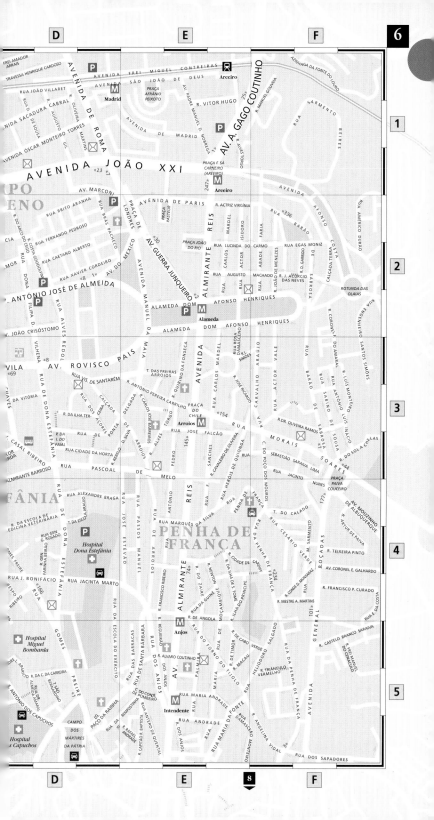

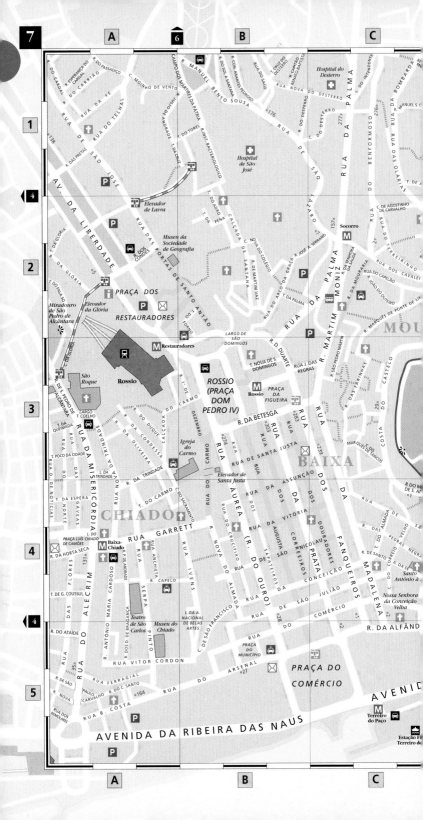

CENTRAL
PORTUGAL

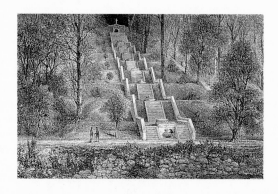

Central Portugal at a Glance

B ETWEEN PORTUGAL'S CAPITAL and
its second city, Oporto, can be
found some of the country's most
impressive architecture and important
historical sights. Near Lisbon are the
fine palaces of Sintra and Queluz, and
in Estremadura are several of Portugal's
foremost religious sites. Estremadura
and Beira Litoral mix empty beaches
with quaint fishing villages and stylish
resorts, while the lush country stretching
inland to the banks of the Tagus supports livestock and crops from grapes
to fruit and rice. Farther north, the Beiras
are more varied, with the historic university town
of Coimbra, the vine-clad valleys of the Dão wine
region, and the bleak highlands and fortress towns of
Beira Alta and Beira Baixa. Dominating this remote
region is the granite range of the Serra da Estrela.

Batalha *means "battle," and the
monastery of Santa Maria da
Vitória at Batalha was built
to give thanks for victory over
the Spanish at the Battle of
Aljubarrota in 1385. Its delicate style makes it one
of Portugal's finest Gothic
buildings (see pp182–3).*

Alcobaça *is principally
known for its abbey, founded in the 12th century by
Portugal's first king, Afonso
Henriques. The graceful,
contemplative air of this
great Cistercian house (see
pp178–9) is exemplified by
its huge vaulted dormitory.*

Sintra, *just west of Lisbon, is
a cool wooded retreat from the
heat of the capital. This is where
the Portuguese monarchs chose
to spend their summers. The
Palácio Nacional is full
of remarkable deco-
rative effects, such
as this painted
"magpie" ceiling
(see pp158–9).*

Beira
Litoral

Estremadura

**ESTREMADURA
AND RIBATEJO**
(See pp170–93)

LISBON
(See pp58–139)

THE LISBON COAST
(See pp148–69)

The Palácio de Queluz,
*a masterpiece of Rococo
architecture (see pp164–5),
lies just outside Lisbon. The
Lion Staircase leads up to
the colonnaded pavilion
named after its architect,
Jean-Baptiste Robillion.*

| 0 kilometers | | 5 |
| 0 miles | 25 | |

◁ **Tomar's Templar fortress of Convento de Cristo overlooking the town**

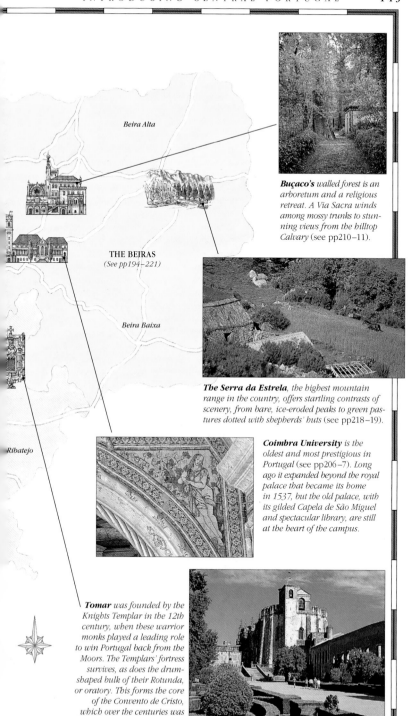

Beira Alta

***Buçaco's** walled forest is an arboretum and a religious retreat. A Via Sacra winds among mossy trunks to stunning views from the hilltop Calvary (see pp210–11).*

THE BEIRAS
(See pp194–221)

Beira Baixa

***The Serra da Estrela**, the highest mountain range in the country, offers startling contrasts of scenery, from bare, ice-eroded peaks to green pastures dotted with shepherds' huts (see pp218–19).*

Ribatejo

***Coimbra University** is the oldest and most prestigious in Portugal (see pp206–7). Long ago it expanded beyond the royal palace that became its home in 1537, but the old palace, with its gilded Capela de São Miguel and spectacular library, are still at the heart of the campus.*

***Tomar** was founded by the Knights Templar in the 12th century, when these warrior monks played a leading role to win Portugal back from the Moors. The Templars' fortress survives, as does the drum-shaped bulk of their Rotunda, or oratory. This forms the core of the Convento de Cristo, which over the centuries was built up around the original church (see pp184–7).*

Horsemanship and Bullfighting

Advertising a summer bullfight in Santarém

CLASSICAL DRESSAGE and bravura bullfighting in Portugal are linked to the Marquês de Marialva, the King's Master of Horse from 1770 to 1799. He made famous the most advanced and difficult dressage techniques, including some in which the horse lifts itself off the ground like a ballet dancer. The Art of Marialva, as it is called, is of great use to horsemen in the bullring, and they will usually demonstrate some dressage movements for the entertainment of the crowd. The Ribatejo is the traditional center of bullfighting, with events held from spring to autumn at annual fairs and towns such as Santarém, Vila Franca de Xira, and Coruche. In Portugal, the bull is never killed in the arena.

Horseman at the national fair in Golegã

Ribatejan berdsmen or campinos, *who round up the fighting bulls, here demonstrate their skills.*

Leading bullfighter João Moura salutes the crowd at a *tourada* with his tricorne hat.

The mane is braided with ribbons for a beautifully groomed effect.

THE CAVALEIRO

The bullfighter or *cavaleiro* wears traditional 18th-century costume, including the satin coat of a grandee, and rides an elaborately adorned horse. He has to plant a number of darts *(farpas)* in the bull's shoulders, and his performance is judged on style and courage.

The costly saddle cloth is embroidered with João Moura's initials.

Tail tidying and decoration go back to the ornate French style of Louis XV.

Box stirrups are traditional, stylish, and secure.

TRADITIONAL EQUESTRIAN SKILLS

Plaque of Lezíria Grande Equestrian Center *(see p192)*

Lisbon's Escola Portuguesa de Arte Equestre, and equestrian centers in the Ribatejo, still maintain the standards set by Marialva. The Lisbon school performs several times a year around the country. On Lusitanian horses of Alter Real stock *(see p296)*, riders in 18th-century costume give superb dressage displays. Their movements resemble these illustrations of 1790 from a book on equestrianism, dedicated to Dom João (later João VI), himself an avid horseman.

The Marquês de Marialva trains his horse in the *croupac* its hind le tucked u beneath as it sprin into the a

THE BULLFIGHT

The *corrida* or *tourada* combines drama and daring. First, a team of bullfighters on foot (*peões de brega*) distracts the bull with capes, preparing it for the *cavaleiro*. He is followed by eight volunteer *forcados*, who aim to overcome the bull with their bare hands in what is known as the *pega*. Finally the bull is herded from the ring among a group of farm oxen.

At this opening ceremony in Montijo, the two cavaleiros *line up with the* forcados *on either side.*

The *cavaleiro* lodges long darts in the bull's shoulders.

The bull charges, provoked by the *cavaleiro* and the prancing horse. The bull's horns are blunted and sheathed in leather.

Partnership between *man and horse is paramount. Most cavaleiros* ride a Lusitanian, *the world's oldest saddle horse and a classic warrior steed, famed for its courage, grace, and strength. Its agility and speed are essential in the ring, and defenders of bull-fighting believe the spectacle has helped preserve the breed.*

The horse's lower legs are strapped for support.

The leader of the *forcados* tackles the bull head on, throwing himself between its horns and gripping it around the neck.

The next in line assists the front man, while the others prepare to lend support.

The bullfight ends with the pega. *The leader of the* forcados *challenges the bull to charge, then launches himself over its head. The others try to hold him in place and use their combined weight to bring the bull to a standstill, with one of the men holding onto its tail. Eight times out of ten the* forcados *get tossed in all directions, then re-form to repeat the challenge. The crowd laughs, but applauds the men's skill and courage.*

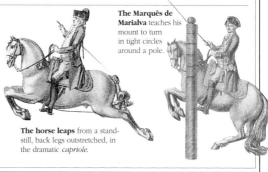

Dom João himself demonstrates the *galope*, a difficult exercise with a change of direction at each step.

The Marquês de Marialva teaches his mount to turn in tight circles around a pole.

The horse leaps from a standstill, back legs outstretched, in the dramatic *capriole*.

Regional Food: Central Portugal

Ceramic honey pot

GASTRONOMICALLY, the central region of Portugal is immensely varied. Aveiro specializes in eel stews and the sweet delicacy of *ovos moles (see p200)*, while suckling pig is a feature on menus around Coimbra. Along the coast, shellfish is varied and abundant; inland, kid and lamb are succulent, spiked with *colorau* (paprika), and cooked in the region's rich red wines. Milk from sheep and goats is turned into a variety of local cheeses, the most famous being Serra, from the Serra da Estrela. The Ribatejo's melons are famous for their sweetness, and Setúbal grows muscat grapes for the table and for wines.

Pataniscas *are tasty salt-cod fritters. Rissois, half-moons filled with a seafood sauce, are favorites as party snacks.*

Papo seco

Pãezinhos

Queijo de ovelha **(ewe's milk cheese)**

Requeijão

Sopa de pedra, *"stone soup," derives from a legend about a beggar monk. Full of vegetables and meats, it is tasty and filling.*

Fresh cheeses *made from ewe's or goat's milk are enjoyed with a variety of fresh rolls. Especially prized is Requeijão.*

Leitão à Bairrada, *roasted suckling pig with crisp crackling, is relished hot or cold, and can be bought in good delicatessens.*

Bife à café, *café-style steak, is tender steak with a creamy sauce, served with fries and topped with a fried egg.*

Frango à piri-piri, *a great favorite from Portugal's former colonies in Africa, is barbecued chicken with chili.*

Bacalhau à Brás *binds shreds of salt cod (bacalhau), potato, and onion with scrambled egg to make a highly esteemed dish.*

CHEESES

Most cheeses are made with ewe's or goat's milk or both. The best (and most expensive) is undoubtedly the buttery Serra, which becomes harder and more piquant as it ages *(see p215)*. Rabaçal is a mild cheese from Coimbra; Azeitão, from near Setúbal, is quite pungent; and Saloio, dried fresh cheese, is favored for its milky taste. Individual small cheeses may be kept in oil.

Rabaçal

Serra

Azeitão

Saloio

Shellfish *is plentiful and much enjoyed in Portugal. Lisbon is full of specialty seafood restaurants with artistic displays of lobsters, shrimp of all sizes, crayfish, oysters, and crabs, including the spiny-shelled spider crab. Lesser-known delicacies such as goose-necked barnacles will also appear on menus. Cockles and clams find their way into a variety of dishes, such as the rich seafood rice,* arroz de marisco.

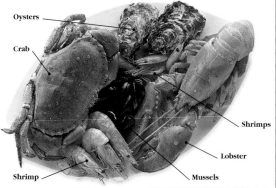

Oysters

Crab

Shrimps

Lobster

Shrimp

Mussels

Açorda de marisco *is a special and unusual dish: shellfish are added to a thick soup of mashed bread, oil, garlic, and coriander.*

Salmonete grelhado, *grilled red mullet, is a specialty in Setúbal, where it is served with a lemony butter sauce.*

Mousse de chocolate *needs to be made with really good dark chocolate, but can be excellent.*

Arroz doce, *creamy rice pudding rich with egg, is flavored with lemon rind and vanilla.*

LOCAL DRINKS

Central Portugal produces a number of wines *(see pp28–9)*, from which *aguardente* (brandy) is distilled. There are also local liqueurs, such as the herb-based Licor Beirão. From the region's many spas come a variety of mineral waters, of which Luso *(see p209)* is one of the most popular. Less known is the Lisbon area's beer-making tradition, and Lisbon itself has several *cervejarias* (beer houses).

Aguardente
Velha
Reserva

Mineral
water
from Luso

Licor
Beirão

Sagres
beer

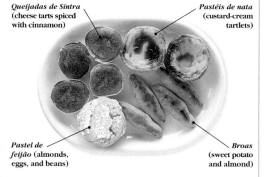

Queijadas de Sintra
(cheese tarts spiced
with cinnamon)

Pastéis de nata
(custard-cream
tartlets)

*Pastel de
feijão* (almonds,
eggs, and beans)

Broas
(sweet potato
and almond)

Tartlets *such as* pastéis de nata *epitomize the region's infinite variety of cakes, many based on egg yolks, almonds, and spices.*

THE LISBON COAST

ITHIN AN HOUR'S DRIVE *northwest of Lisbon you can reach the rocky Atlantic coast, the wooded slopes of Sintra, or countryside dotted with villas and royal palaces. South of Lisbon you can enjoy the sandy beaches and fishing towns along the coast or explore the lagoons of the Tagus and Sado river estuaries.*

Traders and invaders, from the Phoenicians to the Spanish, have left their mark in this region, in particular the Moors, whose forts and castles, rebuilt many times over the centuries, can be found all along this coast. After Lisbon became the capital in 1256, Portuguese kings and nobles built summer palaces and villas in the countryside west of the city, particularly on the cool, green heights of the Serra de Sintra.

Across the Tagus, the less fashionable southern shore (Outra Banda) could be reached only by ferry, until the suspension bridge was built in 1966. Now, the long sandy beaches of the Costa da Caparica, the coast around the fishing town of Sesimbra, and even the remote Tróia peninsula have become popular resorts during the summer months. Fortunately, large stretches of coast and unspoiled countryside are being protected as conservation areas and nature preserves.

Despite the region's rapid urbanization, small fishing and farming communities still flourish. Lively fish markets offer a huge variety of fresh fish and seafood; Colares and Palmela are noted for their wine; flocks of sheep still roam the unspoilt Serra da Arrábida, providing milk for Azeitão cheese; and rice is the main crop in the Sado estuary. Traditional industries also survive, such as salt panning near Alcochete and marble quarries at Pero Pinheiro.

Although the sea is cold and often rough, especially on west-facing coasts, the beaches are among the cleanest in Europe. As well as surfing, fishing, and scuba diving, the region provides splendid golf courses, horseback riding facilities, and a Formula 1 racing track. Arts and entertainment range from music and film festivals to bullfights and country fairs where regional crafts like hand-painted pottery and baskets are displayed.

Tiled façades of houses in Alcochete, an attractive town on the Tagus estuary

◁ Brightly painted fishing boats moored in the harbor at Sesimbra

Exploring the Lisbon Coast

North of the Tagus, the beautiful hill town of Sintra is dotted with historic palaces and surrounded by wooded hills, at times enveloped in an eerie sea mist. On the coast, cosmopolitan Cascais and the traditional fishing town of Ericeira are both excellent bases from which to explore the rocky coastline and surrounding countryside. South of the Tagus, the Serra da Arrábida and the rugged coast around Cabo Espichel can be visited from the small port of Sesimbra. Inland, the nature preserves of the Tagus and Sado estuaries offer a quiet retreat.

Torres Vedras
VILA FRANCA DO ROSÁRIO
ERICEIRA 2
1 PALÁCIO DE MAFRA
N116
A8
N247
N9
N8
LOURES
MONSERRATE 5
COLARES 3
6 SINTRA
N117
A9
IC17
CABO DA ROCA
4
SERRA DE SINTRA
N249
PALÁCIO DE QUELUZ 9
LISBO
A5
8 ESTORIL
CASCAIS 7
COSTA DA CAPARICA 11
0 kilometers 10
0 miles 5
Lagoa de Albufeira
CABO ESPICHEL
12
KEY
Highway
Major road
Minor road
Scenic route
River
Ferry route
Vista

Sights at a Glance

Alcácer do Sal 18
Alcochete 10
Cabo Espichel 12
Cascais 7
Colares 3
Costa da Caparica 11
Ericeira 2
Estoril 8
LISBON pp58–139
Monserrate 5
Palácio de Mafra 1
Palácio de Queluz pp164–5 9
Palmela 14
Península de Tróia 17
Serra da Arrábida 15
Sesimbra 13
Setúbal 16
Sintra pp156–61 6

Tours

Serra de Sintra 4

Cabo da Roca on the western edge of Serra de Sintra

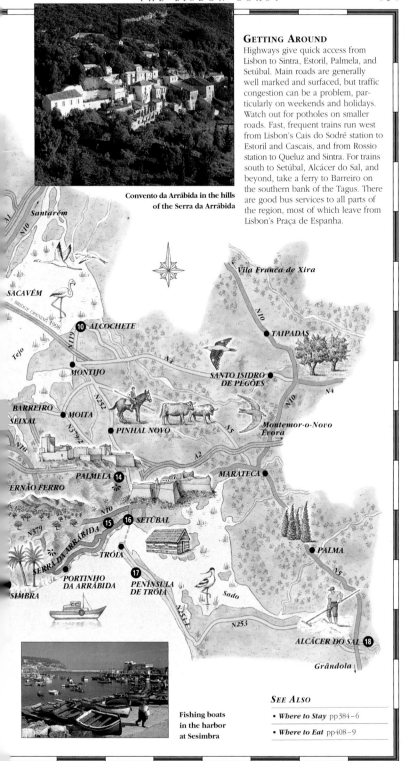

**Convento da Arrábida in the hills
of the Serra da Arrábida**

GETTING AROUND

Highways give quick access from
Lisbon to Sintra, Estoril, Palmela, and
Setúbal. Main roads are generally
well marked and surfaced, but traffic
congestion can be a problem, particularly on weekends and holidays.
Watch out for potholes on smaller
roads. Fast, frequent trains run west
from Lisbon's Cais do Sodré station to
Estoril and Cascais, and from Rossio
station to Queluz and Sintra. For trains
south to Setúbal, Alcácer do Sal, and
beyond, take a ferry to Barreiro on
the southern bank of the Tagus. There
are good bus services to all parts of
the region, most of which leave from
Lisbon's Praça de Espanha.

**Fishing boats
in the harbor
at Sesimbra**

The stunning library in the Palácio de Mafra, paved with checkered marble

Palácio de Mafra ❶

Road map B5. Terreiro de Dom João V, Mafra. ☎ 21-818 15 50.
🚌 *from Lisbon.* ⏰ *10am–5pm Wed–Mon.* ● *Jan 1, Easter, May 1, Dec 25.* ⛪ 🚫 📷 *compulsory.*

THE MASSIVE BAROQUE palace and monastery *(see also pp52–3),* which dwarfs the small town of Mafra, was built during the reign of Portugal's most extravagant monarch, João V. It began with a vow by the young king to build a new monastery and basilica, supposedly in return for an heir (but more likely to atone for his well-known sexual excesses). Work began in 1717 on a modest project to house 13 Franciscan friars but, as wealth began to pour into the royal coffers from Brazil, the king and his Italian-trained architect, Johann Friedrich Ludwig (1670–1752), made ever more extravagant plans.

No expense was spared: 52,000 men were employed and the finished project housed not 13 but 330 friars, a royal palace, and one of the finest libraries in Europe, decorated with precious marble, exotic wood, and countless works of art. The magnificent basilica was consecrated on the king's 41st birthday, October 22, 1730, with festivities lasting for eight days.

The palace was never a favorite with the members of the royal family, except for those who enjoyed hunting deer and wild boar in the adjoining *tapada* (hunting preserve). Most of the finest furniture and art works were taken to Brazil when the royal family escaped the French invasion in 1807. The monastery was abandoned in 1834 following the dissolution of all religious orders, and the palace itself was abandoned in 1910, when the last Portuguese king, Manuel II, escaped from here to the Royal Yacht anchored off Ericeira.

Allow at least an hour for the tour that starts in the monastery, through the pharmacy, with fine old medicine jars and some alarming medical instruments, to the hospital, where 16 patients in private cubicles could see and hear mass in the adjoining chapel without leaving their beds.

Upstairs, the sumptuous palace state rooms extend across the whole of the monumental west façade, with the King's apartments at one end and the Queen's apartments at the other, a staggering 232 m (760 ft) apart. Halfway between the two, the long imposing façade is relieved by the twin towers of the domed basilica. The interior of the church is decorated in contrasting colors of marble and furnished with six early 19th-century organs. Fine Baroque sculptures, executed by members of the Mafra School of Sculpture, adorn the atrium of the basilica. Begun by José I in 1754, many renowned Portuguese and foreign artists trained in the school under the directorship of the Italian sculptor Alessandro Giusti (1715–99). Farther on, the Sala da Caça has a grotesque collection of hunting trophies and boars' heads.

Mafra's greatest treasure, however, is its magnificent library, with a patterned marble floor, Rococo-style wooden bookcases, and a collection of over 40,000 books in gold embossed leather bindings, including a prized first edition of *Os Lusíadas* (1572) by the Portuguese poet, Luís de Camões *(see p46).*

Statue of St. Bruno in the atrium of Mafra's basilica

ENVIRONS: Once a week, on Thursday mornings, the small country town of **Malveira,** 10 km (6 miles) east of Mafra, has the region's biggest market, selling clothes and household goods, as well as food.

At the village of **Sobreiro,** 6 km (4 miles) west of Mafra, Zé Franco's model village is complete with houses, farms, a waterfall, and working windmill – all in minute detail.

The king's bedroom in the Royal Palace

Tractor pulling a fishing boat out of the sea at Ericeira

Ericeira ❷

Road map B5. 🏘 *4,500.* 🚌
🛈 *Rua Mendes Leal (261-86 31 22).*
🛒 *daily.*

Ericeira is an old fishing village that keeps its traditions despite an ever-increasing influx of summer visitors from Lisbon and abroad who enjoy the bracing climate, clean sandy beaches, and fresh seafood. In July and August, when the population soars to 30,000, sidewalk cafés, restaurants, and bars around the tree-lined Praça da República are buzzing late into the night. Red flags warn when swimming is dangerous: alternative attractions include a miniature golf course in Santa Marta park and an interesting local history museum, the **Museu da Ericeira**, exhibiting model boats and traditional regional fishing equipment.

The unspoiled old town, a maze of whitewashed houses and narrow, cobbled streets is perched high above the ocean. From Largo das Ribas, at the top of a 30-m (100-ft) stone-faced cliff, there is a bird's-eye view of the busy fishing harbor below, where tractors have replaced the oxen that once hauled the boats out of reach of the tide. On August 16, the annual fishermen's festival is celebrated with a candlelit procession to the harbor at the foot of the cliffs for the blessing of the boats.

On October 5, 1910, Manuel II, the last king of Portugal *(see pp54–5)*, sailed into exile from Ericeira as the Republic was declared in Lisbon; a tiled panel in the fishermen's chapel of Santo António above the harbor records the event. The banished king settled in Twickenham, southwest London, where he died in 1932.

🏛 Museu da Ericeira
Largo da Misericórdia. 📞 *261-625 36.*
🕐 *Jun–Sep: Tue–Sun; Oct–May: Mon–Sat (pm only).* ⬤ *Jan 1, Dec 25.* 🎫

Colares ❸

Road map B5. 🏘 *6,500.* 🚌
🛈 *Cabo da Roca, 6 km (4 miles) SW (21-928 00 81).*

On the lower slopes of the Serra de Sintra, this lovely village faces toward the sea over a green valley, the Várzea de Colares. A leafy avenue winds its way up to the quiet village, full of beautiful flowers, pine, and chestnut trees. The vineyards here produce the famous Colares wine, which is a robust, velvety red. The older vines grow in a dry, sandy soil, with their roots set deep below in clay. These were the only grapevines in Europe to survive the disastrous phylloxera epidemic, which first appeared in Kew Gardens, England, in 1863. The insect, which destroyed vineyards all over Europe by eating the tender roots, could not penetrate the dense sandy soil of the Atlantic coast and thus spared the vines around Colares. Various wines can be sampled at the Adega Regional de Colares on Alameda de Coronel Linhares de Lima.

Environs: There are several popular beach resorts west of Colares. From the village of Banzão you can ride 3 km (2 miles) to **Praia das Maçãs** on the old tramway, which opened in 1910 and still runs in the summer months from July 1 to September 30. Just north of Praia das Maçãs is the picturesque village of **Azenhas do Mar**, clinging to the cliffs; just to the south is the larger resort of **Praia Grande**. Both have natural swimming pools cut into the rocks that are filled by seawater at high tide. The unspoiled **Praia da Adraga**, 1 km (half a mile) farther south, has a delightful beach café. In the evenings and off-season, fishermen set up their rods and lines to catch bass, bream, and flat fish that swim in on the high tide.

Natural rock pool at Azenhas do Mar, near Colares

Serra de Sintra Tour

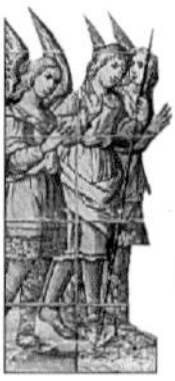

Tiled angels, Peninha chapel

THIS ROUND-TRIP from Sintra follows a dramatic route over the top of the wooded Serra. The first part is a challenging drive with hazardous hairpin bends on steep, narrow roads that are at times poorly surfaced. It passes through dense forest and a surreal landscape of giant moss-covered boulders, with breathtaking views of the Atlantic coast, the Tagus estuary, and beyond. After dropping down to the rugged, windswept coast, the route returns along small country roads passing through hill villages and large estates on the cool, green northern slopes of the Serra de Sintra.

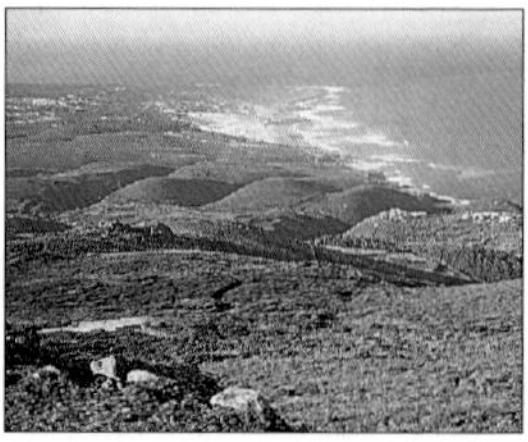

Atlantic coastline seen from Peninha

Colares 6
The village of Colares rests on the lower slopes of the wooded Serra, surrounded by gardens and vineyards *(see p153).*

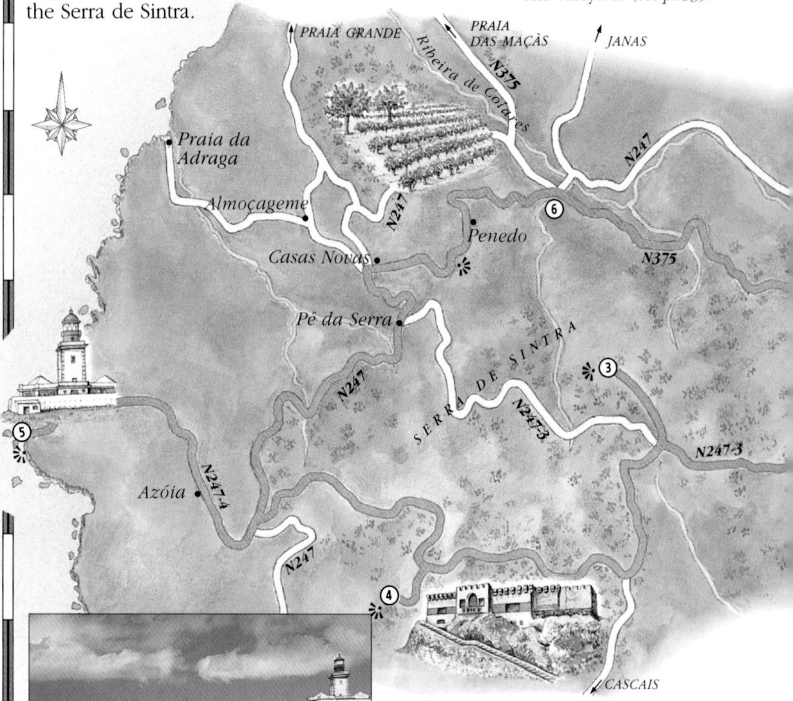

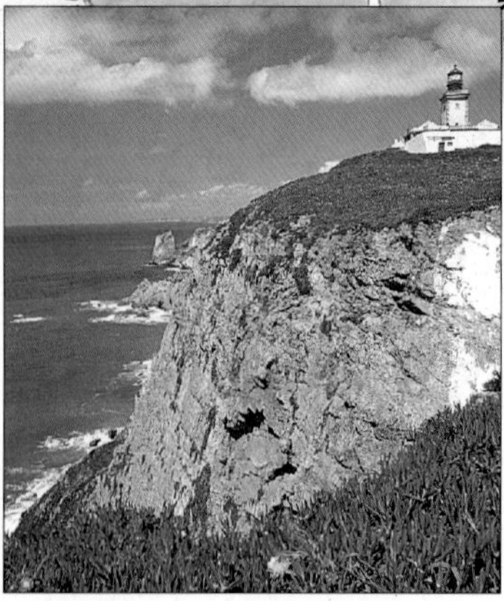

Peninha 4
This 490-m (1,600-ft) high peak affords stunning views toward the coast. A 17th-century chapel decorated with *azulejo* panels is perched high on the gray rocks.

Cabo da Roca 5
A lighthouse at the top of an impressive cliff, 140 m (459 ft) high, marks the most westerly point of the European mainland.

0 kilometers

0 miles 1

KEY

Tour route

Other roads

Vista

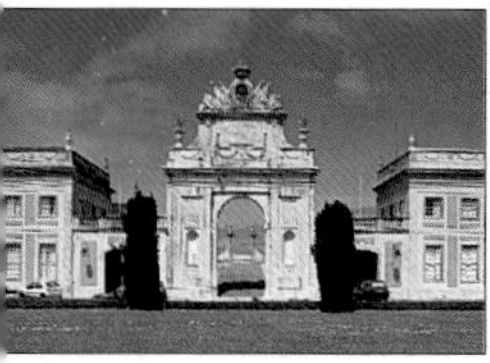

Seteais [8]
The elegant pink palace, now a luxury hotel and restaurant *(see p386 & p409)*, was built in the 18th century for the Dutch Consul, Daniel Gildemeester.

Tips for Drivers

Length: *36 km (22 miles).*
Stopping-off points: *There are wonderful picnic spots in the forests and in the Parque da Pena, with cool springs of drinking water and fountains along the mountain roads. At Cabo da Roca you will find a café, restaurant, and souvenir shops; at Colares there are several delightful restaurants and bars.*
(See also pp444–5.)

Monserrate [7]
The cool, overgrown forest park and elaborate 19th-century palace epitomize the romanticism of Sintra.

Sintra [1]
From the center of the old town the road winds steeply up past magnificent *quintas* (country estates) hidden among the trees.

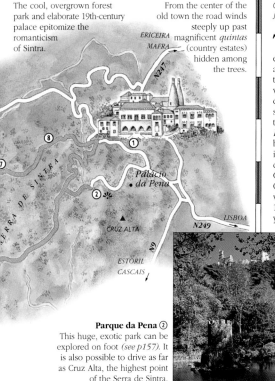

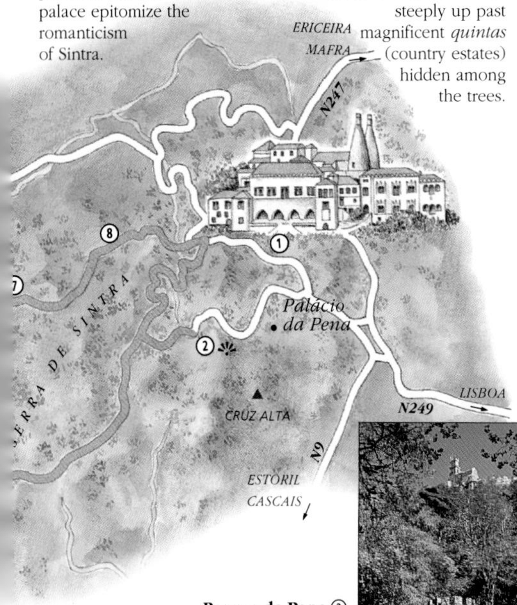
ERICEIRA
MAFRA
N247
8
1
7
SERRA DE SINTRA
Palácio da Pena
2
CRUZ ALTA
LISBOA
N249
N9
ESTORIL
CASCAIS

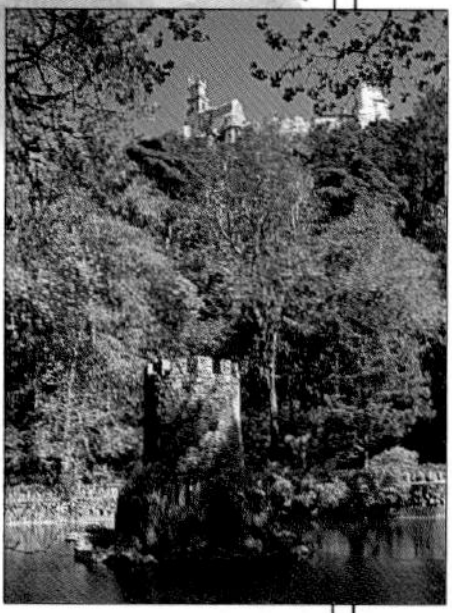

Parque da Pena [2]
This huge, exotic park can be explored on foot *(see p157)*. It is also possible to drive as far as Cruz Alta, the highest point of the Serra de Sintra.

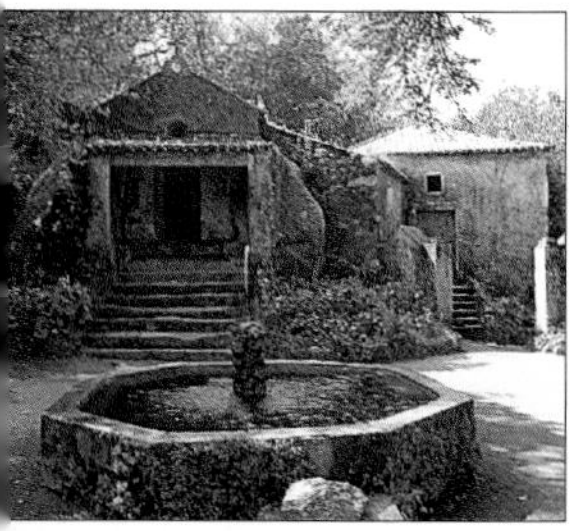

Convento dos Capuchos [3]
Two huge boulders guard the entrance to this remote Franciscan monastery, founded in 1560, where the monks lived in tiny rock-hewn cells lined with cork. There are stunning views of the coast from the hill above this austere, rocky hideaway.

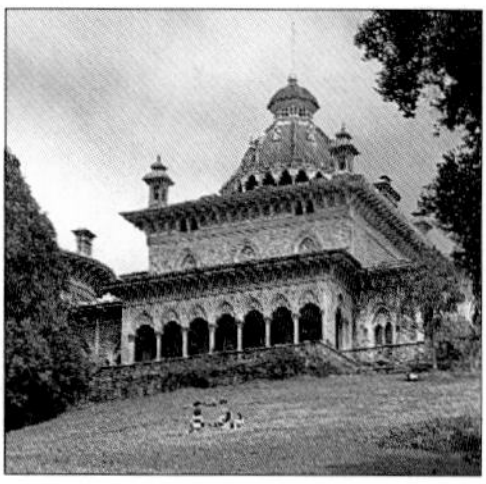

Palace of Monserrate

Monserrate [5]

Road Map B5. Estrada de Monserrate. ☎ *21-923 12 01.* 🚌 *to Sintra then taxi.* ○ *May–Sep: 9:45am–7pm daily; Oct–Apr: 9:45am–5:15pm daily.* ● *Jan 1, Easter, May 1, Dec 25.* ♿

The wild, romantic garden of this once magnificent estate is a jungle of exotic trees and flowering shrubs. Among the subtropical foliage and valley of tree ferns, you will come across a waterfall, a small lake, and a ruined chapel tangled in the roots of a giant *Ficus* tree. Its history dates back to the Moors, but it takes its name from a small 16th-century chapel dedicated to Our Lady of Montserrat in Catalonia, Spain. The gardens were landscaped in the late 18th century by a wealthy young Englishman, the eccentric aesthete William Beckford. They were later immortalized by Lord Byron in *Childe Harold's Pilgrimage* (1812).

In 1856, the abandoned estate was bought by another Englishman, Sir Francis Cook, who built a fantastic Moorish-style palace (which now stands eerily empty) and transformed the gardens with a large sweeping lawn, camellias, and subtropical trees from all over the world. These include the giant *Metrosideros* (Australian Christmas tree, covered in a blaze of red flowers in July), the native *Arbutus* (known as the strawberry tree because of its juicy red berries), from which the *medronheira* firewater drink is distilled, and cork oak, with small ferns growing on its bark.

The Friends of Monserrate is an organization that has been set up to help restore the sadly neglected house and gardens to their former glory.

Sintra 6

Visiting the sights of Sintra by horse-drawn carriage

$\mathcal{S}$INTRA'S STUNNING setting on the north slopes of the granite Serra, among wooded ravines and fresh water springs, made it a favorite summer retreat for the kings of Portugal. The tall conical chimneys of the Palácio Nacional de Sintra *(see pp158–9)* and the fabulous Palácio da Pena *(see pp160–61)*, eerily impressive on its peak when the Serra is blanketed in mist, are unmistakable landmarks.

Today, the town (recognized as a UNESCO World Heritage site in 1995) draws thousands of visitors throughout the year. Even so, there are many quiet walks in the wooded hills around the town, especially beautiful in the cool evenings of the summer months.

Fonte Mourisca on Volta do Duche

Exploring Sintra

Present-day Sintra is in three parts, Sintra Vila, Estefânia, and São Pedro, joined by a confusing maze of winding roads scattered over the surrounding hills. In the pretty cobbled streets of the old town, Sintra Vila, which is centered on the **Palácio Nacional de Sintra**, are the museums and beautifully tiled **post office**. The curving **Volta do Duche** leads from the old town, past the lush **Parque da Liberdade**, north to the Estefânia district and the striking Neo-Gothic **Câmara Municipal** (town hall). To the south and east, the hilly village of São Pedro

spreads over the slopes of the Serra. The Sunday **market** here extends across the broad market square and along Rua 1° de Dezembro.

Exploring Sintra on foot involves a lot of walking and climbing up and down its steep hills. For a more leisurely tour, take one of the horse and carriage rides around the town. The **Miradouro da Vigia** in São Pedro offers impressive views, as does the cozy **Casa de Sapa** café, where you can sample *queijadas*, the local sweet specialty *(see p147)*.

The many fountains dotted around the town are not just ornamental – the locals also fill their bottles here with the fresh spring drinking water. Two of the most striking are the elaborately tiled **Fonte Mourisca** (Arab Fountain), so called for its Neo-Moorish decoration and geometrical tile patterns, and the **Fonte da Sabuga**, where the water spouts from two breasts.

Toy Alfa Romeo, Museu do Brinquedo

🏛 Museu do Brinquedo

Largo Latino Coelho. **(** 21-924 21 71. ◯ 10am–6pm Tue–Sun. 🏷 🔥
This small, bright museum is bursting at the seams with a fine collection of toys from all over the world, including model planes, cars and trains, battalions of toy soldiers, dolls, and dolls' houses, tin toys, and curious clockwork models of cars and soldiers. The museum is fun for a rainy day, particularly for nostalgic adults.

🏛 Museu Regional

Praça da República 23. **(** 21-924 05 91. ◯ Mon–Fri (also: Sat & Sun pm). ● Carnaval, May 1, Dec 22–Jan 2.
Sintra's regional museum is on two floors. The Art Gallery, used for temporary exhibitions, houses a small permanent collection of paintings and old prints showing views of Sintra, including two early views of Palácio da Pena in the 1860s. The Archaeological Museum upstairs has cases filled with finds from the surrounding area, from Neolithic axes to Roman amphorae and mosaics.

Chimneys of the Palácio Nacional de Sintra above the old town

♠ Castelo dos Mouros

Estrada da Pena. 📞 *21-923 51 16.*
🕐 *daily.* ⬤ *Jan 1, Dec 25.*
Standing above the old town
like a sentinel, the ramparts
of the 8th-century Moorish
castle, conquered by Afonso
Henriques in 1147, snake
over the top of the Serra. On
a fine day, there are breathtaking views from the castle
walls of the old town to
Palácio da Pena, on a neighboring peak, and far along

the coast. Hidden inside the
walls are a ruined chapel and
an ancient Moorish cistern. For
hikers, a steep trail threads up
through wooded slopes from
the 12th-century church of
Santa Maria. Follow the
signs to a dark green swing
gate where the trail begins.
The monogram "DFII" carved
on the gateway is a reminder
that the castle walls were
restored by Fernando II *(see
p161)* in the 19th century.

Battlements of the Castelo dos Mouros perched on the slopes of the Serra

VISITORS' CHECKLIST

Road map B5. 🏠 *23,000.*
🚉 🚌 *Avenida Dr Miguel
Bombarda.* 🈯 *Praça da República
23 (21-923 11 57).* 🛍 *2nd &
4th Sun of month in São Pedro.*
🎵 *Festival de Música (Jun–Sep).*

♣ Parque da Pena

Estrada da Pena. 📞 *21-924 08 73.*
🕐 *daily.* ⬤ *Jan 1, Dec 25.* ♿
A huge park surrounds the
Palácio da Pena where trails
wind among a lush vegetation
of exotic trees and shrubs.
Hidden among the foliage are
gazebos, follies, and fountains,
and a Romantic chalet built in
1869 by Fernando II for his
mistress. Cruz Alta, the highest
point of the Serra at 530 m
(1,740 ft), commands spectacular views of the Serra and
surrounding plain. On a nearby
crag stands the statue of Baron
Von Eschwege, architect of the
palace and park.

SINTRA TOWN CENTER

Câmara Municipal ①
Casa de Sapa ②
Castelo dos Mouros ⑩
Fonte Mourisca ⑦
Fonte da Sabuga ⑧
Museu do Brinquedo ⑤
Museu Regional ⑥
*Palácio Nacional de
　Sintra pp158–9* ③
Post office ④
Santa Maria ⑨

0 meters　　　　200
0 yards　　　　　200

KEY

🚉	Train station
🚌	Bus station
🅿	Parking
🈯	Tourist information
🕆	Church
•••	Trail

MAFRA
Estefânia

TRAVESSA DO
MUNICÍPIO
RUA DA RIBEIRA
RUA DO PAÇO
RUA DR. A. COSTA
AVENIDA DR. MIGUEL BOMBARDA
RUA JOÃO DE DEUS
LARGO DR. V. HORTA
RUA PASSEIO DOS VELHOS
RUA CONSELHEIRO SEGURADO
CALÇADA DO RIO DO PORTO
VOLTA DO DUCHE
LARGO RAINHA DONA AMÉLIA
PRAÇA DA REPUBLICA
RUA CONSIGLIERI PEDROSO
RUA F. PIPA
ESTRADA DA PENA
VOLTA DO DUCHE
RUA VISCONDE DE MONSERRATE
RUA MARECHAL SALDANHA
RUA BERNARDIM
PARQUE DA LIBERDADE
RUA DAS MURTAS
MONSERRATE
Palácio da Pena
RIBEIRO
LISBOA
São Pedro
Palácio da Pena

Palácio Nacional de Sintra

Swan panel,
Sala dos Cisnes

AT THE HEART of the old town of Sintra (Sintra Vila), a pair of strange conical chimneys rises high above the Royal Palace. The main part of the palace, including the central block with its plain Gothic façade and the large kitchens beneath the chimneys, was built by João I in the late 14th century, on a site once occupied by the Moorish rulers. The Paço Real, as it is also known, became the favorite summer retreat for the court and continued as a residence for Portuguese royalty until the 1880s. Additions to the building by the wealthy Manuel I, in the early 16th century, echo the Moorish style. Gradual rebuilding of the palace has resulted in a fascinating amalgamation of various different styles.

★ Sala das Pegas
It is said that King João I had the ceiling panels painted as a rebuke to the court women for indulging in idle gossip like chattering magpies (pegas).

The Torre da Meca has dovecotes below the cornice decorated with armillary spheres and nautical rope.

The Sala das Galés (galleons) houses temporary exhibitions.

★ Sala dos Brasões
The domed ceiling of this majestic room is decorated with stags holding the coats of arms (brasões) of 74 noble Portuguese families. The lower walls are lined with 18th-century Delft-like tiled panels.

Jardim da Preta, a walled garden

Sala de Dom Sebastião, the audience chamber

TIMELINE						
10th century Palace becomes residence of Moorish governor	**1281** King Dinis orders restoration of the Palácio de Oliva (as it was then known)	**1495–1521** Reign of Manuel I; major restoration and Manueline additions	**1683** Afonso VI dies after being imprisoned here for nine years by brother Pedro II		**1755** Parts of palace damaged in great earthquake *(see pp62–3)*	
800	**1000**	**1200**	**1400**	**1600**	**1800**	
	1147 Christian reconquest; Afonso Henriques takes over palace		**1385** João I orders complete rebuilding of central buildings and kitchens		**1880s** Maria Pia (grandmother of Manuel II) is last royal resident	
8th century First palace established by Moors		*Siren, Sala das Sereias (c.1660)*			**1910** Palace becomes a national monument	

★ Sala dos Cisnes
The magnificent ceiling of the former banquet hall, painted in the 17th century, is divided into octagonal panels decorated with swans (cisnes).

The Sala dos Árabes
is decorated with fine *azulejos*.

Sala das Sereias
Intricate Arabesque designs on 16th-century tiles frame the door of the Room of the Sirens.

The kitchens, beneath the huge conical chimneys, have spits and utensils once used for preparing royal banquets.

Entrance

Sala dos Archeiros,
the entrance hall

Manuel I added the *ajimece* windows, a distinctive Moorish design with a slender column dividing two arches.

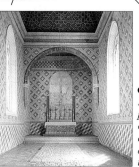

Chapel
Symmetrical Moorish patterns decorate the original 14th-century chestnut and oak ceiling and the mosaic floor of the private chapel.

VISITORS' CHECKLIST

Largo Rainha Dona Amélia.
21-910 68 40. 10am–1pm, 2–5pm Thu–Tue (last adm: 30 mins before closing). Jan 1, Easter, May 1, Jun 29, Dec 25.
compulsory.

STAR FEATURES

★ **Sala dos Brasões**

★ **Sala dos Cisnes**

★ **Sala das Pegas**

Sintra: Palácio da Pena

Triton Arch

O N THE HIGHEST PEAKS of the Serra de Sintra stands the spectacular palace of Pena, an eclectic medley of architectural styles built in the 19th century for the husband of the young Queen Maria II, Ferdinand Saxe-Coburg-Gotha. It stands over the ruins of a Hieronymite monastery founded here in the 15th century on the site of the chapel of Nossa Senhora da Pena. Ferdinand appointed a German architect, Baron Von Eschwege, to build his summer palace filled with oddities from all over the world and surrounded by a park. With the declaration of the Republic in 1910, the palace became a museum, preserved as it was when the royal family lived here. Allow at least an hour and a half to visit this enchanting place.

Entrance Arch
A studded archway with crenellated turrets greets the visitor at the entrance to the palace. The palace buildings are painted the original daffodil yellow and strawberry pink.

Manuel II's Bedroom
The oval-shaped room is decorated with bright red walls and stuccoed ceiling. A portrait of Manuel II, the last king of Portugal, hangs above the fireplace.

In the kitchen the copper pots and utensils still hang around the iron stove. The dinner service bears the coat of arms of Ferdinand II.

★ Ballroom
The spacious ballroom is sumptuously furnished with German stained-glass windows, precious Oriental porcelain, and four life-size turbaned torchbearers holding giant candelabra.

★ Arab Room
Marvelous trompe-l'oeil frescoes cover the walls and ceiling of the Arab Room, one of the loveliest in the palace. The Orient was a great inspiration to Romanticism.

VISITORS' CHECKLIST

Estrada da Pena, 2 km (1 mile) S of Sintra. 21-923 02 27. from Avenida Dr Miguel Bombarda, Sintra (May–mid-Sep) or taxi. 10am–6pm (Oct–May: 5pm) Tue–Sun (last adm: 30 mins before closing). Jan 1, Easter, May 1, Jun 29, Dec 25.

The Triton Arch is encrusted with Neo-Manueline decoration and guarded by a fierce sea monster.

★ Chapel Altarpiece
The impressive 16th-century alabaster and marble retable was sculpted by Nicolau Chanterène. Each niche portrays a scene of the life of Christ, from the manger to the Ascension.

The cloister, decorated with colorful patterned tiles, is part of the original monastery buildings.

Entrance

STAR FEATURES

★ Arab Room

★ Ballroom

★ Chapel Altarpiece

FERDINAND: KING CONSORT

Ferdinand was known in Portugal as Dom Fernando II, the "artist" king. Like his cousin Prince Albert, who married the English Queen Victoria, he loved art, nature, and the new inventions of the time. He was himself a watercolor painter. Ferdinand enthusiastically adopted his new country and devoted his life to patronizing the arts. In 1869, 16 years after the death of Maria II, Ferdinand married his mistress, the opera singer Countess Edla. His lifelong dream of building the extravagant palace at Pena was completed in 1885, the year he died.

Outdoor café in the popular vacation resort of Cascais

Cascais ●

Road map B5. 🏛 *30,000*. 🚉 🚌
ℹ️ *Rua Visconde da Luz 14 (21-486 82 04).* 🛒 *Wed.*

A SAFE HARBOR since prehistoric times, Cascais stands in a sheltered, sandy bay at the mouth of the Tagus River, once heavily defended against invaders. It became a very fashionable resort in the 1870s, when Luís I converted the 17th-century citadel on the southwest corner of the bay into a summer palace. Part of this is now the president of Portugal's summer residence.

Ocean swimming became popular at the turn of the century, and wealthy families built splendid vacation villas here. Now it is a busy cosmopolitan resort, with fashionable shops in the pedestrian streets of the old town. Fishing is still an important activity, and the day's catch is auctioned near the harbor in the afternoon.

The **Museu-Biblioteca** in Gandarinha Park was once the palatial residence of the Conde de Castro Guimarães. Superbly sited on a small creek where the sea sweeps in at high tide, the house was built in 1892, when Cascais was at the height of fashion. The count and his wife died childless in the 1920s, and the house, with its eclectic collection of Indo-Portuguese furniture, paintings, *azulejos*, porcelain, and valuable books, was left to the State. The prize exhibit in the library is a rare 16th-century illustrated book by Duarte Galvão (1455–1517), *Chronicles of Dom Afonso Henriques.* One of the hand-painted illustrations, which purports to show the siege of Lisbon in 1147 *(see pp42–3)*, depicts 16th-century Lisbon in meticulous detail.

On a smaller scale, the **Museu do Mar** focuses on the life and history of Cascais with some fascinating old photographs, painted panoramas, and finds from local shipwrecks.

Nearby, the church of **Nossa Senhora da Assunção** is decorated with paintings by Josefa de Óbidos *(see p51)*.

🏛 **Museu-Biblioteca**
Avenida Rei Humberto de Itália. 📞 *21-482 54 07.* **Museum** 🕐 *Tue–Sun.* 🗓
Library 🕐 *Mon–Fri.* ● *public hols.*
🏛 **Museu do Mar**
Rua Júlio Pereira de Mello. 📞 *21-484 08 61.* 🕐 *Tue–Sun.* ● *public hols.* 🗓

ENVIRONS: At **Boca do Inferno** (Mouth of Hell), about 3 km (2 miles) west on the coast road, the sea rushes into clefts and caves in the rocks making an ominous booming sound and sending up spectacular spray in rough weather. The place is almost obscured by a roadside market and cafés, but a small platform gives a good view of the rocky arch with the sea roaring in below.

The magnificent sandy beach of **Guincho**, 10 km (6 miles) farther west, is backed by sand dunes with clumps of umbrella pines, and a small fort (now a luxury hotel) stands perched on the rocks above the sea. Atlantic breakers rolling in make this a paradise for experienced windsurfers and surfers, but beware of the strong undercurrent.

Spectacular view of the weatherbeaten coastline at Boca do Inferno, near Cascais

Estoril ●

Road map B5. 🏛 *40,000*. 🚉 🚌
ℹ️ *Arcadas do Parque (21-466 38 13).*

E STORIL HAS THE AIR of a once prosperous resort, as indeed it was. Exiled royalty, including Italy's last king, Umberto II, Juan de Borbón of Spain, Karl I, the last Austro-Hungarian Emperor, and King Carol of Romania settled here, and it grew from a small spa village into an elegant town, popular as a chic conference site.

The proximity to Lisbon, the mild climate, and its fame as a haunt of aristocrats have long attracted both summer and winter visitors to this "Portuguese Riviera." Today, grand villas, modern apartments, and five-star hotels line the coast, following the long, breezy promenade behind the sandy beach that links Estoril with the town of Cascais, 3 km (2 miles) to the west.

Sandy beach and promenade along the bay of Estoril

Impressively sited at the top of the central park, the casino is flanked with tall, majestic date palms. Other diversions include several superb golf courses, sailing, and horse-back riding. In September, the drone of Formula 1 racing cars at the nearby Autodromo echoes around the hills.

Palácio de Queluz **9**

See pp164–5.

Alcochete **10**

Road map C5. 🏛 *13,000.* 🚌 ℹ *Largo da Misericórdia (21-234 26 31).*

THIS DELIGHTFUL old town overlooks the wide Tagus estuary from the southern shore. Salt has long been one of the main industries here, and saltpans can still be seen to the north and south of the town, while in the town center a large statue of a muscular salt worker has the inscription: "Do Sal a Revolta e a Esperança" (From Salt to Rebellion and Hope). On the outskirts of town is a statue of Manuel I (*see pp46–7*), who was born here on June 1, 1469 and granted the town a Royal Charter in 1515.

Statue of a salt worker in Alcochete (1985)

ENVIRONS: The **Reserva Natural do Estuário do Tejo** covers a vast area of estuary water, salt marshes, and small islands around Alcochete and is a very important breeding ground for water birds. Particularly interesting are the flocks of flamingos that gather here during the autumn and spring migration, en route from colonies such as the Camargue in France and Fuente de Piedra in Spain. Boat trips are available to see the birdlife and wildlife of the estuary, which includes wild bulls and horses.

🦅 **Reserva Natural do Estuário do Tejo**
Avenida dos Combatentes da Grande Guerra 1. 📞 *21-234 17 42.* ✉

Pilgrims' lodgings, Cabo Espichel

Costa da Caparica **11**

Road map B5. 🏛 *40,000.* 🚊 *to Cacilhas or Trafaria then bus.* ℹ *Av. da República 18 (21-290 00 71).*

LONG SANDY beaches, backed by sand dunes, have made this a popular vacation resort for Lisboetas who come here to swim, sun, and enjoy the seafood res-taurants. A rail-road, with open carriages, runs for 10 km (6 miles) along the coast during the summer months. The first beaches reached from the city are popular with families with children, and the more distant beaches suit those seeking quiet isolation. Farther south, sheltered by pine forests, **Lagoa do Albufeira** is a peaceful wind-surfing center and campsite.

Cabo Espichel **12**

Road map B5. 🚌 *from Sesimbra.*

SHEER CLIFFS DROP straight into the sea at this windswept promontory where the land ends dramatically. The Romans named it Promontorium Barbaricum, alluding to its dangerous location; a light-house warns sailors of the treacherous rocks below. Stunning views of the ocean and the coast can be enjoyed from this bleak outcrop of land, but beware of the strong gusts of wind on the cliff edge.

In this desolate setting stands the impressive **Santuário de Nossa Senhora do Cabo**, a late 17th-century church with its back to the sea. On either side of the church a long line of pilgrims' lodgings facing in-ward form an open courtyard. Baroque paintings, votives, and a frescoed ceiling deco-rate the interior of the church, which otherwise stands aban-doned and derelict. Behind the church is a domed chapel tiled with blue and white *azulejo* panels depicting fishing scenes.

The site became a popular place of pilgrimage in the 13th century when a local man had a vision of the Madonna rising from the sea on a mule. Legend has it that the tracks of the mule can be seen em-bedded in the rock. The large footprints, on Praia dos Lagosteiros below the church, are actually believed to be fossilized dinosaur tracks.

Spring flowers by the saltpans of the Tagus estuary near Alcochete

Palácio de Queluz ❾

I N 1747, PEDRO, younger son of João V, commissioned Mateus Vicente to transform his 17th-century hunting lodge into a Rococo summer palace. The central section, including a music room and chapel, was built, but after Pedro's marriage in 1760 to the future Maria I, the palace was again extended. The French architect Jean-Baptiste Robillion added the sumptuous Robillion Pavilion and gardens, cleared space for the Throne Room and redesigned the Music Room. During Maria's reign, the royal family kept a menagerie and went boating on the *azulejo*-lined canal.

A sphinx in the gardens

Corridor of the Sleeves
Painted azulejo *panels (1784) representing the continents and the seasons, as well as hunting scenes, line the walls of the bright Corredor das Mangas (sleeves).*

Neptune's Fountain

★ Sala dos Embaixadores
Built by Robillion, this stately room was used for diplomatic audiences as well as concerts. The trompe l'oeil *ceiling shows the royal family attending a concert.*

The Lion Staircase is an impressive and graceful link from the lower gardens to the palace.

STAR FEATURES

★ Throne Room

★ Sala dos Embaixadores

★ Palace Gardens

To canal

Lion Fountain

The Robillion Pavilion displays the flamboyance of the French architect's Rococo style.

Don Quixote Chamber
The royal bedroom, where Pedro IV (see p54) was born and died, has a domed ceiling and magnificent floor decoration in exotic woods, giving the square room a circular appearance. Painted scenes by Manuel de Costa (1784) tell the story of Don Quixote.

Music Room

Operas and concerts were performed here by Maria I's orchestra, "the best in Europe" according to English traveler, William Beckford. A portrait of the queen hangs above the grand piano.

VISITORS' CHECKLIST

Road map B5. Largo do Palácio, Queluz. ☎ 21-435 00 39.
🚊 Queluz-Belas then 20-min walk. 🚌 from Lisbon, Colégio Militar. ◻ 10am–1pm, 2–5pm Wed–Mon. ● Jan 1, Easter, May 1, Jun 29, Dec 25. 🎫 📷 ♿
🖥 🍴 Cozinha Velha (see p409).

The royal family's living rooms and bedrooms opened out onto the Malta Gardens.

Chapel

★ Throne Room

The elegant state room (1770) was the scene of splendid balls and banquets. The gilded statues of Atlas are by Silvestre Faria Lobo.

Entrance

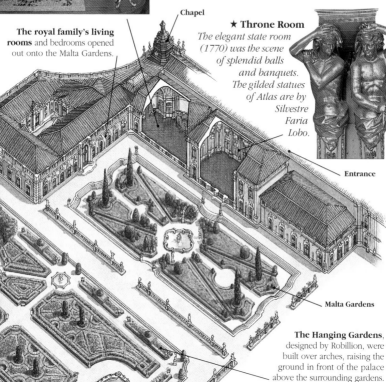

Malta Gardens

The Hanging Gardens, designed by Robillion, were built over arches, raising the ground in front of the palace above the surrounding gardens.

MARIA I (1734–1816)

Maria, the oldest daughter of José I, lived at the palace in Queluz after her marriage to her uncle, Pedro, in 1760. Serious and devout, she conscientiously filled her role as queen, but suffered increasingly from bouts of melancholia. When her son José died from smallpox in 1788, she went hopelessly mad. Visitors to Queluz were dismayed by her agonizing shrieks as she suffered visions and hallucinations. After the French invasion of 1807, her younger son João (declared regent in 1792) took his mad mother to Brazil.

★ Palace Gardens

The formal gardens, adorned with statues, fountains, and topiary, were often used for entertaining. Concerts performed in the Music Room would spill out into the Malta Gardens.

Sesimbra

Road map C5. 27,000.
Largo da Marinha 26–7 (21-223 57 43). 1st & 3rd Fri of month.

A STEEP NARROW ROAD leads down to this busy fishing village in a sheltered south-facing bay. Protected from north winds by the slopes of the Serra da Arrábida, the town has become a popular vacation resort with Lisboetas. It was occupied by the Romans and later the Moors until King Sancho II *(see pp42–3)* conquered its heavily defended forts in 1236. The old town is a maze of steep narrow streets, with the **Santiago Fort** (now a customs post) in the center overlooking the sea. From the terrace, which is open to the public during the day, there are views of the town, the Atlantic, and the wide sandy beach that stretches out on either side. Sesimbra is fast developing as a resort, with apartment hotels mushrooming on the surrounding hillsides and sidewalk cafés and bars that are always busy on sunny days, even in winter.

The fishing fleet of brightly painted boats is moored in the **Porto do Abrigo** to the west of the main town. The harbor is reached by taking Avenida dos Náufragos, a sweeping

Colorful fishing boats in the harbor at Sesimbra

promenade that follows the beach out of town. On the large trawlers *(traineiras)*, the catch is mainly sardines, sea bream, whiting, and swordfish; on the smaller boats, octopus and squid. In the late afternoon, when the fishing boats return from a day at sea, a colorful, noisy fish auction takes place on the dockside. The day's catch can be tasted in the town's excellent fish restaurants along the shore.

High above the town is the **Moorish castle**, greatly restored in the 18th century when a church and small flower-filled cemetery were added inside the walls. There are wonderful views from the ramparts, especially at sunset.

Palmela

Road map C5. 14,000.
Castelo de Palmela (21-233 21 22). every other Tue.

T HE FORMIDABLE castle at Palmela stands over the small hill town, high on a northeastern spur of the wooded Serra da Arrábida. Its strategic position dominates the plain for miles around, especially when floodlit at night. Heavily defended by the Moors, it was eventually conquered in the 12th century and given by Sancho I to the Knights of the Order of Santiago *(see p43)*. In 1423, João I transformed the castle into a monastery for the Order, which has now been restored and converted into a splendid *pousada (see p385)*, with a restaurant in the monks' refectory and a swimming pool for residents, hidden inside the castle walls.

From the castle terraces, and especially from the top of the 14th-century keep, there are fantastic views all around, over the Serra da Arrábida to the south and, on a clear day, across the Tagus to Lisbon. In the town square below, the church of **São Pedro** contains 18th-century tiles of scenes from the life of St. Peter.

The annual wine festival, the Festa das Vindimas, is held in September in front of the 17th-century Paço do Concelho (town hall). The villagers, dressed in traditional costume, press the wine barefoot. On the final day there is a spectacular fireworks display.

The castle at Palmela with views over the wooded Serra da Arrábida

Serra da Arrábida

Road map C5. 🚍 *Setúbal.*
🛈 *Parque Natural da Arrábida, Praça da República, Setúbal (265-52 40 32).*

T HE PARQUE NATURAL da Arrábida covers the small range of limestone mountains that stretches east-west along the coast between Sesimbra and Setúbal. It was established to protect the wild, beautiful landscape and rich variety of birds and wildlife, including eagles, wildcats, and badgers.

The name Arrábida is from Arabic meaning a place of prayer, and the wooded hillsides are indeed a peaceful, secluded retreat. The sheltered, south-facing slopes are thickly covered with aromatic and evergreen shrubs and trees such as pine and cypress, more typical of the Mediterranean. Vineyards also thrive on the sheltered slopes, and the town of **Vila Nogueira de Azeitão** is known for its wine, especially the Moscatel de Setúbal.

The **Estrada de Escarpa** (the N379-1) snakes across the top of the ridge and affords astounding views. A narrow road winds down to **Portinho da Arrábida**, a sheltered cove with a beach of fine white sand and crystal clear sea, popular with amateur fishermen. The sandy beaches of **Galapos** and **Figueirinha** are a little farther east along the coast road toward Setúbal. Just east of Sesimbra, the Serra da Arrábida drops to the sea in the sheer 380-m (1,250-ft) cliffs of Risco, the highest in mainland Portugal.

Portinho da Arrábida on the dramatic coastline of the Serra da Arrábida

🏛 Convento da Arrábida
Serra da Arrábida. 📞 21-218 05 20.
🕐 *by appt only (21-352 70 02).* 📷
Half hidden among the trees on the southern slopes of the Serra, overlooking the sea, this large 16th-century building was once a Franciscan monastery. The five round towers, perched along the slope of the hillside, were probably used for solitary meditation.

🏛 Museu Oceanográfico
Fortaleza de Santa Maria, Portinho da Arrábida. 📞 265-52 40 32.
🕐 *Tue–Fri.* 📷
The small fort, just above Portinho da Arrábida, was built by Pedro, the Prince Regent, in 1676 to protect local communities from attacks by Moorish pirates. It now houses a Sea Museum and Marine Biology Center where visitors can see aquariums containing local sea creatures, including sea urchins, octopus, and starfish.

🏛 Quinta da Bacalhoa
Vila Fresca de Azeitão. 📞 21-218 00 11. **Gardens** 🕐 11am–1pm Mon–Sat. ⬤ *public hols.* 📷
📷 *compulsory.* ♿
Hidden by a thick hedge, this beautiful manor was built in 1480, in the early Renaissance style. In 1528 it was enlarged with a graceful loggia, overlooking a formal garden of low topiary hedges around a fountain. The sunken garden, with orange and lemon trees, leads to an ornamental pool and arched pavilion with a tile panel of *Susannah and the Elders*, dated 1565 *(see p22)*. In 1937 the estate was bought by an American, Mrs. Scoville, whose family still owns it.

KEY

━━━ Major road
═══ Minor road
── Other road

0 kilometers   5

0 miles   3

Manueline interior of Igreja de Jesus, Setúbal

Setúbal ⓰

Road map C5. 🏙 120,000. 🚋 🚌
🚢 🛈 Casa do Corpo Santo, Praça
do Quebedo (265-53 42 22).

ALTHOUGH THIS is an important
industrial town and the
third largest port in Portugal
(after Lisbon and Oporto),
Setúbal is a good place to stay
for a few days to explore the
area. To the south of the central gardens and fountains are
the fishing harbor, marina and
ferry port, and a lively covered
market. North of the gardens
is the old town, with attractive
pedestrian streets and squares
full of shops and cafés.

The 16th-century **cathedral**,
dedicated to Santa Maria da
Graça, has glorious tiled panels
dating from the 18th century,
and gilded altar decorations.
Street names commemorate
two famous Setúbal residents:
Manuel Barbosa du Bocage
(1765–1805), whose satirical
poetry landed him in prison,
and Luísa Todi (1753–1833),
a celebrated opera singer.

In Roman times, fish-salting
was the most important industry here. Rectangular tanks,
carved from stone, can be
seen under the glass floor of
the Regional Tourist Office at
No. 10 Travessa Frei Gaspar.

🔒 Igreja de Jesus
Praça Miguel Bombarda. 🕻 265-52
41 50. ◯ Tue–Sun. 🚹 **Museum**
◯ Tue–Sat. ● public hols.
To the north of the old town,
this striking Gothic church is
one of Setúbal's architectural
treasures. Designed by the
architect Diogo Boitac in 1494,

**Fisherman's boat on the shallow mud flats of
the Reserva Natural do Estuário do Sado**

the lofty interior is adorned
with twisted columns, carved
in three strands from pinkish
Arrábida limestone, and rope-
like stone ribs decorating the
roof, recognized as the earliest
examples of the distinctive
Manueline style (see pp20–21).

On Rua do Balneário, in
the now-abandoned monastic
quarters adjacent to the church,
a **museum** houses 14 remarkable paintings of the life of
Christ. Painted in glowing
colors, the works are attributed to the followers of Jorge
Afonso (1520–30), influenced
by the Flemish school.

🏛 Museu de Arqueologia e Etnografia
Avenida Luísa Todi 162. 🕻 265-393
65. ◯ Tue–Sat. ● public hols.
The archaeological museum
displays a wealth of finds from
digs around Setúbal, including
Bronze Age pots, Roman coins,
and amphorae made to carry
wine and garum, a sauce
made from fish marinated in
salt and herbs considered a
great delicacy in Rome. The
ethnography display shows
local arts, crafts, and industries,
including the processing of salt
and cork over the centuries.

⚓ Castelo de São Filipe
Estrada de São Filipe. 🕻 265-52 38
44. ◯ daily.
The star-shaped fort was built
in 1595 by Philip II of Spain
during the period of Spanish
rule (see pp50–51) to keep a
wary eye on pirates, English
invaders, and the local population. A massive gateway
and stone tunnel lead to the
sheltered interior, which now
houses a pousada (see p385)
and an exquisite small chapel,
tiled with scenes from the life
of São Filipe by Policarpo de
Oliveira Bernardes
(see p22). A broad
terrace offers mar-
velous views of the
city and the Sado
estuary.

ENVIRONS: Setúbal is
an excellent starting
point for a tour by
car of the unspoiled
**Reserva Natural
do Estuário do
Sado**, a vast stretch
of mud flats, shallow

lagoons, and salt marshes with patches of pine forest, which has been explored and inhabited since 3500 BC. Otters, water birds (including storks and herons), oysters, and a great variety of fish are found in the preserve. The old tidal water mill at Mouriscas, 5 km (3 miles) to the east of Setúbal, uses the different levels of the tide to turn the grinding stones. Rice-growing and fishing are the main occupations today, and pine trees around the lagoon are tapped for resin.

✖ Reserva Natural do Estuário do Sado
ℹ *Praça da República, Setúbal (265-52 40 32).*

Península de Tróia ⑰

Road map C5. 🚌 🛳 *Tróia.* ℹ *Complexo Turístico de Tróia (265-49 41 51).*

Thatched fisherman's cottage in the village of Carrasqueira

HIGH-RISE VACATION apartments dominate the tip of the Tróia peninsula, easily accessible from Setúbal by ferry. The Atlantic coast, stretching south for 18 km (11 miles) of untouched sandy beach, lined with dunes and pinewoods, is now the haunt of sun-seekers in the summer.

Near Tróia, in the sheltered lagoon, the Roman town of **Cetóbriga** was the site of a thriving fish-salting business; the stone tanks and ruined buildings are open to visit. To the south, chic new vacation villas and golf clubs are springing up along the lagoon.

Farther on, **Carrasqueira** is an old fishing community where you can still see traditional reed houses, with walls and roofs made from thatch. The narrow fishing boats

moored along the mud flats are reached by walkways raised on stilts. From here to Alcácer do Sal, great stretches of pine forest line the road, and there are the first glimpses of the cork oak countryside, typical of the Alentejo.

⋔ Cetóbriga
N253-1. 📞 *265-49 43 18.* ◻ *daily.*

Alcácer do Sal ⑱

Road map C5. 🏘 *15,000.* 🚉 🚌 ℹ *Praça Pedro Nunes (265-62 25 65).* 🛒 *1st Sat of month.*

BYPASSED by the main road, the ancient town of Alcácer do Sal (*al-kasr* from the Arabic for castle, and *do sal* from its trade in salt) sits peacefully on the north bank of the Sado River. The imposing castle was a hill fort as early as the 6th century BC.

View over Alcácer do Sal and the Sado River from the castle

The Phoenicians established an inland trading port here, and the castle later became a stronghold for the Romans. Rebuilt by the Moors, it was finally conquered by Afonso II in 1217. The restored buildings have now taken on a new life as a *pousada (see p384)*, with sweeping views of the rooftops and untidy storks' nests on the town's church roofs.

There are pleasant cafés along the riverside promenade and several historic churches. The small church of Espírito Santo now houses a **Museu Arqueológico** exhibiting local finds, and the 18th-century **Santo António** holds a marble Chapel of the 11,000 Virgins. The bullring is a focus for summer events and hosts the agricultural fair in October.

🏛 Museu Arqueológico
Igreja do Espírito Santo, Praça Pedro Nunes. 📞 *265-62 25 65.* ◻ *Mon–Fri.*

BIRDS OF THE TAGUS AND SADO ESTUARIES

Many waterbirds, including black-winged stilts, avocets, Kentish plovers, and pratincoles are found close to areas of open water and mud flats as well as the dried-out lagoons of the Tagus and Sado estuaries. Reed beds also provide shelter for nesting and support good numbers of little bitterns, purple herons, and marsh harriers. From September to March, the area around the Tagus estuary is extremely important for wildfowl and wintering waders.

Black-winged stilt, a wader that feeds in the estuaries

ESTREMADURA AND RIBATEJO

ETWEEN THE TAGUS *and the coast lies Estremadura, an area of rolling hills that tumble down to rugged cliffs and sandy beaches. In contrast, the Ribatejo is a vast alluvial plain stretching along the banks of the Tagus. Portugal's finest medieval monasteries bear witness to the illustrious if turbulent past of these regions.*

The name Estremadura comes from the Latin *Extrema Durii*, "beyond the Douro," once the border of the Christian kingdoms in the north. As Portugal expanded southward in the 12th century, land taken from the Moors *(see pp42–3)* was given to the religious orders. The Cistercian abbey at Alcobaça celebrates Afonso Henriques's capture of the town of Santarém in 1147, and the Knights Templar began their citadel at Tomar *(see p185)* soon after.

Spanish claims to the Portuguese throne brought more fighting: Batalha's magnificent abbey was built near the site of João I's victory over the Castilians at Aljubarrota in 1385. More recently, in 1808–10, Napoleonic forces sacked many towns in the region, but were stopped by Wellington's formidable defenses, the Lines of Torres Vedras.

Nowadays, Estremadura is an area of expanding commerce, where vineyards, wheatfields, and market gardens flourish. In the Ribatejo (the name means Banks of the Tagus) the river's vast flood plain provides fertile soil for agriculture and grazing land for Portugal's prized black fighting bulls and fine horses.

The area around Tomar and the river towns along the Tagus have thriving industries, while on the Zêzere River the dam built at Castelo de Bode in the 1940s heralded a new era of hydroelectric power. The Atlantic coast is a popular vacation destination, especially the fishing village of Nazaré and the sandy beaches along the Pinhal de Leiria forest. Visitors also flock to Portugal's most important religious shrine at Fátima, scene of celebrated visions of the Virgin Mary in 1917.

Posters advertising the local bullfighting events in Coruche

◁ **Austere Gothic columns in the nave of the Cistercian abbey church at Alcobaça**

Exploring Estremadura and the Ribatejo

THE IMPRESSIVE MONUMENTS in Estremadura recall the important role the region has played in Portugal's history. Leiria's charming old town is a convenient base from which to visit the great abbeys at Batalha and Alcobaça or the modern shrine at Fátima. Tomar is also a good place to stay, and it is possible to make day trips from Lisbon. Those in search of more leisurely pursuits can enjoy boating on the Castelo de Bode lake or relaxing on the coast's stunning beaches. The fertile Lezíria plain of the Ribatejo is an area famous for cattle and horse breeding. Here visitors can enjoy bullfights at Santarém and lively local festivals.

SIGHTS AT A GLANCE

GETTING AROUND

Trains connect all the major towns in the region, and there is a good local bus service. Buses from Lisbon offer day trips to popular destinations like Alcobaça and Tomar. The A1 highway allows easy north-south access, and side roads, including the IP6, link the rest of the region. The older N1 (IC2), however, is often congested. East of the Tagus, in the Lezíria, roads are few but adequate.

Colorful beach huts at São Martinho do Porto, near Nazaré

0 kilometers   25

0 miles   15

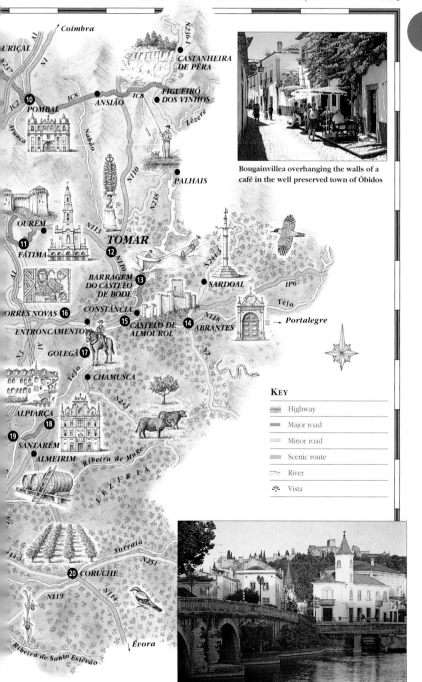

Coimbra

CASTANHEIRA
DE PÊRA

URIÇAL

IC8

POMBAL **10**

ANSIÃO

IC8

FIGUEIRÓ
DOS VINHOS

Zêzere

Nabão

N110

PALHAIS

N238

OURÉM **11**

N113

FÁTIMA

TOMAR

12

N110

BARRAGEM
DO CASTELO
DE BODE

13

N2443

SARDOAL

IP6

Tejo

ORRES NOVAS **16**

CONSTÂNCIA

Portalegre

ENTRONCAMENTO

CASTELO DE
ALMOUROL

15

N118

ABRANTES

14

Tejo

N2

GOLEGÃ **17**

CHAMUSCA

N243

ALPIARÇA **18**

19

SANTARÉM

ALMEIRIM

Ribeira de Muge

L E Z Í R I A

Bougainvillea overhanging the walls of a
café in the well preserved town of Óbidos

KEY

▬▬	Highway
▬▬	Major road
▬▬	Minor road
▬▬	Scenic route
⌇	River
☀	Vista

Sorraia

N251

20 CORUCHE

N119

N114

Ribeira de Santo Estêvão

Évora

SEE ALSO

• *Where to Stay* pp386–8

• *Where to Eat* pp410–11

The Renaissance bridge, Ponte Velha, over the Nabão River
in Tomar, with the Convento de Cristo in the distance

Berlenga Islands ❶

Road map B4. 🚢 *from Peniche.*
ℹ️ *Peniche.*

MONKS, A LIGHTHOUSE keeper, fishermen, and recently, biologists have inhabited this rocky archipelago that juts out from the Atlantic Ocean 12 km (7 miles) from the mainland. Berlenga Grande, the biggest island, can be reached by ferry in about an hour. This island is a nature preserve with nesting sites for seabirds including guillemots and herring gulls.

On the southeast side of the island is the 17th-century pentagonal **Forte de São João Baptista**. This stark, stone fort suffered repeated assaults from pirates and foreign armies over the years. Today it is a basic hostel. Small boats can be rented from the jetty to explore the reefs and marine grottoes around the island. **Furado Grande** is the most spectacular of these: a 70-m (230-ft) tunnel, opening into the Covo do Sonho (Dream Cove) framed by imposing red granite cliffs.

Stone fortress of São João Baptista on Berlenga Grande

Peniche ❷

Road map B4. 🏘️ *20,000.* 🚌
ℹ️ *Rua Alexandre Herculano (262-78 95 71).* 🛒 *Thu (except Jul & Dec).*

SET ON A PENINSULA, this small, pleasant town is partly enclosed by 16th-century walls. Totally dependent on its port, Peniche has excellent fish restaurants and deep-sea fishing facilities. At the water's edge on the south side of town stands the 16th-century **Fortaleza**, used as a prison during the repressive Salazar regime *(see pp56–7)*. The fortress was made famous by the escape in 1960 of the Communist leader Álvaro Cunhal. Inside, the **Museu de Peniche** caters to popular interest with a grim political tour that includes a look into the prison cells. In Largo 5 de Outubro, the **Igreja da Misericórdia** has 17th-century painted ceiling panels depicting the *Life of Christ*, and patterned *azulejo* panels from the same period.

🏛️ Museu de Peniche
Campo da República. 📞 *262-78 27 10.* 🕐 *Tue–Sun.* ⬤ *Dec 25.* 🎟️

Boats anchored in the old harbor at Peniche

ENVIRONS: On the peninsula's western headland, 2 km (1 mile) from Peniche, **Cabo Carvoeiro** affords fine views of the ocean and the strange-shaped rocks along the eroded coastline. Here, the interior of the chapel of **Nossa Senhora dos Remédios** is faced with 18th-century tiles on the *Life of the Virgin* attributed to the workshop of António de Oliveira Bernardes *(see p22)*.

Along the coast, 2 km (1 mile) east of Peniche, **Baleal** is a small community with gorgeous beaches and an idyllic fishing cove across a causeway.

Óbidos ❸

Road map B4. 🏘️ *600.* 🚉 🚌
ℹ️ *Rua Direita (262-95 92 31).*

THIS ENCHANTING hill town with pretty whitewashed houses is enclosed within 14th-century castellated walls. When King Dinis *(see pp44–5)* married Isabel of Aragon in 1282, Óbidos was among his wedding presents to her. At the time Óbidos was an important port, but by the 16th century the river had silted up and its strategic importance declined. It has since been restored and preserved as a picture-postcard town popular with tourists.

The entrance into the town is through the southern gate, **Porta da Vila**, whose interior is embellished with 18th-century tiles. Rua Direita, the main shopping street, leads to Praça de Santa Maria. Here, a Manueline **pelourinho** (pillory) is decorated with a fishing net, the emblem of Dona Leonor, wife of João II. She chose this emblem in honor of the fishermen who tried in vain to save her son from drowning.

Opposite the pillory is the church of **Santa Maria**, with a simple Renaissance portal. The future Afonso V was married to his cousin Isabel here in 1441. He was ten years old, she eight. The interior of the church retains a simple clarity with a painted wooden ceiling and 17th-century tiles. In the chancel, a retable depicting the *Mystic Marriage of St. Catherine* (1661) is by Josefa de Óbidos *(see p51)*. The artist lived most of her life in Óbidos and is buried in the church of **São Pedro** on Largo de São Pedro. Her work is also on display in the **Museu Municipal**.

Dominating the town is the **castle**, rebuilt by Afonso Henriques after he took the town from the Moors in 1148.

View of the castle over the whitewashed houses of Óbidos

Today it is a charming *pousada* *(see p387)*. The sentry path along the battlements affords fine views of the rooftops.

Southeast of town is the Baroque **Santuário do Senhor da Pedra**, begun in 1740 to a hexagonal plan. An early Christian stone crucifix on the altar remains a venerated item.

🏛 Museu Municipal
Praça de Santa Maria. 【 262-95 50 10. ◯ daily. ● Jan 1, Dec 25.

Pillory in front of the Igreja de Santa Maria in Óbidos

Caldas da Rainha ●

Road map B4. 🏠 22,000. 🚃 🚌
🛈 Rua Duarte Pacheco (262-83 10 03). 🚩 Mon.

THE "QUEEN'S HOT SPRINGS" is a sprawling spa town. It owes its prosperity to successes in three quite different fields: thermal cures, fruit farming, and ceramics. The queen who gave her name to the town was Dona Leonor, founder of the **Misericórdia** hospital on Largo Rainha Dona Leonor. The original hospital chapel later became the impressive Manueline **Igreja do Populo**, built by Diogo Boitac *(see pp106–7)*. Inside is the chapel of São Sebastião, built in the 15th century and faced with 18th-century *azulejos*.

The market in Praça da República and shops in Rua da Liberdade sell local ceramics, including the green cabbage-leaf majolica ware *(see pp24–5)* typical of the town. Examples of the religious and humorous work of the caricaturist and potter Rafael Bordalo Pinheiro (1846–1905) can be seen in the **Museu de Cerâmica**, housed in the ceramics factory.

🏛 Museu de Cerâmica
Rua Elídio Amado. 【 262-84 02 80.
◯ Tue–Sun. ● public hols.

ENVIRONS: The saltwater **Lagoa de Óbidos**, 15 km (9 miles) west of Caldas, is a popular lagoon for sailing and fishing.

The fairytale town of Óbidos encircled by medieval crenellated walls ▷

Alcobaça ●

PORTUGAL'S LARGEST CHURCH, the Mosteiro de Santa Maria de Alcobaça, is famous for its simple medieval architecture. Founded in 1153, the abbey is closely linked to the arrival of the Cistercian order in Portugal in 1138 as well as the birth of the nation. In March 1147, Afonso Henriques *(see pp42–3)* conquered the Moorish stronghold of Santarém. To commemorate the victory, the king fulfilled his vow to build a mighty church for the Cistercians. This massive task was completed in 1223. The monarchy continued to endow the monastery, notably King Dinis who built the main cloister. Among those buried here are the tragic lovers King Pedro and his murdered mistress Inês.

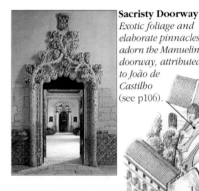

Sacristy Doorway
Exotic foliage and elaborate pinnacles adorn the Manueline doorway, attributed to João de Castilho (see p106).

Tomb of Inês de Castro

Dormitory

The chapterhouse was where the monks met to elect the abbot and discuss issues regarding the monastery.

The kitchen's huge chimney

The octagonal lavabo was where the monks washed their hands.

Refectory and Kitchen
Stairs lead up to the pulpit where one of the monks read from the Bible as the others ate in silence. In the vast kitchen next door, oxen could be roasted on the spit inside the fireplace and a specially diverted stream provided a constant water supply.

★ Cloister of Dom Dinis
Also known as the Cloister of Silence, the exquisite cloister was ordered by King Dinis in 1308. The austere galleries and double arches are in keeping with the Cistercian regard for simplicity.

STAR FEATURES

★ Cloister of Dom Dinis

★ Tombs of Pedro I and Inês de Castro

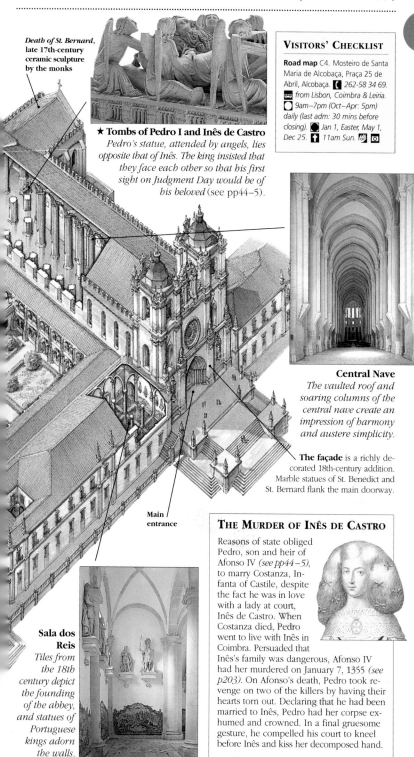

Death of St. Bernard, late 17th-century ceramic sculpture by the monks

★ **Tombs of Pedro I and Inês de Castro**
Pedro's statue, attended by angels, lies opposite that of Inês. The king insisted that they face each other so that his first sight on Judgment Day would be of his beloved (see pp44–5).

VISITORS' CHECKLIST

Road map C4. Mosteiro de Santa Maria de Alcobaça, Praça 25 de Abril, Alcobaça. ☎ *262-58 34 69.* 🚌 *from Lisbon, Coimbra & Leiria.* ◯ *9am–7pm (Oct–Apr: 5pm) daily (last adm: 30 mins before closing).* ● *Jan 1, Easter, May 1, Dec 25.* ✝ *11am Sun.* 📷 📷

Central Nave
The vaulted roof and soaring columns of the central nave create an impression of harmony and austere simplicity.

The façade is a richly decorated 18th-century addition. Marble statues of St. Benedict and St. Bernard flank the main doorway.

Main entrance

Sala dos Reis
Tiles from the 18th century depict the founding of the abbey, and statues of Portuguese kings adorn the walls.

THE MURDER OF INÊS DE CASTRO

Reasons of state obliged Pedro, son and heir of Afonso IV *(see pp44–5)*, to marry Costanza, Infanta of Castile, despite the fact he was in love with a lady at court, Inês de Castro. When Costanza died, Pedro went to live with Inês in Coimbra. Persuaded that Inês's family was dangerous, Afonso IV had her murdered on January 7, 1355 *(see p203)*. On Afonso's death, Pedro took revenge on two of the killers by having their hearts torn out. Declaring that he had been married to Inês, Pedro had her corpse exhumed and crowned. In a final gruesome gesture, he compelled his court to kneel before Inês and kiss her decomposed hand.

The beach at Nazaré viewed from Sítio

Nazaré ❻

Road map C4. 🏘 *10,000.* 🚌
🛈 *Avenida da República 17 (262-56 11 94).* 🚹 *Fri.*

BESIDE A GLORIOUS BEACH in a sweeping bay backed by steep cliffs, this fishing village is a popular summer resort that has maintained some of its traditional character. Fishermen dressed in checked shirts and black stocking caps and fishwives wearing several layers of petticoats can still be seen mending nets and drying fish on wire racks on the beach. The bright boats with tall prows that once were hauled from the sea by oxen are still used, but now they have a proper anchorage south of the beach. According to legend the name Nazaré comes from a statue of the Virgin Mary brought to the town by a monk from Nazareth in the 4th century.

High on the cliff above the town is **Sítio**, reached by a funicular that climbs 110 m (360 ft). At the cliff edge stands the tiny **Ermida da Memória**. According to legend, this is where the Virgin Mary saved Dom Fuas Roupinho, a local dignitary, and his horse from following a deer that leapt off the cliff in a sea mist in 1182. Across the square, the 17th-century church of **Nossa Senhora da Nazaré**, with two Baroque belfries and 18th-century tiles inside, contains an anonymous painting of the miraculous rescue. The church also contains the revered image of Our Lady of Nazaré. In September this statue is borne down to the sea in a traditional procession, a colorful reminder of the town's origins.

ENVIRONS: São Martinho do Porto, 13 km (8 miles) south of Nazaré, is a sandy beach on a curving, almost landlocked bay. The safe location makes it popular with families and children. The Visigothic church of **São Gião**, 5 km (3 miles) farther south, has fine sculpting and well-proportioned arches.

Porto de Mós ❼

Road map C4. 🏘 *6,000.* 🚌
🛈 *Jardim Principal (244-49 13 23).* 🚹 *Fri.*

ORIGINALLY A MOORISH fort, and rebuilt over the centuries by successive Christian kings, the rather fanciful **castle** perches on a hill above the small town of Porto de Mós. Its present appearance, with green cone-shaped turrets and an exquisite loggia, was the inspired work of King Afonso IV's master builders in 1420.

In the town below, the 13th-century church of **São João Baptista** retains its original Romanesque portal. In the public gardens is the richly decorated Baroque church of **São Pedro**. Just off the Praça da República, the **Museu Municipal** displays a varied collection of local finds dating back to Roman remains and dinosaur bones. More modern exhibits include the local *mós* (millstones), as well as present-day ceramics and woven rugs.

🏛 **Museu Municipal**
Travessa de São Pedro. 📞 *244-49 96 00.* 🕐 *Tue–Sun.* 🔴 *public hols.*

Donkey in the Serra de Aire nature preserve, south of Porto de Mós

ENVIRONS: South of the town, the 38,900-ha (96,000-acre) **Parque Natural das Serras de Aire e Candeeiros** covers a limestone landscape of pastures, olive groves, and stone walls and is a nesting place for the red-beaked chough.

The area is also dotted with vast and spectacular underground caverns with odd rock formations and festoons of stalactites and stalagmites. The **Grutas de Mira de Aire**, 17 km (10 miles) southeast of Porto de Mós, are the biggest, descending 110 m (360 ft) into tunnels and walkways around subterranean lakes. A tour through caverns with names such as the "Jewel Room," past bizarre rocks dubbed "Chinese Hat" or "Jellyfish," ends in a theatrical light and water show.

🦇 **Grutas de Mira de Aire**
Mira de Aire, N243. 📞 *244-44 03 22.* 🕐 *daily.* 🖼

Batalha ❽

See pp182–3.

Baroque church of Nossa Senhora da Nazaré in Sítio

Leiria ❾

Road map C4. 🏃 *13,000.* 🚉 🚌
ℹ️ *Jardim Luis de Camões (244-81 47 48).* 🏪 *Tue & Sat.*

EPISCOPAL CITY since 1545, Leiria is set in attractive countryside on the banks of the Lis River. Originally the Roman town of Collipo, it was recaptured from the Moors by Afonso Henriques *(see pp42–3)* in the 12th century. In 1254 Afonso III held a *cortes* here, the first parliament attended by common laymen.

The resplendent hilltop **castle** that crowns the city houses a library and meeting rooms. In the early 14th century, King Dinis restored the castle with a fine keep, the Torre de Menagem, and an elegant loggia; he turned it into a royal residence for himself and his queen, Isabel of Aragon. Within the castle battlements stands the Gothic church of **Nossa Senhora da Pena**, today little more than a roofless shell of dark granite walls. A magnificent view from the castle loggia overlooks the wide expanse of pine forest, the Pinhal de Leiria, and the rooftops of the town below.

The old town below the castle is full of charm, with tiny dwellings over archways, graceful arcades, and the small 12th-century church of **São Pedro** on Largo de São Pedro.

The Romanesque portal is all that remains of the original church. The muted 16th-century **Sé** above Praça Rodrigues Lobo has an elegant vaulted nave and an altarpiece in the chancel painted in 1605 by Simão Rodrigues. From Avenida Marquês de Pombal, climbing the hill opposite the castle, an 18th-century stairway takes you up to the elaborate 16th-century **Santuário de Nossa Senhora da Encarnação**. The small Baroque interior is tightly packed with colorful geometric *azulejo* panels and 17th-century paintings of the *Life of the Virgin*.

⚜ Castle
Largo de São Pedro. 🔔 *244-81 39 82.* ⭕ *daily.* ⬤ *Jan 1, Dec 25.* 📷

ENVIRONS: West of Leiria is the long coastal pine forest, the **Pinhal de Leiria**, planted by King Dinis, "the farmer king," to supply wood for ship building. "A green and whispering cathedral," in the words of the poet Afonso Lopes Vieira (1878–1946), the forest extends northward to the beach of Pedrogão. **São Pedro de Muel**, 22 km (13 miles) to the west of Leiria, is a small resort on a marvelous beach.

Exposed and rugged coastline west of Leiria

Pombal ❿

Road map C4. 🏃 *12,500.* 🚉 🚌
ℹ️ *Largo do Cardal (236-21 32 30).* 🏪 *Mon & Thu.*

CLOSELY ASSOCIATED with the Marquês de Pombal *(see pp52–3)*, who retired here in disgrace in 1777, this small town of whitewashed houses is overlooked by the stately **castle** founded in 1171 by the Knights Templar *(see p185).*

The Marquis lived in what is now Praça Marquês de Pombal. Here the old prison and the *celeiro* (granary) are adorned with the Pombal family crest. The former monastery of Santo António contains the **Museu Marquês de Pombal**. Its collection of documents and art focuses on the Marquis.

🏛 Museu Marquês de Pombal
Largo do Cardal. 🔔 *236-21 20 01.* ⭕ *Mon–Fri.* ⬤ *public hols.* ♿

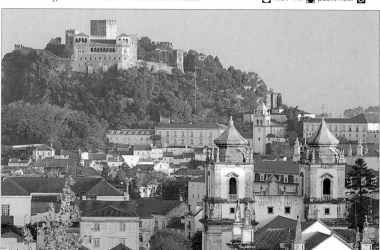

Arcaded loggia and castle towers guarding the town of Leiria

Batalha ❷

João I's coat of arms on portal

T HE DOMINICAN ABBEY of Santa Maria da Vitória at Batalha is a masterpiece of Portuguese Gothic architecture. The pale limestone monastery celebrates the victory at Aljubarrota in 1385. João I had vowed that he would dedicate a magnificent church to the Virgin if he won the battle. Today, the abbey still has military significance: two unknown soldiers from World War I lie in the chapterhouse. The abbey was begun in 1388 under master builder Afonso Domingues, succeeded in 1402 by David Huguet. Over the next two centuries successive kings left their mark on the monastery: João's son, King Duarte, ordered a royal pantheon behind the apse, and Manueline additions include the Unfinished Chapels and much of the decoration of the abbey buildings.

Chapterhouse
Guards keep watch by the Tomb of the Unknown Soldiers beneath David Huguet's striking star-vaulted ceiling.

★ Royal Cloister
Gothic arches by Afonso Domingues and David Huguet around the cloister are embellished by Manueline tracery (see pp20–21) to achieve a harmony of form and decoration.

The lavabo, where monks washed their hands before and after meals, contains a fountain built around 1450.

Refectory

Main entrance

Portal
The portal was decorated by Huguet with religious motifs and statues of the apostles in intricate late Gothic style.

STAR FEATURES
★ **Founder's Chapel**
★ **Royal Cloister**
★ **Unfinished Chapels**

★ **Unfinished Chapels**
Begun under King Duarte, the octagonal mausoleum was abandoned by Manuel I in favor of the Jerónimos monastery in Belém (see pp106–7).

VISITORS' CHECKLIST

Road map C4. Mosteiro de Santa Maria da Vitória, Batalha.
244-76 54 97. *from Lisbon, Leiria, Porto de Mós & Fátima.* 9am–6pm (Oct–Mar: 5pm) daily. Jan 1, Easter, May 1, Dec 24 & 25.

The stained-glass window behind the choir dates from 1514.

Manueline Portal
Most of the decoration of the Unfinished Chapels dates from the reign of Manuel I. This delicate portal was carved in 1509 by Mateus Fernandes.

Lofty nave by Afonso Domingues

The chapel is topped by an octagonal lantern.

★ **Founder's Chapel**
The tomb of João I and his English wife Philippa of Lancaster, lying hand in hand, was begun in 1426 by Huguet. Their son, Henry the Navigator, is also buried here.

THE BATTLE OF ALJUBARROTA

In 1383 Portugal's direct male line of descent ended with the death of Fernando I (*see pp44–5*). Dom João, the illegitimate son of Fernando's father, was proclaimed king, but his claim was opposed by Juan of Castile. On August 14, 1385, João I's greatly outnumbered forces, commanded by Nuno Álvares Pereira, faced the Castilians on a small plateau near Aljubarrota, 3 km (2 miles) south of Batalha. João's spectacular victory ensured 200 years of independence from Spain. The monastery now stands as a symbol of Portuguese sovereignty and the power of the House of Avis.

Commander Nuno Álvares Pereira

João I's motto, *Por bem* (for good), is inscribed on his tomb.

Curved limestone gallery around the vast esplanade in front of the basilica at Fátima

Fátima ⓫

Road map C4. 🏘 *4,000.* 🚌
ℹ *Avenida Dom José Alves Correira da Silva (249-53 11 39).* 🚃 *Sat.*

THE SANCTUARY of Fátima is a devotional shrine on a prodigious scale, a pilgrim destination on a par with Santiago de Compostela in Spain or Lourdes in France. The Neo-Baroque limestone **basilica**, flanked by statues of saints, has a 65-m (213-ft) tower and an esplanade twice the size of St. Peter's Square in Rome.

On May 13 and October 13 thousands of pilgrims arrive to commemorate appearances of the Virgin to three shepherd children. On May 13, 1917, 10-year-old Lucia Santos and her young cousins, Francisco and Jacinta Marta, saw a shining figure in a holm oak tree. She ordered them to return to the tree on the same day for six months, and by October 13 70,000 pilgrims were with the children by the tree. Many spoke of "the miracle of the

sun," yet only Lucia heard the three "Secrets of Fátima" spoken on her last appearance. The first talked of peace (this was during World War I); the second was about Russia; the third was never divulged, since it supposedly prophesied a disaster so terrible "the living would envy the dead." Inside the basilica, begun in 1928, are the tombs of Jacinta and Francisco. Lucia, who became a Carmelite nun, is still alive today. The stained-glass windows show scenes of the sightings. In the esplanade, the **Capela das Aparições** marks the site of the apparition. Inside, the crown of the Virgin holds the bullet extracted from Pope John Paul II after the assassination attempt in 1981. A symbolic holm oak stands outside. East of the sanctuary, the children's homes have been preserved in the **Casa dos Pastorinhos**.

For most people, however, the most impressive sight is the intense emotion and faith of the penitents who approach the shrine on their knees. Wax limbs are burned as offerings for miracles performed by the Virgin, and thousands of candles light the esplanade in the nighttime masses.

🏠 **Casa dos Pastorinhos**
Aljustrel. 📞 *249-53 28 28.*
🕐 *daily.* ♿

Church and clocktower of São João Baptista in Tomar's main square

ENVIRONS: The medieval town of **Ourém**, 10 km (6 miles) northeast of Fátima, is a walled citadel, dominated by the 15th-century castle of Ourém built by Afonso, grandson of Nuno Álvares Pereira *(see p183)*. His magnificent tomb is in the 15th-century Igreja Matriz. The town's name is said to derive from Oureana, a Moorish girl who, before she fell in love with a Christian knight and converted, was called Fátima.

Ruined secret passage connecting the towers of the castle in Ourém

Tomar ⓬

Road map C4. 🏘 *20,000.* 🚉 🚌
ℹ *Avenida Dr Cândido Madureira (249-32 24 27).* 🚃 *Fri.*

FOUNDED IN 1157 by Gualdim Pais, the first Grand Master of the Order of the Templars in Portugal, the town is dominated by the 12th-century castle containing the Convento de Cristo *(see pp186–7)*. The heart of this charming town is a neat grid of narrow streets. The lively shopping street, Rua Serpa Pinto, leads to the Gothic church of **São João Baptista** on Praça da República, the town's main square. The late 15th-century church has an elegant Manueline portal and is capped by an octagonal spire. Inside, there is a carved stone pulpit, and 16th-century paintings including a *Last Supper* by Gregório Lopes (1490–1550). A particularly gory beheading of John the Baptist is also attributed to Lopes.

The area outside the church is the focus of the spectacular Festa dos Tabuleiros, a festival with pagan origins held in July, every two or three years, in which girls in white carry towering platters of bread and flowers on their heads. The festival has similar roots to the Festa do Espírito Santo *(see p366)*, popular in the Azores.

Nearby, in Rua Dr. Joaquim Jacinto, stands one of the oldest **synagogues** in Portugal, built in 1430–60 with four tall columns and a vaulted ceiling. The building was last used as a place of worship in 1497 after which Manuel I *(see pp46–7)* banished all Jews who refused to convert to Christianity. It has since been a prison, a hay loft, and a warehouse. Today, it holds a small Jewish museum, the **Museu Luso-Hebraico de Abraham Zacuto**, named after a famous 15th-century astronomer and mathematician.

Farther south stands the 17th-century church of São Francisco. Its former cloisters now house the **Museu dos Fósforos**, a match museum proudly boasting the largest collection in Europe – over 43,000 matchboxes from 104 countries of the world.

On the east side of the Nabão River, just off Rua Aquiles da Mota Lima, is the 13th-century church of **Santa Maria do Olival**, with a distinctive three-story bell tower. Restored various times through the centuries, the church preserves its Gothic façade and rose window. Inside are the graves of Gualdim Pais (died 1195) and other Templar Masters, and an elegant Renaissance pulpit. The church once had significance far beyond Tomar as the mother church for mariners in the Age of Discovery.

Pulpit in Santa Maria do Olival

Heading north, Rua Santa Iria takes you to the **Capela de Santa Iria**, beside the 15th-century bridge, **Ponte Velha**. This Renaissance chapel is said to have been built where the saint was martyred in the 7th century *(see p191)*. A powerful stone retable depicting *Christ on the Cross* (1536) stands

Tomar's main shopping street, Rua Serpa Pinto, overlooked by the castle

above the altar in the Capela dos Vales. On an island in the river the shaded **Parque do Mouchão** is a pleasant walk; an allegedly Roman water-wheel turns with the passing water. Continuing northward, past the octagonal 16th-century **Ermida de São Gregório** with its wild Manueline doorway, a huge flight of steps leads to a 17th-century chapel **Nossa Senhora da Piedade**.

On the slopes of the hill leading up to the Convento do Cristo is the Renaissance basilica, **Nossa Senhora da Conceição**, built between 1530 and 1550. Its exterior simplicity contrasts with the elegantly proportioned and delicately carved Corinthian columns of the interior. The architect is believed to be Francisco de Holanda (1517–84), who worked for King João III.

🏛 **Museu Luso-Hebraico de Abraham Zacuto**
Rua Joaquim Jacinto. 249-32 26 01. ☐ Thu–Tue. ⬤ public hols.

🏛 **Museu dos Fósforos**
Largo 5 de Outubro. 249-32 26 01. ☐ Sun–Fri. ⬤ public hols. ♿

THE ORDER OF CHRIST

During the 12th and 13th centuries, the crusading Order of the Knights Templar helped the Portuguese in battle against the invading Moorish infidels. In return they were rewarded with extensive lands and political power. Castles, churches, and towns sprang up under their protective mantle. In 1314, Pope Clement V was forced to suppress this rich and powerful Order, but in Portugal King Dinis turned it into the Order of Christ, which inherited the property and privileges of the Templars.

Cross of the Order of Christ

Ideals of Christian expansion were revived in the 15th century when their Grand Master, Prince Henry the Navigator, invested the order's revenue in exploration. The emblem of the order, the squared cross, adorned the sails of the caravels that crossed the uncharted waters *(see pp46–7)*.

Tomar: Convento de Cristo

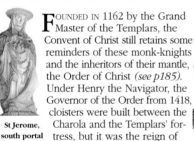

St Jerome, south portal

Founded in 1162 by the Grand Master of the Templars, the Convent of Christ still retains some reminders of these monk-knights and the inheritors of their mantle, the Order of Christ *(see p185)*. Under Henry the Navigator, the Governor of the Order from 1418, cloisters were built between the Charola and the Templars' fortress, but it was the reign of João III (1521–57) that saw the greatest changes. Architects such as João de Castilho and Diogo de Arruda, engaged to express the Order's power and royal patronage in stone, built the church and cloisters with dazzling Manueline flourishes, which reached a pinnacle with the window in the west front of the church.

★ **Manueline Window**
Marine motifs twine round this elaborate window. The carving at the base is thought to be either the architect (see p20) or the Old Man of the Sea.

Cloister of the Crows, flanked by an aqueduct

★ **Great Cloister**
Begun in the 1550s, probably by Diogo de Torralva, this cloister reflects João III's passion for Italian art. Concealed spiral stairways in the corners lead to the Terrace of Wax.

The "Bread" Cloister was where loaves were handed out to the poor who came to beg at the monastery.

The Terrace of Wax, where honeycombs were left to dry

THE CHAROLA

The nucleus of the monastery is the 12th-century Charola, the Templars' oratory. Like many of their temples, its layout is based on the Rotunda of Jerusalem's Holy Sepulchre, with a central octagon of altars. In 1356, Tomar became the headquarters of the Order of Christ in Portugal, and the Charola's decoration reflects the Order's wealth. The paintings and frescoes (mostly 16th-century biblical scenes) and the gilded statuary below the Byzantine cupola have undergone much careful restoration. When the Manueline church was built, an archway was created in the side of the Charola to link the two, making the Charola the church's main chapel.

The gilded octagon

STAR FEATURES

★ **Charola**

★ **Manueline Window**

★ **Great Cloister**

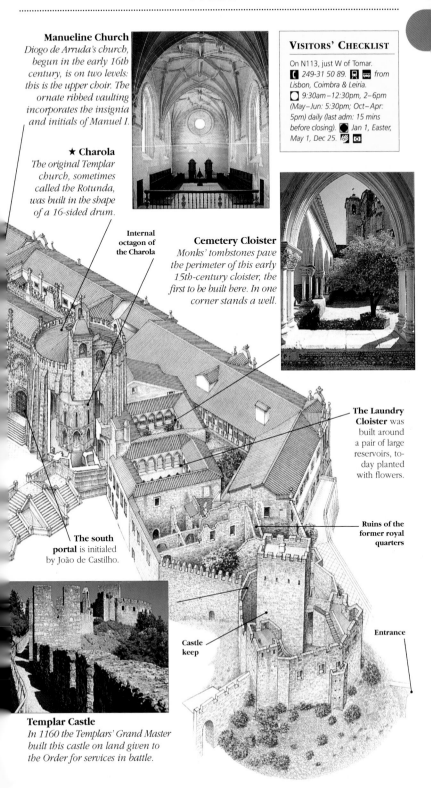

Manueline Church
Diogo de Arruda's church, begun in the early 16th century, is on two levels: this is the upper choir. The ornate ribbed vaulting incorporates the insignia and initials of Manuel I.

VISITORS' CHECKLIST

On N113, just W of Tomar.
249-31 50 89. from Lisbon, Coimbra & Leiria.
9:30am–12:30pm, 2–6pm (May–Jun: 5:30pm; Oct–Apr: 5pm) daily (last adm: 15 mins before closing). Jan 1, Easter, May 1, Dec 25.

★ **Charola**
The original Templar church, sometimes called the Rotunda, was built in the shape of a 16-sided drum.

Internal octagon of the Charola

Cemetery Cloister
Monks' tombstones pave the perimeter of this early 15th-century cloister, the first to be built here. In one corner stands a well.

The Laundry Cloister was built around a pair of large reservoirs, today planted with flowers.

Ruins of the former royal quarters

The south portal is initialed by João de Castilho.

Castle keep

Entrance

Templar Castle
In 1160 the Templars' Grand Master built this castle on land given to the Order for services in battle.

The defensive walls of the early 13th-century fortress at Abrantes

Barragem do Castelo de Bode ⑬

Road map C4. 🚌 to dam. 🚤 from Castanheira. 🛈 Tomar (249-32 24 27).

PERHAPS THERE ONCE was a "Castle of the Billygoat," but today the name refers to a large dam *(barragem)* that blocks the flow of the Zêzere River 10 km (6 miles) upstream from its confluence with the Tagus. Construction of the dam began in 1946 to serve the first of Portugal's hydroelectric power stations. Above the dam, a long, sprawling lake nestles between hills covered in pine and eucalyptus forests in which lie small, isolated villages. The valley is a secluded area popular for boating, fishing, and water sports; it is possible to rent equipment from centers along the lake shore. Canoes, windsurf boards, and water skis can be found at the Centro Naútico

do Zêzere, in Castanheira on the western side of the lake, and yachting facilities are usually available from hotels such as the peaceful Estalagem Lago Azul *(see p386)*. A cruise can also be taken from the hotel, stopping at the sandy beaches and the small islands.

Abrantes ⑭

Road map C4. 🏛 15,000. 🚃 🚌 🛈 Largo 1º de Maio (241-225 55). 🗓 Mon.

GRANDLY SITUATED above the Tagus, the town was once of strategic importance. It had a vital role in the Reconquest *(see pp42–3)*, and during the Peninsular War *(see p54)* both the French General Junot and the Duke of Wellington made it a base. The ruined **fortress** that overlooks the town and the surrounding flatlands is a reminder of its status.

The 15th-century church of Santa Maria do Castelo, within the castle walls, is now the small **Museu Dom Lopo de Almeida**. Besides local archaeological finds, it houses the tombs of the Almeida family, counts of Abrantes. On Rua da República, the **Misericórdia** church, constructed in 1584, has six magnificent religious panels attributed to Gregório Lopes (1490–1550).

🏛 **Museu Dom Lopo de Almeida**
Rua Capitão Correia de Lacerda. 📞 241-37 17 24. 🕐 daily. 🔴 public hols. 🚻

Whitewashed houses in Constância above the banks of the Tagus

ENVIRONS: The 16th-century church of São Tiago e São Mateus, in the town of **Sardoal**, 8 km (5 miles) north of Abrantes, holds a compelling thorn-crowned Christ by a 16th-century painter called the Master of Sardoal. An 18th-century tile panel on the façade of the Capela do Espírito Santo, in Praça da República, honors Gil Vicente, the 16th-century playwright born here.

The attractive whitewashed town of **Constância**, 12 km (7 miles) west of Sardoal, nurtures the memory of the poet Luís Vaz de Camões. Exiled from court, he lived here briefly after 1546. The **Casa Memória de Camões**, the poet's home on the river bank, can be visited.

🏠 **Casa Memória de Camões**
Rua do Tejo. 📞 249-73 95 36. 🔴 until further notice.

LUÍS VAZ DE CAMÕES (1524–80)

The author of Portugal's celebrated epic poem, *Os Lusíadas*, had a passionate nature and was often in trouble. Banished from court, he enlisted in 1547 and set sail for North Africa, where he lost an eye. Imprisoned after another brawl, he agreed to serve his country in India, but his was the only ship from the fleet to survive the stormy seas. This experience gave his subsequent poem its vibrant power. A unique record of the Discoveries, this Classical-style epic charts the voyage of Vasco da Gama to India and recounts events and legends from Portuguese history. There was to be no success for Camões, however, and he spent bleak years in India yearning for Lisbon. His poem was published in 1572, but he died almost unnoticed.

Statue of Camões on the river bank at Constância

Castelo de Almourol 🟤

Road map C4. 🚌 *to Barquinha then taxi.* 🕐 *daily during daylight hours.* ℹ️ *Praça da República, Barquinha (249-72 03 50).*

The evocative ruins of the island fortress of Almourol

DRAMATICALLY SET on a tiny island in the Tagus, this enchanting castle was built over a Roman fortress in 1171 by Gualdim Pais *(see p185)*. Legends about this magical place abound. A 16th-century romance called *Palmeirim de Inglaterra* weaves a tale of giants and knights and the fight of the crusader Palmeirim for the lovely Polinarda. Some say the castle is haunted by the ghost of a princess sighing for the love of her Moorish slave.

Over the centuries, the castle, surrounded by ramparts and nine towers, has never been taken by invading forces.

Torres Novas 🟤

Road map C4. 🏙 *16,000.* 🚌 ℹ️ *Largo do Paço (249-81 29 10).* 🗓 *Tue.*

ANIMATED STREETS and many fine churches cluster beneath the castle walls of this handsome town. The ruins of the 12th-century **fortress**, scene of bitter fighting between Moors and Christians during the Reconquest, now enclose a garden. Just below the castle is the 16th-century **Misericórdia** church with a Renaissance portal and an interior lined with colorful "carpet" *azulejos* from 1674. The **Igreja de Santiago**, on Largo do Paço, was probably built in 1203, although tiles and a gilded retable with a wood carving of the young Jesus assisting Joseph in his carpentry are 17th-century additions.

In the center of town is the **Museu Municipal de Carlos Reis**, named after the painter Carlos Reis (1863–1940) who was born here. The museum contains paintings by 19th- and early 20th-century artists, a 15th-century Gothic figure of Nossa Senhora do Ó, as well as coins and bronze and ceramic artifacts from the Roman ruins at Vila Cardílio.

🏛 **Museu Municipal de Carlos Reis**
Rua do Salvador. 📞 *249-81 25 35.* 🕐 *Tue–Sun.* ⬤ *public hols.*

ENVIRONS: Roman ruins dating from the 4th century AD at **Vila Cardílio**, 3 km (2 miles) southwest of Torres Novas, retain some superb mosaics and baths. On the northeast outskirts of town the **Grutas das Lapas**, large Neolithic caves, can be seen carved out of the rock. The small wetland **Reserva Natural do Paúl de Boquilobo**, 8 km (5 miles) south, between the Tagus and Almondo Rivers, was declared a nature preserve in 1981. The willow trees and aquatic plants along the river shelter wildfowl in winter, and in spring it is an important nesting site for colonies of egrets and herons.

🏛 **Vila Cardílio**
Off N3. 🕐 *daily.* 🏛 **Grutas das Lapas**
Rua José Mota e Silva, Lapas. 🕐 *daily (ask for key in house opposite).* ♿

Remains of the hypocaust, the Roman underfloor heating system, at Vila Cardílio outside Torres Novas

Portal of the Igreja Matriz in Golegã

Golegã ⓱

Road map C4. 🏠 *9,000.* 🚌
🅸 *Largo Dom Manuel I (249-97 63 87).* 🚌 *Wed.*

USUALLY A QUIET town, Golegã is overrun during the first two weeks of November by thousands of horse enthusiasts who throng to the colorful annual horse fair, the Feira Nacional do Cavalo. This coincides with the tasting of the year's new wine on St. Martin's day (November 11). The fair attracts Portugal's finest horses, breeders, and equestrians, while the atmosphere is enlivened by the joyful consumption of the young wine and *agua-pé* (literally, foot water).

In the center of town, the 16th-century **Igreja Matriz**, attributed to Diogo Boitac *(see pp106–7)*, has an exquisite Manueline portal and a calm interior. The small **Museu de Fotografia Carlos Relvas** is housed in the elegant Art Nouveau house and studio of the photographer (1838–94). A vivid modern art collection can be seen in the **Museu de Pintura e Escultura Martins Correia** in the old post office.

🏛 **Museu de Fotografia Carlos Relvas**
Largo Dom Manuel I. 🅲 *249-943 87.*
◯ *daily.* 🈺
🏛 **Museu de Pintura e Escultura Martins Correia**
Largo da Imaculada Conceição.
🅲 *249-943 87.* ◯ *Tue–Sun.*
● *Jan 1, Dec 25.* ♿ *to ground floor.*

Alpiarça ⓲

Road map C4. 🏠 *8,000.* 🚌
🅸 *Rua José Relvas 374 (243-543 54).*
🚌 *Wed.*

SET IN THE VAST, fertile plain known as the Lezíria, which stretches east of the Tagus and is famous for horse breeding, Alpiarça is a small, neat town. The fine twin-towered parish church, on Rua José Relvas, is dedicated to **Santo Eustáquio**, patron saint of the town. Built in the late 19th century, it houses paintings from the 17th century, including a charming *Divine Shepherdess* in the sacristy, in which the young Jesus is shown conversing with a sheep. The stone cross in the courtyard is dated 1515.

On the southern outskirts of town is the striking **Casa Museu dos Patudos** surrounded by vineyards. This was the residence of the wealthy and cultivated José Relvas (1858–1929), an art collector and diplomat as well as a politician and – briefly – premier of the Republic. The exterior of this eye-catching country house, built for him by Raúl Lino in 1905–9, has simple whitewashed walls and a green and white striped spire. The colonnaded loggia, reached by an outside staircase, is lined with colorful *azulejo* panels. The museum contains Relvas's personal collection of fine and decorative art. Renaissance paintings include *Virgin with Child and St. John* by Leonardo da Vinci

and *Christ in the Tomb* by Albrecht Dürer. There are also paintings by Delacroix and Zurbarán, as well as many works by 19th-century Portuguese artists, including 30 by Relvas's friend, José Malhôa *(see p55)*. Relvas also collected exquisite porcelain, bronzes, furniture, and Oriental rugs, as well as early Portuguese Arraiolos carpets, including a particularly fine one in silk.

🏛 **Casa Museu dos Patudos**
2 km (1 mile) S, N118. 🅲 *243-543 21.*
◯ *Wed–Sun.* ● *public hols.* 🈺

Elegant façade of the country manor, Quinta da Alorna, outside Almeirim

ENVIRONS: Almeirim, 7 km (4 miles) to the south, was a favorite abode of the House of Avis *(see pp46–7)*. Today, little of its royal past remains and most visitors come here to sample the famous *sopa de pedra* (stone soup) *(see p146)*.

Many large estates and fine stables extend across the vast flat plains of this fertile horse and cattle breeding area. The **Quinta da Alorna**, a handsome 19th-century manor house within walled gardens and well known for its wines, lies just outside Almeirim.

Tiled loggia of the Casa Museu dos Patudos, Alpiarça

The Tagus seen from the Jardim das Portas do Sol in Santarém

Santarém ⑲

Road map C4. 🏛 30,000. 🚉 🚌
ℹ️ *Rua Capelo e Ivens 63 (243-39 15 12).* 🛒 *2nd & 4th Sun of month.*

THE LIVELY DISTRICT capital of the Ribatejo, overlooking the Tagus, has an illustrious past. To Julius Caesar it was an important bureaucratic center, Praesidium Julium. To the Moors it was the stronghold of Xantarim – from Santa Iria, the 7th-century martyred nun from Tomar *(see pp184–5)* whose body was thrown into the Nabão River and allegedly reappeared here on the Tagus shore. To the Portuguese kings, who ousted the Moors in 1147, Santarém was a pleasing abode and the site of many gatherings of the *cortes* (parliaments).

At the center of the old town, in Praça Sá da Bandeira, is the vast **Igreja do Seminário**, a multiwindowed Baroque edifice built by João IV for the Jesuits in 1640 on the site of a royal palace. The huge interior has a painted wooden ceiling with marble and gilt ornamentation. From here, Rua Serpa Pinto runs southeast past a cluster of older buildings. The lofty **Igreja do Marvila**, built in the 12th century and later altered, has a Manueline portal and is lined with dazzling early 17th-century diamond-patterned *azulejo* panels. The medieval, although much restored 22-m (72-ft) high **Torre das Cabaças**, stands opposite the **Museu Arqueológico**. Formerly the Romanesque church of São João de Alporão, the museum has many fine pieces covering the Roman and Moorish periods of the city's

history. The star display is the elaborate tomb of Duarte de Meneses, heroic governor of Ceuta, a Christian stronghold in Morocco. He was hacked to death in 1464 in a disastrous campaign in Alcácer-Ceguer *(see pp42–3)*. The tomb is said to contain all that could be recovered – a single tooth.

Rua Serpa Pinto leads into Rua 5 de Outubro and up to the **Jardim das Portas do Sol**, built on the site of a Moorish castle. The gardens are enclosed by the city's medieval walls, and a terrace affords a panorama of the river and its vast meadowlands.

Returning to town on Largo Pedro Álvares Cabral, the 14th-century **Igreja da Graça** has a spectacular rose window carved from a single stone. The church contains the tombstone of Pedro Álvares Cabral, who discovered Brazil *(see p48)*. Farther south, the 14th-century **Igreja do Santíssimo Milagre**, on Rua Braamcamp Freire, has a Renaissance interior and 16th-century *azulejos*. A small crystal flask in the sacristy is said to contain the blood of Christ. The belief stems from a 13th-century legend in which a holy wafer intended to help persuade a husband to stop beating his wife was miraculously transformed into blood.

Santarém is an important bullfighting center with a modern bullring at the southwest corner of town. During the first ten days of June, the town hosts the Ribatejo Fair, Portugal's largest agricultural fair, in which there are bullfights and contests between the colorfully dressed herdsmen, or *campinos*.

🏛 **Museu Arqueológico**
Rua Conselheiro Figueiredo Leal. ⭕ *Tue–Sun.* ⬤ *public hols.* 🈹

Tomb of Duarte de Meneses in the Museu Arqueológico, Santarém

Fields and vineyards in the low-lying Lezíria extending beyond Coruche

Coruche ⑳

Road map C5. 🏛 *3,500*. 🚌 🚍
ℹ *Porto João Felicio (243-61 74 88).*
📅 *last Sat of month.*

CORUCHE IS an attractive little town in the heart of the bullfighting country with a riverside location overlooking the Lezíria, the wide open plain that stretches east of the Tagus. The town, inhabited since Palaeolithic times, was razed to the ground in 1180 by the Moors as reprisal against the conquering Christians.

In the central pedestrian street, Rua de Santarém, the **O Coruja** café is lined with vivid modern *azulejo* panels showing bulls in the Lezíria, the town's bullring, and scenes of local life. A short walk up the street stands the tiny church of **São Pedro**. Its interior is completely covered with 17th-century blue and yellow carpet tiles. An *azulejo* panel on the altar front shows St. Peter surrounded by birds and animals. Above the town

Chancel in the church of São Pedro covered in *azulejos*, Coruche

stands the simple 12th-century blue and white church of **Nossa Senhora do Castelo**. From here there are excellent views of the fertile agricultural land and cork oaks of the Sorraia valley and the Lezíria.

Bull-running *(largada)* in Vila Franca de Xira

Vila Franca de Xira ㉑

Road map C5. 🏛 *20,000*. 🚌 🚍
ℹ *Rua Almirante Cândido dos Reis 147 (263-260 53).* 📅 *Wed.*

SITTING BESIDE the Tagus, surrounded by the riverside industries that dominate this area, the town has a reputation larger than its modest appearance suggests. Traditionally the area has been the center for bull and horse rearing communities. Twice a year crowds flock here to participate in the bull-running through the streets and watch the *tourada* and horsemanship. The animated and gaudy Festa do Colete Encarnado (named after the red waistcoat worn by *campinos*, the Ribatejo herdsmen)

takes place over several days in early July. The festival is a lively occasion with folk dancing, boat races on the Tagus, and sardines being grilled in the street. A similar festival, the Feira de Outubro, takes place in October. The brightly colored costumes of the *campinos* and other exhibits related to bullfighting in Portugal are displayed in the small **Museu Etnográfico**.

The town center retains an exuberantly tiled covered **market** dating from the 1920s. Farther east, on Largo da Misericórdia, striking 18th-century *azulejos* adorn the chancel of the **Misericórdia** church. South of town, the **Ponte Marechal Carmona**, built in 1951, is the only bridge across the Tagus River between Santarém to the north and Lisbon to the south.

🏛 **Museu Etnográfico**
Praça de Touros. 📞 *263-230 57.*
🕐 *Tue–Sun.* ⬤ *public hols.*

ENVIRONS: At the **Centro Equestre da Lezíria Grande** in Povos, 3 km (2 miles) south, you can watch stylish displays of dressage on thoroughbred Lusitanian horses *(see p296)*.

⬤ **Centro Equestre da Lezíria Grande**
N1. 📞 *263-252 79.* 🕐 *Tue–Sun.*
⬤ *Jan 1, Easter, Dec 25.* ♿

Alenquer ㉒

Road map C5. 🏛 *4,000*. 🚌
🛈 *Largo Luís de Camões (263-721 97 00)*. 🎪 *Mon after 2nd Sun of month*.

VILA ALTA, the old part of town, climbs steeply up the slopes of the hillside, high above the newer town by the river. In the central Praça Luís de Camões, the 15th-century church of **São Pedro** contains the tomb of the humanist chronicler and native son, Damião de Góis (1501–74). Pêro de Alenquer, a navigator for the explorers Bartolomeu Dias in 1488 and Vasco da Gama in 1497 *(see pp48–9)*, was also born here. Uphill, near the ruins of a 13th-century castle, the monastery church of **São Francisco** retains a Manueline cloister and a 13th-century portal. Founded in 1222, during the saint's lifetime, this was the first Franciscan monastery in Portugal.

ENVIRONS: At **Meca**, 5 km (3 miles) northwest, is the huge pilgrimage church of Santa Quitéria, where a blessing of animals takes place each May.

Defensive walls and the castle overlooking Torres Vedras

Torres Vedras ㉓

Road map B5. 🏛 *30,000*. 🚉 🚌
🛈 *Rua 9 de Abril (261-31 40 94)*.
🎪 *3rd Mon of month*.

THE TOWN IS CLOSELY linked with the Lines of Torres Vedras, fortified defenses built by the Duke of Wellington to repel Napoleon's troops during the Peninsular War *(see p54)*. North of the town, near the restored fort of **São Vicente**, traces of trenches and bastions are still visible, but along most of the lines the forts and earthworks have gone, buried by time and rapid change.

Above the town, the restored walls of the 13th-century **castle** embrace a shady garden and the church of Santa Maria do Castelo. Down in the town, on Praça 25 de Abril, a memorial to those who died in the Peninsular War stands in front of the 16th-century Convento da Graça. Today the monastery houses the well-lit **Museu Municipal**. A room devoted to the Peninsular War displays a model of the lines; other interesting exhibits include a 15th-century Flemish School *Retábulo da Vida da Virgem*. The monastery church, **Igreja da Graça**, contains a monumental 17th-century gilded altarpiece. In a niche in the chancel is the tomb of São Gonçalo de Lagos *(see p320)*.

Beyond the pedestrian Rua 9 de Abril, the Manueline church of **São Pedro** greets the visitor with an exotic winged dragon on the portal. The interior has a painted wooden ceiling and colorful 18th-century *azulejo* panels depicting scenes of daily life adorn the walls. Behind the church, on Rua Cândido dos Reis, is a 16th-century water fountain, the **Chafariz dos Canos**.

🏛 **Museu Municipal**
Praça 25 de Abril. 📞 *261-31 04 84*.
🕐 *Tue–Sun*. ⬤ *public hols*. 📷

THE LINES OF TORRES VEDRAS

Flintlock pistol from Peninsular War

In October 1809, to save Lisbon from Napoleonic invasion, Arthur Wellesley (later the Duke of Wellington) ordered an arc of defensive lines *(Linhas de Torres)* to be built. When complete, over 600 guns and 152 redoubts (masonry forts) lay along two lines stretching from the sea to the Tagus River. One was 46 km (29 miles) long, from the Sizandra River mouth, west of Torres Vedras, to Alhandra, south of Vila Franca de Xira. The second line, running behind the first as far as the sea, was 39 km (24 miles) long. A short third line covered the possibility of retreat and embarkation. Construction of the lines took place in extraordinary secrecy: rivers had to be dammed, earthworks raised, hills shifted, and homes and farms demolished, but within a year the chain of hilltop fortresses was complete. On October 14, 1810, General Masséna, at the head of 65,000 French troops, saw with astonishment the vastly altered and fortified landscape and realized it was impregnable. In November, the invaders fell back to Santarém *(see p191)* and in 1811, suffering hunger and defeat, withdrew beyond the Spanish border.

Portrait of the Duke of Wellington, 1814

THE BEIRAS

S TRETCHING FROM THE SPANISH BORDER *to the sea, the Beiras are a bulwark between the cool green north and the parched south. This diverse region encompasses the heights of the Serra da Estrela and the salt marshes of the Ria de Aveiro, and its towns vary from lively Figueira da Foz to the stately old university town of Coimbra.*

The three provinces of the Beiras may not be a hub of tourism, but their past commercial and defensive significance has left its mark. In Beira Litoral, the elaborate bows of Aveiro's seaweed boats are a legacy of trade with the Phoenicians. All over Beira Baixa, from its capital, Castelo Branco, to little granite villages, there are relics of early foreign occupations, and Viseu, Beira Alta's capital, grew up at a crossroads of trading routes used by the Romans.

The Romans were never as firmly entrenched here as farther south, but the ruins of Conimbriga speak eloquently of the elegant city that once stood here and that gave its name to Coimbra, the principal city of Beira Litoral. Afonso Henriques, as king of the new nation of Portugal *(see p42)*, moved his court to Coimbra, the young country's capital for over a century.

The upheavals of the nation's founding and a hard-won independence have left a rich heritage of castles and fortified towns. Conscious of Spain's proximity and claim on their land, successive Portuguese kings constructed a great defensive chain of forts along the vulnerable eastern border. The seemingly impregnable walls of Almeida still stand as a reminder of the region's unsettled history. These border fortresses continued to prove vital in the fight for independence from Spain in the 17th century, and again against Napoleon's forces *(see p54)*. Even Buçaco, revered for the peace and sanctity of its forest, is known also as the site of Wellington's successful stand against Masséna.

Despite the unforgiving terrain and 20th-century depopulation, the Beiras are the source of some gastronomic treats: Portugal's favorite cheese is made in the Serra da Estrela, and the lush Bairrada district around Mealhada is famous for its *leitão*, suckling pig. The region's wines are some of Portugal's best known: rich, fruity Bairradas and the oaky Dãos *(see pp28–9)*.

Distinctive candy-striped beach houses in Costa Nova, between the Ria de Aveiro and the sea

◁ A stone *pelourinho* (pillory) in a quiet corner of Castelo Mendo, one of the border towns in Beira Alta

Exploring the Beiras

THE BEIRAS, ENCOMPASSING some of Portugal's finest scenery, consist of three regions. Along the Beira Litoral are the sleepy backwaters of the Ria de Aveiro and, in contrast, the busy seaside resort of Figueira da Foz. The stately old university city of Coimbra repays exploration and is a convenient base for visiting the historic forest of Buçaco and several of Portugal's spas.

Inland lies Viseu, the charming capital of Beira Alta, on the route to the medieval strongholds of Guarda, Trancoso, and the border castles. The country's highest mountains, the Serra da Estrela, separate the Beira Alta from the little-visited Beira Baixa, where Monsanto, voted "most Portuguese village," and the handsome little city of Castelo Branco are contrasting attractions.

Coimbra's Museu Nacional Machado de Castro, with a fine sculpture collection

SIGHTS AT A GLANCE

0 kilometers 25

0 miles 15

Summer at the shore in popular Figueira da Foz

Dão vineyards between Viseu and Mangualde

GETTING AROUND

A rail network links the principal cities to smaller towns, but stations are often outside the town. Buses run from Coimbra to outlying areas, and local buses link villages and towns throughout the region. The most convenient way to explore the Beiras, however, is by car. The Oporto-Lisbon A1 highway passes close to Coimbra and Aveiro, and the IP5 provides a fast scenic route between Aveiro and the eastern uplands. All but the major routes are relatively traffic-free and a pleasure to drive, but unpaved surfaces can still be expected.

Steep terraces in the Serra de Açor, around Piódão

KEY

▬▬	Highway
▬▬	Major road
▬▬	Minor road
▬▬	Scenic route
⌒	River
☀	Vista

SEE ALSO

- **Where to Stay** pp388–90
- **Where to Eat** pp411–13

Arouca ❶

Road map C2. 🏚 *2,400.* 🚌
ℹ️ *Praça Brandão de Vasconcelos
(256-94 35 75).* 🏛 *5 & 20 of month.*

THIS SMALL TOWN in a green valley owes its principal attraction, the great **Convento de Arouca**, to its saintly royal benefactor, Mafalda. Princess Mafalda was born in 1195, the daughter of Sancho I. She was betrothed to the teenage Prince Enrique of Castile, but when he died in an accident, Mafalda took the veil in Arouca. Under her, the convent became Cistercian and Mafalda's wealth and dedication made the house highly influential. She died in 1256, and her incorrupt corpse was discovered in 1616, leading to her beatification in 1793.

For a thousand years the convent has stood beside Arouca's church on the main square. In the early 18th century the church underwent redecoration: 104 carved choir stalls are surmounted by paintings in sumptuous gilded panels, and the organ and chancel retable are also heavily gilded. Honored with its own altar is a recumbent effigy of Santa Mafalda in a silver and ebony casket; her mummified remains lie below the casket.

Guided tours take visitors around the convent's museum, in which are displayed some exquisite silver monstrances, furniture, and religious works of art, including two paintings

by 18th-century artist André Gonçalves, showing Mafalda saving the monastery from fire. The Neo-Classical double cloister, begun in 1781, the large refectory and kitchen, and a chapterhouse covered with cheerful Coimbra tiles of rural scenes can also be visited.

🏛 Convento de Arouca
Largo de Santa Mafalda. 📞 *256-94 33 21.* 🕐 *Tue–Sun.* ● *Jan 1, May 2, Dec 25.* 🈲 🎟

Silver and ebony casket in the convent church at Arouca, containing the effigy of Santa Mafalda

Santa Maria da Feira ❷

Road map C2. 🏚 *10,000.* 🚉 🚌
ℹ️ *Mercado Municipal, Avenida das Descobertas (256-37 20 32).*
🏛 *20 of month.*

PROSPEROUS FROM CORK and its thriving markets, Santa Maria derives its name from long tradition – a document from 1117 refers to "Terra de Santa Maria, a place people call Feira," after the fairs held here. A large market each month in the broad Rossio

upholds the town's reputation. A double stairway leads from the Rossio to the **Igreja dos Lóios**, with blue 17th-century tiles decorating the façades of its two symmetrical belltowers. On the opposite side of the Rossio, winding streets of solid merchants' houses from the 18th and 19th centuries lead to a decorative stairway with an ornamental fountain. This rises up to the 18th-century **Misericórdia** church.

Crowning a wooded hill on the southern edge of the town is the fairytale **castle**. Although much is a 20th-century reconstruction, it follows the 15th-century design of a local, Fernão Pereira, and his son. They added crenellations and towers to an 11th-century fort that in turn had been built over a temple to a local god. The title of Conde da Feira was bestowed on Pereira, and the castle remained in his family until 1700. There is not much inside the castle now, but it retains its romantic air.

♣ Castle
Largo do Castelo. 📞 *256-37 22 48.*
🕐 *Tue–Sun.* 🈲 🈳

Ovar ❸

Road map C2. 🏚 *14,000.* 🚉 🚌
ℹ️ *Rua Elias Garcia (256-57 22 15).*
🏛 *Tue, Thu & Sat (general), 3rd Sun of month (antiques).*

VARINAS, the hardworking Portuguese fishwives, take their name from Var, or O Var, this small town that earned its living from the sea and the Ria de Aveiro that spreads out to the south *(see p201).* Industry has arrived in the shape of foundries and steel mills, but oxen still plod along the roads.

Gleaming tiles cover many of the small houses, as well as the twin-towered 17th-century **Igreja Matriz** in Avenida do Bom Reitor. In the town center the Calvary chapel of the 18th-century **Capela dos Passos** is adorned with woodcarvings carrying a shell motif.

Ovar's Carnaval parade is one of the most colorful in Portugal, and its sponge cake,

The pinnacled and crenellated castle crowning Santa Maria da Feira

House façades in Ovar with their traditional eye-catching blue tiles

pão-de-ló, is highly esteemed. Tableaux in the **Museu de Ovar** recreate the lifestyle of a bygone era, alongside displays of regional costume and dolls. There are also mementoes of Júlio Dinis, a popular Portuguese novelist who lived in Ovar in the 19th century.

🏛 **Museu de Ovar**
Rua Heliodoro Salgado 11. 🕻 *256-57 28 22.* ⬜ *Mon–Sat.* ● *public hols.* 📷

Aveiro ➍

See pp200–1.

Praia de Mira ➎

Road map C3. 🏠 *5,000.* 🚌
ℹ *Praça da República (231-45 85 06).* 🗓 *11 & 30 of month.*

Fishing boat on the beach at Praia de Mira

TOURISM IS ONLY NOW making an impact on this stretch of coast backed by a wooded preserve, the Mata Nacional das Dunas de Mira. Praia de Mira, with the dunes and Atlantic on one side and the peaceful lagoon of Barrinha de Mira on the other, is a pretty fishing village developing as a resort. Fishing boats are still drawn up the spectacular beach by oxen, but leisure craft now cruise the shore and the inland waterways, and the fishermen's striped *palheiros* (*see p18*), popular as seaside cottages, are fast vanishing amid shops, bars, and cafés.

Figueira da Foz ➏

Road map C3. 🏠 *35,000.* 🚉 🚌
ℹ *Edifício Atlântico, Avenida 25 de Abril (231-40 28 20).* 🗓 *daily.*

LIVELY AND COSMOPOLITAN, if somewhat timeworn, this popular resort has a bustling marina, a casino, and a wide, curving beach with breakers that attract intrepid surfers.

Although general jollity is the keynote, the town's **Museu Municipal Dr Santos Rocha** has a notable archaeological collection, and an eclectic display extending to Arraiolos carpets (*see p301*), a musical archive, weapons, and photographs.

The **Casa do Paço**, overlooking the river, has an amazing interior. Its walls are lined with 8,000 Delft tiles taken from a shipwreck in the late 17th century. Where the Mondego meets the sea stands the 16th-century triangular fortress of **Santa Catarina**. The Duke of Wellington briefly made this little fort his base when he landed to retake Portugal from Napoleon's forces in 1808 (*see p54*).

🏛 **Museu Municipal Dr Santos Rocha**
Rua Calouste Gulbenkian. 🕻 *233-40 28 40.* ⬜ *Tue–Sun.* ● *public hols.*
🏛 **Casa do Paço**
Largo Professor Vitor Guerra. 🕻 *233-221 59.* ⬜ *Mon–Fri.* ● *public hols.*

Montemor-o-Velho ➐

Road map C3. 🏠 *2,600.* 🚌
ℹ *Castelo de Montemor-o-Velho (239-68 03 80).* 🗓 *every other Wed.*

THIS ATTRACTIVE and historic hillside town rises out of fields of rice and corn beside the River Mondego. Its **castle**, which served as a primary defense of the city of Coimbra (*see pp202–7*) is mostly 14th century, but it had previously been a Moorish stronghold, and the keep has fragments of Roman stonework. The church of **Santa Maria de Alcaçova** within its walls was founded in 1090. Restored in the 15th century, its naves and arches reflect the Manueline style.

Montemor was the birthplace of Fernão Mendes Pinto (1510–83), famous for the colorful accounts of his travels in the east. Another explorer, Diogo de Azambuja (died 1518), is buried here. Columbus is said to have sailed with Azambuja, who intrepidly navigated along the West African coast. His tomb, by the Manueline master Diogo Pires, is in the **Convento de Nossa Senhora dos Anjos** in the square of the same name (ask at the tourist office for key). Its 17th-century façade hides an earlier, more lavish interior, with Manueline and Renaissance influences.

♣ **Castle**
Rua do Castelo. ⬜ *Tue–Sun.*

Enjoying café life in the spring sunshine of Figueira da Foz

Aveiro ❶

THIS LITTLE CITY, once a great sea port, has a long history – Aveiro's salt pans were featured in the will of Countess Mumadona in AD 959. By the 16th century it was a considerable town, rich from salt and the *bacalhoeiros* fishing for cod off Newfoundland. When storms silted up the harbor in 1575 this wealth vanished rapidly, and the town languished beside an unhealthy lagoon, the *ria*. Only in the 19th century did Aveiro regain some of its prosperity; it is now ringed with industry and is home to an important university. The *ria* and canals give Aveiro its individual character.

Wooden barrel of *ovos moles*

Old Quarter
Tucked in between the Canal das Pirâmides and the Canal de São Roque are the neat, whitewashed houses of Aveiro's fishermen. In the early morning the focus of activity is the **Mercado do Peixe**, where the fish from the night's catch is auctioned.

Skirting the Canal Central, along Rua João de Mendonça, are Art Nouveau mansions and some of the many *pastelarias* selling Aveiro's specialty: *ovos moles*. Literally "soft eggs," these are a rich confection of sweetened egg yolk in candied casings shaped like fish or barrels. As so often in Portugal, the original recipe is credited to nuns. *Ovos moles* are sold by weight or in little barrels.

Bridge across the Canal de São Roque

Across the Canal Central
South of the Canal Central and the bustling Praça Humberto Delgado are the principal historic buildings of Aveiro. The **Misericórdia** church in the Praça da República dates from the 16th century, its façade of *azulejos* framing a splendid Mannerist portal. In the same square stands the stately 18th-century **Paços do Concelho**, or town hall, with its distinctive Tuscan-style pilasters.

Nearby, opposite the museum, is Aveiro's modest 15th-century cathedral of **São Domingos**. The figures of the Three Graces over the door on the Baroque façade were added in 1719.

A short walk south lies the **Igreja das Carmelitas**, its nave and chancel decorated with paintings of the life of St. Teresa, the Carmelite reformer.

🏛 Museu de Aveiro
Rua de Santa Joana Princesa.
📞 234-232 97. 🕐 *Tue–Sun.*
⬤ *public hols.* ▨

The former Mosteiro de Jesus is full of mementoes of Santa Joana, who died here in 1490. The daughter of Afonso V, Joana retreated to the convent in 1472 and spent the rest of her life here. She was beatified in 1693, and her ornamental Baroque marble tomb, completed 20 years later, is in the lower choir. Simpler in style are the 18th-century paintings in the chapel, showing scenes of her life. This was once the needlework room where Santa Joana died. Among Portuguese primitive paintings is a superb 15th-century full-face portrait of the princess in court dress.

The museum hosts a superb gilded chancel (1725–9), 15th-century cloisters, and refectory faced in Coimbra tiles. Between the refectory and chapterhouse lies the Gothic tomb of an armored knight, Dom João de Albuquerque.

Colorful seaweed-collecting *moliceiros* moored along the Canal Central

Raking the salt as it dries in the pans fringing the Ria de Aveiro

ENVIRONS: Lying about 8 km (5 miles) south of Aveiro, at Ílhavo, is the modern block of the **Museu Marítimo e Regional de Ílhavo**, where the region's long seafaring history is told through displays of fishing craft and equipment, with maritime memorabilia from shells to model boats.

About 4 km (2 miles) farther south a small sign points to the **Museu Histórico da Vista Alegre**. A name renowned in the world of porcelain (*see p24*), the Vista Alegre factory was established in 1824, and samples of its fine porcelain are for sale in the factory shop. The museum traces the history of the factory, and has displays of porcelain (together with some crystal glass) from the 1850s to the present day.

Museu Marítimo e Regional de Ílhavo
Avenida Rocha Madahil. 234-32 17 97. *Wed–Sat, Tue & Sun pm.* *public hols.*

Museu Histórico da Vista Alegre
Signposted off N109. 234-32 53 65. *Tue–Sun.* *public hols.*

RIA DE AVEIRO

Old maritime charts show no lagoon here, but in 1575 a terrible storm raised a sand bar that blocked the harbor. Denied access to the sea, Aveiro declined, its population cut down by the fever bred in the stagnant waters. It was not until 1808 that the *barra nova* was created, linking Aveiro once more to the sea.

The lagoon that remains covers some 65 sq km (25 sq miles) and is nearly 50 km (30 miles) long, from Furadouro south past Aveiro's salt pans and the nature preserve of São Jacinto to Costa Nova. Of the boats seen here the most elegant is the *moliceiro*. Despite the bright, often humorous, decoration on its high, curving bow, this is a working boat, harvesting *moliço* (seaweed) for fertilizer. Chemical fertilizers have drastically cut demand for *moliço*, but a few of the stately craft survive; the Festa da Ria is a chance to see them in full sail.

In summer a daily boat trip between Aveiro and Torreira explores this unique backwater, known as the Rota da Luz, the "route of light" running between gleaming salt flats, pale beaches, and sparkling ocean.

Intricately painted prow of a *moliceiro* in the Ria

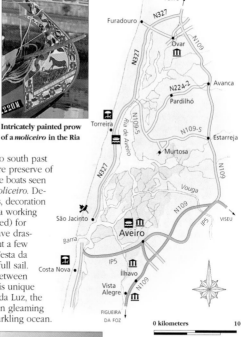

KEY

	Highway
	Major road
	Minor road
	Other road
	Boat trips
	Salt marsh

The seaward waterfront at the fishing village of Torreira

Coimbra ❽

Student in May celebrations

THE BIRTHPLACE OF SIX KINGS and the seat of Portugal's oldest university, Coimbra arouses an affection in the Portuguese shared by no other city. To the Romans the town founded on Alcáçova hill was Aeminium, but as its importance grew it took on the mantle and name of nearby Conimbriga (*see p208*). Coimbra was wrested from the Moors in AD 878, only to come under their control again a century later, until finally freed by Ferdinand the Great of Castile in 1064. When Afonso Henriques, the first king of Portugal, decided to move his capital south from Guimarães in 1139 (*see pp42–3*), his choice was Coimbra, an honor it retained until 1256. For the Portuguese, Coimbra carries the roots of nationhood and, for visitors, a wealth of fascinating historic associations.

Orientation

In the historic heart of the city, high above the Mondego, lie the cathedrals, university, and a fine museum, but a first impression of Coimbra is likely to be of commerce, not culture. Stores, traffic, and the railroad rule the riverside and around the Praça do Comércio. The Largo da Portagem is a useful starting point, and river trips depart from nearby, alongside the Parque Dr Manuel Braga.

Tomb of Portugal's first king, Afonso Henriques, in Santa Cruz

The Lower Town

From Largo da Portagem, Rua Ferreira Borges leads past stores, lively bars, restaurants, and *pastelarias* to the Praça do Comércio. In one corner of this bustling square stands the church of **São Tiago**. Its plain façade is a restoration of the 12th-century original, but inside is an exuberant Rococo altarpiece in gilded wood.

Running north of the Praça do Comércio, Rua Visconde da Luz leads to the Praça 8 de Maio and the historic church of **Santa Cruz** (*see p205*). Portugal's first two kings are buried here, and monks from the adjacent monastery of Santa Cruz tutored the first students at Coimbra university.

Beyond Praça 8 de Maio is Rua da Sofia, the "street of wisdom," named after the theological colleges that once stood here. The convent churches to which they were attached remain: the **Igreja do Carmo** (1597), with a 16th-century retable, and the **Igreja da Graça**, founded by João III in 1543. The nearby Pátio da Inquisição is a reminder that Coimbra, like Lisbon and Évora, was a seat in the 16th century of the fiercely intolerant Inquisition (*see p51*).

Café tables in the Praça do Comércio, overlooked by São Tiago

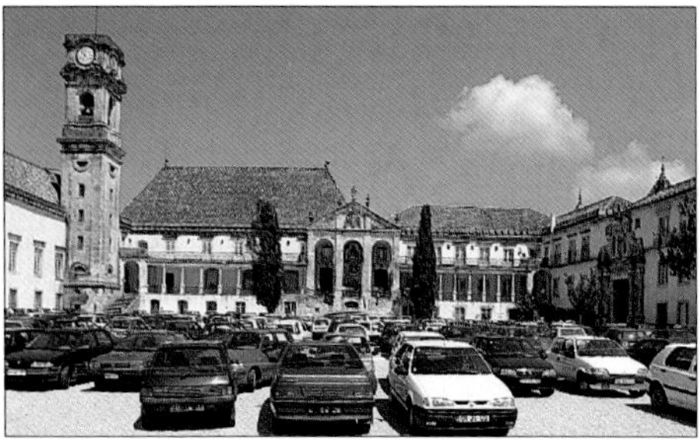

Pátio das Escolas, at the heart of Portugal's oldest university

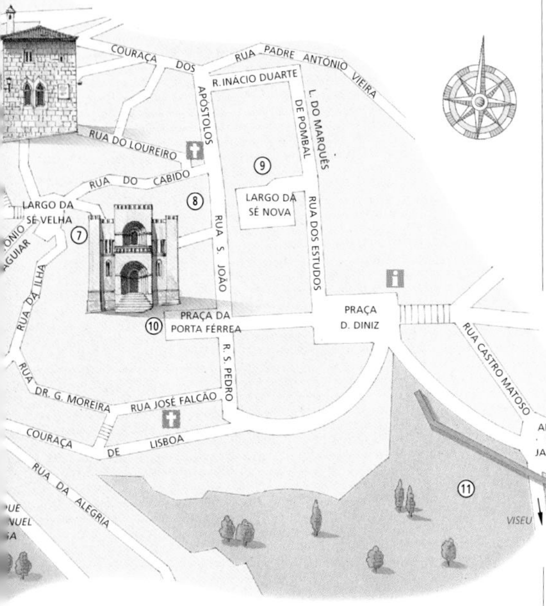

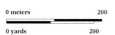

0 meters 200

0 yards 200

Coimbra City Center

Arco de Almedina ⑥
Igreja do Carmo ②
Igreja da Graça ①
Jardim Botânico ⑪
Museu Nacional Machado de Castro ⑧
Portugal dos Pequenitos ⑬
Santa Clara-a-Nova ⑫
Santa Clara-a-Velha ⑭
Santa Cruz ③
São Tiago ④
Sé Nova ⑨
Sé Velha ⑦
Torre de Anto ⑤
University ⑩

The Upper Town

The altered and restored 12th-century **Arco de Almedina**, off the Rua Ferreira Borges, is the gateway to the old city (in Arabic *medina* means town). Steps lead up past the **Torre de Anto**, whose Renaissance windows and medallions are from the workshop of the 16th-century sculptor Jean de Rouen. The tower now houses an arts and crafts gallery.

Among the houses lining the maze of steep alleys that wind up to the top of the hill are a number of *repúblicas*, student lodgings since medieval times.

Coimbra's two cathedrals, **Sé Velha** and **Sé Nova** *(see p204)*, lie in the shadow of the hilltop **university** *(see pp206–7)*. Beyond is the upper town's main square, Praça da República.

Across the Mondego

It is worth crossing the river just to admire the view of old Coimbra. The two convents of **Santa Clara** *(see p205)* on the southern bank have close ties with Santa Isabel, and with Inês de Castro, Pedro I's luckless lover, who was stabbed to death here in 1355 *(see p179)*. A romantic legend tells how a spring, the **Fonte dos Amores**, rose on the spot. This can be seen in the garden of the 18th-century Quinta das Lágrimas, now a hotel *(see p389)*, just south of Santa Clara-a-Velha.

Key

- Train station
- Bus station
- Riverboat service
- Parking
- Tourist information
- Church
- Aqueduct
- Steps

Visitors' Checklist

Road map C3. *150,000.* *Coimbra A, Avenida Emídio Navarro; Coimbra B, N of city, on N11.* *Avenida Fernão de Magalhães.* *Largo da Portagem (239-82 38 86).* *Mon–Sat.* *early May: Queima das Fitas; Jun: Feira Medieval; 1st week in Jul (even years): Festas da Cidade.*

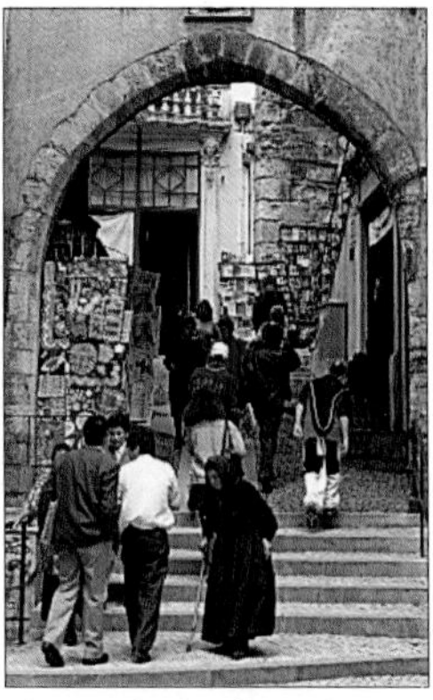

The Arco de Almedina arching over the steps to the upper town

Exploring Coimbra

THAT THE CITIZENS of Coimbra fondly call their river, the Mondego, "O Rio dos Poetas," gives a clue to the affection they have for their vibrant and beautiful city. From the university *(see pp206–7)* at the top of Alcaçova hill, down the narrow streets and stairways to the lower town, the city is crammed with historic buildings and treasures (and, all too often, slow-moving traffic). Most sights are within walking distance of each other, and despite its steep hill, Coimbra is a city best appreciated on foot. Across the Mondego there are further historic sights and an unusual theme park for children.

Elaborate façade of the Sé Nova

The Sé Velha's gilded altarpiece

⌂ Sé Velha

Largo da Sé Velha. [C] 239-82 52 73.
◯ Sat–Thu. 🖼 to cloister.

The fortress-style Old Cathedral is widely regarded as the finest Romanesque building in Portugal, a celebration in stone of the triumph over the Moors in 1064. The nation's first king, Afonso Henriques, made the city of Coimbra his capital, and

his son, Sancho I, was crowned here in 1185, soon after the cathedral was completed.

In the simple interior, square piers lead the eye up the nave to the flamboyant retable over the altar. Colored and gilded, this was the work of Flemish woodcarvers in about 1502 and depicts the birth of Christ, the Assumption, and many saints. A 16th-century altarpiece in the south transept is also highly decorated, as is the Manueline font, thought to be by Diogo Pires the Younger. In contrast is the quiet restraint of the cloister, built in 1218 but much restored in the 18th century.

The tomb of the city's first Christian governor, Sisinando (a Moslem convert who died in 1091), lies in the chapterhouse, and in the north aisle is the tomb of the Byzantine Dona Vetaça (died 1246), who was companion and tutor to the wife of King Dinis, the saintly Queen Isabel *(see p45)*.

⌂ Sé Nova

Largo da Sé Nova. [C] 239-82 31 38.
◯ Tue–Sat. 🖼 public hols except for mass.

New is a relative term, as this church, a short walk from the university, was founded by the Jesuits in 1598. (Their adjacent Colégio das Onze Mil Virgens is today part of the sciences faculty.) The Jesuit Order was banned by the Marquês de Pombal in 1759 *(see p52)*, but their church became the episcopal seat in 1772. Jesuit saints still look out from the façade.

The interior, more spacious than the Sé Velha, is barrel-vaulted, with a dome over the crossing. To the left of the entrance is a Manueline-style octagonal font brought, like the choir stalls, from the Sé Velha. The paintings above the stalls are copies of Italian masters. The altarpiece in the 17th-century chancel, featuring more Jesuit saints, is flanked by a pair of 18th-century organs.

Coimbra seen from the Mondego, with the university's landmark bell tower crowning Alcaçova hill

🏛 Museu Nacional Machado de Castro

Largo Dr José Rodrigues. 📞 *239-82 37 27.* ⬡ *Tue–Sun.* ⬤ *public hols.* 🎫

The elegant 16th-century loggias and lovely courtyards of the former bishops' palace are the setting for the display of some of Portugal's finest sculpture – Joaquim Machado de Castro (1731–1822) was himself a master sculptor. Among the medieval pieces is an endearing knight holding a mace. Also in the collection, together with furnishings and vestments, are paintings from the 12th to 20th centuries, including an early 16th-century work, *The Assumption of Mary Magdalen*, by the Master of Sardoal. An intriguing feature of the museum is the Cripto-portico de Aeminium, a maze of underground Roman passages contianing a dramatic collection of Roman sculpture and stelae, Visigothic artifacts, and earlier discoveries.

Claustro do Silêncio (Cloister of Silence) in the monastery of Santa Cruz

🏠 Santa Cruz

Praça 8 de Maio. 📞 *239-82 29 41.* ⬡ *daily.* 🎫 *to cloister.*

Founded in 1131, the church and monastery of Santa Cruz are rich in examples of the city's own early 16th-century school of sculpture. Carvings by Nicolau Chanterène and Jean de Rouen adorn the church's Portal da Majestade, designed by Diogo de Castilho in 1523. The chapterhouse by Diogo Boitac is Manueline in style, as are the Claustro do Silêncio and the choir stalls, carved in 1518 with a frieze on the theme of exploration. The first two kings of Portugal, Afonso Henriques and Sancho I, were reinterred in the chancel in 1520. Their elaborate tombs are thought to be by Chanterène, who is also buried here.

🌿 Jardim Botânico

Alameda Dr Júlio Henriques. ⬡ *daily.*

These, Portugal's largest botanical gardens, were created in 1772 when the Marquês de Pombal introduced the study of natural history at the University of Coimbra.

The entrance, near the 16th-century aqueduct of São Sebastião, leads into 50 acres devoted to a remarkable collection of some 1,200 plants, including many rare and exotic species. The gardens still play a scientific role, but are laid out as formal pleasure gardens, with a wilder area overlooking the Mondego.

🏠 Santa Clara-a-Velha

Santa Clara. ⬤ *for restoration.*

Santa Isabel, the widow of King Dinis, chose to rebuild the convent of Santa Clara for her retreat. She died in 1336 in Estremoz *(see p300)*, but was buried here in the convent church. The murdered Inês de Castro was also laid to rest here 20 years later, but was re-entombed at Alcobaça *(see pp178–9)*.

Almost from the day it was built, Santa Clara suffered from flooding from the river, and it was finally abandoned in 1677. In 1696 Santa Isabel's remains were moved to safety in the Convent of Santa Clara-a-Nova. The original Gothic church has been in silted ruins since the end of the 17th century, but is now at last being restored.

🏠 Santa Clara-a-Nova

Calçada de Santa Isabel. 📞 *239-44 16 74.* ⬡ *Mon–Fri, Sat am, Sun pm.* ⬤ *public hols.* 🎫 *to cloister.*

The vast "new" convent of the Poor Clares was built between 1649 and 1677 to house the nuns from Santa Clara-a-Velha on drier land uphill. The building was designed by a mathematics professor, João Turriano, and although intended as a convent, it now serves in part as a barracks for the army. In the richly Baroque church, pride

Open-air study in the Jardim Botânico

of place is given to the silver tomb of Santa Isabel, installed in 1696 and paid for by the people of Coimbra. The saint's original tomb, a single stone, lies in the lower choir, and polychrome wooden panels in the aisles tell the story of her life. The convent's large cloister, built by the Hungarian Carlos Mardel, was contributed in 1733 by João V, a generous benefactor who was well known for his charity to nuns.

🏛 Portugal dos Pequenitos

Santa Clara. 📞 *239-44 12 25.* ⬡ *daily.* ⬤ *Dec 25.* 🎫 ♿

Different in mood from the rest of Coimbra, Portugal dos Pequenitos is a children's wonderland. Here, set in a lovely park, is a miniature world, and children and adults alike can explore scaled-down versions of Portugal's finest national buildings, whole villages of typical regional architecture, and pagodas and temples representing the far-flung reaches of the former Portuguese empire.

Child-size model of an Algarve manor house in Portugal dos Pequenitos

Coimbra University

Atlas on the Via Latina

IN RESPONSE to an ecclesiastical petition, King Dinis founded a university, one of the world's oldest and most illustrious, in 1290. Vacillating between Lisbon and Coimbra, it was finally installed in 1537 in Coimbra's royal palace. Study was mostly of theology, medicine, and law until the reforms by the Marquês de Pombal in the 1770s that broadened the curriculum. A number of 19th-century literary figures, including Eça de Queirós *(see p55)*, were alumni of Coimbra. Many buildings were replaced after the 1940s, but the halls around the Pátio das Escolas echo with 700 years of learning.

Museu de Arte Sacra
As well as works of art on religious themes, the four rooms of the museum display vestments, chalices, and books of early sacred music.

★ **Capela de São Miguel**
Although begun in 1517 the chapel's interior is mostly 17th and 18th century. The azulejos, ornate ceiling, and the fine Mannerist altar are eclipsed by the dazzling organ, angels trumpeting its Baroque glory.

The portal of Capela de São Miguel is Manueline in style, the work of Marcos Pires before his death in 1521.

Portrait of João V (c.1730)

STAR FEATURES

★ Biblioteca Joanina

★ Capela de São Miguel

★ **Biblioteca Joanina**
Named after its benefactor, João V (whose coat of arms is over the door), the library was built in the early 18th century. Its rooms, rich in gilt and exotic wood, are lined with 300,000 books.

The bell tower, symbol of the university, can be seen from all over the city. The best-known of its three bells, called *a cabra*, the goat, has summoned generations of students to lectures since the tower was completed in 1733.

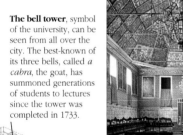

VISITORS' CHECKLIST

Universidade de Coimbra, Largo da Porta Férrea. (*239-84 02 30.* 📷 *1 from Largo da Portagem.* ⏰ *9:30am–noon, 2–5pm daily.* ● *Dec 25.* 📷 ♿ *Biblioteca Joanina only.* ▣

Sala Grande dos Actos

Also known as the Sala dos Capelos, this is where major events such as investitures are celebrated. Dons' benches line the walls below portraits of Portuguese monarchs.

The Via Latina is a colonnaded walkway added to the original palace in the 18th century. The Portuguese coat of arms above the double staircase is crowned by a statue of Wisdom, while below, figures of Justice and Fortitude flank José I, in whose reign (1750–77) the Marquês de Pombal modernized the university.

To ticket office

Sala do Exame Privado

José Ferreira Araújo's exuberant ceiling, painted in 1701, arcs above a frieze of portraits of past rectors in the private examination hall.

STUDENT TRADITIONS

When the university was founded, the only subjects studied were canon and civil law, medicine, and letters – grammar and philosophy. To indicate which college they belonged to, students began to pin colored ribbons to their gowns: red for law, yellow for medicine, dark blue for letters. Much has changed in 700 years, but students are still initiated in rites whose origins are long forgotten, and in May, as the academic year ends, there is a ceremonial burning of ribbons, the Queima das Fitas.

Burning college ribbons in best scholastic tradition

Porta Férrea

Built in 1634, this heavy iron gate to the university pátio is flanked by figures representing the original faculties.

Conimbriga ●

Road map C3. 2 km (1 mile) S of
Condeixa-a-Nova. **C** *239-94 11 77.*
▦ *from Coimbra.* **Site** ◑ *9am–1pm,
2–8pm (Sep–Mar: 6pm) daily.*
● *Dec 25.* **Museum** ◑ *10am–1pm,
2–7pm (Sep–Mar: 6pm) Tue–Sun.*
● *Dec 25.* ▨ ♿ *museum only.*

THIS, THE LARGEST and most
extensively excavated
Roman site in Portugal *(see
pp40–41),* was on the Roman
road between Lisbon (Olisipo)
and Braga (Bracara Augusta).
There is evidence of Roman
habitation as early as the 2nd
century BC, but it was under
Augustus, from
about 25 BC,
that Conimbriga
became a sub-
stantial town:
baths, a forum,
and the aque-
duct have been
uncovered from
this era. The
finest buildings,
however, date
from the 2nd and 3rd centuries
AD, and they provide a vivid
image of a prosperous city.

The site is approached along
a section of Roman road that
led into the city from the east.
Just to the left cluster the out-
lines of shops, baths, and two
once-luxurious houses, both
with exquisite mosaic floors.

At Conimbriga is one of the
largest houses discovered in
the western Roman empire.
This opulent villa, known as
the Casa de Cantaber, is built
around ornamental pools in
superb colonnaded gardens,

**Detail of a bedroom floor in
a house near the entrance**

with its own bath complex and
a sophisticated heating system.
Some of the fine mosaics in
the museum probably came
from this huge residence.

The Casa das Fontes, dating
from the first half of the 2nd
century, is under a protective
cover, but walkways provide a
good view. Its pictorial mosaics
and fountains, rare survivals
that give the house its name,
form a strong image of the
Roman taste for good living.
The city's pools, and the baths
and steam rooms of Trajan's
thermae, were fed by a spring
3.5 km (2 miles) away via an
aqueduct, mostly subterranean,
built in the time
of Augustus.

Official exca-
vation was begun
here in 1912, but
a considerable
part of the 13-ha
(32-acre) site has
yet to be fully ex-
plored, including
an amphitheater
north of the city.

In the 3rd or early 4th century,
buildings were plundered for
stone as defensive walls were
hastily raised against barbarian
hordes. In a successful assault
in AD 468, the Suevi burned
the city and murdered the inhabitants. Excavated skeletons
may date from this episode.

Just outside the ruins is an
informative museum that
explains the history and layout
of the site, and has exhibits
of Roman busts, mosaics, and
coins alongside more ancient
Celtic artifacts. There is also
a restaurant and picnic site.

**View of the church of São Miguel
within the castle walls at Penela**

Penela ●

Road map C3. 🚶 *620.* ▦
🅸 *Largo Marquesa dos Fornos de
Algodres (239-56 93 26).* ▲ *Thu.*

PENELA'S THICKSET **castle** was
built in 1087 by Sisinando,
governor of Coimbra, as part
of the line of defenses of the
Mondego valley. Its squat
towers provide wonderful
views of the village and, to the
east, of the wooded Serra da
Lousã. The church within the
castle walls, **São Miguel**,
dates back to the 16th century.
Below, in Penela itself, **Santa
Eufémia**, dated 1551 above
its decorative doorway, has a
Roman capital used as a font.

ENVIRONS: Among walnut and
olive groves 5 km (3 miles) to
the west, is the tiny village of
Rabaçal, whose tasty cheese,
made with a mixture of sheep
and goat milk, is a regional
specialty *(see p146).* Some
village women still age the
cheese rounds in darkened
rooms in their homes.

Lousã ●

Road map C3. 🚶 *9,000.* 🚃 ▦
🅸 *Câmara Municipal, Rua Dr João
Cáceres (239-99 35 02).* ▲ *Tue & Sat.*

THE PAPER FACTORY at Lousã,
on the forested banks of
the River Arouce, was opened
in 1716 and is still working.
Skilled papermakers imported
from Italy and Germany by the
Marquês de Pombal *(see p52)*
brought prosperity, still evident
in the handsome 18th-century

The central garden of the Casa das Fontes in Conimbriga

The castle at Arouce, near Lousã, oddly defenseless in its deep valley

houses. Most elegant of these is the **Palácio dos Salazires**, a private home in Rua Viscondessa do Espinhal. Also notable is the **Misericórdia**, with a 1568 Renaissance portal, in Rua do Comércio.

ENVIRONS: From the outskirts of Lousã, a road leads to the **Castelo de Arouce**, deep in a valley 3 km (2 miles) south. Legend says it was built in the 11th century by a King Arunce who took refuge in the valley when fleeing from raiders. Beside the dark schist castle three shrines tucked into a fold of the hills form the **Santuário de Nossa Senhora da Piedade**.

A viewpoint on the tortuous road south toward Castanheira de Pêra gives a splendid view across the wooded valley. A turning east leads up to **Alto do Trevim** which, at 1,204 m (3,950 ft), is the highest point in the Serra de Lousã.

Buçaco ⑫

See pp210–11.

Luso ⑬

Road map C3. ⚐ 3,000. ▦
🛈 *Rua Emídio Navarro (231-93 91 33).*
⚑ *Mon–Sat.*

IN THE 11TH CENTURY Luso was just a village linked to a monastery at Vacariça, but it developed into a lively spa town in the 18th century as its hot-water springs became a focus for tourism. The thermal waters, which originate from a spring below the **Capela de São João**, are said to be of therapeutic value in the treatment of a wide range of conditions, from bad circulation and muscle tone to renal problems and arthritis.

There are a number of grand, if somewhat faded, hotels here, and an elegant Art Nouveau lobby adorns the former casino, but the main reason for visiting the resort is to enjoy its spa facilities. An additional attraction of Luso is the proximity of the treasured national forest of Buçaco, which is a powerful presence above the town.

Taking the spa waters at the Fonte de São João, Luso

ENVIRONS: Between Luso and Curia, **Mealhada** is an attractive small town in the heart of a region famous for *leitão*, suckling pig *(see p146)*. This enormously popular dish is prominently advertised at numerous hotly competing restaurants in the area.

Arganil ⑭

Road map D3. ⚐ 3,000. ▦
🛈 *Avenida das Forças Armadas (235-20 48 23).* ⚑ *Thu.*

TRADITION SAYS that this was a Roman city called Argos. In the 12th century, Dona Teresa, the mother of Afonso Henriques *(see pp42–3)*, gave the town to the bishopric of Coimbra, whose incumbent also acquired the title of Conde de Arganil. Most of the town's architecture is unremarkable, but the church of **São Gens**, the Igreja Matriz in Rua de Visconde de Frias, dates back perhaps to the 14th century.

ENVIRONS: One of the most unusual local sights is kept in the sanctuary of Mont'Alto, 2 km (1 mile) above the town. Here, the **Capela do Senhor da Ladeira** harbors the Menino Jesus, a Christ Child figure in a bicorne hat (part of a full wardrobe). He comes out for *festas*, but the chapel key is otherwise available from the last house on the right.

Menino Jesus in Mont' Alto sanctuary, Arganil

THERMAL SPAS

In response to the Portuguese enthusiasm for thermal waters and health-oriented vacations, spa resorts have developed across the northern half of the country, with several of them in the Beiras, near Luso. All offer extensive sports facilities and a calm ambience as well as treatments for all the body's major systems. Most spas close for the winter, but Curia, 16 km (10 miles) northwest of Luso, is open all year for relaxation and treatments. Luso itself produces the country's best-known bottled mineral water.

Buçaco ⑫

PART ANCIENT WOODLAND, part arboretum, the National Forest of Buçaco is a magic place. As early as the 6th century it was a monastic retreat, and in 1628 the Carmelites built a house here, walling in the forest to keep the world at bay (women had already been banned by the pope in 1622). In their secluded forest the monks established contemplative walks, chapels – and trees. The trees, added to by Portuguese explorers, gained papal protection in 1632, and the 105 ha (260 acres) contain some 700 native

Viewpoint of Cruz Alta

and exotic species, including the venerable "Buçaco cedar." The peace of the forest was disturbed in 1810 as British and Portuguese troops fought the French on Buçaco ridge. In 1834 the monastery closed, but the forest endures, with its shady walks, hermits' grottoes, and the astonishing Buçaco Palace Hotel at its center.

★ Fonte Fria

This impressive cascade, fed by the greatest of the forest's six spring tumbles down to a magnolia-fringed pool.

LUSO →

N234-3 LUSO

RUA DOS FETOS

AVENIDA [

Porta dos Degraus and steps leading to Luso

Vale dos Fetos

Leading down to a small lake, the Valley of Ferns is lined with luxuriant specimens collected worldwide. The magnificent tree ferns give the valley a tropical air.

The Portas de Coimbra incorporate the papal bulls defending the trees and forbidding entry to women.

BUÇACO PALACE HOTEL

King Carlos, who commissioned this extravaganza in 1888, never lived to see his creation. His son, Manuel II, visited only briefly before his exile in 1910 *(see p55)* – he is said to have brought the French actress, Gaby Deslys, here for a romantic interlude. Its rebirth as a luxury hotel, serving its own renowned wines, was the inspiration of the royal chef, and it became a fashionable rendezvous for socialites. In World War II it was also rumored to be frequented by spies. It is now one of the great hotels of Portugal *(see p388).*

Gaby Deslys, with whom Manuel II reputedly had a brief romance

KEY

▬	Wall
• • •	Route of Via Sacra
P	Parking
⛪	Chapel
☀	Vista

STAR SIGHTS

★ Buçaco Palace Hotel

★ Fonte Fria

Monastery
Only the cloisters, chapel and a few monks' cells of the Carmelite monastery remain. A plaque records that Wellington slept in one of the cork-lined cells.

VISITORS' CHECKLIST

Road map C3. 3 km (2 miles) SE of Luso. 🚍 🚶 *Luso (231-93 91 33)*. **Monastery** ○ *Sat–Thu.* **Forest** ○ *daily.* 🚗 *for vehicles (May–Oct).* **Museu Militar** Almas do Encarnadouro. 📞 *231-93 93 10.* ○ *Tue–Sun.* ● *Jan 1, Easter, Dec 25.* 🎫 *except Wed.* ♿ 🎉 *Sep 27: Anniversary of Battle of Buçaco.*

Porta da Rainha was made for Catherine of Bragança, but when her visit in 1693 was cancelled the gateway was sealed up for 11 years.

Museu Militar, devoted to the Peninsular War

Tasmanian eucalyptus (1876)

★ Buçaco Palace Hotel
Completed in 1907, the Neo-Manueline folly of a hunting lodge built by Luigi Manini includes murals and tiles by prominent artists. Azulejos in the hall feature scenes of the Battle of Buçaco.

The Monument to the Battle of Buçaco marks Wellington's victory on the ridge of Buçaco on September 27, 1810. As the nearby Museu Militar explains, this decisive battle halted the French march on Coimbra.

Cruz Alta, the forest's highest point, has glorious views as far as the sea.

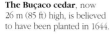

Porta da Cruz Alta

The Buçaco cedar, now 26 m (85 ft) high, is believed to have been planted in 1644.

Via Sacra
Chapels containing life-size figures mark the Stations of the Cross along this winding pathway. They were installed by the Bishop of Coimbra in 1693.

0 meters	250
0 yards	250

The village of Piódão, blending with the granite of the surrounding Serra de Açor

Piódão ⑮

Road map D3. 🏃 60. 🚌 to Coja 20 km (12 miles) away. ℹ️ Arganil (235-20 48 23).

As ITS NAME SUGGESTS, the Serra de Açor, hills of the goshawk, is a place of bleak beauty where solitary villages cling to precipitous terraces. Piódão, nestling in its valley, is the most striking of these dark schist and slate hamlets. Seemingly remote, Piódão was, until the late 19th century, on the main commercial route from Coimbra to Covilhã, but with newer roads the village was forgotten. With help from EU funds, it is now coming back to life: stores are opening, houses are being repainted with traditional blue trim, and in the main square the bright white **Igreja Matriz** stands out against the surrounding dark stone. Happily, Piódão still retains its old-world charm.

Oliveira do Hospital ⑯

Road map D3. 🏃 3,500. 🚌 ℹ️ Casa da Cultura, Rua do Colégio (238-591 19). 🔄 2nd Mon of month.

THESE LANDS ONCE belonged to the Knights Hospitallers, a gift in 1120 from the mother of Afonso Henriques. The 13th-century **Igreja Matriz** in Largo Ribeira do Amaral, houses a magnificent reminder of the era of these warrior monks. One of the founders of the

town, Domingues Joanes, lies in a large tomb surmounted by a charming equestrian statue.

Today, this lively industrial town is perfectly situated for exploring the valleys of the Mondego and the Alva.

ENVIRONS: At Lourosa, 12 km (7 miles) to the southwest, the 10th-century church of **São Pedro** reflects the changing fate of Portugal over the centuries. A cemetery excavated beneath the church dates from the Roman era; the porch is Visigothic, while inside are ten impressive Roman arches and an *ajimece* (Moorish window).

Caramulo ⑰

Road map C3. 🏃 1,700. 🚌 ℹ️ Avenida Jerónimo Lacerda (232-86 14 37).

IN A GRASSY ROLLING serra west of Viseu, this town was once, with its clear mountain air, a center for sanatoriums.

Interior of São Pedro at Lourosa, near Oliveira do Hospital

It is better known today for two very disparate museums in one institutional building.

In the art collection of the **Fundação Abel de Lacerda**, the exhibits on display range across 16th-century Flemish tapestries, sculpture, porcelain, silver, and ivory to Egyptian bronzes from 1580 to 900 BC. The paintings are as varied: from Portuguese primitives to the 20th century. Chagall and Dalí are represented, as is the Portuguese Maria Helena Vieira da Silva (1908–92). One of Picasso's haunting still lifes was donated by the artist in 1947.

The collection in the **Museu do Automóvel** is just as eclectic: a working 1899 Peugeot, Bugattis and Rolls-Royces, and a bullet-proof 1938 Mercedes-Benz ordered for Salazar when he was prime minister *(see pp56–7)* but never used.

🏛 **Fundação Abel de Lacerda and Museu do Automóvel**
Caramulo. 🎫 232-86 12 70. 🕐 daily (may close early in winter). 🚫 Easter, Dec 24 & 25. 🎦

ENVIRONS: From the museum the road winds southwest up to two viewpoints and picnic spots in the Serra do Caramulo. About 4 km (2 miles) from Caramulo are the wildflower pastures of **Cabeça da Neve**, at 970 m (3,200 ft). A little farther on, signposted to the west, is the boulder-strewn upland of **Caramulinho**, rising to 1,074 m (3,524 ft). The views from here are magnificent.

Viseu ⑱

Road map D3. 👥 *19,500.* 🚌
ℹ *Avenida Calouste Gulbenkian
(232-42 20 14).* 🍴 *Tue.*

A<small>N ENTHRALLING</small> old town is
at the heart of this lively
regional capital. Viseu has been
a major northern crossroads
since the time of the Romans
and is the center of the Dão
wine-growing region *(see p29).*

On a visit to Viseu it is hard
to miss that this was the home
town of one of Portugal's great
16th-century artists. The name
of Grão Vasco graces a hotel,
a museum, even a wine label.

On the western side of the
old town is the striking 15th-
century **Porta do Soar de
Cima**, a remnant of the original walls. In the Rossio, the
main square, the **Igreja dos
Terceiros de São Francisco**
(1773) has an Italianate façade
and gilded interior. The 1887
town hall on the west side has
a grand stairway and *azulejos*
featuring the history of Viseu
and its personalities. Just north
is Rua Augusto Hilário, named
after the originator of Coimbra-
style *fado (see pp66–7)* who
was born here.

**The two-towered 17th-century
façade of Viseu's cathedral**

🏛 Sé

Largo da Sé. 📞 *232-42 29 84.*
⏱ *daily.* 🎫 *to treasury.*
Viseu's cathedral still retains a
few Romanesque features, but
it has been altered over the
centuries in a variety of styles
that work together surprisingly
well. The façade is a 17th-
century replacement of a
Manueline frontage that fell
down in 1635. Inside, the
vaulted roof is supported by
16th-century knotted ribs on
13th-century columns. In the

The graceful Rococo façade of the church of the Misericórdia, Viseu

north chapel are fine *azulejos*
from the 18th century, while
those in the two-story cloister
date from a century earlier. The
sacristy has a lavishly painted
ceiling and early "carpet" tiles
(see p22). In the chancel, choir
stalls in Brazilian jacaranda
contrast with a startling modern
altar, an inverted pyramid in
polished granite and steel.

The Sé's treasury, housed
in the chapterhouse, includes
a 12th-century Gospel and a
13th-century Limoges coffer.

Facing the cathedral is the
Misericórdia church, with its
beautifully proportioned 18th-
century Rococo façade; the
interior is unexceptional.

🏛 Museu de Grão Vasco

Largo da Sé. 📞 *232-42 20 49.*
⏱ *Tue–Sun.* 🔴 *public hols.* 🎫
In the 16th-century
former bishops' palace
abutting the cathedral
is the Museu de Grão
Vasco, Viseu's "great
Vasco." The paintings
of Vasco Fernandes
(c.1475–1540) and his
fellow artists of the
Viseu School are highly
esteemed for their
naturalism, back-
ground landscapes,
drapery, and attention
to detail. Their treat-
ment of light betrays
the marked influence
of Flemish painters.

On the top floor of
the three-story mu-
seum are exhibited

the masterpieces that once
adorned the chancel altarpiece
in the cathedral. Predominant
are Vasco's monumental *St.
Peter* and, from a series of
14 panels on the life of Christ,
The Adoration of the Magi.
Painted in about 1503–5, it
is memorable for the inclusion
of a Brazilian Indian among
those paying homage to the
newborn Christ *(see p48).*
Some of the other panels are
thought to be by fellow artists
in the Viseu School.

Among other masterpieces
hung here are works by Grão
Vasco's great rival, Gaspar Vaz,
including a *Last Supper.* On
the lower floors are works
by Portuguese artists from the
19th and 20th centuries, including the brilliant Columbano
Bordalo Pinheiro.

***St. Peter* (1503–5) by Vasco Fernandes in
the Museu de Grão Vasco, Viseu**

Sernancelhe ⑲

Road map D2. 🏠 *1,100.* 🚌
ℹ️ *Avenida das Tílias (254-551 03).*
🕑 *every other Thu.*

SMALL WHITEWASHED houses cluster around the granite heart of this modest Beira town, which was established on the banks of the Távora in the 10th century. In the central Praça da República stands the Romanesque **Igreja Matriz.** The granite statues in its façade niches, survivors from the 12th century, flank a notable arched portal embellished by a semicircle of carved angels. The pillory that stands across the square is dated 1554.

The grandest house here is the Baroque **Solar dos Carvalhos**, behind the church. Long and low, with carved granite portals against whitewashed walls, it is where the local noble family lived in the 18th century. It is still a private house.

Carved arch over the portal of the Igreja Matriz, Sernancelhe

Only a few stubs of castle wall remain on the rocky outcrop overlooking the square, but a small battlemented house has been built into them.

ENVIRONS: In the Serra da Lapa, which rises to the south of Sernancelhe, stands a popular shrine known as the **Santuário de Nossa Senhora da Lapa**. The story tells of a mute shepherd girl, Joana, who found a statue of the Virgin Mary on a large boulder and took it home. Irritated, her mother threw it on the fire, at which moment the child miraculously spoke: "Don't burn it," cried Joana. "It is the Senhora da Lapa." A chapel was built to enshrine the boulder, and the image, now with a slightly scorched face, looks down from an ornamental recess. The space below her niche is packed with images and offerings left by pilgrims.

The castle at **Penedono** is captivating. Perched on rocks in the middle of this small town 17 km (11 miles) northeast of Sernancelhe, it has survived since at least the 10th century. The castle is mentioned in the medieval tale of a knight known as O Magriço, who went to England with 11 other knights to joust in honor of 12 English ladies. There is little to see inside the castle – if closed, the key is in the store beside the *pelourinho* (pillory), but there are splendid views from the walls.

🏛 **Santuário de Nossa Senhora da Lapa**
Quintela da Lapa, 11 km (7 miles) SW of Sernancelhe.
📞 *232-68 89 93.* 🕑 *daily.*

The castle of Penedono, near Sernancelhe, with its imposing medieval battlements

The main gateway into the old walled town of Trancoso

Trancoso ⑳

Road map D2. 🏠 *6,000.* 🚌
ℹ️ *Avenida Herois de São Marcos (271-81 11 47).* 🕑 *Fri.*

WHEN KING DINIS married Isabel here in 1283 *(see pp44–5)*, he gave her Trancoso as a wedding gift. He was also responsible for the impressive walls that still encircle the town and, in 1304, established here the first unrestricted fair in Portugal. Left in peace after 1385, the town became a lively commercial center. Trancoso once had a large Jewish population, and in the old Judiaria, houses survive with one broad and one narrow door, separating domestic life from commerce.

From the southern gate, Rua da Corredoura leads to **São Pedro**, restored after 1720. A tombstone in the church commemorates Gonçalo Anes, a local shoemaker who, in the 1580s, wrote the celebrated *Trovas* under the name of Bandarra. These prophesied the return of the young King Sebastião *(see p107).*

ENVIRONS: Tumbledown ruins above a humble village are all that remain of the medieval citadel of **Marialva**, 24 km (15 miles) to the northeast of Trancoso. Granite walls, fragments of stone carvings, and a striking 15th-century pillory emanate an aura of lost grandeur. Probably founded by Ferdinand of León and Castile early in the 11th century and fortified by Sancho I, it is not known why Marialva fell into ruin. No battle destroyed it, and it seems merely to have been abandoned as townsfolk moved to more fruitful lands.

SERRA CHEESE

Serra, made from the milk of ewes grazing in the Serra da Estrela *(see pp218–19)*, is Portugal's finest cheese. It is made in the winter – its success was once governed by the temperature of the women's hands as they worked in their cool granite kitchens – and traditionally the milk is coagulated with *flor do cardo*, thistle. Now the small factories producing the cheese, in rounds of 1.5–2 kg (about 3–5 lb), are certified to ensure quality and authenticity (fakes are not uncommon). Young Serra is pale and slightly runny, with a thin rind. A longer curing produces a harder, more seasoned cheese.

A shepherd with his flock on the slopes of the Serra da Estrela

Celorico da Beira ㉑

Road map D3. 🏠 *3,000.* 🚉 🚌
🛈 *Estrada Nacional 16 (271-74 21 09).*
🛒 *Tue (general), Dec–May: Fri (cheese).*

IN THE LEE OF the Serra da Estrela, the pastures around Celorico da Beira have long been a source of the region's famous Serra cheese. From December to May the cheese market in the Praça Municipal is a local attraction, and every February Celorico holds a lively fair dedicated to cheeses.

Around Rua Fernão Pacheco, running from the main road up to the castle, is the old center of Celorico, a cluster of granite houses with Manueline windows and Gothic doors. Of the 10th-century **castle**, battered by a long succession of frontier disputes with Spain, only a tower and the outer walls remain. Its stark silhouette is less dramatic at close quarters. The **Igreja Matriz**, restored in the 18th century, has a painted coffered ceiling. During the Peninsular War, the church served briefly as a makeshift hospital for the English forces.

Almeida ㉒

Road map E2. 🏠 *1,600.* 🚌
🛈 *Portas de São Francisco (271-57 42 04).* 🗓 *8 & last Sat of month.*

FORMIDABLE defenses in the form of a 12-pointed star guard this small, delightfully preserved border town.

Almeida was recognized by Spain as Portuguese territory under the Alcañices Treaty on September 12, 1297, but this did not stop further incursions. The present Vauban-style stronghold *(see p297)* was designed in 1641 by Antoine Deville after Spain's Philip IV, in post-Restoration rage, destroyed the earlier defenses protecting the town and its medieval castle.

From 1742 to 1743 Almeida was in Spanish hands again; during the Peninsular War it was held in turn by the French under Masséna and the British under the Duke of Wellington. In 1810, a French shell lit a powder trail that destroyed the castle.

To breach the town's fortifications today, you must cross a bridge and pass through a tunnel. The **casamatas**, soldiers' barracks, can be visited, and an armory in the main gateway, the Portas de São Francisco, holds mementos of Almeida's military past. In the town are a 17th-century parish church and a **Misericórdia** church of similar age, attached to one of Portugal's oldest almshouses. A walk around the grassy walls gives rewarding views of the town.

Almeida's complex fortifications, still discernible despite the incursion of grass and wildflowers

Border Castles Tour [23]

DEFENDING PORTUGAL'S FRONTIERS was a vital priority of the nation's early kings. The greatest period of castle-building was in the reign of King Dinis (1279–1325). All along the shakily held border, Spanish incursions were frequent and loyalties divided. Castles were constantly being assaulted, besieged, and rebuilt, and those that survived are a lasting reminder of this long period of dispute. Much of the terrain, especially in the Serra da Marofa, is bleak and rocky, but near Pinhel and beyond Castelo Mendo the scenic valley of the Côa River provides a dramatic backdrop.

Castelo Rodrigo ②
This tiny fortified village still has its encircling walls built by King Dinis in 1296. But the fine palace of its lord, the Spanish sympathizer Cristóvão de Moura, was burned down at the Restoration in 1640 *(see pp50–51)*.

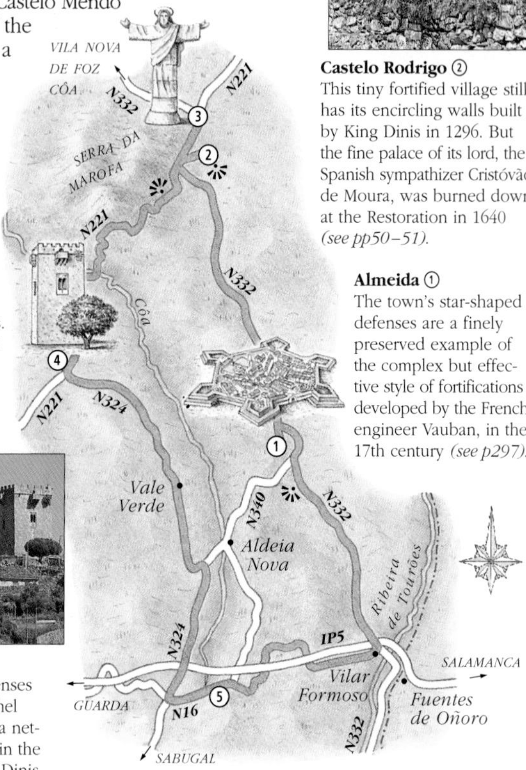
VILA NOVA
DE FOZ
CÔA
N332
N221
SERRA DA
MAROFA
N221
N332
Côa
N221
N324
N340
N332
Vale
Verde
Aldeia
Nova
Ribeira
de Tourões
IP5
Vilar
Formoso
Fuentes
de Oñoro
SALAMANCA
GUARDA
N16
N324
N332
SABUGAL

Figueira de Castelo Rodrigo ③
From the 18th century, Castelo Rodrigo was largely abandoned in favor of less isolated Figueira, now a flourishing little town known for its almond blossoms. Just to the south, topped by a huge stone Christ the King, is the highest point of the Serra da Marofa, 977 m (3,205 ft).

Almeida ①
The town's star-shaped defenses are a finely preserved example of the complex but effective style of fortifications developed by the French engineer Vauban, in the 17th century *(see p297)*.

Pinhel ④
Part of the region's defenses since Roman times, Pinhel formed the fulcrum for a network of fortresses, and in the early 14th century King Dinis built it up into an impressive citadel. Much of this ring of walls survives, as do two towers. Today, Pinhel is noted for its wine.

> ## TIPS FOR DRIVERS
>
> ***Length:*** *115 km (72 miles).*
> ***Stopping-off points:*** *Most villages have cafés, and Pinhel and Almeida have restaurants.*
> ***Road conditions:*** *The tour uses well-surfaced roads but short cuts are deceptive and are not recommended.* (See also pp444–5.)

KEY

- Tour route
- Other roads
- International border
- Vista

0 kilometers **10**
0 miles **5**

Castelo Mendo ⑤
Beyond the main gate, guarded by two stone boars, little survives of the castle here, but the distant views make its role as a frontier fort easy to appreciate.

The soaring triple-aisled interior of Guarda's Gothic cathedral

Guarda ㉔

Road map D3. 🏔 20,000. 🚉 🚌
ℹ️ *Rua Infante Dom Henrique (271-22 18 17).* 📅 *1st & last Wed of month.*

Sᴘʀᴇᴀᴅ ᴏᴠᴇʀ a bleak hill on the northeast flank of the Serra da Estrela, Guarda is Portugal's highest city, at 1,056 m (3,465 ft). Founded in 1197 by Sancho I, the city's original role as border guard explains its name and its rather forbidding countenance. Some of its arcaded streets and squares are lively and interesting, but the great fortresslike **Sé**, with its flying buttresses, pinnacles, and gargoyles, could never be described as lovely. Master architects who worked on the cathedral, begun in 1390 and completed in 1540, included Diogo Boitac (from 1504 to 1517) and the builders of Batalha *(see pp182–3).* The interior, by contrast, is light and graceful. The 100 carved figures high on the altarpiece in the chancel were worked by Jean de Rouen in 1552.

On display in the nearby **Museu de Guarda** are two floors of paintings, artifacts, archaeological discoveries, and a section on the city's own poet, Augusto Gil (1873–1929).

From the cathedral square, Rua do Comércio leads down to the 17th-century **Misericórdia** church. Inside the ornamental portal are Baroque altars and pulpits. Just north of the cathedral, in the historic town center, is the 18th-century

church of **São Vicente**, which has 16 elaborate *azulejo* panels depicting the life of Christ.

Guarda used to support a thriving Jewish community; in Rua Dom Sancho I is a key shop that may once have served as a synagogue. History records that João I, on a visit to Guarda, was smitten by Inês Fernandes, the beautiful daughter of a Jewish shoemaker. From their liaison a son, Afonso, was born. In 1442 the title of first Duke of Bragança was bestowed on Afonso, and 200 years later his descendant would take the throne as João IV, first of the Bragança monarchs *(see p299).*

Cabral family crest in the chapel, Belmonte

Centum Cellas, an unusual Roman landmark near Belmonte

🏛 **Museu de Guarda**
Rua Alves Roçadas 30. 📞 *271-21 34 60.* 🕐 *Tue–Sun.* ⚫ *public hols.* 📷

Serra da Estrela ㉕

See pp218–19.

Belmonte ㉖

Road map D3. 🏔 *3,600.* 🚉 🚌
ℹ️ *Praça da República 18 (275-91 14 88).* 📅 *1st & 3rd Mon of month.*

Bᴇʟᴍᴏɴᴛᴇ was for generations the fiefdom of the Cabral family, a name associated with heroic exploits. Pedro Álvares Cabral, who in 1500 was the first navigator to land in Brazil, had forebears who fought at Ceuta *(see p48)* and Aljubarrota *(see p183).* Fernão, an earlier ancestor known as the Giant of the Beiras, was famed for his feats of strength. The family crest, incorporating a goat *(cabra)* as a play on words, can be seen in the castle and adjacent chapel. The **castle**, begun in 1266, retains its keep and, a later addition, an ornate Manueline window. The little church of **São Tiago** nearby has preserved its Romanesque simplicity: the frescoes above the altar and, in a tiny side chapel, a serene granite pietà date from the 13th century. Beside the church is the 15th-century **Capela dos Cabrais** that holds the Cabral family tombs.

On the opposite side of the village is the modern **Igreja da Sagrada Família** (1940). It is the repository for a treasured statue of Nossa Senhora da Esperança, which, according to tradition, accompanied Cabral on his voyage to Brazil.

Eɴᴠɪʀᴏɴꜱ: Just northeast of Belmonte is a Roman tower, **Centum Cellas**, also called Torre de Colmeal. The role of this square, three-storied structure is uncertain; archaeologists' theories have suggested a range of functions from hostel or military base to mansion and temple.

Serra da Estrela 🚱

Haymaking near
the town of Linhares

THESE "STAR MOUNTAINS" are the highest range on mainland Portugal, with much of the Serra over 1,500 m (5,000 ft). The highest point rises to 1,993 m (6,539 ft) but is topped by a small stone tower – the Torre – to "stretch" it to 2,000 m. The exposed granite of the upper slopes is good for little but grazing sheep, and stone shepherds' huts form part of the landscape, their thatched roofs renewed each year after the harsh winter. Sheep have shaped the fortunes of the area, providing wool for a textile industry and supplying milk for Portugal's best-known cheese. A designated nature preserve, the Serra's long-distance paths and stunning flora attract walkers and nature enthusiasts, while a winter snowfall brings skiers to the slopes around Torre.

Cabeça do Velho
The granite of the mountain tops has been eroded into many weird shapes, such as this "old man's head" near Sabugueiro. It is matched by an "old woman's head" south of Seia.

Valezim
In Valezim are several old water mills of a type not often found in Portugal. Two of them are still used to grind grain.

Seia is one of the main entry points to the Parque Natural da Serra da Estrela.

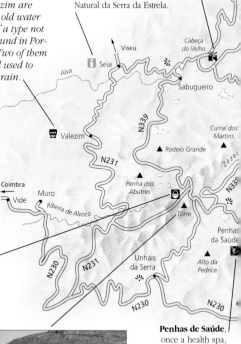

Serra Cheese Shop
The best Serra cheese, prized for its rich flavor (see p215), is still made by hand. Farmers sell their produce at cheese fairs and from stands or small shops such as this one near the summit of Torre.

Penhas de Saúde,
once a health spa, is now popular with skiers.

Torre
Despite the unpredictability of snow, the slopes below Torre are used for skiing, tobogganing, or just fun in the snow.

STAR SIGHTS

★ Zêzere Valley

★ Linhares

★ Linhares

*Guarded by the towers
of its medieval castle,
Linhares is like a living
museum. The forum,
from which medieval
justice was dispensed,
survives, as do many
fine houses from its
15th-century heyday.*

VISITORS' CHECKLIST

Road map D3. 🚦 *Praça da
República 28, Seia (238-222 72);
Covilhã (275-32 21 70); Gouveia
(238-424 11); Manteigas (275-
98 00 60).* 🚃 *Covilhã, Guarda.*
🚌 *to Covilhã, Seia & Guarda.
Limited local service within park.*
🚏 *Sat in most villages & towns.*
🎭 *Feb: Carnaval & annual
cheese fairs; Dec: Santa Luzia.*

KEY

═	Major road
─	Minor road
🚦	Tourist information
☀	Vista

Celorico
da Beira

Prados

Linhares ⛫

Cabeça Alta ▲

Folgosinho

Galhardos ▲

Mondego

Videmonte

Guarda

Guarda

🚦
Manteigas

N232

Zêzere

Valhelhas

N18-1

Belmonte

Poço
do Inferno
☀

Manteigas,
at the heart of
the Serra, is a
textile center. Just
to the west there is
a *pousada (see p390).*

★ Zêzere Valley

*The Zêzere eventually joins the
Tagus, but here, near its source,
the young river flows through a
classic glacier-cut valley. The
golden broom growing here is
used to thatch mountain huts.*

0 kilometers 5

0 miles 2

Poço do Inferno

*This cascade in a gorge
of the Leandros River is a
spectacular sight, especially
when it freezes in winter.*

🚦
hã

:elo
nco

Covilhã, the
largest and live-
liest town in
the area, has a
busy morning
market. It is
also known for
its fine textiles
woven from
locally pro-
duced wool.

SHEEPDOG OF THE SERRA

Intelligent, loyal, and brave, the Serra da
Estrela sheepdog embodies all the qualities
required in this wild region. Its heavy coat,
as shaggy as its charges, helps it survive the
bitter high-altitude
winters. In the past
its strength was
called upon to de-
fend the flock from
wolves. Pedigree Serra
da Estrela dogs (repu-
tedly with some wolf's
blood introduced in their
breeding) are raised at
kennels near Gouveia
and west of Manteigas.

Sabugal ㉗

Road map E3. 🏃 *2,500.* 🚌
ℹ️ *Câmara Municipal, Praça da República (271-75 10 40).*
🛒 *1st Thu & 3rd Tue of month.*

IN 1296, WHEN THIS small town beside the River Côa was confirmed as Portuguese in the Treaty of Alcañices, the **castle** was refortified by the ever-industrious King Dinis *(see p44)*. Its imposing towered walls and unusual five-sided keep survive from this era, although the castle suffered in peacetime from villagers raiding it for building stone.

Peopled since prehistoric times, Sabugal still has part of its medieval walls, reinforced in the 17th century and now ringed by newer houses. In the Praça da República stands a granite **clock tower**, reconstructed in the 17th century.

ENVIRONS: Wrapped in its ring of walls, **Sortelha**, 20 km (12 miles) west, is enchanting. It sits on a granite outcrop and the views from the high keep of its gem of a 13th-century castle are stunning. In front of the arched castle entrance is a 16th-century pillory with an armillary sphere on top. In the tiny citadel are a school and stony lanes of granite houses, some discreetly converted into restaurants *(see p413)*.

The local fondness for bullfights *(see pp144–5)* is reflected in names of nearby villages

The castle at Sabugal, with its distinctive five-sided keep

such as **Vila do Touro**. In a local variation, the *capeia*, bulls were taunted into charging into a huge fork of branches.

Penamacor ㉘

Road map D3. 🏃 *3,200.* 🚉 🚌
ℹ️ *Rua 25 de Abril (277-39 43 16).*
🛒 *1st & 3rd Wed of month.*

FOUGHT OVER by successive waves of Romans, Visigoths, and Moors, this frontier town was fortified in the 12th century by Gualdim Pais, Master of the Knights Templar *(see pp184–5)*. Today the weather-beaten castle walls rise above a quiet town in the heart of a hardy, sparsely inhabited countryside where the main attraction is the hunting of small game.

From the main square, the road up to the old town passes beside the former town hall, built over a medieval archway. Beyond lie the restored **castle keep** and the 16th-century **Igreja da Misericórdia**, with an elegant Manueline portal capped by armillary spheres.

ENVIRONS: Penamacor is the headquarters of the **Reserva Natural da Serra da Malcata**. These 20 sq km (8 sq miles) of forested wilderness shelter not only wolves and otters, but the Reserva is one of the last refuges of the Iberian lynx. Visitors should first call at the information center for advice.

🦌 **Reserva Natural da Serra da Malcata**
🚌 *to Penamacor or Sabugal.* ℹ️ *Rua dos Bombeiros Voluntários, Penamacor (277-39 44 67).* 🎟️ *by appt.*

Monsanto ㉙

Road map E3. 🏃 *1,500.* 🚌
ℹ️ *in Penamacor (277-943 16).*
🛒 *3rd Sat.*

AN ODD FAME hit Monsanto in 1938 when it was voted "most Portuguese village in Portugal." The village is at one with the granite hillside on which it perches: its lanes blend into the gray rock, the houses squeezed between massive boulders. Tiny gardens sprout from the granite, and dogs drink from granite bowls.

The ruined **castle** began as a *castro*, a Lusitanian fortified settlement, and suffered a long history of sieges and battles for its commanding position. It was finally destroyed by a 19th-century gunpowder

Monsanto's houses, dwarfed by immense granite boulders

explosion. Cars cannot venture beyond the village center, but the view alone is worth the walk up to the ruined walls.

A story is told of how a long siege by the Moors drove the hungry villagers to a desperate ploy. They threw their last calf, full of their last grain, over the walls, a show of profligacy that convinced the Moors to give up. Each May there is a mock reenactment of this victory with much music and singing.

Idanha-a-Velha ⑳

Road map D3. 🏃 90. 🚌 ℹ️ *Rua da Senhora do Almortão, Idanha-a-Nova (277-32 29 15).*

THIS MODEST HAMLET among the olive groves encapsulates the history of Portugal. Discreet signs and explanations in Portuguese, French, and English guide visitors around the landmarks of this fascinating living museum.

Idanha-a-Velha was, it is said, the birthplace of the Visigothic King Wamba and had its own bishop until 1199. The present appearance of the **cathedral** comes from early 16th-century restoration, but in the echoing interior are stacked inscribed and sculpted Roman stones.

In the middle of the village stand a 17th-century pillory and the Renaissance **Igreja Matriz**, and near an early 20th-century olive press is a ruined **Torre dos Templários**, a relic of the Templars. This order of religious knights held sway in Idanha until the 14th century *(see pp184–5)*.

Statue-lined Stairway of the Apostles in the unusual Jardim Episcopal, Castelo Branco

Castelo Branco ㉛

Road map D4. 🏃 35,000. 🚉 🚌 ℹ️ *Alameda da Liberdade (272-34 10 02).* 🛒 *Mon.*

THIS HANDSOME, busy old city, overlooked by the vestiges of a Templar castle, is the most important in the Beira Baixa.

Much the greatest attraction is the extraordinary **Jardim Episcopal** beside the former bishops' palace. Created by Bishop João de Mendonça in the 18th century, the garden's layout is conventionally formal; its individuality lies in its dense population of statues. Baroque in style and bizarre in character, stone saints and apostles line the boxwood-edged paths, lions peer at their reflections in pools, and monarchs stand guard along the balustrades – the hated kings of the 60-year Spanish rule *(see p50)* conspicuously half-size.

The 17th-century Paço Episcopal itself now houses the **Museu Francisco Tavares Proença Júnior**. Its collection includes archaeological finds, displays of 16th-century tapestries, and Portuguese primitive art. Castelo Branco is also well known for its fine silk-embroidered bedspreads, called *colchas*, and examples of these are in the museum.

In the mainly 18th-century Convento da Graça opposite there is a small **Museu de Arte Sacra** with a varied collection of religious art, including an ivory Christ. Beside the road back to the town center stands a 15th-century cross known as the **Cruzeiro de São João**.

🌿 **Jardim Episcopal**
Rua Bartolomeu da Costa. 🔲 *daily.*
⬤ *Jan 1, Good Fri, Dec 25.* 🏷️
🏛️ **Museu Francisco Tavares Proença Júnior**
Rua Bartolomeu da Costa.
📞 *272-34 42 77.* ⬤ *for restoration.*
🏛️ **Museu de Arte Sacra**
Rua Bartolomeu da Costa.
📞 *272-34 44 54.* 🔲 *Mon–Fri.*
⬤ *public hols.* ♿

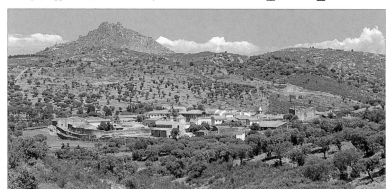

The historic little village of Idanha-a-Velha, among its olive groves beside the Ponsul River

Northern Portugal

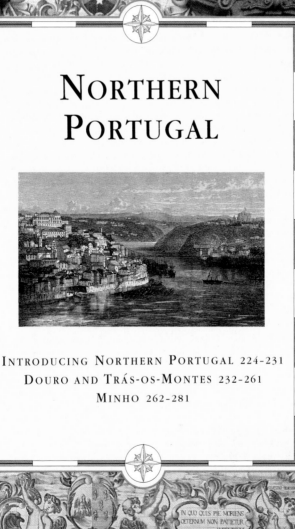

Northern Portugal at a Glance

PORTUGAL NORTH of the Douro River is rural and unspoiled, yet offers splendid opportunities for cultural sightseeing, walking, and water sports. Beyond the cultivated valley of the Douro and the fertile Minho rises the remote and romantically named Trás-os-Montes ("Behind the Mountains"), with its tracts of wilderness and tiny medieval townships. It could be said the nation was conceived between the Minho and the Douro, and historic cities such as Oporto, Bragança, and Braga give fascinating insights into the country's past.

*In the **Parque Nacional da Peneda-Gerês** scenery ranges from dramatic forested valleys to flowery meadows. Local farmers store their grain in unusual stone* espigueiros *(see pp270–71).*

Viana do Castelo, *at the mouth of the Lima River, is elegant and relaxed (see pp274–5). The stately buildings in the Praça da República, including the arcaded* Paços do Concelho *(the old town hall), reflect the town's wealthy past.*

MINHO
(See pp262–81)

Bom Jesus do Monte, *near Braga, attracts worshipers, penitents, and tourists, who all come to climb 116 m (380 ft) up the Baroque staircase (see pp278–9). This is the Staircase of the Five Senses, with fountains depicting each of the senses.*

Douro Litoral

Oporto, *set on Penaventosa Hill above the Douro River, is Portugal's second city (see pp236–47). Alongside a wealth of historic sights and sophisticated shopping, it offers the charm of its steep medieval alleys tumbling down to the lively riverside docks, and a chance to taste port at its point of origin.*

◁ **Azulejos** on the Igreja do Carmo in Oporto, depicting the founding of the Carmelite Order

The Casa de Mateus, familiar to many from the Mateus Rosé wine label, lies in the hills above the valley of the Douro. This Baroque *solar*, or manor house, is set in beautifully manicured formal gardens, its distinctive pinnacles rising above the orchards and vineyards that surround it (see pp254–5).

Bragança, capital of Trás-os-Montes, gave its name to Portugal's last and longest-ruling royal dynasty. The keep and walls of this remote citadel, founded in the 12th century, look out over the valley of the Fervença River (see pp258–9).

Trás-os-Montes

DOURO AND TRÁS-OS-MONTES
(See pp232–61)

Alto Douro

0 kilometers   25

0 miles   10

Port Country, as the scenic valley of the Upper Douro is commonly called, is the nursery of Portugal's port industry. A tour of a *quinta*, or wine estate, with its steeply terraced riverside vineyards, is highly recommended (see pp252–3).

The Festivals of the North

PORTUGUESE CITIES, towns, and villages all have their own particular saints' days. These are primarily religious occasions, especially in the Minho and across the devout north, but are also a chance to put aside the cares of life for a day or two. It is a popular maxim that a holy day is best celebrated by eating, drinking, dancing, and merrymaking, as well as worshiping and giving thanks. The most solemn and spectacular celebrations of Holy Week, Semana Santa, can also be seen in the north, especially in Braga *(see pp276–7)*, Portugal's ecclesiastical capital.

Dressing up for Holy Week

Street procession during the Festa das Cruzes in Barcelos

A solemn moment as Easter candles are lit in Braga

EASTER

HOLY WEEK, culminating in Easter Sunday, is the major religious festival of the year. In Braga, processions snake around the city walls to the great cathedral, and every village has its own ceremonies.

The start of Holy Week is heralded by Palm Sunday, when branch-bearing faithful line the streets to commemorate the entry of Christ into Jerusalem. Good Friday evening is palpably solemn, as innumerable processions follow the 14 Stations of the Cross, many believers doing public penance. In some villages an effigy of the lifeless and bleeding Christ is carried through the streets.

On Easter Sunday, after a mass proclaiming the risen Christ, every parish priest processes around his village with a crucifix on a tall staff for parishioners to kiss the feet of Jesus. While the priest takes a customary glass of wine, his entourage ecstatically set off rockets. Families then traditionally lunch on roast kid *(cabrito)*.

After Easter, the passion of Christ is recalled in Barcelos *(see p273)*. Crosses are erected the length of a petal-strewn route for the **Festa das Cruzes**.

SÃO JOÃO

OPORTO's celebration of São João *(Jun 23–24)* is one of Portugal's most exuberant festivals. It coincides with the summer solstice, and to celebrate, people eat, drink, and dance all night, playfully hitting each other over the head with giant garlic-leeks (or sometimes, even more strangely, with squeaky plastic hammers). Bonfires are lit, and a spectacular display of fireworks explodes over the Douro.

Wielding a São João hammer

Gold necklets

Embroidered apron pockets

COSTUME IN THE MINHO

Festivals are important vehicles for keeping alive tradition, particularly regional costume. These days, rock music and designer clothes are as much part of young people's lives in Minho villages as elsewhere in Western Europe, but traditional dress is worn with pride on days of celebration. The Minho's costume is the most colorful in Portugal, with exquisitely embroidered scarves and aprons in colors denoting village loyalties. Messages of love and friendship are stitched onto pockets, and bodices are lost under tiers of gold filigree.

A new tradition, which has become a part of São João over the last decade, is the annual regatta of the *barcos rabelos*, the boats in which port used to be shipped down the Douro *(see p252)*.

ROMARIAS

A NY KIND of celebration or party can be described as a *festa*, but one billed as a *romaria* implies a religious dimension. Most *festas* in the north are *romarias*; they begin with a special mass, then saints' statues are brought from the church to be paraded through the streets on litters. Blessings are dispensed in all directions – fire engines and ambulances frequently also getting the treatment – followed by a spraying with some Raposeira sparkling wine. Many *romarias* take place in the summer, and in August few days go by without a celebration. **Assumption Day** *(Aug 15)*

Nossa Senhora da Agonia, Viana do Castelo

is celebrated all over Portugal with dancing and music. *Gigantones*, grotesque giants of pre-Christian origin, join street processions, and fireworks light the sky. A few days later, one of the year's most spectacular *romarias* takes place in Viana do Castelo *(see pp274–5)*. The festivities celebrating **Nossa Senhora da Agonia** include a bullfight and an afternoon devoted to a kaleidoscopic display of regional costume,

STICK DANCING

Stick dancers, or *pauliteiros*, can still be seen at village festivals in Trás-os-Montes. The dances are of ancient origin, probably associated with fertility rites, and the sticks may once have been swords. The most famous troupe comes from the village of Duas Igrejas, near Miranda do Douro *(see p260)*.

Dancers performing at a *festa*

which may include more than a thousand participants. As a finale, fireworks are set off from the bridge over the Lima River to cascade down into the water as a fiery waterfall.

On the coast just to the west of Braga, villagers in São Bartolomeu do Mar mark the end of their *romaria* *(Aug 22–24)* by dipping their children in the sea, as a mock sacrifice to the waves.

Outlandish costumes and masks donned for the Dia dos Rapazes

CHRISTMAS AND WINTER

O N CHRISTMAS EVE, families gather to enjoy enormous quantities of *bacalhau* (salt cod) and mulled port, and to exchange presents, before attending midnight mass.

Between Christmas and Epiphany, Trás-os-Montes village boys dress in weird, fringed suits to take part in the rite-of-passage **Dia dos Rapazes**.

The Christmas season ends on **Dia de Reis** *(Jan 6)*, when the *bolo rei*, or "king cake," rich with crystallized fruit "jewels," is eaten *(see p33)*.

Comical giants leading an Assumption Day parade in Peso da Régua

The Story of Port

T HE "DISCOVERY" OF PORT dates from the 17th century, when British merchants, eager to build up trade with Portugal, doctored the wine of the Douro with brandy to stop it from turning sour in transit. It was found that the stronger and sweeter the wine, the better flavor it acquired. Over the years, methods of maturing and blending were refined and continue today in the port lodges of Vila Nova de Gaia *(see p247)*. Croft was one of the first big shippers, followed by other English and Scottish firms, and much of the port trade is still in British control.

Barco rabelo (see p250) ferry-ing port down the Douro

OPORTO • Vila Real •
Peso da Régua • • Tua
Pinhão •
Lamego
Douro
Corgo Pinhão Tua Sabor Douro

THE PORT REGION

Port comes only from a demar-cated region of the upper Douro valley, stretching 100 km (62 miles) to the Spanish border. Régua and Pinhão are the main centers of production, but most top-quality vineyards lie on estates or *quintas* in the harsh eastern terrain *(see pp252–3)*.

STYLES OF PORT

A classic after-dinner drink, port is rich, full-bodied, and high in alcohol. The tawnies are lighter in taste and color than ruby or vintage, but all are blended from several wines, selected from dozens of samples.

WARRE'S
1980 VINTAGE PORT

The star *of any shipper's range is made from wines of a single vintage year, from the best vine-yards. Blended and bottled after two years in oak casks, vintage port is then matured in tall black bottles.*

Vintage

DOW'S PORT
1989

LBV (Late Bottled Vintage) *is wine of a single year that has been matured in wood for four to six years before being bottled ready for drinking. The label gives the year of vintage and when it was bottled.*

LBV

GRAHAM'S PORT
10

This light port, *so-called because it pales to an am-ber color as it ages, is less full-bodied than vintage or ruby ports. It may be labeled as 10, 20 or 30 years old, referring to the average age of its blend of old and young wines.*

Aged Tawny

COCKBURN'S.
Fine Tawny

Less sweet *and lighter than ruby or vintage ports, tawny often appeals for those very reasons. It is blended from wines of different years after aging in wood, or may even be a clever mixture of red and white.*

Tawny

GRAHAM'S FINE RUBY PORT

The full-bodied, *fruity port named after its deep red color is matured in wood until ready to drink. The younger ones take no more than three years. All are blended from wines of various ages.*

Ruby

FERREIRA PORT

The two styles *of white port – dry and sweet – differ from the others as they are drunk as an aperitif, and are at their best chilled. White port is made only from white Malvasia grapes, hence the color.*

White

Collecting grapes in tall wicker baskets for transport to the wineries

How Port is Made

The climax of the Douro farmers' year comes in late September. Bands of pickers from the outlying provinces congregate in the Douro valley to harvest the grapes. More than 40 varieties are used in the making of port.

Treading the grapes in stone tanks or lagares *to extract the juice is a feature of very traditional* quintas. *Some shippers believe it adds a special quality.*

Fermentation *in cement or steel tanks is a more common method. Carbon dioxide builds up within the tank, forcing the fermenting must (juice from the grapes) up a tube into an open trough at the top. The gas is released and the must sprays back over the pits and skins, in a process similar to treading.*

In the fortification *process, the semifermented must is run into a second vat where brandy – actually grape spirit – is added. This arrests the fermentation, leaving the wine sweet from natural grape sugar.*

Thousands of bottles of Graham's vintage port from 1977, one of the best years, await full maturation at the lodge in Vila Nova de Gaia.

All ports *apart from vintage are matured in oak casks in the port lodges. Once bottled, they are ready for drinking and do not require decanting.*

VINTAGE PORT

In years of outstanding quality, shippers may declare their best wine as "vintage" 18 months after the harvest. It is bottled six months later and begins its long, slow maturation. Shippers usually declare a "Vintage Year" about three times per decade. The minimum period for a good vintage to mature is about 15 years, but the best ones continue to improve indefinitely. Always decant vintage port before drinking it.

The following vintages are now ready to drink:

1960 Hard to find these days, but soft, mellow, and mature if you do.

1963 A classic, full-bodied, rich vintage.

1966 A high-quality, low-yielding vintage; in short supply, but perhaps currently at its peak.

1970 All-time great vintage; magnificent now and will go on improving.

1975 Comparatively thin, unlikely to improve.

Vintages not ready for drinking yet:

1977 A superb vintage, possibly a second great from the 1970s.

1980 Initially viewed as mediocre by the experts, some of whom are now changing their minds.

1983 Full and powerful; may turn out to be excellent.

1985 Maturing quite rapidly; could be drinkable within a few years.

1991 Declared by most shippers, though a few maintain the quality was not high enough.

1994 The most recent declaration, confidently expected to prove the best vintage year in a decade.

Graham's 1980 vintage

Regional Food: Northern Portugal

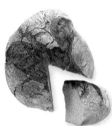

THE LUSH MINHO IS CREDITED with the invention of many recipes that have been adopted nationally, the ubiquitous *caldo verde* soup being just one example. The coast is rich in fish, although salt cod *(bacalhau)* is actually imported, and lamprey and salmon from the Minho's rivers are popular. Cumin, oddly enough, is used to spice dishes. The robust diet of Trás-os-Montes echoes the austere landscape: pork, both fresh and cured, features widely, and nuts and dried beans often add body to dishes. The local sweet tooth ensures the *pastelarias* have delicious pastries.

Walnuts

Broa *is a golden, close-textured corn-bread with a thick, crunchy crust.*

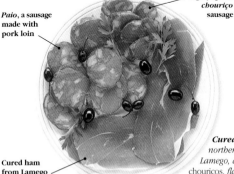

Highly spiced chouriço sausage

Paio, a sausage made with pork loin

Monte, *from Trás-os-Montes, is a smooth, creamy cheese made with cow's and ewe's milk.*

Cured ham from Lamego

Cured meats *play an important role in northern dishes. The best hams are from Lamego, and Trás-os-Montes produces fine chouriços, flavored with paprika and often wine.*

Bola *is popular at Easter and for picnics. A rich bread dough is layered with a mixture of cured meats into a kind of pie.*

Pastéis de bacalhau *are a national addiction. These little salt-cod cakes are eaten cold as a snack or hot as a main dish.*

Caldo verde, *Portugal's most famous soup, gets its vibrant color from its main ingredient: couve galega, a type of kale.*

Sopa de castanhas piladas, *a winter soup from Trás-os-Montes, is made with dried chestnuts, beans, and rice.*

Bacalhau à Gomes de Sá *is a creation from Oporto of salt cod, potato, and onion layers, topped with egg and olives.*

Truta de Barroso *uses local trout stuffed with ham and then fried in bacon fat. It is served with boiled potatoes.*

Feijoada, *popular throughout Portugal, is a stew of kidney or butter beans and cured meats, with many local variations.*

Vitela no espeto *is loin of veal barbecued (ideally on a spit), then sprinkled with oil and covered to draw out the juices.*

Rojões, *a widely popular and variable dish, uses cumin to spice pork, which is then cooked in wine and garlic to a rich stew.*

Chouriço

Morcela

Pork

Chicken

Beef

Cozido à portuguesa *is a national dish with its origins in Trás-os-Montes, where it is a Carnaval specialty. A variety of meats, sausages, and vegetables are served in their own broth.*

Morcela

Farinheira

These sausages *are two of the many types of cured meats used in dishes such as* cozido à portuguesa. *Farinheira is made from pork, wine, and flour, while morcela is a well-seasoned blood sausage. It is good sliced and fried or barbecued.*

Torta de Viana *is a sponge cake roll with a sweetened egg filling.*

Toucinho do céu *is a rich almond and cinnamon cake; it means "bacon from heaven."*

Papos de anjo (angel's breasts) *take their curious name from their delicate shape.*

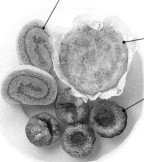

Sopa dourada, *sponge cake under a blanket of ground almonds and egg yolk, was created in Viana do Castelo.*

Cakes *fulfill the Portuguese passion for sweet things. Northern specialties are rich and velvety smooth, addictively sugary, and often flavored with cinnamon.*

Pudim Abade de Priscos, *named after the abbot who invented it, is flavored with port, spices, and lemon.*

DRINKS

Wine and port apart, northern grapes produce *bagaceira*, a clear distillation of wine lees, and Portuguese spirit, *aguardente*. The region has many spa towns, such as Pedras Salgadas, that provide excellent mineral waters.

Mineral water from Pedras Salgadas   **Aguardente**

DOURO AND TRÁS-OS-MONTES

O N ITS WAY TO THE ATLANTIC, *the Douro or "Golden River" weaves its scenic path through deep-cleft gorges, terraced with thousands of vineyards, to the historic city of Oporto, home of port wine. To the northeast, the plateaus and mountain ranges of Trás-os-Montes, "Behind the Mountains," form Portugal's wildest region.*

As early as the 9th century BC, Phoenician merchants arrived in the Douro estuary to trade. The Romans later developed the settlements of Portus and Cale on either side of the river, and the names subsequently united, as Portucale, to denote the region between the Minho and Douro rivers. This was the nucleus of the kingdom of Portugal *(see pp42–3)*. The estuary and coastal strip, or Douro Litoral, is now a mix of fishing ports, beach resorts, and industrial zones, while Portus, at the river's mouth, became Oporto, the regional capital and Portugal's second city.

Rich from centuries of trade, cosmopolitan Oporto is at once modern and steeped in the past, its waterfront and higgledy-piggledy streets a delight to explore. From its hillside, Oporto looks across the Douro to the lodges that nurture the precious wine to which the city gave its name: port.

The upper reaches of the river are devoted to the cultivation of grapes for port, the landscape shaped by endless vineyards and wine estates *(quintas)*.

In contrast with the thriving Douro valley, Trás-os-Montes is remote and untamed, a refuge in the past of religious and political exiles. The hard life and lack of opportunity to better it have depopulated the land; those who remain till the fields and herd their flocks in the unforgiving climate, according to the rhythm of the seasons.

The rural north clings closely to tradition, and local *festas* are some of the country's most colorful *(see pp226–7)*. Outside influences are beginning to make an impact on Trás-os-Montes, but for the visitor it remains a land of quiet stone villages amid fields of rye and moorland, where the wild Parque Natural de Montesinho stretches from Bragança to the Spanish border.

Terraced vineyards covering the hillsides between Pinhão and Alijó, in the valley of the Upper Douro

◁ **Oporto's Barredo district, where houses are squeezed into the steep maze of ancient alleys**

Exploring the Douro and Trás-os-Montes

OPORTO ITSELF IS SO FULL OF INTEREST that many visitors venture no farther. But to follow the Douro upstream is to discover a world of neat terraced vineyards and prosperous *quintas*, all dedicated to producing wine and port. Besides Oporto, either Peso da Régua or the pilgrimage town of Lamego would make a convenient base from which to explore the area.

Trás-os-Montes is Portugal's poorest and least-known region. Its isolated capital, Bragança, is full of historic associations and lies on the edge of the wild terrain of the Montesinho preserve. Between here and Chaves is spectacular country seldom visited by tourists.

Rocky outcrops of the Parque Natural do Alvão

SIGHTS AT A GLANCE

Oporto's dockside, the Cais da Ribeira, in the early morning

KEY

▰▰▰	Highway
▰▰	Major road
▭	Minor road
◿	Scenic route
〜	River
☆	Vista

Port country near Pinhão, where vineyards clothe the banks of the Douro

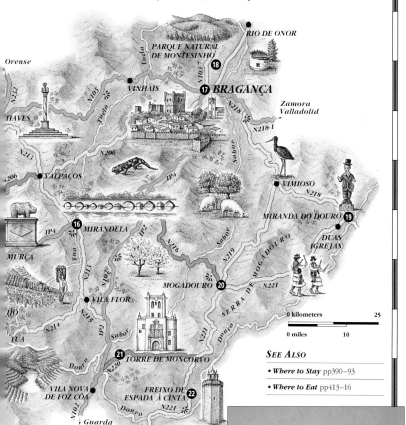

Orense

RIO DE ONOR

PARQUE NATURAL
DE MONTESINHO

N103-7 **18**

VINHAIS

17 **BRAGANÇA**

*Zamora
Valladolid*

CHAVES

N218-1

VALPAÇOS

IP4

VIMIOSO
N218

16 MIRANDELA

MIRANDA DO DOURO **19**

DUAS
IGREJAS

MURÇA

MOGADOURO **20**

VILA FLOR

0 kilometers   25

0 miles   10

SEE ALSO

• **Where to Stay** pp390–93

• **Where to Eat** pp413–16

21 TORRE DE MONCORVO

VILA NOVA
DE FOZ CÔA

FREIXO DE
ESPADA À CINTA **22**
N221

↓ *Guarda*

GETTING AROUND

With the frenetic tempo of traffic in Oporto, it is best
to negotiate the inner city by bus, taxi, or on foot. Boat
trips from Oporto are a good way to see the varied
Douro landscape at a relaxed pace. Trains link Oporto
to the major towns of the north and also run along
the Douro valley. Services are less frequent beyond
Peso da Régua, but a trip alongside the Douro is highly
recommended. In Trás-os-Montes, public transportation is minimal and driving is the most convenient
way to explore this region, especially now that the IP4
links Vila Real and Bragança. However, the state of
repair of many minor roads leaves a lot to be desired.

**The Sabor near Bragança, on the southern
edge of the Parque Natural de Montesinho**

Oporto ●

Ｅ VER SINCE THE ROMANS built a fort here, where their trading route crossed the Douro, Oporto has prospered from commerce. Quick to expel the Moors in the 11th century and to profit from provisioning crusaders en route to the Holy Land, resourceful Oporto took advantage of the wealth generated by Portugal's maritime discoveries in the 15th and 16th centuries. Later, the wine trade with Britain compensated for the loss of the lucrative spice trade. Still a thriving industrial center and the country's second largest city, Oporto successfully blends commercial hubbub with unpretentious charm. Known locally as Porto, it has acquired the Anglicized name of Oporto (literally, "the port").

Lion and eagle statue, Rotunda da Boavista

Market stalls set up in the shadow of the cathedral

The Cathedral District

Oporto's cathedral *(see p240)* crowns the city's upper level, and in the surrounding streets are a variety of monuments to the city's past, including the Renaissance church of Santa Clara *(see p239)* and the turn-of-the-century train station of São Bento *(see p239)*, alongside bustling street markets.

Beneath the towering cathedral lies the crowded Barredo, a quarter seemingly unchanged since medieval days, where balconied houses cling to each other and to the vertiginous hillside, forming a maze of ancient alleys; some are no more than outside staircases.

Ribeira

This riverside quarter is a warren of narrow, twisting streets and shadowy arcades. Behind brightly tiled or pastel-painted façades, many in faded glory, a working population earns its living, hangs out the wash, chats, and mixes in lively street scenes. Restoration of this atmospheric district is attracting a growing number of restaurants and nightclubs.

Washing hanging out to dry in a typical street in the Ribeira district

Cordoaria

The Cordoaria gardens, popular with students at the nearby university, lie in the lee of the Torre dos Clérigos *(see p241)*. The steep streets around are full of interesting shops.

A shop in the Cordoaria area specializing in *bacalhau* (salt cod)

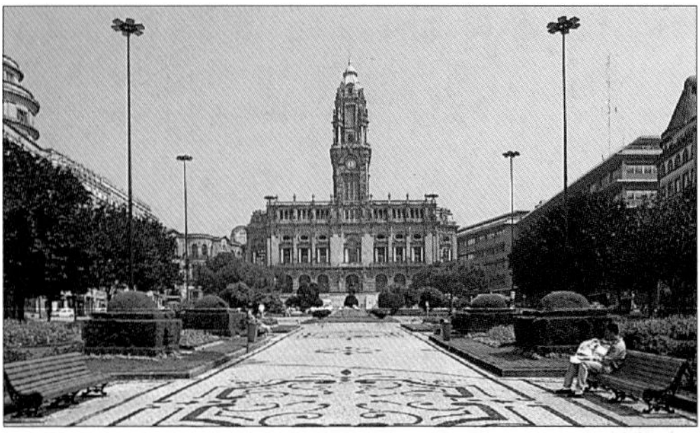

Looking north up the Avenida dos Aliados to the Câmara Municipal

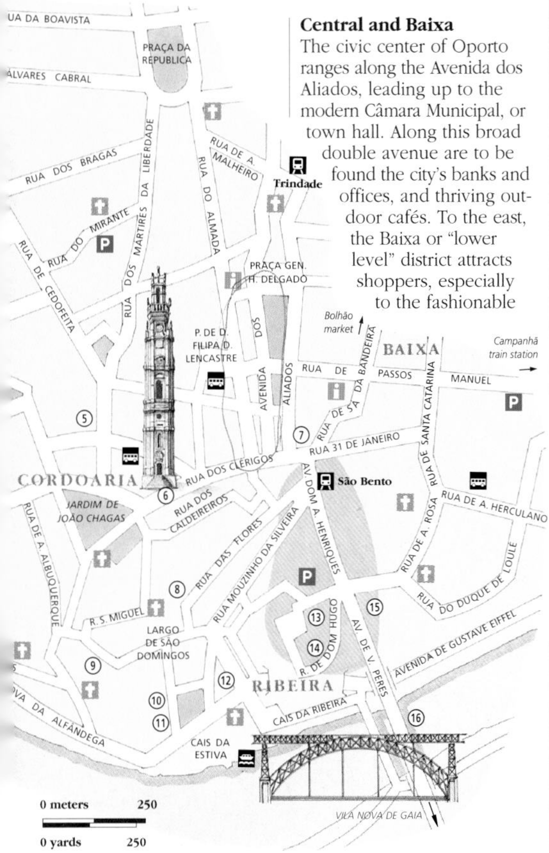

Central and Baixa

The civic center of Oporto ranges along the Avenida dos Aliados, leading up to the modern Câmara Municipal, or town hall. Along this broad double avenue are to be found the city's banks and offices, and thriving outdoor cafés. To the east, the Baixa or "lower level" district attracts shoppers, especially to the fashionable leather and jewelry shops in and around the pedestrian Rua de Santa Catarina and the parallel Rua Sá da Bandeira. Between them lies the two-tier covered Bolhão market. Noisy and exuberant, it provides an entertaining view of Oporto daily life. Everything can be bought here, from fresh fruit and vegetables to household goods and pets.

Key

- Cathedral District *pp238–9*
- 🚆 Train station
- 🚌 Main bus terminal
- ⛴ Riverboat service
- [P] Parking
- ℹ Tourist information
- ✝ Church

Visitors' Checklist

Map C2. 👥 *300,000.*
✈ *Francisco Sá Carneiro 10 km (6 miles) N (22-948 21 41).*
🚆 *National: Campanhã (22-536 41 41); Regional: São Bento (22-200 27 22); Trains to Póvoa de Varzim and Guimarães: Trindade (22-200 52 24).* 🚌 *Praça Dona Filipa de Lencastre; Rua Alexandre Herculano; Praça da Galiza.*
ℹ *Rua Clube dos Fenianos 25 (22-200 58 70); Rua Infante Dom Henrique 63 (22-200 97 70).*
🎉 *Jun 10–29: Festas da Cidade; Jun 23–24: São João do Porto.*

Boavista

The busy traffic artery of the Avenida da Boavista is lined with hotels, residential blocks, and shops. In the center of the Rotunda da Boavista, as Praça de Mouzinho de Albuquerque is known locally, a statue of a jaunty lion (the Luso-British forces) crushing an eagle (the French) marks the victory in the Peninsular War. South of the rotunda is one of the best shopping centers in the city.

Oporto City Center

Casa-Museu Guerra Junqueiro (14)
Feitoria Inglesa (12)
Igreja do Carmo (5)
Igreja dos Clérigos (6)
Igreja dos Congregados (7)
Igreja da Misericórdia (8)
Jardim do Palácio de Cristal (3)
Museu de Etnografia e História (9)
Museu Romântico (2)
Museu Soares dos Reis (4)
Palácio da Bolsa (10)
Ponte de Dom Luís I (16)
Santa Clara (15)
São Francisco (11)
São Martinho de Cedofeita (1)
Sé (13)

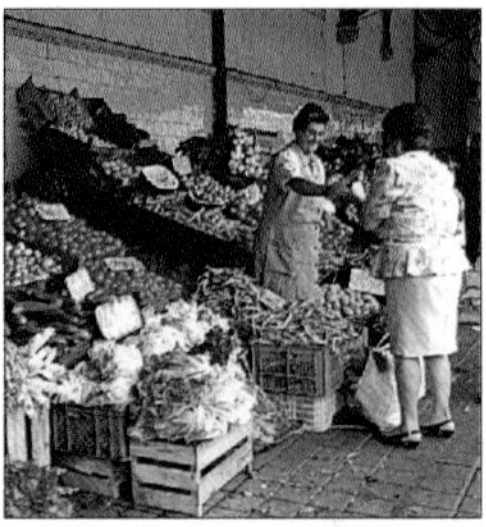

Fresh fruit and vegetables in the colorful Bolhão market

Street-by-Street: Oporto's Cathedral District

ARCHAEOLOGICAL EXCAVATIONS show that Penaventosa Hill, now the site of Oporto's cathedral, or Sé, was inhabited as early as 3,000 years ago. In its elevated position, the cathedral is a useful landmark, and its terrace provides an excellent orientation point. The broad Avenida de Vímara Peres, named after the military hero who expelled the Moors from the city in AD 868, sweeps south past the huddle of steep alleys and stairways of the Barredo. The view to the north is toward the extraordinarily embellished São Bento station and the busy commercial heart of the city.

Rua das Flores
Behind the traditional store-fronts in the Street of Flowers are many of the city's best jewelers and goldsmiths.

Street markets near the Sé offer fresh fish, fruit, and vegetables alongside household goods, bric-a-brac, and souvenirs.

RUA DAS FLORES

R. MOUZINHO D. SILVE

RUA ESCURA

CALÇADA DE VANDOMA

RUA DE DOM HUGO

Terreiro da Sé
This broad open terrace offers a wonderful panorama of the city. In one corner stands a Manueline pillory, complete with hooks.

TERREIRO DA SÉ

Former bishops' palace

★ Sé
Although imposing and perhaps a little forbidding, Oporto's cathedral contains many small-scale treasures. This 17th-century gilded painting of the Last Supper is in the Capela de São Vicente (see p240).

The Casa-Museu Guerra Junqueiro is a charming museum in a house that once belonged to the 19th-century poet *(see p240)*.

Ponte de Dom Luís I

Praça da
Liberdade

Praça de Almeida Garrett
*Traffic hurries by oblivious to
the architectural diversity of
this busy square in the
center of Oporto.*

PRAÇA
DE
ALMEIDA
GARRETT

RUA DO LOUREIRO

AVENIDA DOM AFONSO HENRIQUES

RUA CHÃ

★ São Bento Station
*Oporto's central railroad station, on the site
of an earlier monastery, was completed in
1916. Inside is a feast of* azulejos *by Jorge
Colaço (see p23), depicting early modes of
transport, rural festivities, and historic scenes.*

**The Fernandine
Walls**, named
after Fernando I,
were built in the
14th century;
only fragments
remain here and
along the Cais
da Ribeira *(see
p236).*

Santa Clara
*The Renaissance
church of Santa Clara
presents a strong con-
trast between its simple
external façade and the
opulent gilded wood-
work of its interior.*

RUA SARAIVA DE CARVALHO

0 meters   50

0 yards   50

KEY

– – – Suggested route

STAR SIGHTS

★ **Sé**

★ **São Bento Station**

Exploring Oporto

THROUGHOUT OPORTO THERE IS EVIDENCE of the wealth that flowed into the city from the 15th century onward. Trade in the commodities from Portugal's newly claimed lands *(see pp48–9)* brought Brazilian gold and exotic woods to embellish Oporto's churches, and prosperous merchants spent prodigiously on paintings and *azulejos*. The extravagant stock exchange, the Palácio da Bolsa, and the exclusive Feitoria Inglesa are later reminders of the city's continued importance as a trading center.

🔒 Sé

Terreiro da Sé. **[** 22-205 48 37. **○** Mon–Sat. **●** public hols. **▨** to cloisters.

Built as a fortress church in the 12th and 13th centuries, the cathedral has since been so modified that it lacks a unified style. The only noteworthy survival from the 13th century is the beautiful rose window in the west front. In the small chapel to the left of the chancel is a silver retable of dazzling workmanship, saved from invading French troops in 1809 by means of a hastily raised plaster wall. The south transept gives access to the 14th-century cloisters and the Capela de São Vicente. Niccolò Nasoni's graceful 18th-century staircase leads to the upper levels. Here, vibrant *azulejo* panels depict the life of the Virgin and Ovid's *Metamorphoses*, and there is a splendid panorama of the city.

Portuguese water jug, Museu Guerra Junqueiro

The Gothic cloisters on the south side of the Sé

🏛 Casa-Museu Guerra Junqueiro

Rua de Dom Hugo 32. **[** 22-200 36 89. **○** Tue–Sat. **●** public hols. **▨**

The former home of the poet and fiery Republican activist, Guerra Junqueiro (1850–1923), is an 18th-century Baroque gem. From the tranquil courtyard, visitors enter the poet's private collection, which ranges from Portuguese furniture and rare ceramics to Flemish tapestries and a remarkable set of Spanish alabaster sculptures. On elegant tables in the Dom João V Room there is a colorful parade of Chinese dogs.

♨ Feitoria Inglesa

Rua do Infante Dom Henrique 8. **[** 22-339 29 80.

Closed to the public unless by invitation from a member, the "English factory" is the headquarters of the port-shippers' British Association. It was built to the design of a Robert Adam town house in 1790. A sweeping staircase leads up to the Map Room and a grand ballroom. This exclusive, male domain invited its first ladies to dinner in 1843.

♨ Palácio da Bolsa

Rua Ferreira Borges. **[** 22-339 90 00. **○** May–Oct: daily; Nov–Apr: Mon–Fri. **●** public hols in winter. **▨ ▮** compulsory.

Where the monastery of São Francisco once stood, the city's merchants built the stock exchange, or Bolsa, in 1842. The Tribunal do Comércio, where Oporto's mercantile

The magnificently gilded Arabian Room in Oporto's Palácio da Bolsa

law was upheld, is full of historic interest, and has a small adjoining picture gallery. But the glittering highlight is the Arabian Room. This galleried salon, its convoluted blue and gold arabesques inspired by Granada's Alhambra, makes a setting fit for Scheherazade.

🏛 Museu de Etnografia e História

Largo de São João Novo 11. **[** 22-200 20 10. **●** for restoration.

Housed in an imposing 18th-century palace, the museum covers the life and customs of the Douro. As well as archaeological discoveries and exhibits of local ceramics, there are displays of rural costumes, animal traps, coins, and such curiosities as the city's first elevator (1910). Adding to the interest of this collection are reconstructions of an old wine cellar and a weaver's workshop.

🔒 Casa da Misericórdia

Rua das Flores 15. **[** 22-200 09 41. **○** Mon–Fri. **●** public hols. **▨ ♿**

This religious hospice, alongside its imposing church, was founded in the 16th century. Its most precious possession is the masterful *Fons Vitae* (Fountain of Life), donated by Manuel I in about 1520. The artist's identity remains unproven, but Van der Weyden and Holbein have both been suggested. The picture shows the king with his family and nobles kneeling before the crucified Christ.

SÃO FRANCISCO'S TREE OF JESSE

Illustrating biblical episodes, either in stained-glass windows or as elaborate carvings, was a common form of "Bible teaching" before literacy became widespread. A popular subject was Christ's genealogy, showing his descent from the kings of Judah and Israel. This was commonly rendered as an actual tree, tracing the family line back through Joseph to the father of King David, Jesse of Bethlehem.

São Francisco's Tree, in gilded and painted wood, was carved between 1718 and 1721 by Filipe da Silva and António Gomes. Its sinuous branches and trunk, sprouting from a reclining Jesse, support a dozen expressive figures, culminating in Christ flanked by his mother, Mary, and St. Joseph.

Virgin Mary

Jesus Christ

Joseph

Solomon, who succeeded his father, David, was famed for his wisdom and for the building of the Temple in Jerusalem.

Jesse is shown with the roots of the Tree springing from his loins. His youngest son was David, the slayer of Goliath, who became king of Israel and Judah.

King David, identified by his harp

🅰 São Francisco

Rua da Bolsa 7. ☏ 22-200 64 93.
⭘ Mon–Sat. **Catacombs** ⭘ May–Sep: Mon–Sat. 🎦

Construction of São Francisco began in the 14th century, but it is the 18th-century interior that amazes visitors. Over 200 kg (450 lb) of gold encrusting the high altar, columns, and pillars is wrought into cherubs, garlands, and cavorting animals, reaching a crescendo with the Tree of Jesse on the north wall. A tour includes the catacombs and treasures from the church's monastery, destroyed in 1832.

🅰 Igreja dos Congregados

Praça de Almeida Garrett. ☏ 22-200 29 48. ⭘ daily. ⬤ public hols (pm).
♿ via side entrance.

The modern tiles clothing the façade of this 17th-century church are by Jorge Colaço (see p23). They depict scenes from the life of St. Antony, and provide a dignified presence amid the traffic that clogs this part of the city.

🅰 Igreja dos Clérigos

Rua São Filipe Néri. ☏ 22-200 17 29. ⭘ Thu–Tue.
Tower ⭘ daily. 🎦

This hilltop ensemble of church and tower is an unmistakable landmark. Built in the 18th century by Niccolò Nasoni, the church's oval interior was the first in Portugal.

The soaring Torre dos Clérigos with which the architect complemented his design is, at 75 m (246 ft), still one of the tallest buildings in Portugal. The dizzying 240-step climb is worth it for the superb views of the river, the coastline, and the Douro valley.

Torre dos Clérigos, Oporto's landmark and panoramic vista

São Francisco's extravagant interior

Detail of the *azulejo* panel on the side wall of the Igreja do Carmo

🔒 Igreja do Carmo
Rua do Carmo. **📞** 22-207 84 00.
⭕ *daily.* ♿
This characteristic example of Portuguese Baroque architecture was constructed by José Figueiredo Seixas between 1750 and 1768. Its most notable feature is the immense *azulejo* panel covering one outside wall. Designed by Silvestro Silvestri, it depicts the legendary founding of the Carmelite order on Mount Carmel.

The earlier Igreja das Carmelitas next door was completed in 1628 in a combination of Classical and Baroque styles. It is now part of a barracks.

🏛 Museu Soares dos Reis
Rua Dom Manuel II. **📞** 22-339 37 70.
⭕ *Tue–Sun.* ⚫ *public hols.*
The elegant Carrancas Palace, built in the 18th century, has been a Jewish textile workshop, a royal abode, and, in the Peninsular War, a military headquarters. In 1809 Oporto was in French hands, and Marshal Soult and his troops were quartered here. They were ousted in a surprise attack by Arthur Wellesley, later Duke of Wellington, who then calmly installed himself at the marshal's dinner table.

Today, the palace provides an appropriate setting for an outstanding museum, named after António Soares dos Reis, the country's leading 19th-century sculptor. Prominently featured is the display of Portuguese art. This includes paintings by the 16th-century master Frey Carlos, and the Impressionist Henrique Pousão. Also hung here are landscapes of Oporto by the French artist Jean Pillement (1728–1808). The star sculpture exhibit, *O Desterrado* (The Exile), is Soares dos Reis's own marvel of pensive tension in marble, completed in

O Desterrado b
Soares dos Rei

A River View of Oporto

FLOWING OVER 927 km (576 miles) from its source in Spain to the Atlantic, the Douro has been linked with the fortunes of Oporto since time immemorial. There is an unsubstantiated story that Henry the Navigator, patron of Portuguese explorers, *(see p49)*, was born in the waterfront Casa do Infante. The days are long since gone when ships laden with port or goods from overseas would moor here, but the river continues to be a focal point of the city. A river cruise is a chance to appreciate Oporto from a different viewpoint.

Most riverboat operators are based in the shadow of the swooping curve of the splendid two-tier Ponte de Dom Luís I, linking the city to Vila Nova de Gaia on the southern bank. Designed by an assistant of Gustave Eiffel, it was opened in 1886. The Dona Maria Pia railroad bridge to the east was built by Eiffel himself in 1877, and the river is now spanned by three more bridges, including the concrete Ponte da Arrábida, completed in 1963.

Vila Nova de Gaia
is home of the port lodges *(see p247).*

Ponte da Arrábida

Dockside of the Cais da Estiva

1874. Further sections display Portuguese pottery, Limoges enamels, porcelain, and decorative art. Historical exhibits in the museum include a 15th-century silver bust of São Pantaleão, patron saint of Oporto, and a sword owned by the first king of Portugal.

⌂ São Martinho de Cedofeita

Rua Aníbal Cunha 193. **C** *22-200 56 20.* ◯ *daily.* ♿

Constructed in Romanesque style in the 12th century, this plain little church is the oldest in the city. One explanation of its name is that an earlier church on the site was raised in much haste (*cedo feita* means "soon built") when St. Martin converted Theodomir, the King of the Suevi, to Christianity in the 6th century.

🏛 Museu Romântico

Rua de Entre-Quintas 220. **C** *22-609 11 31.* ◯ *Tue–Sat & Sun pm.* ◯ *public hols.* ♿

The Quinta da Macieirinha was briefly the residence of the abdicated King Carlo Alberto of Sardinia (1798–1849), who lived here for the final two months of his life. In 1972 the upper floor of the mansion

Temporary exhibits in the billiards room of the Museu Romântico

was converted into a museum. The well-proportioned rooms looking out over the river display to advantage delicately finished French, German, and Portuguese furniture, as well as rugs, ceramics, and miscellaneous exhibits. Among the oil paintings and watercolors displayed here are portraits of Baron Forrester *(see p252)* and Almeida Garrett, the great Portuguese Romantic poet, playwright, and author.

On the ground floor of the Quinta da Macieirinha, the Port Wine Institute operates the Solar do Vinho do Porto. In this unexpected bar it is possible to

choose from a tasting list of over 150 varieties of port, then relax in the secluded garden and enjoy the view across the Douro.

♣ Jardim do Palácio de Cristal

Rua Dom Manuel II. ◯ *daily.*

Inspired by the Crystal Palace of London's Great Exhibition in 1851, Oporto's own crystal palace was begun in 1861. The steel and glass structure of the original was replaced in the 1950s by the Sports Pavilion, an ungainly shape dubbed "the half-orange" by local wits. Concerts are occasionally held here, and the leisure gardens around the dome are enlivened by a fair at *festa* time.

Cyclists in the Jardim do Palácio de Cristal

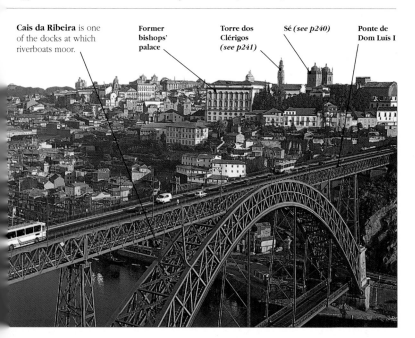

Cais da Ribeira is one of the docks at which riverboats moor.

Former bishops' palace

Torre dos Clérigos *(see p241)*

Sé *(see p240)*

Ponte de Dom Luís I

Oporto: Farther Afield

Away from the city center, Oporto has many additional places of interest. Crossing the Ponte de Dom Luís I brings you to Vila Nova de Gaia, the home of port, and the Mosteiro da Serra do Pilar, with one of the finest views of the old city. In the northern and western suburbs are several fascinating attractions, from the great church of the Hospitallers at Leça do Bailio, north of Oporto, to the latest developments in Portuguese art exhibited in the palatial Art Deco setting of the Casa de Serralves.

Along the coast, beyond the river-mouth castle at Foz do Douro, lies Matosinhos. Despite its industrial port, Matosinhos is famous for its seafood. The beaches are the main draw along the coast south of Oporto.

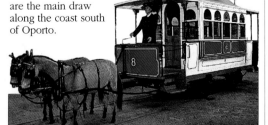

A trolley, once a feature of Oporto, in the Museu do Carro Eléctrico

⛪ Mosteiro da Serra do Pilar

Serra do Pilar. 【 22-379 53 85. ○ by appt only.

It is a steep walk up to this circular 16th-century church, but worth it. From the terrace, the future Duke of Wellington planned his surprise attack on the French in 1809. It is easy to see the advantage gained, for the panoramic view takes in the port lodges below, the sweep of the Douro River, and the old city on the far side.

🏛 Museu do Carro Eléctrico

Alameda Basílio Teles 51. 【 22-606 40 54. ○ Tue–Sun. ⚄

Trolleys, once the backbone of the city's transit system, have been trundled into retirement, but this museum keeps their memory alive. Among the gleaming beauties preserved here are No. 22, introduced in 1895 as the first electric trolley on the Iberian Peninsula, and No. 8, from 1872, which relied on mules for traction.

Special excursions are run for a substantial charge, but you can enjoy a similar experience on the No. 18, Oporto's last trolley, which leaves from near the museum, looping north to end at Boavista (see pp236–7).

🏛 Fundação de Serralves

Rua de Serralves 977. 【 22-617 26 94. ○ Tue–Fri (pm), Sat & Sun. ● Jan 1, Dec 25. ⚄

The clean Art Deco lines of the 1930s Casa de Serralves, surrounded by its magnificent garden, provide the perfect setting for displaying contemporary art. Regularly changing exhibitions by the foundation offers insights into the modern developments in Portuguese art, including new trends in sculpture and architecture.

🏛 Casa-Museu Fernando de Castro

Rua Costa Cabral 716. 【 22-509 46 25. ○ daily.

The former residence of the businessman, collector, and poet, Fernando de Castro (1888–1950), was donated to the state by his sister in 1951. His collection ranges from religious sculpture saved from disbanded churches to works by modern artists and includes a painting of the infant Jesus attributed to Josefa de Óbidos (see p51). Also of special interest are figurines from the 19th and 20th centuries by Teixeira Lopes, both father and son.

Environs: Forts around the river mouth, such as **Castelo da Foz** at Foz do Douro and **Castelo do Queijo** just to the north, are reminders that for centuries the coast and ships were under constant threat from the Spanish and pirates.

The church of **Bom Jesus**, near Matosinhos, was reconstructed by Niccolò Nasoni in the 18th century. Each June, pilgrims come here to honor a wooden statue of Christ. Found on the beach in the 10th century, it was allegedly carved by the disciple Nicodemus.

The 14th-century fortified **Igreja do Mosteiro** at Leça do Bailio, 8 km (5 miles) north of Oporto, was Portugal's first headquarters of the Order of Hospitallers. The church is graced with elegant Gothic arches, finely sculpted capitals, and a splendid rose window.

The Art Deco Casa de Serralves, a forum for modern art

◁ *Barcos rabelos* moored beside the dock at Vila Nova de Gaia

Vila Nova de Gaia

Taylor's port

AFONSO III, IN DISPUTE with the Bishop of Oporto over shipping tolls, established a rival port at Vila Nova de Gaia. In 1253, they reluctantly agreed to share the levies. Today the heart of Vila Nova de Gaia is devoted mostly to the maturation and shipping of port *(see pp252–3)*. Although the regulation that port could be made only in Vila Nova de Gaia was relaxed in 1987, this is still very much the center of production. Every alley is lined with the lodges or *armazéns* (there are no cellars here) in which port is blended and aged.

Guided tours *are a chance to see how port is made* (see pp228–9) *and usually end with a tasting to demonstrate the different styles.*

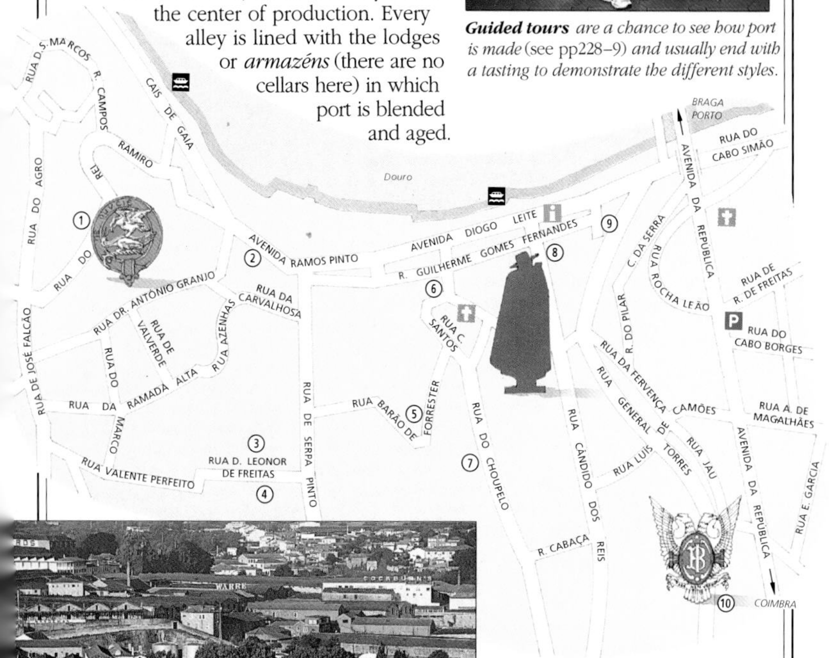

The port lodges *dominate Vila Nova de Gaia. Over 50 port companies are based in these narrow streets, aging and blending most of the world's supply of port beneath a sea of red roofs emblazoned with world-famous names.*

PORT LODGES

Barros (4)	Graham (1)
Borges (10)	Ramos Pinto (6)
Cálem (9)	Sandeman (8)
Cockburn (3)	Taylor (7)
Ferreira (2)	Vasconcelos (5)

VISITING THE LODGES

Joining a tour: Lodges listed here are among those offering tours. Booking is not usually necessary, but contact a lodge beforehand to confirm times; the tourist office at Avenida Diogo Leite 242 (22-30 19 02) can supply addresses and telephone numbers.

Opening times: Variable. Usually Mon–Fri; some also on weekends. Most close on public holidays.

KEY

- ⛴ Boat trips
- [P] Parking
- [i] Tourist information
- ✝ Church

0 meters 250

0 yards 250

The former monastery of São Bento at Santo Tirso, now a college

Santo Tirso ❷

Road map C2. 🏃 *12,000.* 🚊 🚌
ℹ️ *Praça 25 de Abril (252-85 11 34).*
🏛️ *Mon.*

SANTO TIRSO, a major textile center, lies beside the River Ave. The town's most notable building is the former monastery of **São Bento**. Founded by the Benedictines in the 8th century, the monastery was later rebuilt, then modified in the 17th century. The pairs of columns in the 14th-century Gothic cloister are graced with richly carved capitals.

The monastery is now an agricultural college, but houses the **Museu Abade Pedrosa**, featuring local archaeological finds, including stone axes, bronze armlets, and ceramics.

🏛️ Museu Abade Pedrosa
Rua Unisco Godiniz. 📞 *252-83 04 00.* 🕐 *Tue–Sun.* ⬤ *public hols.*

The sanctuary of Nossa Senhora da Piedade in Penafiel

ENVIRONS: At Roriz, 13 km (8 miles) east of Santo Tirso, the Romanesque church of **São Pedro** perches above the Vizela valley. A date of 1228 is carved in the porch, although there are claims that a church may have stood here as early as the 8th century. Above the portal is a fine rose window. Set apart from the church are an attractive bell tower and the ruins of the monastic cloister.

Sanfins de Ferreira, 5 km (3 miles) farther east, is the hilltop site of a *citânia*, an Iron Age citadel, probably inhabited from around the 6th century BC. Traces remain of a triple ring of defensive walls around about 100 huts, and there is also a small museum on the site. The guard next door will let you in on public holidays.

♄ Sanfins de Ferreira
Sanfins, signposted off N209.
📞 *255-86 20 29.* 🕐 *Tue–Sun.*

Penafiel ❸

Road map C2. 🏃 *8,000.* 🚌
ℹ️ *Avenida Sacadura Cabral 90 (255-712 561).* 🏛️ *10 & 20 of month.*

THE GRANITE TOWN of Penafiel stands on a hilltop above the River Sousa. Apart from an elegant Renaissance-style **Igreja Matriz**, there is also a sanctuary, **Nossa Senhora da Piedade**, built in 1908 in a curious medley of Neo-Gothic and Byzantine styles. Penafiel is chiefly known, however, as the regional center for *vinho verde* production *(see pp28–9).*

ENVIRONS: One of the region's foremost estates producing *vinho verde* is the picturesque **Quinta da Aveleda**, which lies just north of Penafiel.

Boelhe, around 17 km (11 miles) south of Penafiel, merits a detour for the 12th-century church of São Gens. Only 10 m (33 ft) high, and a mere 7 m (23 ft) in width and length, it is claimed to be the smallest Romanesque church in the country. Its simple design enhances the aesthetic appeal.

In the 13th-century church of São Salvador at **Paço de Sousa**, 8 km (5 miles) southwest of Penafiel, is the tomb of Egas Moniz. A figure of legendary loyalty, he was counselor to Afonso Henriques (1139–85), the first king of Portugal.

🍷 Quinta da Aveleda
Signposted from N115. 📞 *255-71 10 41.* 🕐 *Mon–Fri.* ⬤ *public hols.* 🎥 ♿ 📷 *compulsory.*

The tiny church of São Gens at Boelhe, south of Penafiel

Amarante ❹

Road map D2. 🏃 *10,000.* 🚊 🚌
ℹ️ *Alameda Teixeira de Pascoaes (255-43 22 59).* 🏛️ *Wed & Sat.*

THE PRETTY, RIVERSIDE town of Amarante is one of the gems of northern Portugal. Rows of 17th-century mansions with brightly painted wooden balconies line Amarante's narrow streets, and restaurants seat diners on terraces overhanging the river. The origins of the town are uncertain, but the first settlement here was probably around 360 BC. Much of the town was burned down in 1809, after a two-week siege by the French forces under Marshal Soult.

A recurring name in Amarante is that of São Gonçalo, a very popular saint born at the end of the 12th century. There are many stories of the dancing and festivities he organized to keep ladies from temptation by finding them husbands, and he has become associated with matchmaking and fertility. On the first weekend in June, the Festa de São Gonçalo begins with prayers for a marriage partner, followed by dancing, music, and the giving of phallic-shaped cakes.

When the old Roman bridge across the Tâmega collapsed during floods in the 13th century, it was São Gonçalo who was credited with replacing it. The present Ponte de São Gonçalo crosses to the 16th-century **Mosteiro de São Gonçalo**, where his memory lives on. In the chapel to the left of the chancel, the image on his tomb has been eroded through the embraces of thousands of devotees in search of his intercession.

Displayed in the **Museu Amadeo de Sousa-Cardoso** is a pair of exhibits linked with a fertility cult predating even São Gonçalo. The *diabo* and *diaba* are a pair of bawdy devils carved in black wood, 19th-century replacements for a more ancient duo destroyed in the Peninsular War. They became the focus of a type of local fertility rite, and were

The Ponte de São Gonçalo across the Tâmega at Amarante

threatened with burning by an outraged bishop of Braga; the *diabo* was "castrated" instead.

The museum's other prized possession is the collection of Cubist works by the artist after whom the museum is named. Amadeo de Sousa-Cardoso (1887–1918), one of Portugal's leading 20th-century artists, was a native of Amarante.

Enthusiasts of folk-dancing should not miss the *arraial*, or barn dance, held in Amarante every Thursday and Saturday between June and October.

🏛 Mosteiro de São Gonçalo
Praça da República. **☎** 255-42 20 50.
○ daily. **&**

🏛 Museu Amadeo de Sousa-Cardoso
Alameda Teixeira de Pascoaes.
☎ 255-43 26 63. **○** Tue–Sun.
⊘ public hols. **🎫**

Cinfães ❺

Road map D2. **🏠** 4,000. **🚌**
ℹ Rua Dr Flavio Resende 40 (255-56 22 32). **🎪** 10 & 26 of month.

CINFÃES LIES just above the Douro, tucked below the foothills of the Serra de Montemuro whose peaks rise over 1,000 m (3,300 ft). The town is a gateway to Lamego and the Upper Douro to the east (see pp252–3) and is surrounded by verdant scenery. Cinfães itself is an agricultural center, and local handicrafts include weaving, lacework, basketry, and the production of miniature *rabelos*, the boats that used to ship port down the river to Oporto (see p250).

ENVIRONS: Around 16 km (10 miles) west of the town, at Tarouquela, is the 12th-century church of **Santa Maria Maior**. Romanesque columns flank the portal, while later additions include the 14th-century Gothic mausoleum beside the chancel.

In the village of **Cárquere**, between Cinfães and Lamego, stands another church dedicated to the Virgin Mary. Legend tells how the sickly young Afonso Henriques, future king of Portugal, was healed at Cárquere by his devoted aide, Egas Moniz. In about 1110, guided by a dream, Moniz unearthed a buried statue of the Virgin and built a church for her. Miraculously, his young charge was cured overnight. The present church dates from the 14th or 15th century, but the finest of its treasures is a minute ivory carving of the Virgin, of unknown date.

The 12th-century church of Nossa Senhora de Cárquere, near Cinfães

Painted ceiling panels in São Nicolau, Mesão Frio's Igreja Matriz

Mesão Frio ⑥

Road map D2. 👥 *700.* 🚌
🅸 *Avenida José Maria Alpoim (254-89 01 00).* 🗓 *Fri.*

THIS SCENIC GATEWAY to the port wine-growing region enjoys a fine setting above the Douro River. Around it, the majestic tiers of the Serra do Marão rise to form a natural climatic shield for the vineyards to the east. Mesão Frio itself is known for its wickerwork and a culinary specialty, *falachas*, or chestnut cakes.

The Igreja Matriz of **São Nicolau** was rebuilt in 1877 but has fortunately retained its magnificent late 16th-century ceiling panels, each one featuring an individual portrait of a saint. The tourist office and town hall are housed in the 18th-century **cloisters** of a former Franciscan monastery.

On the western edge of the town, the lavish Baroque **Casa da Rede** can be seen from the roadside but not visited.

Peso da Régua ⑦

Road map D2. 👥 *5,500.* 🅿 🚌
🅸 *Rua da Ferreirinha (254-238 46).* 🗓 *Wed.*

DEVELOPED from the villages of Peso and Régua in the 18th century, Peso da Régua is the major hub for rail and road connections in the region.

In 1756, Régua, as the town is invariably called, was chosen by the Marquês de Pombal as the center of the demarcated region for port production. From here, *rabelos*, the traditional wooden sailing ships, transported the barrels of port through hazardous gorges to Vila Nova de Gaia *(see p247).* They continued to ply the river even after the advent of the Douro railroad in the 1880s offered a faster and safer means of travel. Régua suffered frequently in the past from severe floods, and these are still a threat, although they have lessened since dams were built across the Douro in the 1970s and 1980s.

Visitors to Régua usually pause only briefly on their way to explore the "port country" *(see pp252–3)*, but it is worth seeking out the **Casa do Douro**, the administrative headquarters of the Port Wine Institute. Its modern stained-glass windows, created by Lino António, vividly depict the history and production of port. Also displayed is a fine map of the Douro valley drawn in the mid-19th century by Baron Forrester *(see p252).*

🏦 **Casa do Douro**
Rua dos Camilos. 📞 *254-32 08 11.*
🕐 *Mon–Fri.* ⬤ *public hols.* ♿

ENVIRONS: In the surrounding countryside are some beautiful *quintas*, the country estates where port is produced. One of the nearest to Régua is the attractive **Quinta da Pacheca** at Cambres, 4 km (2 miles) to the southwest. The **Enoteca de Granjão**, in a village on the road to Mesão Frio, will organize visits to this and other port lodges, and can collect visitors from hotels or the bus or train station in Régua.

🍷 **Enoteca de Granjão**
Granjão (on N108). 📞 *254-32 27 88.*
🕐 *Tue–Sun.* ⬤ *Jan 1, Dec 25.*

Stained-glass window of the Casa do Douro, Peso da Régua, showing loaded *rabelos*

Lamego ⑧

Road map D2. 👥 *12,000.* 🚌
🅸 *Avenida Visconde Guedes Teixeira (254-620 05).* 🗓 *Thu.*

AN ATTRACTIVE TOWN within the demarcated port area, Lamego also produces wines, including Raposeira, Portugal's premier sparkling wine. This fertile region is also known for its fruit and choice hams.

In its more illustrious past, Lamego claims to have been host in 1143 to the first *cortes*, or national assembly, to recognize Afonso Henriques as first king of Portugal. The town's later economic decline was halted in the 16th century, when it turned to wine and textile production, and handsome Baroque mansions from this prosperous period are still a feature of the town. Today, the main focus of Lamego is as a pilgrimage town.

Vineyards on the slopes of the Serra do Marão around Mesão Frio

The grand staircase leading up to Nossa Senhora dos Remédios, Lamego

🏛 Nossa Senhora
dos Remédios

Monte de Santo Estêvão. ⭘ daily.

A small hilltop chapel, originally dedicated in 1391 to St. Stephen, became the focus of pilgrims devoted to the Virgin, and in 1761 Nossa Senhora dos Remédios was built on the spectacular site. The church is reached via an awe-inspiring double stairway, similar to Braga's even larger Bom Jesus (see pp278–9). Its 686 steps and nine terraces, embellished with azulejos and urns, rise to the Pátio dos Reis, a circle of noble granite figures beneath the twin-towered church. The church itself is of marginal interest, but there is a well-earned view across the town to the Douro and its tributaries.

In early September pilgrims arrive in their thousands for Lamego's Romaria de Nossa Senhora dos Remédios (see p32), many of them climbing the steps on their knees.

🏛 Sé

Largo da Sé. 🄲 254-627 66. ⭘ daily.

Lamego's Gothic cathedral, founded in 1129, retains its original square tower, while the rest of the architecture reflects modifications between the 16th and 18th centuries, including a fine Renaissance cloister graced with a dozen well-proportioned arches.

🏛 Museu de Lamego

Largo de Camões. 🄲 254-620 08. ⭘ Tue–Sun. ⭘ public hols. 🎫

One of the country's best local museums is housed in the former bishops' palace. Prominently displayed is the strikingly original Criação dos Animais (Creation of the Animals), part of a series of altar panels attributed to the great 16th-century Portuguese artist Grão Vasco (see p213). Finely worked 16th-century Flemish tapestries include a detailed life of Oedipus.

ENVIRONS: At the foot of the valley 4 km (2 miles) east, the **Capela de São Pedro de Balsemão** is said to be the oldest church in Portugal. Although much modified, the 7th-century sanctuary, of Visigothic origins, remains. Here, in an ornate tomb, lies Afonso Pires, a 14th-century bishop of Oporto. A statue of Nossa Senhora do Ó, the pregnant Virgin, is from the 15th century.

The 12th-century monastery of **São João de Tarouca**, the first Cistercian house in Portugal, lies 16 km (10 miles) south of Lamego. The interior of the church has many fine 18th-century azulejo panels, notably those in the chancel depicting the founding of the monastery, and in the sacristy, where none of the 4,709 tiles has the same design. The church also contains a remarkable St. Peter by Grão Vasco. The Count of Barcelos, bastard son of King Dinis, is buried here, his tomb adorned with vigorous scenes of a boar hunt.

Just to the northeast, **Ucanha** is famed for its fortified tollgate and bridge, imposing survivals from the 12th century.

🏛 São João de Tarouca

Signposted from N226. ⭘ Tue–Sun. ♿

The monastery church of São João de Tarouca in its peaceful setting

Port Country Tour ❾

Bottles of Graham's port

THE BARRELS OF PORT maturing in the port lodges of Vila Nova de Gaia *(see p247)* begin their life here, on the wine estates *(quintas)* of the Upper Douro *(see pp228–9)*. Centuries of toil on the poor schist have created thousands of terraces along the steep river banks, many no wider than a person's outstretched arms. An EU-funded program to dynamite and bulldoze tractor access to the terraces is labor saving, but set to change the face of the land. Many traditional *quintas*, including those indicated on the map, welcome visitors. Early autumn is the most rewarding time to tour; workers sing as they pick and celebrate a successful *vindima* or harvest.

The village and vineyards of Vale de Mendiz just before sunset

Peso da Régua ①
Régua's role as an administrative center for port and, later, for the wines of the region, goes back to 1756. The *rabelos* moored here are a reminder of how port used to be transported down to the lodges of Vila Nova de Gaia.

VILA REAL

São Martinho

N.

Paradela de Guiães

N322-2

Estrada

Corgo

Galafura

Ferrã

Quinta do Crasto

PORTO

Quinta São Domingos

N108

①

N108

Barragem da Régua

Douro

N222

Quinta São Luís

N222

N313

Folgosa

JOSEPH JAMES FORRESTER, PORT BARON

In 1831, Joseph Forrester arrived from Britain to join his uncle's wine company in Oporto, and enthusiastically set about reforming the port trade. In his 1844 treatise, *A Word or Two on Port*, he waged war on shippers who adulterated the wine. He also studied the vine blight *oidium tuckeri*, drew up remarkably detailed maps of the Douro valley, and found time to become a talented watercolorist. His contribution was such that in 1855 Pedro V bestowed on him the title of Barão. In 1862, Forrester's boat capsized at Cachão de Valeira. Dragged down by his moneybelt, he drowned, but the ladies in his company survived, buoyed up by their crinolines.

0 kilometers   5

0 miles   3

KEY

▦	Tour route
	Other roads
▬	Railroad
※	Vista

Pinhão ②
Many of the most famous names in port production have *quintas* close to this small town. Its train station is decorated with 24 dazzling *azulejo* panels depicting local scenes and folk culture.

Tips for Drivers

Tour length: *125 km (78 miles). Beyond Pinhão, steep, narrow roads can make the going slow.*
Stopping-off points: *The drive beside the Douro has several fine vistas. Alijó, Régua, and Sabrosa make good overnight stops* (see pp390–93), *and many* quintas *offer tours and port tasting.* (See also pp444–5.)

Sabrosa ③
The village of Sabrosa, set among vineyards above the Pinhão River, has a wealth of 15th-century houses. It was in one of these that the explorer Magellan *(see p48)* was born in about 1480.

Sanfins do Douro
N212
Cheires
N322
N212
Pinhão
Quinta do Bucheiro
Quinta do Casal de Celeirós
São Mamede de Ribatua
Tua
Vale de Mendiz
N322-3
N214
N214
MIRANDELA
N323
Douro
Linhares
Quinta do Castelinho
N222
Valença do Douro
Quinta do Panascal
Cachão de Valeira
N222-3
N222
Távora
Tabuaço
VILA NOVA DE FOZ CÔA

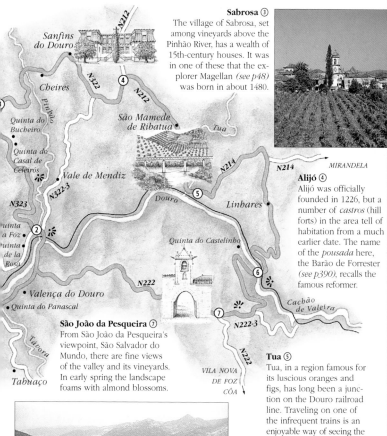

Alijó ④
Alijó was officially founded in 1226, but a number of *castros* (hill forts) in the area tell of habitation from a much earlier date. The name of the *pousada* here, the Barão de Forrester *(see p390)*, recalls the famous reformer.

São João da Pesqueira ⑦
From São João da Pesqueira's viewpoint, São Salvador do Mundo, there are fine views of the valley and its vineyards. In early spring the landscape foams with almond blossoms.

Tua ⑤
Tua, in a region famous for its luscious oranges and figs, has long been a junction on the Douro railroad line. Traveling on one of the infrequent trains is an enjoyable way of seeing the valley's terraced vineyards.

Barragem de Valeira ⑥
Until the end of the 18th century the Douro was unnavigable beyond Cachão de Valeira. Even when engineers had bypassed the worst of the rapids, this stretch of water remained treacherous – it was here that Baron Forrester met his death – until the water was tamed by the Valeira dam in 1976.

Casa de Mateus

T HE SPLENDID MANOR HOUSE, or *solar*, depicted on the labels of Mateus Rosé (*see p28*) epitomizes the flamboyance of Baroque architecture in Portugal. It was built in the early 18th century, probably by Niccolò Nasoni, for António José Botelho Mourão, among whose titles was 3rd Morgado de Mateus. His descendants still live here, but visitors can tour the gardens and part of the house, and buy the estate's produce (but not Mateus wine, which is a separate concern).

English 17th-century cupboard in the Tea Salon

The wood-paneled library, repository of many valuable works

The Manor House

Inside and out, the Casa de Mateus was conceived to present carefully created vistas and series of mirror images. A formal pool added in the 1930s continues this spirit of harmonious repetition, reflecting the main façade and its two wings.

Tours start in the first-floor entrance salon, a well-proportioned room graced by a pair of sedan chairs and with a magnificent wooden ceiling featuring family coats of arms. Doorcases and ceilings throughout the house are of richly carved chestnut. The Tea Salon has a 17th-century William and Mary cupboard and

Coat of arms on the entrance hall ceiling

matching longcase clock from England, while the Salon of the Four Seasons gets its name from the large 18th-century paintings on its walls. Many of the paintings in the house were contributed by the 4th Morgado's uncle, an archdeacon in Rome who was also responsible for the original gardens. The library, remodeled in the mid-20th century, contains volumes dating back to the 16th century, but the rarest book is in the small museum: an 1817 copy of *Os Lusíadas* (*see p188*), with engravings by leading artists. It is one of a

limited edition produced by the colorful diplomat grandson of the 3rd Morgado (his tomb is in the family chapel beside the house). Also on display in the museum is family correspondence with famous figures of the era, including Frederick the Great and Wellington.

The Gardens

Beneath the entrance staircase a dark passageway leads between the stables to an inner courtyard and out to the formal gardens on the far side of the house. Little remains of the original gardens planted by the horticultural archdeacon, and the present gardens were laid out in the 1930s and 1940s. The style, however, is of an earlier, romantic era and the complex parterres and formal beds edged with tightly clipped dwarf boxwood hedges form a living tapestry

The principal façade of the Casa de Mateus, its pinnacled symmetry reflected in a rectangular pool

Immaculate boxwood-edged flower beds in the Casa de Mateus gardens

that reflects perfectly the ornate symmetry of the house. In winter the camellias, relics from the 19th century, are a highlight of the gardens, but for most visitors the lasting memory is of the vast cedar tunnel, greatest among the many pieces of topiary here.

Beyond the formal gardens lie the well-ordered orchards and fields of the estate.

THE CEDAR TUNNEL

This celebrated feature in the Casa de Mateus garden was formed from cedars planted in 1941. It is 35 m (115 ft) long and 7.5 m (25 ft) high, the tight-knit greenery providing an aromatic walk in summer. To keep it in shape, gardeners have to scale specially fashioned outsize ladders.

Vila Real ⓫

Road map D2. 14,000. Avenida Carvalho Araújo (259-32 28 19). Tue & Fri.

PERCHED OVER a gorge cut by the confluence of the Cabril and Corgo Rivers, Vila Real is a busy commercial center. As the communications hub of the Upper Douro, it makes a convenient starting point to explore the valley of the Douro to the south and the Parque Natural do Alvão to the northwest. Vila Real also has a car-racing circuit, which hosts major events each year during June and July.

Midway along the main street, Avenida Carvalho Araújo, is the 15th-century **Sé**. This fine Gothic cathedral was originally the church of a Dominican friary. The other monastic buildings burned down under suspicious circumstances in the mid-19th century.

At the southern end of the avenue, a plaque on the wall at No. 19 marks the birthplace of Diogo Cão, the explorer who discovered the mouth of the Congo in 1482 *(see pp48–9)*.

The **Igreja dos Clérigos**, in nearby Rua da Portela, is also known as Capela Nova or Capela de São Pedro. It presents a pleasing Baroque façade attributed to Niccolò Nasoni and an interior of fine blue and white *azulejos*.

ENVIRONS: The small village of **Bisalhães**, 6 km (4 miles) to the west, is famed for its boldly designed black pottery *(see p25)*. Examples can be

seen displayed for sale at the annual Festa de São Pedro, celebrated in Vila Real each year on June 28–9. Also seen at this time is the fine embroidery from nearby Agarez.

Parque Natural do Alvão ⓬

Road map D1. to Ermelo via Campeã. Praceta do Tronco, Cruz das Almas, Vila Real (259-32 41 38).

The scenic Parque Natural do Alvão

WITHIN THE 72 sq km (28 sq miles) of the nature reserve between the Corgo and Tâmega rivers, the scenery ranges from verdant, cultivated lowlands to bleak heights that reach 1,339 m (4,393 ft) at **Alto das Caravelas**. Despite hunters and habitat encroachment, hawks, dippers, and otters can still be spotted. Between the picturesque hamlets of **Ermelo** and **Lamas de Olo**, where corn is still kept in *espigueiros (see p271)*, the Olo drops in a spectacular cascade, the **Fisgas de Ermelo**. From **Alto do Velão**, just southwest of the park, are splendid views west of the Tâmega valley.

Vila Real seen across the deep gorge of the Corgo and Cabril Rivers

A farmer and his grazing ox near
Carvalhelhos, Serra do Barroso

Serra do Barroso ⑬

Road map D1. 🚌 *to Montalegre
or Boticas.* 🛈 *Praça do Município,
Montalegre (276-51 22 54).*

JUST SOUTHEAST of the Parque
Nacional da Peneda-Gerês
(see pp270–71) is the wild
and remote Serra do Barroso.
The landscape of heathery hillsides is split by the immense
Barragem do Alto Rabagão,
the largest of many reservoirs
in the area created by the
damming of rivers for hydroelectric power. Water is a main-
stay of the local economy: a
high rainfall enables farmers
to eke out an existence on the
poor soil, and the artificial
lakes attract fishing and water
sports enthusiasts. The source
of one of the country's most
popular bottled mineral waters
is at **Carvalhelhos**.

The village of **Boticas** nearby produces a beverage with
a more original claim to fame.
In 1809, the locals buried their
wine rather than have it fall
into the hands of the invading
French. When the enemy de-
parted, the wine was retrieved
and found to have improved.
The bottles were colloquially
termed *mortos* ("dead"), hence
the name of the wine – *vinho
dos mortos.* The practice continues, and bottles are usually
buried for up to two years.

The area's principal town is
Montalegre, on a plateau to
the north. Its most notable
feature is the imposing keep,
27 m (88 ft) high, of the
ruined 14th-century castle.

Oxen are bred in the Serra,
and inter-village *chegas dos
bois* (ox fights) are a popular
pastime. The contest is usually
decided within half an hour,
when the weaker ox takes to
its heels – champions are fêted
by hordes of adoring fans.

Chaves ⑭

Road map D1. 🚶 *18,000.* 🚌
🛈 *Terreiro da Cavalaria (276-33 30
29).* 🛒 *Wed.*

BESIDE THE UPPER REACHES of
the Tâmega stands historic
Chaves, attractively sited in the
middle of a fertile plain.

Thermal springs and nearby
gold deposits encouraged the
Romans to establish Aquae
Flaviae here in AD 78. Its strategic position led to successive
invasion and occupation by
the Suevi, Visigoths, and Moors,
before the Portuguese gained
final possession in 1160. The
name Chaves ("keys") is often
associated with the keys of the
north awarded to Nuno Álvares
Pereira, hero of Aljubarrota
(see p183). A likelier but more
pedestrian explanation is that
Chaves is simply a corruption
of the Latin "Flaviae."

Today Chaves is famous for
its spa and historic center,
and for its smoked hams. A
curiosity of the north, the distinctive black pottery *(see p25),*
is made in nearby Nantes.

The old town focuses on the
Praça de Camões. The 14th-
century **keep** overlooking this
pleasant medieval square is all
that remains of the castle given
to Nuno Álvares Pereira by
João I. On the south side of
the square stands the **Igreja
Matriz** with its fine Romanesque portal. The Baroque

Tiled and gilded Misericórdia church at Chaves

Misericórdia church opposite
has an exquisite interior lined
with 18th-century *azulejos.*
Attributed to Policarpo de
Oliveira Bernardes *(see p22),*
the huge panels depict scenes
from the New Testament.

The 14th-century keep of Chaves
castle, set in formal gardens

🏛 Museu Militar and
Museu da Região Flaviense
Praça de Camões. 🕭 *276-33 29 65.*
⏰ *Tue–Fri, Sat & Sun pm.* ⬤ *public
hols.* 🎟 *joint ticket.*
Within the castle keep is a
small military museum, where
suits of armor, uniforms, and
associated regalia are on display. Also exhibited are military
memorabilia from the city's
defense against the attack by
Royalists from Spain in 1912.

In the flower-filled
garden surrounding
the keep are a few
archaeological finds
from Chaves's long
history, but most are
to be found in the
Museu da Região
Flaviense behind the
keep. Here, in the
Paço dos Duques de
Bragança, are dis-
played a variety of
local archaeological
discoveries. Items of
interest include sou-
venirs of the Roman
occupation, such as
milestones and
coins, alongside an
oxcart and a straw
mantle of the type
worn by shepherds
for protection in the
rain or the hot sun.

Ponte Romana

The 16-arch Roman bridge across the Tâmega was completed around AD 100, at the time of the Emperor Trajan. Its construction brought added importance to Chaves as a staging post on the route between Braga and Astorga (in northwestern Spain). On the bridge are Roman milestones telling that funds to build it were raised locally.

Thermal springs

Largo Tito Flávio Vespasiano.
276-33 24 45. daily.
A few minutes on foot from the city center is one of the hottest springs in Europe. Water here bubbles up at a temperature of 73°C (163°F), and the spa's facilities attract both vacationers and patients seeking treatment (see p209). Chaves water is recommended for the treatment of ailments as diverse as arthritis, kidney dysfunction, and hypertension.

The huge cleft Pedra Bolideira near Chaves

ENVIRONS: Close to the village of Soutelo, 4 km (2 miles) northwest of Chaves (the route is marked), is the strange **Outeiro Machado Boulder**. It measures 50 m (165 ft) in length and is covered with mysterious hieroglyphs and symbols of unknown meaning. These may be Celtic in origin.

Another gigantic boulder, the **Pedra Bolideira**, lies near Bolideira, 16 km (10 miles) east of Chaves. Split in two, the massive larger section balances lightly, needing only a gentle push to rock it to and fro.

The spa town of **Vidago**, 17 km (11 miles) southwest of Chaves, is well known for its therapeutic water. The Vidago Palace Hotel (see p393), once the haunt of royalty, has been renovated in recent years, but retains the regal charm of its park, lakes, and pump room.

Murça's Misericórdia church, with its vine-embellished pillars

Murça

Road map D2. 3,000.
Rua Militão Bessa Ribeiro (259-51 15 08). 13 & 28 of month.

THE MARKET TOWN of Murça is famed for its honey, goat cheese, and sausage. Its major attraction, and the focal point of the garden in the main square, is its **porca**, an Iron Age granite pig with a substantial girth of 2.8 m (9 ft) (see p40). The role of *berrões*, as beasts such as these are called, is enigmatic, but they may have been linked to fertility cults. Smaller versions survive in Bragança, Chaves, and elsewhere. In more recent times the Murça *porca* has been pressed into service at elections, when the winning political parties would paint her in their colors.

The **Misericórdia** church on the main street is notable for its early Baroque façade, attractively ornamented with designs of vines and grapes.

Mirandela

Road map D1. 8,000.
Praça do Mercado (278-26 57 68).
3, 14 & 25 of month.

MIRANDELA, at the end of the Tua narrow-gauge railroad line, has pretty gardens running down to the Tua River and an elegant Roman bridge with 20 asymmetrical arches. Built for the deployment of troops and to aid the transport of ore from local mines, it was rebuilt in the 16th century and is now for pedestrians only.

Displayed in the **Museu Municipal Armindo Teixeira Lopes** are sculpture, prints, and paintings, including views of Lisbon and Mirandela by the local 20th-century artist after whom the museum is named.

The 17th-century **town hall** once belonged to the Távoras, but the family was accused of attempted regicide in 1759 and all trace of them vanished.

Museu Municipal Armindo Teixeira Lopes

Rua Coronel Sarmento Pimente.
278-26 57 68. Mon–Fri; May–Oct: also Sat & Sun pm. public hols.

ENVIRONS: In a lovely valley 15 km (9 miles) northeast of Mirandela lies **Romeu**. Its **Museu das Curiosidades**, as the name implies, is a hodgepodge of exhibits from the turn of the century onward. The collection of the local Menéres family, it includes Model-T Fords, music boxes, and early photographic equipment. Next door is the famed Maria Rita restaurant (see p415).

Museu das Curiosidades

Jerusalém do Romeu. Tue–Sun.
public hols.

The Tua River at Mirandela, with its Roman bridge and waterside parks

Bragança: the Citadel ⑰

THIS STRATEGIC HILLTOP was the site of a succession of forts before Fernão Mendes, brother-in-law of King Afonso Henriques, built a walled citadel here in 1130. Like several predecessors, it was named Brigantia. Within the walls still stand Sancho I's castle, built in 1187, with its watchtowers and dungeons, and the pentagonal 12th-century Domus Municipalis beside the church of Santa Maria.

The town gave its name to Portugal's final royal dynasty, descended from an illegitimate son of João I who was created first Duke of Bragança in 1442 *(see p299).*

Bragança's walled citadel on its isolated hilltop

Porta da Traição

The Museu Militar in the robust Gothic keep includes memorabilia from the Africa campaigns (1895) of a local regiment. The keep is 33 m (108 ft) high.

The medieval pillory has the appearance of skewering a hapless *porca,* an ancient stone pig *(see p40),* to the pedestal.

★ Castle
The castle's Torre da Princesa, scene of many tragic tales, was refuge to Dona Sancha, unhappy wife of Fernão Mendes and prison to other mistreated wives.

RUA DOM FERNÃO O BRAVO

Porta da Vila

To town

Porta de Santo António

Santa Maria
The church's elaborately carved portal dates from its 18th-century restoration.

★ Domus Municipalis
This, the only surviving example of Romanesque civic architecture in Portugal, served as a hall where the homens boms ("good men") settled disputes. Below was the town's cistern.

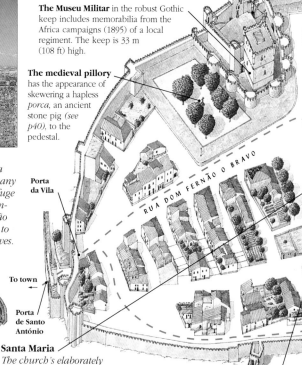

STAR SIGHTS

★ **Castle**

★ **Domus Municipalis**

VISITORS' CHECKLIST

Road map E1. 🏘 *35,000.*
🚌 *Agência de Viagens e Turismo
Sanvitura, Avenida João da Cruz.*
🚶 *Avenida Cidade de Zamora
(273-38 12 73).* 🚃 *3, 12 & 21
of month.* 🎪 *mid-Aug: Nossa
Senhora das Graças.* **Castle** *and*
Museu Militar 🕻 *273-223 78.*
🕐 *Fri–Wed.* ⬤ *public hols.* 🈂

KEY

– – – Suggested route

```
0 meters                    50
0 yards                     50
```

Porta do Sol

Houses within the Citadel
*Bragança had outgrown the
citadel by the 15th century,
but streets of small houses
still cluster within the walls.*

Museu Abade de Baçal gardens, where archaeological finds are displayed

Beyond the Citadel
By the 15th century, Bragança
had expanded west along the
banks of the Fervença River.
The Jewish quarter in Rua dos
Fornos survives from this era,
when Jews from North Africa
and Spain settled here and
founded the silk industry.

Despite its royal links, the
town never overcame its isolation, the Bragança monarchs
preferring Vila Viçosa *(see
pp298–9)*. Only now are the
investments of returning emigrants and the completion of
the Oporto-Spain highway
reviving trade. A new cathedral "for the millennium" was
inaugurated in 1996, another
indicator of the city's rebirth.
Near the modest old cathedral in the town center is a
lively covered market where
delicacies such as smoked
hams and *alheiras* (chicken
sausages) are sold.

🏛 Museu Abade de Baçal
Rua Abílio Bessa 27. 🕻 *273-33 15 95.*
🕐 *Tue–Sun.* ⬤ *public hols.* 🈂
The Abbot of Baçal (1865–
1947) was a prodigious scholar
whose definitive researches
into the region's history and
customs, including its Jewish
connections, were published
in 11 volumes. Bragança's
museum is named after him.

Highlights among the paintings are *The Martyrdom of St.
Ignatius*, an unsigned triptych
of the 16th century, and watercolors by Aurélia de Sousa
(1865–1922), including her impressionist *A Sombra* (In the
Shade). In another section are
displayed colorful *pauliteiros*
costumes *(see p227)* and gruesome instruments of torture.

In the garden are a variety
of archaeological discoveries
including *porcas* and tablets
with Luso-Roman inscriptions.

🛕 São Bento
Rua de São Francisco.
🕐 *variable hours.* 🚻
Founded in 1590 by Bishop
António Pinheiro, São Bento
has two startlingly contrasting
ceilings: a splendid canopy of
Moorish-influenced geometric
carving in the chancel, and a
richly colored 18th-century
trompe l'oeil over the nave.

🛕 São Vicente
Largo do Principal. 🕐 *variable hours.*
The secret wedding between
Inês de Castro and Dom Pedro
is reputed to have taken place
here in 1354 *(see p179)*. The
original 13th-century church
was reconstructed in the 17th
century with the addition of a
great deal of sumptuous gilt-
work. The *azulejo* panel to the
right of the main door depicts
General Sepúlveda exhorting
the citizens of Bragança to
free themselves from French
occupation in 1809.

**Street in the old Jewish quarter,
sloping steeply down to the river**

The sparsely inhabited landscape of the Parque Natural de Montesinho

Parque Natural de Montesinho ⑱

Road map E1. 🚌 *to Rio de Onor & Vinhais*. ℹ️ *Bairro Salvador Nunes Teixeira 5, Bragança (273-38 14 44).*

O NE OF THE WILDEST areas in Europe, the preserve covers 175,000 acres between Bragança and the border with Spain. The region, understandably, is known as Terra Fria (Cold Land). Bleak mountains rise to 1,481 m (4,859 ft) above heather and broom, descending to oak forests and valleys of alder and willow.

Spectacular views of the park can be enjoyed from **Vinhais**, on its southern fringe, and the wilderness attracts walkers and riders – mountain bikes and horses can be rented locally.

The population clusters in farming communities on the lowlands, leaving much of the Serra an undisturbed habitat for such rare species as wolves and golden eagles, as well as boars, otters, and falcons.

Little changed from medieval times, villages such as **França** and **Montesinho** are typical in their stone houses and cobblestone streets. Ancient practices such as herbal cures and reverence for the supernatural linger, and ties are communal rather than national. In **Rio de Onor** Spanish and Portuguese have been fused into a unique dialect, Rionorês.

Farm parlor, Museu da Terra de Miranda

Miranda do Douro ⑲

Road map E1. 🚹 *3,000.* 🚌 ℹ️ *Largo do Menino Jesus da Cartolinha (273-43 11 32).* 🛒 *1st of month.*

T HIS MEDIEVAL OUTPOST stands on top of the Douro gorge, which here forms an abrupt border with Spain. Its key position and the establishment of a bishopric here in 1545 paved the way for the town's development into the cultural and religious center of Trás-os-Montes. But in 1762, during the Seven Years' War against France and Spain, the powder store exploded, claiming 400 lives and destroying the castle (only the keep remains). This mishap, compounded by the transfer of the bishopric to Bragança, led the town into a deep economic decline, only recently halted by new trade links with the coast and Spain.

The lovely twin-towered **Sé** was founded in the 16th century. The graceful wood carvings of the chancel retable depict, among other themes, the Apostles and the Virgin attended by angels. But the cathedral's most original feature is a wooden figure in the south transept of the Boy Jesus. The Menino Jesus da Cartolinha represents a boy who, legend tells, appeared during a Spanish siege in 1711 to rally the demoralized Portuguese to miraculous victory. Devotees dressed the statue in 17th-century costume and later gave him a top hat *(cartolinha)*.

The excellent **Museu da Terra de Miranda** houses an eclectic display of archaeological finds, folk costume, a reconstruction of a Mirandês farmhouse parlor, and curious rural devices such as an inflated pig-bladder blackjack.

🏛 Museu da Terra de Miranda
Largo Dom João III. 📞 *273-43 11 64.* 🕙 *Tue–Sat & Sun am.* ⚫ *public hols.* 🅿️

ENVIRONS: Just southwest of Miranda, the village of **Duas Igrejas** is famed for its stick dancers, or *pauliteiros*, who perform at local festivals and overseas *(see p227)*. The tradition is in decline, but for the Festa de Santa Bárbara, on the third Sunday in August, the dancers don their distinctive black and white costumes and are accompanied in their energetic display by drums and *gaita de foles* (bagpipes).

A distinctive *pombal*, or dovecote, still found around Montesinho

THE DOVECOTES OF MONTESINHO

Doves supply not only food, but also droppings, which are highly prized as fertilizer. In this part of Trás-os-Montes the traditional horseshoe-shaped dovecote or *pombal* is still a familiar sight, although many are now disused. The birds nest in rough cells inside the whitewashed schist walls and enter and leave through gaps in the tile or slate roof. They are fed via a small raised door at the front of the *pombal*.

The church and town of Mogadouro, viewed from beside the ruins of its 13th-century castle

Mogadouro 🔁

Road map E2. 🏠 *3,000.* 🚌
ℹ️ *Largo Santo Cristo (279-34 38 47).*

APART FROM the hilltop tower, little remains of the great castle founded here by King Dinis and presented to the Templars in 1297. From the top there are fine views over the drowsy little market town known for its handicrafts, particularly leather goods and articles of silk, linen, and wool.

Mogadouro's 16th-century **Igreja Matriz** features a 17th-century tower, while lavishly gilded retables from the 18th century decorate the altars.

Torre de Moncorvo 🔁

Road map E2. 🏠 *2,500.* 🚌
ℹ️ *Rua Manuel Seixas (279-25 22 89).*
🗓️ *8 & 23 of month.*

FAMED FOR the white mantle of almond blossoms that fleetingly covers the valleys in early spring (egg-shaped *amêndoas cobertas*, sugared almonds, are an Easter treat), Moncorvo also offers an atmospheric stroll through its maze of medieval streets. Its name is variously attributed to a local nobleman, Mendo Curvo, or perhaps to his raven (*corvo*).

The ponderous 16th-century **Igreja Matriz**, the largest in Trás-os-Montes, boasts a 17th-century altarpiece depicting scenes from the life of Christ.

ENVIRONS: The fate of the Côa valley, south of Moncorvo, was finally decided in 1996 when plans for a dam were dropped to preserve the world's largest collection of open-air Stone Age engravings. The rock art, first discovered in 1933 and estimated to be 20,000 years old, features bulls, horses, fish, and a naked man, the Homem de Pisco. Visitor facilities in the 20-km (12-mile) long **Parque Arqueológico do Vale do Côa** are still being improved, but tours can be arranged in Vila Nova de Foz Côa.

🏛️ Parque Arqueológico do Vale do Côa
Avenida Gago Coutinho 19a, Vila Nova de Foz Côa. 📞 *279-76 43 17.*
🕐 *Tue–Sun.* ⬤ *public hols.* 🎫 🚫

Rich interior of the Igreja Matriz at Freixo

Freixo de Espada à Cinta 🔁

Road map E2. 🏠 *2,300.* 🚌
ℹ️ *Avenida do Emigrante (279-65 33 04).* 🗓️ *2nd Sat of month.*

SEVERAL STORIES try to explain the curious name of this remote border town. "Ash tree of the girt sword" may derive from the arms of a Spanish nobleman, or a Visigoth called Espadacinta, or from a tale that, when founding the town in the 14th century, King Dinis strapped his sword to an ash.

Dominating the skyline is the heptagonal **Torre do Galo**, a relic from the 14th-century defenses. Views from the top are splendid, especially in spring when the almond blossoms attract a great many tourists. A newer cultivation is that of silkworms, a revival of an 18th-century industry.

The intricate 16th-century portal of the **Igreja Matriz** leads into a splendid small-scale version of Belém's Mosteiro dos Jerónimos (*see pp106–7*). Panels of the altarpiece, attributed to Grão Vasco (*see p213*), include a fine *Annunciation*.

⛪ Torre do Galo
Praça Jorge Álvares. 🕐
Tue–Fri. ⬤ *public hols.*

MINHO

·····························

KNOWN AS THE BIRTHPLACE *of the nation, the Minho has two of Portugal's most historic cities: its first capital, Guimarães, and Braga, the country's main religious center. Life in the province is still firmly rooted in tradition. Agriculture thrives thanks to the abundant rainfall that makes this the greenest area in Portugal.*

The province of Minho occupies land between the Douro River in the south and the Minho River in the north. Fortified hilltop stone forts *(castros)* remain as evidence of the Neolithic history of the region. When Celtic peoples migrated into the area in the first millennium BC, these sites developed into *citânias* (settlements) such as Briteiros.

During the 2nd century BC, advancing Roman legions conquered the land, introduced vine-growing techniques, and constructed a network of roads. Roman milestones are still visible in Peneda-Gerês National Park. When Christianity became the official religion of the Roman empire in the 4th century AD, Braga became an important religious center, a position it holds to this day. The Suevi swept aside the Romans in the 5th century, followed by the Visigoths, who were ousted in turn by the Moorish invasion of 711. The Minho was won back from the Moors in the 9th century. The region rose to prominence in the 12th century under Afonso Henriques *(see pp42–3)*, who proclaimed himself the first king of Portugal and chose Guimarães as his capital.

The Minho's fertile farms and estates have been handed down within families for centuries, each heir traditionally receiving a share of the land. This custom results in plots of land too small to support their owners, many of whom emigrate in search of work. The economy of the Minho, under pressure from high local unemployment, concentrates on medium-scale industry around Braga and Guimarães. Agriculture in the valleys includes production of the area's distinctive *vinhos verdes* or "green wines." Despite the growth of tourism, the Minho has maintained its strong folk traditions. Carnivals and street markets pervade everyday life, and ox-drawn carts are still in use.

Cows being herded across a bridge near the Brejoeira Palace, south of Monção

◁ The sanctuary of Nossa Senhora da Peneda, in the Parque Nacional da Peneda-Gerês

Exploring the Minho

I N THE SOUTH of the Minho lie Braga and Guimarães, the two major cities of the region, both rich in historic sights. From Braga, the Baroque splendor of Bom Jesus or the ruins of Citânia de Briteiros, the country's largest Iron Age site, are within easy reach. Between Braga and the coast lies Barcelos, the ceramics center of the region, famed for its weekly market. Traveling north, the pretty town of Viana do Castelo is a useful base from which to explore the coast. Turning inland again, the picturesque market town of Ponte de Lima, beside the Lima River, is one of many places in the Minho that provide accommodations in traditional manor houses. In the north of the Minho, the Minho River forms the border with Spain. Along the river, fortified towns offer magnificent views into Spain. To the northeast, hikers and wildlife enthusiasts should not miss the dramatic mountain ranges of the Parque Nacional da Peneda-Gerês.

Foal grazing in the Parque Nacional da Peneda-Gerês

SEE ALSO

- **Where to Stay** pp393–4
- **Where to Eat** pp416–17

Manueline portal on the 16th-century parish church, Vila do Conde

MONÇÃO ❸

Vigo
Pontevedra

❷ VALENÇA DO MINHO

N13

VILA NOVA DE CERVEIRA

N101

N301

N303

PAREDES DE COURA

Minho

❶ CAMINHA

N303

N201

N306

ARCOS DE VALDEVEZ

PONTE DA BARCA

VILA PRAIA DE ÂNCORA

BRAVÃES

❻ PONTE DE LIMA

N202

Lima

❼ VIANA DO CASTELO

N13

N204

N201

N103

Cávado

ESPOSENDE

BRAGA

❾ BARCELOS

N13

N205

N206

VILA NOVA DE FAMALICÃO

A3

A7

PÓVOA DE VARZIM

❽ VILA DO CONDE

N14

Ave

Porto

Porto

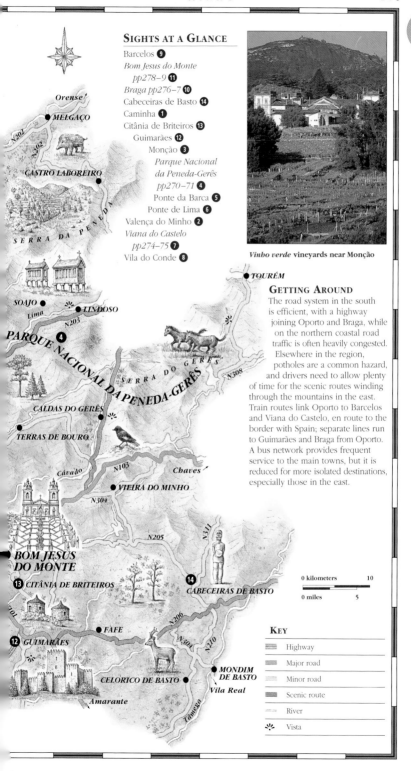

SIGHTS AT A GLANCE

Vinho verde vineyards near Monção

GETTING AROUND

The road system in the south
is efficient, with a highway
joining Oporto and Braga, while
on the northern coastal road
traffic is often heavily congested.
Elsewhere in the region,
potholes are a common hazard,
and drivers need to allow plenty
of time for the scenic routes winding
through the mountains in the east.
Train routes link Oporto to Barcelos
and Viana do Castelo, en route to the
border with Spain; separate lines run
to Guimarães and Braga from Oporto.
A bus network provides frequent
service to the main towns, but it is
reduced for more isolated destinations,
especially those in the east.

| 0 kilometers | | 10 |
| 0 miles | 5 | |

KEY

▬▬▬	Highway
▬▬▬	Major road
▬▬▬	Minor road
▬▬▬	Scenic route
═══	River
☼	Vista

Popular cafés in Praça do Conselheiro Silva Torres, Caminha's attractive main square

Caminha ❶

Road Map C1. 🏚 *2,000.* 🚌 🚍 🚐
🚹 *Rua Ricardo Joaquim de Sousa (258-92 19 52).* 🛒 *Wed.*

THIS ANCIENT FORTRESS town perches beside the Minho with fine views across the river to Spain. Occupied in Celtic and Roman times for its strategic position, Caminha developed into a major port until the diversion of its trade to Viana do Castelo in the 16th century. Today it is a small port, with a daily ferry connection to A Guarda in Spain.

On the main square is the 15th-century **Torre do Relógio** clock tower, once a gateway in the medieval defensive walls, and the 17th-century **Paços do Concelho** with its attractive loggia supported by pillars. Cross to the other side of the square, past the Renaissance fountain, to admire the seven Manueline windows on the upper story of the **Solar dos Pitas** mansion (15th century).

The Rua Ricardo Joaquim de Sousa leads to the Gothic **Igreja Matriz**. Begun in the late 15th century, it has a superb inlaid ceiling of panels carved in Mudéjar (Moorish) style. Renaissance carvings above the side doors depict the Apostles, the Virgin, and several figures in daring poses, including one man with his posterior bared toward Spain.

ENVIRONS: Foz do Minho, the mouth of the Minho, lies 5 km (3 miles) southwest of town. From here local fishermen will take groups (by prior arrangement) to the ruined island fortress of **Forte da Ínsua**.

The small walled town of **Vila Nova de Cerveira**, 12 km (7 miles) northeast of Caminha on the road to Valença, has a 16th-century castle, refurbished as the luxurious Pousada Dom Dinis *(see p394)*. The tranquil atmosphere is ideal for a stroll in narrow streets lined with 17th- and 18th-century mansions, or along the river-front, where a car ferry runs to the Spanish town of Goián.

Valença do Minho ❷

Road Map C1. 🏚 *3,000.* 🚍 🚐
🚹 *Avenida de Espanha (251-233 74).* 🛒 *Wed & 2nd Sun of month.*

SET IN A COMMANDING position on a hilltop overlooking the Minho River, Valença is an attractive border town with an old quarter set in the narrow confines of two double-walled forts, shaped like crowns and linked by a causeway. During the reign of Sancho I (1185–1211), the town was named *Contrasta*, due to its position facing the Spanish town of Tui.

The **forts** date from the 17th and 18th centuries and were designed according to the principles of the French architect Vauban. There are fine views from the ramparts across the river into Galicia. Although the town was briefly captured by Napoleonic troops in 1807, its formidable bastions resisted subsequent shelling and attacks from across the river in 1809.

Lining the cobblestone alleys of the old quarter are shops full of linen, wickerwork, pottery, and handicrafts to tempt the thousands of Spanish visitors who stroll across the bridge to shop. South of the ramparts is the newer part of town.

In Praça de São Teotónio, **Casa do Eirado** (1448) boasts a crenellated roof and late Gothic window, adorned with the builder's signature. The 18th-century **Casa do Poço** presents symmetrical windows and wrought-iron balconies.

A quiet sunlit corner in the old quarter of Valença do Minho

ENVIRONS: The **Convento de Ganfei**, 5 km (3 miles) east of Valença on the N101, was reconstructed in the 11th century by a Norman priest. It retains pleasing Romanesque features, including ornamental animal and plant motifs and vestiges of medieval frescoes. To visit the chapel, ask for the key at the house opposite.

Part of the walls and ramparts surrounding Valença do Minho

Monção ❸

Road Map C1. 🏛 *2,500.* 🚌
ℹ️ *Praça Deu-la-Deu (251-65 27 57).*
🗓 *Thu.*

A REMOTE and charming town, Monção once formed part of the string of fortified border posts standing sentinel on the Minho River. Both the town's main squares are lined with old houses and decorated with chestnut trees, flowerbeds, and mosaic paths.

The 13th-century **Igreja Matriz** in Rua João de Pinho boasts an outstanding Romanesque doorway of sculpted acanthus flowers. Inside, to the right of the transept is the cenotaph of the valiant Deu-la-Deu Martins, the town's heroine, erected in 1679 by a descendant. A leafy avenue east of the town leads to the hot mineral springs used for the treatment of arthritis.

A colorful element in the June Corpus Christi festival is the Festa da Coca, when St. George engages the dragon *(coca)* in comic ritual combat before giving the final blow.

ENVIRONS: The countryside around Monção produces excellent *vinho verde (see p29)*, one of the best-known estates is **Palácio de Brejoeira**. The Neo-Classical palace stands 5 km (3 miles) south of town.

About 7 km (4 miles) southeast of Monção, the monastery of **São João de Longos Vales** was built in Romanesque style

Bridge across the Lima at Ponte da Barca, with the town behind

in the 12th century. The exterior capitals and interior apse have fantastical sculpted figures, including serpents and monkeys. Visits are arranged by the tourist office in Monção.

The town of **Melgaço**, 24 km (15 miles) east of Monção provides a useful gateway to the Peneda-Gerês National Park.

Parque Nacional da Peneda-Gerês ❹

See pp270–71.

Ponte da Barca ❺

Road Map C1. 🏛 *2,000.* 🚌
ℹ️ *Largo da Misericórdia (258-45 28 99).* 🗓 *every other Wed.*

T HE TOWN OF Ponte da Barca derives its name from the graceful 15th-century bridge that replaced the boat once used to ferry pilgrims across the Lima River *(ponte* means

bridge, and *barca* means boat). A stroll through the tranquil town center leads past the pillory (crowned with sphere and pyramid), the graceful arcades and noble mansions from the 16th and 17th centuries. The Jardim dos Poetas (Poets' Garden) and riverside parks are ideal for picnics, and the huge open-air market along the river is well worth a visit.

Carved relief on the tympanum of the small parish church at Bravães

ENVIRONS: Some of Portugal's finest Romanesque carvings are on the 13th-century church at **Bravães**, 4 km (2 miles) west of Ponte da Barca. Sculpted monkeys, oxen, and birds of prey decorate the columns of its main portal; the tympanum shows Christ in majesty flanked by two angels.

The town of **Arcos de Valdevez**, 5 km (3 miles) north of Ponte da Barca, nestles by the banks of the Vez River and lies within convenient reach of Peneda-Gerês National Park. The impressive church of **Nossa Senhora da Lapa** was built in 1767 by André Soares. This Baroque showpiece has an oval exterior, yet transforms the interior into an octagon.

Hiking enthusiasts should ask the tourist office for directions to follow the circuit of elevated viewpoints and local villages from the hamlet of **São Miguel**, 11 km (7 miles) east of Ponte da Barca.

DEU-LA-DEU MARTINS

In 1368, when a Spanish army had besieged Monção to the verge of starvation, Deu-la-Deu Martins used the last of the town's flour to bake rolls that she flung over the walls to the Spaniards, with taunts that there were plenty more

The heroic Deu-la-Deu Martins on Monção's coat of arms

to throw at them. Thinking their time was being wasted in a futile siege, the troops soon withdrew. In gratitude for saving the town, Deu-la-Deu (the name means "God gave her") is remembered on the town's coat of arms, where she is shown with a loaf of bread in each hand. *Pãezinhos* (bread rolls) *de Deu-la-Deu* used to be baked to honor her memory, but the tradition is no longer followed.

Vinho verde **vineyards around village of Lapela, near Monção** ▷

Parque Nacional da Peneda-Gerês 🔾

Broom in Peneda Mountains

PENEDA-GERÊS National Park, one of Portugal's greatest natural attractions, stretches from the Gerês Mountains in the south to the Peneda range and the Spanish border in the north. Established in 1971, it extends over about 700 sq km (270 sq miles) of wild, dramatic scenery, with windswept peaks and wooded valleys of oak, pine, and yew. It is home to rare wolves and golden eagles among its rich variety of fauna. In the villages, everyday life remains rooted in tradition.

Lamas de Mouro, at the northern entrance to the park, serves as an information center and offers accommodations.

Castro Laboreiro is best known for the breed of sheepdog to which it gives its name. The ruins of a medieval castle can be seen in the village.

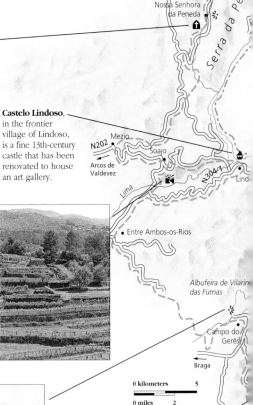

Castelo Lindoso, in the frontier village of Lindoso, is a fine 13th-century castle that has been renovated to house an art gallery.

★ Nossa Senhora da Peneda
Surrounded by massive rocks, this elaborate sanctuary is a replica of Bom Jesus (see pp278–9). The site is visited in early September by pilgrims from all over the region.

Soajo
The traditional village of Soajo, surrounded by terraced hillsides, is known for its collection of espigueiros. The village's local festival takes place in the middle of August.

0 kilometers 5

0 miles 2

Vilarinho das Furnas
Beautifully set in a rocky landscape, the Vilarinho das Furnas reservoir was formed by damming the Homem River. The reservoir is good for swimming as well as hiking along its shores.

Caldas do Gerês, known since Roman times for its spa, now serves as an information center and base for excursions from the center of the park.

Pitões das Júnias Monastery
Dating to 1147, the picturesque ruins of this monastery lie approximately 3 km (2 miles) south of the road leading into Pitões das Júnias village.

Visitors' Checklist

Road map C1. *from Braga to Caldas do Gerês; from Arcos de Valdevez to Soajo & Lindoso; from Melgaço to Castro Laboreiro & Lamas de Mouro.* *Caldas do Gerês: on main road (253-39 01 10); Lamas do Mouro: next to camp site; Arcos de Valdevez: Rua Padre Manuel Himalaia (258-653 38). Information on camp sites, hiking & pony trekking is available at these offices and at Montalegre* (see p256). **Castelo Lindoso** *Tue–Sun.* *public hols.*

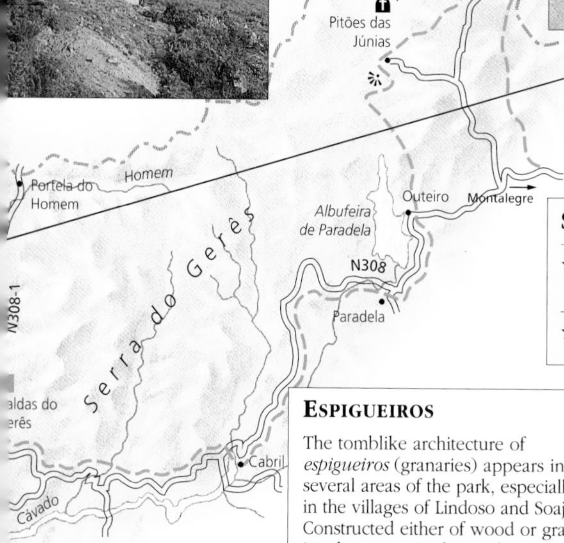

Inverneiras in Sedra
Migration during the summer from these solidly built winter houses to brandas, *stone shelters high in the mountains, is still practiced in some villages.*

★ Roman Road
Sections of the old Roman road that ran from Braga to Astorga in Spain can still be seen at points along the Homem River valley.

Star Sights

- ★ **Nossa Senhora da Peneda**
- ★ **Roman Road**

Key

- Road
- Long trail
- International border
- Tourist information
- Vista

Espigueiros

The tomblike architecture of *espigueiros* (granaries) appears in several areas of the park, especially in the villages of Lindoso and Soajo. Constructed either of wood or granite, they are raised on columns and slatted for ventilation. The design keeps grain and corn at the right humidity as well as off the ground, out of reach of hens and rodents. Topped with an ornamental cross or pyramid, the design of *espigueiros* has scarcely changed since the 18th and 19th centuries.

Granite *espigueiro*, Lindoso

Ponte de Lima 6

Road Map C1. 👥 *3,200.* 🚌
🛈 *Praça da República (258-94 23 35).*
📅 *every other Mon.*

THIS ATTRACTIVE riverside
town takes its name from
the ancient bridge over the
Lima River. During the Middle
Ages, the town played a pivotal role in the defense of the
Minho against the Moors.

The Roman **bridge** has only
five of its original stone arches;
the rest were rebuilt or restored
in the 14th and 15th centuries.
The 15th-century church of
Santo António now houses the
Museu dos Terceiros, a museum of sacred art with a fine
display of carvings.

The remaining medieval fortifications of Ponte de Lima
include the former prison
tower and the 15th-century
**Palácio dos Marqueses de
Ponte de Lima**, a fortress-
palace which now func-
tions as the town hall.

The town's market,
a tradition dating back
to 1125, takes place
on the river's wide and
sandy left bank. In mid-
September crowds gather
in the town to celebrate
the *Feiras Novas* (new
fairs), a combined
religious festival and
folkloric market.

**Stone carving of
a musician, Museu
dos Terceiros**

🏛 **Museu dos Terceiros**
Avenida Dom Luís Filipe. 📞 *258-94
25 63.* 🕐 *Wed–Mon.* ● *public hols.*

Viana do Castelo 7

See pp274–5.

Former dormitory of the Mosteiro de Santa Clara, Vila do Conde

Vila do Conde 8

Road map C2. 👥 *21,000.* 🚉 🚌
🛈 *Rua 25 de Abril (252-64 27 00).*
📅 *Fri.*

THE SMALL TOWN of Vila
do Conde enjoyed its
boom years as a ship-
building center in the
Age of Discovery *(see
pp46–7)*; today it is
a quiet fishing port.
By the river, in the
historic center, the main
attraction is the **Mosteiro
de Santa Clara**, founded
in 1318. The principal
dormitory building,
dating from the 18th
century, is now a
correctional institu-
tion for teenagers.
The church and cloisters, however, are open to the public.
The Gothic church has Renaissance additions and contains
the tombs of the nunnery's
founders, Dom Afonso Sanches
(son of King Dinis) and his
wife Dona Teresa Martins.

Near the Mosteiro de Santa
Clara are parts of the imposing
5-km (3-mile) **aqueduct**, built
in 1705–14, with 999 arches.

At the heart of the historic
center is Praça Vasco da Gama,
with an unusual pillory in the
shape of an arm with thrusting
sword – a vivid warning to
potential wrongdoers. Bordering the square by the pillory is
the 16th-century **Igreja Matriz**,
notable for its wonderfully
ornate Manueline portico,
attributed to João de Castilho.

The town is a center for lace-
making (bone lace or *rendas
de bilros*). Visitors can buy
samples and see the skills at
the **Escola de Rendas** (lace-
making school). The same
building also houses the Museu
de Rendas (lace museum).

♨ **Mosteiro de Santa Clara**
Largo Dom Afonso Sanches. 📞 *252-
63 10 16.* 🕐 *Mon–Fri.* ● *public hols.*
🏛 **Escola de Rendas**
Rua de São Bento 70. 📞 *252-64 30
70.* 🕐 *mid Jun–Sep: daily; Oct–mid
Jun: Mon–Fri.* ● *public hols.*

ENVIRONS: The town of **Póvoa
de Varzim**, 3 km (2 miles)
north of Vila do Conde, is a
resort with sandy beaches,
amusements, and nightlife.

In the village of Rates, 10 km
(6 miles) northeast, the 13th-
century church of **São Pedro
de Rates** boasts a portal surmounted by gracefully sculpted
statues of saints, and a rose
window. Its nearby counterpart
at Rio Mau, the church of **São
Cristóvão de Rio Mau**, was
finished in 1151. Above the
door is a bishop (possibly St.
Augustine) flanked by helpers.

Ponte de Lima's Roman bridge, leading to the church of Santo António

THE LEGEND OF THE BARCELOS COCK

A Galician pilgrim, as he was leaving Barcelos en route to Santiago de Compostela, was accused of stealing silver from a landowner and sentenced to death by hanging. As a final plea to save himself, the prisoner requested a meeting with the judge, who was about to dig into a meal of roast rooster. The Galician vowed that as proof of his innocence the rooster would stand up on the plate and crow.

The judge pushed aside his meal and ignored the plea. But as the prisoner was hanged, the rooster stood up and crowed. The judge, realizing his mistake, hurried to the gallows and found that the Galician had miraculously survived thanks to a loose knot. According to legend, the Galician returned years later to carve the Cruzeiro do Senhor do Galo, now housed in the Museu Arqueológico in Barcelos.

Traditional Barcelos cock

Azulejos of St. Benedict's miracle of the sickle, Nossa Senhora do Terço

Barcelos ❾

Road map C1. 🏚 *10,000.* 🚍 🚌
ℹ️ *Torre de Menagem, Largo da Porta Nova, (253-81 18 82).* 🔔 *Thu.*

A PLEASANT riverside town, Barcelos is famed as the country's leading ceramics and crafts market and the source of the legendary cock that has become Portugal's national symbol. From its origins as a settlement in Roman times, the town of Barcelos developed into a flourishing agricultural center and achieved political importance during the 15th century as the seat of the First Duke of Bragança. The town's star attraction is the Feira de Barcelos, a huge weekly market held on Campo da República. Anything from clothes to livestock can be bought here. Pottery enthusiasts can browse among bright designs including pagan figurines and the famous clay roosters.

North of the square stands **Nossa Senhora do Terço**, the 18th-century church of a former Benedictine nunnery. In contrast to its plain exterior, the interior is beautifully decorated with panels of *azulejos* illustrating St. Benedict's life.

In the southwest corner of the square, a graceful cupola crowns the **Igreja do Senhor da Cruz**, built around 1705 on the site where two centuries earlier João Pires, a cobbler, had a miraculous vision of a cross etched into the ground. The Festa das Cruzes (festival of crosses), the town's most spectacular event, is held at the beginning of May to celebrate the vision. During the celebrations thousands of flowers are laid on the streets to welcome a procession to the church, and events include magnificent displays of local folk costumes, dancing, and fireworks.

The other historic attractions in the town are clustered together in a tranquil setting beside the 15th-century granite bridge that crosses over the Cávado River. The privately owned **Solar dos Pinheiros** is an attractive mansion on Rua Duques de Bragança, built in 1448. The sculpted figure plucking his beard on the south tower is known as Barbadão, the "bearded one." So incensed was this devout Jew when his daughter bore a child to a gentile (King João I) that he vowed never to shave again.

A rich Gothic pillory stands in front of the ruined Counts' Palace or Paço dos Condes, destroyed by the earthquake of 1755. The ruins provide an open air setting for the **Museu Arqueológico**, which displays stone crosses, sculpted blazons, sarcophagi, and its famous exhibit, the Cruzeiro do Senhor do Galo, a cross paying tribute to the Barcelos cock legend. Next to the palace, the **Igreja Matriz** is Romanesque with Gothic influences and dates from the 13th century. There are 18th-century *azulejos* inside as well as an impressive rose window. The nearby **Museu de Olaria** illustrates the history of ceramics in the region.

🏛 **Museu Arqueológico**
Largo do Município. 📞 253-82 47 41.
🕐 *daily.*
🏛 **Museu de Olaria**
Rua Cónego J. Gaiolas. 📞 253-82 47 41. 🕐 *Tue–Sun.* ⬤ *Jan 1, Easter, Aug 15, Nov 1, Dec 25 & 26.* 🈲 ♿

16th-century pillory on terrace overlooking the Cávado River at Barcelos

Street-by-Street: Viana do Castelo ●

VIANA DO CASTELO lies in a beautiful setting on the Lima estuary. During the 15th century, the town gained prominence as a fishing center and provided ships and seafarers for the great maritime discoveries of the 16th century *(see pp48–9)*. From here João Velho set off to explore the Congo, and João Álvares Fagundes charted the rich fishing grounds of Newfoundland. Wealth derived from trade with Europe and Brazil funded the town's many opulent mansions built in Manueline, Renaissance, and Baroque styles. Today the main interest lies in the winding streets and intimate squares of the city center, easily explored on foot.

The fountain, constructed in 1553 by João Lopes the Elder, forms the focal point of the square.

Casa dos Lunas was once the home of the Luna family.

Train and bus stations

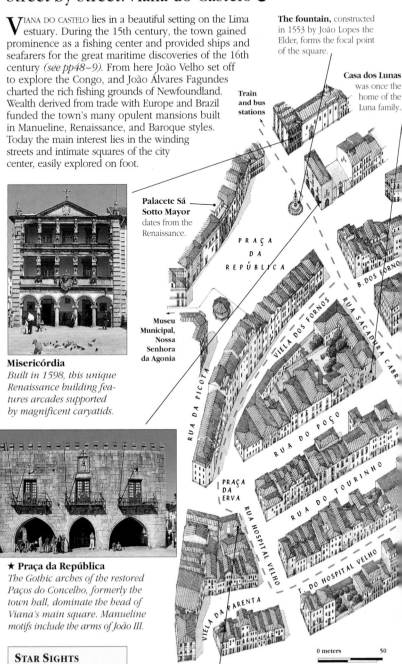

Palacete Sá Sotto Mayor dates from the Renaissance.

PRAÇA DA REPÚBLICA

Museu Municipal, Nossa Senhora da Agonia

Misericórdia
Built in 1598, this unique Renaissance building features arcades supported by magnificent caryatids.

RUA DA PICOTA

VIELA DOS FORNOS

B. DOS FORNOS

RUA SACADURA CABRAL

RUA DO POÇO

RUA DO TOURINHO

PRAÇA DA ERVA

RUA HOSPITAL VELHO

T. DO HOSPITAL VELHO

VIELA DA PARENTA

★ **Praça da República**
The Gothic arches of the restored Paços do Concelho, formerly the town hall, dominate the head of Viana's main square. Manueline motifs include the arms of João III.

STAR SIGHTS
★ **Igreja Matriz**
★ **Praça da República**

The Hospital Velho was originally a pilgrims' hospice. It now houses the Alto Minho tourist office.

0 meters   50
0 yards   50

KEY

– – – Suggested route

VISITORS' CHECKLIST

Road Map C1. 🏠 25,000. 🚉 Largo da Estação. 🚌 Avenida Capitão Gaspar de Castro. 🛈 Edifício do Hospital Velho (258-82 26 20); Castelo de Santiago da Barra (258-82 02 71). 🅿 Fri. 🎭 2nd Sun in May: Festa das Rosas; mid-Aug: Romaria de Nossa Senhora da Agonia.

Casa da Praça, a magnificent Baroque mansion

Casa de João Velho is a 15th-century house, said to have belonged to the town's most famous navigator.

The fountain in Praça da República, the center of daily life in Viana

Exploring Viana do Castelo

Both a busy fishing port and vacation resort, Viana is overlooked by the peak of Monte de Santa Luzia. The town is the capital of Minho folk culture, playing host to lively festivals and supporting a thriving handicrafts industry.

🏛 Museu Municipal

Largo de São Domingos. 📞 258-82 03 77. 🕐 Tue–Sun. 🔴 public hols. 🈺 & new wing only.

Viana's Museu Municipal is housed in the 18th-century Palacete dos Barbosas Macéis and has an excellent collection of rare ceramics, furniture, archaeological finds, and paintings. In one of the upstairs rooms, the walls are tiled with animated allegorical depictions of the continents, while the chapel is lined with tiles signed by the 18th-century artist Policarpo de Oliveira Bernardes, (see p22). Among the exhibits are a 17th-century Indo-Portuguese cabinet magnificently decorated with inlaid ivory, and pieces of Oporto faïence from the Massarelos district, embellished with fine brushwork.

Early 19th-century ceramic, Museu Municipal

🏠 Nossa Senhora da Agonia

Campo de Nossa Senhora da Agonia. 📞 258-82 40 67. 🕐 daily. &

Northwest of the center, the mid-18th century chapel of Nossa Senhora da Agonia houses a statue of Our Lady of Sorrows (agonia). The chapel, with façade and altar designed by André Soares, draws enormous crowds for the romaria of Nossa Senhora da Agonia, a three-day festival held each year in the month of August (see p227). The statue is carried in procession through the town amid much feasting and carnival celebration.

ENVIRONS: In order to enjoy exceptional views, take the zigzag road to **Monte de Santa Luzia**, 3 km (2 miles) north of the town center. (A funicular runs regularly from the station.) The basilica, completed in 1926 and modeled on the Sacré Coeur in Paris, is a pilgrimage site with little aesthetic appeal. The steep climb, however, is well rewarded by the superb views from the top of the dome. Behind the church you can wander along woodland paths or visit the imposing Pousada de Santa Luzia (see p394). From the pousada it is a short walk to the top of the hill, where there are traces of a Celtiberian settlement (citânia).

The excellent beach of **Praia do Cabedelo** lies to the south of the town. The beach is accessible by road via the bridge or by a five-minute ferry crossing from the riverside dock on Avenida dos Combatentes da Grande Guerra. To the north lies **Vila Praia de Âncora**, another popular beach resort.

★ **Igreja Matriz**
The arch surrounding the west door of Viana's 15th-century, fortresslike parish church is adorned with Gothic reliefs of the apostles.

Braga ⑩

The west façade of the Sé, with its 15th-century galilee, or porch

CHURCHES, GRAND 18TH-CENTURY HOUSES, and fine gardens provide the focus for the charm and interest of Braga's center, once past the urban development on the city outskirts.

Known in Roman times as Bracara Augusta, Braga has a long history as a religious and commercial center. In the 12th century, it became the seat of Portugal's archbishops and the country's religious capital. The city lost some influence in the 19th century, but today continues as the ecclesiastical capital of Portugal and main city of the Minho.

Symbol of the city, Our Lady of the Milk

Not surprisingly, Braga hosts some of Portugal's most colorful religious festivals. Semana Santa (Holy Week) is celebrated with dramatic, solemn processions, while the lively festival of São João in June sees dancing, fairs, and fireworks.

Exploring Braga

The compact historic center borders **Praça da República**, the central square. Within the square stands the 14th-century **Torre de Menagem**, all that remains of the city's original fortifications. A short walk leads to Rua do Souto, a narrow pedestrian street lined with elegant shops and cafés, including the **Café Brasileira**, furnished in 19th-century salon style. Toward the end of the road stands the impressive **Sé**, the cathedral of Braga. Other churches worth a visit include the small, 16th-century **Capela dos Coimbras** and the 17th-century Baroque **Santa Cruz**. Many of the finest mansions in Braga also date from the Baroque period, such as the **Palácio do Raio** and the **Câmara Municipal** (the town hall). Both buildings are attributed to the 18th-century architect André Soares da Silva.

The blue-tiled façade of the Palácio do Raio, also known as the Casa do Mexicano

🔒 Sé

Rossio da Sé. ◯ *daily.*
Museu de Arte Sacra 🔋 *253-26 33 17.* ◯ *daily.* 📷

Braga's cathedral was begun in the 12th century, when Henry of Burgundy decided to build on the site of an older church, destroyed in the 6th century. Since then the building has seen many changes, including the addition in the late 15th century of a graceful galilee (porch). The church now exhibits a range of styles from Romanesque to Baroque. Outstanding features include the chapel to the right, just inside the west door, housing the ornate 15th-century tomb of the first-born son of João I (*see pp46–7*), Dom Afonso, who died in childhood. Also of interest are the upper choir with its elaborately carved wooden stalls, and the ornate, gilded Baroque organ cases.

The cathedral also houses the Treasury or **Museu de Arte Sacra**, which contains a rich collection of ecclesiastical treasures as well as, statues, carvings, and *azulejo* tiles.

Several chapels can be seen in the courtyard and cloister. The Capela dos Reis houses the tombs of the founders, Henry of Burgundy and his wife Dona Teresa, as well as the preserved body of the 14th-century archbishop Dom Lourenço Vicente.

From Rua de São João you can admire a statue of Nossa Senhora do Leite (Our Lady of the Milk), symbol of the city of Braga, sheltered under an ornate Gothic canopy.

🏛 Antigo Paço Episcopal

Praça Municipal. 🔋 *253-61 22 34.*
Library ◯ *Mon–Fri.*

Near the Sé is the former archbishops' palace. The façades date from the 14th, 17th, and 18th centuries, but

The Jardim de Santa Bárbara by the walls of the Antigo Paço Episcopal

a major fire destroyed the interior in the 18th century. The palace is now used as a library and archives. Beside it are the immaculate gardens of the Jardim de Santa Bárbara.

⚏ Palácio dos Biscainhos

Rua dos Biscainhos. 253-21 76 45.
☐ Tue–Sun. ● Jan 1, Easter, May 1, Jun 24, Dec 25. 🖾

To the west of the city center is the Palácio dos Biscainhos. Built in the 16th century and modified over the centuries, this aristocratic mansion features ornate, terraced gardens, and grand salons with lavish stucco ceilings. It now houses the city's Museu Etnográfico e Artístico (Ethnography and Arts Museum) with displays of foreign and Portuguese furniture. An unusual detail is the ribbed, paved ground floor, designed to allow carriages inside the building to deposit guests and drive on to the stables beyond.

ENVIRONS: The attractively simple chapel of **São Frutuoso de Montélios**, 3.5 km (2 miles) northwest of Braga, is one of the very few remaining examples of pre-Romanesque architecture to be found in Portugal. Built in about the 7th century, it was destroyed by the Moors and rebuilt in the 11th century.

VISITORS' CHECKLIST

Road map C1. 🏠 160,000.
🚉 Largo da Estação. 🚌 Praça da Galiza. 🛈 Avenida da Liberdade 1 (253-26 25 50). 🚆 Tue. 🎭 Holy Week (week before Easter); Jun 23–24: Festa de São João.

West of Braga, 4 km (2.5 miles) from the center and on the road to Barcelos, is the former Benedictine **Mosteiro de Tibães**. Dating back to the 11th century, this magnificent architectural complex with its gardens and cloisters was rebuilt in the 19th century and is being refurbished to house a historical center.

At Falperra, 6 km (4 miles) southeast of Braga, stands the church of **Santa Maria Madalena**. Designed by André Soares da Silva in 1750, it is known for its ornate exterior, perhaps the country's finest expression of the Rococo.

⛪ São Frutuoso de Montélios

Av. São Frutuoso. ☐ Tue–Sun (Oct–Mar: Wed–Sun). ● public hols. 🖾

🏛 Mosteiro de Tibães

Lugar de Tibães. 253-62 26 70.
☐ Tue–Sun. ● Jan 1, Easter, May 1, Dec 25. 🖾 to museum. ♿

Interior of the old coach stable at the Palácio dos Biscainhos

BRAGA CITY CENTER

Antigo Paço Episcopal ⑤
Câmara Municipal ③
Capela dos Coimbras ⑧
Jardim de Santa Bárbara ⑥
Market ①
Palácio dos Biscainhos ②
Palácio do Raio ⑩
Santa Cruz ⑨
Sé ④
Torre de Menagem ⑦

KEY

🚌	Bus station
🅿	Parking
🛈	Tourist information
✝	Church

0 meters   250

0 yards   250

Bom Jesus do Monte

O N A FORESTED SLOPE east of Braga stands Portugal's most spectacular religious sanctuary. In 1722 the Archbishop of Braga devised the giant Baroque Escadaria (stairway) of Bom Jesus as the approach to a small existing shrine. The stairway and the church of Bom Jesus were completed by Carlos Amarante in 1811. The lower section features

Fountain on Staircase of the Three Virtues

a steep Sacred Way with chapels showing the 14 Stations of the Cross, the scenes leading up to Christ's crucifixion. The Escadório dos Cinco Sentidos, in the middle section, depicts the five senses with ingenious wall-fountains and statues of biblical, mythological, and symbolic figures. This is followed by the similarly allegorical Staircase of the Three Virtues.

At the summit, an esplanade provides superb views and access to the church. Close by are several hotels, a café, and a boating lake hidden among the trees. Both a pilgrimage site and tourist attraction, the sanctuary attracts large festive crowds on weekends.

★ Escadaria
The staircase is built of granite accentuated by whitewashed walls. The steps represent an upward spiritual journey.

Chapel of the Crucifixion

Chapel of Jesus before Pilate

Chapel of the Road to Calvary

Chapel of the Flagellation

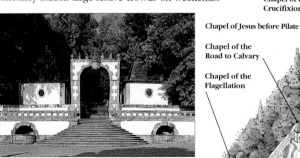

Entrance Portico
At the foot of the giant stairway stands a portico bearing the coat of arms of Dom Rodrigo de Moura Teles, the archbishop who commissioned the work.

★ Funicular
The funicular (elevador) *dates back to 1882. Hydraulically operated, it makes the ascent to the terrace beside the church in three minutes.*

Chapel of Christ's Agony in the Garden

Chapel of the Last Supper

Chapel of the Kiss of Judas

Chapel of Darkness

The Hotel do Elevador (*see p393*) stands near the top of the funicular.

Hotel do Parque

Pelican fountain

VISITORS' CHECKLIST

Road map C1. 5 km (3 miles) E of Braga. ☎ 253-67 66 36. 🚌 funicular to the top. ⭘ daily. 🔲 🔲 🔲 🔲 daily exc Sat.

The church of Bom Jesus was built on the site of a 15th-century sanctuary. In front of it stand eight statues of people who condemned Christ, including Herod and Pilate.

Chapel of the Descent from the Cross *Each chapel has a tableau of life-size terra-cotta figures in a scene from Christ's last journey.*

On the Staircase of the Five Senses are five fountains, each representing a bodily sense: sight, hearing, smell, taste, and touch.

Statues, symbols and inscriptions elaborate on the theme of the senses.

Chapel of Simon the Cyrenian

Staircase of the Three Virtues *The final stretch of staircase represents the gaining of Faith, Hope, and Charity, symbolized by fountains and various allegorical figures.*

Chapel of the Crown of Thorns

Fountain of the Five Wounds of Christ *The fountains positioned at various points on the long ascent symbolize the water of life and purification of the body and spirit. In the fountain at the foot of the Staircase of the Five Senses, water spills from the five bezants on the Portuguese coat of arms, a symbolic reference to Christ's wounds.*

0 meters 25

0 yards 25

STAR FEATURES

★ **Escadaria**

★ **Funicular**

Guimarães

FRAMED BY GENTLY RISING HILLS, the town of Guimarães is celebrated as the birthplace of the nation. When Afonso Henriques proclaimed himself king of Portugal in 1139 *(see pp42–3)*, he chose Guimarães as his capital, and the distinctive outline of its proud castle appears on the Portuguese coat of arms. In the well preserved city center, the narrow streets of the medieval quarter are ideal for exploration on foot. The cobbled Rua de Santa Maria, lined with old town houses embellished with ornate statuary, leads up from the main square, the Largo da Oliveira, past the Paço dos Duques to the castle. To feel the hustle and bustle of the Middle Ages, visit the town in the first week of August for the Festas Gualterianas, a festival of medieval art and costume.

Baroque candle-holder, Paço dos Duques

♠ Castelo de São Miguel

Rua Conde Dom Henrique. **(** 253-41 22 73. ◯ *daily.* ● *Jan 1, Apr 25, May 1, Dec 25.* 🖼

The castle's huge square keep, encircled by eight crenellated towers, dominates the skyline. First built to deter attacks by Moors and Normans in the 10th century, it was extended by Henry of Burgundy two centuries later and, according to tradition, was the birthplace of Portugal's first king, Afonso Henriques. The font where he was reputedly baptized is kept in the tiny Romanesque church of **São Miguel**, situated at the western end of the castle.

♛ Paço dos Duques

Rua Conde Dom Henrique. **(** 253-41 22 73. ◯ *daily.* ● *Jan 1, Apr 25, May 1, Dec 25.* 🖼

Constructed in the 15th century by Dom Afonso (first Duke of Bragança), the Burgundian style of the Paço dos Duques reflects Dom Afonso's taste acquired on his travels through Europe. The palace fell into disuse when the Bragança family moved to Vila Viçosa *(see pp298–9)*. In 1933, under the Salazar dictatorship *(see pp56–7)*, it was renovated as an official residence for the president.

On view in a small museum inside the palace are lavish displays of Persian rugs, Flemish tapestries, and paintings such as the impressive *O Coreiro Pascal* (Paschal Lamb) by Josefa de Óbidos *(see p51)*. Paying unusual homage to the nation's maritime exploits, the chestnut ceiling in the banquet hall imitates the upturned hull of a Portuguese caravel.

♛ Museu de Alberto Sampaio

Rua Alfredo Guimarães. **(** 253-41 24 65. ◯ *Tue–Sun.* ● *Jan 1, Easter, May 1, Dec 25.* 🖼

This museum, housed in the beautiful Romanesque cloister and adjoining rooms of Nossa Senhora da Oliveira, displays some outstanding religious art, *azulejos*, and ceramics, all from local churches.

The star exhibits, donated to the church by João I, are his tunic worn at the battle of Aljubarrota in 1385 *(see p183)* and a 14th-century silver altarpiece, comprising a triptych of the Visitation, Annunciation, and Nativity, reportedly taken from the defeated Spanish king. The Santa Clara room contains gilt carving, the work of local craftsmen, taken from the former convent of Santa Clara, now the town hall.

Largo da Oliveira, center of old Guimarães

♦ Nossa Senhora da Oliveira

Largo da Oliveira. **(** 253-41 61 44. ◯ *daily.*

This former monastery lies on the square's east side. Founded by Afonso Henriques, the church was restored by João I in gratitude to Our Lady of the Olive Tree for his victory at Aljubarrota *(see p183)*. The Manueline tower is from 1515.

In front of it is the Padrão do Salado, a 14th-century Gothic shrine housing a cross. It commemorates the legend of how the church and square acquired their name. An olive tree was transplanted here to supply the altar lamp with oil, but it withered. In 1342, the merchant Pedro Esteves placed the cross on it, whereupon the tree flourished. The tree that stands in the square today dates only from 1985.

The massive battlements surrounding the keep of Castelo de São Miguel

VISITORS' CHECKLIST

Road map C1. 🏛 60,000.
🚉 Avenida Dom João IV.
🚌 Alameda Mariano Felgueiras.
ℹ️ Praça de São Tiago (253-51
51 23). 🎪 Fri. 🎉 first weekend
in Aug: Festas Gualterianas.

🏛 Museu Martins Sarmento

Rua Paio Galvão. [253-41 59 69.
🕐 Tue–Sun. 🔒 public hols. 🎟️
Named after the archaeologist
who excavated major Iron
Age sites in the north, notably
Citânia de Briteiros, the museum is housed in the Gothic
cloister of the 14th-century
convent of São Domingos. Specializing in finds from these
sites, some dating to the Stone
Age, the museum contains
a wealth of archaeological,
ethnological, and numismatic
exhibits. These include a rare
pair of Lusitanian granite
warriors, a bronze votive oxcart, and the Pedras Formosas,
two stone slabs inscribed with
human figures. The most striking exhibit is the Colossus of
Pedralva, a stone figure that
stands 3 m (10 ft) tall.

🏛 São Francisco

Largo de São Francisco. [253-51
79 26. 🕐 Tue–Sun. 🔒 public hols.
Built in 1400 in Gothic style,
the elegant church of São Francisco was reconstructed in the
18th century. The interior of
the church boasts a chancel
covered in magnificent 18th-
century *azulejos* with scenes
from the life of St. Antony.

ENVIRONS: The former monastery of **Santa Marinha da
Costa** is one of Portugal's top
pousadas (see p379). It stands
5 km (3 miles) southeast of
Guimarães and was founded
in 1154. The gardens and
chapel are open to the public.

Renaissance stone fountain at Santa
Marinha da Costa monastery

Reconstructed huts at the Iron Age site of Citânia de Briteiros

Citânia de Briteiros ⑬

Road map C1. 15 km (9 miles) N of
Guimarães, off N101. [253-41 59
69. 🚌 from Guimarães & Braga.
🕐 May–Sep: 9am–7:30pm daily;
Oct–Apr: 9am–6pm daily. 🎟️

THE IRON AGE settlement
of Citânia de Briteiros
is one of Portugal's most
impressive archaeolog-
ical sites. Excavated by
Martins Sarmento (1833–
99), who devoted his life
to the study of Iron Age
sites, are the foundations
of 150 stone dwellings,
a number of which have
since been reconstructed.
From about the 4th
century BC to the
4th century AD, the
site was inhabited by
Celtiberians, but was
most probably under
Roman rule from c.20
BC. A network of
paths leads visitors
past paved streets,
subterranean cisterns,
sewers, and water supply ducts.
The Museu Martins Sarmento
in Guimarães displays various
excavated artifacts.

**The *basto* statue
of Cabeceiras
de Basto**

Cabeceiras de Basto ⑭

Road map D1. 🏛 17,000. 🚌
ℹ️ Paços do Concelho, Praça da
República (253-66 22 16). 🎪 Mon.

THE TERRAS DE BASTO, once
a region of refuge from
Moorish invasion, lie east of
Guimarães among mountains
and forests. Statues known as
bastos, believed to represent
Celtic warriors, are found in
various parts of the Terras de
Basto, where they served as
territorial markers. In the main
town, Cabeceiras de Basto,
the prime attraction is the
Baroque **Mosteiro de
Refojos**, with its splendid
dome 33 m (108 ft) high,
surrounded by statues of
the Apostles, and sur-
mounted by a statue of
the archangel Michael.
The town also owns the
best of the *basto* statues,
albeit with a French
head; it was changed by
troops as a joke during
the Napoleonic Wars.

ENVIRONS: The fine
hiking country of
the Terras de Basto,
carpeted with flowers
in spring, has other
villages worth visiting.
Mondim de Basto,
overlooking the
Tâmega River some
25 km (15 miles) south
of Cabeceiras, is a convenient
base for climbing **Monte
Farinha**, which, at 966 m
(3,169 ft), is the highest peak
in the region. Then climb the
steps to the top of the church
of Nossa Senhora da Graça on
the summit for splendid views.
Over the Tâmega, the village
of **Celorico de Basto** has a
small castle and several manor
houses in the surrounding area.
Most are private, but some,
such as the **Casa do Campo**
(see p393), are part of the
Turismo de Habitação program
(see p376) and take in guests.

SOUTHERN
PORTUGAL

Southern Portugal at a Glance

SOUTH OF THE TAGUS the vast wheatfields and parched plains of the Alentejo stretch almost uninterrupted to the horizon. There is a rich legacy of early civilization here, dating back to prehistory, but visitors to Elvas, Beja, or the World Heritage city of Évora will not be troubled by mass tourism – until they reach the southern coast. Many visitors know nothing of Portugal except the tourist playground of the Algarve, yet it is least typical of the country. The sandy beaches are a year-round attraction, but historic towns like Faro and the quieter hinterland are well worth exploring.

Évora, *the Alentejo's historic university city, has monuments dating back to the Roman era. Gleaming white arcades and balconies of finely wrought ironwork are reminders that for over 450 years, until 1165, Évora was inhabited by the Moors (see pp302–5).*

Beja *flourished under the Moors, and its museum is housed in a former convent resplendent with Hispano-Arab tiles, such as these in the chapterhouse (see p311).*

Baixo Alentejo

Lagos, *principal town of the western Algarve, is flanked by inviting cove beaches, such as Praia de Dona Ana, which make it easy to understand why sun worshipers flock here (see pp320–21).*

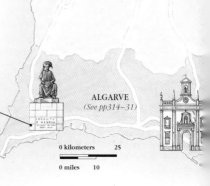

ALGARVE
(See pp314–31)

0 kilometers 25

0 miles 10

◁ **Sandy beach and calm waters at the popular resort of Albufeira**

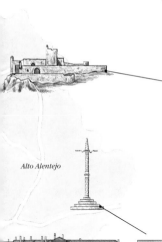

Alto Alentejo

Marvão, *within a stone's throw of the Spanish border, sits like a miniature fortress high in the Serra de São Mamede. The granite walls that protect the tiny town merge imperceptibly with the rock and have kept Marvão safe through centuries of dispute* (see p294).

Elvas *has some of the best-preserved fortifications in Europe* (see p297). *At the center of the walled old town lies the Praça da República, where Elvas's former cathedral looks out over the square's striking geometric mosaics.*

ALENTEJO
(See pp290–313)

Vila Viçosa *was chosen in the 15th century as the seat of the dukes of Bragança. Here they built their vast Paço Ducal* (see pp298–9), *in front of which stands a bronze equestrian statue of the 8th Duke, who became King João IV in 1640.*

Faro, *the gateway to the Algarve thanks to its international airport, is nevertheless bypassed by many visitors. Much was destroyed by the 1755 earthquake, but the town has retained a quiet historic center beside the harbor. In spring the streets and squares are scented with the sweetness of orange blossoms* (see pp326–8).

The Beaches of the Algarve

Sunbathing on the beach

FACING NORTH AFRICA to the south, and exposed to the force of the Atlantic in the west, the Algarve has a varied coastline. The Barlavento (windward side) includes the west coast and the south coast almost as far as Faro. Beaches around the promontory of Sagres are backed by soaring cliffs, and on the west coast many beaches are deserted. The sea here is colder and rougher than the south coast, with dangerous currents. Between Sagres and Lagos is the start of a series of beautiful sandy coves, punctuated with grottoes, overlooked by tightly packed resorts. East of Faro, the Sotavento (leeward side) has long, sandy beaches washed by warm, calm water.

Arrifana ①

🚌 🍴 ☕ ⛑

The gracefully curving beach of Arrifana is one of the most stunning on the west coast. Sheltered below high cliffs, the approach by road offers dramatic views *(see p318).*

Castelejo ②

☕ 🏄

This long, deserted beach of soft sand can be reached only by a dirt road by bicycle, car, or jeep. Its remote location, however, ensures peace and quiet *(see p319).*

Beliche ③

☕ ⛑

Despite being at the "world's end," Beliche is sheltered by Cabo de São Vicente. The sandy beach is backed by fascinating caves and rock formations *(see p320).*

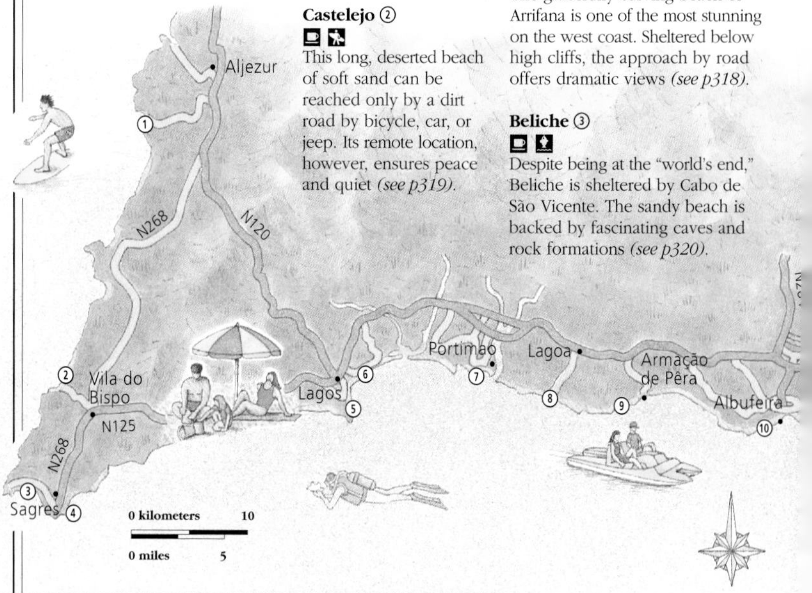
Aljezur
N268
N120
Vila do Bispo
N125
N268
Sagres
Lagos
Portimão
Lagoa
Armação de Pêra
Albufeira
0 kilometers 10
0 miles 5

KEY

Highway

Major road

Minor road

For key to symbols see back flap

Martinhal ④

🍴 🏄 ⛵ 🏊

Martinhal is a wide, sheltered expanse of sand east of Sagres. The area is popular for water sports of all kinds, and the beach boasts an aquatic school with parasailing, waterskiing, and windsurfing *(see p320).*

Dona Ana (5)

🚌 🍴 ⛱ 🚿 ⛺

A tiny cove on the way to Ponta da Piedade, Dona Ana is one of the prettiest beaches in the Algarve, although crowded during the summer. A boat trip to see nearby caves and grottoes is highly recommended *(see p321)*.

Ilha de Tavira (11)

🚗 ☕ ⛱ 🚿 ⛵ 🏊

In summer, boats go from Quatro Águas to the sandy Ilha de Tavira. The beach facing the coast has calm water, whereas the beaches on the ocean side, that run the length of the island, offer good swimming and windsurfing *(see p330)*.

Meia Praia (6)

🚌 ☕ 🍴 ⛱ 🛟 🚿 ⛵ 🏊

A vast expanse of sand stretching for 4 km (2 miles), the sheltered Meia Praia is the longest beach in the Algarve. Easily reached by road, there is also a boat trip from Lagos during the summer months *(see p321)*.

Carvoeiro (8)

🚌 🚗 🚻 🍴 ☕ 🚿

Carvoeiro is a fishing village with a diminutive cove. The whole area is great for cove beaches, and a boat trip or a walk along the cliff will take you to spectacular sandy beaches with excellent swimming and snorkeling.

Praia da Rocha (7)

🚌 🚗 🍴 ⛱ 🛟 🚿 ⛵

Framed by red cliffs and lapped by calm water, this spacious beach is justifiably famous – and crowded in tourist season. Water sports can be practiced here in a gentler sea than the extreme southwest, and visitors are well catered to *(see p322)*.

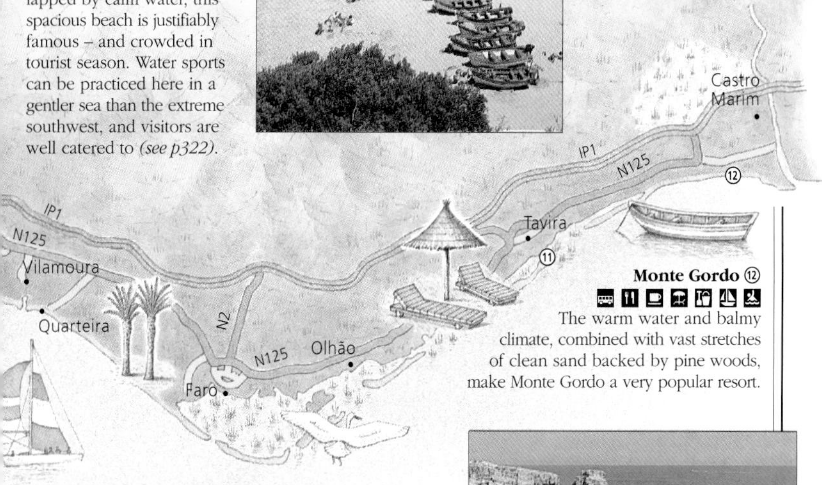

Monte Gordo (12)

🚌 🍴 ☕ ⛱ 🚿 ⛵ 🏊

The warm water and balmy climate, combined with vast stretches of clean sand backed by pine woods, make Monte Gordo a very popular resort.

Senhora da Rocha (9)

🚌 🍴 ☕ ⛱ 🚿 ⛵

Senhora da Rocha, named after a small chapel on its eastern promontory, is actually three small, sheltered beaches. Typical of this part of the coast, these half-moons of sand tucked below eroded yellow cliffs are reached by steep steps.

São Rafael (10)

🚌 🚗 🚻 🍴 ☕ ⛱ 🚿 ⛵

The small, popular beach of São Rafael offers soft sand and shallow water, with spectacular caves and eroded rock formations to explore. For those without a car, it is a steep walk down from the bus stop on the main road *(see p323)*.

Regional Food: Southern Portugal

The **TUNA AND SARDINES** available in the Algarve are unrivaled, but every type of seafood, from cod to clams, is excellent. Inland, fish is replaced by goat, lamb, and, above all, acorn-fed pigs, cooked into delicious stews with local wine. A feature of southern cooking is the *cataplana*, a kind of tightly sealed wok in which the food steams in its own juice. Bread is enjoyed, not just as a snack, but to soak up the herby juices in fish and meat dishes *(ensopados)*. Almonds, oranges, figs, and olives grow in abundance throughout the south.

Peppers

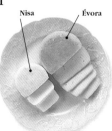

Nisa   Évora

Ewe's milk cheeses *come from all over the Alentejo. Among the best are Évora and the piquant Nisa.*

Chouriço

Spicy *linguiça*

Presunto pata negra

Salpicão, made with pork loin

Empadas (chicken pies)

Pão alentejano, *the peasant loaf of the Alentejo, is served at most meals and used in many bread-based dishes.*

Pork *is used in many guises in the Alentejo, which produces sausages and smoked hams* (presunto) *in delicious variety. Chicken pies are a specialty of Évora.*

Sopa alentejana, *fragrant with garlic, coriander, and olive oil, is a bread-based soup topped with a poached egg.*

Gaspacho, *always served cold, is a garlic-laden tomato soup, incorporating cucumber, sweet peppers, and olive oil.*

Salada mista *usually means a simple salad of lettuce leaves, tomatoes, and onions dressed with olive oil and vinegar.*

Atum de cebolada, *from the Algarve, is a fresh tuna steak that is cooked on a bed of onions with tomato sauce.*

Sardinhas assadas, *charcoal-grilled sardines, are a seaside tradition – a feast in summer when they are at their best.*

Lulas cheias *are succulent squid stuffed with cured meats and rice, then cooked in a onion and tomato mixture.*

Caldeirada *is a stew made with a variety of fish layered with potato. It is extremely popular all along the coast.*

Porco à alentejana, *a curious marriage of pork and clams, is usually cooked in a* cataplana, *which seals in the flavors.*

Borrego ensopado, *an everyday favorite in the Alentejo, is a stew of young lamb served on bread to mop up the gravy.*

Coelho em vinho *is an Alentejan recipe for rabbit, a meat popular all over Portugal. This version is cooked in wine.*

Cabrito assado *is a small kid, roasted whole, with a covering of paprika, garlic, wine, and lard to keep it moist.*

Olive oil (azeite) *enriches dishes from gaspacho to salads.*

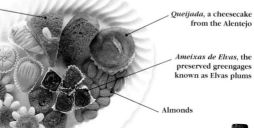

Bolo podre ("rotten cake"), a dark, spiced honey cake

Selection of marzipan *doces de amêndoa*

Figos cheios, figs studded with almonds

Queijada, a cheesecake from the Alentejo

Ameixas de Elvas, the preserved greengages known as Elvas plums

Almonds

Dried figs

Sweetmeats *in the south reflect the rich harvest of figs and almonds from the Algarve, fashioned into mouthwatering honeyed treats.*

FRUIT

As well as the ubiquitous grape, the climate favors greengages, apricots, and citrus fruits. Mild winters help the Algarve grow the best figs, oranges, and strawberries in the country.

Oranges

Grapes

LIQUEURS

The south's best wines are from the Alentejo *(see pp28–9)*, but the Algarve has two local liqueurs: the bitter-almond *amarguinha*, splendid on ice, and *medronheira*, made from the pretty fruit of the strawberry tree *(Arbutus unedo)*.

Amarguinha, an almond liqueur

Medronheira sweetened with honey

ALENTEJO

....

THE SUN-BAKED ALENTEJO *occupies nearly one-third of Portugal, stretching all the way from the Tagus south to the Algarve. Its vast rolling plains, golden with wheat or silver with olive trees, its whitewashed villages, megaliths, and castles, and above all the space and tranquility, are the Alentejo's great attractions for visitors.*

Stone circles, dolmens, and other relics of Stone Age life pepper the Alentejan plain, particularly around Évora, a historical gem of a city at the region's geographical center.

Évora, like Beja, Vidigueira, and other towns, was founded by the Romans, who valued this land beyond the Tagus – *além Tejo* – for its wheatfields. Introducing irrigation systems to overcome the soil's aridity, they established enormous farms to grow grain for the empire. Worked by peasant farmers, these huge estates, or *latifúndios*, still exist, some of them now being run as cooperatives.

Grain apart, the vast plains yield cork from the bark of cork oaks and olives – Elvas is prized for these as well as its candied greengages *(see p289)*. Vineyards around Reguengos and Vidigueira have long produced powerful wines, and the Alentejo has a number of demarcated wine regions *(see pp28–9)*. Since 1986, Portugal's membership of the European Union has increased the rate of investment and modernization, although the region is still sparsely populated, supporting only ten percent of the population. Land tenure has always been a concern here, and communism has a strong appeal – the Alentejans were solid supporters of the 1974 revolution *(see p57)*.

Many towns and villages, especially in the south, carry echoes of the long Moorish occupation in the cubelike white houses, while to the north and east the plains give way to a rocky terrain of fortified villages and scrubland grazed by flocks of sheep.

Portuguese from other regions mock the amiable *alentejanos* for their slow ways, but they are widely admired for their singing and their handicrafts.

An Alentejan house in Odemira, with the traditional blue trim typical of the region

◁ **Cork oaks and olive trees breaking up the wheatfields of the Alentejo plains**

Exploring the Alentejo

THE ANCIENT CITY of Évora, with its exceptional historic center and location in the heart of the Alentejo, is an obvious starting point for exploring this varied and beautiful region.

To the northeast lie the white towns of Estremoz and Vila Viçosa, where local marble has been used in the construction of some fabulous façades, and Alter do Chão, home of Portugal's royal horse, the Alter Real. Nearer the long-disputed Spanish frontier, towns and villages still shelter within massive fortifications, while traveling south the legacy of the Moors becomes ever more apparent: Beja and Mértola, especially, are full of Moorish history.

On the west coast there are some lovely beaches, with many stretches still relatively untouched by tourism.

The cromlech of Almendres, one of many prehistoric sites around Évora

SIGHTS AT A GLANCE

The fertile farmland and orchards of the northern Alentejo, seen from Estremoz

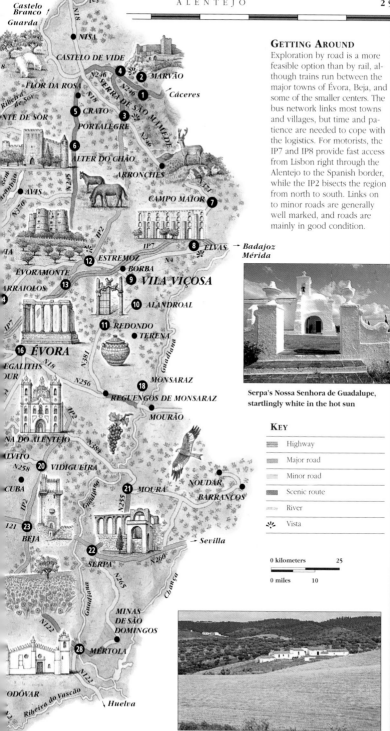

Tejo

NISA

CASTELO DE VIDE

FLOR DA ROSA

Ribeira de Sôr

NTE DE SÔR

SERRA DE SÃO MAMEDE

MARVÃO

Cáceres

CRATO

PORTALEGRE

ALTER DO CHÃO

ARRONCHES

AVIS

CAMPO MAIOR

ESTREMOZ

BORBA

VILA VIÇOSA

ÉVORAMONTE

ARRAIOLOS

ALANDROAL

REDONDO

TERENA

ÉVORA

EGALITHS

OUR

MONSARAZ

REGUENGOS DE MONSARAZ

MOURÃO

NA DO ALENTEJO

ALVITO

VIDIGUEIRA

CUBA

MOURA

NOUDAR

BARRANCOS

BEJA

SERPA

Sevilla

MINAS
DE SÃO
DOMINGOS

MÉRTOLA

ODÔVAR

Ribeira do Vascão

Huelva

Faro

IP7   ELVAS → Badajoz
Mérida
N4

GETTING AROUND

Exploration by road is a more feasible option than by rail, although trains run between the major towns of Évora, Beja, and some of the smaller centers. The bus network links most towns and villages, but time and patience are needed to cope with the logistics. For motorists, the IP7 and IP8 provide fast access from Lisbon right through the Alentejo to the Spanish border, while the IP2 bisects the region from north to south. Links on to minor roads are generally well marked, and roads are mainly in good condition.

Serpa's Nossa Senhora de Guadalupe, startlingly white in the hot sun

KEY

	Highway
	Major road
	Minor road
	Scenic route
	River
☀	Vista

0 kilometers   25

0 miles   10

A sea of wheat surrounding a farmhouse near Moura

Serra de São Mamede ❶

Road map D4. 🚌 *to Portalegre.*
🚹 *Portalegre.*

THE DIVERSE GEOLOGY and
capricious climate of this
remote range, caught between
the Atlantic and the Mediterranean, encourage a fascinating
range of flora and fauna. In
1989, 320 sq km (120 sq miles)
of the Serra were designated
a *parque natural*, and griffon
vultures and Bonelli's eagles
soar overhead. Red deer, wild
boar, and the catlike genet live
among the sweet chestnut trees
and holm oaks, and streams
attract otters and amphibians,
such as the Iberian midwife
toad. The preserve is also
home to one of the largest
colonies of bats in Europe.

The Serra's apparent empti-
ness is deceptive: megaliths
suggest that it was settled in
prehistoric times, and in the
south of the preserve, rock
paintings survive in the Serra
de Cavaleiros and Serra de
Louções. Below Marvão is the
Roman town of Amaia (São
Salvador de Aramenha), and
the Roman network of roads
still winds among the trim
white villages, offering grand
views at every curve.

From Portalegre, the road
climbs for 15 km (9 miles) to
the Pico de São Mamede at
1,025 m (3,363 ft). A minor
road leads south to Alegrete,
a fortified village crowned by
its ruined 14th-century castle.

Sheep in the summer pastures of the Serra de São Mamede

Marvão ❷

Road map D4. 🏰 *270.* 🚉 🚌
🚹 *Rua Dr Matos Magalhães (245-
931 04).* 🏪 *Thu.*

THIS SERENE MEDIEVAL hamlet
is dramatically set at 862 m
(2,828 ft) on a spectacular
escarpment facing Spain. Its
13th-century walls and 17th-
century buttresses blend
seamlessly into the granite of
the mountains, making it an
impregnable stronghold. The
Romans, who called the outcrop Herminius Minor, were
followed by the Moors – the
name may have come from
Marvan, a Moorish leader –
whom the Christians evicted
with difficulty only in 1166.

The walls completely enclose
the little collection of whitewashed houses, a *pousada*
(see p395), and the 15th-century
Igreja Matriz. Rua do Espírito

Santo leads past the former
governor's house (now a bank)
with its 17th-century iron balcony, and a Baroque fountain,
up towards the **castle**.

Built by King Dinis in about
1299, the castle dominates the
village. Its walls enclose two
cisterns and a keep and offer
spectacular views south and
west toward the Serra de São
Mamede and eastward to the
Spanish frontier.

The **Museu Municipal**, in
the former church of Santa
Maria, retains the main altar,
and has an interesting exhibition of traditional remedies,
an ethnological display, and
local archaeological finds
dating from Paleolithic to
Roman times.

🏛 **Museu Municipal**
Largo de Santa Maria. 📞 *245-931
04.* ⬜ *daily.* ⬤ *Dec 25.* 🎫 🚻

Portalegre ❸

Road map D4. 🏰 *15,000.* 🚉 🚌
🚹 *Estrada de Santana 25 (245-30 07
70).* 🏪 *Wed & Sat (food); 2nd Wed
of month (clothes).*

STRATEGICALLY POSITIONED on
a low plateau of the Serra
de São Mamede amid fertile
country, Portalegre is of
Roman origin. Fortified by
King Dinis (see pp44–5), it
acquired city status in 1550.

Textile, tapestry, and silk
industries brought prosperity
in the 16th and 17th centuries,
reflected in the city's fine
Renaissance and Baroque
mansions. These are to be

Looking out over the plain from the heights of Marvão's castle

found along Rua 19 de Junho, the main street of the old town. Near the new town's central square, the Rossio, a former Jesuit monastery is now the only tapestry factory still in use. Cork production is also a tradition here, and the tall chimneys of cork factories on the edge of the city indicate a continuing industry.

Uphill lies the cathedral, or **Sé**. Built in 1556, it acquired its Baroque façade and twin pinnacles in the 18th century. The late Renaissance interior has paintings by anonymous Portuguese artists and a sacristy lined with striking *azulejo* panels. These blue and white tile pictures, dating from the first years of the 17th century, depict scenes from the life of the Virgin Mary and the flight of the Holy Family into Egypt.

In an adjacent 18th-century mansion is the small **Museu Municipal**, where the eclectic collection on display ranges from religious art to Portuguese ceramics.

The home of José Régio (1901–69), the eminent Portuguese poet and dramatist, is near the Praça da República. Now the **Museu José Régio**, it contains some fascinating folk art objects in a variety of media, as well as a recreated Alentejan kitchen.

🏛 **Museu Municipal**
Rua José Maria da Rosa.
📞 245-33 06 16. 🕐 Wed–Mon.
⬤ public hols. 📷
🏛 **Museu José Régio**
Rua José Régio. 📞 245-236 25.
🕐 Tue–Sun. ⬤ public hols. 📷

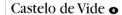

Folk crucifix, Museu
José Régio, Portalegre

Castelo de Vide ❶

Road map D4. 🚶 *3,000.* 🚘 🚌
ℹ Rua Bartolomeu A. da Santa 81
(245-90 13 61). ⬤ Fri (clothes).

SPRAWLED ON a green slope of the Serra de São Mamede, this pretty spa town enjoyed by the Romans has worn well. It is fringed by modern development, but the lower town, around Praça Dom Pedro V, retains its Baroque church of **Santa Maria**, the 18th-century town hall and pillory, and handsome mansions from the same era. In the Largo Frederico Laranjo is one of several sources of the town's curative waters: the **Fonte da Vila**, a carved stone fountain with a pillared canopy. Just above is the maze-like **Judiaria**, where small white houses sprout vivid pots of geraniums. Its cobbled alleys conceal a 13th-century **synagogue** and are lined with fine Gothic doorways. The town's oldest chapel, the 13th-century **Salvador do Mundo** on the Estrada de Circunvalação, has a much admired *Flight into Egypt* by an unknown 18th-century artist.

In the upper town, the tiny **Nossa Senhora da Alegria** offers a feast of 17th-century polychrome floral tiles. It stands within the walls of the **castle** that gave the town its name. This was rebuilt in 1310 by King Dinis, who negotiated here to marry Isabel of Aragon. Much of the castle was lost in an explosion in 1705.

Red-tiled roofs of Castelo de Vide

Crato ❺

Road map D4. 🚶 *2,000.* 🚘 🚌
ℹ Rua 5 de Outubro (245-971 61).
⬤ 3rd Thu of month.

MODEST HOUSES under oversized chimneys give no hint of Crato's past eminence. Part of a gift from Sancho II to the powerful crusading Order of Hospitallers, Crato was the Order's headquarters by 1350. Its prestige was such that Manuel I and João III were both married here, and João III's nephew was Grand Prior.

In 1662, invading Spanish forces sacked and burned the town, a catastrophe from which it never recovered. The Hospitallers' **castle** remains, in ruins, and in the Praça do Município the 15th-century **Varanda do Grão-Prior** marks the entrance to what was the Grand Prior's residence.

Rua de Santa Maria leads, via an avenue of orange trees, to the **Igreja Matriz**, much altered since its 13th-century origins. In the chancel, 18th-century *azulejos* depict fishing, hunting, and traveling scenes.

ENVIRONS: Just north of Crato are the imposing monastery and church of **Flor da Rosa**. Built in 1356 by the Grand Prior of Crato, father of Nuno Álvares Pereira *(see p183)*, the monastery was restored and in 1995 opened as a *pousada (see p395)*. A tapestry in the dining room shows the monastery surrounded by pine forests, as it was until the 20th century.

The crenellated monastery, now a *pousada*, of Flor da Rosa, near Crato

Alter do Chão ⑥

Road map D4. 🏛 *2,700.* 🚌
🛈 *Palácio do Álamo, Largo Barreto Caldeira (245-61 00 04).*
🎪 *1st Thu of month.*

THE ROMANS founded Elteri (or Eltori) in 204 BC but razed it under the Emperor Hadrian after the inhabitants were accused of disloyalty. The town was reestablished in the 13th century.

Dominating the town center is the five-towered **castle** with a Gothic portal built in 1359 by Pedro I. Its forbidding walls contrast with the flower-filled market square, the Largo Doze Melhores de Alter, at its feet.

Several streets northwest of the castle are graced by fine Baroque town houses, many trimmed with yellow paintwork in typical Alentejan style. The elegant 18th-century **Palácio do Álamo** that houses the tourist office, also serves as an art gallery and library.

♣ Castle
Largo Barreto Caldeira. ○ *Jun–Sep: variable hours.*

ENVIRONS: Alter is best known for the **Coudelaria de Alter**, founded in 1748 to breed the Alter Real. The stud farm extends to 740 acres around attractive stables painted in the royal livery of white and ocher.

Spanning the Seda 12 km (7 miles) west along the N369 is the robust, six-arched **Ponte de Vila Formosa**. This bridge carried the Roman road from Lisbon to Mérida in Spain.

♛ Coudelaria de Alter
3 km (2 miles) NW of town. 📞 *245-61 00 60.* ○ *Tue–Sun.* 📷 ♿

Campo Maior's macabre but compelling Capela dos Ossos

Campo Maior ⑦

Road map E5. 🏛 *8,500.* 🚌
🛈 *Rua Major Talaya 104 (268-68 89 96).* 🎪 *2nd Sat of month.*

ACCORDING TO LEGEND, this town got its name when three families settled in *campo maior*, the "bigger field." King Dinis fortified the town in 1310, and the monumental Porta da Vila was added in 1646.

Disaster struck in 1732 when a gunpowder magazine, ignited by lightning, destroyed the citadel and killed 1,500 people. It seems likely that after a decent period, the victims provided the material for the morbid **Capela dos Ossos**, entirely faced in human bones. Dated 1766, it bears an inscription on mortality spelled out in collarbones.

Each September the streets are dressed with paper flowers for the joyful Festa das Flores.

♠ Capela dos Ossos
Largo do Regala. 📞 *268-686 168.*
○ *daily (if closed, ask priest to open).*

Elvas ⑧

Road map D5. 🏛 *15,000.* 🚉 🚌
🛈 *Praça da República (268-62 22 36).*
🎪 *every other Mon.*

ONLY 12 KM (7 miles) from the Spanish border, Elvas feels like a border town. The sprawl of modern Elvas caters to busy cross-border traffic, but the old town's fortifications are among the best preserved in Europe. Within the walls a few architectural features and many of the street names are reminders that for 500 years the town was in Moorish hands.

Elvas was liberated from the Moors in 1230, but for another 600 years its fate was to swing between periodic attacks from Spain and the witnessing of numerous peace treaties.

Despite its dramatic history, Elvas is nowadays associated in Portuguese minds with Elvas plums *(see p289).*

Summer roses brightening an Elvas street

ALTER REAL: HORSE OF KINGS

Most Lusitano horses – Portugal's national breed – are gray, but those called Alter Real ("real" means royal) are purebred bay or brown. King José (1750–77), who yearned for a quality Portuguese horse, imported a stock of Andalusian mares, from which the gracious, nimble Alter Real was bred. The equestrian statue in Lisbon's Praça do Comércio *(see p65)* is of José astride his beloved Alter, Gentil. The stud prospered until the Napoleonic Wars (1807–15), when horse stealing and erratic breeding sent the Alter into decline. By 1930, the royal horse was practically extinct, but years of dedication have finally revived this classic breed.

The Fortifications of Elvas

A walk around the top of the battlements gives a fine view of the old town and a vantage point from which to appreciate the ingenious design of the fortifications. Using the principles of the French military architect the Marquis de Vauban, a series of pentagonal bastions and free-standing angled ravelins form a multifaceted star, protecting the walls from every angle. What survives dates mostly from the 17th century, when the defenses held off Spanish troops in the War of Independence *(see pp50–51)*. Elvas also served as Wellington's base to besiege Badajoz across the Guadiana.

Two surviving satellite forts indicate the strategic importance of Elvas: just to the southeast lies **Forte de Santa Luzia** (1641–87), and 2 km (1 mile) to the north is the 18th-century **Forte de Graça**, which is still a military post.

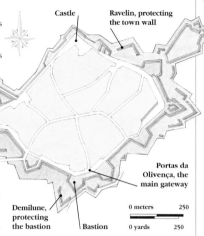

Castle

Ravelin, protecting the town wall

Portas da Olivença, the main gateway

Demilune, protecting the bastion

Bastion

0 meters   250

0 yards   250

♠ Castle
Parada do Castelo. ⬭ *daily.*
Romano-Moorish in origin, the castle that crowns the steep Elvas streets was rebuilt for Sancho II in 1226. It has been subjected to further remodeling over the years, principally by King Dinis and then in the late 15th century under João II, whose arms, which incorporate a pelican, can be seen above the entrance. The great keep was erected in 1488. Until the end of the 16th century the castle was used as the residence of the mayors of Elvas.

♠ Nossa Senhora da Assunção
Praça da República. 🄲 268-62 59 97.
⬭ *Mon–Fri.* 🌑 *public hols.* ♿
Until 1882, this was the cathedral of Elvas. Built in the early 16th century, its architect was Francisco de Arruda, who also designed the town's impressive aqueduct. His Manueline south portal survives, but much of the church has been modified. The *azulejos* in the nave date from the early 17th century.

⬭ Museu Arqueológico and Biblioteca
Largo do Colégio. 🄲 268-62 24 02.
⬭ *daily (library: Mon–Sat).* 🌑 *1 Jan, Easter, 25 Dec.* 🈂 *to museum.*
The archaeological museum's cool rooms display a collection that ranges from Roman water pots to prehistoric artifacts. The building in which the museum has been installed

since 1880 is a former Jesuit college. The associated library, which is entered by a quaint tiled porch, contains more than 50,000 books, including a number of rare early works.

♠ Nossa Senhora dos Aflitos
Largo do Pelourinho. ⬭ *Tue–Sun.*
🌑 *public hols.*
The plain exterior belies the wealth within the walls of this little 16th-century church. The octagonal floor plan originates from the layout of an earlier Templar church, but its appeal is in the fine marble columns and spectacular yellow and blue *azulejos* added in the 17th century. These line the walls and reach up into the cupola.

Just behind the church is the archway of the Arab Porta da Alcáçova, a vestige of Elvas's

Largo de Santa Clara, with its ornate pillory

Moorish fortifications. In the adjacent Largo de Santa Clara is a pillory, carved in typically exuberant Manueline style and still armed with its hooks.

The arches of the great aqueduct

♠ Aqueduto da Amoreira
Until the 16th century the only source of drinking water in Elvas was the Alcalá well in the west of the town. When this began to fail, alarmed citizens conceived the notion of an aqueduct to bring water from the spring at Amoreira, some 8 km (5 miles) away. Work begun in 1498 was not finished until 1622. The great round buttresses and arches of architect Francisco de Arruda march across the valley and still deliver water to the fountain in the Largo da Misericórdia. The aqueduct has a total of 843 arches in up to five tiers and in places towers to over 30 m (100 ft).

Vila Viçosa: Paço Ducal

T HE DUKES OF BRAGANÇA owned vast estates, but the lavish palace at Vila Viçosa, begun by Dom Jaime in 1501, became their favored residence.

When the 8th Duke became king in 1640, many of the furnishings accompanied him to Lisbon, but the long suite of first-floor rooms is still splendid, from the Sala de Cabra-Cega, where royal parties played blind man's buff, to the heroic Sala de Hércules. More intimate are the rooms of King Carlos and his wife, which are much as he left them the day before his assassination in 1908.

Chapel
Despite later additions, the chapel has retained its coffered ceiling and other features from the early 16th century. It was here, on December 3, 1640, that the 8th Duke learned that he was to become king.

Dining room

First floor

★ Sala dos Duques
Lining the ceiling of the Room of the Dukes are portraits of all the dukes of Bragança by the Italian Domenico Dupra (1689–1770), commissioned by João V. On the walls are Brussels tapestries of scenes from the life of Achilles.

The vast kitchen, which once regularly fed several hundred people, gleams with over 600 copper pots and pans, some large enough to bathe in.

Sala de Cabra-Cega

The armories, in a series of vaulted rooms, display swords, crossbows, halberds, and suits of armor.

Ground floor

The library is contained in several rooms and includes precious early works collected by King Manuel II in exile *(see p57).*

Formal Gardens
The Jardim da Duquesa and the Jardim do Bosque are partly enclosed by palace walls but can be seen from the dining-room windows. Their geometric formality reflects the palace's architectural style.

Entrance

STAR FEATURE

★ Sala dos Duques

KEY TO FLOOR PLAN

☐ Royal rooms

☐ Library

☐ Chapel

☐ Armories

☐ Kitchen

☐ Treasury

☐ Public areas

PALACE GUIDE

*Guided tours, which last
about an hour, take in the
royal rooms ranged along the
first floor and ground floor areas
such as the kitchen, armories,
treasury, and library. Entry to
the coach museum, on the
north side of the palace, is
by separate ticket. From
time to time areas
may be closed for
restoration, and
rooms can be shut
off without notice.*

Vila Viçosa ⑨

A FTER THE EXPULSION of the
Moors in 1226, this hill-
side town was named Val
Viçosa – "fertile valley." In the
15th century it became the
country seat of the dukes of
Bragança, and when the 8th
Duke became King João IV,
Vila Viçosa was expanded to
meet the needs of nobles
and visiting ministers. In
streets lined with orange
trees, substantial houses of
local white marble reflect Vila
Viçosa's prosperous royal past.

The town is full of reminders
of the Braganças. Dominating
the west side of the Terreiro do
Paço is the long façade of the
Paço Ducal, which stretches
for 110 m (360 ft). Visitors to
the palace emerge through the
Porta do Nó, a marble and
schist gateway formed into the
knot symbol of the Braganças.

In the center of the square a
statue of João IV on horseback
looks across to the **Igreja dos
Agostinhos** (not open to the
public). Founded in 1267 but
rebuilt in the 17th century, the
church was intended as the last
resting place of the dukes, but
despite their affection for Vila
Viçosa, most Bragança monarchs are buried in Lisbon, at
São Vicente de Fora *(see p72)*.

**View from the castle at Vila Viçosa,
looking toward the Paço Ducal**

In the Renaissance **Convento
das Chagas**, on the south side
of the square, are the tombs of
the Bragança wives. Founded
by the 4th Duke's second wife
in 1530, the convent is being
converted to a *pousada*.

Alongside the Paço Ducal, an
18-km (11-mile) wall rings the
tapada real, or royal chase.
Uphill from the Terreiro do
Paço is the **castle**, where an
exhibition explains the history
of the hunt. The castle, built by
King Dinis, was the Braganças'
residence from 1461 until the
Paço Ducal became habitable.

In the nearby 14th-century
church of **Nossa Senhora da
Conceição** stands a Gothic
image of the Virgin, said to be
from England. During the 1646
cortes João IV crowned her as
patron saint of Portugal, after
which no Portuguese monarch
ever wore a crown.

♠ Castle

THE ROYAL HOUSE OF BRAGANÇA

**Catherine, born at
Vila Viçosa in 1638**

Afonso, illegitimate son of João I, was
created Duke of Bragança in 1442,
first of an influential but bloodstained
dynasty. Fernando, the 3rd Duke, was
executed in 1483 by his cousin, João
II, who feared his power. Jaime, the
unstable 4th Duke, locked up his wife
in Bragança castle *(see p258)*, then
killed her at Vila Viçosa. It was Dom
Jaime who initiated the building of
the palace at Vila Viçosa, an ambitious
work embellished by later dukes to
reflect their aspirations and affluence.
The 8th Duke only reluctantly relinquished a life of music
and hunting here to take up the throne *(see p50)*.

The Braganças ruled Portugal for 270 years, accumulating
wealth and forging alliances (João IV's daughter, Catherine,
married Charles II of England), but inbreeding enfeebled the
bloodline *(see p165)*. The last monarch, Manuel II, fled to
exile in 1910, two years after his father and brother were shot
by Republicans. The present duke farms quietly near Viseu.

**The Porta do Nó, its carved knots
the symbol of the Braganças**

Alandroal, surrounded by groves of cork oaks

Alandroal

Road map D5. 🏘 *2,100.* 🚌
🛈 *Largo da Misericordia (268-44 91 50).* 🛒 *Wed.*

THE LOW-LYING little town of Alandroal, wrapped neatly around its **castle** ruins, was built by the Knights of Avis, who settled here from 1220. Little remains inside, but a surviving inscription shows it was completed in 1298. The **Igreja Matriz** within its walls dates from the 16th century.

The **Misericórdia** church near the castle walls contains beautiful *azulejos* reputed to be the work of Policarpo de Oliveira Bernardes (1695–1778).

ENVIRONS: Terena, 10 km (6 miles) south of Alandroal, is well known for its pottery. The 14th-century sanctuary of **Nossa Senhora de Boa Nova** has frescoes covering its walls and ceiling; dating from 1706, these depict saints and Portuguese kings. For access ask at the house opposite the church.

MARBLE: ALENTEJO'S WHITE GOLD

Portugal is the world's second largest exporter of marble, and even Italy, the biggest producer, buys Portugal's quality stone. Around 90 percent – over 550,000 tons a year – is quarried around Estremoz. The marble from Estremoz and nearby Borba is white or pink, while the quarries at Viana do

Quarrymen near Estremoz, working on elephantine blocks of prized marble

Alentejo yield green stone. Marble has been used for construction since Roman times, and in towns such as Évora *(see pp302–5)* and Vila Viçosa *(see pp298–9)*, palaces and humble doorsteps alike gleam with the stone often referred to as Portugal's "white gold."

Redondo

Road map D5. 🏘 *3,600.* 🚌
🛈 *Praça da República (266-98 92 10).* 🛒 *2nd Thu of month.*

THE CENTER OF ONE of the Alentejo's wine regions *(see p29)*, medieval Redondo is also famous for its pottery. Whole families work to produce Roman-style water jugs, casseroles, and bowls painted with humorous folk-art motifs *(see p25)*. These are sold from the tiny white houses leading up to the ruins of the **castle** founded by King Dinis.

ENVIRONS: The Convento de São Paulo in the Serra de Ossa, 10 km (6 miles) north, was built in 1376; Catherine of Bragança stayed here on her return home in 1692 after the death of her husband, King Charles II of England. It is now a luxury hotel *(see p396)*, but retains its wonderful 16th- to 18th-century *azulejos*.

Estremoz

Road map D5. 🏘 *8,000.* 🚌
🛈 *Praça da República 26 (268-33 35 41).* 🛒 *Sat.*

A KEY STRONGHOLD in the War of Restoration *(see p50)* and then in the War of the Two Brothers *(see p54)*, Estremoz looks out from its hilltop over groves of gnarled olive trees.

The medieval upper town, set within stout ramparts, is dominated by a 13th-century marble keep, rising to 27 m (89 ft). This is the **Torre das Três Coroas**, the Tower of the Three Crowns, recalling the kings (Sancho II, Afonso III, and Dinis) in whose reigns it was built. The adjoining castle and palace complex, built for Dona Isabel, is now restored as a *pousada (see p395)*. The saintly Isabel *(see p45)*, wife of King Dinis, died here in 1336, and the **Capela da Rainha Santa** dedicated to her is lined with *azulejos* recording her life.

Today the bustling weekly market in the Rossio, the main square in the lower town, is a reflection of local farming life. Across the square are the remains of King Dinis's once-fine palace and the town's **Museu Municipal**, with a display of archaeological finds, restored living rooms, and a parade of *bonecos*, the charming pottery figurines for which Estremoz is famous *(see p25)*.

🏛 **Museu Municipal**
Largo Dom Dinis. 📞 268-33 92 00.
🕐 *Tue–Sun.* ⬤ *public hols.* 📷
🏛 **Capela da Rainha Santa**
Pousada da Rainha Santa, Largo Dom Dinis. 🕐 *Apr–Sep: Tue–Sun.*
⬤ *public hols.*

Évoramonte ⑬

Road map D5. 🏃 *1,000.* 🚌
ℹ️ *Junta de Freguesia (268-95 91 51).*

Stone "rope" embellishing the castle walls at Évoramonte

ABOVE THE DOORWAY of No. 41, along Évoramonte's single street, is a historic plaque. It records that here, on May 26, 1834, Dom Miguel ceded the throne, ending the conflict with his older brother *(see p54)*.

Évoramonte's eye-catching **castle**, its walls bound by bold stone "ropes," largely replaced an earlier castle that fell in an earthquake in 1531. The 16th-century walls, however, have been controversially restored with concrete. An exhibition explains the castle's history.

♟ **Castle**
🕐 *Wed–Mon.* ⬤ *public hols.* 📷

Arraiolos ⑭

Road map D5. 🏃 *2,400.* 🚌
ℹ️ *Praça Lima e Brito (266-49 91 05).*
📅 *Sat (food), 1st Sat of month (general).*

THE FOUNDATION of Arraiolos is attributed either to Celts or perhaps to local tribes in about 300 BC. Its 14th-century **castle** seems overwhelmed

by the town walls and looming 16th-century **Igreja do Salvador**. Typically, houses in Arraiolos are low and white, with a blue trim to ward off the devil.

The principal sight in Arraiolos, however, is of women stitching at their bright wool rugs in the shadowy rooms behind the main street. Carpets from Arraiolos decorate countless manor houses and palaces throughout Portugal. The craft may have begun with the Moors, but floral designs of the 18th century are thought to be the finest. The **Câmara Municipal** has a fine display of locally made carpets from different eras.

🏛 **Câmara Municipal**
Praça Lima e Brito. 📞 266-49 91 05.
🕐 *Mon–Fri.* ⬤ *public hols.*

ENVIRONS: At **Pavia**, 18 km (11 miles) to the north, is the startling sight of a tiny chapel built into a dolmen. It is marked as Anta de São Dinis; if closed, ask at the café.

Montemor-o-Novo ⑮

Road map C5. 🏃 *7,000.* 🚌
ℹ️ *Largo Calouste Gulbenkian (266-820 71).* 📅 *2nd Sat of month.*

MONTEMOR WAS fortified by the Romans and then by the Moors – the Arab warrior Al-Mansur is remembered in the name of the nearby

The view down the nave of the Igreja Matriz in Montemor-o-Novo

Almançor River. The town, regained from the Moors in the reign of Sancho I, was awarded its first charter in 1203. The **castle**, rebuilt in the late 13th century, is now a ruin crowning the hill.

Montemor's 17th-century **Igreja Matriz** stands in Largo São João de Deus, named after the saint who was born nearby in 1495. The Order of Brothers Hospitallers that St. John of God founded evolved from his care for the sick, especially foundlings and prisoners.

A former convent in the upper town is now the **Museu de Arqueologia**. There are numerous agricultural exhibits, from old farm pumps to implements for carving cork.

🏛 **Museu de Arqueologia**
Convento de São Domingos, Largo Professor Dr Banha de Andrade.
📞 266-802 35. 🕐 *Tue–Sun.*
⬤ *Jan 1, Dec 25.* 📷 ♿

Arraiolos, crowned by its castle and the Igreja do Salvador

Street-by-Street: Évora ⑯

Rising out of the Alentejan plain is the enchanting walled city of Évora. The town rose to prominence under the Romans and flourished throughout the Middle Ages as a center of learning and the arts. It was a popular residence of Portuguese kings but fell out of favor after Spain's annexation of Portugal in 1580. Its influence waned even more when the Jesuit university closed in the 18th century. Students once again throng Évora's streets, joined by visitors who come to discover its many historical sites and enjoy the atmosphere of the old town. The city's historic legacy was officially recognized in 1986, when UNESCO declared Évora a World Heritage Site.

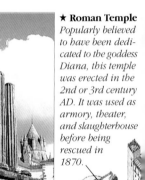

★ **Roman Temple**
Popularly believed to have been dedicated to the goddess Diana, this temple was erected in the 2nd or 3rd century AD. It was used as armory, theater, and slaughterhouse before being rescued in 1870.

Rua 5 de Outubro
The shops along this street sell curios and handicrafts, from painted chairs to carved cork.

| 0 meters | 50 |
| 0 yards | 50 |

KEY

– – – Suggested route

PRAÇA DO GIRALDO

Tourist information

To train and bus stations

Praça do Giraldo
The fountain in Évora's main square was erected in 1571. Its marble predecessor received the first water delivered by the town's aqueduct (see p305).

STAR SIGHTS

★ Sé

★ Roman Temple

★ Museu de Évora

RUA DO SALVADOR
RUA DE DONA ISABEL
RUA DAS CASAS PINTADAS
PRAÇA DO SERTÓRIO
RUA DE VASCO DA GAMA
RUA JOÃO DE DEUS
RUA NOVA
RUA 5 DE OUTUB
RUA DA REPÚBLICA

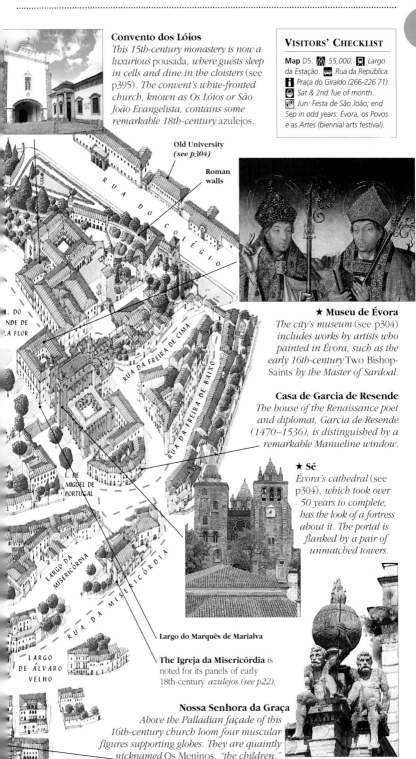

Convento dos Lóios

This 15th-century monastery is now a luxurious pousada, *where guests sleep in cells and dine in the cloisters* (see p395). *The convent's white-fronted church, known as Os Lóios or São João Evangelista, contains some remarkable 18th-century azulejos.*

Old University (see p304)

Roman walls

R U A   D O   C O L É G I O

L. DO NDE DE A FLOR

RUA DA FREIRA DE CIMA

RUA DA FREIRA DE BAIXO

L. DE MIGUEL DE PORTUGAL

LARGO DA MISERICÓRDIA

RUA DA MISERICÓRDIA

LARGO DE ÁLVARO VELHO

★ Museu de Évora

The city's museum (see p304) *includes works by artists who painted in Évora, such as the early 16th-century* Two Bishop-Saints *by the Master of Sardoal.*

Casa de Garcia de Resende

The house of the Renaissance poet and diplomat, Garcia de Resende (1470–1536), is distinguished by a remarkable Manueline window.

★ Sé

Évora's cathedral (see p304), *which took over 50 years to complete, has the look of a fortress about it. The portal is flanked by a pair of unmatched towers.*

Largo do Marquês de Marialva

The Igreja da Misericórdia is noted for its panels of early 18th-century *azulejos* (see p22).

Nossa Senhora da Graça

Above the Palladian façade of this 16th-century church loom four muscular figures supporting globes. They are quaintly nicknamed Os Meninos, *"the children."*

Exploring Évora

SQUEEZED WITHIN ROMAN, medieval, and 17th-century walls, Évora's web of streets is an architectural and cultural cornucopia. From the forbidding cathedral, a stroll down past the craft shops of Rua 5 de Outubro leads to Praça do Giraldo, the city's lively main square, whose arcades are a reminder of Moorish influence. Évora's religious dedication is reflected in the number and variety of its churches – over 20 churches and monasteries, including a grisly chapel of bones. On a happier note, Évora's restaurants are excellent, and the pleasure of wandering the historic streets is enhanced by evocative names such as Alley of the Unshaven Man and Street of the Countess's Tailor.

Azulejos at the Old University, depicting Aristotle teaching Alexander

🏛 Sé

Largo do Marquês de Marialva.
266-269 10. ⭘ daily (museum Tue–Sun). 🎟 to cloister & museum.
Begun in 1186 and consecrated in 1204, the granite cathedral of Santa Maria was completed by 1250. Romanesque blends with Gothic in this castlelike cathedral whose towers, one turreted, one topped by a blue cone, give the façade an odd asymmetry. Flanking the portal between them are superb 14th-century sculpted Apostles. The 18th-century high altar and marble chancel are by JF Ludwig, the architect of the monastery at Mafra *(see pp52–3)*. A Renaissance portal in the north transept is by Nicolau Chanterène. In the cloisters, which date from about 1325, statues of the Evangelists stand watch at each corner.

A glittering treasury houses sacred art. The most intriguing exhibit here is a 13th-century ivory Virgin whose body opens out to become a triptych of tiny carved scenes: her life in nine episodes.

🏛 Museu de Évora

Largo do Conde de Vila Flor.
266-226 04. ⭘ Tue–Sun. ● some public hols. 🎟
This 16th-century palace, once the residence of governors and bishops, is now the regional museum. Évora's long history is represented here, from Roman columns to modern sculpture in creamy local marble. A beautiful Moorish window came from the old town hall, and a stone frieze probably from the Roman temple. Notable upstairs are *The Life of the Virgin*, a 16th-century

Carved figures of the Apostles decorating the Gothic entrance to the Sé

Flemish polyptych in 13 panels and works by the Portuguese painter known as the Master of Sardoal, especially his *Two Bishop-Saints* and a *Nativity*.

🏛 Old University

Largo dos Colegiais. 266-255 72.
⭘ Mon–Sat. ● public hols.
With the establishment of the Jesuits' Colégio do Espírito Santo, Évora, already noted for its architecture and sacred art, became a seat of learning. The school, which was inaugurated in 1559 by Cardinal Henrique, brother of João III, flourished for 200 years, but was closed in 1759 when the reforming Marquês de Pombal banished the Jesuits *(see p53)*.

Today part of the University of Évora, the school still has a graceful cloister and notable *azulejos* – in the classrooms they depict suitably studious themes such as Plato lecturing to disciples (1744–9). The 18th-century Baroque chapel, now the Sala dos Actos, is used for graduation ceremonies.

🏛 Praça do Giraldo

Évora's bustling main square is bounded along its eastern side by a series of graceful Moorish arcades. The name Giraldo, some say, stems from Geraldo Sem-Pavor (the Fearless), an outlaw who in 1165 ousted the Moors for King Afonso Henriques.

The square has witnessed some bloody acts: João II watched the beheading of his brother-in-law, the Duke of Bragança, here in 1483, and it was the site in 1573 of an Inquisitional burning. Today, it is a favorite meeting place, especially on market days.

🏛 São Francisco

Praça 1° de Maio. 266-245 21.
⭘ daily. 🎟 to Capela dos Ossos.
The principal fascination of this 15th-century church is its Capela dos Ossos. This gruesome chapel of bones was created in the 17th century from the remains of 5,000 monks. Two leathery corpses, one of a child, dangle from a chain, and a mordant reminder at the entrance reads: *Nós ossos que aqui estamos, pelos vossos esperamos* (We bones that are here await yours).

Largo da Porta de Moura, with its striking Renaissance fountain

🏛 Largo da Porta de Moura

The western entrance to this square is guarded by the vestiges of a Moorish gateway. Both the domed Casa Soure and the double arches of the belvedere on Casa Cordovil at the opposite end show the Arab influence on architecture in Évora. The central fountain, looking like some futuristic orb, surprisingly dates back to 1556. Just south of the square, the portal of the Convento do Carmo features the knot symbol, denoting it once belonged to the Braganças (see p299).

🌳 Jardim Público

🚪 daily. ♿

On the southern edge of the old town, Évora's public gardens are set out on the site of the grandiose Palácio de Dom Manuel, built for Afonso V (1438–81) and embellished by successive kings. It was the venue for grand banquets and ceremonies but fell into disrepair and finally disappeared in 1895. All that remains is the graceful Galeria das Damas, a 20th-century reconstruction of a walkway and pavilion built for Manuel I (1495–1521).

THE ROMANS IN THE ALENTEJO

Once the Romans gained dominance over Lusitania (see pp40–41), they turned the Alentejo into a vast wheatfield: their very name for the principal town – Ebora Cerealis (Évora) – reflects the importance of the region's grain supply. Latifúndios, large farms instigated by the Romans, survive to this day, as do Roman open-cast copper and iron mines. Local marble was used in the construction of the finest villas, and Roman remains are to be found scattered throughout the region, particularly in Évora and Beja (see p311) and in more isolated sites such as São Cucufate, near Vidigueira (see p310) and Miróbriga, near Santiago do Cacém (see p312).

Roman bridge over the Odivelas, near Vidigueira

⚓ Walls

The fortifications that have protected Évora down the centuries form two incomplete concentric circles. The inner ring, of which only fragments are discernible, is Roman, from perhaps as early as the 1st century AD, with Moorish and medieval additions – the two stubby towers that give the Largo da Porta de Moura its name mark an Arab gate.

In the 14th century, new walls were built to encompass the growing town. Completed under Fernando I, these had 40 towers and ten gates, including the Porta de Alconchel, which still faces the Lisbon road.

When João IV was defiantly declared king in 1640 (see p50), major fortifications were erected on this outer ring in anticipation of Spanish attack, and it is these 17th-century walls that are most evident today. The fear of attack was not unfounded, and the walls withstood much battering from the besieging Spanish in 1663.

Surviving arches of Évora's 16th-century aqueduct

🏛 Aqueduto da Água de Prata

Évora's aqueduct, evocatively called "of the silver water," was built between 1531 and 1537 by the town's own eminent architect, Francisco de Arruda. The construction was regarded with wonder, and is even described in Os Lusíadas, the epic by Luís de Camões (see p188). It originally carried water as far as the Praça do Giraldo. Like the walls, it was damaged in the 17th century during the Restoration War with Spain, but a surviving stretch, some 9 km (5 miles) long, can still be seen approaching from the northwest: there is a good view of it from Rua Cândido dos Reis.

Megaliths Tour 17

ARCHAEOLOGISTS DATE the *pedras talhas*, hewn stones, near Évora to between 4000 and 2000 BC. Their symbolism remains mysterious. Dolmens are thought to be where Neolithic communities buried their dead, together with their possessions – more than 130 have been found in the region. Tall, phallic menhirs jutting from olive groves immediately suggest fertility rites, while cromlechs, carved stones standing in regulated groups, probably had religious significance. This tour includes examples of each; more can be found farther east, near Monsaraz, and the museum in Montemor-o-Novo *(see p301)* has finds related to the area.

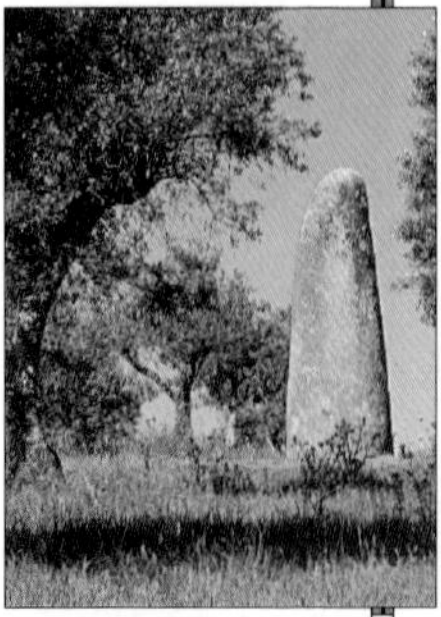

Menhir of Almendres 2
Standing 2.5 m (8 ft) tall, this solitary stone is located away from the cromlech, in an olive grove behind a row of tall Cooperativa Agrícola storage bins.

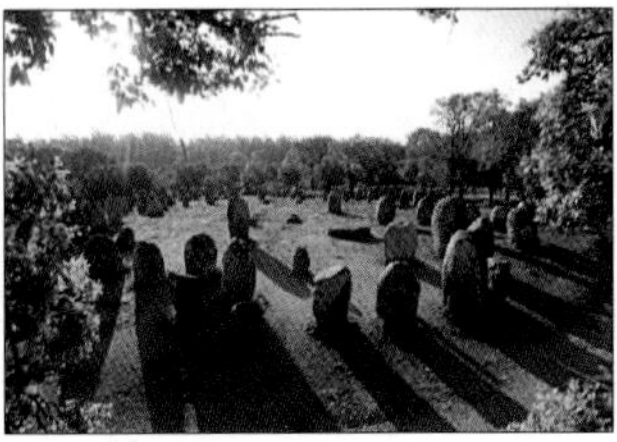

Cromlech of Almendres 3
This oval, made up of 95 ellipitical stones, is believed to have been a temple dedicated to a solar cult. The route to the cromlech is marked from the N114.

Évora 1
In the undulating farmland around the historic city of Évora *(see pp302–5)* at least 150 megalith sites have been found.

Grutas do Escoural 6
Discovered in 1963, these caves contain paintings about 15–20,000 years old.

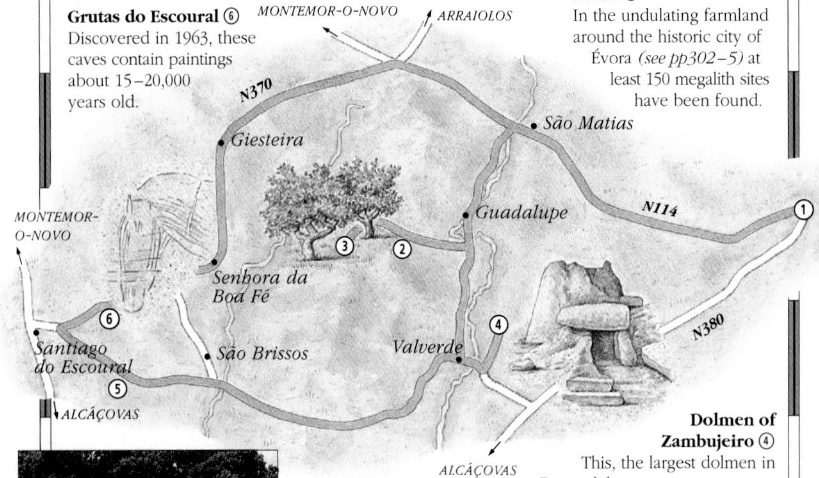
MONTEMOR-O-NOVO
ARRAIOLOS
N370
Giesteira
São Matias
Guadalupe
N114
MONTEMOR-O-NOVO
Senhora da Boa Fé
Santiago do Escoural
São Brissos
Valverde
N380
ALCÁÇOVAS
ALCÁÇOVAS

Dolmen of Zambujeiro 4
This, the largest dolmen in Portugal, has an entrance passage 14 m (46 ft) long leading to a chamber built of enormous stones. It is off the beaten track; the route from Valverde leads across farmland.

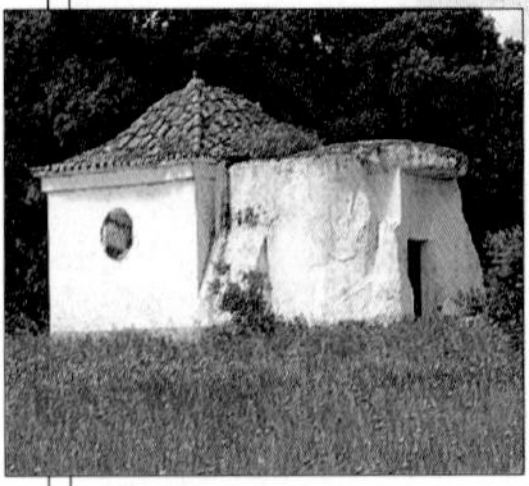

Dolmen-chapel of São Brissos 5
Beyond the hamlet of Brissos, this tiny chapel has been created from an *anta* or dolmen. Another is to be found at Pavia *(see p301)*.

KEY

▬	Tour route
═	Other roads

0 kilometers 5
0 miles 3

TIPS FOR DRIVERS

Tour length: *80 km (50 miles).*
Access to sites: *The only guarded site is Escoural. The caves are closed at lunchtime, on Mondays, and at some other times. Access roads to the sites are often no more than tracks, and signs can be erratic.* (See pp444–5.)

Riding through the narrow streets of Monsaraz on the day of a bullfight

Monsaraz ⓰

Road map D5. 👥 150. 🚌
🛈 Largo Dom Nuno Álvares Pereira (266-55 71 36).

T HE TINY MEDIEVAL walled town of Monsaraz perches above the River Guadiana on the frontier with Spain. Now a placid backwater, it has known more turbulent times. Regained from the Moors in 1167 by the intrepid adventurer Geraldo Sem-Pavor (the Fearless), the town was handed over to the militant Knights Templar. Its border position continued to expose it to Spanish attack, but in 1381 assault came from an unexpected quarter. Troops of the Earl of Cambridge, Portugal's ally, were enraged by lack of pay and the annulment of the earl's betrothal to Fernando I's daughter, and unleashed their wrath on Monsaraz.

Principal access to the town is through the massive Porta da Vila. Rua Direita, the main street, leads up to the **castle**. Built by Afonso III and Dinis in the 13th century as part of the border defenses, it was reinforced in the 17th century. The keep commands glorious views in all directions, and at its foot is the garrison court-yard that today serves on occasion as a bullring.

The 16th-century **Igreja Matriz** in Rua Direita is worth visiting for its tall gilded altars and painted pillars. The 17th- and 18th-century houses along here display coats of arms. In

the Gothic Paços da Audiência, now the **Museu de Arte Sacra,** is a collection of vestments, religious books, and sculpture. Its earlier role as a law court is reflected in an unusual secular fresco: *O Bom e o Mau Juiz* (The Good and Bad Judge).

🏛 Museu de Arte Sacra
Largo Dom Nuno Álvares Pereira.
🕙 9am–6pm daily. 🈂

ENVIRONS: Surrounded by vineyards, **Reguengos de Monsaraz**, 16 km (10 miles) west, lies at the heart of one of the region's demarcated wine areas *(see p29).* Its 19th-century church, Santo António, was built in flamboyant Neo-Gothic style by the architect of Lisbon's bullring *(see p120).*

A number of striking megaliths are found near Monsaraz. Signs in Telheiro, just north of Monsaraz, point to the spectacular **Menhir of Outeiro**, 5.6 m (18 ft) and the strangely inscribed **Menhir of Bulhôa**. About 4 km (2 miles) south is the **Cromlech of Xerez**, a menhir in a square of lesser stones.

Mourão, some 8 km (5 miles) farther on, is noted for the huge pepperpot chimneys on its tiny houses. The town's 14th-century castle looks out over the Guadiana River.

Viana do Alentejo ⓲

Road map D6. 👥 3,500. 🚌
🛈 Rua Brito Camacho 13 (266-931 06). 🗓 2nd & last Thu of month.

T HE NATURAL SPRINGS of Viana do Alentejo have offered an abundant water source in the Alentejo's dry heartland since Roman times. Its **castle**, begun in 1313, was built to the precise plans of King Dinis, the height of the outer wall exactly calculated to protect soldiers from attacking lancers. The unusual cylindrical towers show a Moorish influence, and much of the later remodeling dates from João II, who held a *cortes* here in 1481–2.

Mirroring the castle walls are the crenellations and pinnacles of the adjacent 16th-century **Igreja Matriz**. The highly carved Manueline entrance to this splendid fortified church leads into a majestic triple-naved interior.

Ten minutes' walk east of the town stands the vast pil-grimage church of **Nossa Senhora de Aires**, rebuilt in the 1700s. Inside, the chancel's golden canopy contrasts with pilgrims' humble ex votos.

ENVIRONS: The Moorish-style castle at **Alvito**, 10 km (6 miles) south of Viana, was built in 1482 for the newly ennobled Barão de Alvito; it now oper-ates as a *pousada (see p395).*

The low roofs and distinctive pepperpot chimneys of Mourão, near Monsaraz

A bullfight in the shadow of the 13th-century keep of Monsaraz castle ▷

The vineyards around Vidigueira caught in the evening light

Vidigueira ⓴

Road map D6. 🏃 *2,800*. 🚌
🅸 *Praça da República (284-43 61 02)*.
🅰 *2nd Sat of month*.

Fᴵɴᴇ ᴡɪɴᴇꜱ from Vidigueira make it a leading center of wine production in the Alentejo. Less well known is the fact that the explorer Vasco da Gama was Conde de Vidigueira. His remains, now in the Mosteiro dos Jerónimos *(see pp106–7)*, lay from 1539 to 1898 in the Convento do Carmo, now private property. A mediocre statue of the town's most famous son stands in the flowery square named after him. The main features of this unpretentious little town are a **Misericórdia** church dated 1620 and a clock tower from Vasco da Gama's time.

Environs: One of Portugal's most notable Roman sites, **São Cucufate**, named after a later monastery, lies 4 km (2 miles) west. The vaulting belonged to a 4th-century villa, but excavations have revealed the baths of a 2nd-century house, whose wine presses, reservoir, and temple indicate a sumptuous Roman residence.

Moura ㉑

Road map D6. 🏃 *12,000*. 🚌
🅸 *Largo de Santa Clara (285-25 13 75)*. 🅰 *1st Sat of month*.

Lᴇɢᴇɴᴅ ᴍɪɴɢʟᴇꜱ with history in this quiet town among oak and olive trees. Salúquia, daughter of a Moorish governor is said to have thrown herself from the castle tower on learning that her lover had been killed. From this tragedy the town acquired its name – Moura, the Moorish girl. The town's old Moorish quarter is an area of narrow streets and low, whitewashed houses.

Even after the Reconquest in the 12th century, Moura's frontier position left it open to attack. A siege in 1657, during the War of Restoration *(see pp50–51)*, leveled much of it. The 13th-century **castle** survived, only to be blown up by the Spanish in 1707 – just a skeletal keep and wall remain.

Nossa Senhora do Carmo, near the castle, was founded in 1251, the first Carmelite convent in the country. Its two-story cloister shows Gothic and Renaissance influence, and the chancel ceiling frescoes are early 18th century.

View over Moura's quaint Moorish quarter

Serpa ㉒

Road map D6. 🏃 *4,800*. 🚌
🅸 *Largo Dom Jorge de Melo 2–3 (284-537 27)*. 🅰 *last Tue of month*.

Aꜰᴛᴇʀ ᴘᴇᴀᴄᴇꜰᴜʟ ᴠɪꜱᴛᴀꜱ of olive trees, Serpa's stout walls, topped by an arched aqueduct, come as a surprise. Beside the monumental **Porta de Beja** is a *nora*, or Arab water wheel. Won from the Moors in 1232, Serpa successfully resisted foreign control until a brief Spanish occupation in 1707.

Today, Serpa is a quiet agricultural town that produces an esteemed ewe's-milk cheese. Pleasing squares and streets of houses that dazzle with the brilliance of their whitewash are overlooked by a **castle** of Moorish origin, rebuilt by King Dinis in the late 13th century. The **Convento de Santo António** in Rua da Ladeira was founded in the 15th century and is noted for its flamboyant 18th-century *azulejos*.

Serpa's great Porta de Beja

Environs: Serpa is just 35 km (22 miles) from the Spanish border. The Moors, and later Spain, fought for control of the region, which was finally ceded to Portugal in 1295. Continued disputes have left the legacy of a chain of watch towers and a peppering of fortresses across these hills. One of the most remote, the deserted fort at **Noudar**, was built in 1346, but even in this isolated corner, evidence of pre-Roman habitation has been uncovered.

On the border at **Barrancos**, an incomprehensible mix of Spanish and Portuguese is spoken. A speciality here is *perna preta* (black leg), a ham from the local black pigs.

LOVE LETTERS OF A HEARTSICK NUN

Mariana's window

Lettres Portugaises, published in French in 1669, are celebrated for their lyric beauty. They are the poignant letters of a nun whose French lover deserted her: she was Mariana Alcoforado, born in Beja in 1640; he was the Comte de Saint-Léger, later Marquis de Chamilly, fighting in the Restoration wars with Spain. The true authorship of the five letters may be in doubt, but the story of the lovelorn nun endures – Matisse even painted her imaginary portrait. Sentimental visitors to the convent of Nossa Senhora da Conceição (now the Museu Regional) in Beja still sigh over "Mariana's window."

Beja ㉓

Road map D6. 🏠 *18,000.* 🚗 🚌
🛈 *Rua Capitão João Francisco de Sousa 25 (284-236 93).* 📅 *1st & 3rd Mon of month.*

CAPITAL OF the Baixo (lower) Alentejo, Beja is a city of historic and social importance. It is also a major center for the production of wheat, olives, and cork, which are grown on the Bejan plains and provide the city's lifeblood.

The town became a regional capital under Julius Caesar, who called it Pax Julia after the peace made here with the Lusitani *(see p40).* The Praça da República marks the site of the Roman forum. The Moors arrived in AD 711, giving the town its present name and a lively, poetic culture until they were forced out in 1162.

More recently, Beja has been the scene of struggles against oppressive regimes. In 1808, occupying French troops massacred the inhabitants and sacked the city, and in 1962, during the Salazar regime *(see pp56–7),* General Delgado led an unsuccessful uprising here.

Beja's old town, an area of narrow, often cobbled, streets, stretches from the castle keep southeast to the 13th-century convent of São Francisco, now a superb *pousada (see p395).*

🏛 Museu Regional Rainha Dona Leonor

Largo da Conceição. 📞 *284-32 33 51.* 🕐 *Tue–Sun.* ⚫ *public hols.* 📷
In the heart of the old town, the former Convento de Nossa Senhora da Conceição houses the regional museum. A little marble ossuary near the entrance contains the bones of the convent's first abbess. Exhibits are mostly paintings and coats of arms, but the building itself is a remarkable blend of architectural styles, with a Gothic church portal, Manueline windows, and a dazzling Baroque chapel. Its *azulejos* are especially beautiful, the most notable being the Hispanic-Arab tiles in the chapterhouse and the early 16th-century examples in the cloister. Upstairs is a section on local archaeology and the romantic "Mariana's window."

♣ Torre de Menagem

Largo do Lidador. 📞 *284-31 18 00.* 🕐 *Tue–Sun.* ⚫ *public hols.* 📷
The unmistakable landmark of the castle keep marks the northwest limit of the old quarter. This work of King Dinis in the late 13th century towers 36 m (118 ft) high. The 183-step climb up through its three stories provides a rewarding panorama from the top.

Beja's landmark castle keep

🏛 Museu Visigótico

Largo de Santo Amaro. 📞 *284-32 14 65.* 🕐 *Tue–Sun.* ⚫ *public hols.* 📷 *joint ticket with Museu Regional.*
Just beyond the castle keep stands Beja's oldest church, Santo Amaro, its columns surviving from its Visigothic origins. Appropriately, the church now serves as an exhibition area for the Museu Regional's collection of relics from this early but important period of Portugal's history.

ENVIRONS: The remains of the luxurious **Roman villa** at Pisões, 10 km (6 miles) southwest of Beja, date from the 1st century AD. Excavation is far from complete, but extensive floor mosaics and fragments of decorated walls, baths, a bathing pool, and hypocaust have been uncovered.

⋔ Roman villa

Herdade de Almocreva, Estrada de Aljustrel (follow signs). 🕐 *daily.*

Chapterhouse of the former convent, now Beja's Museu Regional

Igreja Matriz, Santiago do Cacém

Santiago do Cacém ㉔

Road map C6. 🏘 *6,000.* 🚌
ℹ️ *Largo do Mercado (269-82 66 96).*
🛒 *2nd Mon of month.*

SANTIAGO DO CACÉM's Moorish castle was rebuilt in 1157 by the Templars *(see pp184–5).* Its walls, which enclose the cemetery of the adjacent 13th-century **Igreja Matriz**, afford panoramic views of the Serra de Grândola to the northeast. The attractive main square is enhanced by the elegant 18th-century mansions built by rich landowners who came here to escape the heat of the plains.

The **Museu Municipal** still retains some cells from its days as a Salazarist prison *(see p56).* Exhibits here include Roman finds from nearby Miróbriga.

🏛 **Museu Municipal**
Largo do Município. 🎫 269-82 73 75.
🕐 *Tue–Fri, Sat & Sun (pm only).*
🌑 *public hols.*

ENVIRONS: On a hill just to the east of Santiago do Cacém lies the site of the Roman city of **Miróbriga.** Excavations, still in progress, have uncovered a forum, two temples, thermal baths, and a circus which had seating for 25,000 spectators.

🏚 **Miróbriga**
Signposted off N121. 🎫 269-238 03. 🕐 *Tue–Sun.* 🌑 *public hols.* 🅿️

Sines ㉕

Road map C6. 🏘 *9,300.* 🚌 🚌
ℹ️ *Jardim das Descobertas (269-63 44 72).* 🛒 *1st Thu of month.*

THE BIRTHPLACE of Vasco da Gama *(see p108)* is now a major industrial port and tanker terminal ringed with refinery pipelines. Once past this heavy industrial zone visitors reach the old town with its popular sandy beach, but it is not always possible to escape the haze of pollution.

A prominent landmark above the beach is the modest medieval **castle,** restored in the 16th century by King Manuel. It was here that Vasco da Gama, son of the *alcaide-mor,* or mayor, is thought to have been born in 1469, and a museum dedicated to the great navigator is to be housed in the castle keep. A modern statue of Vasco da Gama stands looking out over the bay.

The **Museu Arqueológico** in the town displays striking jewelry, perhaps Phoenician, found on a nearby estate.

🏛 **Museu Arqueológico**
Rua Francisco Luís Lopes 38. 🎫 269-63 23 30. 🕐 *Tue–Sun.* 🌑 *public hols.*

ENVIRONS: North and south of Sines are attractive beaches. About 10 km (6 miles) south, **Porto Covo** is a picturesque village with an old fort above a cove beach. A little farther to the south and a short boat ride offshore is the low hump of **Ilha do Pessegueiro,** Peach Tree Island. Treeless and windswept, with the ruins of a fort, the little island is less romantic than it sounds.

More appealing are two sea-blue lagoons, **Lagoa de Santo André** and **Lagoa de Melides,** set in a long stretch of sandy coast about 20 km (12 miles) north of Sines. The lagoons attract a commune of campers, but vast open spaces remain for seekers of privacy.

Whitewashed houses with the traditional blue trim at Porto Covo, south of Sines

Vila Nova de Milfontes ㉖

Road map C6. 🏘 *3,200.* 🚌 ℹ️ *Rua António Mantas (283-99 65 99).* 🛒 *2nd & 4th Sat of month in Brenheiras.*

ONE OF THE loveliest places on Portugal's west coast is where the River Mira meets the sea. The popular resort of Vila Nova de Milfontes, on the sleepy estuary, is low-key and unassuming but offers many places to stay. Its small castle overlooking the bay once defended the coast against pirates and is now a hotel. In contrast to the quiet river are the grand beaches with their crashing waves, a major summer attraction, especially with surfers.

ENVIRONS: To the south about 10 km (6 miles) is the unspoiled beach of **Almograve,** backed by impressive cliffs.

The calm, sunny face of the sandy coast near Vila Nova de Milfontes

Zambujeira do Mar ㉗

Road map C7. 🏘 *1,000.* 🚌
ℹ️ *Rua Miramar (283-611 44).*

A NARROW STRIP of sheltered land divides the plains of the Alentejo from the bracing Atlantic. Here lies the solitary village of Zambujeira do Mar, the whiteness of its gorgeous beach enhanced by the dark backdrop of high basalt cliffs. Traditionally, families come here for Sunday beach outings, joined nowadays by campers and more adventurous tourists.

Mértola ㉘

Road map D6. 🏘 *1,200.* 🚌
ℹ️ *Largo Vasco da Gama (286-625 73).* 🎪 *1st Thu of month.*

P RETTY, WHITEWASHED Mértola is of great historical interest. The whole of this small town is a *vila museu*, a museum site, with discoveries from different eras exhibited in *núcleos*, or areas where a concentration of treasures from that period can be found. The tourist office has details of each *núcleo*.

Mértola's origins date back to the Phoenicians, who created a thriving port here on the Guadiana, later enjoyed by the Romans and the Moors. Roman artifacts can be seen

Mértola's unusual Moorish-style church, high above the River Guadiana

at the **Núcleo Romano**, based at an excavation beneath the municipal council buildings.

The post-Roman period in Mértola is on display in the **Núcleo Visigótico** and in an early Christian **basilica** whose ruins adjoin the Roman road to Beja *(see p311)*. The influence bequeathed by several centuries of Moorish domination is seen in Mértola's **Núcleo Islâmico**, which houses one of the country's best collections of Portuguese Islamic art and includes ceramics, coins, and jewelry. The **Igreja Matriz** below the Moorish walls was formerly a mosque, unique in Portugal for being so little altered. Among surviving Arab features are the five-nave layout, four horseshoe arches, and a *mihrab* or prayer niche.

Overlooking the town is the crumbling hilltop **castle**, with its keep of 1292, offering lovely views of the river valley.

ENVIRONS: The copper mines at **Minas de São Domingos**, 16 km (10 miles) to the east, were the main employer in the area from 1858 to 1965, when the vein was exhausted. An English company ran the mine under the harshest conditions, with miners' families living in one windowless room. The village's population has now fallen from 6,000 to 800, and the ghost-town atmosphere is relieved only by a reservoir and surrounding lush greenery.

Around Mértola, 600 sq km (230 sq miles) of the wild Guadiana valley is a newly designated **Parque Natural**, home to the black stork, azure-winged magpie, and raptors such as the red kite.

THE VERSATILITY OF CORK

Groves of evergreen cork oak *(Quercus suber)* provide the Alentejo with welcome shade and a thriving industry. It was Dom Pérignon, the wine-making monk, who in the 17th century revived the use of cork as a tasteless, odorless seal for wine. Portugal, the world's largest cork producer, has almost 7,000 sq km (2,700 sq miles) under cultivation and turns out some 30 million corks a day. In rural areas, this versatile bark is fashioned into waterproof, heatproof food containers, and these decorated boxes are a traditional craft of the Alentejo.

Harvesting cork is a skilled task. Mature trees, stripped in summer every ten years or so, reveal a raw red undercoat until their new bark grows.

The glowing red of a stripped tree in an Alentejan cork grove

ALGARVE

ENCLOSED BY RANGES OF HILLS *to the north, the Algarve has a climate, culture, and scenery very different from the rest of Portugal. Its stunning coastline and year-round mild weather, maintained by warm sea and air currents from nearby North Africa, make it one of the most popular vacation destinations in southern Europe.*

The Algarve's fertile soil and strategic headlands and rivers have attracted visitors since the time of the Phoenicians. Five centuries of Arab rule, from AD 711, left a legacy that is still visible in the region's architecture, lattice chimneys, *azulejos*, orange groves, and almond trees. Place names beginning with Al are also of Moorish origin; Al-Gharb ("the West") denoted the western edge of the Islamic empire.

When the Algarve was reclaimed by the Christians in 1249, the Portuguese rulers designated themselves kings "of Portugal and of the Algarves," emphasizing the region's separateness from the rest of the country. It was the Algarve, however, that shot Portugal to prominence in the 15th century, when Henry the Navigator *(see p49)* is said to have set up a school of navigation at Sagres, and launched the age of exploration from these southern shores.

The earthquake of 1755 *(see pp62–3)* had its epicenter just south of Lagos, then the region's capital. Virtually all the towns and villages were destroyed or badly damaged, which explains why very few buildings in the region predate this period.

Since the 1960s, when Faro airport was opened, international tourism has replaced agriculture and fishing as the region's main industry. A few stretches of the southwestern seashore are now cluttered with high-rise complexes catering to the yearly influx of tourists. However, the whole western seaboard exposed to the Atlantic and the lagoons east of Faro have been barely touched by development. Trips inland, to the pretty whitewashed village of Alte or the border town of Alcoutim in the east, provide a welcome reminder that, in places, the Algarve's rural way of life continues virtually uninterrupted.

Colorful ceramic plates for sale outside a local craft shop in Alte

◁ Strolling along the sandy Praia da Rocha near Portimão

Exploring the Algarve

T HE ALGARVE IS A DELIGHT to visit all year round. In summer the coast between Faro and Lagos attracts thousands of visitors, but even near popular resorts such as Albufeira and Portimão it is possible to escape the crowds. Though often bypassed, Faro itself is well worth a visit. Picturesque Tavira is an ideal center for the lagoons of the eastern Algarve, while from Lagos you can reach the beaches on the rugged southwest coast. Inland, the hillside villages are peaceful, with lush vegetation, both wild and cultivated. The wooded Serra de Monchique is an area of outstanding beauty offering lovely walks.

Wooded slopes around the vast lake created by the Bravura dam, north of Lagos

KEY

▨	Highway
▨	Major road
▨	Minor road
▨	Scenic route
═	River
☀	Vista

Brightly painted fishing boats in the harbor at Sagres

SIGHTS AT A GLANCE

One of the delightful sandy coves near Albufeira

GETTING AROUND

The IP1 divided highway from Albufeira to Spain has relieved the N125, which can become very congested in summer. Roads branch off to beaches, coastal towns, and inland villages.

A frequent but slow rail service connects the main towns, but stations are sometimes far from the center. Reliable buses link coastal resorts and inland towns, although progress can be slow.

0 kilometers 10

0 miles 5

SEE ALSO

Whitewashed house and lattice-work chimney in Cacela Velha

Commanding view of the countryside from Aljezur's Moorish castle

Aljezur ❶

Road map 7C. 2,500.
Largo do Mercado (282-982 29).
3rd Mon of month.

THE SMALL VILLAGE of Aljezur is overlooked by a 10th-century **Moorish castle**, reached via the old quarter. Although now in ruins, a cistern and towers remain, and there are splendid views toward the Serra de Monchique.

Aljezur's **Igreja Matriz**, much rebuilt after the earthquake of 1755 *(see pp62–3)*, has a fine Neo-Classical altarpiece. Dating from about 1809, it was probably executed in the workshop of José da Costa of Faro.

ENVIRONS: From Aljezur, the wild and deserted beaches of the Algarve's west coast are easily explored, but a car is essential. Open to the strong currents of the Atlantic, **Praia de Arrifana** 10 km (6 miles) southwest and **Praia de Monte Clérigo**, 8 km (5 miles) northwest, are sandy, sweeping beaches backed by cliffs. On the Alentejo border, **Praia de Odeceixe** is a sheltered cove that is popular with surfers.

Serra de Monchique ❷

Road map 7C. Monchique.
Monchique.

PROVIDING SHELTER from the north, this volcanic mountain range helps to ensure the mild southern climate of the Algarve. The highest point is **Fóia** at 902 m (2,959 ft). This, however, is less pleasantly wooded than **Picota**, which, at 773 m (2,536 ft), is the second highest peak. An impressive 4-km (2-mile) walk to this peak from Monchique passes among chestnut trees and fields of wild flowers. A spectacular panorama sweeps down to the Ponta de Sagres *(see p320)*, and there are stunning views of the rest of the range. Whether you explore the Serra on foot or by car, there is a wonderful variety of vegetation to enjoy, with rhododendron, mimosa, chestnut, pine, cork oak, and patches of terraced fertile land in the valleys.

In recent years, the increased planting of fast-growing eucalyptus trees has given cause for concern. This highly flammable species is one of the reasons for the serious fires that break out all too often in the Serra.

The 68-km (42-mile) run along the N267 from Nave, just below Monchique, to Aljezur in the west, leads through a beautiful part of the Serra. The landscape is a mixture of woods and moorland, kept fertile by an abundant water supply. Cork oak grows here, home to the nuthatch and lesser-spotted woodpecker.

Monchique ❸

Road map 7C. 7,000.
Largo dos Chorões (282-91 11 89). 2nd Fri of month.

Manueline portal of the Igreja Matriz in Monchique

THE SMALL market town of Monchique is primarily famous for its altitude, 458 m (1,500 ft), and consequently spectacular views. It is also known for its wooden handicrafts, particularly the folding chairs which are believed to date back to Roman times.

The 16th-century **Igreja Matriz**, on the cobbled Rua da Igreja behind the main square, has an impressive Manueline doorway whose knotted columns end in unusual pinnacles. Above the town is the ruined monastery of **Nossa Senhora do Desterro**. This Franciscan house, founded in 1632 by Dom Pero da Silva, is now only a shell, but it is worth visiting for the stunning views across to the peak of Picota.

The mountains of the Serra de Monchique rising above meadows of wild flowers

ENVIRONS: A delightful, tiny spa, 6 km (4 miles) south, **Caldas de Monchique** is set in the foothills of the Serra in peaceful wooded surroundings.

The hot, curative waters have attracted the ailing since Roman times, and even though João II died soon after taking them in 1495, their reputation has remained undiminished. In the summer, people come to be treated for skin, digestive, and rheumatic complaints. As well as the wholesome spring water, the bars here offer the local firewater, *medronheira*.

The shady main square has a large, attractive handicraft center. The woods offer good walking trails.

Vila do Bispo ❹

Road map 7C. 🏛 7,000. 🚌
🚹 *Câmara Municipal (282-63 91 06).*
🎪 *1st Thu of month.*

THE GRAND NAME of "The Bishop's Town" today refers to a peaceful village, rather remote in feel, which makes the crowds of central Algarve seem very far away. It acquired its name in the 17th century when it was donated to the see of Faro. The town's parish church, **Nossa Senhora da Conceição**, has a delightful interior decorated with 18th-century *azulejos* from the floor up to the wooden, painted ceiling, and a Baroque altarpiece dating from 1715.

ENVIRONS: The beaches in the area are remote and unspoiled. **Praia do Castelejo**, 5 km (3 miles) to the west, is accessible by a dirt road that

Baroque altarpiece inside Nossa Senhora da Conceição, Vila do Bispo

Promontory of Cabo de São Vicente jutting into the Atlantic Ocean

winds up from the village over moorland. The beach, set at the foot of steep cliffs, is large, sandy, and surf-fringed. The intrepid can turn off this track for the 6 km (4 miles) journey to **Torre de Aspa**, an obelisk at 156 m (512 ft) marking the spot for spectacular views over the ocean. The road is quite rough, so it is advisable to walk the last 2 km (1 mile).

Cabo de São Vicente ❺

Road map 7C. 🚌 *to Sagres then taxi.* 🚹 *Lighthouse (282-62 42 34).*

IN THE MIDDLE AGES, this windblown cape at the extreme southwest of Europe was believed to be the end of the world. The Romans called it the *Promontorium Sacrum* (Sacred Promontory), and today, with its 60-m (200-ft) cliffs fronting the Atlantic, it still presents a most awe-inspiring aspect. The ocean waves have created long, sandy beaches and carved deep caves into the cliffs.

Since the 15th century, Cabo de São Vicente has been an important reference point for shipping, and its present lighthouse has a 95-km (60-mile) range, said to be the most powerful in Europe. For even longer it has had religious associations, and its name arises from the legend that the body of St. Vincent was washed ashore here in the 4th century. Prince Henry the Navigator *(see p49)* was also reputed to have lived here, but, if so, all traces of his Vila do Infante have disappeared. A number

of important naval battles have taken place off the Cape, including the defeat of a Spanish fleet in 1797 by the British admirals Jervis and Nelson.

Since 1988 the coast from Sines in the north to Burgau in the east has been made a nature preserve, providing important nesting grounds for Bonelli's eagle, kestrel, white stork, heron, and numerous other bird species. There is also a colony of sea otters.

Clump of scented thyme near Cabo de São Vicente

FLOWERS OF THE WESTERN ALGARVE

The remote headlands of Cabo de São Vicente and Sagres are renowned in botanical circles for their flowers, which put on a strikingly colorful and aromatic display from February to May. The climate, underlying rock and comparative isolation of these headlands have given an intriguing, stunted appearance to the local vegetation. There is a great array of different species, including cistuses, squills, an endemic sea pink, junipers, lavenders, narcissus, milk-vetches, and many other magnificent plants.

The enormous Rosa dos Ventos wind compass on Ponta de Sagres

Sagres ⓺

Road map 7C. 🏔 *3,500.* 🚍
ℹ *Praça Central (open from summer 1997).* ⛴ *1st Fri of month.*

THE SMALL TOWN of Sagres has little to offer except a picturesque harbor. Essentially it is a good base from which to explore the superb beaches *(see p286)* and isolated peninsula west of the town. Henry the Navigator *(see p49)* built a fortress on this windswept promontory and, according to tradition, a school of navigation and a shipyard. From here he realized his dream "to see what lay beyond the Canaries and Cape Bojador … and attempt the discovery of things hidden from men." From 1419–60, he poured his energy and the revenues of the Order of Christ *(see p185)*, of which he was master, into building caravels and sending his fear-stricken sailors into unknown waters.

In 1434 Gil Eanes of Lagos was the first sailor to round the dreaded Cape Bojador, in the region of Western Sahara. With this feat, the west coast of Africa was opened up for exploration *(see pp48–9)* and Portugal poised for expansion.

Little remains of Prince Henry's original fortress; the walls that can be seen today are part of a 17th-century fort. Still visible is the giant pebble wind compass, the **Rosa dos Ventos**, 43 m (141 ft) in diameter, said to have been used by Henry. The simple chapel of **Nossa Senhora da Graça** was also built by him. The whole site, looking across to Cabo de São Vicente and out toward the open Atlantic, is exhilarating and atmospheric.

ENVIRONS: The town is also within easy reach of many superb beaches. Some, such as **Telheiro**, 9 km (5 miles) west of Sagres, and **Ponta Ruiva** 2 km (1 mile) up the west coast, are accessible only by car. Nearer to Sagres, **Beliche** is surprisingly sheltered, **Tonel**, on the tip of the promontory, has wonderful surf and **Martinhal**, 1 km (half a mile) east, has a water sports school offering water-skiing, surfing, and wind surfing.

Lagos ⓻

Road map 7C. 🏔 *20,000.* 🚉 🚍
ℹ *Largo Marquês de Pombal (282-76 30 31).* ⛴ *1st Sat of month.*

SET ON ONE of the largest bays in the Algarve, Lagos is an attractive, bustling town. In the 8th century it was conquered by the Arabs, who left

Moorish archway leading onto Avenida dos Descobrimentos, Lagos

behind fortifications that were extended in the 16th century. A well-preserved section and archway can be seen near Rua do Castelo dos Governadores, where there is a monument to the navigator Gil Eanes.

The discoveries of the 15th century *(see pp48–9)*, pioneered by Henry the Navigator, whose statue gazes scowlingly out to sea, turned Lagos into an important naval center. At the same time a most deplorable period of history began, with the first slaves brought back from the Sahara in 1441 by Henry's explorer Nuno Tristão. The site of the first **slave market** in Europe is marked by a plaque under the arcades on Rua da Senhora da Graça.

The city was the capital of the Algarve from 1576–1756. Extensive damage was caused by the earthquake of 1755 *(see pp62–3)*, so that today the center consists primarily of pretty 18th- and 19th-century buildings. The citizens of Lagos continue to make their living from fishing, which helps the town to retain a character independent of the tourist trade.

São Gonçalo in Santa Maria, Lagos

The chic new marina on the east side of town provides the first safe anchorage on the south coast for boats coming in from the Atlantic.

♣ Forte Ponta da Bandeira
Avenida dos Descobrimentos.
📞 *282-76 14 10.* 🕐 *Tue–Sun.*
⊘ *public hols.* ♿
On the seafront stands the 17th-century fortress which defended the entrance to the harbor. Its imposing ramparts afford far-reaching views over the town and the bay.

⛪ Santa Maria
Praça Infante Dom Henrique.
📞 *282-76 27 23.* 🕐 *Tue–Sun.* ♿
The parish church of Lagos originated in the 16th century, and still retains a Renaissance doorway. Of local interest is a statue of São Gonçalo of Lagos, a fisherman's son born in 1360 who became an Augustinian monk, preacher, and composer of religious music.

⛪ Santo António

Rua General Alberto Silveira. 📞 *282-76 23 01.* ⭕ *Tue–Sun.* ⚫ *public hols.*

This 18th-century church is an Algarvian jewel. The lower section of the walls is covered in blue and white *azulejos*, the rest in carved, gilded, and painted woodwork, an inspirational and riotous example of Baroque carving. Cherubs, beasts, flowers, and scenes of hunting and fishing, surround eight panel paintings of miracles performed by St. Anthony.

A statue of the saint stands above the altar, surrounded by gilded pillars and arches adorned with angels and vines. St. Anthony was patron and honorary colonel-in-chief of the local regiment and, according to tradition, this statue accompanied it on various campaigns during the Peninsular War (1807–11) *(see p54).*

Nearby is the grave of Hugh Beatty, an Irish colonel who commanded the Lagos regiment during the 17th-century wars with Spain. He died here in 1709 and his motto "Non vi sed arte" (Not with force but with skill) adorns the tomb.

🏛 Museu Regional

Rua General Alberto Silveira. 📞 *282-76 23 01.* ⭕ *Tue–Sun.* ⚫ *public hols.* 📷 ♿

Next door to the church of Santo António, an eclectic ethnographic museum displays local handicrafts and artifacts, traditional costumes and – most oddly – pickled creatures, including animal freaks such as an eight-legged goat kid. The custodian provides an informal guided tour.

Ocher sandstone rocks on the sheltered beach of Praia de Dona Ana, Lagos

ENVIRONS: The promontory, called the **Ponta da Piedade**, sheltering the bay of Lagos to the south has a series of wonderful rock formations, caves, and calm, transparent waters. Accessible by road and sea, and most spectacular at sunset, this area is not to be missed. The nicest beach is **Praia de Dona Ana**, 25 minutes' walk from the center of town, but **Praia do Camilo**, farther on to the tip of the promontory, may be less crowded. The long **Meia Praia** stretches for 4 km (2 miles) east of Lagos. A regular bus service leaves from the center of town.

A 10-km (6-mile) drive due north of Lagos leads to the huge **Barragem de Bravura** reservoir. It is peaceful and especially picturesque seen from a viewpoint high up.

Alvor ❽

Road map 7C. 🏘 *7,000.* 🚉 🚌
ℹ *Portimão (282-41 91 31).*
📅 *1st Tue of month.*

T HIS LOVELY FISHING town of white houses is popular with vacationers, but in offseason retains its charm. It was a Roman port, and later the Moorish town of Al-Bur. By the 16th century it was again a prosperous town, but it suffered much damage in the earthquake of 1755. The town was rebuilt with stone from the Moorish castle, so little of that fortress remains.

At the top of the town the 16th-century church, **Divino Salvador**, has a Manueline portal, carved with foliage, lions, and dragons. The outermost arch is an octopus tentacle.

Church of Divino Salvador overlooking the whitewashed houses and the harbor at Alvor

Nossa Senhora da Conceição, Portimão

Portimão

Road map 7C. 40,000.
*Largo 1º de Dezembro 33 (282-41
91 31).* 1st Mon of month.

O NE OF THE LARGEST towns in
the Algarve, Portimão is
not renowned for its beauty
but has plenty of character and
a long history as a port. The
Romans settled here, attracted
by the natural harbor on the
wide estuary of the Rio Arade.

While Portimão's outskirts
are modern and sprawling,
its town center dates from the
18th century and has excellent
shopping facilities as well as
a large, bustling market.

The center lies around the
pedestrianized **Rua Vasco da
Gama**, with numerous shops
specializing in leather goods.
Along Rua Diogo Tomé, the
church of **Nossa Senhora da
Conceição** occupies a low
hill. Rebuilt after the earthquake of 1755 *(see pp62–3),*
its 14th-century origins are still
visible in the portico with its
carved capitals. Inside, there

are 17th- and 18th-
century *azulejo* panels.
In Largo 1º de Dezem-
bro there are benches
adorned with brightly
colored 19th-century
tiles. The waterfront is
always lively, and res-
taurants serve fresh
sardines and sea bass.

ENVIRONS: Just 3 km
(2 miles) south lies
Portimão's touristic
neighbor, **Praia da
Rocha**, a series of
sandy coves among protruding red and ocher rocks. At its
east end is the **Fortaleza de
Santa Catarina**, a castle built
in the 16th century to protect
Portimão and Silves. From here
there is a superb view of the
lovely, sweeping beach backed
by 70 m (230 ft) cliffs and
overlooked by a swath of
high-rise hotels. These are
multiplying, and visitors will
find themselves fighting for
space in tourist season.

Silves

Road map 7C. 10,000.
*Rua 25 de Abril 26–28 (282-44
22 55).* 3rd Mon of month.

S ILVES'S COMMANDING position
made it the ideal fortified
settlement. The Romans built
a castle here, but it was under
the Arabs that the city flourished, becoming the Moorish
capital, Xelb. In the mid-12th
century the Arab geographer
Idrisi praised its beauty and
its "delicious, magnificent" figs.

Silves was renowned as a
center of culture in Moorish
Al-Gharb, home of poets,
orators, and historians until
the Knights of Santiago *(see
pp42–3)* took the city in 1242.

Until the 15th century, when
the Arade River silted up, Silves
was a prosperous port. Today,
the city's economy is largely
based on oranges and lemons,
grown to picturesque effect
in the surrounding orchards.
Above the town, the red walls
of the impressive castle stand
out against the skyline.

Quiet cobblestone street in Silves

♣ Castle
Castelo de Silves. **(** 282-44 56 24.
☐ *daily.* ☑ &
The red sandstone castle dates
back mainly to Moorish times,
though it has done duty as a
Christian fortress and, more
recently, a jail. It was the site
of the Palace of the Verandahs,
abode of Al-Mu'tamid from
1053 when he was ruler of
Seville and Wali of Al-Gharb.

There are superb views of
the town and countryside from
the massive, polygonal ramparts. Inside, the huge, vaulted
Moorish **Cisterna da Moura
Encantada** (Cistern of the
Enchanted Moorish Girl), now
holds the town's water supply.

The castle and town of Silves rising above a fertile valley of orange groves

🔒 Sé

Largo da Sé. ☐ *daily.* ● *public hols.*
Built on the site of a mosque,
the cathedral dates from the
13th century, but has been
much altered over the years.
In the chancel, light falls from
lovely double windows with
stained-glass borders onto a
jasper statue of Nossa Senhora
da Conceição, believed to date
from the 14th century.

Opposite the Sé, the 16th-
century **Misericórdia** church
has a Manueline side door and
a Renaissance altarpiece.

🏛 Museu Arqueológico

Rua das Portas de Loulé. 📞 *282-44
48 32.* ☐ *daily.* ● *public hols.* 🖼
Situated down the hill from
the cathedral, the Municipal
Museum was opened in 1990.
Its exhibits include Stone and
Iron Age tools, sculpted Roman
capitals, surgical instruments
from the 5th–7th centuries, a
13th-century anchor, and 18th-
century ceramic items. The
museum is built around its
star exhibit, a large Arab
well-cistern of about the
12th century that was
uncovered here in
1980. The staircase
built into the structure
descends 15 m (49 ft) to
the bottom of the well.

ENVIRONS: One kilometer
(half a mile) east of Silves
is the **Cruz de Portugal**,
an ornate 16th-century
granite cross. This may have
been given to the city by
Manuel I when João II's
body was transferred   *Silves's Cruz*
from Silves Cathedral to   *de Portugal*
Batalha *(see pp182–3).*
The faces are intricately carved
with the Crucifixion and the
Descent from the Cross.

Albufeira ⓫

Road map *7C.* 👥 *20,000.* 🚊 🚌
🛈 *Rua 5 de Outubro (289-58 52 79).*
📅 *1st & 3rd Tue of month.*

IT IS HARDLY surprising that
this charming fishing town
of whitewashed houses, overlooking a sheltered beach, has
become the tourist capital of
the Algarve. The Romans liked
it too and built a castle here.
For the Arabs it was Al-Buhar

Colorful fishing boats on the beach at Albufeira

(The Castle on the Sea), and
under them it prospered from
trade with North Africa. The
Knights of Santiago *(see p43)*
took it in the 13th century,
but the consequent loss of
trade almost ruined it. In
1833 it was set on fire by
supporters of Dom
Miguel during the
War of the Two
Brothers *(see p54).*
Much of the town center
is pedestrianized, including the oldest part around
Rua da Igreja Velha, where
some of the buildings still
have original Moorish
arches. The church of **São
Sebastião**, on Praça Miguel
Bombarda, has a Manueline
doorway. Rua 5 de Outubro
leads through a tunnel
to the beach, east of
which is the **Praia dos
Barcos**, where the fishermen
ply their trade. From **Praia de
São Rafael**, 2 km (1 mile) west
of Albufeira, to **Praia da Oura**
due east, the area is punctuated by small sandy coves set
between eroded ocher rocks.

Alte ⓬

Road map *7C.* 👥 *500.* 🚊 🚌
🛈 *Estrada da Ponte 17 (289-47 82
00).* 📅 *3rd Thu of month.*

PERCHED ON A HILL, Alte is one
of the loveliest villages of
the Algarve. The approach
from the east along the N124

is the most picturesque, with
sweeping views of rolling hills.
The focus of this steep, white
village is the 16th-century
Nossa Senhora da Assunção,
which has a Manueline doorway and baptismal fonts, and
a fine gilded altarpiece celebrating the Assumption. The
chapel of São Sebastião has
beautiful, rare, 16th-century
Sevillian *azulejos.*

About ten minutes' walk
from the church, and clearly
marked, is the Alte River, over-
hung with trees, and a water
source known as the **Fonte
Grande**. This leafy setting is
ideal for picnicking. On the
steep slopes, about 700 m (half
a mile) from the village is a
mill (converted into a restaurant) and a 5-m (16-ft) high
waterfall, **Queda do Vigário**.

**One of many filigree chimneys
that adorn the rooftops of Alte**

Vilamoura

Road map C7. **⚐** *9,000.* **▭**
ℹ *Praça Cupertino Miranda (289-31 47 54).*

THE COAST between Faro and Lagos has effectively become a strip of villa complexes and high-rise hotels. Vilamoura is a prime example of this kind of development and is set to become Europe's largest leisure complex. Its 4,000 acres encompass three golf courses, several tennis courts, a riding school, and fishing and shooting facilities. There is even a small landing strip. Its hotels and apartment blocks are still on the rise, and the already well-established complex is scheduled to be finished by the year 2000.

The focal point is the large **marina**, which bristles with powerboats and is fronted by restaurants, cafés, and shops. It makes a diverting excursion, and even the Portuguese have been known to spend a Sunday afternoon here. Due east is the crowded **Praia da Marina**. You can also visit the nearby Roman ruins of **Cerro da Vila**, which date from the 1st century AD and include a bath complex and a house with mosaics depicting fish.

ℍ Cerro da Vila
Avenida Cerro da Vila. **☎** *289-38 00 88.* **◯** *daily (Sep–Mar: Mon–Fri).*
▨ &

Luxury yachts and powerboats moored at the chic marina at Vilamoura

18th-century tile panels and gilded altar in São Lourenço, Almancil

Almancil

Road map D7. **⚐** *2,000.* **▯ ▭**
ℹ *Loulé.* **⚑** *1st & 4th Sun of month.*

OUTSIDE the undistinguished village of Almancil lies one of the Algarve's gems, the 18th-century **Igreja Matriz de São Lourenço**. Its interior is an outstanding masterpiece of decoration in *azulejo* panels. The church was commissioned by local inhabitants in gratitude to St. Laurence, who answered their prayers for water.

The copious blue and white tiles were probably designed by master craftsmen in Lisbon and shipped down. They cover the cupola, the walls of the chancel and nave, and the nave vault to stunning effect. The wall panels illustrate episodes from the life of St. Laurence; on one side of the altar the saint is shown healing two blind men, and on the other side he gives money to the poor. Along the nave arches, the tiled scenes show the saint conversing with Pope Sixtus II; arguing for his Christian belief with the Roman Emperor Valerian; and refusing to give up his faith. The story culminates in his martyrdom. In the last panel on the right, in which the saint is placed on a grill to be burned, an angel comforts him. The nave vault depicts the *Coronation of St. Laurence*,

and the cupola has decorative, *trompe-l'oeil* effects of exceptional quality. The last tiles were put in place in 1730.

The altarpiece, dated about 1735, was the work of Manuel Martins and was gilded by leading local painters. Astonishingly, the 1755 earthquake (*see pp62–3*) dislodged only five tiles from the vault.

St. Laurence's feast day is celebrated on August 10. In the 18th century, worshipers would flock to the church, "not only due to their devotion to St. Laurence, but also for the grandeur of his feast . . . and for the dancing and singing of all those present."

Loulé

Road map D7. **⚐** *20,000.* **▯ ▭**
ℹ *Edifício do Castelo (289-46 39 00).*
⚑ *Sat.*

LOULÉ IS AN ATTRACTIVE market town and thriving craft center. Its Moorish origins are still visible in the bell tower of the church of São Clemente. The **castle**, on the north side of town, is also Moorish in origin, rebuilt in the 13th century. Remnants of the walls behind the castle provide an overview of the town and the many lovely filigree chimneys, typical of the Algarve.

The heart of the town lies immediately south of Praça da República and encompasses the busy, pink-domed market. On Saturdays the area is particularly lively when gypsies run a simultaneous outdoor market. From Rua 9 de Abril to the Igreja Matriz you can watch handicraft workers carving wood, weaving hats, making lace, decorating horse tackle, and painting pottery and tiles.

The 13th-century **São Clemente**, on Largo da Silva, was badly damaged in three earthquakes, the last in 1969, but its triple nave, defined by Gothic arches, has been conserved. There are two beautiful side chapels dating from the early 16th century. The Capela de Nossa Senhora da Consolação is decorated from floor to vault with superb blue and white *azulejo* panels, and the Capela de São Brás, has a Manueline arch and a blue and gold Baroque altarpiece.

Other churches of note are the **Igreja da Misericórdia**, on Avenida Marçal Pacheco, which has a Manueline doorway, and the chapel of **Nossa Senhora da Conceição**, close to Praça da República. Here, the Baroque altarpiece (1745) by Miguel Nobre of Faro is complemented by scenes in blue and white *azulejos*.

ENVIRONS: The 16th-century, hilltop chapel of **Nossa Senhora da Piedade**, adorned with *azulejo* panels, lies 2 km (1 mile) west of Loulé. Behind it stands a modern white church of the same name, built to replace the old chapel but which never became a popular place of worship. The spot also affords spectacular views.

Colorful tiled fountain on the terrace of the Patamar da Casa do Presépio, Estoi

Estoi ⑯

Road map D7. 👥 *4,300.* 🚌
🚉 *Faro (289-80 36 04).* 🛒 *daily.*

THE QUIET VILLAGE of Estoi has two notable sights, separated by a short distance and about 1,800 years. Just off the main square is the **Palácio de Estoi**, an unashamedly pretty Rococo pastiche, unique to the region. The palace was the brainchild of a local nobleman who died soon after work was begun in the mid-1840s. Another wealthy local later acquired the place and completed it in 1909. For the vast amount of money and energy he expended on his new home, he was made Viscount of Estoi. The work was supervised by the architect

Domingos da Silva Meira, whose interest in sculpture is evident everywhere.

The palace now belongs to Faro Council, and its interior – a feast of pastel and stucco – is slowly being restored.

🌷 Palace gardens

Rua do Jardim. 📞 *289-972 82.* ⏰ *Tue–Sat.* 🚫 *public hols.* ♿
Dotted with orange trees and palms, the gardens are well worth visiting and continue the joyful Rococo spirit of the palace. The lower terrace has a blue and white tiled pavilion, the Casa da Cascata, inside of which is a copy of Canova's *Three Graces*. The main walled terrace above, the Patamar da Casa do Presépio, has a large pavilion with stained-glass windows, fountains adorned with nymphs, and niches covered in charming pastoral scenes in *azulejos*.

Detail of fish mosaic in the baths of the Roman ruins at Milreu

🏛 Milreu

N2-6. ⏰ *Tue–Sun.* 🚫 *public hols.*
A ten-minute walk downhill from the other end of the main square leads to Estoi's second sight: the Roman complex of Milreu, which dates from the 1st or 2nd century AD. The buildings probably began as a large farmhouse that was converted in the 3rd century into a luxurious villa, built around a central courtyard.

Ebullient fish mosaics still adorn the baths, alongside the living quarters, but most portable archaeological finds are now housed in Faro's Museu Municipal *(see p327).* The importance of the villa, which may have belonged to a wealthy patrician, is indicated by the remains of a temple overlooking the site. This was converted into a Christian basilica in the 5th century.

Pink Rococo façade of the Palácio de Estoi

Faro 🔟

Azulejo **crucifix in exterior chapel of Nossa Senhora do Pé da Cruz**

CAPITAL OF THE ALGARVE since 1756, Faro has been reborn several times over the centuries – following invasion, fire, and earthquake. A prehistoric fishing village, it became an important port and administrative center under the Romans, who named it Ossonoba. Captured from the Moors in 1249 by Afonso III, Faro prospered until 1596, when it was sacked and burned by the Earl of Essex, favorite of Elizabeth I of England. A new city rose from the ashes, only to be badly damaged in the earthquake of 1755 *(see pp62–3)*. Although vestiges of the ancient city walls are still standing, the finest buildings date mainly from the late 18th and 19th centuries.

Statue of Dom Francisco Gomes do Avelar in Largo da Sé

Exploring the Old City

The center of Faro is attractive and easily explored on foot. It fans out from the small harbor to encompass the compact Old City to the southeast. Partly encircled by ancient walls, this is reached via the

Arco da Vila. The arch was built on the site of a medieval castle gate in the 19th century for the bishop, Dom Francisco Gomes do Avelar, who had taken it upon himself to redesign the city in decline. The portico is originally Moorish, and a statue of St. Thomas Aquinas, patron saint of Faro, surveys the scene. At the heart of the Old City, the Largo da Sé is a peaceful square, lined with orange trees and flanked by the elegant 18th-century seminary and **Paço Episcopal** (bishops' palace), still in use and closed to the public. Just outside the walls, through another archway of Moorish origin, the Arco do Repouso, is the 18th-century church of **São Francisco**, impressively decorated with tiled scenes of the life of St Francis. Farther north is the 17th-century **Nossa Senhora do Pé da Cruz** with

fanciful oil panels of stories from Genesis, such as the creation of the sun and stars. At the rear is an interesting exterior chapel or *humilhadero*.

🔒 Sé

Largo da Sé. ☎ 289-80 66 32. ◻ *daily.* ● *public hols.*

The first Christian church here, built on the site of a mosque, was all but destroyed in the attack by the English in 1596. The base of the bell tower, its medieval doorway, and two chapels survived, and long-term reconstruction resulted in a mixture of Renaissance and Baroque styles.

By the 1640s a finer building had emerged that included a chancel decorated with *azulejos* and the Capela

Orange trees in front of the 18th-century bishops' palace along the Largo da Sé

de Nossa Senhora dos Prazeres, decorated with ornate gilded woodcarving. One of the cathedral's most eccentric features is the large 18th-century organ decorated with Chinese motifs. Its stop list includes an echoing horn and a nightingale's song, and it has often been used by leading European organists for recitals.

🏛 Museu Municipal

Largo Dom Afonso III. 📞 *289-82 20 42.* 🕐 *Mon–Fri.* ⬤ *public hols.* 🎟

Since 1973 the Municipal Museum has been housed in the former convent of Nossa Senhora da Assunção, founded for the Poor Clares by Dona Leonor, sister of Manuel I. Her emblem, a fishing net, adorns the portico.

A variety of local archaeological finds are displayed in the museum, partly in the lovely two-story Renaissance cloister built by Afonso Pires in 1540. The collection contains Roman,

17th-century chancel of Faro's Sé

medieval, and Manueline stone carvings and statuary. However, the most attractive exhibit is a huge, Roman floor mosaic featuring a magnificently executed head of the god Neptune (3rd century AD), found near the train station.

🏛 Museu Marítimo

Rua da Comunidade Lusiada. 📞 *289-80 36 01.* 🕐 *Mon–Fri (pm).* ⬤ *public hols.* 🎟

The Museu Marítimo is housed in part of the harbormaster's building on the waterfront. Its small and curious collection of maritime exhibits centers on models of boats from the Age of Discovery (see pp46–9) onward, including the square-rigged *nau*, prototype of the galleon. One example is Vasco da Gama's *São Gabriel*, the flagship on his voyage to India in 1498. There are also displays of traditional fishing methods from the Algarve.

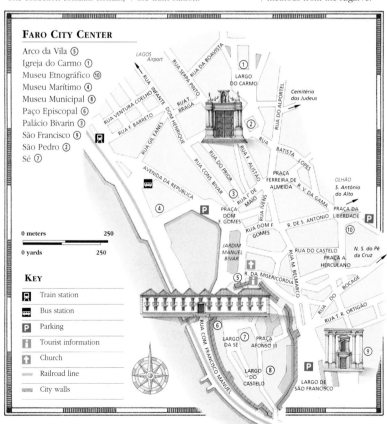

FARO CITY CENTER

Arco da Vila ⑤
Igreja do Carmo ①
Museu Etnográfico ⑩
Museu Marítimo ④
Museu Municipal ⑧
Paço Episcopal ⑥
Palácio Bivarin ③
São Francisco ⑨
São Pedro ②
Sé ⑦

0 meters 250
0 yards 250

KEY

🚉 Train station
🚌 Bus station
🅿 Parking
🛈 Tourist information
⛪ Church
▬ Railroad line
▬ City walls

Exploring Faro

The lively center of Faro along Rua de Santo António is a stylish, pedestrian area full of shops, bars, and restaurants. Between here and the Largo do Carmo are some fine 18th-century buildings, such as the **Palácio Bivarin**. The early morning market on Largo de Sá Carneiro, to the north, offers fresh produce, clothing, and local crafts. From here, a brisk walk uphill to the **Ermida de Santo António do Alto** brings a panorama of Faro with the sea and saltpans to the south.

🏛 Museu Etnográfico

Praça da Liberdade 2. 289-82 76 10.
◯ Mon–Fri. ◉ public hols.
The Ethnographic Museum takes a nostalgic look at the Algarve's traditional way of life showing ceramics, looms, and decorative horse tackle. Old photographs document peasant farming techniques, with their heavy reliance on manpower, donkeys, and oxen. The most charming exhibit is the cart used by the last water seller in Olhão, in operation until 1974.

Imposing twin-towered façade of the Baroque Igreja do Carmo

⛪ Igreja do Carmo

Largo do Carmo. 289-82 44 90.
◯ Mon–Fri. to Capela dos Ossos.
The impressive façade of this church was begun in 1713. Inside, the decoration is Baroque run wild, with every scroll and twist covered in precious Brazilian gold leaf.

In somber contrast, the Capela dos Ossos (Chapel of Bones), built in 1816, has walls lined with skulls and large bones taken from the friars' cemetery. It is a stark reminder of the transience of human life.

Sumptuous Baroque decoration of the main altarpiece in São Pedro

⛪ São Pedro

Largo de São Pedro.
289-80 54 73. ◯ daily.
The parish church of Faro is dedicated to St. Peter, patron saint of fishermen. Though restored with Italianate columns after the earthquake of 1755, much original Baroque decoration has survived, including the main altarpiece (1689).

Highlights include the chapel of the Santíssimo Sacramento, with a dazzling altarpiece (c.1745) featuring a bas-relief of the Last Supper and a sculpture of St. Anne teaching the young Virgin Mary to read. The altar of the Capela das Almas is surrounded by stunning *azulejos* (c.1730) showing the Virgin and other saints pulling souls out of purgatory.

⛼ Cemitério dos Judeus

Estrada da Penha. 282-41 67 10.
◯ Mon–Fri (am). ◉ public hols.
At the far northeast corner of town is the Jewish cemetery, created for the Jewish community brought here in the 18th century by the Marquês de Pombal *(see pp52–3)* to revitalize the economy. The cemetery is laid out in the traditional Sephardic way with children buried nearest the entrance, women in the center, and the men in back. It served from 1838 until 1932, during which time 60 families prospered in the area. They gradually moved away, so that there is no Jewish community in Faro today.

Olhão 🔞

Road map D7. 🏛 *15,000.* 🚉 🚌
ℹ️ *Largo da Lagoa (289-71 39 36).*
🅰️ *daily (fish); Sat (general).*

OLHÃO HAS BEEN involved in fishing since the Middle Ages, and today it is one of the largest fishing ports and tuna and sardine canning centers in the Algarve. In 1808 the village was elevated to the status of town, after 17 of its fishermen crossed the Atlantic Ocean to Rio de Janeiro without charts, expressly to bring to exiled King João VI the news that Napoleon's troops had been forced out of the country.

Olhão's square, whitewashed houses with their flat roof terraces and boxlike chimneys are reminiscent of Moorish architecture. The best view is from the top of the bell tower of the parish church, **Nossa Senhora do Rosário**, on Praça da Restauração, built between 1681 and 1698 with donations from the local fishermen. The custodian lets visitors through the locked door leading from the nave. In 1758 the parish priest remarked on the fishermen's great devotion to "Our Lady of the Rosary in their grief and danger at sea, especially in summertime when North African pirates often sail off this coast." At the rear of the church is the external chapel of **Nossa Senhora dos Aflitos**, where women pray for their men's safety in stormy weather.

The narrow, pedestrian streets of the old town wind down from here to the waterfront, lined with shops and also the scene of

Whitewashed chapel of Nossa Senhora dos Aflitos behind the parish church in Olhão

The wide lagoon of the Parque Natural da Ria Formosa

one of the region's most lively and picturesque markets. The noisy covered fish market sells the catch that has come in that morning, while on Saturdays outside stalls line the dock, with local farmers selling other produce such as fruit, nuts, honey, and live chickens.

Shop selling local basketware in Olhão

ENVIRONS: At the eastern end of the dock, beyond the market, boats take you out to the islands of **Armona** (15 min), **Culatra** (30 min), and **Farol** (45 min). These flat, narrow bars of sand provide shelter to the town and excellent sandy beaches for visitors, particularly on the ocean side. The islands are part of the Parque Natural da Ria Formosa.

Parque Natural da Ria Formosa ⑲

Road map D7. Quinta de Marim, Marim (289-70 41 34). along N125. from Faro, Olhão & Tavira.

STRETCHING from Praia de Faro to Cacela Velha (see p331), the Ria Formosa Nature Reserve follows 60 km (37 miles) of coastline. It was created in 1987 to protect the valuable ecosystem of this area, which was under serious threat from uncontrolled building, sand

extraction, and pollution, all by-products of the massive rise in tourism. The lagoon area of marshes, salt pans, islets, and channels is sheltered from the open sea by a chain of barrier islands – actually sand dunes above sea level. Inlets between the islands allow the tide to ebb and flow into the lagoon.

The lagoon waters are warm and highly nutritious, and therefore rich in shellfish, such as oysters, cockles, and clams. These are also bred here and make up 80 percent of the nation's mollusk exports. The fish life and warm climate attract numerous wildfowl and waders; snakes, toads, and chameleons also live here. Apart from fish and shellfish farming and salt panning, all other human activities that might encroach on the park's ecosystem are strictly controlled or forbidden.

Quinta de Marim, about 3 km (2 miles) east of Olhão, is an environmental education center. Its 148 acres of dune and pinewoods are home to various recovery projects, including a restored traditional farmhouse, a tidal mill, and a recuperation center for injured birds. The web-footed Portuguese water dog, once much used by fishermen, has been bred back from near-extinction here. At the eastern end of the park are Roman tanks where fish was salted before being transported all over the empire.

Quinta de Marim
Marim. 289-70 41 34. daily.
Jan 1, Dec 25.

WATER BIRDS OF THE RIA FORMOSA

The Ria Formosa is an important area for breeding wetland birds such as cattle egrets, red-crested pochard, and purple herons. On drier areas of land, both pratincoles and Kentish plovers can be found. Some northern European species, such as the wigeon and dunlin, winter here, and it is a stopover for migrant birds en route to Africa. Among the resident species is the rare purple gallinule, symbol of the park.

Cattle egrets feed among cattle and are often seen perched on their backs pecking off insects and flies.

The purple gallinule is a dark-colored relative of the moorhen. It can run fairly quickly on its extremely long legs but is a poor flier.

The red-crested pochard is a brightly colored duck originally from central Europe.

Houses with four-sided roofs, "Telhados de Quatro Águas," along the Gilão River in Tavira

Tavira ⑳

Road map D7. 🏠 10,000. 🚉 🚌
🛈 Rua da Galeria 9 (281-32 53 98).
📅 3rd Mon of month.

THE LOVELY TOWN of Tavira, full of historic churches and fine mansions with filigree balconies, lies along both sides of the Gilão River, linked by a **bridge** of Roman origin. This was part of the coastal Roman road between Castro Marim and Faro (see pp326–8).

Tavira's early ascendancy began with the Moors, who saw it as one of their most important settlements in the Algarve, along with Silves and Faro. It was conquered in 1242 by Dom Paio Peres Correia, who was outraged at the murder of seven of his knights by the Moors during a truce. The proximity of Tavira to the coast of Morocco ensured its importance, formally recognized in 1282 by King Dinis, who gave its seamen equal rights with those of Lisbon. The town became an ideal base for the control of piracy and the support of Portuguese positions in North Africa.

Tavira flourished until the 16th century, after which a slow decline set in, aggravated by a severe plague (1645–6) and the silting up of the harbor. Fishing for tuna became a major enterprise, but since the fish have moved away, the town now accommodates tourists without compromising either its looks or atmosphere.

The best view of the town is from the walls of the **Moorish castle**, in the old Arab center on top of the hill. From here the four-sided "Telhados de Quatro Águas" (roofs of four waters) that line Rua da Liberdade are clearly visible. An architectural feature that seems to have originated in Tavira, these pyramid-like roofs possibly evolved to allow the sudden torrential rain of the Algarve to run off easily. From the castle walls, the nearby clock tower of the church of **Santa Maria do Castelo** also acts as a landmark. The church itself occupies the site of what was once the biggest mosque in the Algarve. Its façade retains a Gothic doorway and

Beach on Ilha de Tavira, one of the many islands off the Algarve's eastern coast

windows, and its interior, restored in the 19th century, houses the tombs of Dom Paio Peres Correia and his seven knights. Santa Maria do Castelo is the only one of Tavira's 21 churches to be open outside service hours. Below the castle, the delicately arcaded church of **Nossa Senhora da Graça** was built in 1568 for the Order of St. Augustine.

Renaissance architecture was pioneered in the town by André Pilarte and can be seen on the way up to the castle, in the **Igreja da Misericórdia** (1541–51), with its lovely doorway topped by Saints Peter and Paul, and in the nearby **Palácio da Galeria** (open for temporary exhibitions). Rua da Liberdade and Rua José Pires Padinha have a sprinkling of 16th-century houses. The river embankments are graced by 18th-century mansions, in particular along the east bank next to the Roman bridge. A stroll along Rua do Cais takes you past a small public garden to the market and fish auction.

♣ **Moorish castle**
Alto de Santa Maria. ◯ daily. ♿

ENVIRONS: The sandy, offshore **Ilha de Tavira**, 11 km long by 500 m wide (7 miles by 550 yards), provides excellent swimming. In the summer it is a popular resort reached by ferry from Quatro Águas, 2 km (1 mile) southeast of Tavira. The area, part of the Ria Formosa nature park (see p329), is popular for bird-watching.

Cacela Velha 🜲

Road map D7. 🏚 *50.* 🛈 *Junta de Vila Nova de Cacela (281-95 12 28).*

THIS HAMLET perches on a cliff overlooking the sea, reached via a landscape of fields and olive trees. It is uniquely pretty, and bypassed by tourism, with a peaceful, self-contained air. Immaculate blue and white fishermen's houses cluster around the remains of a fort and a white-washed 18th-century church.

On the beach, which is sheltered by a long spit of sand, fishing boats are dotted about. The Phoenicians and later the Moors adopted this protected, attractive site until it was taken over by the Knights of Santiago in 1240 *(see p43).*

Blue and white houses, Cacela Velha

Castro Marim 🜳

Road map D7. 🏚 *4,000.* 🚌 🛈 *Praça 1° de Maio 2 (281-53 12 32).*

CASTRO MARIM has attracted "visitors" since ancient times. The Phoenicians, Greeks, and Romans all made use of its commanding location above the Guadiana River. It was the gateway to the Moorish Al-Gharb, and later, successive Christian kings granted it privileges in order to expand the population and ensure its strategic value. For centuries it became a sanctuary for fugitives from the Inquisition *(see p51).* The **castle** with round turrets above the town is of Moorish origin, the outlying walls a 13th-century addition.

Moorish castle and the abandoned Misericórdia church, Castro Marim

ENVIRONS: The town was also a center for salt production and the surrounding *salinas* are now home to valuable wildlife in the **Reserva Natural do Sapal**, established in 1975. Extending for 5,160 acres south of the town, this is a damp area of marshes and salt pans with a large variety of plant and bird species including flamingos, white storks (which make their large, untidy nests here), and black-winged stilts, symbol of the preserve.

Alcoutim 🜴

Road map D7. 🏚 *1,300.* 🚌 🛈 *Praça da República (281-54 61 79).*

THE TINY, GEMLIKE, unspoiled village of Alcoutim lies 15 km (9 miles) from the border with the Alentejo, and on the natural border with Spain, the Guadiana River. The drive there along the N122-2, a rough, winding road that sometimes runs alongside the Guadiana, provides stunning views of the countryside and across the river to Spain.

The size of Alcoutim belies its history. As a strategic location and river port, it was seized on by the Phoenicians, Greeks, Romans, and, of course, the Moors, who stayed until the reconquest in 1240. Here, in 1371, on flower-decked boats midway between Alcoutim and its Spanish counterpart, Sanlúcar de Guadiana, King Fernando I of Portugal signed the peace of Alcoutim with Enrique II of Castile. By the late 17th century, when its political importance had waned, the town had acquired a new reputation – for smuggling tobacco and snuff from Spain.

The walls of the 14th-century **castle** give an excellent view of the small village and its idyllic setting. Near the main square, by the river, is the refreshingly simple 16th-century church of **San Salvador**.

ENVIRONS: Visitors can take a scenic trip 15 km (9 miles) downriver to **Foz de Odeleite** by fishing boat from the jetty. The boat passes orchards and orange groves, and at Álamo there is a Roman dam.

View from Alcoutim across the Guadiana to Sanlúcar in Spain

PORTUGAL'S ISLANDS

Portugal's Islands at a Glance

O NCE REMOTE OUTPOSTS of a maritime empire, today
Madeira and the Azores are easily accessible by
air from mainland Portugal. The fertile islands of
Madeira and Porto Santo, 650 km (400 miles) off the
African coast, are popular holiday destinations, with
subtropical flora and high mountains. The Azorean
archipelago lies farther west, close to the Mid-Atlantic
Ridge. The climate here is more temperate, and the
active volcanoes have created a fascinating scenery
of moonlike landscapes and collapsed craters.

***Terceira** is a relatively flat island
famous for its bull-running festivals,
the "tourada à corda." On the southern
coast, the twin-towered church of São
Mateus, built at the turn of the century,
overlooks the harbor of São Mateus.*

Corvo

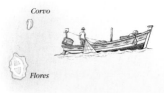

Flores

THE AZORES
(See pp358–71)

Graciosa

São Jorge

Faial　　Pico

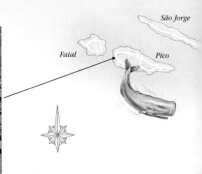

*__Pico__ is the summit of a
steep volcano protruding
from the sea. On the lower
slopes of the mountain
that fall toward the sea,
the fields are crisscrossed
with a patchwork of stone
walls made from black
volcanic basalt.*

◁ **Fertile pastures sloping down to volcanic cones and the sea on the Azorean island of Faial**

MADEIRA
(See pp340–57)

Funchal *is the capital of Madeira, famous for its flowers. Exotic blooms are sold along the main street, Avenida Arriaga, which is lined with tall jacaranda trees.*

Porto Santo

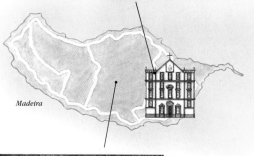

Madeira

Ilbas Desertas

| 0 kilometers | 20 |
| 0 miles | 10 |

Pico Ruivo, *at 1,861 m (6,105 ft), is the highest point on the island of Madeira. Its slopes, covered in giant heather, offer stunning views.*

Terceira

| 0 kilometers | 50 |
| 0 miles | 25 |

São Miguel

São Miguel *is popular for its therapeutic spa treatments in hot pools of mineral water. At Caldeira das Furnas, in the east of the island, steaming mud springs bubble from the ground.*

Santa Maria

The Landscape and Flowers of Madeira

MADEIRA HAS A MILD, moist climate that promotes a rich cover of vegetation. At first glance, the flowers and foliage appear to harmonize with the environment. The well traveled botanist, however, will soon become aware of the strange assortment of flowers from around the world. For example, over the past few centuries, many plants from South Africa's Cape region and from South America have been introduced, which now thrive alongside indigenous plants.

Pride of Madeira

(see p346)

MADEIRA'S GARDENS

The subtropical climate and mixture of indigenous and imported plants combine to produce gardens that are the envy of horticulturists all over the world. Gardens such as the Botanical Gardens in Funchal *(see p346)* are awash with color all year. Here are some of the most striking plants that can be found in Madeira's gardens.

Magnolia in bloom

AROUND THE COAST

In many coastal areas the cliffs are spectacular, such as this stretch at Ponta de São Lourenço *(see p350)*. A rich and varied flora, both native and introduced, can be found along Madeira's coast despite the dry and stony habitat.

Hottentot fig *is a coastal groundcover plant originating from South Africa.*

Lampranthus spectabilis *is a South African plant that flowers on the coast between May and July.*

Canary Island date palms *are a familiar sight, especially along the sunny south coast.*

AGRICULTURAL AND WAYSIDE GROUND

An irrigation system using man-made channels called *levadas,* such as this one near Curral das Freiras *(see p354),* allows the islanders to cultivate many otherwise unpromising areas. The borders of agricultural land are often rich with flowers.

Mimosa trees *grow especially well in wooded parts of Madeira, where they bloom in winter.*

Parrot's Beak *is a large, striking flower that appears in March and April.*

Hibiscus syriacus, *from the Far East, flowers between June and October.*

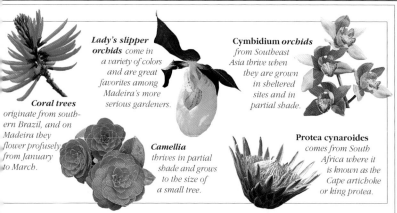

Lady's slipper orchids *come in a variety of colors and are great favorites among Madeira's more serious gardeners.*

Cymbidium orchids *from Southeast Asia thrive when they are grown in sheltered sites and in partial shade.*

Coral trees *originate from southern Brazil, and on Madeira they flower profusely from January to March.*

Camellia *thrives in partial shade and grows to the size of a small tree.*

Protea cynaroides *comes from South Africa where it is known as the Cape artichoke or king protea.*

HIGH GROUND

The views from the summit of Pico Ruivo, the island's highest point *(see p354)*, are spectacular. In upland areas, the vegetation harbors a higher proportion of native species than in the lowlands.

TERRACED PLANTATIONS

Plantations, such as this one growing bananas near Calheta *(see p356)*, are made by digging terraces into the hillside. A wide range of crops are grown, for home consumption and export.

Isoplexis sceptrum, *known as the yellow foxglove, is a flowering shrub native to Madeira.*

Sweet chestnuts *grow well in Madeira and produce an abundant autumn harvest.*

Broom *flowers are colorful and popular with pollinating insects.*

Papayas *produce fruit all year round. The plant originates from South America.*

Prickly juniper *is a hardy, spiny evergreen shrub covered in tough red berries.*

Sword aloe *has spiky leaves that provide a good physical barrier around plantations.*

The Azores: Volcanic Islands Rising from the Ocean Bed

SITUATED ON EITHER SIDE of the Mid-Atlantic Ridge, the Azores are a result of 20 million years of volcanic activity. As the plates of the earth's crust pull apart, volcanic eruptions form a giant ridge of mountains beneath the Atlantic. In places, the ridge is buckled and cut by perpendicular fractures, known as transform faults. Molten rock (magma) has been forced through these faults to form the Azores. These islands, among the youngest on earth, emerged above the waves less than five million years ago. Their striking landscape tells of their volcanic past and is still shaped by volcanic activity today.

The Mid-Atlantic Ridge *is a line of submarine volcanoes that runs the whole length of the Atlantic Ocean.*

Corvo

Terceira lies directly above a major transform fault.

Graciosa

Flores

Transform fault

The Mid-Atlantic Ridge marks the spot where the African, Eurasian, and American plates of the earth's crust are being pulled apart.

Faial

Pico

A mantle plume is a mass of partially molten mantle that has welled upwards, pooling beneath the rocky lithosphere. The magma it produces seeks fissures through which to erupt.

São Jorge

São Miguel has several spectacular water-filled calderas and hot springs.

Santa Maria

VOLCANIC RESOURCES OF THE AZORES

The dramatic formation of the Azores has left the islands with abundant natural resources. Hot springs, strong building materials, and, eventually, fertile soil, are all the result of the ongoing volcanic activity. A wet, temperate climate gradually breaks down the volcanic rocks into fertile soils. Older soils support luxuriant vegetation and are excellent for arable farming, but younger soils, like those found on Pico, support little agriculture.

These stone cottages *on Pico, like many on the islands, make use of the plentiful basalt rock as a durable building material.*

Furnas, on São Miguel, *is an area of sulfur and hot mud springs used for bathing and medicinal purposes.*

Rising high above the clouds, the still-active volcanic peak of Pico Alto dominates the island of Pico, which is itself the top of a giant underwater volcano. At 2,350 m (7,700 ft) above sea level, Pico Alto is the highest peak in the whole of Portugal.

THE GEOLOGY OF THE AZORES

The Azores lie along transform fault lines, cracks in the earth's crust that cross the Mid-Atlantic Ridge. These faults are weak points through which magma can rise. Successive volcanic eruptions have formed hundreds of undersea mountains on either side of the ridge. The highest peaks of these mountains are the nine islands of the Azores. Their emergence above the sea has been aided by the swelling of the mantle plume beneath the ocean crust, which lifts the sea floor closer to the surface of the sea.

Thin ocean crust

Atlantic Ocean

The upper mantle is a layer of dense rock. With the crust above, it forms the lithosphere, a series of semirigid moving plates.

The lower mantle, or asthenosphere, is a deep layer of partially molten rock that surrounds the earth's core.

Basalt lava blocks used for stone walls provide shelter for vines and protect against soil erosion on Pico. Volcanic soil here is of relatively recent formation and suitable for few crops except grapes.

THE FORMATION OF A CALDERA

A caldera is a large crater that forms during or after a volcanic eruption, when the roof of the magma chamber collapses under the weight of the volcano's cone. Water collecting in the natural bowl of a caldera can form a crater lake.

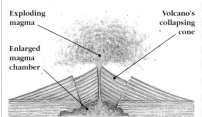

Caldeira das Sete Cidades on the island of São Miguel

Gas and volcanic ash

Alternate layers of lava flows and volcanic ash

Vent

Magma chamber

In an active volcano, the magma chamber below the cone is full of molten rock. As pressure forces this magma up through the volcano's vent, it is expelled to the surface as a volcanic eruption.

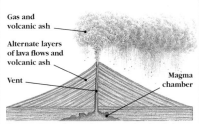

Exploding magma

Volcano's collapsing cone

Enlarged magma chamber

As magma is expelled, the level in the magma chamber drops. This may cause the volcano's cone to collapse under its own weight, leaving behind the characteristic bowl-shaped crater, or caldera.

Caldera lake

Eroded crater

Residual hot rock

After the volcano has died down and is eroded, the caldera can fill with water and form a lake. Residual hot rock near the magma chamber may continue to heat the surrounding ground water.

MADEIRA

MADEIRA IS A GREEN, SUBTROPICAL *paradise of volcanic origin, its soils formed from lava and ash, completely different in character from the Portuguese mainland. Blessed with a uniform daytime temperature that varies only by a few degrees either side of 20° C (68° F), the island has an all-year-round appeal.*

Madeira is a mere dot in the Atlantic Ocean, 608 km (378 miles) from Morocco and nearly 1,000 km (621 miles) from Lisbon. Despite this, Madeira and Porto Santo appear on a Genoese map of 1351, so there is no doubt that sailors had long known about the islands. They remained unclaimed, however, until 1418, when João Gonçalves Zarco was blown out into the Atlantic by violent storms while exploring the coast of Africa. Zarco counted his blessings at having found safe harbor in Porto Santo, set up the Portuguese flag, and returned to Lisbon. A year later he returned on a voyage of discovery sponsored by Henry the Navigator *(see p49)*. Early in 1420, after a winter on Porto Santo, he set sail for the mist-shrouded land on the horizon. He found a beautiful, thickly wooded island (*madeira* means wood) with abundant fresh water.

The bird-of-paradise flower *(Strelitzia reginae)*

Within seven years the island had attracted a pioneer colony, and the early settlers exploited the fertile soil and warm climate to grow sugar-cane. The islanders grew rich on this "white gold," and slaves were brought in to work the land and create the terraced fields and irrigation channels (*levadas*) that still cling to the steep hillsides. Today, despite the gradients, Madeirans make use of every spare patch of land, and wine, bananas, and exotic flowers form the backbone of the economy.

In the late 19th century, Madeira became a popular winter vacation spot for northern Europeans. The start of commercial flights in 1964 introduced the rest of the world to its charms. Today Madeira appeals to eager walkers, plant lovers, and sun seekers, although it lacks the sandy beaches of its sister island, Porto Santo.

Triangular shaped houses, typical of the town of Santana on the north coast of Madeira

◁ Path winding through the spectacular mountain scenery of Pico do Arieiro

Exploring Madeira

Funchal is the island's capital and the only town of any size. This is where most of the museums and historic buildings are to be found, as well as the best hotels, restaurants, and shops. Most of Madeira's agricultural crops are grown along the sunny, prosperous south coast. The cooler, wetter north side has fewer settlements and more cattle. Many parts of the mountainous and volcanic interior remain wild, and some are accessible only on foot. Pico Ruivo, the highest peak on the island, is a favorite destination for walkers.

Terraces near Boa Ventura, on the road from Santana to São Vicente

15 PORTO MONIZ

ACHADAS DA CRUZ

R101

PONTA DO PARGO

SEIXAL

R101

PONTA DELGADA

BOA VENTURA

14 SÃO VICENTE

RABAÇAL WALKS
13

PRAZERES

RABAÇAL

R204

PAUL DA SERRA
12

SERRA DE ÁGUA

CURRAL DAS FREIRAS

1

16 CALHETA

R222

R209

R101

PONTA DO SOL

ESTREITO DE CÂMARA DE LOBOS

RIBEIRA BRAVA **17**

CABO GIRÃO

CÂMARA DE LOBOS **18**

0 kilometers   5
0 miles   3

Early morning view across the rooftops of Funchal, with the mountainous interior beyond

GETTING AROUND

Madeira's one international airport, Santa Catarina, is at Santa Cruz, 18 km (11 miles) northeast of Funchal. Buses operate to all corners of the island from Funchal but are not geared to tourists. Taxis can be used, but for flexibility car rental is best. From north to south the island is 19 km (12 miles) wide and from east to west just 56 km (35 miles) long. Even so, traveling times are magnified by the mountainous terrain. To reach the nearby island of Porto Santo, you can either fly from Santa Cruz or take the ferry from Funchal to Porto Abrigo (near Vila Baleira). *(See also pp444–5.)*

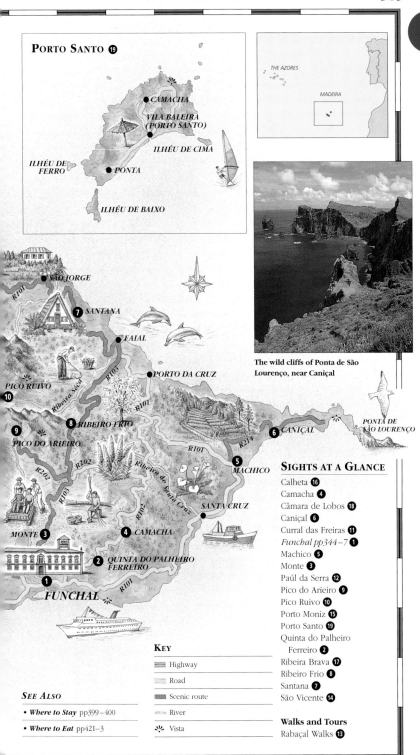

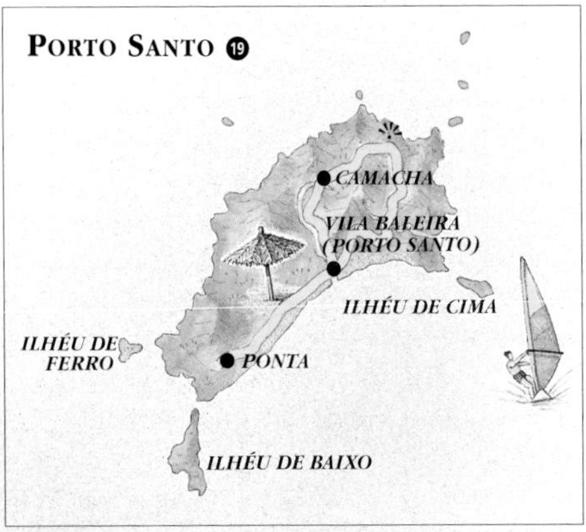
PORTO SANTO 19
CAMACHA
VILA BALEIRA
(PORTO SANTO)
ILHÉU DE CIMA
ILHÉU DE
FERRO
PONTA
ILHÉU DE BAIXO

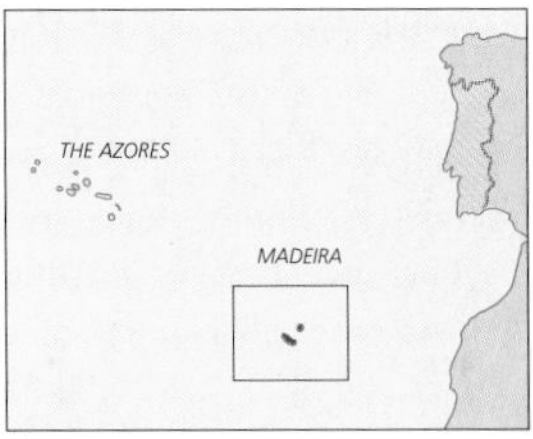
THE AZORES
MADEIRA

The wild cliffs of Ponta de São Lourenço, near Caniçal

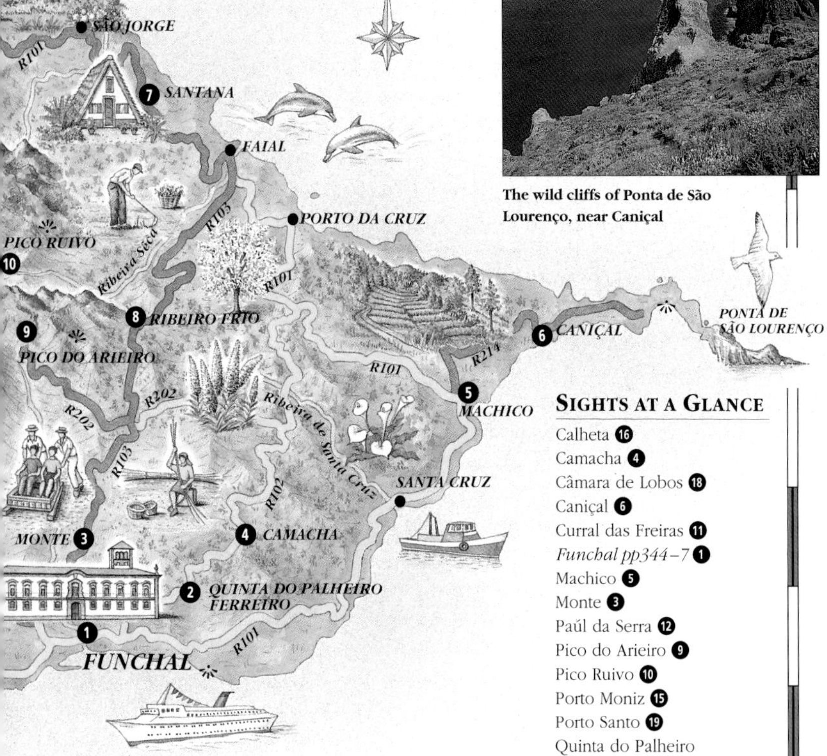
SÃO JORGE
R101
7 SANTANA
FAIAL
R103
PORTO DA CRUZ
PICO RUIVO
10
Ribeira Seca
R101
8 RIBEIRO FRIO
9
PICO DO ARIEIRO
R202
R202
R101
R214
6 CANIÇAL
PONTA DE
SÃO LOURENÇO
5
MACHICO
Ribeira de Santa Cruz
R103
R102
SANTA CRUZ
MONTE 3
4 CAMACHA
2 QUINTA DO PALHEIRO
FERREIRO
1
FUNCHAL
R101

Sights at a Glance

Calheta 16
Camacha 4
Câmara de Lobos 18
Caniçal 6
Curral das Freiras 11
Funchal pp344–7 1
Machico 5
Monte 3
Paúl da Serra 12
Pico do Arieiro 9
Pico Ruivo 10
Porto Moniz 15
Porto Santo 19
Quinta do Palheiro Ferreiro 2
Ribeira Brava 17
Ribeiro Frio 8
Santana 7
São Vicente 14

Walks and Tours

Rabaçal Walks 13

Key

- Highway
- Road
- Scenic route
- River
- Vista

See Also

- ***Where to Stay*** pp399–400
- ***Where to Eat*** pp421–3

Street-by-Street: Funchal **①**

Tiling on Palácio do Governo Regional, Avenida M. Arriaga

THE DEEP NATURAL HARBOR of Madeira's capital, Funchal, attracted early settlers in the 15th century. The historic core of the capital still overlooks the harbor and boasts fine government buildings and 18th-century houses with shady courtyards and decorative iron balconies. Visitors have called Funchal a "little Lisbon" because of the town's steep cobblestone streets, carved black basalt doorways, and air of grandeur.

The Igreja do Colégio (Collegiate Church) was founded by the Jesuits in 1574. The plain exterior contrasts with the richly decorated high altar, framed by carved, gilded wood (1641–60).

Rua da Carreira and Rua do Surdo have preserved many of their original elegant balconied houses.

São Pedro church

The Museu Municipal houses an aquarium and is a favorite with children.

RUA DAS PRETAS

RUA DO SURDO

RUA DA CARREIRA

RUA S. FRANCISCO

AVENIDA

Adegas de São Francisco (see p347)

The monument to João Gonçalves Zarco, the man who claimed Madeira for Portugal, was created by the sculptor Francisco Franco in 1927.

Toyota Showroom
The building's exterior is decorated with 20th-century tiles depicting various Madeiran scenes including the famous Monte toboggan (see p348).

M. ARRIAGA

AVENIDA

RUA DAS FONTES

| 0 meters | 50 |
| 0 yards | 50 |

The Palácio de São Lourenço is a 16th-century fortress housing Madeira's military headquarters.

Yacht Marina
Lined with seafood restaurants, the yacht marina on Avenida do Mar is ideal for an evening stroll. The sea wall around the marina offers good views.

Avenida do Mar

STAR SIGHTS

★ **Sé**

★ **Praça do Município**

Câmara Municipal
*Funchal's city hall is an
imposing 18th-century
mansion with a fountain
in its courtyard
depicting Leda
and the Swan.
Inside, a small
museum traces
the history of
Funchal in
photographs.*

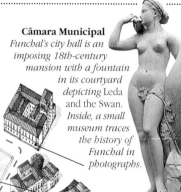

**The Museu
de Arte Sacra**
includes Flemish
paintings, embroi-
dered vestments, and
statues among the
displays of religious
art *(see p346)*.

★ Praça do Município
*Contrasting black and white stones
pave the attractive municipal
square. On the northeast side of the
square is the Câmara Municipal.*

**Bus
station**

Rua do Aljube
*Alongside the Sé, flower
sellers in traditional
costumes offer a colorful
array of exotic flowers.*

**Palácio
do Governo
Regional**

The Alfândega Velha (Old
Customs House) was built in
1477 and is now home to the
island's regional parliament.

★ Sé
*São Tiago (St. James) is one
of many gilded figures that
adorn the wonderfully
carved wooden choir stalls
in Funchal's 15th-century
cathedral (see p346).*

KEY

- - - Suggested route

Exploring Funchal

F UNCHAL HAS THREE MAIN AREAS: to the west lies the so-called "tourist zone" where all the major hotels are located, and to the east is the Zona Velha, the Old Town, a warren of former fishermen's houses, some now turned into lively restaurants. The central downtown area (*see pp344–5*) is characterized by its historic buildings and stylish shops. Linking all three areas is the Avenida do Mar, the harborside promenade. Funchal is also divided by three rivers, though these flow along concrete channels and are virtually hidden from view by trellises covered with scarlet and purple bougainvillea.

Carved Manueline-style lions in the garden at Quinta das Cruzes

🏛 Sé

Largo da Sé. 📞 *291-22 81 55.*
🕐 *daily.*

The cathedral is one of the few buildings in Madeira to have survived virtually untouched since the early days of the island's colonization. In the 1490s, King Manuel I (*see pp46–9*) sent the architect Pêro Anes from the mainland to work on the design of the colony's cathedral. The Sé was finally completed in 1514.

The highlights are the ceiling and the choir stalls, although neither is easy to see in the dark interior. The ceiling of inlaid wood is best seen from the south transept, where enough light filters in to illuminate the intricate patterning. The choir stalls depict saints, prophets and apostles in 16th-century costume. Aspects of Madeiran life feature in the decorative details of the armrests and seats: one cherub carries a bunch of bananas, another a goatskin full of wine.

Clock tower of Funchal's Sé

🏛 Museu de Arte Sacra

Rua do Bispo 21. 📞 *291-22 89 00.*
🕐 *Tue–Sat & Sun am.*
⬤ *public hols.* 🈺

Madeiran merchants, who grew rich on the profitable sugar trade, sought to secure their salvation by commissioning paintings, statues, embroidered vestments, and illuminated hymn books for their local churches. Hundreds of examples now fill this museum, which is housed in the former bishops' palace, a building dating from 1600. There are some masterpieces in the collection, including the late-Gothic processional cross donated by King Manuel I and religious paintings by major Flemish artists of the 15th and 16th centuries. Some works include portraits of the dignitaries who commissioned them. *Saints Philip and James* is a 16th-century painting showing Simão Gonçalves de Câmara, Zarco's (*see p341*) grandson.

🏛 Quinta das Cruzes

Calçada do Pico 1. 📞 *291-74 13 88.*
🕐 *Tue–Sun.* ⬤ *public hols.* 🈺

It is said that Zarco, the man who claimed Madeira for Portugal (*see p341*), built his house where the Quinta das Cruzes now stands. The elegant 19th-century mansion is now the Museum of Decorative Arts, furnished as a merchant's house with Indian silk wall hangings, Regency sideboards, and oriental carpets. In the basement is furniture made from mahogany crates used in the 17th century for shipping sugar, and turned into chests and cupboards when the sugar trade died.

The garden is dotted with ancient tombstones and architectural fragments. These include two window frames from 1507 carved with rope motifs, acrobatic figures, and man-eating lions in a Madeiran version of the Manueline style of architecture (*see pp20–21*).

🏛 Convento de Santa Clara

Calçada de Santa Clara. 📞 *291-74 26 02.* 🕐 *daily.*

Opposite Quinta das Cruzes is the Convento de Santa Clara, founded in 1496 by João Gonçalves de Câmara, one of Zarco's grandsons. Zarco himself is buried under the high altar, and Martim Mendes Vasconcelos, his son-in-law, has a tomb at the rear of the church. Precious 17th-century *azulejo* tiles cover the walls.

🌿 Jardim Botânico

Quinta do Bom Sucesso, Caminho do Meio. 🕐 *daily.* ⬤ *Dec 25.* 🈺 🈺

Opened to the public in 1960, the Botanical Gardens display plants from all over the world. Desert cacti, rainforest orchids, and South African proteas grow here as well as native Madeiran dragon trees. There are contrasting sections: formal areas of bedding plants, quiet carp ponds, and wild wooded parts.

The intricately patterned formal gardens of the Jardim Botânico

♥ Adegas de São Francisco

Avenida Arriaga 28. ☎ 291-74 01 10.
🕐 Mon–Fri, Sat am. ● public hols.
📷 ☑ compulsory.

In the cobbled courtyards of the St. Francis wine lodge, visitors are greeted by the scents of ancient wood and Madeira. Some of the buildings in this maze of coopers' yards, wine vaults, and sampling rooms go back to the 17th century when the site was part of Funchal's Franciscan friary. You sample wines made on the premises more than 150 years ago as well as more recent (and less expensive) vintages. Included in the guided tour is a visit to the warming rooms where Madeira is "cooked" by hot water pipes *(see p349)*.

Tasting Madeira wine at the Adegas de São Francisco

⊖ Mercado dos Lavradores

Rua Dr Fernão Ornelas. ☎ 291-22 25 84. 🕐 Mon–Sat. ● public hols.

The Mercado dos Lavradores is where flower growers, basket weavers, farmers, and fishermen from all over Madeira bring their products to market. The covered market building, situated on three floors around an open courtyard, is full of the color and bustle of island life. Stall-holders offer slices of mango or custard fruit to prove that theirs are the sweetest and best. In the basement, marble tables are draped with great slabs of tuna and black-skinned scabbard fish with huge eyes and razor-sharp teeth.

On Fridays the market spills out into the back streets of the Zona Velha (Old Town), the former fishermen's quarter and now an area of small shops,

lively sidewalk cafés, and bars. The simple, single-story dwellings situated at the pedestrian eastern end of Rua Dom Carlos I, are said to date from the 15th century. The little Corpo Santo chapel was built by 16th-century fishermen in honor of their patron, St. Peter, and is said to be the oldest such building in Funchal.

⚓ Fortaleza de São Tiago

Rua do Portão de São Tiago. ☎ 291-22 64 36. **Museum** 🕐 Tue–Sun.
● public hols. 📷

Along the seafront is the newly restored Fortaleza de São Tiago, built in 1614, with additions dating from 1767. The fortress, with its maze of passages and staircases, commands extensive views of Funchal and houses a Museum of Contemporary Art.

House and gardens of the Quinta do Palheiro Ferreiro

Quinta do Palheiro Ferreiro ❷

Palheiro Ferreiro. ☎ 291-79 24 22.
🚌 🕐 9am–12:30pm Mon–Fri.
● Jan 1, Easter, May 1, Dec 25. 📷 ♿

THE QUINTA DO PALHEIRO Ferreiro is Madeira's finest garden and a place of pilgrimage for flower-loving visitors. A French landscape architect laid out the gardens in the 18th century for the wealthy Count of Carvalhal, who built the elegant mansion (not open to visitors) overlooking the garden and the little Baroque chapel in the garden itself.

The estate was acquired in 1885 by the long-established Anglo-Madeiran Blandy family, hence its English name: Blandy's Gardens. New species were introduced from South Africa, China, and Australia, resulting in a garden that combines the clipped formality of late 18th-century layout with the profusion of English-style herbaceous borders, plus the combination of tropical and temperate climate varieties.

Quite apart from its horticultural interest, the garden is a peaceful wildlife haven, full of beauty and contrast as you pass from the formality of the Ladies' Garden to the tropical wilderness of the ravine ominously marked as "Inferno" (Hell).

Fish seller chopping tuna into huge steaks in the basement of Funchal's Mercado dos Lavradores

The contrasting façade of Nossa Senhora do Monte, created by basalt against whitewash

Monte ❸

🏃 10,000. 🚌 ℹ️ Caminho de Ferro 182 (291-78 25 55).

MONTE HAS BEEN a favorite destination for visitors to Madeira since the late 19th century, when a rack-and-pinion railroad was built to haul cruise liner passengers up the hillside from Funchal. Coming down they would take the famous **Monte toboggan** ride. The railroad closed in 1939, but the station and a viaduct survive, now forming part of the luxuriant **Jardim do Monte** public gardens. It is a short stroll through the gardens to the church of **Nossa Senhora do Monte**, whose twin-towered façade looks down on the island's capital. The present church was built in 1818 on the site of a chapel built in 1470 by Adam Gonçalves Ferreira (Adam and his twin sister Eve were the first children to be born on Madeira).

The Virgin of Monte is Madeira's patron saint, and this church is the focal point of the pilgrimage that takes place annually on August 15 (the Feast of the Assumption) when penitents climb the church's 74 steps on their knees. The object of their worship is a tiny statue of the Virgin kept in a silver tabernacle on the high altar. Devout Madeirans believe that the Virgin herself gave this statue to a Madeiran shepherd girl in the 15th century.

Left of the nave is a chapel housing a mortuary chest containing the remains of the last Hapsburg Emperor, Karl I, who was crowned in 1916 but deposed in 1918. He sought exile in Madeira and died of pneumonia in 1922, at the age of 35.

Toboggan drivers in straw hats wait for passengers every day on the corner of Caminho do Monte, and they run (for a fee) to Livramento and on to Funchal. From the church steps, past the drivers' corner, a left turn marked "Old Monte Gardens" leads to the entrance of the **Monte Palace Gardens**. These superb gardens, laid out in 1894, will delight children with their maze of pathways and bridges, follies, fountains, cascades, and tame black swans. The gardens extend for 7 ha (17 acres) down a lushly planted valley with areas devoted to Madeiran flora, South African proteas, plants from Japan and China, azaleas, camellias, and orchids.

🌷 **Monte Palace Gardens**
Caminho do Monte 174.
📞 291-78 23 39. 🕐 Mon–Sat.
📷 ♿ limited.

One of the skilled wicker workers of Camacha constructing a table

Camacha ❹

🏃 9,000. 🚌 ℹ️ Junta da Freguesia, Urbanização dos Casais de Além (291-92 24 66).

MOST OF THE wicker products sold in Funchal are made in and around Camacha, and the sole attraction in this otherwise sleepy village is a large store packed with everything wicker, from picture frames, bedsteads, and cradles to peacock-backed armchairs. It is often possible to see weavers at work, bending the pliant stripped willow around a frame to produce a linen basket or plant container. A Noah's Ark full of paired animals is displayed on the middle floor, along with a full-sailed galleon, as an advertisement of the local wicker weavers' skills.

THE MONTE TOBOGGAN

Sliding in a wicker basket mounted on wooden runners, it is possible to cover the 4-km (2-mile) descent from Monte to Funchal in 20 minutes. The trip is made by thousands every year, fascinated by the experience of traveling at speed down a public highway on a wooden sled. Ernest Hemingway once described it as "exhilarating." A cushioned seat softens the ride, and passengers are in the safe hands of the toboggan drivers, who push and steer from the rear, using their rubber-soled boots as brakes. Madeiran tobogganing was invented as a form of transportation in 1850.

The famous Monte tobggan ride

Madeira Wine

Wicker-covered Madeira bottle

From the middle of the 16th century, ships stopping at Madeira would take on barrels of local wine, which helped sailors to avoid scurvy because of its vitamin and mineral content. It was found that the wine tasted better at the end of an equatorial voyage, and so people started sending Madeira on long voyages to be heated by the tropical sun. By the 18th century, a simpler, artificial means of heating the wine had been developed. This process, known as *estufagem*, is still used today.

The Madeira is "cooked" for six months using the heat of the sun, assisted by hot water pipes. A Madeira will typically spend six months at temperatures of 40–50°C (104–122°F) before it is fortified with brandy. The grape variety used to make the wine determines its character. Four main varieties are cultivated, resulting in four types of Madeira. These can be drunk at different stages in a meal.

Making barrels for Madeira, Funchal

The Four Types of Madeira

Sercial *is made from white grapes grown at about 800 m (2,600 ft). It is an amber-colored dry wine drunk as an aperitif, with soup, or with fish, and is best served lightly chilled. A good-quality Sercial is aged for at least eight years.*

Verdelho *grapes are white, grown at 400–600 m (1,300–2,000 ft), and make a medium-dry tawny wine for drinking with meat. Sweeter than Sercial, Verdelho goes well with a slice of Madeira cake (invented by the English for just this purpose).*

The barrels *in the Adegas de São Francisco (see p347), where Madeira is warmed, need frequent repair as do the wooden floors that bear their huge weight.*

These casks of Verdelho *are being aged after the addition of brandy to the wine. Vintage wine must spend at least 20 years in the cask and two in the bottle.*

Bual *is a dark, rich, and nutty wine made from white grapes grown on terraces below 400 m (1,300 ft). It is a medium-sweet wine that can be served as an alternative to port. It makes an excellent accompaniment to cheeses and dessert.*

Malmsey, *the most celebrated Madeira, is made from Malvasia grapes grown in sunny vineyards backed by cliffs, where the heat absorbed by the rock by day warms the grapes by night. The result is a rich dark wine drunk as an after-dinner digestive.*

Vintage Madeira *from every decade as far back as the mid-19th century is still available for sale. The oldest surviving bottle of Madeira dates from 1772.*

Machico [5]

👥 22,000. 🚌 ℹ *Forte do Amparo, Rua Dr José A. Almada (291-96 22 89).* 🛒 *Mon–Fri (fish).*

LEGEND HAS IT that Machico was named after Robert Machim, a merchant from Bristol, who eloped with the aristocratic Anne of Hertford and set sail for Portugal. Caught in a storm and shipwrecked on Madeira, the two lovers died from exposure and were buried. The rest of the crew repaired the boat and sailed to Lisbon, where their story inspired Prince Henry the Navigator *(see p49)* to send João Gonçalves Zarco *(see p341)* in search of this mysterious wooded island.

Machico has been Madeira's second most important town since the first settlements, when the island was divided into two captaincies: Zarco ruled the west from Funchal, and Tristão Vaz Teixeira ruled the east from Machico. However, Funchal's superior location and harbor soon ensured its development as the capital of Madeira while Machico became a sleepy agricultural town.

The **Igreja Matriz** on Largo do Município, Machico's main square, dates from the 15th century. Above the high altar is a statue of the Virgin Mary, donated by Manuel I *(see pp46–9)*, as were the three marble pillars used in the construction of the Gothic south portal. Inside, there is a fine example of Manueline-style stone masonry in the Capela de São João Baptista, whose arch shows Teixeira's coat of arms, with a phoenix rising from the flames.

Main altar in the Capela dos Milagres, Machico

Across the River Machico, on Largo dos Milagres, is the **Capela dos Milagres** (Chapel of the Miracles). The present structure dates from 1815, but it stands on the site of Madeira's first church, where Robert Machim and Anne of Hertford are supposedly buried. The earlier church of 1420 was destroyed in a flood in 1803, but the 15th-century crucifix was found floating out at sea. Machico celebrates the return of its cross with a procession every year on October 8.

Fishing boats hauled up on the beach at Caniçal

View from Ponta de São Lourenço promontory, east of Caniçal

Caniçal [6]

👥 5,000. 🚌 ℹ *Serrado da Igreja (291-96 17 55).*

CANIÇAL WAS ONCE the center of Madeira's whaling industry: the whaling scenes for John Huston's film version of *Moby Dick* (1956) were shot here. Whaling only ceased in June 1981, and since then the waters around Madeira have been declared a marine mammal sanctuary, where the killing of whales, dolphins, and seals is forbidden. Local fishermen who once hunted whales now work with the Society for the Protection of Sea Mammals, helping marine biologists understand whale migrations.

The old whaling company's office is now the **Museu da Baleia** (Whaling Museum). It shows a 45-minute video on whale hunting with commentaries by retired fishermen.

Caniçal is still a busy fishing port, and the stony beach is used by tuna fishermen to repair their colorful boats.

🏛 Museu da Baleia

Largo da Lota. ☎ *291-96 14 07.* ○ *Tue–Sun.* ● *public hols.* 📷 ♿

ENVIRONS: The easternmost tip of Madeira, the **Ponta de São Lourenço**, is characterized by dramatic wave-battered cliffs plunging 180 m (590 ft) to the Atlantic. Hikers are attracted by trails that meander from one clifftop to another, with wildflowers growing in sheltered hollows. The treeless landscape contrasts totally with the island's wooded interior.

On the road from Caniçal to Ponta de São Lourenço, watch out for the sign to the bay of **Prainha**, Madeira's only naturally sandy beach.

Santana ❼

🏛 10,500. 🚌 ℹ *Câmara Municipal, Sítio do Serrado (291-57 21 13).*

Santana (named after St. Anne, mother of the Virgin) has more than 100 thatched triangular houses, several of which, restored and brightly painted, can be visited by the public. The hillsides above the broad valley in which Santana sits are also dotted with triangular thatched byres, where cows are tethered to stop them from wandering along narrow terrace paths and harming themselves or crops.

The valley is intensively farmed both for fruit and vegetables, and osiers, the willow branches that are the raw material for the wicker workers of Camacha *(see p348)*.

Ribeiro Frio ❽

🏛 45. 🚌 *from Funchal.*

Bridge across a *levada* on the walk from Ribeiro Frio to Balcões

Ribeiro Frio is a pretty spot consisting of a couple of restaurants, a store, and a trout farm fed by the "cold stream" after which the place is named.

Surrounding the trout farm is an attractive garden full of native trees and shrubs. This is the starting point for two of the island's best *levada* walks *(see p355)*. The 12-km (7-mile) path marked to **Portela** (on the right heading downhill past the restaurants) passes through dramatic mountain scenery but is best left to experienced hikers because of the long tunnels and steep drops in places. Far easier is

Sunrise over the mountains, seen from Pico do Arieiro

the 20-minute walk on the left (going downhill) marked **Balcões** (Balconies). This vista gives panoramic views across the valley of the River Ametade to Penha de Águia (Eagle Rock), the sheer-sided hill that projects from Madeira's northern coast.

Pico do Arieiro ❾

🚌 *to Camacha, then taxi.* **Pousada do Pico do Arieiro** 📞 *291-23 01 10 (reservations: 291-76 56 58).*

From Funchal it is about a 30-minute drive up the Pico do Arieiro, Madeira's third highest mountain at 1,810 m (5,938 ft). The route leads through steep hillsides cloaked in fragrant eucalyptus and bay laurel. At around 900 m (2,950 ft), you will often meet the cloudline and pass for a few minutes through swirling mists, and possibly rain, before emerging into a sunlit landscape of volcanic rocks. At the top, the view is of clouds in the valleys and dramatic mountain ridges with knife-edge peaks. Just visible on a clear day is Pico Ruivo *(see p354)*, connected to Pico do Arieiro by a 10-km (6-mile) path. The Pousada do Pico do Arieiro guesthouse on the mountaintop allows hikers to see a spectacular sunrise.

THE TRIANGULAR HOUSES OF SANTANA

Simply constructed from two A-shaped wooden frames, with a wood-paneled interior and thatched roof, these triangular houses are unique to Madeira. They are first mentioned in the 16th century, but most of the surviving examples are no more than 100 years old. Today their doors and windows are often painted a cheerful red, yellow, or blue. In the warm year-round climate of Madeira, cooking and eating take place out of doors, and the toilets are placed well away from the house. To the inhabitants, therefore, the triangular houses serve principally as shelter from the rain and for sleeping. The interior is deceptively spacious, with a living area downstairs and sleeping space up in the loft.

Panoramic view of the mountains from the Pico Ruivo summit

Pico Ruivo ❿

🚌 *to Santana or Faial, then taxi to Achada do Teixeira, then walk.*

MADEIRA'S HIGHEST mountain at 1,861 m (6,105 ft), Pico Ruivo is accessible only on foot. The easiest way to scale its heights is via a well-marked trail that begins at the village of Achada do Teixeira and leads visitors on a 45-minute walk to the top.

Alternatively, follow the walk from the top of Pico do Arieiro *(see p351)* along one of the island's most spectacular trails. Awe-inspiring mountain scenery and glorious views can be enjoyed all along the 10-km (6-mile) walk. This takes two to three hours and is really suitable only for experienced, well-equipped hikers. Vertigo sufferers should not attempt the path, as it involves negotiating narrow ridges with sheer drops on either side.

Curral das Freiras ⓫

👥 3,000. 🚌 🛈 *Câmara de Lobos (291-94 20 71).*

CURRAL DAS FREIRAS means "Nuns' Refuge," and the name refers to the nuns of the Santa Clara convent who fled to this idyllic spot when pirates attacked Funchal in 1566. The nuns have left now, but the village remains. Visitors first glimpse Curral das Freiras from a viewpoint known as the **Eira do Serrado**, perched some 800 m (2,625 ft) above the scattered village.

The valley is surrounded on all sides by jagged mountain peaks. Until 1959 the only access to the village was by a steep, zigzagging path, but road tunnels now make the journey much easier and allow local people to transport their produce to the capital. Television arrived in 1986.

The sweet chestnuts that grow in profusion around the village are turned into sweet chestnut bread, best eaten still warm from the oven, and *licor de castanha*, a chestnut-flavored liqueur. Both can be sampled in local bars.

Paúl da Serra ⓬

🚌 *to Canhas, then taxi.*

Sheep grazing on the wide plateau of Paúl da Serra, east of Rabaçal

THE PAÚL DA SERRA (literally "high moorland") is a large, boggy plateau, 17 km (11 miles) long and 6 km (4 miles) wide. The plain contrasts dramatically with the jagged mountains that characterize the rest of Madeira.

Electricity for the north of the island is generated here by wind turbines. Only gorse and grass grow on the thin soil, and the spongelike volcanic substrata act as a natural reservoir for rainfall. Water filters through the rock to emerge as springs that then feed the island's *levada* system.

THE LEVADAS OF MADEIRA

Madeira possesses a unique irrigation system that enables the plentiful rainfall of the north of the island to be distributed to the dry, sunny south. Rainfall is stored in reservoirs and lakes, or channeled from natural springs, and fed into

the network of *levadas* that ring the island. These narrow channels carry water long distances to banana groves, vineyards, and market gardens. Altogether there are 2,150 km (1,335 miles) of canals, some dating back to the 1500s. Maintenance paths run alongside the *levadas*, providing a network of trails reaching into remote parts of the island that are inaccessible by road.

Levada do Risco, one of many walking routes across Madeira

◁ **Terraced hillsides around the village of Curral das Freiras**

Rabaçal Walks ⓭

REACHED DOWN a single-track road from the Paúl da Serra plateau, Rabaçal is the starting point for two equally magical *levada* walks. One is a simple 30-minute, there-and-back stroll to the Risco waterfall, while the other is a more demanding two- to three-hour walk to the beauty spot known as Vinte e Cinco Fontes (25 Springs).

Tips for Walkers

***Length**: These two walks can be combined to create a circular trail of 8 km (5 miles), taking around three and a half hours.*

***Note**: The levadas can be slippery and sometimes very narrow. In places the path is only 30 cm (1 ft) wide, but the channel runs at waist height and you can hold on.*

Levada da Rocha Vermelha ⑥
Wild, mountainous terrain forms the backdrop to the steep path down to the lower *levada*.

25 Fontes ⑤
A 30-minute walk brings you to a mossy, fern-hung area with a main cascade and many smaller ones.

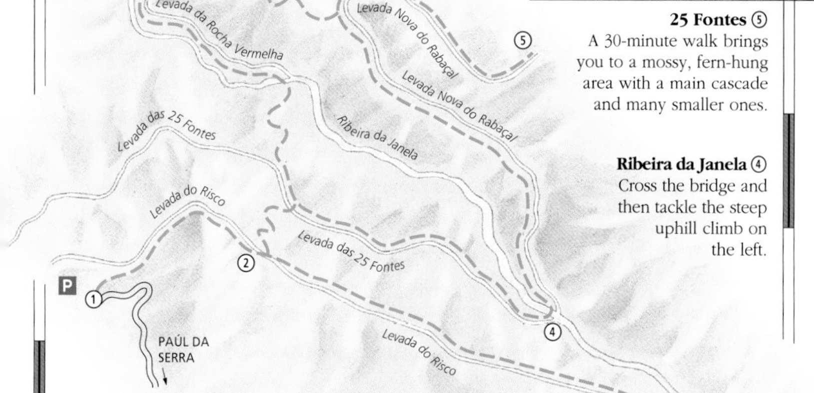

Ribeira da Janela ④
Cross the bridge and then tackle the steep uphill climb on the left.

Rabaçal ①
The starting point of the walk has a parking lot and government rest house with picnic tables and views down the secluded valley. Follow the marked path down to the right to meet the Levada do Risco.

Risco Waterfall ③
At this magnificent spot, a torrent of water cascades from the rocky heights down into the green depths of the Risco valley far below.

Levada do Risco ②
The course of the *levada*, which leads to the waterfall, is shaded by tree heathers draped with hairlike lichens.

Key

- Trail
- Road
- River
- Levada
- [P] Parking

0 meters 250
0 yards 250

Simple stone font in the attractively tiled baptistry of the Igreja Matriz in São Vicente

São Vicente ⑭

🏃 8,000. 🚌 ℹ️ *Câmara Municipal, Vila de São Vicente (291-84 21 35).*

T HE AGRICULTURAL town of São Vicente has grown prosperous over the years by tempting travelers to break their journeys here as they explore Madeira's northern coast.

To see how the village looked before development began, visit the **Igreja Matriz** (originally built in the 17th century), and look at the painting on the ceiling of St. Vincent blessing the town. St. Vincent appears again over the elaborately carved and gilded main altar, this time blessing a ship.

Around the church, cobblestone, traffic-free streets are lined with boutiques, bars, and shops selling sweet cakes, including the popular

Madeiran specialty *bolo de mel*, the so-called "honey cake" (actually made with molasses and fruit).

São Vicente marks the starting point of the coastal road northwest to Porto Moniz, one of the island's most exhilarating drives. The road, little more than a ledge cut into the sheer cliffs, sometimes passes through tunnels, sometimes through waterfalls. The 19-km (12-mile) road took 16 years to build by hand.

The only village along this lonely road is **Seixal**. Despite the Atlantic storms that can batter the island's northern coast, Seixal occupies a remarkably sheltered spot where vineyards cling to the hillside terraces, producing excellent wine.

Porto Moniz ⑮

🏃 4,000. 🚌 ℹ️ *Porto, Vila Porto Moniz (291-85 25 94).*

A LTHOUGH IT IS only 75 km (47 miles) from Funchal, visitors arriving in Porto Moniz feel a great sense of achievement after the long journey to this remote coastal village, on the northwest tip of Madeira.

Porto Moniz is surrounded by a patchwork pattern of tiny fields. The fields are protected by fences made from tree heather and dried bracken, a necessary precaution against the heavy, salt-laden air that blows in off the Atlantic.

Apart from its picturesque charm, the main attraction at Porto Moniz is the series of natural rock pools joined by concrete paths on the foreshore, where you can paddle or immerse yourself in sun-warmed water while being showered by spray as waves break against the nearby rocks.

Calheta ⑯

🏃 3,500. 🚌 ℹ️ *Câmara Municipal Vila da Calheta (291-82 25 39).*

Bananas, a prolific crop in Calheta

C ALHETA STANDS among flourishing vineyards and banana plantations. It is also at the center of what little sugarcane production survives on Madeira, and the sweet smell of cane syrup being extracted and turned into rum hangs around the village from the **factory** (visitors are welcome; the best time is March to April).

The **Igreja Matriz** looks unpromisingly modern, but it dates from 1430 and contains a large ebony and silver tabernacle donated by Manuel I *(see pp46–7)*. There is also a fine wooden ceiling.

🏭 Factory
Vila da Calheta. 📞 291-82 22 64.
🕐 *daily.* ⬤ *public hols.*

ENVIRONS: About 2 km (1 mile) east of Calheta, at **Loreto**, the 15th-century chapel has a Manueline south portal and geometrically patterned ceiling. Outside Estreito da Calheta, 3 km (2 miles) northwest of Calheta, is **Lombo dos Reis**. Here the Capela dos Reis Magos (Chapel of the Three Kings) has a lively 16th-century Flemish altar carving of the *Adoration of the Magi*.

The warm, natural rock pools at Porto Moniz

Part of Porto Santo's splendid sandy beach

Ribeira Brava ⑰

🏚 *13,500.* 🚌 🛈 *Forte de São Bento (291-95 16 75).* 🅿 *daily.*

R IBEIRA BRAVA is a small, attractive resort town situated on the sunny south coast of Madeira. It has a pebble beach and a fishing harbor, which is reached through a tunnel to the east of the main town.

Overlooking the principal square, **São Bento** remains one of the most unspoiled churches on Madeira. Despite restoration and reconstruction, several of its 16th-century features are still intact. These include a stone-carved font and ornate pulpit decorated with wild beasts such as wolves, the Flemish painting of the *Nativity* in the side chapel, and the wooden statue of the Virgin over the main altar. The church's clock tower has a beautifully tiled roof.

São Bento's clock tower, Ribeira Brava

This is one of Madeira's main centers for catching scabbard fish *(peixe espada)*, which are featured on every Madeiran menu. Long lines are baited with octopus to catch these unusual fish that dwell at depths of 800 m (2,600 ft). The fishermen live in single-story dwellings along the harbor front, and their tiny **chapel** dates from the 15th century, but was rebuilt in 1723. The chapel is dedicated to St. Nicholas, the patron saint of seafarers, and is decorated with scenes from the saint's life, as well as vivid portrayals of drownings and shipwrecks.

ENVIRONS: The second highest sea cliff in Europe is **Cabo Girão**, located 10 km (6 miles) west of Câmara de Lobos. It peaks at a dramatic 589 m (1,932 ft) above sea level.

Câmara de Lobos ⑱

🏚 *15,000.* 🚌 🛈 *Câmara Municipal, Largo da República (291-94 21 08).* 🅿 *Mon–Sat.*

V ISITORS TO this pretty fishing village are not allowed to forget that it was several times painted by Winston Churchill, who often visited Madeira in the 1950s. Bars and restaurants are named in his honor, and a plaque marks the spot on the main road, east of the harbor, where the great statesman set up his easels. The town has not changed greatly since then.

Porto Santo ⑲

🏚 *5,000.* ✈ 🚢 🛈 *Avenida Henrique Vieira de Castro, Vila Baleira (291-98 23 61).* 🅿 *Mon–Sat, Sun am.*

P ORTO SANTO, the island that lies 37 km (23 miles) to the northeast of Madeira, is seen by visitors as they fly in to Madeira's airport. A rough sea journey by ferry leaves from Madeira's harbor in Funchal for Porto Abrigo, near Vila Baleira, Porto Santo's capital. You can also fly to the island by helicopter or scheduled TAP (Air Portugal) flight.

Madeirans like to visit their sister island for the one thing that their own island lacks: a sandy beach that runs for 9 km (6 miles) along the entire south coast of the island. The beach and the surrounding seas are ideal for all sorts of water sports, from windsurfing and snorkeling to yachting and deep sea diving.

The one historic site of note on the island is the **Casa de Colombo** (house of Christopher Columbus), located behind Nossa Senhora da Piedade in Vila Baleira. The house is built from rough stone and was restored for the 500th anniversary of his landing in America. It contains an account of what is known of Columbus's life, along with maps, paintings, and engravings.

🏛 **Casa de Colombo**
Travessa da Sacristia, Vila Baleira.
📞 *291-98 34 05.* 🕐 *Mon–Fri & Sat am.* ⬤ *public hols.*

CHRISTOPHER COLUMBUS ON PORTO SANTO

Historical records vouch for the fact that Christopher Columbus came to Madeira in 1478, probably as an agent for sugar merchants in his native Italian town of Genoa. He went to Porto Santo to meet Bartolomeu Perestrelo, also from Genoa and the island's governor. There he met Filipa Moniz, Perestrelo's daughter. The two were married in 1479, but Filipa died soon after while giving birth to their son. Nothing else is known about Columbus's visit to the island, though this has not prevented local people from identifying his house.

***Christopher Colombus* by Ridolfo Ghirlandaio (1483–1561)**

THE AZORES

F AR OUT IN THE ATLANTIC, *1,300 km (800 miles) west of Portugal's mainland, the nine islands of the Azores are known for their spectacular volcanic scenery, abundant flora, and peaceful way of life. Once wild and remote, they are now a popular destination for travelers who enjoy walking, sailing, and getting away from it all.*

Santa Maria was the first island discovered by the Portuguese in 1427; the archipelago was named after the buzzards the early explorers saw flying overhead and mistook for goshawks *(açores)*. The islands were settled during the 15th and 16th centuries by colonists from Portugal and Flanders who introduced cattle, corn, and grapevines.

Império chapel on Pico

The Azores have profited from their far-flung position in the Atlantic. Between 1580 and 1640, when Portugal came under Spanish rule *(see pp50–51)*, the ports of Angra do Heroísmo on Terceira and Ponta Delgada on São Miguel prospered from the trade with the New World. In the 19th century the islands were a regular port of call for American whaling ships. During the 20th century they have benefited from their use as stations for transatlantic cable companies, meteorological observatories, and military air bases.

Today the majority of islanders are involved in either dairy farming or tuna fishing, and close links are maintained with both mainland Portugal and the sizeable communities of emigrant Azoreans in the United States and Canada. Many emigrants return to their native island for the traditional annual festivals, such as the *festas* of the Holy Spirit, celebrated in the colorful *impérios*. With few beaches, a capricious, often wet climate and no large-scale resorts, the Azores have escaped mass tourism. Most travelers come here to explore the green mountains embroidered with blue hydrangeas and relax in quiet ports adorned with cobbled streets and elegant Baroque churches. Once a brave new world of pioneer communities, the Azores are now an autonomous region of Portugal and an exotic corner of the European Union, where life remains refreshingly civil and unhurried.

Small fishing boats on the dockside at Lajes on the southern coast of Pico

◁ **Terceira's walled pastures sloping down to the sea with the two small Ilhéus das Cabras in the distance**

Exploring the Azores

THE ISLANDS OF THE AZORES are spread 650 km (400 miles) apart and fall into three distinct groups. In the east lie Santa Maria and São Miguel, the largest island and home to the regional capital, Ponta Delgada. The main towns in the central group of five islands are Horta on Faial, a popular stop-over port for boats crossing the Atlantic, and Angra do Heroísmo on Terceira, a busy cosmopolitan city. From here visitors can travel to the other islands of São Jorge, Graciosa, and Pico, the last dominated by a towering volcanic peak 2,350 m (7,700 ft) high. Farther west lie the remote, weather-beaten islands of Flores and Corvo.

9 CORVO
Vila Nova do Corvo

8 FLORES
R1-2
Santa Cruz das Flores
R1-2
Lajes

Transatlantic sailing boat moored in Faial's fine marina at Horta

Santa Cruz da Graciosa
R1-1
Praia
4 GRACIOSA

SIGHTS AT A GLANCE

Corvo **9**
Faial **7**
Flores **8**
Graciosa **4**
Pico **6**
Santa Maria **2**
São Jorge **5**
São Miguel pp362–3 **1**
Terceira **3**

7 FAIAL
R1-1
Capelo
Horta

Madalena
São Roque do Pico
São Mateus
R1-2
R2-2
6 PICO
Lajes do Pico
Piedade

R2-1
Velas
R1-2
Calbeta
R2-3
5 SÃO JORGE
Santo Antão

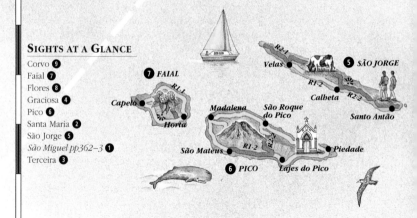

Walking among Pico's black volcanic lava rock

0 kilometers   25
0 miles   10

KEY

Road

Scenic route

Vista

SEE ALSO

• *Where to Stay* pp400–1

• *Where to Eat* p423

GETTING AROUND

São Miguel, Faial, and Terceira have international airports and the local airline, SATA, has internal flights between all the islands. Ferry services connect the five central islands several times a week in summer. There is a daily summer service between Flores and Corvo, but no service between Santa Maria and São Miguel. All ferry services are subject to the weather. Bus services on the islands are designed for the locals and therefore not very useful for tourists. Car rental is more convenient and available on all islands except Corvo. *(See also p447.)*

THE AZORES

MADEIRA

Angra do Heroísmo, capital of Terceira

3 *TERCEIRA*

Biscoitos

R1-7 *R3-1*

Praia da Vitória

Santa Bárbara *Angra do Heroísmo*
São Mateus

R1-1

Ribeira Grande

Porto Formoso

R1-1

Sete Cidades

R6-2

Furnas

Lagoa

Vila Franca do Campo

Povoação

Ponta Delgada

R1-1

1 *SÃO MIGUEL*

Ponta Delgada's elegant waterfront, São Miguel

2 *SANTA MARIA*

Anjos *Santa Bárbara*

Vila do Porto

São Miguel ❶

W ITH ITS HISTORIC maritime capital, rich green fields, and dramatic volcanic scenery, this *ilha verde* (green island) provides a rewarding introduction to the Azores. The largest and most populated of the archipelago's nine main islands, São Miguel is 65 km (40 miles) long and was originally two separate islands. The capital, Ponta Delgada, is a good base from which to make day tours of the rugged coast or visit the volcanic crater lakes and steaming thermal springs in the interior of the island.

The 18th-century city gates leading onto Ponta Delgada's central square

Ponta Delgada

Lined with many impressive churches, convents, and trim white houses, the cobblestone streets of the Azorean capital recall the wealthy days when the port was a crucial staging post between Europe and the New World *(see pp48–9)*. Its hub is the arcaded Praça de Gonçalo Velho Cabral, named after the first governor of the island in 1444, which looks out onto the sea. It is dominated by three imposing arches, dating from 1783, that once marked the entrance to the city. To the north, in Largo da Matriz, stands the parish church of **São Sebastião**. Founded in 1533 it has a graceful Manueline portal intricately carved in limestone. The sacristy is decorated with *azulejo* panels and beautiful 17th-century furniture made of jacaranda wood from Brazil.

A short walk west lies the Praça 5 de Outubro, a shaded, tree-lined square overlooked by the **Forte de São Brás**. This Renaissance fortress, built on a spur overlooking the sea, was greatly restored in the 19th century. Also on the square, the immense **Convento da Esperança** becomes the focus

of intense festivities when the city celebrates the festival of Santo Cristo dos Milagres on the fifth Sunday after Easter. A statue of Christ, wearing a red robe decorated with sumptuous diamond and gold ornaments, leads the procession through the streets. The statue can be seen in the lower church along with other religious treasures, including reliquaries, monstrances, and precious jewels. Colorful tiles, dating from the 18th century, by António de Oliveira Bernardes *(see p22)* decorate the choir.

The principal museum in the Azores, the **Museu Carlos Machado**, occupies the former monastery of Santo André. Its exhibits reflect the fishing and farming industries that have ruled life on the islands. Of particular interest are the paintings by Domingos Rebelo (1891–1975) showing scenes of Azorean life. The natural history wing is packed with an encyclopedic array of stuffed animals, varnished fish, skeletons, and a large relief model of the island.

🏛 **Museu Carlos Machado**
Rua João Moreira. 🎫 296-28 38 14. 🕐 *Tue–Sun.* ⬤ *public hols.* 🈲

West of the Island

The northwest of São Miguel is punctured by a giant volcanic crater, **Caldeira das Sete Cidades**, with a 12-km (7-mile) circumference. In places its sheer walls drop like green curtains for 300 m (1,000 ft). When not obscured by cloud, the crater is best seen from the vantage point of **Vista do Rei** from which a walk leads west around its rim. The crater floor contains the small village of Sete Cidades and three dark green lakes separated by a thin strip of land. The crater is believed to have been formed in the 1440s when an eruption destroyed the volcanic peak that had formed the western part of the island. In contrast to the lush vegetation that covers the crater now, the first settlers described the area as a burned-out shell.

The main town on the north coast, **Ribeira Grande** has a small **Casa da Cultura** (cultural center) housed in the restored 17th-century Solar de São Vicente. *Azulejos* from the 16th to 20th century are on display, and in other rooms the crafts and rural lifestyle of the islanders are recorded, including a period barbershop rescued from Ponta Delgada.

🏛 **Casa da Cultura**
Rua São Vicente Ferreira 10, Ribeira Grande. 🎫 *296-47 21 18.* 🕐 *Mon–Fri.* ⬤ *most public hols.* **Donation.**

KEY

═══ Main road

─── Other road

🔆 Vista

Turquoise waters of the crater lake, Lagoa do Fogo

East of the Island

The **Lagoa do Fogo**, "Lake of Fire," was formed in the island's central mountains by a volcanic eruption in 1563. On sunny days its remote sandy beach is a tranquil picnic spot.

Farther east, the spa resort of **Furnas** is the perfect place to admire the geothermal activity taking place beneath the surface of the Azores (see pp338–9). Scattered around the town are the **Caldeiras das Furnas**, where visitors will see the steaming geysers and hot bubbling springs that provide the therapeutic mud and mineral water used for the spa's treatments. In the 18th century, Thomas Hickling, a prosperous merchant from Boston, laid out gardens in Furnas that have now grown into the glorious **Parque Terra Nostra**. Covering 30 acres, the gardens have a rich collection of mature trees and plants, including hibiscus and hydrangeas, as well as a bizarre swimming pool with warm, mustard-colored water.

The volcanic ground on the northern shores of the **Lagoa das Furnas**, 4 km (2 miles) south, is so hot the islanders come here to cook *cozido*

VISITORS' CHECKLIST

👥 125,000. ✈ 6 km (4 miles) W of Ponta Delgada. 🚢 🚌 Avenida Infante Dom Henrique, Ponta Delgada. 🚌 Avenida Infante Dom Henrique, Ponta Delgada (296-28 57 43). 🎉 5th Sun after Easter: Santo Cristo dos Milagres (Ponta Delgada); Festas do Espírito Santo (see p366); Jun 29: São Pedro Cavalcade (Ribeira Grande).

(see p231). The rich meat and vegetable stew is placed underground in a huge pot, where it simmers for five hours.

The far east of São Miguel is a quiet, staggeringly beautiful area of deep valleys. Two immaculately kept vistas, **Miradouro do Sossego** and **Miradouro da Madrugada**, have wonderful gardens – the latter is a favorite spot for watching the sunrise.

🏛 Caldeiras das Furnas
Off R1-1. 📞 296-58 43 85. ⏰ daily.

Pristine gardens and picnic area of the Miradouro da Madrugada

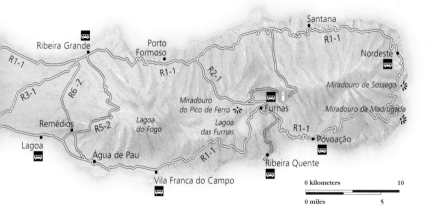

The wide bay of São Lourenço on Santa Maria

Santa Maria ➋

🏠 6,000. ✈ 3 km (2 miles) NW
of Vila do Porto. 🚢 Vila do Porto.
🚌 Rua Dr Luis Bettencourt, Vila do
Porto. 🛈 Aeroporto de Santa Maria,
Vila do Porto (296-88 63 55).
🎭 Festas do Espírito Santo (see p366);
Aug 15: Nossa Senhora da Assunção
(Vila do Porto).

Lying 55 km (34 miles) south
of São Miguel, Santa Maria
was the first island in the archipelago to be discovered by
the Portuguese, around 1427.
Though only 18 km (11 miles)
long, it has great scenic variety
and boasts sandy beaches,
tranquil countryside, and the
warmest climate in the Azores.

**Nossa Senhora da Purificação studded with
black basalt in Santo Espírito, Santa Maria**

The island's capital, **Vila do
Porto**, is on the south coast
and consists of a long main
street that runs down to a small
harbor. The west of the island
is a dry, flat plateau with a vast
airstrip built in World War II.
To the north lies the fishing
town of **Anjos**, where a statue
commemorates a visit made by
Christopher Columbus in 1493
on his return from his first
trip to the New World. Next
to it, the small, whitewashed
chapel of **Mãe de Deus** is the
oldest in the Azores.

The highest point of Santa
Maria is the central **Pico Alto**,
590 m (1,935 ft) above sea
level, which on a clear day
offers fine views of the green
and hilly east side of
the island. Toward the
east coast, the village
of **Santo Espírito** is
worth visiting for the
white Baroque façade
of its church of Nossa
Senhora da Purificação
adorned with black
lava decoration, while
the vine-covered half-
crater of **Baía de São
Lourenço**, north of
here, is a delightful
summer beach resort.

Terceira ➌

🏠 60,000. ✈ 3 km (2 miles) NW
of Praia da Vitória. 🚢 Angra do
Heroísmo. 🚌 Avenida 1º de Maio,
Angra do Heroísmo. 🛈 Rua Direita,
Angra do Heroísmo (295-21 33 93).
🎭 Festas do Espírito Santo (see
p366); last 2 weeks in Jun: Festas
de São João.

Terceira, meaning "third"
in Portuguese, is so named
because it was the third island
to be discovered, in 1427. It is
the most developed of the five
central islands – a result in
part of the large American-run
airbase that has been operating
at Lajes since World War II.
Terceira is famous for its unusual form of bull-running,
known as the *tourada à corda*
(bullfight with a rope), which
takes place from spring to autumn. A bull is let loose in the
street and taunted while tied
to a rope held tight by teams
of men. It is also well known
for the brightly painted chapels
devoted to the cult of the Holy
Spirit *(see p366)*. Terceira's
interior is predominantly green
pastureland, while the coast
has barren areas of black lava.

**Taunting a bull with umbrellas
during a *tourada à corda*, Terceira**

Angra do Heroísmo

The most cosmopolitan city in
the Azores, Angra do Heroísmo
was declared a UNESCO World
Heritage site in 1983, in recognition of the role the port has
played in the Atlantic. For over
three centuries the town was a
stopover point on the routes
between Europe, America, and
Africa. It was here in 1499 that
Vasco da Gama *(see p108)*
buried his brother Paulo after
their journey to India, and in
the early 17th century its
harbor glittered with Spanish
fleets returning laden with
treasure from the Americas.

The 16th-century Sé (cathedral) at the center of Terceira's capital, Angra do Heroísmo

Maria II gave the town its name for the bravery *(heroísmo)* it demonstrated during the struggles for Liberalism in the early 19th century *(see pp54–5)*. Despite the severe damage caused by an earthquake in 1980, the city's wealthy past is reflected in the fine streets lined with monumental churches and balconied houses.

The best view of the harbor is from **Monte Brasil**, a volcanic crater on the western side of the bay. Beside this popular picnic spot stands the fort, **Castelo de São João Baptista**, built during Spain's annexation of Portugal *(see pp50–51)* as a treasure store, and still in military use. A second rewarding vista is from the **Alto da Memória** at the south end of Rua São João de Deus, from which the twin towers of the 16th-century **Sé** (restored after a fire in 1983) are easily seen. A path leads down into the **Jardim Municipal**, the city's restful public gardens. These once formed part of the 15th-century Convento de São Francisco that now houses the **Museu de Angra do Heroísmo**. The museum's exhibits reflect the history of the Azores and the city and include armor, maps, paintings, and sculptures.

Wooden John the Baptist, Museu de Angra

🏛 **Museu de Angra do Heroísmo**
Ladeira de São Francisco. [295-21 31 47. ◯ Tue–Sun (Sat & Sun pm only). ● public hols. 📷 ♿

Around the Island
Terceira is a large, oval-shaped island with a gentle green interior of forested hills and farmland. Its center bears witness to its volcanic origins: the **Caldeira de Guilherme Moniz** is an eroded crater 3 km (2 miles) wide, the largest in the Azores. Nearby, the **Algar do Carvão** is a dramatic volcanic blast hole, thick with dripping moss, where visitors can tour an enormous subterranean cave. West of here, the **Furnas do Enxofre** are hot steaming geysers where the heavy sulfur vapors crystalize into brightly colored formations.

Two vistas overlooking the island can be reached by car: in the west, a road bordered with blue hydrangeas winds up through the **Serra de Santa Bárbara** to a vast lonely crater at 1,022 m (3,353 ft), while the eastern **Serra do Cume**, at 545 m (1,788 ft), overlooks the airport and **Praia da Vitória**. This port has a large bay with a sandy beach. Its name pays tribute to a famous victory in 1581 when the Spanish attempted to seize the island at Baía da Salga, 10 km (6 miles) south, and were thwarted by the release of a herd of cattle onto the shore.

On the north coast, **Biscoitos** (which means biscuits) takes its name from the rubble of biscuitlike lava spread along the shore. Exhilarating swimming pools, popular in the summer, have been created among the rocks. The area is also known for its wine, and the land is covered in a chessboard of stone-walled pens *(curraletas)* built to shelter vines. The friendly **Museu do Vinho** explains the simple production methods used to produce the rich *verdelho* wine that was once exported to the Russian court, and it provides an opportunity to taste and buy today's vintages.

🏞 **Algar do Carvão**
Off R5-2. [295-21 29 92. ◯ daily (Oct–Mar: on request). 📷

🏛 **Museu do Vinho**
Canada do Caldeiro, Biscoitos. [295-90 84 04. ◯ daily. ● Jan 1, Dec 25.

Patchwork of stone-walled fields in the northeast of Terceira, near Praia da Vitória

The Holy Spirit Festivals

FESTIVALS ARE A VIBRANT feature of life in the Azores and have helped foster the deep sense of community that is a hallmark of the islands' culture. Emigrants and relatives from North America and mainland Portugal often return to their native island to celebrate the most popular *festas*.

The islands' most traditional festivals are associated with the Holy Spirit *(Festas do Espírito Santo)*. Brought to the Azores by the first Portuguese settlers, who called upon the Holy Spirit to

A girl wearing the emperor's crown

protect them against natural disasters, the rituals have remained almost unchanged. An "emperor," usually a child, is crowned in the parish church. With a scepter and silver plate as insignia of the Holy Spirit, the "emperor" presides over the festivities that take place each Sunday for seven weeks after Easter. The seventh Sunday, Whit Sunday, or the day of Pentecost when Christ's disciples were filled with the Holy Spirit, is the occasion of a great feast in the village.

The distribution of bread *for the Festival of the Holy Spirit originated in the donation of food to the poor introduced by saintly Queen Isabel (see p45). On the last day of celebrations, the seventh Sunday after Easter, a Holy Spirit soup is made from beef and vegetables and is handed out, along with bread, to everyone outside the local* império.

THE IMPÉRIOS OF THE HOLY SPIRIT

Império **with Gothic windows in Terra Chã, Terceira (1954)**

Flamboyantly decorated *império* **in São Sebastião, Terceira (1918)**

Simple *império* **in Praia da Vitória, Terceira (1861)**

The focus of the ceremonies is a small chapel or *império* (empire), which is used for the distribution of the Holy Spirit soup on the seventh Sunday. Here, the emperor's crown, scepter, and plate are displayed on the altar on the last day of the festivities. On Terceira, where the cult of the Holy Spirit is particularly strong, many of the 58 *impérios* are painted in bright colors every spring. Up to 500 islanders gather for a village feast accompanied by dancing, brass bands, and lavish floral displays. In many places a *tourada à corda* will be held, where a bull, tied to the end of a long rope, is let loose in the street.

An emperor's crown on ceremonial display in an *império* **on São Miguel**

Traditional ox-drawn cart on the island of Graciosa

Graciosa ⑥

🏠 5,500. ✈ 2 km (1 mile) W of Santa Cruz da Graciosa. 🚢 Praia de São Mateus. 🛈 Praça Fontes Pereira de Melo, Santa Cruz (295-71 25 09). 🎊 Festas do Espírito Santo; Aug: Santo Cristo.

THE "GRACIOUS" ISLAND is one of the most peaceful in the Azores. Only 12 km (7 miles) long, most of its low-lying land is given over to farms and vineyards where ox-drawn carts and plows are still in use. The capital, **Santa Cruz da Graciosa**, on the northern coast, has a simple dock backed by rows of whitewashed houses with wrought-iron balconies and oval windows. A small **Museu Etnográfico** recalls life on this sleepy island with toys, sea chests, kitchenware, wine presses, furniture, and mementoes sent back by emigrants to North America. A building next door houses a whaling boat (see pp368–9).

The picturesque Monte da Ajuda that rises behind the town is capped by a 16th-century fortified chapel, **Nossa Senhora da Ajuda**, decorated with 18th-century tiles. Nearby, a small *vigia* (whalers' lookout) faces the sea.

In the southeast lies the island's principal sight, **Furna do Enxofre**, where visitors can descend flights of steps into the bowels of a volcanic crater. At the bottom is a huge cave with a deep, sulphurous lake and peep-holes where bubbling brews of evil gray liquid can be spied beneath the rocks. The best time to visit is late morning when the sun shines through the small cave mouth and lights the interior. Above the cave, at **Furna**

Maria Encantada, a natural tunnel through the rock leads to the edge of the crater. From here there are stunning views over the island. Treatments using the island's geothermal waters are available at the coastal resort of **Carapacho**, at the foot of the volcano.

🏛 **Museu Etnográfico**
Rua das Flores, Santa Cruz. 📞 295-71 24 29. 🕘 daily (Oct–Mar: Mon–Fri). ● public hols. 🎫 ♿ ground floor.

🌋 **Furna do Enxofre**
2 km (1 mile) E of Luz, follow signs to Caldeira. 🕘 Fri–Wed. 🎫

The rich Baroque interior of Santa Bárbara in Manadas, São Jorge

São Jorge ⑨

🏠 11,000. ✈ 7 km (4 miles) E of Velas. 🚢 Velas & Calheta. 🛈 Rua Dr José Pereira 1, Velas (295-41 22 14). 🎊 23 Apr: Festa de São Jorge; Festas do Espírito Santo; Jul: Semana Cultural de Velas (Velas).

SÃO JORGE IS A LONG, thin mountainous island that stretches for 56 km (35 miles) but is only 8 km (5 miles) wide. On its north coast, sheer cliffs

drop 480 m (1,575 ft) to the sea. Over the centuries these cliffs have collapsed in places, creating tongues of land known as *fajãs*. It was on these coastal promontories that the island's Flemish colonists first settled in the mid-15th century.

Today many islanders on São Jorge are engaged in the production of a delicious, cured cheese, *Queijo de São Jorge*, exported to mainland Europe. The pace of life is leisurely, and most visitors come here to enjoy walking along the paths that climb up and down between the *fajãs*. The most popular route is in the northeast of the island from Serra do Topo 10 km (6 miles) down to Fajã dos Cubres.

Most of the settlements lie along the gentler south coast, including the capital, **Velas**, and **Calheta**, where the small **Museu de São Jorge** displays objects of local history such as the ornate breads baked for the Holy Spirit festival, a honey press, agricultural utensils, and religious sculptures. West of Calheta, in the pretty village of **Manadas**, the 18th-century church of **Santa Bárbara** has an atmospheric carved and painted interior. In **Urzelina**, 2 km (1 mile) farther west, the tower of a church buried by lava in 1808 protrudes defiantly from the ground. In the west of the island there is a pleasant forested picnic area at **Sete Fontes**, and on a clear day the nearby summit of **Pico da Velha** offers superb views of the central Azorean islands.

🏛 **Museu de São Jorge**
Rua José Azevedo da Cunha, Calheta. 📞 295-41 63 23. 🕘 Mon–Fri. ● public hols.

Dramatic cliffs along the north coast of São Jorge

Pico

🏠 15,500. ✈ 8 km (5 miles) E of Madalena. ⛴ Madalena. 🚌 Avenida Machado Serpa, Madalena. ℹ Rua Maria Gloria Duarte, Madalena (292-62 35 24). ⛪ Festas do Espirito Santo (see p366); Jul 22: Santa Maria Madalena; Aug 19–25: Festa dos Baleeiros.

THE FULL MAJESTY of Pico, the highest mountain in Portugal, becomes apparent when it is seen from the neighboring central islands.

Rustic house and well on Pico made from black lava rocks

Only then does one realize how gracefully this volcanic peak soars out of the Atlantic, shooting up 2,350 m (7,700 ft) to form the summit of the greatest mountain range in the world, the Mid-Atlantic Ridge *(see pp338–9)*.

The island's capital, **Madalena**, is a relaxed port that lies opposite Faial's capital, Horta. A regular ferry service crosses the 7 km (4 miles) between the two islands, making a day trip feasible. The entrance to the harbor is guarded by two rocks, Em Pé (standing) and Deitado (lying down), where colonies of birds have made their home.

Many people come to Pico to climb its eponymous peak, which in winter is often snow-capped and at other times can be wrapped in cloud. It is a strenuous climb, best done in

The summit of Pico's volcano

the company of a guide, and permission is required in advance. For further details contact the tourist office.

The other main draw to Pico in summer is whale-watching. From **Lajes do Pico** groups are taken out in small boats for three-hour trips organized by the **Espaço Talassa**. They are guided by radio messages

In Pursuit of the Whale

EVERY SUMMER the waters around the Azores are visited by a great variety of whales and dolphins. Until 1984 whaling was a traditional part of Azorean life – in the 19th century American whaling vessels frequently called here to pick up crew for their expeditions, and from the 1870s the Azoreans took up large-scale hunting in their own waters. Flags were waved from clifftop *vigias* (lookouts) giving coded directions so that other villagers would not get to the prize first.

Since whaling was banned in the 1980s, the Azoreans have applied their knowledge gained from hunting to whale-watching and conservation.

Scrimshaws are carvings made on the teeth and bones of whales and often depict whaling scenes. This fine example from the Museu do Scrimshau on Faial (see p370) shows the long, narrow boats called canoas that could hold up to 14 men.

Whale-watching *today takes place in small boats that allow fast and safe access to the whales. As well as trips out to sea, the whales can be observed from the vigias. These land-based towers afford spectacular views of the whales in their natural habitat. Expeditions run from Pico and Faial (see p370).*

from men who scan the sea for a fluke (tail) from the former *vigias* (lookouts). The history of Azorean whaling is recalled at the **Museu dos Baleeiros**, also in Lajes, where boats, tackle, and whalebone artifacts are displayed. The whales were processed at an immense factory on the north side of the island at São Roque do Pico. Closed down in 1981, the **Fábrica da Baleia** has been preserved as a ghostly piece of industrial heritage that still retains the boilers where the blubber was turned into oil.

A coastal road encircles Pico, offering a slow but rewarding drive that reveals the charm of this undeveloped island. Minor eruptions in previous centuries have covered parts of its landscape with black molehills of lava that the islanders christened *mistérios* (mysteries). The black lava has been used to build houses and grids of stone walls that enclose fields or shelter vines.

In some places, notably around **Cachorro** on the north coast, the eroded lava has formed unusual arches in the sea.

Pico's famous *Verdelho* wine, which is similar to the one made in Madeira *(see p349)*, was once regularly exported to mainland Europe. In recent years there has been a revival of viticulture on the island, and the production of new reds and whites – such as the much acclaimed *Terras da Lava* – now means visitors have a refined alternative to the ubiquitous *vinho de cheiro* (wine of smell) traditionally drunk by the Azoreans.

🐟 **Espaço Talassa**
Rua do Saco, Lajes. ☎ 292-67 20 10.
⬜ daily. ▨
🏛 **Museu dos Baleeiros**
Rua dos Baleeiros, Lajes. ☎ 292-67 22 76. ⬜ Tue – Sun. ⬤ public hols. ▨
⚓ **Fábrica da Baleia**
Rua do Poço, São Roque do Pico.
☎ 292-64 20 96. ⬜ daily (Oct – Mar: Mon – Fri). ⬤ public hols. ♿ limited.

West coast of Pico with Faial in the distance

MARINE LIFE IN THE AZORES

Some 20 species of cetaceans can be found in the waters of the Azores. These warm-blooded animals follow the warm currents of the Gulf Stream to feed in the region's abundant, unpolluted waters. Schools of playful and gregarious dolphins are often seen scything through the waves at incredible speeds, but the most impressive sights are sperm whales. These large, sociable animals dive to great depths for giant squid and live in family groups called pods. Like all whales and dolphins they must come to the surface to breathe, and this is when whale-watching expeditions make their sightings.

Atlantic spotted dolphins, fast and graceful swimmers

Sperm whales
are huge, tear-shaped creatures, the largest of the toothed whales. They can be seen breaching (diving out of the water), spy bopping (raising their head to have a look around), and socializing by rubbing bodies.

Pilot whales belong to the dolphin family and are recognizable from their strong blow of up to 1 m (3 ft).

Risso's dolphins have a squat head and light gray coloring. Older ones are often crisscrossed with white scars.

Bottlenose dolphins are the best known. These playful animals love to ride the waves at the bow of a moving vessel.

Loggerhead turtles, born on Florida's beaches, are frequent visitors to the warm Azorean waters.

Transatlantic yachts moored in the marina at Horta, Faial, with the pointed summit of Pico in the distance

Faial ⑦

🏛 16,000. ✈ 10 km (6 miles) SW of Horta. ⛴ Horta. 🚌 Rua Vasco da Gama, Horta. 🛈 Rua Vasco da Gama, Horta (292-222 37). 🎭 Festas do Espírito Santo (see p366); 1st–2nd Sun in Aug: Semana do Mar (Horta).

Faial was settled by Flemish farmers in the 15th century and prospered with the development of the harbor at Horta as a stopover for ships and – more recently – flying boats crossing the Atlantic. Today it is a fertile island with a lively, international atmosphere and a mild climate, famous as a yachting destination and for the endless hedges of hydrangeas that fill it with color when they bloom in June and July.

Horta

Stretching around a wide bay, Faial's capital has been a convenient anchorage for caravels, clippers, and sea planes over the centuries. Captain Cook commented on Horta's fine houses and gardens when he called here in 1775. Today, visiting crews crossing between the Caribbean and Mediterranean paint a calling card on the dockside and celebrate their safe passage in **Peter's Café Sport**. In the upstairs rooms of the café, an engrossing **Museu do Scrimshau** exhibits engraved whales' bones and teeth dating back to 1884 (see p368).

In the **Museu da Horta** displays of antique furniture, portraits, nautical memorabilia, and nostalgic photographs of the island's port are upstaged by miniature sculptures of liners and scenes of daily life, painstakingly carved from the white pith of fig trees. These virtuoso examples of a traditional island craft are by the Faial-born Euclides Silveira da Rosa (1910–79).

Ship's calling card on the dockside in Horta, Faial

Excursions for dolphin- and whale-watching (see pp368–9) in the waters round the island are organized by the **Baleia à Vista** company.

🏛 **Museu do Scrimshau**
Peter's Café Sport, Rua T. Valadim 9.
📞 292-318 37. ⬜ daily. 📷
🏛 **Museu da Horta**
Palácio do Colégio, Largo Duque A. de Bolama. 📞 292-233 48. ⬜ Tue–Sun. ⬤ Jan 1, Easter, May 1, Dec 25. 📷
⚓ **Baleia à Vista**
📞 292-992 35. ⬜ daily. 📷

Barren, ash-covered volcanic landscape at Capelinhos, the westernmost point of Faial

Around the Island

Two vistas overlook Horta – to its south rises the volcanic peak of **Monte da Guia**, while the northern **Miradouro da Espalamaca** is guarded by a huge statue of Nossa Senhora da Conceição. If the cloud cover permits, it is well worth driving 15 km (9 miles) to see Faial's central **Caldeira do Cabeço Gordo** – a vast green crater 2 km (1 mile) wide and 400 m (1,300 ft) deep. The path winding around its rim takes about two hours to walk and has magnificent views.

Faial's other spectacular natural sight is the **Vulcão dos Capelinhos** in the far west of the island. A volcano erupted here in 1957–8, smothering a lighthouse that can now be seen buried in ash. Around it lies a scorched and barren landscape that has, not surprisingly, been used as the location for a German postnuclear holocaust movie. The story of the eruption is told in the nearby **Exposição Fotográfica** where photographs and maps trace the area's geological activity, showing how the black land is gradually coming back to life. Also shown are the lava formations created in the eruption.

🏛 **Exposição Fotográfica**
Canto do Capelo. 📞 292-951 65.
⬜ daily (Oct–Mar: Tue–Sun).
⬤ Jan 1, Dec 24, 25 & 31.

Flores

2,000. *1 km (half a mile) N of Santa Cruz.* *Lajes.* *Rua da Conceição, Santa Cruz.* *Rua Dr Almas da Silveira, Santa Cruz (292-523 69).* *Festas do Espírito Santo (see p366); Jun 24–26: Festas de São João; Jul 19–22: Festa do Emigrante (Lajes).*

OFTEN CUT OFF by stormy weather, the island of Flores is a romantic outpost that was not permanently settled until the 16th century. A notorious hideout for pirates waiting to raid the treasure-laden Spanish galleons on their return to Europe, Flores was the scene of an epic battle in 1591 between the ship of the English commander Sir Richard Grenville and a fleet of Spanish ships. The battle was immortalized in a poem by Alfred Tennyson, "The Revenge" (the name of Grenville's ship).

This westernmost island of the Azores is 17 km (10 miles) long and extremely mountainous. Its name derives from the abundance of flowers growing in its ravines, and the prospect of wilderness draws adventurous walkers here during the summer. The capital, **Santa Cruz**, is enlivened by the **Museu das Flores**, housed in the former Franciscan convent. Its displays include shipwreck finds, Azorean pottery, furniture, agricultural tools, fishing rods, and a guitar made from whalebone. The convent church of **São Boaventura**, erected in 1641, has a beautiful, carved cedarwood chancel.

Hydrangeas growing in the mountains of Flores

The southern half of the island is the most scenic. The deep, verdant valleys are punctuated with dramatic peaks and volcanic crater lakes and caves. Yams and sweet potatoes grow in the fertile soil. The tranquil **Lagoa Funda** (Deep Lake), 25 km (15 miles) southwest of Santa Cruz, is a large crater lake at the base of a mountain. Visible from the main road just west of the lake, are the strange vertical rock formations of the **Rocha dos Bordões** formed by solidified basalt.

The winding road continues northward over the mountains and, as the road descends towards the west coast, there are stunning views of the green valley and village of **Fajãzinha**. The resort of **Fajã Grande**, ringed by cliffs, is a

popular base for walkers, and impressive waterfalls plunge into the sea from the high cliffs. A short walk north from the town is the **Cascata da Ribeira Grande**, a towering jet of water that divides into smaller waterfalls before collecting in a still pool.

🏛 **Museu das Flores**
Largo da Misericórdia, Santa Cruz. *292-521 59.* *Mon–Fri.* *public hols*

Corvo ❾

370. *Vila Nova.* *Rua da Matriz, Vila Nova.* *Câmara Municipal, Rua J. da Bola, Vila Nova (292-561 15).* *Festas do Espírito Santo (see p366); 3rd Sun in Jul: Sagrada Família.*

CORVO LIES 24 km (15 miles) northeast of Flores. The smallest island in the Azores, it has just one settlement, **Vila Nova**, and is blissfully undeveloped, with only two taxis and one policeman. The entire island is the blown top of the marine volcano Monte Gordo. An ethereal green crater, the **Lagoa do Caldeirão**, squats at its northern end. Its rim can be reached by road, after which there is a steep descent down to the crater floor 300 m (984 ft) below. In its center, the crater is dotted with serene lakes and islands; a patchwork of stone-walled fields covers part of the slopes.

The island of Corvo seen from the rocky shore of Flores

TRAVELERS' NEEDS

WHERE TO STAY

PORTUGAL OFFERS a wide range of accommodation, from luxury hotels and restored palaces to family-run hostels and efficiency apartments. The majority of the country's hotels are in Lisbon, Oporto, and on the Algarve and Estoril coasts. Elsewhere, outside of the main towns, hotels are relatively scarce. This shortage is made up for by a number offering accommodations in traditional or historic buildings often set in lovely countryside. These all require advance booking, as rooms are in short supply. Other

Porter at Lisbon's luxurious Hotel da Lapa (see p382)

options include efficiency apartments in cities and resorts, and converted country villas and farmhouses, all offering flexibility and a good value. It is worth remembering that all rooms are cheaper outside tourist season. Accommodations in Lisbon divide between top-flight hotels and basic lodging with little choice in between. The hotels listed on pages 380–401 have been selected from every price category and represent the best value in each area.

TYPES OF HOTEL

HOTELS VARY considerably in quality, price, and facilities. Not surprisingly, the highest concentration can be found in Lisbon and the Algarve, where there are hotels to suit most budgets. In towns and cities elsewhere in the country, there is usually a satisfactory range of accommodations.

There are several other types of lodging in addition to the conventional hotel, and the range of categories on offer can at first appear confusing.

An *albergaria* (inn) is usually found in towns or cities and offers lodging in pleasant, friendly surroundings, usually at a lower price than a hotel of a similar quality. The regional equivalent is an *estalagem*, which is often an old restored building of great character, set in its own grounds.

The modern *apart-hotels* consist of self-contained apartments including a kitchen, combined with some hotel facilities, such as restaurants, bars, and a swimming pool. This type of lodging offers great flexibility and good value, and is particularly well suited to families. *Apart-hotels* are mostly found in the tourist resort areas of the Algarve and the Estoril coasts.

POUSADAS

POUSADAS ARE country inns run by the state, of which there are around 40 throughout Portugal (see pp378–9), with two on Madeira. Staying in a *pousada* is an excellent way to savor Portugal's history,

Bedroom at the York House Hotel in Lisbon, a converted 16th-century convent (see p382)

scenery, and culture; all *pousadas* offer very comfortable accommodation. They fall broadly into two categories. "Historical" *pousadas* are converted national monuments or other buildings such as palaces, which can sometimes have a very illustrious background. "Regional" *pousadas* are set in areas of local interest or fine scenery, such as in parks or preserves, and vary from the traditional to the very modern.

HOTEL CHAINS

AT THE TOP END of the hotel market, two small hotel chains offer the most luxurious surroundings and facilities. The grand **Hotéis Alexandre de Almeida** is the oldest chain in Portugal founded in 1917. This group boasts the Buçaco Palace Hotel, a magnificent retreat built for the Portuguese monarchy. The **Hotéis Tivoli** have seven luxurious hotels in converted palaces in Lisbon, Sintra, Coimbra, and Oporto.

Hotel Almansor in the resort of Carvoeiro, the Algarve (see p397)

◁ **Breakfasting beneath the wisteria at the Pousada de Palmela**

More modest accommodations are offered by **Choice Hotels,** who run two modern hotel chains: Comfort Hotels and Quality Suites. The latter offers better facilities and service, but Comfort Hotels have better facilities for disabled travelers. **Best Western** offers individually styled properties with quality service. **IBIS** hotels offer pleasant, simply furnished rooms with air-conditioning and a standardized level of comfort throughout their hotels.

PENSÕES

P ENSÕES or guesthouses generally fall into the lowest price range and can often be an excellent value, as well as offering a more relaxed environment. At its simplest, accommodations in a *pensão* consist of a clean, basic room with a shared bathroom. At the more luxury end of the market, 4-star *pensões* can rival top hotels for comfort and service. *Pensões* usually offer full-board accommodations that includes meals. A *pensão* that offers only bed and breakfast is called a *residencial*.

GRADINGS

M OST CATEGORIES of tourist accommodations are graded with a star rating, which ranges from one to five (five being the most luxurious). In theory, the stars awarded indicate the size, degree of comfort, and facilities offered. The establishment has to adhere to a set of criteria to achieve and maintain its star rating. The system can be very misleading, however, with quality varying a great deal within each star rating and from one type of lodging to another. For instance, a three-star *pensão* will often be more comfortable and stylish than a one- or two-star hotel.

View from the Seteais Palace, Sintra, now a luxury hotel *(see p386)*

PRICES

I N PORTUGAL, establishments are free to decide their own prices, but tariffs must be clearly displayed. It is sometimes possible to bargain for a better rate, especially outside the tourist season. As a rule, the cost of a single room is around 60 to 75 percent of the cost of a double. The most expensive areas to stay are the Algarve and Estoril coasts, and Madeira and the Azores, but on the mainland, prices drop outside the summer. *Pousadas* charge three

Reid's Hotel in Funchal, Madeira *(see p400)*

different rates: between July and September is the most expensive, April to June and October are mid-priced, and the off season runs from November to March.

NATIONAL TOURIST AGENCIES

A DVANCE BOOKING is essential for locations in tourist season, when resort accommodations in the Algarve and around the Estoril coast are booked by tour operators.

Pousadas can be booked easily through the **Portuguese National Tourist Office** *(see pp426–7)* or **Enatur**, the Portuguese national tourism agency. Advance booking is essential for rural residences, as they often have only a few rooms. You can reserve rooms through the owners' associations listed in the directory on page 377 or through a travel agent. A deposit may be required, and guests must stay a minimum of 3 days.

Portugal has few roadside inns, so motorists should stay in towns; book rural lodging in advance. The **Direccão-Geral do Turismo** (State Tourist Office) publishes two annual guides that are available through National Tourist Offices: *Guia do Alojamento Turístico* (The Official Guide to Tourist Accommodation) and *Turismo no Espaço Rural* (The Official Guide to Tourism in the Countryside).

Casa do Campo, a manor house in Celorico de Basto *(see p393)*

RURAL ACCOMMODATIONS

THREE PROGRAMS operated by *Turismo no Espaço Rural* (TER) enable visitors to stay with a family in rural Portugal. Properties in these programs have to be registered with the State Tourist Office and will display the TER logo.

In the program run by the *Associação de Turismo de Habitação*, visitors are welcomed as guests of the owners, often in private stately homes and manor houses. The highest concentration of properties is in the Minho, and there are also a handful in Madeira and the Azores. They vary from surroundings of antique opulence with four-poster beds to more modest farmhouses, and prices also vary accordingly. *Turismo Rural* (TR) offers visitors a chance to stay in rustic houses built in the local regional style, and *Agroturismo* (AT) offers rooms on family-run farms,

where guests can join in with the work if they wish. Many of these country properties are well off the beaten track, and it is important to obtain clear directions before setting out.

Each of the properties in these programs is represented by one of three owners' associations, **ANTER**, **PRIVETUR**, and **TURIHAB**, all of which can send you information.

RESORT ACCOMMODATIONS

PORTUGAL'S RESORT accommodations are situated mainly along the Algarve and Estoril coasts. The most convenient way to book accommodations is to make prior arrangements through a travel agent or tour operator. Hotel prices can drop considerably in the off season, and it is often possible to get a very good deal at less popular times of the year, when there are also fewer crowds to contend with.

The tourist village or *Aldeamento Turístico* is a unique feature of resort areas such as the Algarve. These self-contained complexes offer well-furnished and fitted private apartments and usually provide a range of sports facilities, beaches, pools, restaurants, bars, and sometimes a supermarket.

These complexes are rated as follows: Luxury (L), First Class (1ª) or Second Class (2ª).

Apartamentos Turísticos (Tourist Apartments) do not have the hotel-style facilities of the tourist villages but are ideal for those who want flexibility. They are generally built-to-order modern buildings in resort areas that offer efficiency accommodations. These Tourist Apartments also carry one of three quality gradings.

The luxurious Marinotel at the resort of Vilamoura in the Algarve *(see p399)*

BUDGET ACCOMMODATIONS

YOUTH HOSTELS in Portugal (*Pousadas de Juventude*) are dotted mainly along the coast and include two in the Azores. There are 22 in all, and they are open all year, but advance booking is advisable in the summer. They require a valid IYHF card, which can be obtained from any Youth Hostel Association. Facilities may include the use of a kitchen, bar, and swimming pool. Some also offer facilities for the disabled. Information is available from **Movijovem**, the head office of the Portuguese Youth Hostel Association.

Almost as cheap as youth hostels, and offering greater privacy, rooms *(quartos)* in private houses will invariably cost less than a *pensão*. This type of accommodation is often rented out in resorts, and lists of *quartos* are available from the local tourist office.

Dining room at Casa de Esteiró, rural lodging in Caminha *(see p393)*

CAMPING, CAMPSITES, AND RVING

THERE ARE OVER 100 official campsites in Portugal. Most are along the coast, usually in attractive locations. The largest is at Albufeira in the Algarve, but most are small and quiet. A chain of campsites is run by the company **Orbitur**.

Generally you pay a rate for the tent and per person, and an extra charge for showers and parking. The Portuguese Tourist Office will provide lists of campsites and information. You will need an international camping card, available from the **Family Campers and RVers Association**. The card is good for one year and costs $35. This provides third party insurance cover and entitles holders to some out-of-season discounts.

Provided you show due consideration for the environment, it is possible to camp outside official sites in the

São Miguel campsite, near Odemira in the Alentejo region

countryside, except for the Algarve, where it is strictly forbidden to stray from the sites.

CHILDREN

CHILDREN ARE as welcome as adult visitors to Portugal and families are well catered to. Most hotels give children under eight years old a 50 percent discount on the price of accommodations and meals.

DISABLED TRAVELERS

HOTELS WITH facilities for the disabled are listed by the Portuguese Tourist Office, which also produces an informative leaflet. Some campsites and youth hostels provide special facilities; these are listed by relevant organizations, and in a guide published by the **Secretariado Nacional de Reabilitação**.

DIRECTORY

HOTEL CHAINS

Tivoli Hotels
US 【 *(800) 223-5652.*
Lisbon 【 *21-319 89 00.*

Hotéis Alexandre de Almeida
Lisbon 【 *21-793 10 24.*

TOURS

Pinto Basto Tours International
24 S. Main St., 2nd Fl.,
New City, NY 10956.
【 *(800) 345-0739.*
FAX *(914) 639-8017.*

Alta Tours
870 Market St., Ste. 784,
San Francisco, CA 94102.
【 *(800) 338-4191.*
FAX *(415) 434-2684.*

Relvas Travel Center
188 Pequeonnock St.,
Bridgeport, CT 06604.
【 *(800) 359-7358.*
FAX *(203) 332-1229.*

NATIONAL TOURIST AGENCIES

Direcção-Geral de Turismo
Avenida António Augusto de Aguiar 86,
1050 Lisbon.
【 *21-357 50 15.*
FAX *21-357 52 20.*

Enatur S.A.
Avenida Santa Joana Princesa 10,
1070 Lisbon.
【 *21-848 90 78.*
FAX *21-848 92 57.*

Direcção Regional de Turismo dos Açores
Casa do Relógio Colónia Alemã,
9900 Horta, Azores.
【 *292-29 38 01.*
FAX *292-29 20 04.*

Direcção Regional de Turismo da Madeira
Avenida Arriaga 18,
9000 Funchal.
【 *291-22 90 57.*
FAX *291-23 21 51.*

RURAL ACCOMMODATIONS

ANTER
Associação Nacional de Turismo no Espaço Rural,
Travessa Megue 4, 1º,
7000 Évora.
【 & FAX *266-74 45 55.*

PRIVETUR
Associação Portuguesa de Turismo de Habitação,
Largo das Pereiras,
4990 Ponte de Lima.
【 & FAX *258-74 14 93.*

TURIHAB
Associação de Turismo de Habitação,
Praça de República,
4990 Ponte de Lima.
【 *258-74 16 72.*
FAX *258-74 14 44.*

RURAL ACCOMMODATIONS

Movijovem
Pousadas de Juventude,
Avenida Duque d'Avila 137,
1050 Lisbon.
【 *21-313 88 20.*
FAX *21-352 86 21.*

CAMPING AND RVING

Family Campers and RVers Association
4804 Transit Rd.,
Depew, NY 14043.
【 & FAX *(716) 668-6242.*
fcrvnat@local net.com

Portugal: Camping and Caravanning Albufeira
Estrada de Ferreiras, 8200
Albufeira, Algarve.
【 *289-58 95 05.*
FAX *289-58 76 33.*

Orbitur Intercambio de Turismo
Rua Diogo de Couto 1, 8º,
1100 Lisbon.
【 *21-815 48 71.*
FAX *21-814 80 45.*

DISABLED TRAVELERS

Secretariado Nacional de Reabilitação
Avenida Conde de Valbom 63,1050 Lisbon.
【 *21-793 65 17.*
FAX *21-796 51 82.*

The Pousadas of Portugal

Pousada symbol

THE CONCEPT of the *pousada* dates from the 1940s, when the Portuguese government decided to establish a national network of state-run country inns, offering "hospitality in keeping with the style and tradition of the region." *Pousadas* are often set in remote, scenic locations, and most have fewer than 30 rooms, so visitors can expect friendly, personalized service and a high degree of comfort. This map does not show all of Portugal's *pousadas*, just the 35 that are described in the listings on pages 380–401.

Pousada da Ria *near the port of Aveiro has 19 bedrooms, most of which have balconies overlooking the sheltered lagoon of Ria de Aveiro (see p388).*

Vale do Mir

Vila Nova de Cerveira

Viana do Castelo

Pousada de São Pedro *lies 13 km (8 miles) southeast of the picturesque town of Tomar and was originally built in the 1940s to house engineers working on the nearby Castelo de Bode dam. Overlooking the Zêzere River below the dam, the pousada reopened in 1993 after closing for extensive renovation (see p386).*

Condeixa-a-Nova

Pousada do Castelo, *in the walled town of Óbidos, is situated in a beautifully restored palace inside the 15th-century castle keep. The pousada combines a medieval atmosphere with all modern comforts and a highly recommended restaurant (see p387).*

Batalha

ESTREMADURA AND RIBATEJO

Queluz

THE LISBON COAST

LISBON

Setúbal

Pousada de Palmela *boasts an elegant interior, commanding hilltop views of the town of Palmela and the Atlantic Ocean and an illustrious history. It is a thoughtful conversion of a monastery, which was the headquarters of the Portuguese Knights of Santiago in the 13th century (see p385).*

Santiago do Cacém

Santa Clara-a-Velh

Pousada do Infante *occupies a spectacular clifftop position in the most southwesterly town of Europe, Sagres. The terrace restaurant of this specially built pousada has magnificent views of the Atlantic Ocean (see p399).*

ALGARVE

Pousada de Santa Marinha da Costa, housed in a medieval monastery near the city of Guimarães, is one of Portugal's most impressive and historic pousadas (see p393).

MINHO

Bragança 🅿

Vieira do Minho 🅿

DOURO AND TRÁS-OS-MONTES

Miranda 🅿 do Douro

🅿
Amarante

0 kilometers 50

0 miles 25

Pousada de Barão de Forrester, named after JJ Forrester, an influential figure in 19th-century port production (see p252), enjoys a peaceful setting among vineyards in the small Douro town of Alijó (see p390).

Almeida 🅿

Caramulo 🅿

🅿 Guarda

🅿
Oliveira do Hospital

🅿 Monsanto

THE BEIRAS

Pousada da Rainha Santa Isabel dominates the town of Estremoz and the surrounding countryside. In the 13th century, the site of the pousada was home to King Dinis and his wife, Queen Isabel (see p395).

Marvão 🅿

Crato 🅿

🅿 Sousel

🅿
Elvas

🅿

Pousada dos Lóios in Évora has been converted from a 15th-century monastery. Adjacent to the remains of a Roman temple of Diana, it features an elegant dining room set in the original monastic cloisters and a Neo-Classical façade that dates from the mid-18th century (see p395).

🅿 Alvito

🅿
🅿
Serpa

ALENTEJO

São Brás de Alportel 🅿

Pousada de São Francisco is located in the heart of the old Roman town of Beja at the center of the sunbaked plains of the southern Alentejo. The building incorporates parts of a former Franciscan convent, dating back to the 13th century. It was opened as a pousada in 1994 (see p395).

Choosing a Hotel

THE HOTELS in this guide have been selected across a wide price range for their good value or exceptional location. The chart gives a brief description of each hotel, highlighting factors that may influence your choice. Entries are listed by price category within the towns with color-coded thumb tabs to indicate the regions covered on each page.

	CREDIT CARDS	RESTAURANT	GARDEN	SWIMMING POOL	NUMBER OF ROOMS
LISBON					
BAIRRO ALTO: *Camões* $ Travessa do Poço da Cidade 38, 1º E, 1200. **Map** 7 A3. **(** *21-346 75 10.* **FAX** *21-346 40 48.* Conveniently located in the heart of the Bairro Alto, this light and airy hotel offers comfortable rooms and a friendly atmosphere.					18
BAIRRO ALTO: *Borges* $$ Rua Garrett 108, 1200. **Map** 7 A4. **(** *21-346 19 51.* **FAX** *21-342 66 17.* The Borges, one of the few places to stay in the stylish Chiado area, successfully combines elegant furnishings with pleasant surroundings.	AE DC MC V				100
BAIRRO ALTO: *Suíço Atlântico* $$ Rua da Glória 3–19, 1250. **Map** 7 A2. **(** *21-346 17 13.* **FAX** *21-346 90 13.* Tucked away in a small side street, this hotel has large old-fashioned rooms and public areas with stone arches and wooden beams.	AE DC MC V				90
BAIXA: *Alegria* $ Praça da Alegria 12, 1250. **Map** 4 F1. **(** *21-347 55 22.* **FAX** *21-347 80 70.* This small, bargain *pensão* offers clean and homey rooms and is set in a pleasant parklike square with a central fountain.					25
BAIXA: *Beira Minho* $ Praça da Figueira 6, 2º E, 1100. **Map** 7 B3. **(** *21-346 18 46.* **FAX** *21-886 78 11.* The spectacular views up toward the Bairro Alto from this simple *pensão* make up for the lack of facilities.					24
BAIXA: *Coimbra e Madrid* $ Praça da Figueira 3, 3º, 1100. **Map** 7 B3. **(** *21-342 17 60.* **FAX** *21-342 32 64.* A plain and simple *pensão* with rather sparse decoration. Some of the rooms, however, have magnificent views of the Castelo de São Jorge.					36
BAIXA: *Norte* $ Rua dos Douradores 159, 1100. **Map** 7 B3. **(** *21-887 89 41.* Centrally located near Praça da Figueira, this *pensão* has few facilities and no breakfast but the rooms are neat and comfortable. Good value.					36
BAIXA: *Restauradores* $ Praça dos Restauradores 13, 4º, 1250. **Map** 7 A2. **(** *21-347 56 60.* A very small and fairly basic *pensão* on the fourth floor of a building that has a great location in the busy center of the city. No breakfast.					30
BAIXA: *Duas Nações* $$ Rua da Vitória 41, 1100. **Map** 7 B4. **(** *21-346 07 10.* **FAX** *21-347 02 06.* The "Two Nations" is a friendly place to stay, right in the heart of the Baixa, but the rooms overlooking Rua Augusta can be noisy.	AE DC MC V				66
BAIXA: *Florescente* $$ Rua das Portas de S. Antão 99, 1150. **Map** 7 A2. **(** *21-342 66 09.* **FAX** *21-342 77 33.* For a *pensão* the rooms of the Florescente are extremely well equipped. This street is famous for its many fine restaurants. No breakfast.	AE MC V				70
BAIXA: *Internacional* $$ Rua da Betesga 3, 1100. **Map** 7 B3. **(** *21-346 64 01.* **FAX** *21-347 86 35.* Centrally located between Praça da Figueira and Rossio, this hotel features modern and spacious rooms. Residents can relax in the hotel's large, comfortable TV lounge and small bar.	AE DC MC V				53
BAIXA: *Nova Goa* $$ Rua do Arco do Marquês de Alegrete 13, 1100. **Map** 7 C3. **(** *21-888 11 37.* **FAX** *21-886 78 11.* Just around the corner from Praça da Figueira, this *pensão* is like many in the vicinity: clean, comfortable, and fairly basic.					42

Price categories for a standard double room per night, including breakfast:
$ under 7,000$00
$$ 7–12,000$00
$$$ 12–20,000$00
$$$$ 20–30,000$00
$$$$$ over 30,000$00.

RESTAURANT
The hotel has one or more restaurants open for lunch and supper, sometimes reserved for residents.
GARDEN
A garden, courtyard, or large terrace for the use of hotel guests.
SWIMMING POOL
The hotel has its own indoor or outdoor pool.
CREDIT CARDS
Major credit cards accepted: *AE* American Express, *DC* Diners Club, *MC* MasterCard and *V* VISA.

	CREDIT CARDS	RESTAURANT	GARDEN	SWIMMING POOL	NUMBER OF ROOMS
BAIXA: *Portugal* $$ Rua João das Regras 4, 1100. **Map** 7 C3. ☎ *21-887 75 81.* [FAX] *21-886 73 43.* Though plain on the outside, this hotel situated off Rua Martim Moniz is surprisingly elegant with stylish old-fashioned decor. 🛁 [TV] ❄	AE DC MC V				58
BAIXA: *Roma* $$ Travessa da Glória 22a, 1°, 1250. **Map** 7 A2. ☎ *21-346 05 57.* [FAX] *21-346 05 57.* This simple *pensão* has a fine location just off Avenida da Liberdade, convenient for shops and sightseeing. There is a 24-hour bar service. 🛁 [TV] ♿	AE MC V				24
BAIXA: *Metrópole* $$$ Praça Dom Pedro IV 30, 1100. **Map** 7 B3. ☎ *21-346 91 64.* [FAX] *21-346 91 66.* This turn-of-the-century building has been renovated in a style reminiscent of the 1920s. The result is a charming and elegant hotel. The famous Buçaco wines *(see p210)* can also be bought here. 🛁 [TV] ❄ ♿	AE DC MC V				36
BAIXA: *Orion Eden* $$$ Praça dos Restauradores 24, 1250. **Map** 7 A2. ☎ *21-321 66 00.* [FAX] *21-321 66 66.* The modern Orion Eden has apartments and studios, all with private kitchen. Three studios have been adapted for the disabled. 🛁 [TV] ❄ [P] ♿	AE DC MC V			●	137
BAIXA: *Avenida Palace* $$$$ Rua 1° de Dezembro 123, 1200. **Map** 7 B3. ☎ *21-346 01 51.* [FAX] *21-342 28 84.* The Avenida Palace hotel, with its Neo-Classical façade and enviable central location, offers both elegance and convenience. The luxurious interior decoration retains many charming original details. 🛁 [TV] ❄ [P]	AE DC MC V				100
BAIXA: *Sofitel Lisboa* $$$$ Av. da Liberdade 123–5, 1250. **Map** 4 F1. ☎ *21-342 92 02.* [FAX] *21-342 92 22.* The comfortable, modern Sofitel features an attractive piano bar called the "Molière," situated just off the lobby. 🛁 [TV] ❄ [P] ♿	AE DC MC V	●			170
BAIXA: *Tivoli Jardim* $$$$ Rua J. César Machado, 1250. **Map** 4 F1. ☎ *21-353 99 71.* [FAX] *21-355 65 66.* The rooms of this stylish hotel are well appointed with spacious bathrooms and a minibar. An unusual round pool graces the garden behind the hotel and there are extensive sports facilities. 🛁 [TV] ❄ [P]	AE DC MC V	●	■	●	119
BAIXA: *Tivoli Lisboa* $$$$$ Av. da Liberdade 185, 1250. **Map** 4 F1. ☎ *21-319 89 00.* [FAX] *21-357 94 61.* This large and elegant hotel has modern rooms and a huge two-level central lobby. The suites are particularly spacious. 🛁 [TV] ❄ [P]	AE DC MC V	●	■	●	300
CAMPO PEQUENO: *Lar do Areeiro* $$ Praça Francisco Sá Carneiro 4, r/c, 1000. **Map** 6 E1. ☎ *21-849 31 50.* Conveniently located close to many shops, this *pensão* offers bargain accommodations that are clean and comfortable. 🛁	MC V				43
CASTELO: *Ninho das Águias* $ Costa do Castelo 74, 1100. **Map** 7 C3. ☎ *21-886 70 08.* The simple "Eagle's Nest" *pensão* sits below the castle walls. A stuffed eagle greets visitors on the terrace, that has amazing views. No breakfast.			■		16
ENTRECAMPOS: *Quality Hotel Lisboa* $$$ Campo Grande 7, 1700. ☎ *21-795 75 55.* [FAX] *21-795 75 00.* A pleasant hotel that caters to the business traveler. Features include a health club, gymnasium, and jacuzzi. 🛁 [TV] ❄ [P] ♿	AE DC MC V	●			83
ESTEFÂNIA: *Caravela* $ Rua Ferreira Lapa 38, 1150. **Map** 6 D4. ☎ *21-353 90 11.* [FAX] *21-357 17 51.* The rooms in this *pensão* have a slightly old-fashioned ambience. Each room has a direct outside line, and there is a bar and TV room. 🛁 [TV]	AE DC MC V				45

Price categories for a standard double room per night, including breakfast:

Ⓢ under 7,000$00
ⓈⓈ 7–12,000$00
ⓈⓈⓈ 12–20,000$00
ⓈⓈⓈⓈ 20–30,000$00
ⓈⓈⓈⓈⓈ over 30,000$00.

RESTAURANT
The hotel has one or more restaurants open for lunch and supper, sometimes reserved for residents.

GARDEN
A garden, courtyard, or large terrace for the use of hotel guests.

SWIMMING POOL
The hotel has its own indoor or outdoor pool.

CREDIT CARDS
Major credit cards accepted: *AE* American Express, *DC* Diners Club, *MC* MasterCard and *V* VISA.

Hotel	Credit Cards	Restaurant	Garden	Swimming Pool	Number of Rooms
ESTEFÂNIA: *Sol Lisboa* ⓈⓈⓈⓈⓈ Av. Duque de Loulé 45, 1050. **Map** 5 C4. **[** 21-353 21 08. **FAX** 21-353 18 65. The modern Sol hotel has 84 well-equipped suites with kitchens, as well as a small shopping arcade and a rooftop pool and sauna. ⌂ TV ▤ P ♿	AE DC MC V	●	▨	●	84
GRAÇA: *Mundial* ⓈⓈⓈ Rua Dom Duarte 4, 1100. **Map** 7 B3. **[** 21-886 31 01. **FAX** 21-887 91 29. This hotel, located centrally off Praça da Figueira, has plain but comfortable rooms. The restaurant offers marvelous views. ⌂ TV ▤ P ♿	AE DC MC V	●	▨		147
GRAÇA: *Senhora do Monte* ⓈⓈⓈ Calçada do Monte 39, 1100. **Map** 7 D1. **[** 21-886 60 02. **FAX** 21-887 77 83. This *albergaria* is somewhat off the beaten track, but it is well worth the effort to find it. The rooms are fairly plain but the views, especially from the rooftop bar and garden, are simply the best in town. ⌂ TV ▤	AE DC MC V		▨		28
LAPA: *As Janelas Verdes* ⓈⓈⓈⓈ R. das Janelas Verdes 47, 1200. **Map** 4 D3. **[** 21-396 81 43. **FAX** 21-396 81 44. A delightful *pensão* housed in an 18th-century ivy-covered mansion, once owned by the Portuguese novelist Eça de Queirós *(see p55)*. It has Neo-Classical decor and a peaceful, charming patio. ⌂ TV ▤ P	AE DC MC V		▨		17
LAPA: *York House* ⓈⓈⓈⓈ Rua das Janelas Verdes 32, 1200. **Map** 4 D4. **[** 21-396 24 35. **FAX** 21-397 27 93. This enchanting *pensão* is housed in the 17th-century Convento dos Marianos. Set around a shady, plant-filled patio, the elegant rooms have wooden or terra-cotta floors and elegant antique furniture. ⌂ TV	AE DC MC V	●	▨		34
LAPA: *Hotel da Lapa* ⓈⓈⓈⓈⓈ R. do Pau da Bandeira 4, 1200. **Map** 3 C3. **[** 21-395 00 05. **FAX** 21-395 06 65. A gracious and charming hotel located in the city's diplomatic area. Each room in the Palace Wing is uniquely decorated in its own Portuguese style – from 18th-century Neo-Classical to Art Deco. ⌂ TV ▤ P ♿	AE DC MC V	●	▨	●	94
RATO: *13 da Sorte* Ⓢ Rua do Salitre 13, 1100. **Map** 4 F1. **[** 21-353 18 51. **FAX** 21-353 18 51. This well located *pensão* has some individual suites but no breakfast. The terrace bar "Gaivota" (meaning seagull) offers splendid views. ⌂ TV ♿	DC MC V				24
RATO: *Amazónia* ⓈⓈⓈ T. da Fábrica dos Pentes 12–20, 1250. **Map** 5 B5. **[** 21-387 70 06. **FAX** 21-387 90 90. Conveniently close to the city center, this stylish hotel has elegant public rooms, large bedrooms, and a piano bar. ⌂ TV ▤ ♿	AE DC MC V		▨	●	192
RATO: *Lisboa Plaza* ⓈⓈⓈ Travessa do Salitre 7, 1250. **Map** 4 F1. **[** 21-346 39 22. **FAX** 21-347 16 30. Built in 1953, and situated off Praça da Alegria, the traditional decor of this hotel is by the Portuguese interior designer, Graça Viterbo. ⌂ TV ▤	AE DC MC V	●			112
RATO: *Altis* ⓈⓈⓈⓈⓈ Rua Castilho 11, 1250. **Map** 4 F1. **[** 21-314 24 96. **FAX** 21-354 86 96. This huge hotel has every expected facility, including a rooftop grill and well-equipped health club with an indoor pool. ⌂ TV ▤ P ♿	AE DC MC V	●	▨	●	303
RATO: *Ritz Intercontinental* ⓈⓈⓈⓈⓈ Rua R. da Fonseca 88, 1093. **Map** 5 B5. **[** 21-383 20 20. **FAX** 21-383 17 83. The legendary Ritz is an elegant, comfortable hotel. Many of the rooms have balconies that overlook the Parque Eduardo VII. ⌂ TV ▤ P ♿	AE DC MC V	●	▨		284
ROTUNDA: *Castilho* Ⓢ Rua Castilho 57, 1250. **Map** 4 F1. **[** 21-386 08 22. **FAX** 21-386 29 10. An excellent-value *pensão* with good facilities and clean and comfortable rooms, some of which have three or four beds. ⌂ TV ♿	MC V				25

ROTUNDA: *Jorge V* $$ Rua Mouzinho da Silveira 3, 1250. **Map** 5 C5. ☎ *21-356 25 25.* FAX *21-315 03 19.* This pleasant, comfortable hotel offers good value for the area. Roughly half the rooms have balconies, so request one when checking in. 🛁 [TV] ❄	AE DC MC V				49
ROTUNDA: *Britânia* $$$ Rua R. Sampaio 17, 1100. **Map** 5 C5. ☎ *21-315 50 16.* FAX *21-315 50 21.* Housed in a building designed by the architect Cassiano Branco in 1944, this delightful hotel has a beautiful marble lobby. 🛁 [TV] ❄ [P]	AE DC MC V				30
ROTUNDA: *Capitol* $$$ Rua Eça de Queirós 24, 1050. **Map** 5 C4. ☎ *21-353 68 11.* FAX *21-352 61 65.* A comfortable hotel just off Avenida de Duque de Loulé. The rooms overlooking the market can be noisy early in the morning. 🛁 [TV] ❄ [P] ♿	AE DC MC V	●			57
ROTUNDA: *Diplomático* $$$ Rua Castilho 74, 1250. **Map** 5 B5. ☎ *21-386 20 41.* FAX *21-386 21 55.* The Diplomático has spacious rooms with modern facilities and offers complimentary tea, coffee, and chocolate in the rooms. 🛁 [TV] ❄ [P] ♿	AE DC MC V	●	■		90
ROTUNDA: *Le Méridien Lisboa* $$$$$ Rua Castilho 149, 1070. **Map** 5 B4. ☎ *21-383 09 00.* FAX *21-383 32 31.* Overlooking the Parque Eduardo VII from one of the city's seven hills, this hotel has comfortable rooms and spectacular views. 🛁 [TV] ❄ [P] ♿	AE DC MC V	●			330
ROTUNDA: *Nacional* $$$ Rua Castilho 34, 1250. **Map** 5 B5. ☎ *21-355 44 33.* FAX *21-356 11 22.* This interesting glass-fronted hotel has comfortable rooms and extensive facilities. There are also two suites available. 🛁 [TV] ❄ [P] ♿	AE DC MC V				61
ROTUNDA: *Rex* $$$ Rua Castilho 169, 1070. **Map** 5 B4. ☎ *21-388 21 61.* FAX *21-388 75 81.* The Rex is located close to the Parque Eduardo VII. The rooftop restaurant has good views and offers a buffet breakfast. 🛁 [TV] ❄ [P] ♿	AE DC MC V	●			36
ROTUNDA: *Veneza* $$$ Avenida da Liberdade 189, 1250. **Map** 5 C5. ☎ *21-352 67 00.* FAX *21-352 66 78.* The ornate staircase decorated with modern murals by Pedro Luiz-Gomes is the highlight of this spacious and comfortable hotel. 🛁 [TV] ❄ [P] ♿	AE DC MC V				36
SALDANHA: *Horizonte* $$ Av. António A. de Aguiar 42, 1050. **Map** 5 B4. ☎ *21-353 95 26.* FAX *21-353 84 74.* This large *pensão* offers good value for the money for this area. The rooms at the front look out over Avenida da Liberdade and can be noisy. 🛁 [TV] ❄ ♿	AE DC MC V				53
SALDANHA: *Marisela* $$ Rua Filipe Folque 19, r/c, 1050. **Map** 5 C3. ☎ *21-353 32 05.* FAX *21-316 04 23.* Located in a quiet street very close to the gardens of Parque Eduardo VII, this bargain *pensão* has rather basic but adequate rooms. 🛁 ♿ [TV]	AE MC V	●			34
SALDANHA: *Príncipe* $$ Avenida Duque de Ávila 201, 1050. **Map** 5 B3. ☎ *21-353 61 51.* FAX *21-353 43 14.* Most of the rooms in this modern hotel have their own balcony. There is a small bar and lounge just off the lobby. 🛁 [TV] ❄ [P] ♿	AE DC MC V	●			67
SALDANHA: *VIP* $$ Rua Fernão Lopes 25, 1000. **Map** 5 C3. ☎ *21-352 19 23.* FAX *21-315 87 73.* A simple hotel built over shops in a busy part of the city, the VIP is neat and tidy, although the decor is somewhat old-fashioned. 🛁 [TV] ❄	AE DC MC V	●			54
SALDANHA: *Impala* $$$ Rua Filipe Folque 49, 1050. **Map** 5 C3. ☎ *21-314 89 14.* FAX *21-357 53 62.* All the rooms in the quiet Impala hotel are suites, each with its own living room, kitchen, bar, and refrigerator. 🛁 [TV] ♿	AE DC MC V				26
SALDANHA: *Real Parque* $$$$$ Avenida L. Bivar 67, 1050. **Map** 5 C3. ☎ *21-357 01 01.* FAX *21-357 07 50.* This impressive modern hotel, located on a quiet side street, has seven rooms designed especially for the disabled. 🛁 [TV] ❄ [P] ♿	AE DC MC V	●			153
SALDANHA: *Sheraton Lisboa* $$$$$ Rua L. Coelho 1, 1069. **Map** 5 C3. ☎ *21-357 57 57.* FAX *21-354 71 64.* On one of the city's vantage points, Lisbon's Sheraton offers spacious rooms, a communications center, and a health club. 🛁 [TV] ❄ [P] ♿	AE DC MC V	●		●	384

<table>
<tr><td colspan="6">

Price categories for a standard double room per night, including breakfast:

$ under 7,000$00
$$ 7–12,000$00
$$$ 12–20,000$00
$$$$ 20–30,000$00
$$$$$ over 30,000$00.

</td></tr>
</table>

RESTAURANT
The hotel has one or more restaurants open for lunch and supper, sometimes reserved for residents.

GARDEN
A garden, courtyard, or large terrace for the use of hotel guests.

SWIMMING POOL
The hotel has its own indoor or outdoor pool.

CREDIT CARDS
Major credit cards accepted: *AE* American Express, *DC* Diners Club, *MC* MasterCard and *V* VISA.

	CREDIT CARDS	RESTAURANT	GARDEN	SWIMMING POOL	NUMBER OF ROOMS
THE LISBON COAST					
ALCÁCER DO SAL: *Pousada de Vale do Gaio* $$$$ Torrão, 7595. **Road map** C5. 【 265-66 96 10. FAX 265-66 95 45. This peaceful and intimate *pousada* on the lakeside, converted from the dam engineer's residence, offers excellent country walks. 🔲 TV 🔳 P 🔲	AE DC MC V	●			14
CARCAVELOS: *Praia Mar* $$$ Rua Gurué 16, 2775. **Road map** B5. 【 21-457 31 31. FAX 21-457 31 30. This delightful hotel overlooks the Estoril coast's largest sandy beach. Modern and elegant throughout, the rooms are spacious and comfortable. The famed wines from Buçaco *(see p210)* are also available. 🔲 TV P 🔲	AE DC MC V	●	■	●	148
CASCAIS: *Arco Bandeira* $$ Avenida Valbom 15, 2750. **Road map** B5. 【 21-342 34 78. This is a quiet hotel, with welcoming, tourist-friendly staff, a homely atmosphere, and comfortable, clean rooms. 🔲 TV	MC V		■	●	8
CASCAIS: *Baía* $$$ Avenida Marginal, 2750. **Road map** B5. 【 21-483 10 33. FAX 21-483 10 95. The modern Baía hotel has a fantastic location overlooking the long, sandy beach that runs parallel to the Avenida Marginal. 🔲 TV 🔳 P 🔲	AE DC MC V	●	■	●	113
CASCAIS: *Casa da Pérgola* $$$ Avenida Valbom 13, 2750. **Road map** B5. 【 21-484 00 40. FAX 21-483 47 91. This Mediterranean-style mansion has rooms with stucco ceilings and marble floors. It closes from November until a week before Easter. 🔲 🔳			■		11
CASCAIS: *Cidadela* $$$ Avenida 25 de Abril, 2750. **Road map** B5. 【 21-482 76 00. FAX 21-486 72 26. A short walk from the town center, the Cidadela is surrounded by gardens. Most of the rooms have spectacular views of the bay. 🔲 TV 🔳 P	AE DC MC V	●	■	●	128
CASCAIS: *Albatroz* $$$$$ Rua F. Arouca 100, 2750. **Road map** B5. 【 21-483 28 21. FAX 21-484 48 27. Built in the 19th century as a retreat for the Portuguese royal family, the Albatroz sits perched on the rocks directly overlooking the ocean. Inside, the luxurious decoration is matched by excellent service. 🔲 TV 🔳 P 🔲	AE DC MC V	●	■	●	40
CASCAIS: *Estoril Sol* $$$$$ Parque de Palmela, 2750. **Road map** B5. 【 21-483 28 31. FAX 21-483 22 80. As well as marvelous views of the bay of Cascais, the Estoril Sol has a saltwater pool and a health club with Turkish baths. 🔲 TV 🔳 P 🔲	AE DC MC V	●		●	310
COSTA DA CAPARICA: *Praia do Sol* $ Rua dos Pescadores 12a, 2825. **Road map** B5. 【 21-290 00 12. FAX 21-290 25 41. A small hotel, the Praia do Sol offers well-appointed rooms conveniently located close to the beach in this popular resort town. 🔲 TV 🔳	AE DC MC V				53
COSTA DA CAPARICA: *Costa da Caparica* $$$ Av. Gen. Delgado 47, 2825. **Road map** B5. 【 21-291 03 10. FAX 21-291 06 87. This hotel, with an unusual semicircular entrance, overlooks the beach. It has seven rooms adapted for the disabled. 🔲 TV 🔳 P 🔲	AE DC MC V	●		●	353
ERICEIRA: *Vilazul* $$ Calçada da Baleia 10, 2655. **Road map** B5. 【 261-868 00 00. FAX 261-629 27. Only 500 m (550 yds) from the sea, this bright and airy *pensão* has panoramic views from the terrace and some of the bedrooms. 🔲 TV 🔳	AE DC MC V	●	■		21
ESTORIL: *Hotel Alvorada* $$ Rua de Lisboa 3, 2675. **Road map** B5. 【 21-468 00 70. FAX 21-468 72 50. Only a few minutes' walk from the beach, this newly decorated hotel offers friendly service and bright, well-appointed rooms. 🔲 🔳 P	AE DC MC V				54

ESTORIL: *São Cristóvão* $$ Av. Marginal 7079, 2765. **Road map** B5. ☎ *21-468 09 13.* [FAX] *21-468 09 13.* This charming *pensão* is housed in an interesting old villa. Located on the ocean side of the Avenida Marginal, it offers spectacular views. 🛏 [P] ♿			■		14
ESTORIL: *Hotel de Inglaterra* $$$ Rua do Porto 1, 2765. **Road map** B5. ☎ *21-468 44 61.* [FAX] *21-468 21 08.* Many rooms in this impressive early 20th-century mansion have private balconies with views of the Bay of Cascais or the Sintra Hills. 🛏 [TV] ☰ ♿	AE DC MC V	●	■	●	52
ESTORIL: *Lennox Country Club* $$$ Rua Eng. A. de Sousa 5, 2765. **Road map** B5. ☎ *21-468 04 24.* [FAX] *21-467 08 59.* Situated in its own lush gardens with panoramic views, this *estalagem* is perfect for golfers. Even the bar resembles a clubhouse. 🛏 [TV] ☰ [P]	AE DC MC V	●	■	●	34
ESTORIL: *Palácio* $$$$$ Rua do Parque, 2765. **Road map** B5. ☎ *21-468 04 00.* [FAX] *21-468 48 67.* An elegant hotel with a prime location between the ocean and the casino. It has an 18-hole golf course and tennis courts. 🛏 [TV] ☰ [P]	AE DC MC V	●	■	●	162
GUINCHO: *Estalagem Muchaxo* $$$ Praia do Guincho, 2750. **Road map** B5. ☎ *21-487 02 21.* [FAX] *21-487 04 44.* This rustic *estalagem*, with exposed beams and open brickwork, overlooks the ocean. The saltwater pool is built into the cliffs. 🛏	AE DC MC V	●	■	●	24
GUINCHO: *Senhora da Guia* $$$ Estrada do Guincho, 2750. **Road map** B5. ☎ *21-486 92 39.* [FAX] *21-486 92 27.* Set in its own grounds with a saltwater pool, this charming *estalagem* is housed in a comfortable and relaxing manor house. 🛏 [TV] ☰ [P]	AE DC MC V	●	■	●	42
GUINCHO: *Hotel do Guincho* $$$$ Praia do Guincho, 2751. **Road map** B5. ☎ *21-487 04 91.* [FAX] *21-487 04 31.* Perched on a clifftop overlooking the ocean, this atmospheric hotel with arched ceilings and medieval decor was once a fortress. 🛏 [TV] ☰ [P]	AE DC MC V	●	■		31
MAFRA: *Castelão* $$ Avenida 25 de Abril, 2640. **Road map** B5. ☎ *261-81 20 50.* [FAX] *261-516 98.* Convenient as a base when visiting the fabulous monastery in Mafra, this fairly small hotel is comfortable and clean. 🛏 [TV] [P]	AE DC MC V	●			35
MONTE ESTORIL: *Comfort Hotel* $$$ Rua Belmonte 1, 2765. **Road map** B5. ☎ *21-468 02 02.* [FAX] *21-468 11 17.* This modern hotel, 2 km (1 mile) north of Estoril, has excellent sea views as well as an ice-cream parlor and a solarium. 🛏 [TV]	AE DC MC V		■	●	48
PAÇO D'ARCOS: *Sol Palmeiras* $$$$ Avenida Marginal, 2780. **Road map** B5. ☎ *21-441 66 21* [FAX] *21-443 07 68.* Housed in a 19th-century manor house, many of the rooms in the Sol Palmeiras are suites with views of the Tagus estuary. 🛏 [TV] ☰ [P] ♿	AE DC MC V	●	■	●	35
PALMELA: *Pousada de Palmela* $$$$ Castelo de Palmela, 2950. **Road map** C5. ☎ *21-235 12 26.* [FAX] *21-233 04 40.* The fortified walls of this 12th-century castle now enclose a tranquil *pousada* with whitewashed rooms and many plants. 🛏 [TV] ☰	AE DC MC V	●	■		28
QUELUZ: *Pousada da Dona Maria I* $$$$ L. do Palácio Nacional, 2745. **Road map** B5. ☎ *21-435 61 58.* [FAX] *21-435 61 89.* Once used by staff of the marvelous 18th-century Palácio de Queluz, today the "Clock Tower" is an impressive *pousada.* 🛏 [TV] ☰ [P] ♿	AE DC MC V	●			26
SESIMBRA: *Hotel do Mar* $$$ R. Gen. Delgado 10, 2970. **Road map** C5. ☎ *21-223 33 26.* [FAX] *21-223 38 88.* This hotel, built on different levels on the cliffside, is surrounded by lush gardens. The presidential suite has a private pool. 🛏 [TV] ☰ [P] ♿	AE DC MC V	●	■	●	169
SETÚBAL: *IBIS Setúbal* $$ N10, Vale de Rosa, 2910. **Road map** C5. ☎ *265-77 22 00.* [FAX] *265-77 24 47.* Featuring the usual combination of IBIS comforts and economy, this hotel is surrounded by its own peaceful gardens. 🛏 [TV] ☰ [P] ♿	AE DC MC V	●	■	●	102
SETÚBAL: *Pousada de São Filipe* $$$$ Castelo de Setúbal, 2900. **Road map** C5. ☎ *265-52 38 44.* [FAX] *265-53 25 38.* This historic castle, built by Philip II of Spain *(see p50)* in 1590, is a friendly *pousada* with fine views of the estuary. 🛏 [TV] ☰ [P]	AE DC MC V	●	■		14

For key to symbols see back flap

Price categories for a standard double room per night, including breakfast:

$ under 7,000$00
$$ 7–12,000$00
$$$ 12–20,000$00
$$$$ 20–30,000$00
$$$$$ over 30,000$00.

RESTAURANT
The hotel has one or more restaurants open for lunch and supper, sometimes reserved for residents.
GARDEN
A garden, courtyard, or large terrace for the use of hotel guests.
SWIMMING POOL
The hotel has its own indoor or outdoor pool.
CREDIT CARDS
Major credit cards accepted: *AE* American Express, *DC* Diners Club, *MC* MasterCard and *V* VISA.

Column headers: CREDIT CARDS · RESTAURANT · GARDEN · SWIMMING POOL · NUMBER OF ROOMS

Hotel	Credit Cards	Restaurant	Garden	Swimming Pool	Number of Rooms
SINTRA: *Central* $$ — Praça da República 35, 2710. Road map B5. 21-923 09 63. Heavy furniture and peeling paint give this hotel an old-fashioned atmosphere. It has an excellent position opposite the Palácio Nacional.	AE MC V	●	■		10
SINTRA: *Residencial Sintra* $$ — T. dos Avelares 12, 2710. Road map B5. & FAX 21-923 07 38. Located just east of Sintra town center, in the residential area of São Pedro, this rambling old *pensão* is friendly and full of character.	MC V		■	●	10
SINTRA: *Tivoli Sintra* $$$$ — Praça da República, 2710. Road map B5. 21-923 35 05. FAX 21-923 15 72. The modern Tivoli Sintra, tucked away in a corner of Sintra's main square, has wonderful views across the valley, a bar, and a boutique.	AE DC MC V	●			75
SINTRA: *Caesar Park* $$$$$ — Estr. da Lagoa Azul, Linhó, 2710. Road map B5. 21-924 90 11. FAX 21-924 90 07. This huge, luxurious complex in the Sintra hills has an 18-hole golf course, designed by Robert Trent Jones Jr. and a health club.	AE DC MC V	●	■	●	174
SINTRA: *Palácio de Seteais* $$$$$ — R. B. du Bocage 8, 2710. Road map B5. 21-923 32 00. FAX 21-923 42 77. Just outside town, this elegant hotel occupies a delightful 18th-century palace with tastefully decorated interiors and a topiary garden.	AE DC MC V	●	■	●	30

ESTREMADURA AND RIBATEJO

Hotel	Credit Cards	Restaurant	Garden	Swimming Pool	Number of Rooms
ABRANTES: *Hotel de Turismo* $$ — Largo de Santo António, 2200. Road map C4. 241-212 61. FAX 241-252 18. This hotel, decorated in bright, classic colors, is found in a very pleasant location surrounded by attractive gardens.	AE DC MC V	●	■	●	41
BALEAL: *Casa das Marés* $$ — Peniche, 2520. Road map B4. 262-76 92 55. The family-run "House of Tides" is set on a promontory with dramatic ocean views. Breakfast is served on the terrace above a cove.			■		12
BARRAGEM DO CASTELO DE BODE: *Estalagem Lago Azul* $$ — Lago Azul, Ferreira do Zêzere, 2240. Road map C4. 249-36 16 54. FAX 249-36 16 64. The rooms of this *estalagem* are functional, but there are tennis courts and sailing boats, and the lakeside setting is spectacular.	AE DC MC V	●	■	●	20
BARRAGEM DO CASTELO DE BODE: *Pousada de São Pedro* $$$$ — Castelo de Bode, Tomar, 2300. Road map C4. 249-38 11 59. FAX 249-38 11 76. Overlooking the River Zêzere, this pleasant *pousada* offers simple but tastefully furnished rooms and excellent regional cooking.	AE DC MC V	●	■		25
BATALHA: *Pousada do Mestre Afonso Domingues* $$$ — L. do Mestre A. Domingues 6, 2440. Road map C4. 244-76 52 60. FAX 244-76 52 47. This *pousada* stands next to the town's abbey, Batalha, and is named after its architect. The rooms are traditionally furnished.	AE DC MC V	●	■		21
CALDAS DA RAINHA: *Caldas Internacional* $$ — Rua Dom F. Rego 45, 2500. Road map B4. 262-83 23 07. FAX 262-84 44 82. Patterned floor tiles in the lobby welcome the visitor to the modern Caldas Internacional Hotel close to the city center.	AE DC MC V	●	■	●	83
CONSTÂNCIA: *Quinta Santa Bárbara* $$ — 2250. Road map C4. 249-73 92 14. FAX 249-73 93 73. A splendid 15th-century manor house, the Quinta Santa Bárbara has been converted into a distinguished hotel, with cozy, rustic rooms. The Gothic stone vaults of the former refectory now house the restaurant.	MC V	●	■	●	7

FÁTIMA: *Dom Gonçalo* $$
Rua Jacinto Marto 100, 2495. **Road map** C4. 🅒 *249-53 30 62.* **FAX** *249-53 20 88.*
A delightful *estalagem* that is set in charming, well-kept gardens and woods and yet is still very close to the sanctuary. 🚗 📺 🍴 🅿 ♿
DC MC V — 42

FÁTIMA: *Verbo Divino* $$
Praça Paulo VI, 2495. **Road map** C4. 🅒 *249-53 93 30.* **FAX** *249-53 22 63.*
Built to guarantee a revenue for the Divine Word Missionaries, this is a large, simply decorated hotel for pilgrims to Fátima. 🚗 📺 🍴 🅿 ♿
MC V — 208

GOLEGÃ: *Casa da Azinhaga* $$$
Azinhaga, 2150. **Road map** C4. 🅒 *249-95 71 46.* **FAX** *249-95 71 46.*
This classic manor house, 7 km (4 miles) south of horse-loving Golegã, offers comfortable rooms in a pleasant ambience. 🚗 🅿
— 7

LEIRIA: *Leiriense* $
Rua A. de Albuquerque 8, 2400. **Road map** C4. 🅒 *244-82 30 54.* **FAX** *244-82 30 73.*
Found tucked away in the narrow side streets of the old area of Leiria, this *pensão* is clean, welcoming, and quite charming. 🚗 📺 🍴 ♿
MC V — 24

LEIRIA: *Dom João III* $$
Avenida Dom João III, 2400. **Road map** C4. 🅒 *244-81 25 00.* **FAX** *244-81 22 35.*
The modern, well-equipped rooms of this hotel have views to the splendid *loggia* of the castle and over the River Liz. 🚗 📺 🍴 🅿 ♿
AE DC MC V — 64

LOURINHÃ: *Estalagem da Areia Branca* $$
Praia da Areia Branca, 2530. **Road map** B4. 🅒 *261-41 24 91.* **FAX** *261-41 31 43.*
This very comfortable *estalagem*, perched on the cliffs overlooking the quiet beach of Areia Branca, offers many sports facilities. 🚗 📺 🅿 ♿
AE DC MC V — 29

NAZARÉ: *Mar Bravo* $$$
Praça S. Oliveira 70, 2450. **Road map** C4. 🅒 *262-55 11 80.* **FAX** *262-55 39 79.*
In the heart of Nazaré this *albergaria* has panoramic views of this picturesque town and the beach. All rooms have balconies. 🚗 📺 🍴 🅿 ♿
AE DC MC V — 16

ÓBIDOS: *Rainha Santa Isabel* $$
Rua Direita, 2510. **Road map** B4. 🅒 *262-95 93 23.* **FAX** *262-95 91 15.*
Enclosed within the walls of this lovely town, the attractive wood-paneled rooms of this *albergaria* contain lovely *azulejos*. 🚗 📺 🍴
AE DC MC V — 20

ÓBIDOS: *Estalagem do Convento* $$$
Rua D. José D'Ornelas, 2510. **Road map** B4. 🅒 *262-95 92 14.* **FAX** *262-95 91 59.*
Once a convent, the rooms of this tastefully converted *estalagem* are traditionally and elegantly furnished. Some have marvelous views. 🚗
AE MC V — 31

ÓBIDOS: *Pousada do Castelo* $$$$
Paço Real, 2510. **Road map** B4. 🅒 *262-95 91 05.* **FAX** *262-95 91 48.*
The novelist Graham Greene stayed in this stunning *pousada*, converted from a 15th-century royal castle. Book early as it is very popular. 🚗 📺 🍴
AE DC MC V — 9

PENICHE: *Hotel Vasco da Gama* $
Rua José Estevão 23, 2520. **Road map** B4. 🅒 & **FAX** *262-78 19 02.*
In the charming town center, this snug hotel is just a few steps from the fortress, fishing port, and the town's main churches. 🚗 📺 🅿
AE DC MC V — 13

SANTARÉM: *Casa de Nossa Senhora da Assunção* $$
Azóia de Baixo, 2000. **Road map** C4. 🅒 *243-42 92 64.*
An attractive guesthouse in the heart of the town. The traditionally furnished rooms of the Casa de Nossa Senhora face an inner courtyard. 🚗 🅿
— 3

SANTARÉM: *Vitória* $$
R. 2º Visconde de Santarém 21, 2000. **Road map** C4. 🅒 *243-30 91 30.* **FAX** *243-282 02.*
A modest *pensão* handy for Santarém's main sights, the Vitória offers small rooms that are nevertheless neat, cozy, and welcoming. 🚗 📺
MC V — 25

SÃO MARTINHO DO PORTO: *Americana* $
Rua Dom J. Saldanha 2, 2460. **Road map** B4. 🅒 *262-98 91 70.* **FAX** *262-98 93 49.*
Conveniently located close to the sandy, sheltered beach popular with families, this friendly *pensão* offers pleasant rooms. 🚗 📺 🍴
AE MC V — 25

SÃO PEDRO DE MUEL: *Mar e Sol* $$
Avenida da Liberdade, 2430. **Road map** C4. 🅒 *244-59 91 82.* **FAX** *244-59 94 11.*
Right beside the ocean and spectacular beach, this neat and unpretentious hotel offers rooms with sea views in this popular resort. 🚗 📺 🍴 🅿 ♿
AE DC MC V — 63

For key to symbols see back flap

<table>
<tr><td>

Price categories for a standard double room per night, including breakfast:

$ under 7,000$00
$$ 7–12,000$00
$$$ 12–20,000$00
$$$$ 20–30,000$00
$$$$$ over 30,000$00.

</td><td>

RESTAURANT
The hotel has one or more restaurants open for lunch and supper, sometimes reserved for residents.
GARDEN
A garden, courtyard, or large terrace for the use of hotel guests.
SWIMMING POOL
The hotel has its own indoor or outdoor pool.
CREDIT CARDS
Major credit cards accepted: *AE* American Express, *DC* Diners Club, *MC* MasterCard and *V* VISA.

</td></tr>
</table>

	CREDIT CARDS	RESTAURANT	GARDEN	SWIMMING POOL	NUMBER OF ROOMS
TOMAR: *Santa Iria* $$ Parque do Mouchão, 2300. **Road map** C4. 📞 & FAX 249-32 12 38. Wonderfully situated on an island park on the River Nabão, this discreetly elegant *estalagem* is near many of the city's sights. 📶 TV P	AE MC V	●	▓		13
TOMAR: *Hotel dos Templários* $$$ L. Cândido dos Reis 1, 2300. **Road map** C4. 📞 249-32 17 30. FAX 249-32 21 91. Overlooking the Nabão River and conveniently located in the city center, this hotel offers tennis courts, a gym, and a health club. 📶 TV 📋 P ♿	AE DC MC V	●	▓	●	174
VILA FRANCA DE XIRA: *Lezíria Parque* $$$ N10, 2600, Povos. **Road map** C5. 📞 263-266 70. FAX 263-269 90. Close to the Lisbon to Oporto highway (the A1), this attractive hotel has pleasant views of the Tagus River. 📶 TV 📋 P ♿	AE DC MC V	●	▓	●	71
THE BEIRAS					
ALMEIDA: *Morgado* $ Bairro de São Pedro, 6350. **Road map** E2. 📞 271-57 44 12. Found just outside the walls of the fortress at Almeida, this modern *pensão* is clean and comfortable, and a very good value. 📶 TV P ♿		●	▓		12
ALMEIDA: *Pousada da Senhora das Neves* $$$ Rua da Muralha, 6350. **Road map** E2. 📞 271-57 42 83. FAX 271-57 43 20. Inside the star-shaped fortifications that enclose the town, this *pousada* has pleasantly furnished rooms, some with four-poster beds. 📶 TV 📋 P	AE DC MC V	●			21
AVEIRO: *Arcada* $$ Rua Viana do Castelo 4, 3800. **Road map** C3. 📞 234-230 01. FAX 234-218 86. Located in a Neo-Classical arcaded building overlooking the central canal, the Arcada has character as well as all modern comforts. 📶 TV ♿	AE DC MC V				49
AVEIRO: *Pomba Branca* $$ Rua L. G. de Carvalho 23, 3800. **Road map** C3. 📞 234-225 29. FAX 234-38 18 44. A plant-filled *loggia* overlooks the small subtropical garden of this charming hotel. The cozy interior is decorated with wood paneling. 📶 TV 📋 P ♿	AE DC MC V	●	▓		50
AVEIRO: *Pousada da Ria* $$$ Bico do Muranzel, Torreira, 3870. **Road map** C3. 📞 234-483 32. FAX 234-483 33. This modern *pousada* has a peaceful location on the banks of the Ria de Aveiro. Most of the rooms have balconies overlooking the lagoon where the local painted boats *(moliceiros)* are moored. 📶 TV 📋 P	AE DC MC V	●	▓	●	19
BUÇACO: *Palace Hotel do Buçaco* $$$$ Mealhada, 3050. **Road map** C3. 📞 231-93 01 01. FAX 231-93 05 09. This extraordinary Neo-Manueline hotel, set in a luxuriant forest, was built as a hunting lodge for the last Portuguese kings. The grand interior offers attractive rooms, some with decorative *azulejos*. 📶 TV 📋 P	AE DC MC V	●	▓		64
CARAMULO: *Pousada de São Jerónimo* $$$ 3475. **Road map** C3. 📞 232-86 12 91. FAX 232-86 16 40. This modern *pousada*, covered in ivy, offers well-appointed rooms and a delightful setting high up in the Serra do Caramulo. 📶 TV 📋 P	AE DC MC V	●	▓	●	12
CASTELO BRANCO: *Rainha Dona Amélia* $$$ Rua de Santiago 15, 6000. **Road map** D4. 📞 272-32 63 15. FAX 272-32 63 90. This pleasant modern hotel has comfortable rooms and an excellent location in the city center close to the historical sights. 📶 TV 📋 P ♿	AE MC V	●	▓		64
CASTRO DAIRE: *Montemuro* $ Termas do Carvalhal, 3600. **Road map** D2. 📞 232-311 54. FAX 232-311 12. Located in the mountains between Viseu and the Douro, this modern hotel offers facilities for hunting, fishing, and canoeing. 📶 TV 📋 P ♿	AE DC MC V	●	▓		80

CELORICO DA BEIRA: *Mira Serra* $)$)$ AE   42
Bairro de S. Eufémia, 6360. **Road map** D3. 271-74 26 04. **FAX** 271-74 13 82.   DC
As the name Mira Serra suggests, this attractive and pleasant hotel has   MC
stunning views of the Serra da Estrela mountain range. 🔒 TV 🍽 P ⚕   V

COIMBRA: *Internacional* $)   22
Avenida Emídio Navarro 4, 3000. **Road map** C3. 239-82 55 03.
Conveniently located close to the train station, and overlooking the
Mondego River, this *pensão* is welcoming but very basic. 🔒 TV

COIMBRA: *Bragança* $)$)   MC   83
Largo das Ameias 10, 3000. **Road map** C3. 239-82 21 71. **FAX** 239-83 61 35.   V
A slightly old-fashioned but very comfortable hotel located in the heart of
Coimbra. The suites have marble bathrooms. 🔒 TV 🍽 P

COIMBRA: *Astória* $)$)$ AE   64
Av. Emídio Navarro 21, 3000. **Road map** C3. 239-82 20 55. **FAX** 239-82 20 57.   DC
A charming Art Deco hotel with a somewhat faded splendor, the Astória   MC
has stylish rooms with fine views across the Mondego. 🔒 TV 🍽 ⚕   V

COIMBRA: *Tivoli Coimbra* $)$)$ AE   100
Rua João Machado 5, 3000. **Road map** C3. 239-82 69 34. **FAX** 239-82 68 27.   DC
This modern hotel in the heart of the city boasts an excellent health club   MC
with a Turkish bath, massage, and gymnasium. 🔒 TV 🍽 P ⚕   V

COIMBRA: *Quinta das Lágrimas* $)$)$)$ AE   39
Santa Clara, 3000. **Road map** C3. 239-44 16 15. **FAX** 239-44 16 95.   DC
A handsome 18th-century country house, famous for the "Fountain of Love"   MC
where Pedro and Inês *(see p179)* used to meet in secret. 🔒 TV 🍽 P ⚕   V

CONDEIXA-A-NOVA: *Pousada de Santa Cristina* $)$)$ AE   45
Rua Francisco Lemos, 3150. **Road map** C3. 239-94 40 25. **FAX** 239-94 30 97.   DC
This modern *pousada*, situated in its own gardens, is a good base for   MC
visits to Coimbra and the Roman ruins of Conimbriga. 🔒 TV 🍽 P ⚕   V

COVILHÃ: *Hotel Serra da Estrela* $)$)$ AE   40
Penhas da Saúde, 6200. **Road map** D3. 275-31 38 09. **FAX** 275-32 37 89.   DC
Set in the Serra da Estrela, this modern hotel offers lodging in triangular   MC
bungalows and facilities for horseback riding and winter sports. 🔒 TV 🍽 P   V

CURIA: *Curia Palace Hotel* $)$)$ AE   114
Tamengos, 3780. **Road map** C3. 231-51 21 31. **FAX** 231-51 55 31.   DC
This elegant Art Nouveau palace is set in manicured gardens and features a   MC
tennis court, miniature golf, and a chapel. 🔒 TV 🍽 P ⚕   V

FIGUEIRA DA FOZ: *Hotel Costa de Prata* $)   70
Largo Coronel Galhardo 1, 3080. **Road map** C3. 233-42 66 20. **FAX** 233-42 66 10.
Overlooking the sea, this hotel is brightly decorated throughout and has a
bar and breakfast room with panoramic views. 🔒

FIGUEIRA DA FOZ: *Casa da Azenha Velha* $)$)   6
Caceira de Cima, 3080. **Road map** C3. 233-42 56 41. **FAX** 233-42 97 04.
This welcoming hotel has large, airy bedrooms and a lounge with an
open fire. The hotel provides bicycles for visitors. 🔒 TV 🍽 P ⚕

GUARDA: *Solar de Alarcão* $)$)   3
Rua Dom Miguel de Alarcão 25-27, 6300. **Road map** D3. 271-21 43 92.
This *turismo de habitação* occupies an intriguing granite house built in
1686. There is a chapel, and the rooms are full of antiques. 🔒 TV P

LUSO: *Astória* $)   AE   8
Rua Emídio Navarro, 3050. **Road map** C3. 231-93 91 82.   MC
This small *pensão* is a delight. The rooms are simply furnished but   V
comfortable, and the bar has a friendly atmosphere. 🔒

LUSO: *Grande Hotel de Luso* $)$)$ AE   143
Rua dos Banhos, 3050. **Road map** C3. 231-93 04 50. **FAX** 231-93 03 50.   DC
Dominating the skyline of this attractive spa town, this graceful, elegant   MC
hotel has sports facilities as well as access to the spa. 🔒 TV 🍽 P ⚕   V

MANGUALDE: *Casa d'Azurara* $)$)$ AE   15
Rua Nova 78, 3530. **Road map** D3. 232-61 20 10. **FAX** 232-62 25 75.   DC
Built in the 18th century, today the Casa d'Azurara is a friendly *estalagem*,   MC
set in its own gardens, with many original features. 🔒 TV 🍽 P ⚕   V

For key to symbols see back flap

<table>
<tr><td>

Price categories for a standard double room per night, including breakfast:

$ under 7,000$00
$$ 7–12,000$00
$$$ 12–20,000$00
$$$$ 20–30,000$00
$$$$$ over 30,000$00.

</td><td>

RESTAURANT
The hotel has one or more restaurants open for lunch and supper, sometimes reserved for residents.
GARDEN
A garden, courtyard, or large terrace for the use of hotel guests.
SWIMMING POOL
The hotel has its own indoor or outdoor pool.
CREDIT CARDS
Major credit cards accepted: *AE* American Express, *DC* Diners Club, *MC* MasterCard and *V* VISA.

</td></tr>
</table>

	CREDIT CARDS	RESTAURANT	GARDEN	SWIMMING POOL	NUMBER OF ROOMS
MANTEIGAS: *Pousada de São Lourenço* $$$ Penhas Douradas, 6260. **Road map** D3. **(** 275-98 24 50. **FAX** 275-98 24 53. This traditional granite *pousada*, high in the Serra da Estrela, is ideal for hikers and others seeking a secluded retreat. ⊟ TV ▤ P	AE DC MC V	●			22
MONSANTO: *Pousada de Monsanto* $$$ Rua da Capela 1, 6060. **Road map** D3. **(** 277-31 44 71. **FAX** 277-31 44 81. A friendly and attractive *pousada* in a typical granite village where the hillside houses are squeezed between giant boulders. ⊟ TV ▤ P	AE DC MC V	●			10
OLIVEIRA DO HOSPITAL: *Pousada de Santa Bárbara* $$$ Povoa das Quartas, 3400. **Road map** D3. **(** 238-595 51. **FAX** 238-596 45. A log fire and traditional decor add rustic charm to this modern *pousada* with views of the snow-capped Serra da Estrela. ⊟ TV ▤ P	AE DC MC V	●	■	●	16
SABUGUEIRO: *Casas do Cruzeiro* $$ Apartado 85, 6270 Seia. **Road map** D3. **(** 238-228 25. **FAX** 238-252 82. Tucked in a village in a Serra da Estrela valley, the granite cottages of the Casa do Cruzeiro offer simple rooms and homemade food. ⊟ TV P		●			26
VISEU: *Grão Vasco* $$ Rua Gaspar Barreiros, 3510. **Road map** D3. **(** 232-42 35 11. **FAX** 232-42 64 44. Located right in the center of town, the comfortable Grão Vasco hotel has traditional decor and is surrounded by an attractive garden. ⊟ TV ▤ P	AE DC MC V	●	■	●	115
DOURO AND TRÁS-OS-MONTES					
ALIJÓ: *Pousada de Barão de Forrester* $$$ Rua José Rufino, 5070. **Road map** D2. **(** 259-95 92 15. **FAX** 259-95 93 04. This *pousada* is in the heart of the port wine country and was named after the Englishman James Forrester (1809–62), an advocate of "pure wine" *(see p252)*. Its sports facilities include tennis courts. ⊟ TV ▤ P &	AE DC MC V	●	■	●	21
AMARANTE: *Pousada de São Gonçalo* $$$ Serra do Marão, 4600. **Road map** D2. **(** 255-46 11 13. **FAX** 255-46 13 53. Set in tranquil pine forests, the unusual semicircular shape of this friendly *pousada* affords spectacular views of the Marão hills. ⊟ TV P &	AE DC MC V	●			15
BRAGANÇA: *Classis* $$ Av. João da Cruz 102, 5300. **Road map** E1. **(** 273-33 16 31. **FAX** 273-234 58. A pleasant, modern, and comfortable *pensão* just a short walk from the city center, the Classis is a particularly good value. ⊟ TV ▤ &	AE DC MC V				20
BRAGANÇA: *Estalagem do Caçador* $$$ Largo Manuel Pinto de Azevedo, Macedo de Cavaleiros, 5340. **Road map** E1. **(** 278-42 63 56. **FAX** 278-42 63 81. Located in the Serra de Nogueira, southwest of Bragança, this friendly and welcoming country inn has a pleasant interior. ⊟ TV ▤ P	AE DC MC V	●		●	24
BRAGANÇA: *Pousada de São Bartolomeu* $$$ Estrada do Turismo, 5300. **Road map** E1. **(** 273-33 14 93. **FAX** 273-234 53. This popular *pousada* offers a panoramic view of the city of Bragança. Wooden furniture and stone walls add rustic charm. ⊟ TV ▤ P	AE DC MC V	●	■	●	28
CHAVES: *Aquae Flaviae* $$$ Praça do Brasil, 5400. **Road map** D1. **(** 276-330 90 00. **FAX** 276-330 90 10. An impressive hotel that dominates the skyline of Chaves, the modern Aquae Flaviae has health and beauty facilities. ⊟ TV ▤ P &	AE DC MC V	●	■	●	170
CINFÃES: *Casa do Rebolfe* $$ Porto Antigo, 4690. **Road map** D2. **(** & **FAX** 255-56 23 34. Located east of Cinfães, near Porto Antigo, this 18th-century house beside the Douro has been converted into a welcoming hotel. ⊟ TV ▤ P &			■	●	5

ESPINHO: *Praiagolfe* $$$ — AE DC MC V — 139
Rua 6, 4500. **Road map** C2. 22-731 33 85. **FAX** 22-731 33 97.
Situated on the wide sandy beach, with views of the ocean, this hotel has a delightful location. There is a health club upstairs.

LAMEGO: *Hotel do Parque* $$ — AE DC MC V — 28
Parque N. S. dos Remédios, 5100. **Road map** D2. 254-60 91 40. **FAX** 254-652 03.
Set in a grand whitewashed house next to the Santuário dos Remédios, this hotel offers rustic rooms overlooking a chestnut forest.

LAMEGO: *Villa Hostilina* $$ — 8
Almocave, 5100. **Road map** D2. 254-623 94. **FAX** 254-65 51 94.
Housed in a 19th-century farmhouse, Villa Hostilina offers tranquility and charm and the use of a health club and tennis court.

LAMEGO: *Casa de Santo António* $$$ — AE — 4
Britiande, 5100. **Road map** D2. 254-69 93 46. **FAX** 254-69 93 46.
Converted from a 17th-century manor house, with *azulejo* panels in the chapel, Santo António offers quiet rural accommodations.

MESÃO FRIO: *Casa do Além* $$ — 4
Oliveira, 5040. **Road map** D2. 254-32 19 91. **FAX** 254-32 19 91.
Originally a port wine growing country estate built in the 1920s, this family-run *quinta* has attractive interiors with original decor.

MIRANDA DO DOURO: *Pousada de Santa Catarina* $$$ — AE DC MC V — 12
5210. **Road map** E1. 273-43 10 05. **FAX** 273-43 10 65.
The spacious rooms of this *pousada*, converted from the engineers' residence, overlook the peaceful Miranda do Douro dam.

MURÇA: *Miradouro* $ — V — 13
Curvas de Murça, 5090. **Road map** D2. 259-524 61.
This clean, simple, and bargain *pensão* has a peaceful location in the small town of Murça and features excellent views.

OPORTO: *Residencial Santa Cruz* $ — AE V — 17
Rua Santa Catarina 876, 4000. **Road map** C2. 22-205 71 99.
This bargain *albergaria* is extremely basic, but it has both style and character. The rooms have splendid views of the city center.

OPORTO: *Hotel da Bolsa* $$ — AE DC MC V — 36
Rua F. Borges 101, 4050. **Road map** C2. 22-202 67 68. **FAX** 22-205 88 88.
The "Stock Exchange" hotel has an attractive façade and well-appointed rooms, and is convenient for both shopping and tourist areas.

OPORTO: *Nave* $$ — AE DC MC V — 81
Av. Fernão de Magalhães 247, 4300. **Road map** C2. 22-537 61 31. **FAX** 22-536 12 16.
This modern hotel is conveniently situated ten minutes walk from the center of town. The bedrooms have recently been renovated.

OPORTO: *Malaposta* $$ — AE DC MC V — 37
Rua da Conceição 80, 4050. **Road map** C2. 22-200 62 78. **FAX** 22-200 62 95.
Tucked away on a quiet side street and centrally located, the attractive and modern Malaposta is a friendly, bargain hotel.

OPORTO: *Pensão dos Aliados* $$ — DC MC V — 38
Rua Elísio de Melo 27, 4000. **Road map** C2. 22-200 48 53. **FAX** 22-200 27 10.
This excellent *pensão* with well-equipped rooms is located in the center of town in an impressive building recognized as a city landmark.

OPORTO: *São José* $$ — AE DC MC V — 43
Rua da Alegria 172, 4000. **Road map** C2. 22-208 02 61. **FAX** 22-332 04 46.
One of several hotels in this busy street, close to the city center, the São José has a very pleasant style and ambience.

OPORTO: *Boa-Vista* $$$ — AE MC V — 39
Esplanada do Castelo 58, 4100. **Road map** C2. 22-618 00 83. **FAX** 22-617 38 18.
As the name suggests, the charming Boa-Vista hotel has superb views of the ocean. An enchanting trolley takes guests into town.

OPORTO: *Mercure da Batalha* $$$ — AE DC MC V — 149
Praça da Batalha 116, 4000. **Road map** C2. 22-200 05 71. **FAX** 22-200 24 68.
A delightful hotel in a convenient location. There is a terrace with panoramic views and rooms adapted for the disabled.

<table>
<tr><td>

Price categories for a standard double room per night, including breakfast:

$ under 7,000$00
$$ 7–12,000$00
$$$ 12–20,000$00
$$$$ 20–30,000$00
$$$$$ over 30,000$00.

</td><td>

RESTAURANT
The hotel has one or more restaurants open for lunch and supper, sometimes reserved for residents.
GARDEN
A garden, courtyard, or large terrace for the use of hotel guests.
SWIMMING POOL
The hotel has its own indoor or outdoor pool.
CREDIT CARDS
Major credit cards accepted: *AE* American Express, *DC* Diners Club, *MC* MasterCard and *V* VISA.

</td></tr>
</table>

	CREDIT CARDS	RESTAURANT	GARDEN	SWIMMING POOL	NUMBER OF ROOMS
OPORTO: *Internacional* $$$ Rua do Almada 131, 4050. **Road map** C2. (22-200 50 32. FAX 22-200 90 63. A curious but pleasing combination of Baroque and modern styles in the reception rooms make this an interesting place to stay. 🔲 TV ☰	AE DC MC V	●			35
OPORTO: *São João* $$$ Rua do Bonjardim 120, 4000. **Road map** C2. (22-200 16 62. FAX 22-31 61 14. This small but immaculate hotel, on a busy shopping street that leads into the center, is decorated in a style reminiscent of the 1950s. 🔲 TV	AE DC MC V	●			14
OPORTO: *Dom Henrique* $$$$ Rua G. de Azevedo 179, 4000. **Road map** C2. (22-200 57 55. FAX 22-201 94 51. Located right in the heart of the city, this hotel has 22 floors – one designated non-smoking – and a bar with a panoramic view. 🔲 TV ☰	AE DC MC V	●			112
OPORTO: *Infante de Sagres* $$$$$ P. Dona F. de Lencastre 62, 4050. **Road map** C2. (22-200 81 01. FAX 22-205 49 37. This is a beautifully appointed city-center hotel with public rooms full of antiques, a refined atmosphere, and bedrooms that offer everything a discerning traveler would expect from such a highly rated hotel. 🔲 TV ☰	AE DC MC V	●	■		74
OPORTO: *Ipanema Park* $$$$$ R. de Serralves 124, 4150. **Road map** C2. (22-610 41 74. FAX 22-610 28 09. An elegant hotel in which each room has a view over either the city, river, or Atlantic Ocean. Enjoy every conceivable convenience and a health club that includes an indoor pool and hydromassage. 🔲 TV ☰ P 🅖	AE DC MC V	●		●	281
OPORTO: *Porto Sheraton* $$$$$ Av. da Boavista 1269, 4150. **Road map** C2. (22-608 66 00 . FAX 22-609 14 67. The elegant Sheraton, situated in an affluent suburb of Oporto, offers all modern facilities including a comprehensive health club. 🔲 TV ☰ P 🅖	AE DC MC V	●		●	250
OPORTO: *Tivoli Porto Atlântico* $$$$ Rua A. L. Vieira 66, 4100. **Road map** C2. (22-609 49 41. FAX 22-606 74 52. The modern Tivoli Porto, situated in the elegant suburb of Boavista, has comfortable rooms, all of which have a balcony. 🔲 TV ☰ P 🅖	AE DC MC V		■	●	58
PESO DA RÉGUA: *Império* $ Av. Vasques Osório 8, 5050. **Road map** D2. (254-32 01 20. FAX 254-32 14 57. In the heart of the port region, this modern *pensão* is located near Peso da Régua's harbor and has lovely views of the Douro River. 🔲 TV P	AE DC MC V				33
PINHÃO: *Casa das Pontes* $$ Quinta da Foz, 5085. **Road map** D2. (254-723 53. FAX 254-723 54. Set within the vineyards of the Quinta da Foz, a large estate that produces port, the Casa das Pontes offers rural lodging and can arrange wine tasting and a visit to the cellars where the barrels are kept. 🔲 P	AE DC MC V		■		4
SABROSA: *Quality Inn Sabrosa* $$$ Avenida dos Combatentes da Grande Guerra, Casa dos Barros, 5060. **Road map** D2. (259-93 02 40. FAX 259-93 02 60. Located in the town center in a 17th-century manor (with a new wing added) the Quality Inn has all expected modern facilites. 🔲 TV ☰ P 🅖	AE DC MC V	●	■	●	50
SANTO TIRSO: *Quinta da Picaria* $$ Guimarei, 4780. **Road map** C2. (252-89 12 97. Attractive and traditionally decorated rooms can be rented on this farm. It is an ideal base for those who prefer to stay out of town. 🔲 P			■		4
TORRE DE MONCORVO: *Brasília* $$ N220, 5160. **Road map** E2. (279-25 42 56. FAX 279-25 42 55. This neat and tidy *pensão*, offering all modern conveniences, is conveniently located on the main road through town. 🔲 TV ☰ P 🅖	AE DC MC V	●	■	●	29

VIDAGO: *Vidago Palace Hotel* $$$ | AE DC MC V | 91
5425. **Road map** D1. **(** 276-973 58. **FAX** 276-973 59.
This truly magnificent turn-of-the-century spa hotel, surrounded by forest, has a grandiose façade and a beautiful inside staircase flanked by marble columns. The bedrooms are also charming. 🛏 📺 🍴 P ♿

VILA REAL: *Casa Agrícola da Levada* $$ | 8
Timpiera, 5000. **Road map** D2. **(** 259-32 21 90. **FAX** 259-34 69 55.
Constructed in 1922 by the Portuguese architect Raúl Liria, this charming Art Deco house has elegant rooms and a lovely rose garden. 🛏 📺 P ♿

VILA REAL: *Mira Corgo* $$ | AE DC MC V | 166
Av. 1° de Maio 78, 5000. **Road map** D2. **(** 259-32 50 01. **FAX** 259-32 50 06.
The modern Mira Corgo is tastefully decorated and has superb views from the terrace of the deep ravine and river below. 🛏 📺 🍴 P ♿

MINHO

BARCELOS: *Quinta de Santa Comba* $$ | 9
Freguesia da Várzea, Lugar de Crujães, 4750. **Road map** C1. **(** & **FAX** 253-83 21 01.
A spectacular 18th-century residence with wooden beams and granite stonework, this manor house has an elegant rustic charm. 🛏 P ♿

BOM JESUS DO MONTE: *Hotel do Elevador* $$$ | AE DC MC V | 24
Tenões, Braga, 4700. **Road map** C1. **(** 253-67 66 11. **FAX** 253-67 66 79.
A luxurious hotel that derives its name from the 19th-century water-operated funicular that still takes visitors up to the sanctuary. 🛏 📺 🍴 P ♿

BRAGA: *Comfort Inn* $$ | AE DC MC V | 72
N14, Ferreiros, 4700. **Road map** C1. **(** 253-67 38 65. **FAX** 253-67 38 72.
Located a short distance from the city center, and convenient for a quick stopover, this hotel offers the usual Comfort Inn amenities. 🛏 📺 🍴 P ♿

BRAGA: *Dona Sofia* $$ | MC V | 34
L. São João do Souto 131, 4700. **Road map** C1. **(** 253-26 31 60. **FAX** 253-61 12 45.
Adjacent to a small square with a lovely fountain, this modern hotel is in the center of Braga, close to the city's cathedral. 🛏 📺 P ♿

BRAGA: *Largo da Estação* $$ | AE DC MC V | 51
Largo da Estação 13, 4700. **Road map** C1. **(** 253-21 83 81. **FAX** 253-27 68 10.
Located just outside the town center, close to the train station, this hotel offers some rooms with Jacuzzi bathtubs. 🛏 📺 🍴 P ♿

BRAGA: *Turismo de Braga* $$$ | AE DC MC V | 132
Praceta João XXI, 4710. **Road map** C1. **(** 253-61 22 00. **FAX** 253-61 22 11.
This large hotel dominates a small square in the center of town. Facilities include a solarium and there are panoramic views. 🛏 📺 🍴 P ♿

CAMINHA: *Casa de Esteiró* $$ | AE DC MC V | 3
Vilarelho, 4910. **Road map** C1. **(** 258-92 13 56. **FAX** 258-72 13 33
A restored 18th-century house set in its own magnificent garden, the Casa de Esteiró offers comfortable apartments and a cozy log fire. 📺 P ♿

CELORICO DE BASTO: *Casa do Campo* $$$ | AE MC V | 8
Molares, 4890. **Road map** D1. **(** 255-36 12 31. **FAX** 255-36 12 31
A granite gateway welcomes visitors to this elegant 17th-century country house. The camellia garden is one of the oldest in Portugal. 🛏 P ♿

GUIMARÃES: *Hotel de Guimarães* $$$ | AE DC MC V | 72
Rua E. Almeida, 4810. **Road map** C2. **(** 253-51 58 88. **FAX** 253-51 62 34.
A modern, well-equipped hotel in the city center that boasts a health club, gymnasium, sauna, and massage facilities. 🛏 📺 🍴 P ♿

GUIMARÃES: *Pousada de Nossa Senhora da Oliveira* $$$ | AE DC MC V | 15
Rua de Santa Maria, 4800. **Road map** C2. **(** 253-51 41 57. **FAX** 253-51 42 04.
This *pousada* was once a distinguished aristocratic mansion in the old district of town. Inside, beamed ceilings, leather armchairs, and antique paintings help preserve the original character of the house. 🛏 📺 P

GUIMARÃES: *Pousada de Santa Marinha da Costa* $$$$ | AE DC MC V | 51
Lugar da Costa, 4810. **Road map** C2. **(** 253-51 44 53. **FAX** 253-51 44 59.
This marvelous building, once the 12th-century Santa Marinha da Costa monastery, has been carefully adapted to house this beautiful *pousada*. Original *azulejo* decoration adorns the sumptuous rooms. 🛏 📺 🍴 P

Price categories for a standard double room per night, including breakfast:

$ under 7,000$00
$$ 7–12,000$00
$$$ 12–20,000$00
$$$$ 20–30,000$00
$$$$$ over 30,000$00.

RESTAURANT
The hotel has one or more restaurants open for lunch and supper, sometimes reserved for residents.

GARDEN
A garden, courtyard, or large terrace for the use of hotel guests.

SWIMMING POOL
The hotel has its own indoor or outdoor pool.

CREDIT CARDS
Major credit cards accepted: *AE* American Express, *DC* Diners Club, *MC* MasterCard and *V* VISA.

	CREDIT CARDS	RESTAURANT	GARDEN	SWIMMING POOL	NUMBER OF ROOMS
PONTE DE LIMA: *Casa de Sabadão* $$ Arcozelo, 4990. **Road map** C1. ☎ 258-94 19 63. An enchanting 18th-century country house set among vineyards. Rooms include a charming, isolated apartment in a converted mill. 🖼 P ♿			■		4
PÓVOA DE VARZIM: *Grande Hotel Sopete da Póvoa* $$ L. do Passeio Alegre, 4490. **Road map** C2. ☎ 252-61 54 64. FAX 252-61 55 65. An elegant hotel in the center of Póvoa de Varzim, right next to the casino and overlooking the beach. Guests can make use of the nearby Estrela golf course for discounted greens fees. 🖼 TV 🍽 P ♿	AE DC MC V	●			92
VALENÇA DO MINHO: *Vale Flores* $ Esplanada, 4930. **Road map** C1. ☎ 251-82 41 06. FAX 251-82 41 29. Located in the new part of town, outside the town's fortifications, this *pensão* is clean, functional, and inexpensive. 🖼 TV ♿	AE DC MC V				32
VALENÇA DO MINHO: *Casa do Poço de Valença* $$$ T. da Gaviarra 4, 4930. **Road map** C1. ☎ 251-82 52 35. FAX 251-82 54 69. Inside the Vauban-style fort, this handsome house has a spectacular interior that combines modern decor with antique furniture. 🖼 TV	AE	●	■		7
VALENÇA DO MINHO: *Pousada de São Teotónio* $$$ Baluarte do Socorro, 4930. **Road map** C1. ☎ 251-82 42 42. FAX 251-82 43 97. The traditionally furnished rooms of this small *pousada* have enchanting views of the valley, across the Minho River to Tuy, in Spain. 🖼 TV 🍽	AE DC MC V	●	■		16
VIANA DO CASTELO: *Calatrava* $$ Rua M. Fiúza Júnior 157, 4900. **Road map** C1. ☎ 258-82 89 11. FAX 258-82 86 37. Located conveniently close to the old center of Viana do Castelo, this *pensão* is neat and tidy and has old-fashioned decor. 🖼 TV	AE DC MC V				15
VIANA DO CASTELO: *Casa dos Costa Barros* $$ Rua de São Pedro 22–28, 4900. **Road map** C1. ☎ 258-82 37 05. FAX 258-243 83. This delightful house, which was constructed in the 16th century and has been owned by the same family since 1765, has an elegant interior and handsome stone carvings over the outside windows. 🖼 TV	MC V				10
VIANA DO CASTELO: *Hotel do Parque* $$$ Praça da Galiza, 4900. **Road map** C1. ☎ 258-82 86 05. FAX 258-82 86 12. A welcoming hotel located just outside the old town within its own gardens. The rooftop restaurant has stunning views. 🖼 TV 🍽 P ♿	AE DC MC V	●	■	●	124
VIANA DO CASTELO: *Pousada de Santa Luzia* $$$ Monte de S. Luzia, 4990. **Road map** C1. ☎ 258-82 88 89. FAX 258-82 88 92. Surrounded by eucalyptus and pine trees, this luxurious *pousada* has a spectacular vantage point over the town of Viana. 🖼 TV 🍽 P ♿	AE DC MC V	●	■	●	48
VIEIRA DO MINHO: *Pousada de São Bento* $$$$ Caniçada, 4850. **Road map** D1. ☎ 253-64 71 90. FAX 253-64 78 67. Set in the nature preserve of the Peneda-Gerês National Park, and overlooking the Cávado River, this ivy-clad *pousada* was converted from a hunting lodge. The rustic interior is tranquil and relaxing. 🖼 TV 🍽 P	AE DC MC V	●	■	●	29
VILA DO CONDE: *Motel Sant'Ana* $$$ Azurara, 4480. **Road map** C2. ☎ 252-64 17 17. FAX 252-64 26 93. Within easy reach of Oporto airport, this motel has a magnificent location on the banks of the lovely River Ave. The complex, which resembles a country club, offers well-equipped apartments and a sauna. 🖼 TV P	AE DC MC V	●	■	●	34
VILA NOVA DE CERVEIRA: *Pousada Dom Dinis* $$$ Terreiro, 4920. **Road map** C1. ☎ 251-79 56 01. FAX 251-79 56 04. Built within the walls of the medieval castle at Vila Nova, this tranquil and charming *pousada* has spacious and pleasant rooms. 🖼 TV 🍽 P	AE DC MC V	●	■		28

ALENTEJO

ALVITO: *Pousada do Castelo de Alvito* $$$$
Apartado 9, 7920. **Road map** D6. 284-48 53 43. **FAX** 284-48 53 83.
This elegant *pousada*, housed in a restored 15th-century fortress, has stunning Gothic vaulting in the dining room and Manueline details on the windows. Peacocks roam the tranquil gardens. 📺 ▤ &
AE DC MC V — 20

BEJA: *Hotel Melius* $$
Av. Fialho de Almeida, 7800. **Road map** D6. 284-32 18 22. **FAX** 284-32 18 25.
At the southern edge of the medieval town of Beja, this modern hotel is pleasant and comfortable and offers exceptional value. 📺 ▤ P &
AE DC MC V — 60

BEJA: *Pousada de São Francisco* $$$$
L. Dom N. Álvares Pereira, 7800. **Road map** D6. 284-32 84 41. **FAX** 284-32 91 43.
Originally a Franciscan convent founded in 1268, this attractive white building is now a beautiful and luxurious *pousada*. 📺 ▤ P &
AE DC MC V — 35

CASTELO DE VIDE: *Garcia d'Orta* $$$
Estrada de São Vicente, 7320. **Road map** D4. 245-90 11 00. **FAX** 245-90 12 00.
A discreet and attractive hotel with all the modern amenities and a handsome restaurant offering good Alentejan cooking. 📺 ▤ P &
AE DC MC V — 53

CRATO: *Pousada de Flor da Rosa* $$$$
Flor da Rosa, 7430. **Road map** D4. 245-99 72 10. **FAX** 245-99 72 12.
An architecturally outstanding adaptation of the 14th-century Mosteiro de Santa Maria Flor da Rosa houses this elegant *pousada*. 📺 ▤ &
AE DC MC V — 24

ELVAS: *Elxadai Parque* $$
N4, Varche, 7353. **Road map** D5. 268-62 13 97. **FAX** 268-62 19 21.
A well-equipped complex situated on top of a hill just west of Elvas, with a water park, sports facilities, and an equestrian center. 📺 ▤ P
AE DC MC V — 41

ELVAS: *Pousada de Santa Luzia* $$$
Avenida de Badajoz, 7350. **Road map** D5. 268-62 21 94. **FAX** 268-62 21 27.
The pleasantly decorated Santa Luzia was the first *pousada* to open (1942). Located close to the aqueduct, it has a pool and tennis courts. 📺 ▤ P
AE DC MC V — 25

ELVAS: *Quinta de Santo António* $$$
7353. **Road map** D5. 268-62 84 06. **FAX** 268-62 50 50.
This splendid *estalagem* has elegant 18th-century gardens. The long buildings offer attractive, rustic accommodations. 📺 ▤ P &
AE DC MC V — 30

ESTREMOZ: *Pousada da Rainha Santa Isabel* $$$$
Largo Dom Dinis, 7100. **Road map** D5. 268-33 20 76. **FAX** 268-33 20 79.
This grandiose *pousada* has been beautifully integrated into the 13th-century castle in Estremoz. The 17th- and 18th-century style furniture of the rooms includes four-poster beds and coats of arms. 📺 ▤ &
AE DC MC V — 33

ÉVORA: *IBIS Évora* $$
Quinta da Tapada, Muralha, 7000. **Road map** D5. 266-74 46 20. **FAX** 266-74 46 32.
Located just outside the walls that encircle the old town, this modern hotel is basic, but has all of the usual comforts of an IBIS hotel. 📺 ▤ P &
AE DC MC V — 87

ÉVORA: *Évorahotel* $$
N114, Quinta do Cruzeiro, Apartado 93, 7001. **Road map** D5.
266-73 48 00. **FAX** 266-73 48 06.
On the outskirts of the old town, this is an impressive modern hotel. The well-equipped rooms all have a balcony. 📺 ▤ P &
AE DC MC V — 114

ÉVORA: *Solar Monfalim* $$$
Largo da Misericórdia 1, 7000. **Road map** D5. 266-75 00 00. **FAX** 266-74 23 67.
In the heart of the old town, this Renaissance house offers visitors well-appointed rooms and a delightful atmosphere. 📺 ▤ P &
AE MC V — 26

ÉVORA: *Pousada dos Lóios* $$$$
L. do Conde de Vila Flor, 7000. **Road map** D5. 266-240 51. **FAX** 266-272 48.
Originally a 15th-century monastery, the simple rooms in this elegant *pousada* were converted from the monks' cells. 📺 ▤ P
AE DC MC V — 32

MARVÃO: *Pousada de Santa Maria* $$$
Rua 24 de Janeiro 7, 7330. **Road map** D4. 245-932 01. **FAX** 245-934 40.
This charming *pousada* is set in a cozy, whitewashed town house with traditional painted furniture and friendly staff. 📺 ▤ P
AE DC MC V — 29

For key to symbols see back flap

	CREDIT CARDS	RESTAURANT	GARDEN	SWIMMING POOL	NUMBER OF ROOMS

Price categories for a standard double room per night, including breakfast:

$ under 7,000$00
$$ 7–12,000$00
$$$ 12–20,000$00
$$$$ 20–30,000$00
$$$$$ over 30,000$00.

RESTAURANT
The hotel has one or more restaurants open for lunch and supper, sometimes reserved for residents.

GARDEN
A garden, courtyard, or large terrace for the use of hotel guests.

SWIMMING POOL
The hotel has its own indoor or outdoor pool.

CREDIT CARDS
Major credit cards accepted: *AE* American Express, *DC* Diners Club, *MC* MasterCard and *V* VISA.

MÉRTOLA: *Casa das Janelas Verdes* $
Rua Dr M. Gomes 38–40, 7750. **Road map** D6. 286-621 45.
A pleasant hotel in a whitewashed Alentejan house in the center of town. Water sports facilities are available on the Guadiana River.

| | | | ■ | | 3 |

REDONDO: *Convento de São Paulo* $$$$
Aldeia da Serra, 7170. **Road map** D5. 266-99 91 00. **FAX** 266-99 91 04.
Set in the remote Serra de Ossa, this former 14th-century monastery now houses an elegant hotel. *Azulejo* panels and frescoes adorn the rooms, and water from a Baroque fountain cools the delightful patio.

| AE DC MC V | ● | ■ | ● | 21 |

SANTA CLARA-A-VELHA: *Pousada de Santa Clara* $$$
Barragem de Santa Clara, 7665. **Road map** C7. 283-88 22 50. **FAX** 283-88 24 02.
Overlooking the vast Santa Clara-a-Velha lake, this peaceful *pousada* is ideal for water sports, hiking, and shooting.

| AE DC MC V | ● | ■ | ● | 19 |

SANTIAGO DO CACÉM: *Pousada de São Tiago* $$$
Estrada de Lisboa, 7540. **Road map** C6. & **FAX** 269-224 59.
This ivy-clad *pousada*, set in its own pleasant gardens, resembles a country villa and is an ideal base from which to explore the area.

| AE DC MC V | ● | ■ | ● | 8 |

SANTIAGO DO CACÉM: *Quinta da Ortiga* $$$
IP8, Apartado 67, 7540. **Road map** C6. 269-228 71. **FAX** 269-220 73.
This delightful farmhouse, just north of town and very close to the sea, is surrounded by 10 acres of land with stables.

| AE DC MC V | ● | ■ | ● | 11 |

SERPA: *Pousada de São Gens* $$$
Alto de São Gens, 7830. **Road map** D6. 284-54 47 24. **FAX** 284-54 43 37.
A modern *pousada* located high on a hill overlooking the town of Serpa, the São Gens has spectacular views of the wide Alentejo plains.

| AE DC MC V | ● | ■ | ● | 18 |

SOUSEL: *Pousada de São Miguel* $$$
Serra de São Miguel, 7470. **Road map** D5. 268-55 00 50. **FAX** 268-55 11 55.
This rustic *pousada* is ideal for those in search of peace or outdoor pursuits. There are facilities for hunting and fishing.

| AE DC MC V | ● | ■ | | 32 |

VILA NOVA DE MILFONTES: *Moinho da Asneira* $$
Quinta do Rio Mira, 7645. **Road map** C6. 283-99 61 82. **FAX** 283-99 71 38.
Rooms in the manor house and hillside cottages of this country estate overlook the estuary of the Mira River and are close to the beach.

| AE DC MC V | ● | ■ | | 40 |

VILA VIÇOSA: *Casa de Peixinhos* $$$
7160. **Road map** D5. 268-98 04 72. **FAX** 268-98 01 48.
This extravagant 18th-century building with grand rooms is decorated in shades of ocher and red with Baroque statues in the pebbled patio.

| | | ■ | | 8 |

ALGARVE

ALBUFEIRA: *Alfagar* $$$$
Alfagar, Semina Balaia, 8200. **Road map** C7. 289-54 02 20. **FAX** 289-54 27 70.
On a cliff top overlooking the ocean, this attractive complex offers apartments with direct access to the Santa Eulália beach.

| AE DC MC V | ● | ■ | ● | 210 |

ALBUFEIRA: *Falésia* $$$$
Pinhal do Concelho, Praia da Falésia, 8200. **Road map** C7.
289-50 12 37. **FAX** 289-50 12 70.
Located on Falésia beach, this hotel has brightly furnished and airy rooms and an atrium decorated with hanging plants.

| AE MC V | ● | ■ | ● | 169 |

ALBUFEIRA: *Montechoro* $$$$
Av. Dr F. Sá Carneiro, 8200. **Road map** C7. 289-58 94 23. **FAX** 289-58 99 47.
A modern and stylish hotel surrounded by its own gardens, this hotel has extensive sports facilities and a health club.

| AE DC MC V | ● | ■ | ● | 362 |

ALBUFEIRA: *Sheraton Algarve Pine Cliffs* $$$$$ AE DC MC V — 215
Apartado 644, 8200. **Road map** C7. 289-50 01 00. **FAX** 289-50 19 50.
A pleasing hotel with *azulejo* decoration on the bedsteads, the elegant Sheraton offers sports facilities and an elevator to the beach.

ALJEZUR: *O Palazim* $ — 12
N120, Aldeia Velha, 8670. **Road map** C7. 282-982 49. Nov–Mar.
This boarding house is in an attractive building with a terrace offering wonderful views. The lounge is decorated with *azulejo* panels.

ALMANCIL: *Quinta dos Rochas* $$$ — 8
Fonte Coberta, Caixa Postal 620-A, 8135. **Road map** D7.
289-39 31 65. **FAX** 289-39 91 98.
This small *quinta* (country estate) is conveniently situated close to the beach and offers visitors the comforts of home, a friendly welcome, and peaceful, rural surroundings.

ALMANCIL: *Quinta do Lago* $$$$$ AE DC MC V — 141
8135. **Road map** D7. 289-39 66 66. **FAX** 289-39 63 93.
This stylish hotel has delightful rooms with views of the ocean, a health club, golf concessions, and many other facilities.

ALTE: *Alte* $$$ AE DC MC V — 25
Montinho, 8100. **Road map** C7. 289-47 85 23. **FAX** 289-47 86 46.
In a peaceful inland location away from the teeming crowds on the coast, the charming Hotel Alte boasts excellent views, pleasant gardens and a shuttle bus that takes residents to the beach.

ALVOR: *Alvor Praia* $$$$$ AE DC MC V — 198
Praia dos Três Irmãos, 8500. **Road map** C7. 282-45 89 00. **FAX** 282-45 89 99.
A large, superbly situated luxury hotel complex with gardens that lead directly down to the beach, a heated saltwater swimming pool, and easy access to nearby golf courses.

ARMAÇÃO DE PÊRA: *Vila Vita Parc* $$$$$ AE DC MC V — 182
Apartado 196, 8365. **Road map** C7. 282-31 53 10. **FAX** 282-31 53 39.
Set along a beautiful stretch of coastline in its own gardens with tropical flowers, this luxurious hotel has direct access to the beach.

CARVOEIRO: *Colina Sol* $$$ AE MC V — 124
Vale de Centianes, Praia do Carvoeiro, 8400. **Road map** C7.
282-35 80 64. **FAX** 282-35 86 51.
This large Neo-Moorish hotel complex with well-equipped apartments is set in its own attractive gardens, overlooking the sea.

CARVOEIRO: *Almansor* $$$$ AE DC MC V — 293
Praia Vale Covo, 8400. **Road map** C7. 282-35 80 26. **FAX** 282-35 87 70.
This hotel has a dramatic location perched above a small cove. The secluded beach can be reached by a stairway at low tide.

ESTÓI: *Monte do Casal* $$$ DC MC V — 13
Cerro do Lobo, 8000. **Road map** D7. 289-99 01 40. **FAX** 289-99 13 41.
The elegant Monte do Casal has separate apartments set in a delightful Mediterranean garden with eucalyptus and bougainvillea.

FARO: *Alnacir* $$ AE DC MC V — 53
Estr. Senhora da Saúde 24, 8000. **Road map** D7. 289-80 36 78. **FAX** 289-80 35 48.
A tidy, modern hotel, Alnacir is located on a quiet street close to the center of this busy town. Some rooms have a terrace.

FARO: *Casa de Lumena* $$ AE DC MC V — 8
Praça A. Herculano 27, 8000. **Road map** D7. 289-80 19 90. **FAX** 289-80 40 19.
The Casa de Lumena is a lovely old house with attractive, pleasantly furnished rooms, a courtyard bar, and a relaxed, friendly atmosphere.

FARO: *Hotel Faro* $$ AE DC MC V — 52
Praça Dom F. Gomes 2, 8100. **Road map** D7. 289-80 32 76. **FAX** 289-80 35 46.
Close to the old town, the Hotel Faro has pleasant rooms, and the first floor lounge has a terrace that looks out over the small harbor.

FARO: *Hotel Eva* $$$$ AE DC MC V — 148
Av. da República 1, 8000. **Road map** D7. 289-80 33 54. **FAX** 289-80 23 04.
A modern and comfortable hotel with shops and a barber. Ask for a room that looks out over the marina and the ocean beyond.

For key to symbols see back flap

Price categories for a standard double room per night, including breakfast:

$ under 7,000$00
$$ 7–12,000$00
$$$ 12–20,000$00
$$$$ 20–30,000$00
$$$$$ over 30,000$00.

RESTAURANT
The hotel has one or more restaurants open for lunch and supper, sometimes reserved for residents.

GARDEN
A garden, courtyard, or large terrace for the use of hotel guests.

SWIMMING POOL
The hotel has its own indoor or outdoor pool.

CREDIT CARDS
Major credit cards accepted: *AE* American Express, *DC* Diners Club, *MC* MasterCard and *V* VISA.

	CREDIT CARDS	RESTAURANT	GARDEN	SWIMMING POOL	NUMBER OF ROOMS
LAGOA: *Parque Algarvio* $$ Sítio do Carmo, N125, 8400. **Road map** C7. 282-522 65. **FAX** 282-522 78. Although located alongside the main Algarvian highway, this is a charming and bargain hotel with rooms around the pool.	AE DC MC V	●	■	●	42
LAGOS: *Rubi-Mar* $ Rua da Barroca 70, 8600. **Road map** C7. 282-76 31 65. **FAX** 282-76 77 49. The English-run Rubi-Mar is a friendly hotel overlooking the sea. Generous continental breakfast is served in the rooms.	AE DC MC V				8
LAGOS: *Belavista da Luz* $$$ Praia da Luz, 8600. **Road map** C7. 282-78 86 55. **FAX** 282-78 86 56. This well-equipped hotel overlooks the sandy Praia da Luz. Facilities include a health club, children's area, and game room.	AE DC MC V	●	■	●	45
LAGOS: *Marina Rio* $$$ Av. dos Descobrimentos, Apartado 388, 8600. **Road map** C7. 282-76 98 59. **FAX** 282-76 99 60. Located in the eastern part of Lagos, this *albergaria* is modern and pleasant and has attractive views of the marina.	AE MC V		■	●	36
LAGOS: *Hotel de Lagos* $$$$ Rua A. C. dos Santos, 8600. **Road map** C7. 282-76 99 67. **FAX** 282-76 99 20. This pleasant complex has five restaurants, a health club, a disco, and, during the summer, barbeques are prepared on the beach.	AE DC MC V	●	■	●	317
LOULÉ: *Loulé Jardim* $$ Praça Manuel da Arriaga, 8100. **Road map** D7. 289-41 30 95. **FAX** 289-46 31 77. This small hotel on a quiet garden square is an appealing conversion of a classic town house, including a discreet rooftop pool.	AE DC MC V	●	■	●	52
MONCHIQUE: *Abrigo da Montanha* $$ Estrada da Fóia, 8550. **Road map** C7. 282-91 21 31. **FAX** 282-91 36 60. This attractive *estalagem*, made from wood and bare stone, makes a peaceful retreat and a good base for walks in the Serra de Monchique.	AE DC MC V	●	■	●	16
MONTE GORDO: *Vasco da Gama* $$$ Avenida Infante Dom Henrique, 8900. **Road map** D7. 281-51 13 21. **FAX** 281-51 16 22. Set on the beach, this hotel has spacious rooms, each with its own balcony. There is also a children's pool and playground.	AE DC MC V	●	■	●	168
PORTIMÃO: *Bela Vista* $$$$ Avenida Tomas Cabreira, 8500. **Road map** C7. 282-45 04 80. **FAX** 282-41 53 69. An attractive hotel situated above the popular Praia da Rocha, the Bela Vista is tastefully decorated with relaxing sofas and *azulejo* panels. Breakfast is served on a terrace overlooking the sea.	AE DC MC V	●	■		14
PORTIMÃO: *Le Méridien* $$$$$ Caixa Postal 146, 8502. **Road map** C7. 282-41 54 15. **FAX** 282-41 50 00. This hotel is a golfers' paradise. Set in a lush garden, it has practice facilities, lessons, and a championship course.	AE DC MC V	●	■	●	196
QUARTEIRA: *Estalagem da Cegonha* $$ Centro Hípico de Vilamoura, 8125. **Road map** D7. 289-30 25 77. **FAX** 289-32 26 75. This 17th-century flower-covered *estalagem* offers rustic but well-equipped rooms in a tranquil setting. Horseback riding is available.	AE DC MC V	●	■		9
SAGRES: *Navegante* $$$ Rua Infante D. Henrique, 8650. **Road map** C7. 282-62 43 54. **FAX** 282-62 43 60. This hotel on the Sagres promontory has spectacular views. The rooms are individual apartments with all modern conveniences.	AE DC MC V	●	■	●	56

SAGRES: *Pousada do Infante* $$$
Sagres, 8650. **Road map** C7. 282-62 42 22. FAX 282-62 42 25.
Named after Henry the Navigator *(see p49)*, this *pousada* has a superb
location overlooking the ocean on the Sagres promontory.
AE DC MC V — 39

SÃO BRÁS DE ALPORTEL: *Pousada de São Brás* $$$
Poço dos Ferreiros, 8150. **Road map** D7. 289-84 23 05. FAX 289-84 17 26.
This peaceful *pousada* is housed in a country manor north of Faro, with
spectacular views of the hills and the sea.
AE DC MC V — 33

TAVIRA: *Convento de Santo António* $$$
Atalaia 56, 8800. **Road map** D7. 281-32 56 32.
This charming whitewashed guesthouse offers elegant rooms around the
shady patio, or lovely rooms converted from the monks' cells.
AE — 7

TAVIRA: *Quinta do Caracol* $$$
São Pedro, 8800. **Road map** D7. 281-32 24 75. FAX 281-32 31 75.
This 17th-century whitewashed country house, surrounded by the spacious
gardens of the *quinta* (estate), is a practical base from which to explore
the coast and hilly interior of the eastern Algarve.
AE DC MC V — 7

VILA DO BISPO: *Os Gambozinos* $$
Praia do Martinhal, 8650. **Road map** C7. 282-62 43 18. FAX 282-62 43 48.
This attractive hotel, located on the isolated Sagres peninsula, stretches
along the sandy Martinhal beach, popular with windsurfers. — 17

VILAMOURA: *Atlantis* $$$$$
Quarteira, 8125. **Road map** C7. 289-38 99 77. FAX 289-38 99 62.
A stylish and modern hotel with views of the sea and extensive facilities
including tennis courts and a horseback-riding club.
AE DC MC V — 305

VILAMOURA: *Marinotel* $$$$$
8126. **Road map** C7. 289-38 99 88. FAX 289-38 99 69.
This large hotel, with views of the marina and the ocean, offers many
sports facilities and an exclusive "Presidential Suite."
AE DC MC V — 385

VILA REAL DE SANTO ANTÓNIO: *Guadiana* $$$
Avenida da República 94, 8900. **Road map** D7. 281-51 14 82. FAX 281-51 14 78.
A nicely refurbished 19th-century town house, this hotel is right in the
center of town and has good views of the Guadiana River.
AE DC MC V — 40

MADEIRA

CANIÇO: *Roca Mar* $$$
Caixa Postal 23, 9125. 291-93 43 34. FAX 291-93 40 44.
All rooms at the clifftop Roca Mar have large balconies that offer good
views of the wate. The hotel offers lively evening entertainment, as well
as sports facilities and a free minibus to Funchal.
AE DC MC V — 103

CANIÇO: *Quinta Splendida* $$$$
Sítio da Vargem, 9125. 291-93 04 00. FAX 291-93 04 01.
The rooms of the Quinta Splendida, a villa complex set in the gardens
of a 16th-century mansion, are tastefully furnished.
AE DC MC V — 111

FUNCHAL: *Monte Carlo* $$
Calçada da Saúde 10, 9000. 291-22 61 31. FAX 291-22 61 34.
Housed in a gracious building with fine views from the rooms at the front,
this dignified hotel is a steep walk uphill from the center.
AE DC MC V — 53

FUNCHAL: *Residencial Santa Clara* $$
Calçada do Pico 16b, 9000. 291-74 21 94. FAX 291-74 32 80.
Only a five-minute walk from the center of town, this small, quiet hotel
has grand interiors and splendid views of the sea and mountains. — 14

FUNCHAL: *Windsor* $$
Rua das Hortas 4c, 9000. 291-23 30 81. FAX 291-23 30 80.
A friendly, modern hotel located in the maze of narrow streets at the
heart of Funchal. Most rooms in this quiet hotel face inwards to a shady
central courtyard; there is also a tiny rooftop pool. — 67

FUNCHAL: *Quinta da Penha de França* $$$
Rua Penha de França 2, 9000. 291-22 90 87. FAX 291-22 92 61.
Decorated with old-fashioned elegance and surrounded by a walled
garden, this fine traditional mansion has grand rooms.
AE DC MC V — 73

For key to symbols see back flap

Price categories for a standard double room per night, including breakfast:

$ under 7,000$00
$$ 7–12,000$00
$$$ 12–20,000$00
$$$$ 20– 30,000$00
$$$$$ over 30,000$00.

RESTAURANT
The hotel has one or more restaurants open for lunch and supper, sometimes reserved for residents.

GARDEN
A garden, courtyard, or large terrace for the use of hotel guests.

SWIMMING POOL
The hotel has its own indoor or outdoor pool.

CREDIT CARDS
Major credit cards accepted: *AE* American Express, *DC* Diners Club, *MC* MasterCard and *V* VISA.

	CREDIT CARDS	RESTAURANT	GARDEN	SWIMMING POOL	NUMBER OF ROOMS
FUNCHAL: *Quinta Bela Vista* $$$ Caminho Avista Navios 4, 9000. 291-76 41 44. FAX 291-76 41 43. Located 15 minutes by car from central Funchal, this elegant 19th-century mansion has stylish antique furnishings and polite service.	AE DC MC V	●	■	●	67
FUNCHAL: *Quinta Perestrelo* $$$$ Rua do Dr Pita 3, 9000. 291-76 37 20. FAX 291-76 37 77. This mid-19th-century mansion filled with antiques and set in manicured gardens offers luxurious accommodations.	AE DC MC V	●	■	●	30
FUNCHAL: *Casino Park* $$$$$ Quinta da Vigia, 9000. 291-23 31 11. FAX 291-23 20 76. Madeira's liveliest hotel, with a casino, a theater, cabaret, and disco, was designed by Oscar Niemeyer (architect of the Brazilian capital, Brasília). The comfortable rooms have fine harbor views.	AE DC MC V	●	■	●	375
FUNCHAL: *Reid's Palace Hotel* $$$$$ Estrada Monumental 139, 9000. 291-71 71 71. FAX 291-71 71 77. Founded in 1891, this elegant hotel is the haunt of wealthy and famous patrons. Furnished like a stately home, with chandeliers in the dining room, it enjoys prime clifftop views and palm-fringed pools.	AE DC MC V	●	■	●	168
FUNCHAL: *Savoy* $$$$$ Rua Imperatriz D. Amelia 108–112, 9000. 291-22 20 31. FAX 291-22 31 03. Unobtrusive service is the hallmark of this luxury hotel with spacious rooms and leisure facilities such as a water sports center.	AE DC MC V	●	■	●	336
PICO DO ARIEIRO: *Pousada do Pico do Arieiro* $$$ Santana, 9230. 291-23 01 10. FAX 291-76 10 44. Located on top of Madeira's third-highest mountain, this *pousada* has stunning dawn views for those willing to rise early.	AE DC MC V	●	■	●	21
PORTO MONIZ: *Residencial Orca* $ Vila Porto Moniz, 9270. 291-85 00 00. FAX 291-85 00 19. Atlantic waves batter the shore in front of this isolated hotel. Natural tidal pools below the hotel are sometimes suitable for bathing.	AE DC MC V	●	■		12
PORTO SANTO: *Porto Santo* $$$ Campo de Baixo, 9400. 291-98 23 81. FAX 291-98 26 11. The premier hotel on Porto Santo makes up for the island's low-key attractions by providing a full range of sports facilities.	AE DC MC V	●	■	●	97
RIBEIRA BRAVA: *Brava Mar* $$ Rua Comandante Camacho de Freitas, 9350. 291-95 22 20. FAX 291-95 11 22. An ideal base for exploring the western part of the island, the Brava Mar is a modern hotel with balconied rooms and friendly staff.	AE DC MC V	●	■	●	70
SERRA DE ÁGUA: *Pousada dos Vinháticos* $$ Ribeira Brava, 9350. 291-95 23 44. FAX 291-76 10 44. Book well in advance for this charming *pousada* geared to walkers and set in woodland just below the Encumeada Pass.	AE DC MC V	●	■		21

THE AZORES

	CREDIT CARDS	RESTAURANT	GARDEN	SWIMMING POOL	NUMBER OF ROOMS
CORVO: *Casa de Hóspedes* $ Estrada para o Caldeirão, Vila do Corvo, 9980. 292-561 30. Apart from private homes, this is the only accommodation available on the tiny island of Corvo. The rooms are clean but very basic.			■		5
FAIAL: *Estalagem Santa Cruz* $$$ Rua Vasco da Gama, Horta, 9900. 292-29 30 21. FAX 292-29 39 06. Overlooking the sea, this 16th-century fort, which once protected Horta, has been turned into a cozy hotel adorned with antiques.	AE DC MC V	●	■		25

FAIAL: *Fayal* $$$ AE DC MC V • ■ • 114
Rua Cônsul Dabney, Horta, 9900. **(** 292-221 81. **FAX** 292-220 81.
Built in the 1920s for the staff of transatlantic cable companies, this
complex is now a prestigious hotel in the center of Horta. ⌂ TV ▤ P ⌕

FAIAL: *Quinta das Buganvílias* $$$ AE MC V ■ 10
Castelo Branco, Horta, 9900. **(** 292-94 32 55. **FAX** 292-94 37 43.
This family-run *quinta* near the airport has a rose garden, fruit orchard,
and commercial greenhouses filled with flowers. ⌂ TV ▤ P ⌕

FLORES: *Ocidental* $$ • ■ • 36
Sítio do Boqueirão, Santa Cruz, 9970. **(** 292-521 42. **FAX** 292-523 53.
The main hotel on Flores is a functional block on the outskirts of Santa
Cruz. Rooms are plain but most have balconies facing the sea. ⌂ TV P ⌕

GRACIOSA: *Santa Cruz* $$ ■ 19
L. Barão de Gaudalupe, S. Cruz da Graciosa, 9880. **(** 295-71 23 45. **FAX** 295-71 28 28.
A friendly hotel on a quiet square near the town center. Accommodations
on Graciosa are very limited so reserve well in advance. ⌂ TV

PICO: *L'Escale de l'Atlantic* $$ • ■ 5
Calhau Piedade, Piedade, 9930. **(** 292-66 62 60. **FAX** 292-66 62 60.
On the eastern tip of the island with views of São Jorge, this is a highly
individual designer hotel with stylish rooms. ● *Dec–Jan.* ⌂ P ⌕

PICO: *Pico* $$$ AE MC V • ■ • 68
Rua dos Biscoitos, Madalena, 9950. **(** 292-62 84 00. **FAX** 292-62 84 07.
A modern, well-equipped hotel offering some rooms with balconies and
views of the spectacular blackened peak of the island. ⌂ TV ⌕

SANTA MARIA: *Praia de Lobos* $$ AE MC V • 34
Rua M, Vila do Porto, 9580. **(** 296-88 22 77. **FAX** 296-88 24 82.
A stylish, efficiently run hotel in the center of Vila do Porto, the Praia do
Lobos offers modern facilities and a friendly welcome. ⌂ TV ▤

SÃO JORGE: *Estalagem das Velas* $$$ AE DC MC V ■ 24
Relvão, Velas, 9800. **(** 295-41 26 33. **FAX** 295-41 27 36.
On the outskirts of Velas, this is the only modern hotel on the island.
The attractive rooms have balconies facing the sea. ⌂ TV P

SÃO MIGUEL: *Solar de Lalém* $$ • ■ • 10
Estrada de São Pedro, Maia, 9625. **(** 296-44 20 04. **FAX** 296-44 21 64.
An elegant 19th-century manor house on the north coast, which has been
decorated in a simple style by its easy-going German owners. ⌂ P

SÃO MIGUEL: *Casa Nossa Senhora do Carmo* $$$ • ■ 5
Rua do Pópulo Decima 220, Livramento, 9500. **(** 296-64 20 48 **FAX** 296-64 20 38.
A lovingly restored and secluded *quinta*, to the east of Ponta Delgada.
The rooms are full of antiques and family treasures. ● *Nov–Dec.* ⌂ P

SÃO MIGUEL: *São Pedro* $$$ AE DC MC V • ■ - 26
L. Almirante Dunn, Ponta Delgada, 9500. **(** 296-28 22 23. **FAX** 296-62 93 19.
Built in 1812 for the American merchant Thomas Hickling, the São Pedro
is now a gracious harborside hotel furnished with antiques. ⌂ TV P

SÃO MIGUEL: *Bahia Palace* $$$$ AE DC MC V • ■ • 101
Água d'Alto, Vila Franco do Campo, 9680. **(** 296-58 25 61. **FAX** 296-58 26 15.
A large, isolated complex on the south coast with sports and conference
facilities, the Bahia is often used by business travelers. ⌂ TV ▤ P ⌕

TERCEIRA: *Beira Mar* $$$ AE MC V • ■ 23
L. Miguel Corte-Real, Angra do Heroísmo, 9700. **(** 295-21 51 88. **FAX** 295-62 82 48.
Overlooking the harbor, this hotel has small, basic rooms but is
excellently located for exploring the old heart of the city. ⌂ TV

TERCEIRA: *Quinta do Martelo* $$$ AE MC V • ■ • 10
Canada do Martelo 24, A. do Heroísmo, 9700. **(** 295-64 28 41. **FAX** 295-64 28 41.
An idyllic rural hotel with rooms exquisitely decorated with island crafts
and a restaurant specializing in Azorean dishes. ⌂ TV ▤ P ⌕

TERCEIRA: *Quinta da Nasce-Água* $$$ AE MC V • ■ • 13
Vinha Brava, Angra do Heroísmo, 9700. **(** 295-62 85 01. **FAX** 295-62 85 02.
Overlooking Angra do Heroísmo, this luxurious modern *quinta* in private
grounds has large gardens, tennis, and miniature golf. ⌂ TV ▤ P

For key to symbols see back flap

WHERE TO EAT

PORTUGAL IS the country to feast on all kinds of fish and seafood, from clams, lobster, and sardines to tuna, swordfish, and *bacalhau* (salted cod), the national favorite. All along the coast are restaurants dedicated to cooking freshly caught fish. The Portuguese are great meat eaters too and justifiably proud of such dishes as roast kid and suckling pig. Inland, meat is more

Sign for roast sucking pig at Mealhada *(see p412)*

plentiful and generally of better quality, with specialties varying according to region. Most restaurants are reasonably priced and offer generous portions. Lisbon has plenty of cheap cafés and restaurants, as well as international ones, as does the Algarve. This introduction gives tips on types of eating places, menus, drinks, and ordering to help you enjoy eating out in Portugal.

Waiter at the Palácio de Seteais, near Sintra *(see p409)*

TYPES OF RESTAURANTS

EATING PLACES come in all shapes and sizes and at all price levels. Among the most reasonable is the local *tasca* or tavern, often just a room with half-a-dozen tables presided over by a husband-and-wife team. These are frequented by locals and professionals at lunch time,

which is a good lead to follow. The *casa de pasto* offers a budget three-course meal in a large dining room, while a *restaurante* is more formal and offers a wider choice of dishes. At a *marisqueira* (found all along the coast), the emphasis is on fresh fish and seafood. The *churrasqueira*, a very popular concept imported from Brazil, specializes in spit-roasted foods, while a *cervejaria* (beerhouse) is the ideal place to go for a beer and a snack. As a rule, hotel restaurants in Portugal are of surprisingly good quality. *Pousadas (see pp378–9)*, found throughout the country, offer a network of traditional restaurants, with the focus on local specialties.

Sign for Maria Rita's *(see p415)*

EATING HOURS

LUNCH IS USUALLY served between noon and 2pm when many restaurants, especially in cities, get very crowded. Dinner is served from 7–10pm in most places but can be later in restaurants and *cervejarias* in major cities and resort areas such as Lisbon, Oporto, and the Algarve. Another choice for a very late dinner would be to combine a meal with a show at a *fado* house *(see pp66–7)*, open from about 9:30pm to 3 or 4am.

RESERVATIONS

IT IS A GOOD IDEA to book ahead for expensive restaurants and for those in popular locations in tourist season. Those with disabilities should check in advance on facilities and access. Special facilities for the disabled are generally lacking, but most places will try to be helpful.

THE MENU

MANY RESTAURANTS, especially in tourist areas, offer an *ementa turística*, a cheap, daily-changing three-course menu served with coffee and a drink (glass of wine, beer, water, or soft drink). This provides a full meal at a good price with no hidden costs. Lunch, *almoço*, is often a two-course fixed menu, consisting of a fish or meat main course with potatoes or rice and an appetizer or

The impressive interior of the Cozinha Velha *(see p407)* **at Queluz**

Sharing the local veal specialty at Gabriela's, in Sendim (see p413)

dessert. To sample a local specialty, ask for the *prato do dia* – dish of the day.

Dinner *(jantar)* may be two or more courses, perhaps followed by ice cream, fruit, a simple dessert, or cheese. Casserole-style dishes, such as fish or meat stews or *porco à alentejana* (pork with clams), are brought to the table in a pot for people to share, as are large fish such as sea bass, which are sold by weight. One serving can easily be shared by two people, and it is perfectly acceptable to ask for a *meia dose* or half-portion. Peculiar to Portugal is the plate of assorted appetizers – olives, cheese, and sardine pâté – brought with bread at the start of a meal. Not included in the menu price, these are charged per item consumed in most restaurants.

VEGETARIANS

VEGETARIANS WILL not eat as well as fish lovers, although local cheeses and breads can be excellent. In Lisbon or along the Algarve, vegetarians will benefit from ethnic restaurants. Chefs will usually be happy to provide something meatless, though this will probably mean simply an omelette or a salad.

WINE AND DRINKS

IT WOULD BE a shame to visit Portugal without sampling its two most famous fortified wines: port *(see pp252–3)* and Madeira *(see p349)*. Wherever you are, it is safe to order a bottle or jug of house wine to wash down your meal.

Otherwise, ask for the wine list, and choose one of Portugal's many native wines *(see pp28–9)*. Sagres and Super Bock are good beers, and the bottled water is recommended. This comes either *com gás* (sparkling) or *sem gás* (still).

Relaxing at a waterfront bar at Póvoa de Varzim in the Minho

CAFÉS AND CAKE SHOPS

CAFÉS ARE FUNDAMENTAL to Portuguese daily life and vary from modern white rooms to splendidly decorated, tiled, and mirrored places where you can sit and talk or read the paper for hours. Most have tables outside. They make perfect meeting points and usually offer a range of snacks and sandwiches. At any time of the day a café is the obvious choice for a coffee break with a roll, croissant, or cake. Do not miss the *pastelarias* (cake shops); the sweet-toothed Portuguese adore cakes, and the selections are excellent *(see pp147, 231 & 289)*.

PAYING THE BILL

IN MOST RESTAURANTS you have to pay a cover charge and it is normal to give a 10 per-cent tip where service is not included. It is wise to check in advance whether or not a restaurant accepts credit cards.

CHILDREN

IN PORTUGAL, children are viewed as a blessing rather than a nuisance, so it is an ideal country for families to eat out together. Children's portions or half-portions at reduced prices are advertised or will be provided on request.

SMOKING

SMOKING IS WIDESPREAD and permitted in all public places in Portugal, unless there is a sign saying *proibido fumar*. No-smoking areas in restaurants are very rare.

COFFEE DRINKING IN PORTUGAL

Coffee is widely drunk in Portugal and served in many forms. The most popular is a small cup of strong black coffee, like an espresso. In Lisbon and the South this is called *uma bica*; elsewhere ask for *um café*. A strong one is called *uma italiana*; for a weaker version, try *um carioca de café*. *Uma meia de leite* is half coffee, half milk. Strong coffee with a dash of milk is known as *um garoto escuro* (*um garoto claro* is quite milky). If you like your coffee with plenty of milk, ask for *um galão* (a gallon). This is served in a tall glass, and again you can order *um galão claro* (very milky) or *escuro* (strong).

Uma bica   Um galão

Choosing a Restaurant

THE RESTAURANTS in this guide have been selected for their good value, exceptional food, or interesting location. This chart highlights some of the factors that may influence your choice. This chart lists the restaurants by region; the thumb tabs on the side of the page are color-coded to correspond with the regional areas in the guide.

	CREDIT CARDS	LATE OPENING	OUTDOOR TABLES	GOOD WINE LIST

LISBON

ALCÂNTARA: *Espalha Brasas* $$$
Doca de Santo Amaro, Armazém 12. **Map** 3 A5. **(** 21-396 20 59.
A restaurant with architectural style and a lighthearted menu that includes daily
specials and cocktails. Enjoy the live music in the summer. ● *lunch (Aug); Sun.* ▤
| AE DC MC V | ▪ | ● | ▪ |

ALFAMA: *Hua-Ta-Li* $$
Rua dos Bacalhoeiros 109–115a. **Map** 7 C4. **(** 21-887 91 70.
This large Chinese restaurant close to the docks serves all the
regular rice and noodle favorites. Fast and efficient service. ▤
| | ▪ | | |

ALFAMA: *Lautasco* $$
Beco do Azinhal 7 (off Rua de São Pedro). **Map** 8 E4. **(** 21-886 01 73.
Rustically decorated with wooden paneling and wagon-wheel chandeliers,
Lautasco specializes in typical Portuguese cuisine. ● *Sun; Dec 20–Jan 15.*
| AE DC MC V | | ● | |

ALFAMA: *Sol Nascente* $$
Rua de São Tomé 86. **Map** 8 D3. **(** 21-886 16 33.
On the main road up to the castle from Alfama, this restaurant has fine views
of the Tagus. Try the seafood rice or the pork with clams. ● *Mon.* ▤ ⬚
| AE DC MC V | ▪ | ● | |

ALFAMA: *Senhor Leitão do Arco da Conceição* $$
Rua dos Bacalhoeiros 4. **Map** 7 C4. **(** 21-886 98 60.
As its name suggests, this attractive restaurant with antiques around the
walls specializes in *leitão* (roast suckling pig). ● *Sun.* ♫ *Tue, Thu & Fri.*
| AE MC V | ▪ | ● | |

ALFAMA: *Gargalhada Geral* $$$
Costa do Castelo 7. **Map** 7 C3. **(** 21-886 14 10.
Part of the Chapitô artistic complex *(see p64)*, this cheerful restaurant with a
bar and fine views of the harbor serves innovative cuisine. ● *Sun.* ♫ ⬚
| AE DC MC V | ▪ | ● | ▪ |

ALFAMA: *Casa do Leão* $$$$
Castelo de São Jorge. **Map** 8 D3. **(** 21-888 01 54.
Beneath arched brick ceilings, inside part of Castelo de São Jorge *(see pp78–9)*,
this restaurant offers superb service and excellent traditional Portuguese
cuisine. Sit outside to enjoy the magnificent views. ▤ ♫ *Wed–Fri.*
| AE DC MC V | | ● | ▪ |

ALFAMA: *Faz Figura* $$$$
Rua do Paraíso 15b. **Map** 8 F2. **(** 21-886 89 81.
A chic restaurant, where panoramic views of the river and city can be
enjoyed from the covered terrace. Specialties include *cataplana* dishes *(see
p288)* and *picanha* (steak grilled over an open fire). ● *Sat lunch; Sun.* ▤
| AE DC MC V | | ● | ▪ |

ALMADA: *Atira-te ao Rio* $$$
Cais do Jinjal 69–70. **(** 21-275 13 80.
View Lisbon from the other bank of the Tagus and enjoy the restaurant's
Brazilian specialties. Live samba music on Fridays and Saturdays. ● *Mon.* ♫
| | ▪ | ● | ▪ |

BAIRRO ALTO: *Bota Alta* $$$
Travessa da Queimada 37. **Map** 7 A3. **(** 21-342 79 59.
The "High Boot" is an attractive restaurant with original paintings on the
walls. The menu consists of traditional Portuguese dishes. ● *Sat lunch; Sun.*
| AE DC MC V | | | |

BAIRRO ALTO: *Casanostra* $$$
Travessa do Poço da Cidade 60. **Map** 7 A3. **(** 21-342 59 31.
Within the green, white, and black interior of this Italian restaurant you
can choose from a six-page menu full of Italian delicacies. ● *Mon.* ▤
| AE DC MC V | ▪ | | |

BAIRRO ALTO: *El Último Tango* $$$
Rua Diário de Notícias 62. **Map** 7 A4. **(** 21-342 03 41.
In this Argentinian restaurant the most popular choice is meat grilled over an
open fire. It also has interesting cocktails. ● *Sun; 2 weeks in Jun; 2 weeks in Oct.* ▤
| MC V | ▪ | | ▪ |

Price categories are for a three-course meal for one with half a bottle of wine, including cover charge, service, and VAT:

Ⓢ under 2,000$00
ⓈⓈ 2,000–3,000$00
ⓈⓈⓈ 3,000–4,500$00
ⓈⓈⓈⓈ 4,500–6,000$00
ⓈⓈⓈⓈⓈ over 6,000$00.

LATE OPENING
The kitchen stays open after 10pm, and you can usually have a meal up until at least 11pm.

OUTDOOR TABLES
Tables for eating outdoors, in a garden, or on a balcony, often with a pleasant view.

GOOD WINE LIST
The restaurant will have a good selection of quality wines.

CREDIT CARDS
This indicates which of the major credit cards are accepted: *AE* American Express, *DC* Diners Club, *MC* MasterCard, and *V* VISA.

	CREDIT CARDS	LATE OPENING	OUTDOOR TABLES	GOOD WINE LIST
BAIRRO ALTO: *Canto do Camões* ⓈⓈⓈⓈ Travessa da Espera 38. **Map 7 A4.** ☎ 21-346 54 64. This small, tiled *fado (see pp66–7)* restaurant has traditional Portuguese food and international dishes with a Scandinavian influence. ◗ *Sun (Nov–Mar).* ▤ ♫ ♿	AE DC MC V			
BAIRRO ALTO: *Massima Culpa* ⓈⓈⓈⓈ Rua da Atalaia 35–7. **Map 4 F2.** ☎ 21-342 01 21. This restaurant has a simple, uncomplicated decor with a very Italian atmosphere, and offers numerous antipasti and pasta dishes. ◗ *lunch; Wed.* ▤ ♿	AE DC MC V	▪		▪
BAIRRO ALTO: *Pap'Açorda* ⓈⓈⓈⓈⓈ Rua da Atalaia 57. **Map 4 F2.** ☎ 21-346 48 11. Both Lisboetas and tourists come here for the *açorda de mariscos* (bread and seafood), served in a sunny dining room. The menu is traditional Portuguese with some novel touches. ◗ *Mon lunch; Sun; 2 weeks in Jul; 2 weeks in Oct.* ▤ ♿	AE DC MC V	▪		▪
BAIRRO ALTO: *Tavares* ⓈⓈⓈⓈⓈ Rua da Misericórdia 37. **Map 7 A4.** ☎ 21-342 11 12. Lisbon's oldest restaurant, Tavares, dates from 1784. Its reputation is maintained with dishes, like breast of partridge on toast with *foie gras* and fillets of sea bass *au gratin* with shrimp sauce. ◗ *Sat; Sun lunch.* ▤ ♿	AE DC MC V	▪		▪
BAIXA: *Casa do Alentejo* ⓈⓈ Rua das Portas de Santo Antão 58. **Map 7 A2.** ☎ 21-346 92 31. Set in a fine 17th-century house, this restaurant specializes entirely in Alentejan food like *açorda alentejana* (coriander and bread soup). ◗ *Aug 1–19.*				
BAIXA: *Paris* ⓈⓈ Rua dos Sapateiros 126. **Map 7 B4.** ☎ 21-346 97 97. Open for nearly half a century, Paris offers a delicious mixture of Portuguese and Galician cuisine. Try the swordfish steak or the Alentejan pork. ▤ ♿	AE DC MC V			
BAIXA: *Lagosta Real* ⓈⓈ Rua das Portas de Santo Antão 37. **Map 7 A2.** ☎ 21-342 39 95. Fish, and particularly shellfish, is the order of the day here. Shellfish casserole, lobster stew, and a grilled seafood platter are house specialties. ▤ ♿	AE DC MC V	▪	●	
BAIXA: *Ribadouro* ⓈⓈⓈ Rua do Salitre 2–12. **Map 4 F1.** ☎ 21-354 94 11. Popular with the locals who flood in for a drink after work, this restaurant is part café and part bar and offers a tremendous shellfish menu. ▤	AE DC MC V	▪		▪
BAIXA: *Solar dos Presuntos* ⓈⓈⓈⓈ Rua das Portas de Santo Antão 150. **Map 7 A2.** ☎ 21-342 43 53. An enticing window display of fish and shellfish draws diners inside. Caricatures of famous soccer players adorn the walls. ◗ *Sun; 1 week in Jun; 1 week in Oct.* ▤	AE DC MC V	▪		
BAIXA: *Gambrinus* ⓈⓈⓈⓈⓈ Rua das Portas de Santo Antão 23–5. **Map 7 A2.** ☎ 21-342 14 66. Renowned throughout Portugal, this is an exceptional and expensive restaurant. The service is impeccable, the cuisine delectable, and the extensive wine list includes an array of vintage ports. ◗ *May 1.* ▤ ♿	AE DC MC V	▪		▪
BELÉM: *Ja Sei* ⓈⓈⓈ Avda Brasilia 22. **Map 1 C4.** ☎ 21-301 59 69. This has a beautiful location, right on the river, so it is particularly good in the summer; the seafood-based menu is good all-year-round.	AE DC MC V	▪		▪
BELÉM: *São Jerónimo* ⓈⓈⓈⓈ Rua dos Jerónimos 12. **Map 1 C4.** ☎ 21-364 87 97. São Jerónimo is an elegant, spacious restaurant with 1930s decor. The excellent mixed menu of Portuguese and French cuisine includes skate in peach sauce and duck with nuts in wine sauce. ◗ *Sat lunch; Sun.* ▤	AE DC MC V	▪		

For key to symbols see back flap

<table>
<tr><td>

Price categories are for a three-course meal for one with half a bottle of wine, including cover charge, service, and VAT:

$ under 2,000$00
$$ 2,000–3,000$00
$$$ 3,000–4,500$00
$$$$ 4,500–6,000$00
$$$$$ over 6,000$00.

</td><td>

LATE OPENING
The kitchen stays open after 10pm, and you can usually have a meal up until at least 11pm.

OUTDOOR TABLES
Tables for eating outdoors, in a garden, or on a balcony, often with a pleasant view.

GOOD WINE LIST
The restaurant will have a good selection of quality wines.

CREDIT CARDS
This indicates which of the major credit cards are accepted: *AE* American Express, *DC* Diners Club, *MC* MasterCard, and *V* VISA.

</td></tr>
</table>

	CREDIT CARDS	LATE OPENING	OUTDOOR TABLES	GOOD WINE LIST
BELÉM: *Vela Latina* $$$$ Doca do Bom Sucesso. **Map** 1 B5. 21-301 71 18. On the waterfront, this restaurant has a bar and terrace overlooking the Torre de Belém. The specialty is *cataplana rica do mar* (seafood). Sun.	AE DC MC V	■	●	■
BELÉM: *O Nobre* $$$$$ Rua das Mercês 71a–b. **Map** 2 D3. 21-362 21 06. Worth searching out on a day trip to Belém, O Nobre serves crab soup, game stew, partridge, fish with olives, and roast pork with grapes. Sat lunch; Sun.	AE MC V	■		■
CAMPO PEQUENO: *Chimarrão* $$$$ Campo Pequeno 79. **Map** 5 C1. 21-793 97 60. This Brazilian restaurant specializes in dishes grilled on an open fire. Try *rodízio* (unlimited amount of grilled meat) with salad, rice, and black beans.	AE DC MC V	■		■
CAMPO PEQUENO: *António Clara – Clube dos Empresários* $$$$$ Avenida da República 38. **Map** 5 C1. 21-796 63 80. This wonderful old mansion offers a French-influenced menu in dining areas that were once individual rooms in the house. Sun.	AE DC MC V	■		■
CHIADO: *Adega do Ribatejo* $$ Rue Diário de Noticias 23. **Map** 7 B5. 21-346 83 43 This charming tavern, whose menu is strong on steak and fried fish, offers frequent and unmissable fado extravaganzas. Sat lunch; Sun.	MC V	■		
CHIADO: *Tágide* $$$$$ Largo da Academia Nacional de Belas Artes 18–20. **Map** 7 B5. 21-342 07 20. An elegant restaurant with 18th-century tiles, a 17th-century fountain, and a superb view over the Tagus. Luxurious dishes include marinated salmon, baby octopus in red wine sauce, and partridge in port sauce. Sat lunch; Sun.	AE DC MC V	■		■
ENTRECAMPOS: *A Gondôla* $$$ Avenida de Berna 64. **Map** 5 B2. 21-797 04 26. A Gondôla is a charming restaurant offering a wide choice of dishes ranging from stuffed trout to roast pork and Italian specialties. In the summer enjoy your meal in the pleasant surrounding gardens. Sat, Sun.	MC V		●	
ESTEFÂNIA: *Espiral* $ Praça da Ilha do Faial 14a–b. **Map** 6 D3. 21-357 35 85. This vegetarian restaurant, set in a pleasant square, has a plain interior but a large menu, with fresh juice drinks and organic wine. Jan 1; May 1. Fri & Sat.	AE DC MC V			
ESTEFÂNIA: *Clara Restaurante* $$$$$ Campo dos Mártires da Pátria 49. **Map** 6 D5. 21-885 30 53. This is a spacious and luxurious restaurant in a green-tiled mansion, complete with garden terrace and a fountain. The excellent menu is predominantly French. Sat lunch; Sun; Aug 1–15.	AE DC MC V	■	●	■
ESTRELA: *Conventual* $$$$ Praça das Flores 45. **Map** 4 E2. 21-60 91 96. Decorated with religious antiques, this restaurant has an interesting menu that includes fried baby eels and ox tongue in egg sauce. Sat lunch; Sun.	AE DC MC V	■		■
GRAÇA: *Via Graça* $$$ Rua Damasceno Monteiro 9b. **Map** 8 D1. 21-887 08 30. Via Graça offers some fine views of the castle and the Baixa, and well-presented traditional Portuguese cuisine. Sat lunch; Sun.	AE DC MC V?	■		■
LAPA: *Café d'Arte* $ Rua das Janelas Verdes, Museu de Arte Antiga. **Map** 4 D4. 21-396 41 51. An excellent opportunity to combine lunch with a museum trip in this fantastic riverside setting. lunch (Jun–Aug); Mon; Tue.	MC V		●	

LAPA: *Picanha* $$$
Rua das Janelas Verdes 96. **Map 4 D4.** 21-397 54 01.
Picanha sells one dish: *picanha*, which is rump steak grilled on an open fire,
served with potatoes, rice, salad, and beans. ● *Sat; Sun lunch.* 🍽 ♿

LAPA: *Restaurante Virtual* $$$ AE MC DC V
Rua da Esperança 100. **Map 4 E3.** 21-397 64 51.
Located on a quiet street, this restaurant has great style. A relatively inexpensive
menu includes duck supreme, monkfish, and garlic shrimp. ● *Sat; Sun.* 🍽 ♿

LAPA: *Sua Excelência o Conde* $$$$ AE MC DC V
Rua do Conde 34. **Map 4 D3.** 21-390 36 14.
The owner here can recite the menu in five languages. Classical Portuguese
dishes served in a relaxed atmosphere. ● *Sat & Sun lunch; Wed; Sep.* 🍽 ♿

LAPA: *York House* $$$$ AE DC MC V
Rua das Janelas Verdes 32. **Map 4 D4.** 21-396 24 35.
This delightful hotel restaurant has a varied menu. Sit inside and admire
the tiled walls, or outside below a palm on the flower-laden terrace.

LAPA: *Embaixada Restaurant* $$$$$ AE DC MC V
Hotel da Lapa, Rua do Pau da Bandeira 4. **Map 3 C3.** 21-395 00 05.
This restaurant is as refined and classical as the hotel. It offers a lunch buffet
and Sunday brunch with a typical *cozido* (hearty meat casserole). 🍽 ♿

RATO: *Os Tibetanos* $$ AE MC V
Rua do Salitre 117. **Map 4 F1.** 21-314 20 38.
This vegetarian restaurant, in a Tibetan Buddhist center, has much character
and offers a tasty and inexpensive Tibetan menu. ● *Sun.* 🍽

RATO: *Casa da Comida* $$$$$ AE DC MC V
Travessa das Amoreiras 1. **Map 5 B5.** 21-388 53 76.
A refined Lisbon restaurant with a charming patio and an exquisite menu
offering caviar, frogs' legs, goat, duck, and pheasant. ● *Sat lunch; Sun.* 🍽 ♿

ROTUNDA: *Restaurante 33A* $$$$ AE DC MC V
Rua Alexandre Herculano 33. **Map 5 C5.** 21-354 60 79.
Offering traditional Portuguese cuisine, this restaurant also has a small lounge
with a country ambience and decor to match. ● *Sat lunch; Sun.* 🍽 🎵 ♿

ROTUNDA: *Pabe* $$$$$ AE DC MC V
Rua do Duque de Palmela 27a. **Map 5 C5.** 21-353 74 84.
Pabe looks like a Tudor house and specializes in grilled dishes. A medieval
atmosphere is accentuated by wooden-beamed ceilings and copper tables. 🍽 ♿

ROTUNDA: *O Terraço* $$$$$ AE DC MC V
Hotel Tivoli Lisboa, Avenida da Liberdade 185. **Map 4 F1.** 21-319 89 00.
This delightful restaurant serves an innovative lunchtime special each day
of the week. The dinner menu offers international dishes. 🍽 🎵 ♿

SALDANHA: *António* $$ V
Rua Tomás Ribeiro 63. **Map 5 C3.** 21-353 87 80.
This restaurant is a good stop for lunch. The cooking is straightforward
and includes steak and fries and roast chicken. ● *eve; Sun.* 🍽

OLAIAS: *Navegadores* $$$ AE DC MC V
Altis Park Hotel, Avenida Engenheiro Arantes e Oliveira. 21-846 08 66.
Northeast of the city center, Navegadores offers a terrific, reasonably priced
buffet. Choose from salads, smoked fish, and Portuguese specialties. 🍽 🎵 ♿

SALDANHA: *O Polícia* $$$ AE MC V
Rua Marquês Sá da Bandeira 112a. **Map 5 B3.** 21-796 35 05.
A pleasant restaurant with an attractive bar, so named because the owner's
father was a policeman. The menu changes daily. ● *Sat eve; Sun.* 🍽 🎵 ♿

SALDANHA: *Café Creme* $$$$ AE DC MC V
Avenida Conde de Valbom 52a. **Map 5 B2.** 21-796 43 60.
An attractive, open, and airy restaurant, Café Creme offers a wide choice of
pastas, salads, cod, beef, and grilled dishes. ● *Sat lunch; Sun.* 🍽 🎵 ♿

XABREGAS: *D'Avis* $$$ DC MC V
Rua do Grilo 98. 21-868 13 54.
Specialties at this restaurant, located east of the city center, include cod with
coriander and *migas* (bread dish with spareribs). ● *Sun; 2 weeks in Aug.* 🍽 ♿

For key to symbols see back flap

Price categories are for a three-course meal for one with half a bottle of wine, including cover charge, service, and VAT:

$ under 2,000$00
$$ 2,000–3,000$00
$$$ 3,000–4,500$00
$$$$ 4,500–6,000$00
$$$$$ over 6,000$00.

LATE OPENING
The kitchen stays open after 10pm, and you can usually have a meal up until at least 11pm.

OUTDOOR TABLES
Tables for eating outdoors, in a garden, or on a balcony, often with a pleasant view.

GOOD WINE LIST
The restaurant will have a good selection of quality wines.

CREDIT CARDS
This indicates which of the major credit cards are accepted: *AE* American Express, *DC* Diners Club, *MC* MasterCard, and *V* VISA.

	CREDIT CARDS	LATE OPENING	OUTDOOR TABLES	GOOD WINE LIST
THE LISBON COAST				
CASCAIS: *Dom Manolo* $ Avenida Marginal 11. **Road map** B5. 21-483 11 26. A good-value mixed menu; the house specialty is *frango no churrasco* (spit-roast chicken). *Pastéis de bacalhau* (cod croquettes) are also good. ● *Jan.* ▤		■	●	
CASCAIS: *O Dragão* $$ Rua Frederico Arouca 72. **Road map** B5. 21-486 86 31. This Chinese restaurant offers chicken with almonds, beef chop suey, and sweet-and-sour pork. Glass doors overlook the beach. ● *Mon; 2 weeks in Nov.* ▤	AE DC MC V			
CASCAIS: *Estrela da India* $$ Rua Freitas Reis 15b. **Road map** B5. 21-484 65 40. Some distance from the waterfront, this unpretentious Indian restaurant has a good choice of vegetarian dishes and a take-out service. ● *Mon.* ▤	AE MC V		●	
CASCAIS: *Casa Velha* $$$ Avenida Valbom 1. **Road map** B5. 21-483 25 86. With a regional menu and decor that includes a boat in the dining room, Casa Velha also boasts a table always reserved for the president. ● *Wed.* ▤ ♿	AE DC MC V	■	●	■
CASCAIS: *Novomar* $$$ Beco Torto 1. **Road map** B5. 21-484 42 96. A wide range of fish and shellfish dishes. Watch for the house specialties, both for two people: *cataplana à moda de Cascais* (fish and shellfish steamed in their own juice) and *caldeirada à Novomar* (fresh fish stew). ● *Wed (Oct–Mar).* ▤	AE DC MC V	■	●	■
CASCAIS: *Reijos* $$$ Rua Frederico Arouca 35. **Road map** B5. 21-483 03 11. Located on a busy shopping street, Reijos offers a good selection of grilled fish and shellfish. Also worth trying are the baked Virginia ham, the roast beef, and the spareribs with mushrooms and cream. ● *Sun; Dec.* ▤	AE DC MC V	■	●	■
CASCAIS: *Eduardo's* $$$$ Largo das Grutas 3. **Road map** B5. 21-483 19 01. Tucked away in a quiet corner, Eduardo's serves a mix of Belgian cuisine and Portuguese dishes, many of which are flambéed at the table. ● *Wed.*	AE MC V	■	●	■
CASCAIS: *O Pescador* $$$$$ Rua das Flores 10b. **Road map** B5. 21-484 60 37. A well known seaside restaurant, decorated with old boats, nets, and pictures of famous people who have eaten here. Specializes in seafood. ● *Sun.* ▤	AE MC V	■	●	■
ERICEIRA: *O Barco* $$$ Rua Capitão João Lopes 14. **Road map** B5. 261-86 27 59. O Barco has excellent ocean views. The fish specialties include *feijoada de marisco* (seafood and bean stew) and seafood curry. ● *Thu; Dec.* ▤	AE MC V			■
ESTORIL: *Pinto's* $$ Arcadas do Parque 18b. **Road map** B5. 21-468 72 47. Close to the Palácio Hotel, Pinto's is a mix of bar, cafeteria, and restaurant. It serves pizzas and pastas, as well as a large selection of shellfish. ▤	AE DC MC V	■	●	
ESTORIL: *Four Seasons* $$$$$ Hotel Palácio Estoril, Rua do Parque. **Road map** B5. 21-468 04 00. Exposed beams and leather seats furnish this luxurious restaurant. Try the flambéed shrimp with Pernod, cream, and hollandaise sauce. ▤ ♫ ♿	AE DC MC V			■
GUINCHO: *Estalagem Muchaxo* $$$$ Praia do Guincho. **Road map** B5. 21-487 02 21. Overlooking Cabo da Roca, Muchaxo offers an extensive seafood menu. A popular dish is lobster in a tomato, cream, and port sauce. ▤ ♫ *Sat & Sun.* ♿	AE DC MC V			■

GUINCHO: *Porto de Santa Maria* $$$$
Estrada do Guincho. **Road map** B5. (21-487 02 40.
This is one of the best seafood restaurants in the area. Choose your meal from
the fish tanks and marble table where the best fish is displayed. ● *Mon.* 目 &
AE MC DC V

MONTE ESTORIL: *O Sinaleiro* $
Avenida de Sabóia 595. **Road map** B5. (21-468 54 39.
O Sinaleiro serves excellent food and is popular with locals. Try *escalopes à
Zíngara* (in Madeira wine sauce with cream). ● *Wed; 2 weeks in Apr & Oct.* &
AE MC V

MONTE ESTORIL: *O Festival* $$$$
Avenida de Sabóia 515d. **Road map** B5. (21-468 85 63.
This delightful restaurant serves traditional dishes with interesting touches.
Try the duck à l'orange or the seafood casserole. ● *Mon; Tue lunch; Jan.* 目 &
MC V

PAÇO D'ARCOS: *La Cocagne* $$$$
Avenida Marginal (Curva dos Pinheiros). **Road map** B5. (21-441 42 31.
One of the best French restaurants in Portugal, La Cocagne has refined decor,
impeccable service, exquisite dishes, and magnificent views of the ocean. 目 &
AE DC MC V

PALMELA: *Pousada de Palmela* $$$
Pousada de Palmela, Castelo de Palmela. **Road map** C5. (21-235 12 26.
The converted refectory of the 15th-century monastery offers such delicacies as
trout stuffed with smoked ham and pears in Muscatel wine. 目 ♫ *Fri & Sat.* &
AE DC MC V

PORTINHO DA ARRÁBIDA: *Beira-Mar* $$$
Portinho da Arrábida. **Road map** C5. (21-218 05 44.
Enjoy specials like *arroz de tamboril* (monkfish rice) and *arroz de marisco*
(seafood rice) in this stunning seaside setting. ● *Wed (Oct–Mar); Dec 15–Jan 15.* &
AE DC MC V

QUELUZ: *Cozinha Velha* $$$$$
Largo Palácio Nacional de Queluz. **Road map** B5. (21-435 07 40.
Set in the old kitchens of the Queluz Royal Palace, this spacious restaurant is
famous for its typical Portuguese fare, like pork with clams. 目 ♫ &
AE DC MC V

SESIMBRA: *Ribamar* $$
Avenida dos Náufragos 29. **Road map** C5. (21-223 48 53.
Right next to the sea and offering fantastic views, Ribamar serves some
unusual specialties; try fish with seaweed, or cream of sea-urchin soup. 目 &
AE MC V

SETÚBAL: *Copa d'Ouro* $$
Rua João Soveral 12. **Road map** C5. (265-52 37 55.
A superb fish menu here features *caldeirada à Setubalense* (seafood stew)
and *cataplana de cherne* (stone bass steamed in its own juice). ● *Tue; Sep.* 目
AE MC V

SETÚBAL: *Pousada de São Filipe* $$$
Pousada de São Filipe, Castelo de São Filipe. **Road map** C5. (265-52 38 44.
This restaurant is part of a *pousada* that overlooks Setúbal and the Sado estuary.
Its regional dishes include pumpkin cream soup and aromatic pork loin. 目
AE DC MC V

SINTRA: *Tulhas Bar* $$
Rua Gil Vicente 4–6. **Road map** B5. (21-923 23 78.
This rustic restaurant, decorated with blue and yellow Sintra *azulejos*, serves
superb traditional dishes like veal steaks in Madeira sauce. ● *Wed.* 目
AE DC MC V

SINTRA: *Solar de São Pedro* $$$
Praça Dom Fernando II 12, São Pedro de Sintra. **Road map** B5. (21-923 18 60.
French and Portuguese specialties, like lobster crepes and *açorda de marisco* (a
seafood bread dish), are served in this marketplace restaurant. ● *Wed.* 目 &
AE MC V

SINTRA: *Panorâmico* $$$$
Hotel Tivoli Sintra, Praça da República. **Road map** B5. (21-923 35 05.
Overlooking the lush, verdant Sintra valley, this restaurant offers a different
specialty as a main dish each evening, as well as a regular menu. 目 &
AE DC MC V

SINTRA: *Restaurante Palácio de Seteais* $$$$$
Avenida Barbosa du Bocage 8, Seteais. **Road map** B5. (21-923 32 00.
Set in an 18th-century palace that is now a hotel, this restaurant has a daily-
changing menu of international and traditional Portuguese cuisine. 目 ♫ &
AE DC MC V

VILA FRESCA DE AZEITÃO: *O Manel* $$
Largo Dr Teixeira 6a. **Road map** C5. (21-219 03 36.
A family-run restaurant with a good-value menu. Specialties here are cod in
cream sauce and *feijoada de gambas* (seafood and bean stew). ● *Sun; Oct.* 目
MC V

<table>
<tr><td>

Price categories are for a three-course meal for one with half a bottle of wine, including cover charge, service, and VAT:

$ under 2,000$00
$$ 2,000–3,000$00
$$$ 3,000–4,500$00
$$$$ 4,500–6,000$00
$$$$$ over 6,000$00.

</td><td>

LATE OPENING
The kitchen stays open after 10pm, and you can usually have a meal up until at least 11pm.
OUTDOOR TABLES
Tables for eating outdoors, in a garden, or on a balcony, often with a pleasant view.
GOOD WINE LIST
The restaurant will have a good selection of quality wines.
CREDIT CARDS
This indicates which of the major credit cards are accepted: *AE* American Express, *DC* Diners Club, *MC* MasterCard, and *V* VISA.

</td></tr>
</table>

	CREDIT CARDS	LATE OPENING	OUTDOOR TABLES	GOOD WINE LIST
ESTREMADURA AND RIBATEJO				
ABRANTES: *O Pelicano* $$ Rua Nossa Senhora da Conceição 1. **Road map** C4. 241-223 17. Situated on the busy main square, O Pelicano serves bargain regional food like *migas com entrecosto* (bread dish with spareribs).	MC V	■	●	■
ALCOBAÇA: *Trindade* $$ Praça Dom Afonso Henriques 22. **Road map** C4. 262-58 23 97. Located in a beautiful square next to the north wing of the monastery. Specials are *sole au meunier* and *frango na púcara* (chicken stew). ● *3 weeks in Nov.*	AE MC V	■	●	■
ALMEIRIM: *Toucinho* $$ Rua Timor 20. **Road map** C4. 243-522 37. A family-run restaurant with a reputation for fine country cooking. Try the home-made bread and the real *sopa de pedra (see p146).* ● *Thu; Aug.* ▤ ♿				
BARRAGEM DO CASTELO DE BODE: *São Pedro* $$$ Pousada de São Pedro. **Road map** C4. 249-38 11 59. In a *pousada* dating from the 1950s, this restaurant has a regional menu that includes fried trout and almonds and braised kid with white bean stew. ▤	AE DC MC V			■
BATALHA: *Mestre Afonso Domingues* $$$$ Largo Mestre Afonso Domingues. **Road map** C4. 244-76 52 60. This restaurant, found in the *pousada* named after the architect of the nearby monastery, serves such regional dishes as fried pork with turnip tops. ▤	AE DC MC V		●	■
CALDAS DA RAINHA: *Pateo da Rainha* $$ Rua Camões 39. **Road map** B4. 262-356 58. Situated on the main road, this restaurant is lined with wood and leather, and offers grilled meat and steaks, fresh fish, and monkfish rice. ● *Mon.* ▤	AE DC MC V	■		■
CALDAS DA RAINHA: *A Lareira* $$$ Rua da Lareira, Alto do Nobre. **Road map** B4. 262-234 32. Located in a pine wood, A Lareira offers typical traditional Portuguese food like *ensopado de enguias* (eel stew), *perdiz à Lareira* (partridge with chestnuts, fruits, and vegetables), and homemade desserts. ▤ ♿	MC V	■		
FÁTIMA: *Dom Gonçalo* $$$ Rua Jacinta Marto 100. **Road map** C4. 249-53 93 30. Set in a charming hotel surrounded by its own grounds, not far from the sanctuary. Try the fillet of fish with shrimp rice or the roast suckling pig. ▤ ♿	AE DC MC V			■
FÁTIMA: *Tia Alice* $$$$ Rua do Adro. **Road map** C4. 249-53 17 37. One of the best restaurants in the area. The service is excellent and house specialties are Trás-os-Montes-style rice and duck rice. ● *Mon; Sun eve; Jul.* ▤	AE MC V			■
LEIRIA: *Tromba Rija* $$$$$ Rua Professores Portelas 22, Marrazes. **Road map** C4. 244-85 50 72. Well known thoughout Portugal, this excellent restaurant serves particularly good appetizers. Other dishes include *ovos verdes* (a specialty egg dish), and the famous stone soup (in winter). ● *Mon lunch; Sun; Aug 8–31.* ♪ *Fri & Sat.*	AE MC DC V	■		■
NAZARÉ: *Beira-Mar* $$ Avenida da República 40. **Road map** C4. 262-56 13 58. Beira-Mar has a delightful seafront setting. House specialties include *parrilhada de mariscos* (grilled seafood with garlic, butter, and lemon). ● *Dec–Feb.* ♿	AE DC MC V		●	
ÓBIDOS: *O Alcaide* $$ Rua Direita. **Road map** B4. 262-95 92 20. Try *coelho à Alcaide* (rabbit stew) or *bacalhau à Alcaide* (cod with potatoes and olive oil) at this rustic restaurant with panoramic views of the town. ● *Mon; Nov.*	AE DC MC V		●	■

ÓBIDOS: *Castelo* $$$$ AE DC MC V
Paço Real. **Road map** B4. (262-95 91 05.
Located in the *pousada*, which is part of the fairy-tale medieval castle,
Castelo serves such regional delights as asparagus with smoked ham,
cabrito (braised kid) and *trouxas de ovos* (egg and sugar rolls). ▤

PENICHE: *Estelas* $$$$ AE MC V
Rua Arquitecto Paulino Montês 21. **Road map** B4. (062–78 24 35.
Estelas has a large seafood menu and a selection of meat dishes. Try octopus
salad, seafood rice, or a monkfish kebab. ● *Wed; 2 weeks in Sep.* ▤ ⟁

PENICHE: *Marisqueira Cortiçais* $$$$ AE DC MC V
Porto d'Areia Sul. **Road map** B4. (262-78 72 62.
Popular with locals, this rustic restaurant overlooks the beach and specializes
in seafood and shellfish dishes. ● *Wed (Sep–Jun); 2 weeks in Sep.* ♫ ⟁

SANTARÉM: *Central* $$ AE MC V
Rua Guilherme de Azevedo 32. **Road map** C4. (243-223 03.
This Art Deco restaurant has been open since 1933 and is popular with
locals. Try the delicious *bife à Central* (steak in mustard sauce). ● *Sun.* ▤

SANTARÉM: *Mal Cozinhado* $$ AE DC MC V
Campo Emílio Infante da Câmara. **Road map** C4. (243-235 84.
Do not be put off by the name, Mal Cozinhado (badly cooked). Dishes include
bacalhau com magusto (baked cod with green broth). ● *Sun (Jul–Aug).* ▤

SÃO MARTINHO DO PORTO: *A Casa* $$$ AE DC MC V
Avenida Marginal, Casa Azul. **Road map** B4. (262-98 96 33.
Located at a pretty seaside resort with stunning views of the bay, this
charming restaurant specializes in seafood and shellfish dishes. ▤

TOMAR: *A Bela Vista* $$
Fonte do Choupo 3–6. **Road map** C4. (249-31 28 70.
A Bela Vista offers beautiful views of the river and castle, and excellent regional
specialties like roast kid and *caldeirada* (fish stew). ● *Mon eve; Tue; Nov.*

TOMAR: *Calça Perra* $$$ MC V
Rua Pedro Dias 59. **Road map** C4. (249-32 16 16.
This is a charming restaurant in the gardens of a 16th-century house in the
historic part of town. Specialties are grilled steak and duck with rice. ● *Tue.* ▤

TORRES VEDRAS: *O Pátio do Faustino* $
Largo do Choupal. **Road map** B5. (261-32 43 46.
This rustic restaurant specializes in grilled fish. Decorated with antiques
and Roman-style amphorae, it has a pleasant atmosphere. ● *Sun eve.* ▤

VILA FRANCA DE XIRA: *O Redondel* $$$ AE DC MC V
Praça de Touros Palha Blanco. **Road map** C5. (263-229 73.
The high, curved ceiling of this 100-year-old house lends an elegance to the
restaurant. Traditional Ribatejo dishes like *açorda de sável* (bread and shad fish
soup) are served. Arrange in advance for vegetarian meals. ● *Mon.* ⟁

THE BEIRAS

ALMEIDA: *A Tertúlia* $
Bairro de São Pedro. **Road map** E2. (271-57 42 84.
Located on the main road, this delightful restaurant's specialties include
bacalhau à Tertúlia (cod with potatoes and onion) and roast kid. ● *Fri.* ▤

ALMEIDA: *Senhora das Neves* $$$ AE DC MC V
Pousada da Senhora das Neves. **Road map** E2. (271-57 42 83.
This new restaurant, in the *pousada* inside Almeida's star-shaped fort,
serves dishes like grilled cod in olive oil and braised kid. ▤

AVEIRO: *Marisqueira O Mercantel* $$ AE MC V
Rua António Santos Lé 16. **Road map** C3. (234-280 57.
Offering romantic views of the canal, this restaurant serves specialty seafood
and shellfish dishes. A good meat selection is also available. ● *Mon.*

AVEIRO: *Cozinha do Rei* $$$ MC V
Rua Doutor Manuel Neves 66. **Road map** C3. (234-268 02.
The Cozinha do Rei, one of the best restaurants in Aveiro, is often rented out
for functions, so check availability in advance. Dishes include seafood salad,
roast sea bass, and *ovos moles de Aveiro* (egg and sugar dessert). ▤

For key to symbols see back flap

Price categories are for a three-course meal for one with half a bottle of wine, including cover charge, service, and VAT:

$ under 2,000$00
$$ 2,000–3,000$00
$$$ 3,000–4,500$00
$$$$ 4,500–6,000$00
$$$$$ over 6,000$00.

LATE OPENING
The kitchen stays open after 10pm, and you can usually have a meal up until at least 11pm.

OUTDOOR TABLES
Tables for eating outdoors, in a garden, or on a balcony, often with a pleasant view.

GOOD WINE LIST
The restaurant will have a good selection of quality wines.

CREDIT CARDS
This indicates which of the major credit cards are accepted: *AE* American Express, *DC* Diners Club, *MC* MasterCard, and *V* VISA.

	CREDIT CARDS	LATE OPENING	OUTDOOR TABLES	GOOD WINE LIST
BELMONTE: *Belsol* $$ Quinta do Rio, off N18. **Road map** D3. 275-91 22 06. Situated near the Zêzere river, the pleasant restaurant of the Belsol hotel serves trout fresh from local streams.	DC MC V			
BUÇACO: *Palace Hotel do Buçaco* $$$$$ Palace Hotel do Buçaco. **Road map** C3. 231-93 01 02. The dining room here is a Manueline fantasy, and the intricately carved balcony is unique (*see p210*). Dishes include cod *au gratin* with cream and roast suckling pig from Bairrada. Buçaco's acclaimed wines are bottled in the basement.	AE DC MC V		●	■
CARAMULO: *São Jerónimo* $$ Pousada de São Jerónimo, N230. **Road map** C3. 232-86 12 91. Found in a small *pousada* south of Caramulo, one of Portugal's leading health spas, São Jerónimo offers hearty fare like kid stew and grilled octopus.	AE DC MC V			■
CASTELO BRANCO: *Praça Velha* $$$$ Praça Luís de Camões 17. **Road map** D4. 272-32 86 40. Situated in the old part of town, in an old granary transformed by architects and interior designers, Praça Velha offers ambitious cuisine that combines traditional methods and modern creativity in fish and meat dishes. ● *Mon.*	AE DC MC V		●	■
COIMBRA: *Adega Paço do Conde* $ Rua Paço do Conde 1. **Road map** C3. 239-82 56 05. This bargain restaurant is full of character. Almost everything – meat, chicken, fish, and squid – is barbecued on skewers on a large open grill. ● *Sun.*	DC MC V		●	
COIMBRA: *Democrática* $ Travessa Rua Nova 5. **Road map** C3. 239-82 37 84. Hard to find, but worth the effort. The back room has long benches and is a favorite hangout for university students. The house specialty is *arroz de polvo* (octopus rice). Food is served as long as there are customers. ● *Sun.*	AE DC MC V	■		
COIMBRA: *L'Amphitryon* $$$ Avenida Emídio Navarro 21. **Road map** C3. 239-82 20 55. Set in the fine circular dining room of the Astória hotel amid 1920s decor, L'Amphitryon serves traditional French and Portuguese specialties.	AE DC MC V	■	●	■
COIMBRA: *O Trovador* $$$ Largo da Sé Velha 15–17. **Road map** C3. 239-82 54 75. This rustic restaurant, set in the historic part of the town, offers excellent regional dishes like *chanfana* (kid stew in wine sauce). ● *Sun.*	MC V	■		■
CONDEIXA-A-NOVA: *Santa Cristina* $$$ Rua Francisco de Lemos. **Road map** C3. 239-94 40 25. A modern restaurant, aptly set in a modern *pousada* close to the famous ruins of Conimbriga. Regional specialties include braised kid with turnip tops, cuttlefish and bean stew, and roast chicken with pepper sauce.	AE DC MC V		●	■
GUARDA: *O Telheiro* $$$ N16. **Road map** D3. 271-21 13 56. Set in parkland 1.5 km (1 mile) north of Guarda, O Telheiro specializes in Portuguese grilled dishes, which are reputedly the best meals in the area.	AE DC MC V		●	■
LUSO: *O Cesteiro* $ Rua José Duarte Figueiredo. **Road map** C3. 231-93 93 60. In an attractive setting with pleasant decor, this rustic restaurant serves regional specialties like *chanfana* (kid stew in wine), suckling pig, and cod.	MC V		●	■
MANTEIGAS: *São Lourenço* $$$ N232, Penhas Douradas. **Road map** D3. 275-98 24 50. Set in a *pousada* high in the Serra da Estrela, north of Manteigas, it specializes in local dishes like red bean and cabbage soup and trout in onion marinade.	AE DC MC V			■

MEALHADA: *Pedro dos Leitões* $$$ AE MC V
N1, Sernadelo. **Road map** C3. 231-220 62.
A handy stop for travelers. The specialty here is delicious *leitão* (roast suckling pig) cooked in a wood-burning oven and served with fries. ● *Mon.*

MONSANTO: *Monsanto* $$$ AE DC MC V
Pousada de Monsanto, Rua da Igreja. **Road map** E3. 277-31 44 71.
In a well-preserved village, this traditional restaurant serves regional dishes like fava bean and coriander soup, squid stew, and rabbit with rice.

MONTEMOR-O-VELHO: *Ramalhão* $$$ MC V
Rua Tenente Valadim 24. **Road map** C3. 239-68 94 35.
Dine in a 16th-century manor house surrounded by antiques, and try such local specialties as *ensopado de enguias* (eel stew). ● *Sun eve, Mon; Oct.*

OLIVEIRA DO HOSPITAL: *Pousada Santa Bárbara* $$$ AE DC MC V
Pousada de Santa Bárbara, Póvoa das Quartas. **Road map** D3. 238-595 51.
This restaurant is located in a rustic mountainside *pousada* that looks out over the Serra da Estrela. Regional dishes include roast trout.

TRANCOSO: *O Museu* $$
Largo de Santa Maria. **Road map** D2. 271-81 18 10.
This elegant, stone-walled restaurant is in the old part of town within the castle walls. The roast kid is very popular. ● *Mon; Sep 15–30.*

VISEU: *Casablanca* $$ AE DC MC V
Avenida Emídio Navarro 70–72. **Road map** D3. 232-42 22 39.
Situated in the historic city center, Casablanca is simply decorated with pretty tiles, and serves a variety of fresh fish and seafood as its specialties. ● *Mon.*

VISEU: *Churrascaria Santa Eulália* $$$ AE DC MC V
N2, Repeses. **Road map** D3. 232-262 83.
South of Viseu, Santa Eulália is a bright, spacious restaurant with a seafood-based menu. Try the fish kebab or the *feijoada de marisco* (beans and seafood).

VISEU: *O Cortiço* $$$ AE DC MC V
Rua Augusto Hilário 47. **Road map** D3. 232-42 38 53.
This is a stone-walled restaurant in the center of town. The extensive and sometimes comic menu offers traditional Portuguese dishes, the specialty being *bacalhau podre apodrecido na adega* (rotten cod from the cellar!).

DOURO AND TRÁS-OS-MONTES

ALIJÓ: *Barão de Forrester* $$$ AE DC MC V
Rua José Ruffino. **Road map** D2. 259-95 94 67.
This charming restaurant, in a *pousada* deep in port wine country, has a regional menu that includes Spanish bream and pears with Muscatel wine.

AMARANTE: *O Almirante* $$ AE MC V
Rua António Carneiro. **Road map** D2. 255-43 25 66.
O Almirante combines excellent food with a warm and friendly atmosphere. The house specialties are hake *au gratin* and pork with mushrooms.

AMARANTE: *São Gonçalo* $$$ AE DC MC V
Pousada de São Gonçalo, Ansiães. **Road map** D2. 255-46 11 13.
Northeast of Amarante, São Gonçalo boasts a spectacular view down a long, deep valley, especially at sunset. On the menu are traditional dishes like trout stuffed with ham and pork with chestnuts, as well as some enticing desserts.

AMARANTE: *Zé da Calçada* $$$
Rua 31 de Janeiro. **Road map** D2. 255-42 20 23.
The house specialty here is *bacalhau à Zé da Calçada* (baked cod with mashed potatoes). Also enjoy splendid views of the Tâmega River. ● *Dec 24.*

BRAGANÇA: *Solar Bragançano* $$ AE DC MC V
Praça da Sé 34. **Road map** E1. 273-238 75.
A well-furnished restaurant, Solar Bragançano is housed in an old mansion overlooking the main square. Try the game dishes, like *perdiz com uvas* (partridge with grapes) or *faisão com castanhas* (pheasant with chestnuts).

CHAVES: *Leonel* $$ MC V
Campo da Roda. **Road map** D1. 276-33 31 88.
Popular with the locals, this plainly decorated restaurant offers superbly prepared food. Try baked cod or grilled spareribs. ● *Mon; 2 weeks in Jul; 2 weeks in Nov.*

Price categories are for a three-course meal for one with half a bottle of wine, including cover charge, service, and VAT:
$ under 2,000$00
$$ 2,000–3,000$00
$$$ 3,000–4,500$00
$$$$ 4,500–6,000$00
$$$$$ over 6,000$00.

LATE OPENING
The kitchen stays open after 10pm, and you can usually have a meal up until at least 11pm.

OUTDOOR TABLES
Tables for eating outdoors, in a garden, or on a balcony, often with a pleasant view.

GOOD WINE LIST
The restaurant will have a good selection of quality wines.

CREDIT CARDS
This indicates which of the major credit cards are accepted: *AE* American Express, *DC* Diners Club, *MC* MasterCard, and *V* VISA.

	Credit Cards	Late Opening	Outdoor Tables	Good Wine List
CHAVES: *Carvalho* $$$ Alameda Tabolado, Bloco 4. **Road map** D1. ☎ *276-33 17 27.* Enjoy fine views from this pretty, two-room restaurant with a charming garden. Try the roast kid or *arroz de fumeiro* (rice with smoked meats). ● *Thu.* ▤ ♿	*AE DC MC V*			■
CINFÃES: *Varanda de Cinfães* $$ Rua General Humberto Delgado 20–22. **Road map** D2. ☎ *255-56 12 36.* This cozy informal restaurant serves traditional Portuguese cuisine and is popular with locals. The house specialties are roast lamb and baked cod. ● *Sat (Jan–Mar).*				
ESPINHO: *Terraço Atlântico* $$$ Praia Golfe Hotel, Rua 6. **Road map** C2. ☎ *22-731 33 85.* Few restaurants have such a wonderful panoramic ocean view as this one. Fish dishes are prominent on the menu, although the meats are not forgotten, and there are both red and white wines from every region of Portugal. ▤	*AE DC MC V*			■
GIMONDE: *Dom Roberto* $$$ N218. **Road map** D2. ☎ *273-38 13 02.* This rustic, stone-walled restaurant is located on the riverside in the small town of Gimonde, 7 km (4 miles) east of Bragança. People come from far and wide to try the excellent game dishes and the roast kid. ▤ ♿	*AE DC MC V*	■	●	■
LAMEGO: *O Tonel* $ Estrada de Arneirós. **Road map** D2. ☎ *254-621 61.* A friendly restaurant popular with locals, O Tonel offers good-value Portuguese cuisine, including baked cod and *espetadas* (meat kebabs). ● *Mon; Aug 1–15.*				
LAMEGO: *Restaurante Turisserra* $$$$ Complexo Turístico Turissera, Serra das Meadas. **Road map** D2. ☎ *254-65 61 98.* This charming three-room restaurant, set in the tourist village 6 km (4 miles) north of Lamego, serves excellent traditional Portuguese fare. Enjoy the beautiful views of the Douro and surrounding hills.	*AE DC MC V*			■
LEÇA DA PALMEIRA: *O Chanquinhas* $$$ Rua de Santana 243. **Road map** C2. ☎ *22-995 18 84.* The restaurant is set in a large mansion with elegant dining rooms warmed by a cozy fireplace. The fish and desserts are excellent. ● *Sun; 2 weeks in Aug.* ▤	*AE DC MC V*	■	●	■
LEÇA DA PALMEIRA: *Boa Nova* $$$$ Praia Leça da Palmeira. **Road map** C2. ☎ *22-995 17 85.* This modern restaurant overlooking the sea was built by one of Portugal's most famous architects, Siza Vieira. Try the baked sole or sea bass. ● *Sun.* ▤	*AE DC MC V*	■		■
MIRANDA DO DOURO: *Balbina* $ Rua Rainha Dona Catarina 12. **Road map** E1. ☎ *273-43 23 94.* Well known politicians sit with locals and Spanish vacationers to enjoy traditionally cooked regional cuisine like *bife à Mirandesa* (steak).		■		■
MIRANDA DO DOURO: *Buteko* $ Largo Dom João III. **Road map** E1. ☎ *273-43 12 31.* Set in the historic center of town, Buteko's specialties include *posta Mirandesa* (veal) and *bacalhau à Buteko* (cod in the house style). ● *Sun; 2 weeks in Jan.* ▤	*AE MC V*			
MURÇA: *Miradouro* $$ Pensão Miradouro, Curvas de Murça. **Road map** D2. ☎ *259-51 24 61.* The small, handwritten menu in this plain restaurant changes daily. Dishes include cod Miradouro, kid, and roast suckling pig. ● *Tue; Sep 15–30.* ▤ ♿	*MC V*		●	
OPORTO: *Cardápio* $$ Rua Comércio do Porto 197. **Road map** C2. ☎ *22-208 84 53.* Cardápio, around the corner from the Bolsa (stock exchange), is a bright spot in an unassuming street. Try the *bacalhau com gambas* (cod with shrimp), *arroz de pato* (duck rice), or *bife de pimenta* (peppered steak). ● *Sat & Sun lunch; Mon.*	*AE DC MC V*	■		

OPORTO: *Bule* $$ Rua de Timor 128. **Road map** C2. ☎ *22-617 93 76.* Bule has charming views of a garden sloping down to the ocean, and a mouth-watering self-service table of hors d'oeuvres. ● *Sun; first 2 weeks in Aug.* ▤ ♿	MC V	■	●	
OPORTO: *Tripeiro* $$ Rua de Passos Manuel 195. **Road map** C2. ☎ *22-200 58 86.* Tripeiro – meaning "tripe eater" – is the name for a native of Oporto as well as this famous tripe-serving restaurant. Seafood is also available. ● *Sun.* ▤ ♿	AE DC MC V			
OPORTO: *Adega Vila Meã* $$$ Rua dos Caldeireiros 62. **Road map** C2. ☎ *22-208 29 67.* This busy, family-run restaurant serves daily specials, as well as traditional favorites like baked octopus and roast kid. ● *Sun; 3 weeks in Aug.*				
OPORTO: *Casa Aleixo* $$$ Rua da Estação 216. **Road map** C2. ☎ *22-537 04 62.* Run by the same family since 1948, this friendly restaurant offers excellent value. Traditional dishes in hefty portions include octopus and veal. ● *Sun; Aug.* ▤	AE MC V			
OPORTO: *Chez Lapin* $$$ Rua dos Canastreiros 42. **Road map** C2. ☎ *22-200 64 18.* Beams, stone walls, and numerous antiques give Chez Lapin a rustic feel. The menu features fish and shellfish, plus a different Portuguese special each day. ▤	AE DC MC V	■	●	
OPORTO: *Dom Tonho* $$$ Cais da Ribeira 13–15. **Road map** C2. ☎ *22-200 43 07.* This is one of many restaurants on the historic dockside, in the shadow of the Dom Luís bridge. The menu has a selection of modern Portuguese dishes. ▤ ♿	AE DC MC V	■		■
OPORTO: *Mercearia* $$$ Cais da Ribeira 32. **Road map** C2. ☎ *22-200 43 89.* Very modern, with excellent Portuguese cuisine, Mercearia is set on two floors and has good service, a pleasant atmosphere, and a daily special. ▤	AE DC MC V	■		■
OPORTO: *Taverna do Bebobos* $$$ Cais da Ribeira 21–5. **Road map** C2. ☎ *22-205 35 65.* Located right on the Ribeira waterfront, this restaurant has a real tavern atmosphere and delicious food, especially the octopus rice. ● *Mon; Dec 20–Jan 10.*	MC V	■		
OPORTO: *Dom Manoel* $$$$ Avenida Montevideu 384. **Road map** C2. ☎ *22-617 23 04.* Set in a mansion with views of the Atlantic, Dom Manoel offers *parrilhada mista* (fish and shellfish mixed grill) as the house special. ● *Sun; Aug 8–24.* ▤ ♿	AE DC MC V	■	●	■
OPORTO: *Portucale* $$$$$ Albergaria Miradouro, Rua da Alegria 598. **Road map** C2. ☎ *22-537 07 17.* This is one of the most famous restaurants in the country. It has a wide array of meat, fish, and game dishes, and spectacular views of the area. ▤ ♿	AE DC MC V			■
PESO DA RÉGUA: *Varanda da Régua* $$ Lugar da Boavista, Loureiro. **Road map** D2. ☎ *254-33 69 49.* Enjoy panoramic views from this friendly, family-run place just north of Régua. The menu offers superb Portuguese cuisine like roast kid and baked cod. ▤	MC V			
ROMEU: *Maria Rita* $$ Rua da Capela. **Road map** E1. ☎ *278-931 34.* This homey restaurant in a town house has rustic furniture and stone fireplaces. Try the spicy sausage soup or the stewed duck with rice. ● *Mon; Wed eve.* ▤	MC V			
SENDIM: *Gabriela* $$$ Largo da Praça 27. **Road map** E2. ☎ *273-731 80.* Gabriela boasts a famous chef called Alice, who has appeared on Portuguese TV. The restaurant is attractively furnished with wooden panels and an open fire. ▤				■
TORRE DE MONCORVO: *O Artur* $$ O Lugar do Rebentão, Carviçais. **Road map** E2. ☎ *279-931 84.* Dishes at this charming, friendly restaurant situated just outside Torre include *posta Mirandesa* (thick grilled veal steak), baked cod, and roast kid. ▤	AE MC V	■		
VILA NOVA DE GAIA: *Boucinha* $$$ Avenida Vasco da Gama, Oliveira do Douro. **Road map** C2. ☎ *22-782 77 64.* Set in the stylish surroundings of an old *quinta*, this is an excellent restaurant. Try the *cherne grelhado* (grilled stone bass) with a local wine. ● *Mon.* ▤	AE DC MC V		●	

For key to symbols see back flap

	CREDIT CARDS	LATE OPENING	OUTDOOR TABLES	GOOD WINE LIST
VILA REAL: *Espadeiro* $$ Avenida Almeida Lucena. **Road map** D2. 259-32 23 02. Espadeiro offers superbly prepared regional dishes and local wines. House specials are *cabrito* (roast kid), cod Espadeiro, and roast leg of pork. ● *Wed.* ▤	AE DC MC V		●	
VILA REAL: *Cozinha do Vale* $$$ Casa de Campeã, Torgueda. **Road map** D2. 259-97 96 04. Set in the scenic Campeã valley, 8 km (5 miles) north of Vila Real, this modern restaurant offers local dishes and a good selection of wines. ▤ ♿	AE DC MC V			▪
MINHO				
ARCOS DE VALDEVEZ: *Adega Regional Grill* $$$ N101, Quinta de Silvares. **Road map** C1. 258-661 22. In a pretty setting just north of Arcos, Adega serves carefully prepared traditional cuisine like roast veal and *cozido à portuguesa* (meat stew). ● *Mon; Oct 15–30.*	AE V	▪	●	
BARCELOS: *Bagoeira* $$ Avenida Sidónio Pais 495. **Road map** C1. 253-81 12 36. A very popular restaurant serving Minhoto specialties, including roast kid and stewed duck with rice, prepared with finesse in truly generous portions.	AE DC MC V		●	▪
BARCELOS: *Dom António* $$ Rua Dom António Barroso 87. **Road map** C1. 253-81 22 85. Dom António's is a stone-walled place with rustic decor in the center of town. House specials include *bife na pedra* (steak grilled on a hot stone). ▤	AE DC MC V	▪		
BRAGA: *Abade de Priscos* $$ Praça Mouzinho Albuquerque (Campo Novo) 7. **Road map** C1. 253-27 66 50. Overlooking the leafy square beside the Catholic University, this restaurant offers excellent value and has a large menu ranging from curried shrimp to rabbit and braised veal. ● *Mon lunch; Sun; 2 weeks in Jul or Aug.* ▤				▪
BRAGA: *Ignácio* $$ Campo das Hortas 4. **Road map** C1. 253-61 32 35. Just outside the city walls, Ignácio is full of character. Enjoy a range of regional dishes amid artifacts and antiques. ● *Tue; 2 weeks in Apr; 2 weeks in Sep.* ▤	AE DC MC V			
BRAGA: *São Frutuoso* $$ Rua Costa Gomes 168, Real. **Road map** C1. 253-62 33 72. A friendly restaurant just south of Braga that serves superb country food. Try the cod with maize bread or the stuffed veal. ● *Mon; last 2 weeks in Aug.* ▤	MC V		●	
BRAGA: *Panorâmico do Elevador* $$$ Hotel do Elevador, Bom Jesus do Monte. **Road map** C1. 253-60 34 00. This is one of the most famous restaurants in the area. Enjoy the panoramic views of Braga and Bom Jesus, and its traditional local dishes. ▤ ♿	AE DC MC V			
CAMINHA: *Napoléon* $$$ Lugar de Coura, Seixas. **Road map** C1. 258-72 71 15. Just south of Caminha, Napoléon has a high standard of cooking and offers local, national, and French dishes. ● *Mon; Sun eve; 2 weeks in May; 2 weeks in Dec.* ▤	AE DC MC V		●	▪
GUIMARÃES: *El Rey* $$ Praça Santiago 20. **Road map** C1. 253-41 90 96. El Rey is a cozy place with a good-value menu and a pleasant atmosphere. Try the *bacalhau mistério* (cod surprise) – a house-invented specialty. ● *Sun.* ▤	AE DC MC V	▪	●	
GUIMARÃES: *São Gião* $$$ Lugar de Vinhas, Moreira de Cónegos. **Road map** C1. 253-56 18 53. Found in a small village just south of Guimarães, São Gião offers tasty dishes like duck with olive sauce, shoulder of veal cooked à la São Gião, and *cozido à portuguesa* (meat and vegetable stew with rice). ● *Mon; Sat lunch; Aug.* ▤		▪	●	▪

GUIMARÃES: *Solar do Arco* $$$ AE MC V
Rua de Santa Maria 48–50. **Road map** C1. 253-51 30 72.
This elegant restaurant is located in a charming mansion in the heart
of the city. The house specialty is fresh seafood and fish. ● *Sun dinner.* ▤ ⅃

PONTE DA BARCA: *Bar do Rio* $$ MC V
Praia Fluvial. **Road map** C1. 258-45 25 82.
This is a charming wood-paneled restaurant with stunning views of the Lima
River. Try the specials of *rojões* (fried pork) or cod *au gratin.* ● *Tue.* ▤

PONTE DE LIMA: *A Carvalheira* $$ MC V
Antepaço, Arcozelo. **Road map** C1. 258-74 23 16.
Just south of Ponte de Lima, this friendly place is popular with locals. The
house special is *bacalhau com broa* (cod with cornbread). ● *Mon.* ▤

PONTE DE LIMA: *Encanada* $$ AE MC V
Largo Doutor Rodrigues Alves. **Road map** C1. 258-94 11 89.
This busy restaurant overlooking the river, offers traditional Portuguese fare like
rojões à moda do Minho (pork Minho style) and *vinhos verdes.* ● *Thu; May.* ⅃

PÓVOA DE VARZIM: *O Marinheiro* $$$$ AE DC MC V
Estrada Fontes Novas. **Road map** C2. 252-68 21 51.
An attractive restaurant in the shape of a boat and decorated with fishing
nets and buoys, O Marinheiro offers a fine seafood-based menu. ▤ ♫ ⅃

VALENÇA DO MINHO: *Mané* $$$ MC V
Avenida Miguel Dantas 5. **Road map** C1. 251-234 02.
Above a café-bar, this modern restaurant has a wide, and relatively inexpensive,
array of fish and meat dishes. ● *Sun eve; Mon (except Aug); Jan 1–15.* ▤

VALENÇA DO MINHO: *São Teotónio* $$$ AE DC MC V
Pousada de São Teotónio, Baluarte de Socorro. **Road map** C1. 251-82 42 42.
In a *pousada* within the old fort, São Teotónio offers a fantastic view across
the Minho valley to Tui in Spain, and hearty local dishes like kid stew. ▤

VIANA DO CASTELO: *Camelo* $$$ AE DC MC V
Rua de S. Marta 119–122, S. Marta de Portuzelo. **Road map** C 1. 258-83 05 17.
In a village 1 km (half a mile) from Viana do Castelo, this gem of a restaurant
holds monthly festive banquets and offers summer dining under shady vines.
Try the *bacalhau à camelo* (house cod specialty). ● *Mon; mid-Sep–mid-Oct.* ▤ ⅃

VIANA DO CASTELO: *Casa d'Armas* $$$ MC V
Largo 5 de Outubro 30. **Road map** C1. 258-82 49 99.
Behind a gracious and imposing façade, the stone and wood-paneled interior
of Casa d'Armas is enhanced by medieval-style decor. Expect only the freshest
fish and shellfish and prime quality meats. ● *Wed; 2 weeks in Oct or Nov.* ▤

VIANA DO CASTELO: *Cozinha das Malheiras* $$$ AE DC MC V
Rua Gago Coutinho 19–21. **Road map** C1. 258-82 36 80.
Enjoy good traditional cuisine in this small and intimate restaurant that occupies
a former chapel. The seafood dishes are recommended. ● *Tue; 1 week in Dec.* ▤

VILA PRAIA DE ÂNCORA: *Tasquinha Ibrain* $$$ AE MC V
Rua dos Pescadores. **Road map** C1. 258-91 16 89.
Overlooking the harbor, this cozy place has excellent service and specializes in
seafood. Try the tasty *costeletão* (T-bone steak). ● *1 week in Oct.* ⅃

ALENTEJO

ALANDROAL: *A Maria* $$ AE DC MC V
Rua João de Deus 12. **Road map** D5. 268-43 11 43.
An enchanting restaurant serving Alentejan dishes that include *cozido de grão*
(pork and chickpea stew) and *sopa de cação* (shark soup). ● *Mon; Sep 1–15.* ▤

ALVITO: *Castelo de Alvito* $$$$ AE DC MC V
Pousada do Castelo de Alvito, Apartado 9. **Road map** D6. 284-48 53 43.
A 15th-century castle with beautiful gardens and roaming peacocks
provides the picturesque setting for this fine restaurant. Try the cod
stewed with herbs or roast lamb cooked with spinach. ▤ ⅃

BEJA: *Dom Dinis* $$ AE DC MC V
Rua Dom Dinis 11. **Road map** D6. 284-32 59 37.
Dom Dinis is a country restaurant specializing in grilled food, the most
popular dishes being the meat kebabs and veal chops. ● *Thu.* ▤

For key to symbols see back flap

<table>
<tr><td colspan="2">

Price categories are for a three-course meal for one with half a bottle of wine, including cover charge, service, and VAT:

$ under 2,000$00
$$ 2,000–3,000$00
$$$ 3,000–4,500$00
$$$$ 4,500–6,000$00
$$$$$ over 6,000$00.

</td><td colspan="2">

LATE OPENING
The kitchen stays open after 10pm, and you can usually have a meal up until at least 11pm.

OUTDOOR TABLES
Tables for eating outdoors, in a garden, or on a balcony, often with a pleasant view.

GOOD WINE LIST
The restaurant will have a good selection of quality wines.

CREDIT CARDS
This indicates which of the major credit cards are accepted: *AE* American Express, *DC* Diners Club, *MC* MasterCard, and *V* VISA.

</td></tr>
</table>

	CREDIT CARDS	LATE OPENING	OUTDOOR TABLES	GOOD WINE LIST
BEJA: *Os Infantes* $$ Rua dos Infantes 14. **Road map** D6. 284-32 27 89. Os Infantes has a beautiful setting, fine decor, and a good-value menu. Specialties include traditional Alentejo cuisine, partridge, and hare.	AE DC MC V			
CAMPO MAIOR: *O Faisão* $$ Rua 1° de Maio 19. **Road map** E5. 268-68 61 39. This cozy restaurant, with a fire and pictures of local life on the walls, offers a good selection of traditional dishes like *cozido de grão* (pork and chickpea stew). Try the house beef in mushroom sauce.	AE DC MC V	■	●	■
CRATO: *Flor da Rosa* $$$$ Pousada da Flor da Rosa. **Road map** D4. 245-99 72 10. The restaurant is located in this marvelous *pousada* adapted from the monastery, which is thought to date from the mid-14th century. Traditional regional favorites are served like pig's feet with coriander sauce.	AE DC MC V			■
ELVAS: *Pousada de Santa Luzia* $$$ Avenida de Badajos. **Road map** D5. 268-62 21 94. Not far from the Spanish border, the large restaurant of this *pousada* (see p395) is popular with Portuguese and Spaniards alike. They come here to enjoy the large portions of *bacalhau à bráz* and other traditional treats.	AE DC MC V			
ESTREMOZ: *Águias d'Ouro* $$$ Rossio do Marquês de Pombal 27. **Road map** D5. 268-33 33 26. This cozy restaurant, on the first floor of an attractive town house, serves delicious pig's feet in coriander sauce and lamb in fruit sauce.	AE DC MC V	■		■
ÉVORA: *Cozinha de Santo Humberto* $$$ Rua da Moeda 39. **Road map** D5. 266-242 51. Just off the main square, this is a real delight. A whitewashed cellar is adorned with antiques, and Alentejo dishes and local game are served. ● *Thu; Nov.*	AE DC MC V			
ÉVORA: *Um Quarto Para as Nove* $$$ Rua Pedro Simões 9a. **Road map** D5. 266-267 74. This charming restaurant is situated in the old part of town. Among the menu's highlights are monkfish rice, hare rice, and *açorda alentejana* (bread and coriander dish). ● *Wed; 2 weeks in Sep; 2 weeks in Oct.*	AE MC V	■		
ÉVORA: *O Grémio* $$$$ Alcárcova de Cima 10. **Road map** D5. 266-74 29 31. A wonderful restaurant built into the city's Roman wall. Try the tasty *entrecosto agridoce* (spareribs in a red wine and honey sauce). ● *Wed.*	AE DC MC V			■
ÉVORA: *Fialho* $$$$ Travessa dos Mascarenhas 16. **Road map** D5. 266-230 79. Tucked away in a side street, this tasteful restaurant offers an interesting range of meat, fish, shellfish, and game dishes. ● *Mon; Sep 1–24; last week in Dec.*	AE DC MC V	■		■
MARVÃO: *Sever* $$ Portagem. **Road map** D4. 245-99 31 92. A pretty restaurant with excellent river views. The menu offers immaculately prepared regional specialties like wild boar with clams, and lamb stew.	AE MC V	■	●	
MÉRTOLA: *Alengarve* $ Avenida Aureliano Mira Fernandes 20. **Road map** D6. 286-622 10. This modest restaurant offers good-value regional cuisine like *açorda alentejana* (bread and coriander dish) and roast kid. ● *2 weeks in Oct.*			●	
MONSARAZ: *Casa do Forno* $$ Travessa da Sanabrosa. **Road map** D5. 266-55 71 26. Close to the main road and the town's main tourist attractions, Casa do Forno serves mainly regional dishes, like lamb stew and pork with clams. ● *Fri.*	AE MC V		●	

PORTALEGRE: *O Tarro* ⓈⓈ
Avenida Movimento das Forças Armadas. **Road map** D4. 〖 245-33 12 23.
Popular with the locals, this busy restaurant in the town center serves daily
specials like *bacalhau à Tarro* (cod with ham in a creamy sauce). ▤

| | MC V | ▪ | | |

REDONDO: *Ermita* ⓈⓈⓈⓈ
Convento de São Paulo, Aldeia da Serra. **Road map** D5. 〖 266-99 91 00.
Inside a beautiful hotel, the Ermita offers a wonderful array of dishes such
as avocado with port and duck with olive sauce. There is also an unusual
mixed grill of stone bass, monkfish, shrimp, and squid on the menu. ▤ ▤ ♿

| | AE DC MC V | | | ▪ |

SANTIAGO DO CACÉM: *O Retiro* ⓈⓈ
Rua Machado dos Santos 8. **Road map** C6. 〖 269-226 59.
A charming country restaurant with friendly service. House specialties are
duck rice and *bacalhau com natas* (cod in a creamy sauce). ● *Sun.* ▤ ♫

| | MC V | | | |

SERPA: *Adega Molha O Bico* Ⓢ
Rua Quente 1. **Road map** D6. 〖 284-54 92 64.
A friendly local restaurant where the food is often outstanding. Try the
roast pork or the *cozido de grão* (pork and chickpea stew). ▤

| | | ▪ | | |

SINES: *O Migas* ⓈⓈⓈ
Rua Pero de Alenquer 17. **Road map** C6. 〖 269-63 67 67.
Here a carefully chosen menu includes *mexilhões à moda de Aveiro* (mussels
Aveiro style) and marinated partridge. ● *Sat lunch; Sun; Oct 15–30.* ▤

| | AE MC V | | | ▪ |

VILA NOVA DE MILFONTES: *Porto das Barcas* ⓈⓈⓈ
Estrada do Canal. **Road map** C6. 〖 283-99 92 83.
Menu highlights at this charming restaurant overlooking the sea include
arroz de marisco (seafood rice) and *caldeirada de peixe* (seafood stew).

| | AE DC MC V | ▪ | ● | |

VILA VIÇOSA: *Os Cucos* Ⓢ
Mata Municipal. **Road map** D5. 〖 268-98 08 06.
The setting in the municipal gardens is the main attraction of Os Cucos, though
it offers a good variety of grilled fish dishes as well. ● *2 weeks in Aug.* ▤ ♿

| | AE MC V | ▪ | ● | |

ALGARVE

ALBUFEIRA: *Os Compadres* ⓈⓈ
Avenida Dr Sá Carneiro, Edifício Pateo Sá Carneiro. **Road map** C7. 〖 289-54 18 48.
This restaurant has a good atmosphere and friendly, relaxed service. The owner
is always around to offer advice on what to choose. ● *Thu (Oct–May); Dec.* ▤ ♿

| | AE DC MC V | ▪ | ● | |

ALBUFEIRA: *Marisqueira Santa Eulália* ⓈⓈ
Praia de Santa Eulália. **Road map** C7. 〖 289-54 26 36.
Overlooking the beach, this restaurant serves typical Portuguese seafood
dishes, including grilled monkfish, salmon, and clams. ● *Dec–Jan.* ♿

| | AE DC MC V | ▪ | ● | |

ALBUFEIRA: *Ruína* ⓈⓈⓈⓈ
Rua Cais Herculano. **Road map** C7. 〖 289-51 20 94.
Set in a restored early 19th-century building, Ruína is one of the best
restaurants in town. Specialties of the house are fresh fish and seafood.
Rooms are set aside for coffee and for listening to *fado.*

| | AE DC MC V | ▪ | ● | ▪ |

ALMANCIL: *Chameleon* ⓈⓈ
Rua da República, 40. **Road map** D7. 〖 289-39 75 99.
Chameleon is a pleasant, simply decorated restaurant with a small menu
that is heavily influenced by Indonesian-style cuisine. ● *Mon.* ▤ ♫ ♿

| | AE DC MC V | ▪ | ● | |

ALMANCIL: *Ibérico* ⓈⓈ
Estrada Almancil, Vale do Lobo. **Road map** D7. 〖 289-39 40 66.
Located near the vast Vale do Lobo complex south of Almancil, this place is full
of character and features an eclectic menu, with such dishes as smoked swordfish with horseradish sauce and cannelloni Ibérico (Iberian style). ● *lunch.* ▤

| | AE MC V | ▪ | ● | |

ALMANCIL: *Aux Bons Enfants* ⓈⓈⓈ
Sítio das Areias, Estrada de Almancil. **Road map** D7. 〖 289-39 68 40.
Aux Bons Enfants offers French cuisine and an excellent selection of French
and Portuguese wines from 1945 up to the present day. ● *lunch; Sun.*

| | | | ● | ▪ |

ALMANCIL: *O Tradicional* ⓈⓈⓈⓈⓈ
Estrada da Fonte Santa, Escanxinas. **Road map** D7. 〖 289-39 90 93.
This excellent restaurant, south of Almancil, serves specialties like steak in
Roquefort cheese sauce or duck breast with orange. ● *lunch; Sun; Nov–Dec.* ▤ ♿

| | AE MC V | ▪ | | ▪ |

Price categories are for a three-course meal for one with half a bottle of wine, including cover charge, service, and VAT:

$ under 2,000$00
$$ 2,000–3,000$00
$$$ 3,000–4,500$00
$$$$ 4,500–6,000$00
$$$$$ over 6,000$00.

LATE OPENING
The kitchen stays open after 10pm, and you can usually have a meal up until at least 11pm.

OUTDOOR TABLES
Tables for eating outdoors, in a garden, or on a balcony, often with a pleasant view.

GOOD WINE LIST
The restaurant will have a good selection of quality wines.

CREDIT CARDS
This indicates which of the major credit cards are accepted: *AE* American Express, *DC* Diners Club, *MC* MasterCard, and *V* VISA.

	CREDIT CARDS	LATE OPENING	OUTDOOR TABLES	GOOD WINE LIST
ARMAÇÃO DE PÊRA: *Santola* $$ Largo da Fortaleza. **Road map** C7. 📞 282-31 23 32. With panoramic seaside views, Santola has a pleasant atmosphere and is a reliable choice for seafood and shellfish dishes. ● *Nov 15–Dec 15.*	AE MC V	■	●	
ESTOI: *Monte do Casal* $$$$$ Cerro do Lobo. **Road map** D7. 📞 289-99 15 03. The menu at this old farmhouse restaurant includes a selection of vegetarian dishes and house specialties like salmon in a white wine and dill sauce, and seafood with Monte do Casal sauce. ● *mid-Nov–mid-Feb.* 🍽	MC V		●	■
FARO: *Adega Nortenha* $ Praça Ferreira de Almeida 25. **Road map** D7. 📞 289-82 27 09. This busy, unpretentious place overlooks a pretty square. Daily specials include *feijoada* (bean stew) and *caldeirada* (fish stew). 🍽	AE MC V			
FARO: *Dois Irmãos* $$ Praça Ferreira de Almeida 13–14. **Road map** D7. 📞 289-82 33 37. One of the most popular restaurants in Faro, the Dois Irmãos offers good quality cooking and efficient service. Seafood specialties include fish or meat *cataplana (see p288)* and a variety of fresh fish dishes.	AE MC V	■	●	
FARO: *A Taska* $$ Rua do Alportel 36–8. **Road map** D7. 📞 289-82 47 39. Popular with locals, A Taska is a modest but cozy restaurant decorated as an old tavern. Try the eel stew or the pork with clams. 🍽		■	●	
FARO: *Camané* $$$$$ Avenida Nascente, Praia de Faro. **Road map** D7. 📞 289-81 75 39. Camané is a bright and spacious seafood restaurant located right on the waterfront. The house special is monkfish rice. ● *Mon; 2 weeks in Oct.* 🍽 ♿	MC V	■	●	■
LAGOA: *O Castelo* $$$ Rua do Casino 63, Praia do Carvoeiro. **Road map** C7. 📞 282-35 72 18. Booking is advisable in this cliff-top seafood restaurant surrounded by a pretty garden. Try the monkfish and shrimp rice. ● *Mon; Jan 10–Feb 10.* 🍽 ♿	AE DC MC V	■	●	■
LAGOA: *O Lotus* $$$ Rua Marquês de Pombal 11. **Road map** C7. 📞 282-520 98. O Lotus offers good Portuguese cuisine like marinated sardines, octopus and egg salad, and stone bass in pastry. Desserts include chocolate mousse or *morgado de figo* (fig and almond paste cakes). ● *Sat.* 🍽	AE MC V	■		
LAGOS: *António* $$$ Praia do Porto de Mós. **Road map** C7. 📞 282-76 35 60. António is located in a pretty spot with good views of the ocean. It serves a mainly seafood menu in a friendly and relaxed atmosphere. ● *Jan 1–Feb 7.* ♿	AE DC MC V	■	●	
LAGOS: *Dom Sebastião* $$$ Rua 25 de Abril 20–22. **Road map** C7. 📞 282-76 27 95. This rustic restaurant has an extensive menu offering traditional Portuguese fare like smoked swordfish and kid stew in red wine. ● *Dec 1–25.* 🍽 ♿	AE DC MC V	■	●	
LOULÉ: *Bica Velha* $$ Rua Martim Moniz 17–19. **Road map** C7. 📞 289-46 33 76. The oldest house in Loulé, dating from 1816, is the setting for this rustic, family-run restaurant. Specialties include lamb kebab, pork chop with apple sauce, and orange mousse for dessert. ● *Sun (except Aug); 2 weeks in Nov or Dec.*	AE DC MC V			
LOULÉ: *Casa dos Arcos* $$ Rua Sá de Miranda 23–5. **Road map** D7. 📞 289-41 67 13. Set in Loulé's historic center, this restaurant is popular with tourists and locals alike. It serves good-quality seafood specialties and meat dishes. ● *Sun.* 🍽	AE MC V			

OLHÃO: *Aquário* $$
Rua Doutor João Lúcio 8. **Road map** D7. 289-70 35 39.
Located in the center of town, Aquário offers a selection of tasty seafood dishes like paella, stuffed squid, and shrimp in a cream sauce. ● Mon. 🍽

| | AE DC MC V | | ● |

PORTIMÃO: *Cervejaria Lúcio* $$
Largo Francisco Maurício 33. **Road map** C7. 282-42 42 75.
Overlooking the river, this cheerful, noisy beerhouse is a popular meeting place for locals and serves mainly fish and seafood dishes. ● Nov–Dec. ♿

PORTIMÃO: *A Lanterna* $$$
Rua Foz do Arade Parchal. **Road map** C7. 282-41 44 29.
A variety of Portuguese dishes include smoked swordfish, clams in the house style, and almond mousse dessert. Wines are from the Alentejo. ● Sun; Nov–Dec.

QUARTEIRA: *Restaurante Suisse* $$
Estrada Quarteira-Almancil, Fonte Santa. **Road map** D7. 289-38 01 48.
Do not be put off by this restaurant's location, just south of Quarteira; inside it has a charm all of its own. Among wooden beams and antiques you can order from the varied Swiss-German orientated menu until 2am. ● Tue (Dec–Feb). 🎵

QUINTA DO LAGO: *Cá d'Oro* $$$$$
Hotel Quinta do Lago. **Road map** D7. 289-39 66 66.
This refined and elegant Italian restaurant serves Venetian specialties such as *calamari e gamberi con verdurine di campo* (deep fried shrimp, squid, and seasonal vegetables). ● Tue (Sep–Jun). 🍽 🎵

SAGRES: *O Telheiro* $$
Praia da Mareta. **Road map** C7. 282-62 41 79.
Enjoy the excellent service, and dining room with panoramic views and a terrace. The house specialty is lobster rice. ● Tue; 2 weeks in Nov or Dec. 🍽 ♿

SAGRES: *Pousada do Infante* $$$$
Pousada do Infante. **Road map** C7. 282-62 42 22.
With stunning views of the cliffs and ocean, this restaurant features dishes like fresh fish fillets with mayonnaise and pork with clams. 🍽

SILVES: *Marisqueira Rui* $$
Rua Comendador Vilarinho 23. **Road map** C7. 282-44 26 82.
Popular with the locals, this busy town-center restaurant is open until 2am. Menu highlights are the seafood rice and selection of fresh fish. ● Tue; 2 weeks in Nov. 🍽

TAVIRA: *Quatro Águas* $$
Quatro Águas. **Road map** D7. 281-32 53 29.
Located 1 km (half a mile) south of Tavira, Quatra Águas has superb views of the lagoon. Try the house special "golden octopus." ● Mon; 3 weeks in Nov. 🍽 ♿

VILAMOURA: *Sirius Restaurant* $$$$$
Vilamoura Marinotel. **Road map** D7. 289-38 99 88.
Located in an elegant hotel, Sirius looks out over the marina and serves some superb international and French-orientated cuisine. Indulge in beluga caviar and vodka, escargots bourguignonne, or lobster thermidor. ● Lunch. 🍽 🎵 ♿

MADEIRA

FUNCHAL: *Fim de Século* $
Rua da Carreira 144. 291-22 44 76.
Tiffany lamps help lend this restaurant its fin-de-siècle theme, and the fixed-price menus offer the cheapest eating in downtown Funchal. ● Sun. 🍽 ♿

FUNCHAL: *O Jango* $$
Rua de Santa Maria 166. 291-22 12 80.
O Jango is a cozy restaurant in a converted fisherman's house in the old town. The well priced, fresh food includes bouillabaisse and paella. ● 1–21 Jul. 🍽

FUNCHAL: *Londres* $$
Rua da Carreira 64a. 291-23 53 29.
This downtown restaurant has a typically Portuguese daily special, like *bacalhau* (salt cod) with olives or *cozido*, a hearty meat casserole. ● Sun. 🍽

FUNCHAL: *Marisa* $$
Rua de Santa Maria 162. 291-22 61 89.
An intimate old town restaurant that feels like a private home; as father and son cook delicious paella or seafood rice, and mother takes the orders. 🍽 ♿

For key to symbols see back flap

				CREDIT CARDS	LATE OPENING	OUTDOOR TABLES	GOOD WINE LIST

Price categories are for a three-course meal for one with half a bottle of wine, including cover charge, service, and VAT:

$ under 2,000\$00
$$ 2,000–3,000\$00
$$$ 3,000–4,500\$00
$$$$ 4,500–6,000\$00
$$$$$ over 6,000\$00.

LATE OPENING
The kitchen stays open after 10pm, and you can usually have a meal up until at least 11pm.

OUTDOOR TABLES
Tables for eating outdoors, in a garden, or on a balcony, often with a pleasant view.

GOOD WINE LIST
The restaurant will have a good selection of quality wines.

CREDIT CARDS
This indicates which of the major credit cards are accepted: *AE* American Express, *DC* Diners Club, *MC* MasterCard, and *V* VISA.

FUNCHAL: *Carochinha*　　　$$
Rua de São Francisco 2a. ☎ 291-22 36 95.
Carochinha calls itself an English restaurant, but its eclectic menu includes a wide choice of dishes from various different countries. There is no roast beef, but the bread and butter pudding is excellent. ● *Sun.* 🍽 ♿
Credit cards: AE DC MC V — Good Wine List

FUNCHAL: *O Tapassol*　　　$$
Rua Don Carlos I 62. ☎ 291-22 51 23.
Booking is advised at this excellent small restaurant in the old town. Dine on quail, mussels, limpets, or rabbit, choosing the indoor dining room for style, or the tiny roof terrace for a fun evening. 🍽
Credit cards: AE DC MC V — Late Opening, Outdoor Tables

FUNCHAL: *Caravela*　　　$$$
Avenida das Comunidades Madeirenses. ☎ 291-22 84 64.
This chic seafront restaurant serves good local fish, like tuna, scabbard fish, and turbot, plus more expensive air-freighted seafoods. ● *Dec 25.* 🍽
Credit cards: AE DC MC V — Late Opening, Good Wine List

FUNCHAL: *Casa dos Reis*　　　$$$
Rua Penha de França. ☎ 291-22 51 82.
Small, quiet, sophisticated and one of Funchal's few restaurants to offer vegetarian food on its French-influenced menu. ● *Lunch.* 🍽 🎵 ♿
Credit cards: AE DC MC V — Late Opening, Good Wine List

FUNCHAL: *O Celeiro*　　　$$$
Rua Imperatriz Dona Amélia 101. ☎ 291-23 06 22.
O Celeiro offers candle-lit dining and a fish-based menu featuring several dishes for two, like shellfish and lobster *cataplana* and bouillabaisse. 🍽 ♿
Credit cards: AE DC MC V

FUNCHAL: *Dom Filet*　　　$$$
Rua do Favila 7. ☎ 291-76 44 26.
"King Fillet" specializes in beef served Madeiran style (cubed, skewered on a bay twig and grilled) or char-grilled Argentinian style. ● *Sun lunch.* 🍽 🎵 ♿
Credit cards: AE DC MC V — Late Opening

FUNCHAL: *Marina Terrace*　　　$$$
Marina do Funchal. ☎ 291-23 05 47.
One of a run of outdoor restaurants by the yacht marina, this place serves dishes from simple pizza to lobster or grilled fish. Live *fado* and folk music. 🎵 ♿
Credit cards: AE DC MC V — Late Opening, Outdoor Tables

FUNCHAL: *Dona Amélia*　　　$$$$
Rua Imperatriz Dona Amélia 83. ☎ 291-22 57 84.
Flambé dishes, grilled fish, and *espetadas* (Madeiran beef kebabs) on bay-wood skewers are the specialty of this lovely tiled restaurant. 🍽 ♿
Credit cards: AE DC MC V — Good Wine List

FUNCHAL: *Quinta Palmeira Gourmet Restaurant*　　　$$$$
Avenida do Infante 5. ☎ 291-22 18 14.
In this 19th-century town house, traditional Portuguese dishes are presented with flair, and the homemade ice cream is delicious. 🍽 ♿
Credit cards: AE DC MC V — Late Opening, Outdoor Tables, Good Wine List

FUNCHAL: *Les Faunes*　　　$$$$$
Reid's Palace Hotel, Estrada Monumental 139. ☎ 291-76 30 01.
Madeira's finest restaurant offers stylishly presented international cuisine. Be sure to try one of their delicious desserts like strawberry pancakes or *zabaglione* made with Madeira wine. ● *lunch; Sun; Apr–Oct.* 🍽 🎵 ♿
Credit cards: AE DC MC V — Late Opening, Good Wine List

RIBEIRA BRAVA: *Palheiro Rodízio Grill*　　　$$$
Sítio da Meia Légua. ☎ 291-95 70 46.
This informal restaurant offers a popular Brazilian-style dining experience. Pay a fixed price to eat as much as you like from a constantly replenished buffet of grilled meats (*rodízio*). ● *Mon.* 🍽
Credit cards: MC V — Late Opening, Outdoor Tables

SANTANA: *Quinta do Furão*　　　$$$
Achada do Gramacho. ☎ 291-57 01 00.
Sit next to the fireplace among antiques in this cozy restaurant overlooking the sea. Specials include steak in pastry and seafood kebabs. 🍽 ♿
Credit cards: AE DC MC V — Outdoor Tables

Porto Moniz: *Orca* Hotel Orca, Praia de Porto Moniz. ☎ *291-76 33 22.* Orca is made entirely of wood except for the large windows that enable diners to gaze out over the sea. Try the special of scabbard fish with banana.	$	AE DC MC V		●	
THE AZORES					
Corvo: *O Caldeirão* Rua dos Moinhos. ☎ *292-561 56.* The only restaurant on Corvo, O Caldeirão is the center of its universe. Set on a hill with a view of the sea, it serves fish and meat dishes such as chicken with clams, salted pork, and ham steak. ▤ ♿	$$			●	
Faial: *O Capote* Rua Conselheiro Miguel da Silveira, Horta. ☎ *292-29 32 95.* A lively and often crowded restaurant at the north end of the seafront, it is popular with both locals and yachties celebrating their return to land. ● *Oct.* ▤	$$		■		■
Faial: *Vista da Baía* Avenida Tenente Simas, Varadouro. ☎ *292-94 51 40.* Famous for its barbecued chicken, this is a good lunch stop overlooking a bay on the west coast of the island. ● *Wed; Mon–Fri (Oct–Mar).*	$$			●	■
Flores: *Reis* Rua da Boa Vista, Santa Cruz. ☎ *292-526 97.* Up in the hills above Santa Cruz, this is a clean and simple restaurant attached to the *salsicharia* (sausage shop) run by a local family butcher.	$$	MC V	■		
Graciosa: *A Coluna* Largo Barão de Guadalupe 10, Santa Cruz da Graciosa. ☎ *295-71 23 33.* The owner of this small, idiosyncratic restaurant spent many years in Brazil and serves *feijoada* (bean and meat stew) and other Brazilian favorites. ● *Sun.*	$				■
Pico: *Terra e Mar* Miradouro do Arrife, Terras, Lajes do Pico. ☎ *292-67 27 94.* This small, cliff-top restaurant has a windmill and terrace. Serving simple fish and meat dishes, it is a good place to pause while touring the island.	$			●	
Santa Maria: *O Fontes* Cruz Teixeira, Vila do Porto. ☎ *296-88 23 72.* O Fontes specializes in hearty Azorean dishes like *caldo de nabos* (turnip soup) and *alheira e morcela* (garlic sausage and black pudding). Book a day in advance to be asssured of a table at this popular restaurant. ♿	$$				
São Jorge: *Manezinho* Furna das Pombras, Urzelina. ☎ *295-41 44 84.* A simple seaside restaurant that is popular with locals. Dishes include *ameijoas* (clams) from Fajã da Caldeira de Santo Cristo. ● *Mon.* ♿	$		■	●	
São Miguel: *Tony's* Largo do Teatro 5, Furnas. ☎ *296-58 42 90.* Tony's specializes in *cozido (see p231).* The meat stew is slowly cooked in the hot volcanic rocks found around Furnas. Book at least a day in advance. ▤	$	AE MC V	■	●	
São Miguel: *Alcides* Rua Hintze Ribeiro 67–77, Ponta Delgada. ☎ *296-28 26 77.* An unpretentious but accomplished restaurant serving robust steak and fries fare, close to the Igreja Matriz de São Sebastião. ● *Sun.* ▤	$$				
São Miguel: *Monte Verde* Rua da Areia 4, Ribeira Grande. ☎ *296-47 29 75.* Monte Verde is a small, friendly restaurant with a first-floor dining room decorated with modern *azulejos.* Competent fish dishes include *tigelada de chicharro,* a stew made with thin, sardinelike fish.	$$	MC V	■	●	
Terceira: *Casa do Peixe* Estrada Miguel Corte Real, Angra do Heroísmo. ☎ *295-21 76 78.* Overlooking the harbor, the city's former fish market has been turned into an atmospheric restaurant with a full menu and friendly service. ♿	$	MC V			
Terceira: *Quinta do Martelo* Canada do Martelo 24 , Cantinho, São Mateus. ☎ *295-64 28 42.* This is the place to go to try rich Azorean dishes like Holy Spirit soup (meat and vegetables in white wine) and *alcatra* (meat stew). ● *Wed.* ▤ ♫ ♿	$$$	AE MC V	■	●	■

For key to symbols see back flap

SURVIVAL
GUIDE

PRACTICAL INFORMATION

Tourism in Portugal is not as developed as it is in neighboring Spain, but visitors are well catered to. The major tourist region is the Algarve, where the choice of resorts rivals anywhere in Europe. Portugal has many regional tourist offices

Sign for Tourist Information Office

and a good choice of hotels in cities and resorts. The Portuguese are a hospitable people and are eager for you to experience and enjoy their country. Traveling with a family is encouraged, and restaurants and hotels will offer discounts for children *(see p377)*.

WHEN TO VISIT

In THE SOUTH of the country the winter months are mild, but temperatures in July and August can be very high. The weather conditions in the north may not be suitable for visiting during winter, especially in the mountainous regions where it can be quite cold. Between April and October, the north is pleasantly warm, although rain is not unusual. See pages 34–5 for more detailed information on Portugal's climate.

Christmas, Easter, July, and August are the most popular vacation times in Portugal, for visitors and locals alike. At these times, especially in the south, rooms can be hard to find, and prices are generally higher. At other times of the year, good bargains can be found and the popular tourist areas are far less crowded.

Overall, spring and fall are the best times to visit, when hotel rates are lower, the climate is pleasant throughout the country, and there are not too many people.

CUSTOMS

There is no limit to the amount of goods that visitors can import from one EU member country to another, provided that tax has been paid in the country of purchase. Duty-free allowances exist only for tobacco, alcohol, and perfumes and are the same as for other EU countries. Consulates and customs officials can provide information on allowances. See pages 436–7 for information on VAT and taxes.

Bottles of port

VISAS

American and Canadian nationals may stay without a visa for up to 60 days with a valid passport.

Nationals of the European Union (EU), Australia, and New Zealand need a valid passport or identity card and can stay for up to 90 days without a visa. EU nationals wishing to stay longer than 90 days should contact the local *Serviços de Estrangeiros e Fronteiras* (frontier police) within three days and request an *autorização de residência* (residence permit). Anyone intending to study or work in Portugal needs a letter to prove they will be in college or working.

TOURIST INFORMATION

The PORTUGUESE MINISTRY of Tourism divides the country into a number of touristic regions, which are separate from its administrative districts. All major cities or large towns within each touristic region have a **Government Tourist Office** (Posto de Turismo), as do the larger towns on Madeira and the Azores. This guide gives details of the relevant tourist information office for each sight. Here, visitors can obtain information about the region, town plans, maps, and details on regional events. In some cases they will also sell advance tickets for local shows and concerts. Information about local hotels will be available from the tourist office, although they will not usually book the accommodations.

Tourist season on a beach in the resort of Albufeira, in the Algarve

◁ **Fruit and vegetable stands at the Mercado dos Lavradores, Funchal**

Sign in the village of Marvão

Office opening hours vary as each tourist region is organized independently, but generally they follow the same opening hours as local shops. In more rural areas, offices are often closed on weekends and may not offer the same information and services that can be found in larger towns. There are tourist offices at all the major airports, as well as in all cities and large towns. Visitors can also obtain information prior to traveling, from Portuguese tourist offices abroad. These offices will normally provide visitors planning a trip with a wide range of useful maps, fact sheets, and tourist brochures.

Map of mainland Portugal showing the country's six tourist regions

MUSEUMS

THE MAJORITY of Portugal's museums are run by the state, although there are also a number of private ones. In addition to the main national museums and galleries, there are countless regional ones scattered around the country. These cover a range of topics, from the history of a region to the works of local artists.

ADMISSION CHARGES

MOST MUSEUMS in Portugal charge a small fee, which varies from 200$00 to 500$00. These charges are sometimes reduced or waived altogether (or just in the morning) on Sundays and public holidays. Young people under 14 or seniors (with proof of age) may obtain a 40 percent discount. Those under 26 with a *Cartão Jovem* (youth card) or ISIC card (International Student Identity Card) are entitled to half-price entrance. A convenient ticket system for tourists to Lisbon is the LISBOA card, available from the municipal **Posto Central**. This entitles visitors to entry to 26 of the city's museums (although not private museums, such as the Gulbenkian), and free public transportation for a fixed period of time. LISBOA cards are valid for one, two, or three days.

Museum tickets

OPENING TIMES

MUSEUMS ARE usually open from 10am–5pm from Tuesday to Sunday, with many closing for lunch either from noon to 2pm or from 12:30pm to 2:30pm. Smaller and private museums may have different opening times. Museums and some sights close on Mondays and public holidays. Major churches are open during the day without a fixed timetable, although some may close between noon and 4pm. Smaller churches and those in rural areas may only be open for religious services and in some cases you may need to find the keyholder for admittance.

DIRECTORY

EMBASSIES AND CONSULATES

Canada
Avenida da Liberdade 144, 4º,
1250 Lisbon. **Map** 5 C5.
(21-347 48 92.

US Embassy
Avenida das Forças Armadas,
1600 Lisbon.
(21-726 66 00.

US Consulates:
Azores
Ponta Delgada.
(296-222 16.

Madeira
Avenida Luís de Camões, Apt B4,
Edifício Infante, Funchal, Madeira.
(291-74 34 29.

Oporto
Praça Comandante Samodães 65,
4100 Oporto.
(22-606 30 94.

TOURIST OFFICES

In Portugal:
Coimbra
Largo da Portagem,
3000 Coimbra.
(239-83 30 19.

Faro
Rua da Misericórdia 8,
8000 Faro.
(289-80 36 04.

Lisbon
Palácio Foz,
Praça dos Restauradores,
1200 Lisbon. **Map** 7 A2.
(21-346 36 43.

Oporto
Praça Dom João I 43,
4050 Oporto.
(22-205 75 14.

In US:
New York
590 Fifth Avenue, 4th floor,
New York, NY 10036.
((212) 354-4403,
(800) Portugal.

LISBOA CARD

Posto Central
Rua Jardim do Regedor 50, off
Rua das Portas de Santo Antão.
Map 7 A2.
(21-343 36 72.

Newspaper stand in the Brasileira Café *(see p90)*

LANGUAGE

PORTUGUESE RESEMBLES the Spanish language in many ways, and if you know Spanish you should have little difficulty reading Portuguese. However, Portuguese pronunciation is likely to sound very unfamiliar, and spoken Portuguese sounds nothing like spoken Spanish.

The Portuguese are justifiably proud of their own language and do not take kindly to being addressed in Spanish. Their own language is widely spoken throughout the world as a result of historical ties with Brazil and a number of countries in Africa. A phrase book containing the most useful words and phrases in Portuguese, along with their phonetic pronunciations, can be found on pages 479–80.

MANNERS

THE PORTUGUESE appreciate efforts by visitors, however small, to communicate in their language. A simple attempt at *bom-dia* (good day), *boa-tarde* (good afternoon), or *boa-noite* (good night) will be gratefully received and is sure to elicit a friendly response.

The Portuguese are generally very open and amicable, particularly in the north of the country and in rural areas, and they are unerringly polite. It is considered polite to address

people as *senhor* or *senhora* and this formality extends to many job titles. Arts graduates are addressed as *doutor* and science graduates as *engenheiro.* You are expected to shake hands when introduced to anyone new, although an informal kiss on each cheek between females and among young friends and acquaintances is more commonplace.

Although dress is generally relaxed, decorum should be observed when you visit churches and religious buildings, especially those in strongly Catholic areas: arms should be covered up and shorts should not be worn.

NEWSPAPERS AND MAGAZINES

ENGLISH-LANGUAGE newspapers, including the British *Financial Times,* the weekly *Guardian International,* and the American *International Herald Tribune,* and *USA Today,* are widely available on publication day. Other European papers are on sale a day late, but in the main tourist areas they may be found on the same day. Portuguese daily papers include *Diário de Notícias* and *Público. Correio da Manhã* covers the south and *Jornal de Notícias* the north. English-language

Portuguese dailies and the English APN

papers include the *Anglo-Portuguese News* (APN), aimed at the expatriate population, and the *Algarve Gazette* and *Algarve News.*

RADIO AND TELEVISION

THERE ARE TWO state-owned Portuguese channels, RTP1 and RTP2, and two privately owned, SIC and TVI. Satellite television is available in several languages and the newspaper, *Anglo-Portuguese News,* has lists of programs in English. The Portuguese radio station RDF broadcasts tourist information in English, French, and German during the summer months. Madeira has its own TV channel and a radio service catering to tourists on 96 FM.

FACILITIES FOR THE DISABLED

FACILITIES IN PORTUGAL for the disabled are limited at present, although the situation is gradually improving. Wheelchairs and adapted toilets are now available at most airports and the main stations, reserved car parking is becoming more evident, and ramps and elevators are gradually being installed in public places. In addition, Lisbon and Oporto have a dial-a-ride bus service. To book, phone and indicate when and where you want to be picked up, and your destination. The operators speak only Portuguese, so you may need to ask your hotel for help. There is a special taxi service in Lisbon, but it has to be booked long in advance.

A dial-a-ride bus for the disabled *(transporte especial para deficientes)*

Women travelers admiring the view from the castle in Lisbon

WOMEN TRAVELING ALONE

TRAVELING ALONE in Portugal is fairly safe for women, although common sense, such as keeping to well-lit, public areas after dark, still applies. Some areas of Lisbon, such as the Bairro Alto and the Cais do Sodré, are best avoided after dark, while resorts on the Algarve and Lisbon coasts tend to be the worst for unwanted attentions. Hitchhiking alone is not safe; use taxis or public transportation instead.

STUDENT INFORMATION

YOUNG PEOPLE from 12–25 may buy a *Cartão Jovem*, (youth card), which costs about 1,100$00 and is valid for a year. It offers travel insurance and discounts for shops, museums, travel, and youth hostels *(see p376)*. This card is supplied by the **Instituto Português da Juventude** (Portuguese Youth Institute). The International Student Identity Card (ISIC) provides the same benefits as the *Cartão Jovem* and can be bought in your own country.

RELIGION

ROMAN CATHOLICISM is the dominant religion in Portugal. Church services are held most evenings and every Sunday morning as well as on religious holidays. Sightseeing may be difficult (and is not encouraged) while services are in progress. Churches of other denominations, including the Church of England, Baptist, and Evangelical, can be found in larger towns and cities. **St. Vincent's Anglican Church**, which travels from place to place, holds a number of religious services in the Algarve.

PORTUGUESE TIME

PORTUGAL AND MADEIRA are six hours ahead of Eastern Standard Time (EST) and Eastern Daylight Time. The Azores are five hours ahead. Both Portugal and the Azores use the 24-hour (military) clock, so 1pm = 13:00. Daylight savings may not coincide with the US, so be sure to check.

ELECTRICAL ADAPTORS

VOLTAGE IN PORTUGAL is 220 volts, and plugs have two round pins. Most hotel bathrooms offer built-in adaptors for electric razors, but you will need to supply your own adaptor for other appliances.

Worshipers leaving a church after mass in Trás-os-Montes

CONVERSION CHART

Imperial to Metric
1 inch = 2.54 centimeters
1 foot = 30 centimeters
1 mile = 1.6 kilometers
1 ounce = 28 grams
1 pound = 454 grams
1 US quart = 0.947 liter
1 US gallon = 3.6 liters

Metric to Imperial
1 millimeter = 0.04 inches
1 centimeter = 0.4 inches
1 meter = 3 feet 3 inches
1 kilometer = 0.6 miles
1 gram = 0.04 ounces
1 kilogram = 2.2 pounds
1 liter = 1.1 US quarts

DIRECTORY

PLACES OF WORSHIP

St. George's Church
Rua de São Jorge à Estrela 6,
Lisbon.
【 21-390 62 48.

St. James's Church
Largo da Maternidade de
Júlio Dinis, Oporto.
【 22-606 49 89.

Lisbon Synagogue
Rua A. Herculano 59,
Lisbon.
【 21-385 86 04.

**St. Vincent's Anglican
Church (Algarve)**
Apartado 135,
Boliqueime.
【 289-36 67 20.

STUDENT INFORMATION

**Instituto Português
da Juventude**
Avenida da Liberdade 194,
1250 Lisbon.
【 21-315 19 55.

TAXIS FOR THE DISABLED

Lisbon
【 21-811 90 00 *(needs to be
booked long in advance)*.

BUSES FOR THE DISABLED

Lisbon
【 21-758 56 76.

Oporto
【 22-600 63 53.

Personal Health and Security

Pharmacy sign

IN GENERAL, Portugal is relatively free of crime, but simple precautions should always be taken. When parked, do not leave any valuable possessions in the car, and watch out for pickpockets in crowded areas and on public transit. Should you have serious medical problems, call the emergency service number given in this section. For minor complaints, consult a pharmacy.

Police station at Bragança in the Trás-os-Montes region

WHAT TO DO IN AN EMERGENCY

THE NUMBER to contact in the event of an emergency is 112. Dial the number and then indicate which service you require – the police *(polícia)*, an ambulance *(ambulância)*, or the fire department *(bombeiros)*. If you need medical treatment, the emergency room *(serviço de urgência)* of the closest main hospital will treat you. On highways and main roads, use the orange SOS telephone to call for help. The service is in Portuguese; press the button and then wait for an answer.

Highway SOS telephone

HEALTH PRECAUTIONS

NO VACCINATIONS are needed for visitors, although it is a sensible precaution to have had a typhoid shot and a current polio booster. Tap water is safe to drink throughout the country. If you are visiting during the summer, it is advisable to bring insect repellent, as mosquitoes, while they do not present any serious health problems, can be a nuisance.

MEDICAL TREATMENT

VISITORS FROM the United States should check with their insurance carriers before leaving home, to be sure they are covered if medical care is needed abroad. Travelers may wish to take out additional private travel insurance for the cost of any emergency care,

doctors' fees, and repatriation. Many medical facilities ask you to pay for your treatment in full at the time of service. In some cases, insurance companies require you to provide an official translation of your medical record before they will reimburse you. The **British Hospital** in Lisbon has English-speaking doctors, as do international health centers in Estoril and Cascais, as well as a number of health centers throughout the Algarve. These are advertised in the local English-language press.

PHARMACIES

PHARMACIES *(farmácias)* in Portugal can diagnose simple health problems and suggest appropriate treatment. Pharmacists can dispense a range of drugs that would

normally be available only by prescription in many other countries. The sign for a *farmácia* is a green cross on a white background. They are open from 9am to 1pm and 3pm to 7pm. Each pharmacy displays a card showing the address of the nearest all-night pharmacy and a list of those with late closing (10pm).

PORTUGUESE POLICE

IN ALL MAIN CITIES and towns, the police force is the *Polícia de Segurança Pública* (PSP). Law and order in rural areas is kept by the *Guarda Nacional Republicana* (GNR). The *Brigada de Trânsito* (traffic police) division of the GNR, recognizable by their red armbands, is responsible for patrolling roads.

PERSONAL SECURITY

VIOLENT CRIME is extremely rare in Portugal, and the vast majority of visitors will experience no problems, but sensible precautions should

Traffic policeman

Male PSP officer

Female PSP officer

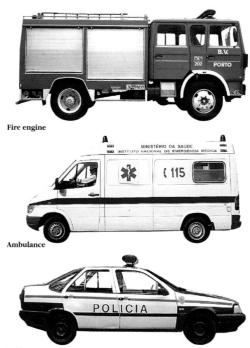

Fire engine

Ambulance

Police car

be taken. It is advisable to arrange travel insurance for your possessions before you leave for Portugal. Thieves do operate, and care should be taken after dark in the Alfama, Bairro Alto, and Cais do Sodré areas of Lisbon, in some of the resorts in the Algarve, and in the Ribeira district of Oporto. Personal belongings should be protected, and leaving anything inside a car, particularly a radio, is not recommended. When walking, hide wallets and carry bags and cameras away from the road so as not to tempt snatchers in cars or on motorbikes. If you are unfortunate enough to encounter thieves during your visit, do not attempt to resist and hand over your possessions immediately.

REPORTING A CRIME

I F YOU HAVE any property stolen, you should immediately contact the nearest police station. Theft of documents, such as a passport, should also be reported to your

consulate. Many insurance companies insist that policy holders report any theft within 24 hours. The police will file a report which you will need in order to claim from your insurance company on your return home. Contact the PSP in towns or cities, or the GNR in rural areas. In all situations, keep calm and be polite to the authorities to avoid delays. The same applies should you be involved in a car accident. In rural areas you may be asked to accompany the other driver to the nearest police station to complete the necessary paperwork. Ask for an interpreter if no one there speaks English.

LEGAL ASSISTANCE

A N INSURANCE POLICY that covers the costs of legal advice, issued by companies such as Europ Assistance or Mondial Assistance, will help with the legal aspects of your insurance claim should you have an accident. If you have not arranged this coverage, call your nearest consulate or the **Ordem dos Advogados** (lawyers' association), who can give you names of English-speaking lawyers and help you with obtaining representation. Lists of interpreters, if you require one, are given in the local Yellow Pages (Páginas Amarelas) under *Tradutores e Intérpretes*, or can be contacted through the **Associação Portuguesa de Tradutores,** which is based in Lisbon.

PUBLIC FACILITIES

T HE PORTUGUESE for toilets is *retretes*. If the usual figures of a man or woman are not shown, look for the words *homens* (men) and *senhoras* (ladies). Toilet facilities are provided at service areas every 40 km (25 miles) and at drive-in rest areas on the highways. In some cases you may have to pay to use ladies' toilets, but men's facilities are free.

Ladies' toilet sign

Men's toilet sign

Banking and Local Currency

BFB Bank Logo

Y̲OU CAN TAKE any amount of money into Portugal, but if you import more than 2,500,000 escudos you must declare it at customs when entering the country. Traveler's checks or Eurocheques are the safest way to carry money in Portugal, but credit cards are the most convenient. They can be used to withdraw Portuguese currency, for a fee, from ATMs (automatic teller machines) displaying the appropriate sign.

A 24-hour bank at Lisbon Airport

BANKING HOURS

B̲ANK OPENING HOURS are from 8:30am to 3pm, Monday to Friday, although many major branches in city centers and in tourist areas close at 6pm. Banks are closed on weekends and on public holidays.

CHANGING MONEY

M̲ONEY CAN be changed at banks, at a foreign exchange desk *(câmbio)*, and in many hotels. Banks are the most convenient way because they are more common than foreign exchange desks and

offer a better rate than hotels. However, service in banks can sometimes be slow and usually involves filling in a number of forms. In addition, some banks restrict currency exchange to their customers.

The quickest and most practical way of changing money is to use the electronic currency exchange machines found outside the branches of most major banks and at the main airports and train stations. They have the added advantage of allowing you to change money outside normal banking hours. The screen in the center of the machine

displays the current exchange rates and gives instructions for use in several languages.

CHECKS AND CARDS

T̲RAVELER'S CHECKS are available from most banks or from branches of Thomas Cook and American Express offices. They are a safe way of carrying money, but in Portugal they are expensive to cash. Commission rates vary from bank to bank, so it is wise to shop around first.

If you have a European bank account, you can use a Eurocheque and a guarantee card. You can write out checks in escudos for up to 30,000$00 per day, and many places will accept them as payment. All banks showing the Eurocheque logo will also cash the checks for you.

The credit cards that are most commonly accepted for payment are Visa, American Express, and MasterCard. They can also be used to withdraw Portuguese currency at banks and foreign exchange desks.

CASH DISPENSERS

A̲ PRACTICAL WAY of obtaining cash advances using your credit card with a PIN number is to use the MB (Multibanco) ATM (automatic teller machine) found outside most banks. Cards accepted are Visa, MasterCard, Amex, Eurocheque, and Eurocard. A transaction tax is charged as well as a commission. It is worth looking around for the best rate first as tax and commission rates vary from bank to bank.

Indicator panel shows which denominations of each currency the machine accepts.

Foreign currency is inserted here.

Exchange rates and instructions are shown on this screen.

Portuguese notes and coins emerge from these slots.

Language and currency is selected using these buttons.

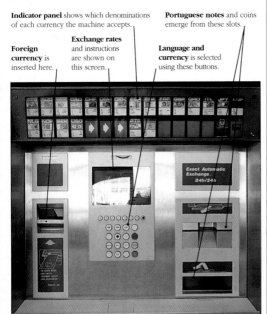

Currency Exchange Machine at Lisbon Airport
These machines provide a convenient way of changing foreign notes into Portuguese currency at any time of day or night.

CURRENCY

T HE BASIC UNIT of currency in Portugal is the escudo ($), pronounced "shkoo-doo." This is divided into 100 centavos. Amounts are written with the escudo sign before the centavos, so 1,000 escudos is shown as 1,000$00. 1,000$00 are usually referred to as a *conto*, this term can be used on checks instead of escudos.

It is advisable to carry smaller denomination notes and coins when traveling in Portugal. Buses, small shops, and kiosks are often unable, or unwilling, to give change for larger bills to pay for small purchases.

On Jan 1, 1999, the Euro became the legal currency in 11 European Union countries including Portugal. Starting Jan 1, 2002, national currencies will be replaced gradually by the Euro. Each state will adorn coins with national designs. The currency can be used in these 11 Member States.

10,000$00

5,000$00

2,000$00

1,000$00

500$00

Bank Notes
Denominations of notes are 10,000$00, 5,000$00, 2,000$00, 1,000$00, and 500$00. Older Portuguese bank notes have been phased out and replaced with new designs, so do not accept old notes if received in change. The smaller replacement designs are shown in the foreground, with the older notes behind. A new design for the 500$00 note was created in 1997.

Coins
The following coins are currently in circulation in Portugal: 200$00, 100$00, 50$00, 20$00, 10$00, 5$00, 2$50 and 1$00. There are no centavo coins in circulation below 1$00; the only coin that incorporates centavos is the 2$50.

200$00

100$00

50$00

20$00

10$00

5$00

2$50

1$00

Using the Telephone

R ECENT YEARS have seen a dramatic improvement in the Portuguese telecommunications system. Formerly, the antiquated equipment caused all kinds of problems for visitors. Thankfully, it has been updated with the help of the latest technology, and visitors should now find that using the telephone in Portugal is relatively free of complications. Public telephones may be used for phoning internally or abroad, either with coins or cards. It is generally much more convenient, especially when making international or long-distance calls, to use card phones instead of coin phones.

Old-style phone booth

Post office *cabine* phone

USING A COIN PHONE

1 Lift receiver and wait for the dial tone.

2 Insert 10$00, 20$00 50$00, 100$00, or 200$00 coins.

3 The display shows amount of credit. If more money is required the message "*Inserir mais moedas por favor*" appears.

4 Enter telephone number and wait to be connected.

5 To make another call, press the follow-on call button.

6 Replace receiver after call. Unused coins will be refunded.

USING A TELECOM CARD PHONE

1 Lift receiver and wait for the dial tone.

2 Insert phonecard arrow side up, or credit card magnetic strip down.

3 The screen will display number of units available, then tell you to enter telephone number.

4 Enter number and wait to be connected.

5 If phonecard runs out in the middle of a call, it will reemerge. Remove it and insert another one.

6 Replace receiver after call. When card reemerges, remove it.

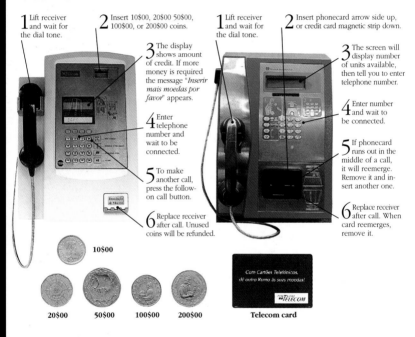

10$00

20$00   50$00   100$00   200$00

Telecom card

TELEPHONING IN PORTUGAL

T HERE ARE SIX different types of pay phone in Portugal. Four use coins and two take cards, although one type of card is being phased out. There are two types of coin-operated phone in the street: the older green phones accept 10$00, 20$00, and 50$00 coins, and the newer beige phones accept these as well as the 100$00 and 200$00 coins. The red phones

found in bars and newsstands accept only 10$00, 20$00, and 50$00 coins, whereas the new blue phones will accept 100$00 and 200$00 coins as well.

Until recently, using a phonecard has been complicated because there were two types of card, the Telecom and the Credifone. Today, only the Telecom card is used. Card phones are more convenient than coin phones, especially when making calls abroad, as they avoid the need to carry

PORTUGAL TELECOM

Telecom logo

pockets full of change. Cards are available in 50 and 120 units from post offices, Portugal Telecom outlets, tobacco shops, and newsstands.

You can also call from post offices. Go to the cashier's window and you will be directed to a booth *(cabine)*. Make your call first and then pay at the counter. The rate is much better than in hotels, which will add on a large surcharge. It is less expensive to call in the evening after 9pm or on weekends, when off-peak rates are charged.

COLLECT CALLS

COLLECT CALLS can be made from any telephone. First dial the *país directo* number for the country you want to call. This number is listed in the opening pages of any telephone directory, after the list of city codes for that country. This number will put you in direct contact with the local telephone operator. There are also separate numbers for calls to the US using services such as AT&T, MCI, and Sprint.

A new-style beige coin telephone covered by a shelter in Oporto

DIALING CODES

- Within each town or region dial the six- or seven-digit number.
- To call Lisbon from outside the city dial 01.
- To call Oporto from outside the city dial 02.
- The Algarve is covered by Portimão (082), Faro (089), and Tavira (081). Madeira's code is 091.
- To call Portugal from the US first dial 011 351, but drop the 0 before dialing the remainder of the city or regional code (eg: 00 351 1 for Lisbon).
- To call abroad from Portugal, dial 00 and then the country code. The code for US and Canada is 1; Ireland: 353; UK: 44; Australia: 61; New Zealand: 64.
- Portugal's directory assistance number is 118. For international directory assistance dial 098.

Postal Services

Correios (postal service) logo

THE POSTAL SERVICE is known as the *Correios*. It is reasonably efficent: a letter sent to a country within the EU should take five to seven days, and a letter sent to the US or farther afield should take about seven to ten days. The *Correios* sign features a horse and rider in white on a red background.

SENDING A LETTER

FIRST CLASS MAIL is known as *correio azul*, and second class mail is called *normal*. First class letters are mailed in blue mailboxes and second class post in red ones. At post offices there may be separate slots for national and international mail. There is also an express mail service called EMS, and for valuable letters, a recorded delivery service *(correio registado)* is available. Stamps *(selos)* can be bought from post offices or from any shop displaying the red and white *Correios* sign, and also from vending machines. These are found in airport terminals and in train stations, as well as on the streets of large towns.

Portuguese stamps

POSTE RESTANTE

A MAIL-HOLDING service *(posta restante)* is available at most major post offices. The envelope should have the name of the recipient in printed capitals, underlined, followed by *posta restante* together with the postcode and the name of the town. To collect the mail, take your passport and look for the counter marked *encomendas.* A fee is charged for this service.

POST OFFICES

POST OFFICES are usually open from 8:30am until 6:30pm from Monday to Friday. Post offices in town or city centers have different opening times. These are 8am–10pm from Monday to Friday and 9am–6pm on Saturdays.

PORTUGUESE ADDRESSES

PORTUGUESE ADDRESSES often include both the story of a building and the location within that floor. The ground floor is the *rés-do-chão* (r/c), first floor *primeiro andar* (1º), the second is expressed as 2º, and so on. Floors are divided into left, *esquerdo* (E or Esqdo), and right, *direito* (D or Dto).

Portugal's Mailboxes
First class letters should be mailed in blue (Correio Azul) *boxes and second class letters in red boxes.*

Information on collection times **First class mailbox**

Second class mailbox

Shops and Markets

Traditional arts and crafts have not been lost as a result of Portugal's modernization. Pottery, ceramics, and tiles *(azulejos)* are produced everywhere with differing styles from town to town, while lace and embroidery are particularly good from Madeira. Cheeses, cured hams, sausages, and wines can all be bought from local shops and markets; port, Madeira, and spirits from wine shops or direct from the producer. Portugal is not an expensive country when compared with the rest of Europe, and prices are likely to be very reasonable for traditional craftwork and produce, especially away from the cities.

Serra cheese from the Serra da Estrela

produce, it also sells pottery, lace, rugs, and clothes. At the regional markets throughout the country a range of local produce is on sale such as cheeses, breads, and hams. In this guide, the market days are given in the information that precedes each town entry. Where a regular date is given, but that date happens to fall on a weekend, the market is held on the nearest weekday.

Choosing fresh, locally grown vegetables and fruit at a typical roadside stall in the Alentejo

RECLAIMING VAT

Value added tax (IVA) can be reclaimed by non-EU residents who stay for less than 180 days. Ask for an *Isenção de IVA* form or invoice in triplicate, describing the goods, quantity, value, and buyer's identity (best done where you see the "Tax Free for Tourists" signs). Present the forms at customs on departure.

OPENING HOURS

Shops open at 9am and close at 7pm, and smaller shops or those in quieter areas normally close for lunch between 1pm and 3pm. Large shopping centers, which usually include a supermarket, restaurants, and banks, have sprouted all over Portugal recently. Opening times for shopping centers are usually from 10am until 11pm daily (including Sunday).

MARKETS

A social and commercial occasion, the street market is integral to Portuguese life. It is usually held in the town's

main square; ask for the *mercado* or *feira* if in doubt. Most markets sell a wide range of goods from food to household items and clothes, but you will also see sites devoted to antiques and local crafts. Roadside stalls are common, often selling produce from smallholdings. Most markets are held in the morning only, but in tourist areas they may go on until late afternoon.

Perhaps Portugal's largest and best-known market is the one in Barcelos *(see p273)* in the Minho, which is held every Thursday in the main square. As well as selling a vast range of household goods and local

CERAMICS

In most cities you can buy as well as commission ceramic tiles and panels. Portugal has a long-standing tradition in ceramics, both for decorative purposes and for home use *(see pp24–5)*. Styles range from elegant Vista Alegre porcelain to simple but classic terra-cotta crockery. Antique *azulejos* are highly sought after and very expensive, but you can buy reproductions of well known historic designs at places such as Lisbon's Museu Nacional do Azulejo *(see pp122–3)*.

OTHER CRAFTS

Portugal is well known for its delicate embroidery and fine lace, and the best-known source is the island of Madeira. On the mainland, the best lace and embroidery comes from towns in the Minho such as Viana do Castelo, also famous for its brightly printed shawls. Embroidered bedspreads are sold in Castelo Branco in the Beira Baixa, and colorful carpets, such as those from Arraiolos *(see p301)*, are sold throughout the Alentejo.

Prices are very reasonable for knitwear, and woolen fishermen's sweaters from Nazaré *(see p180)*, which are often hand-knitted, can be a good value.

Ceramics at the market in Barcelos *(see p273)*

Filigree jewelry (*filigrana*) from the Minho is typically worn at festivals and is sold locally. Gold and silver threads are worked into fine, intricately designed brooches, earrings, and pendants. In theory, all the gold sold in Portugal must be at least 19 carats.

Wickerwork is another specialty of Madeira that is produced in large quantities. Colonial-style lawn chairs are much sought after. Woven baskets are produced throughout the country and make delightful souvenirs. Cork from the Alentejo (*see p313*) is used to make articles such as mats and ice buckets.

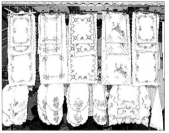

Embroidered handkerchiefs and table mats in Caldas do Gerês, the Minho (*see pp270–71*)

Locally made baskets for sale in the Beiras region (*see p195*)

REGIONAL PRODUCE

IN PORTUGAL every region has its specialties, and it is best to buy fresh items in the region where they are made, although most of the better-known regional produce can be found throughout the country. Cured ham (*presunto*) from the north of the country is particularly good in Chaves (*see pp256–7*), and smoked tongue sausages (*linguiça*) are a specialty of Oporto (*see pp236–41*).

Regional cheeses include the delicious ewe's cheese Serra, which is produced from May to October in the Serra da Estrela (*see pp218–19*). Ilha is a stronger, hard cheese from the Azores, and Queijinhos are small white cheeses produced in Tomar and the surrounding region (*see pp184–5*).

WINES AND SPIRITS

AS WELL AS PRODUCING the well known fortified wines, port (*see pp228–9*) and Madeira (*see p349*), Portugal has a wide range of good table wines (*see pp28–9*). Among the best known are the rich red wines that come from the vineyards of the Dão region and the light *vinhos verdes* from the Minho.

It is usually possible to visit the port lodges and wine producers for tastings and guided tours (*see p247*) as well as to buy produce direct from them. Portugal's best-known spirit is *bagaceira* or *bagaço*, a fiery, clear drink distilled from grapeskins. Other spirits include *figo* (made from figs), *ginginha* (made from red cherries), and *medronheira*, a firewater distilled from arbutus (*see p289*). If these are not to your taste, Portuguese brandies such as *Macieira* and *Constantino* are good and reasonably priced.

CLOTHING AND SHOES

PORTUGAL HAS a thriving textile industry, but much of the country's production in clothes and shoes goes to supply well-known designer brands abroad. These clothes are not usually available in the shops. Some excellent-value seconds are on sale at local markets everywhere; a particularly well-known one is at Carcavelos between Lisbon and Estoril. Leather goods such as shoes, gloves, belts, and bags can be good buys, but prices will reflect the quality of the product (and not all the leather goods on display will be Portuguese).

Shopping for gloves in the Chiado area of Lisbon (*see pp94–5*)

SIZE CHART

Women's dresses, coats, and skirts

Portuguese	34	36	38	40	42	44	46
American	6	8	10	12	14	16	18
British	8	10	12	14	16	18	20

Women's shoes

Portuguese	36	37	38	39	40	41
American	5	6	7	8	9	10
British	3	4	5	6	7	8

Men's suits

Portuguese	44	46	48	50	52	54	56	58 (size)
American	34	36	38	40	42	44	46	48 (inches)
British	34	36	38	40	42	44	46	48 (inches)

Men's shirts

Portuguese	36	38	39	41	42	43	44	45 (size)
American	14	15	15½	16	16½	17	17½	18 (inches)
British	14	15	15½	16	16½	17	17½	18 (inches)

Men's shoes

Portuguese	39	40	41	42	43	44	45	46
American	7	7½	8	8½	9½	10½	11	11½
British	6	7	7½	8	9	10	11	12

Sports Vacations and Outdoor Activities

ALTHOUGH IT IS A SMALL COUNTRY, Portugal offers an amazing variety of terrain, with sports and activities to match. Golf and tennis facilities have been well established for many years, and in the south the mild climate means that both sports can be enjoyed all year round. Other activities such as hiking, cycling, riding, and water sports are also widely enjoyed and easily arranged. Events are often organized on a local basis, so contact the regional tourist offices for the most up-to-date information on sports facilities and events.

Hikers on the summit of Pico Ruivo in Madeira *(see p354)*

Windsurfing at sunset, Viana do Castelo *(see pp274–5)*

WATER SPORTS

SURFING, WINDSURFING, and sailing are extremely popular along Portugal's 500 miles of coastline and around the Atlantic islands. The best beach for surfing is the world-famous Guincho, just outside Cascais *(see pp162–3)*, where international championships have been held. However, the ocean breakers there are suitable only for experienced surfers. More moderate conditons can be found in the Algarve resorts, where windsurfing boards and sailing dinghies can be rented and lessons easily arranged. In the Algarve, the marinas at Lagos and **Vilamoura** are important yachting centers.

For information on scuba-diving centers in mainland Portugal, and ones on Madeira, and the Azores, contact the **Federação Portuguesa de Actividades Subaquáticas**.

Canoeing and kayaking are popular pursuits on many of the country's rivers, especially on the Mondego, the Zêzere and the Cávado. For further details, contact the **Federação Portuguesa de Canoagem**.

HIKING AND CYCLING

BOTH THE PARQUE NATURAL de Montesinho *(see p260)* and the Parque National da Peneda-Gerês *(see pp270–71)* are good areas for hikers, but some of Portugal's best walks are on Madeira and the islands of São Miguel and São Jorge in the Azores. In Madeira you can walk alongside the *levadas* (irrigation channels), some of which date back to the 15th century *(see p354)*. Following *levadas* allows access to parts of the island where no roads can penetrate.

Portugal is well suited to mountain biking, although the country's hilly terrain may deter the less fit. Bikes can be rented in the Parque Nacional da Peneda-Gerês, which has many scenic mountain routes.

GOLF COURSES IN THE ALGARVE

The majority of Portugal's best golf courses are concentrated in the Algarve, which has gained a reputation as one of Europe's prime golfing destinations. The mild climate ensures that a game can be enjoyed all year round, and many courses have been designed by leading professsionals such as Henry Cotton. Some of the top courses insist that players demonstrate a reasonable degree of proficiency, while others welcome golfers of any ability and provide excellent coaching. More serious golfers might consider booking a special package tour.

Immaculate fairway on Vilamoura II golf course

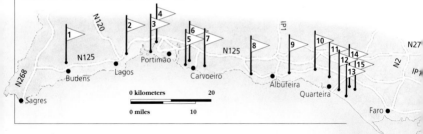

Golfers enjoying a game at Vale do Lobo in the Algarve

TENNIS AND GOLF

TENNIS COURTS are found practically everywhere in Portugal and certainly alongside most tourist facilities. In the Algarve, most of the courts in tourist complexes are hard, although elsewhere many are clay. The larger Algarve resorts and a few other places offer tennis instruction vacations.

Portugal's resorts are famous for their golf courses, which include some of Europe's best. Many offer lessons for golfers of all abilities and special vacations are easy to arrange. Most courses are in the Lisbon area and the Algarve, but there are good facilities elsewhere.

1 Parque da Floresta *(282-653 33)*.
2 Palmares *(282-76 29 53)*.
3 Alto Golf *(282-41 69 13)*.
4 Penina *(282-41 54 15)*.
5 Quinta do Gramacho *(282-526 70)*.
6 Vale da Pinta *(282-526 70)*.
7 Vale de Milho *(282-35 85 02)*.
8 Salgados *(289-59 11 11)*.
9 Sheraton/Pine Cliffs *(289-50 19 19)*.
10 Vilamoura I, II, III *(289-32 16 52)*.
11 Vila Sol *(289-30 21 44)*.
12 Vale do Lobo *(289-39 39 39)*.
13 San Lorenzo *(289-39 65 22)*.
14 Quinta do Lago *(289-39 60 02)*.
15 Pinheiros Altos *(289-39 43 40)*.

Despite its rocky, mountainous terrain, Madeira has two fine courses: Santo da Serra in the east of the island and Palheiro Golf, high above Funchal.

Hoping for a catch at Praia da Adraga, near Colares *(see p153)*

FISHING

ALONG THE COASTS and rivers of Portugal are plenty of opportunities for the fisherman, from deep sea fishing off the shores of the Algarve, Madeira, and the Azores, to angling in the mainland rivers for trout and salmon. You will need to obtain a licence, available from the **Instituto Florestal**.

HORSEBACK RIDING

PORTUGAL ENJOYS a famous riding tradition as a result of the country's fine Lusitano horses. In the Algarve, **Quinta dos Amigos** and **Vale de Ferro** are well known riding schools. Other popular locations include the Alentejo, and the Peneda-Gerês National Park in the north of Portugal.

N125

DIRECTORY

WATER SPORTS

Federação Portuguesa de Actividades Subaquáticas
Rua Frei Manuel Cardoso 39, 1700 Lisbon.
(21-846 01 74.

Federação Portuguesa de Canoagem
Rua António Pinto Machado 60, 4100 Oporto.
(22-606 62 27.

Marina de Vilamoura S.A.
8125 Quarteira.
(289-31 05 60.

GOLF

Adventure Golf Holidays
815 North Road, Westfield, MA 01085.
((800) 628-9655.
FAX (413) 562-3621.

Federação Portuguesa de Golfe
Rua General Ferreira Martins 10, 5°C, Miraflores, 1495 Algés.
(21-410 76 83.

Golf on Tour
300 St. Andrews Trail, Miamisburg, OH 45342.
((513) 866-2523.
FAX (513) 866-8811.

FISHING

Federação Portuguesa de Pesca Desportiva
Rua da Sociedade Farmacêutica 56, 2°, 1150 Lisbon.
(21-356 31 47.

Instituto Florestal
Avenida João Crisóstomo 28, 1050 Lisbon.
(21-312 48 00.

HORSEBACK RIDING

Quinta dos Amigos
8135 Almancil.
(289-39 52 69.

Vale de Ferro
Centro Hípico, Mexilhoeira Grande, 8500 Portimão.
(282-96 84 44.

TRAVEL INFORMATION

PORTUGAL, MADEIRA, and the Azores have airports served by TAP, the national carrier. Major European airlines also fly to Lisbon and Oporto on the mainland. In addition, there are many charter flights operating in summer, especially to the Algarve, which are often sold as part of a package deal. Portugal's mainland rail network varies in speed and luxury, and there are many privatized bus services. Trains are cheap, and it is well worth cracking the complicated system of discounted tickets, although for most journeys, traveling by bus offers greater speed and flexibility. Driving on the mainland and the islands can be a hair-raising experience, both in cities and on twisting mountain roads, and Portugal has one of the highest road accident rates in Europe. On the islands, the smaller distances involved mean that it is sometimes more convenient for visitors to take taxis, but on the mainland driving is the most flexible, albeit risky, means of transportation.

Logo of TAP Air Portugal

Check-in at Lisbon Airport

FLIGHTS TO MAINLAND Portugal arrive at the international airports of Lisbon, Oporto, and Faro. All are served by **TAP Air Portugal**, and the first two are also served by the major European national airlines that run regular scheduled flights from Paris, Frankfurt, Milan, Rome, and Madrid. Four airlines provide direct flights from the US to Lisbon: TAP Air Portugal, **Delta**, **Continental**, and **TWA**.

Many other airlines fly from the US direct to Madrid, where passengers can change for Lisbon. TAP and its partner VARIG link South American cities, such as Rio de Janeiro and Caracas with Lisbon and Oporto. There are no direct flights from Canada, Australia, or New Zealand, and visitors from these countries will need to catch a connecting flight at a European gateway such as London, Zurich, or Paris.

There are no airlines operating direct flights between the US and other Portuguese cities. However, TAP offers connecting flights to passengers traveling on from Lisbon to Faro, Oporto,

Signs at the airport for visitors' facilities

Funchal, or the Azores. There are, in addition, direct charter flights from Boston and Toronto. **Azores Express** and **Relvas Tours** can provide flights into Lisbon, Ponta Delgada, Terceira, and Oporto. These are very popular and should be booked well in advance. **British Airways** and TAP run scheduled flights to Funchal in Madeira from London. Visitors traveling to Madeira and the Azores from other European cities have to change in Lisbon for a domestic flight *(see p441)*.

Because flight arrangements to Portugal can be quite complicated, using a good travel agent is advisable.

AIRPORT	ℂ INFORMATION	DISTANCE TO CITY CENTER	TAXI FARE TO CITY CENTER	PUBLIC TRANSIT TO CITY CENTER
Lisbon	21-81 37 00	6 km (4 miles)	1,500$00	🚌 20 minutes
Oporto	22-948 25 52	11 km (7 miles)	3,000$00	🚌 30 minutes
Faro	289-80 08 00	4 km (2.5 miles)	1,100$00	🚌 15 minutes
Funchal	291-22 50 85	18 km (11 miles)	3,600$00	🚌 30 minutes
Ponta Delgada	296-62 93 85	4 km (2.5 miles)	1,000$00	🚌 10 minutes
Horta	292-935 11	8 km (5 miles)	1,000$00	🚌 15 minutes

AIR FARES

AIRLINES OFFER many options on flights to Portugal, with prices varying according to class, the time of year you choose to travel, and the flexibility that the ticket provides. The least expensive scheduled flights usually have a fixed return date and require you to stay over one Saturday night. Some midweek flights and many package-tour flights may also be offered at reduced prices compared to full-fare flights. All such flights must usually be reserved at least fourteen days in advance, because seats are limited, and it is wise to take out extra insurance against late cancellations, since refunds are not usually given.

Charter flights have fixed outward and return dates, and they allow a maximum stay of one month only, but they are the least expensive way of getting to Portugal. Charter flights to Faro and other resort areas are the most frequent. Students, seniors, and young people should consult their travel agencies because these often have special deals to offer the budget-minded traveler. Ticket prices are usually much higher in the summer as well as at Christmas and over the Easter period.

TAP Air Portugal aircraft on the tarmac at Lisbon Airport

Shuttle service stop, Lisbon Airport

PACKAGE DEALS

SPECIAL INTEREST VACATIONS are just beginning to take off in Portugal. These include stays in manor houses and *pousadas* (see pp378–9), short breaks to Lisbon and Oporto, tennis and golfing vacations in the Algarve, and hiking vacations in the Minho. These, together with package deals including hotel, villa, or apartment accommodations, will often provide inclusive bus service to your destination from the airport. Fly-drive deals are also available, to the Algarve especially, that mean you spend less time at the airport dealing with paperwork. Car rental, when booked as part of a package deal, may be very reasonable. Travel agents sell these vacations, but a list of companies specializing in them on the mainland and the islands is available from **ICEP**, the National Tourist Office.

DOMESTIC FLIGHTS

TAP AND ITS RIVAL, **Portugália**, operate several daily flights between Lisbon and Oporto, and Lisbon and Faro. TAP also flies daily from Lisbon and Oporto to Funchal and from Lisbon to São Miguel, Terceira and Faial in the Azores. It runs daily flights between Funchal and Porto Santo, and between Funchal and Ponta Delgada on São Miguel, and SATA interlinks the Azores (see p447).

(see pp378–9)
(see p447)

DIRECTORY

INTERNATIONAL FLIGHTS

British Airways
US ☎ (800) 247-9297.

TAP Air Portugal
US ☎ (800) 221-7370.

Delta Airlines
US ☎ (800) 241-4141.

Continental Airlines
US ☎ (800) 525-0280.

TWA
US ☎ (800) 892-4141.

CHARTER FLIGHTS

Azores Express
US ☎ (800) 525-0280.

Relvas Tours
US ☎ (800) 359-7358.

PACKAGE TOURS

Portuguese National Tourist Office
590 Fifth Avenue, 4th floor,
New York, NY 10036.
☎ (800) Portugal, (212) 354-4403.

Marketing Ahead
433 Fifth Avenue,
New York, NY 10016.
☎ (800) 223-1356.

DOMESTIC FLIGHTS

Portugália
Lisbon ☎ 21-842 55 61.

SATA
Ponta Delgada ☎ 296-28 22 83.

TAP shuttle bus waiting to leave for central Lisbon

Traveling by Rail

T HE PORTUGUESE STATE RAILROAD, Caminhos de Ferro Portugueses (CP), provides an inexpensive, country-wide network. Quality of service can vary considerably, however, and much modernization to the system is still in the planning stage. The Alfa train between Lisbon and Oporto, via Coimbra, is fast and efficient, but for some other long trips, such as from Lisbon to Évora, it may be quicker and more comfortable to take the bus.

High-speed Alfa train at Santa Apolónia Station in Lisbon

Carved arch over entrance to Lisbon's Rossio station *(see p82)*

ARRIVING BY TRAIN

T HERE ARE TWO main routes into Portugal by train. The first is to travel from Austerlitz station in Paris, changing at Irún on the French-Spanish border, then continuing on to the Portuguese border town of Vilar Formoso in the north. The train splits near Coimbra, heading north for Oporto and south for Lisbon, coming into Santa Apolónia station. The entire journey from London to Lisbon, using the Eurostar to reach Paris, takes 30 hours.

The alternative route is to travel on the overnight train from Madrid, passing through Marvão and Santarém, then on to Lisbon. Travel from Madrid into Lisbon takes 10 hours. This train, called the "hotel-train," has luxurious cars, some of which have showers.

TRAVELING BY TRAIN

M OST AREAS of Portugal are served by rail, although the more remote lines, such as Mirandela to Bragança, have sadly been made obsolete as new roads are built. A bus service covers any gaps in the system, but it is wise to confirm that the service you need actually exists before setting off.

There are several categories of train in Portugal. The most comfortable and quickest is the modern, high-speed Alfa, which travels between Lisbon, Coimbra, and Oporto. The Rápido Inter-Cidades (IC), is only marginally slower, although less luxurious, and connects most important towns and cities. Most smaller towns and villages throughout the country are served by the Regional and the Inter-Regional lines. As you would expect, these local lines are considerably slower than the Rápido and Alfa and the trains are less comfortable, with fewer facilities. However, they stop at a great many more stations.

Logo for Caminhos de Ferro Portugueses

CITY STATIONS

L ISBON HAS FOUR rail terminals. Santa Apolónia station, on Avenida Dom Henrique to the east of the Alfama district, serves the north and all international destinations. A new station, Oriente, close to the Expo site and on the same line as Santa Apolónia, was opened in time for Expo '98. For the south and east (the Algarve and Alentejo) you must cross the Tagus by ferry to catch the train from **Barreiro** station. The ferry departs from the terminal next to Praça do Comércio. West of here is the **Cais do Sodré** station, from where trains leave for Estoril and Cascais. The trip to Cascais takes about 30 minutes.

Rossio station, on Praça dos Restauradores, serves Sintra, about 45 minutes away, and destinations north along the coast as far as Figueira da Foz. However, the Lisbon to Sintra line is not safe at night.

Coimbra has two mainline stations: trains from Lisbon and Oporto stop at **Coimbra B**, a five-minute shuttle ride from the central **Coimbra A**.

Oporto has three mainline stations: trains from the south come into **Campanhã**, to the east of the city, trains from Guimarães, Vila do Conde and Póvoa de Varzim stop in the north of the city at **Trindade**, and trains from Bragança stop at **São Bento** in the center. From here there is a shuttle service to **Campanhã** station.

Exterior of station at Santiago do Cacém with *azulejo* decoration

Time	Destination	Platform	Type of train	Other remarks

Partidas

HORA	DESTINO	LINHA	COMBOIO	OBSERVAÇÕES
13H34	ALVERCA	7	SUBURB	16217 TODAS EST E APEAD
14H00	PORTO CAMP.	1	RAPIDO	123 SERVICO ALFA
14H14	TOMAR	6	REGIONAL	4421
14H34	ALVERCA		SUBURB	16219 SO 3 CARRUAG.FRENT
15H05	PORTO CAMP.		INTERREG	835
15H14	TOMAR		REGIONAL	4423
15H34	ALVERCA		SUBURB	16221 TODAS EST E APEAD
16H00	HENDAYE		INTERNAC	311 SUD EXPRESS
16H03	COVILHA		REGIONAL	4615

INFORMAÇÃO BILHETEIRAS ALFA E IC *** PORTAS 54 E 56

Departures board in Santa Apolónia Station, Lisbon

FARES

FARES WITHIN PORTUGAL are fairly cheap in comparison with other European countries, and there are numerous discounts available. Children under the age of four travel free, and those from four to eleven pay half-fare. There are also discounts for groups, students, and pensioners.

First-class travel on Portugal's trains is 40 percent more expensive than second class, and second-class travel, while fairly basic on some lines, is usually sufficiently comfortable.

Visitors who intend to do much traveling by train might consider buying a tourist ticket *(bilhete turístico)*. This is valid for an unlimited number of trips for 7, 14, or 21 consecutive days and can be used on all the different types of train. Families can save money by using the *cartão de família*, which gives good discounts, but only on trips over 150 km (90 miles). It works as follows: one member of the family pays full fare, other members over 13 years of age pay half the full fare, and those under 13 pay a quarter of the fare. An Interrail pass for young people under 26 gives unlimited travel on all European trains for a month, so will allow travel both to and within Portugal (if it is bought outside the country). The slightly more expensive Interrail 26-plus pass does not allow travel in Spain. For journeys within Portugal only, the Eurodomino pass offers unlimited travel for three, five, or ten days, with a reduced rate for those younger than 26.

PORTUGAL'S PRINCIPAL RAILROAD LINES

Tui
Valença do Minho
Viana do Castelo
BRAGA
Guimarães
Mirandela
Amarante
Vila Real
OPORTO
Pocinho
Peso da Régua
Aveiro
Gouveia
Vilar Formoso
Mangualde
Irún
Guarda
COIMBRA
Covilhã
Figueira da Foz
Pombal
Castelo Branco
Leiria
Tomar
Marvão-Beirã
Caldas da Rainha
Abrantes
Madrid
Santarém
Portalegre
LISBON
Elvas
Badajoz
Cascais
Barreiro
Vendas Novas
Setúbal
Évora
Alcácer do Sal
Beja
Ourique
Silves
Tavira
Portimão
Lagos
Albufeira
FARO
V. R. de Santo António

BUYING TICKETS

TICKETS FOR Alfa and Rápido (IC) trains can usually be booked up to 20 days ahead, although some services only offer 10-day advance bookings, so it is important to check first. Reservations can be made at stations or travel agents. If you want to buy a ticket the day you travel, arrive early as long lines at the ticket office are normal, especially during peak hours and vacation periods. It is important that you buy a ticket before boarding, otherwise you are liable to be fined on the spot by the conductor.

Comboios de amanhã e dias seguintes

Sign at ticket office showing where to buy advance tickets

Só para Comboios de hoje

Sign at ticket office showing where to buy tickets on day of travel

TIMETABLES

MAIN STATIONS in Portugal provide a complete rail timetable, the Guia Horário Oficial. This has details of all routes for IC, Inter-Regional, and Regional trains, and a section in Portuguese only which details the tickets and discounts that are available.

DIRECTORY

TRAIN STATIONS

Coimbra
Coimbra A (239-82 46 32.
Coimbra B (239-82 72 63.

Faro
(289-80 17 26.

Lisbon
Barreiro (21-207 31 18.
Cais do Sodré (21-347 01 81.
Rossio (21-346 50 22.
Santa Apolónia (21-881 62 42.

Oporto
Campanhã (22-536 56 45.
São Bento (22-200 27 22.
Trindade (22-200 52 24.

Driving in Portugal

Automóvel Clube de Portugal logo

PORTUGAL'S ROAD NETWORK includes an expanding highway system, but some older main roads may be in need of repair, while minor roads can be very rough and tortuous. Traffic jams are a problem in and near cities. Never attempt to drive in the rush hour, and watch out for reckless Portuguese drivers. Always carry your passport, license, log book or rental contract, and car insurance. Failure to produce these *documentos* if the police stop you will incur a fine.

A steep road near Gouveia in the Serra da Estrela *(see pp218–9)*

Disembarking at Setúbal after crossing on the car ferry from Tróia

ARRIVING BY CAR

THE QUICKEST ROUTE is to cross the French-Spanish border at Irún and then take the N620 via Valladolid to Vilar Formoso in Portugal. To go to Lisbon or the Algarve, turn off at Burgos, head for Cáceres and then on to Badajoz.

Taking the car ferry to northern Spain from the UK reduces time on the road, but crossings are extremely long: 24 hours to Santander and 35 hours to Bilbao. **Brittany Ferries** travel to Santander leaving from Plymouth (March to November), and from Portsmouth (November to January). **P & O**'s Portsmouth-Bilbao line runs all year round, and all routes operate twice-weekly. There are no ferries traveling to Madeira or the Azores.

Driving time may also be reduced by using the Motorail link from the Gare d'Austerlitz in Paris to Santa Apolónia station in Lisbon, a twice-weekly service. Drivers load their cars one day, travel by passenger train the next, and pick up their cars on the third day.

CAR RENTAL

CAR RENTAL AGENCIES can be found at Lisbon, Faro, and Oporto airports and in main towns, and generally offer very reasonable rates. Local firms usually offer better rates than international ones, but you should check the condition of the car more carefully before you accept it, as well as the insurance coverage. You must have an international license, be over the age of 23, and have had a license for at least one year.

TRAVELING AROUND BY CAR

MAJOR ROADS include EN *(Estrada Nacional)* roads, many of which have been upgraded to IP roads *(Itinerário Principal)* and IC roads *(Itinerário Complementar)*. IP roads are much used by heavy trucks avoiding tolls, and can be slow as a result.

Always fill up with gas in town before setting off, as gas stations can be scarce in remote areas. The best road maps are by Michelin or the Portuguese motoring organization, the ACP *(Automóvel Clube de Portugal)*.

PARKING

FINDING A PARKING space in cities can be difficult. If you do find a spot, leave the car facing the same direction as the traffic on that side of the road. Lisbon and Oporto are building new underground parking lots, while in Coimbra it is best to park on the outskirts and take a bus to the center.

GASOLINE

GAS IS EXPENSIVE and the same price countrywide. Unleaded *(sem chumbo)* is slightly cheaper than 4-star (Super), and diesel is cheaper than both. Some pumps are self-service and color-coded: green for unleaded, blue for leaded, and yellow for diesel.

Traffic lining up for the toll on the Ponte 25 de Abril, Lisbon

RULES OF THE ROAD

TRAFFIC DRIVES on the right hand side, continental rules of the road apply, and the international sign system is used. Unless there are signs to the contrary, traffic from the right has priority at squares, crossroads, and merges. Cars in traffic circles go counterclockwise and have priority over waiting traffic. There is very little advance warning of pedestrian crossings.

Seat belts must be used, and the alcohol limit is 5 ml per liter (.005). Speed limits are 60 kph in towns and 90 kph on other roads (37 mph and 55 mph), and 120 kph (74 mph) on highways. Speeding incurs an on-the-spot fine.

Signs in Lisbon for the coast, south via the Ponte 25 de Abril, and zoo

HIGHWAYS AND TOLLS

PORTUGAL'S EXPANDING highway network *(see map on back endpaper)* links Lisbon with Braga and Guimarães in the north, and Oporto with Amarante. Another section goes all the way from Lisbon to Torres Vedras, and a cross-country stretch runs east to the Spanish border at Elvas. Apart from some sections near Lisbon and Oporto, all

A highway toll – the left lane reserved for users of the Via Verde system

highways have four lanes. Tolls are payable on highways and on Lisbon's bridges, the Ponte 25 de Abril and Ponte Vasco da Gama. Do not use the Via Verde (green lane) at tolls; this is only for the use of drivers who subscribe to an electronic system allowing them to pay automatically.

BREAKDOWN SERVICES

THERE IS a reciprocal breakdown service between **ACP** and other organizations. To qualify, drivers should take out additional coverage with their own organization. Highways have SOS phones, and if you use them, state that you are entitled to ACP. For drivers without coverage, most towns have a garage with a tow truck.

CYCLING

THE SOUTH IS the best area for cycling, but in summer the Alentejo can be too hot. If you plan on doing a lot of cycling, **Instituto Português Cartografia e Cadastro** sells good large-scale maps.

ROAD NUMBERS

Roads in Portugal may have up to three different numbers. Thanks to a building and upgrading program, former EN or *Estrada Nacional* roads can also be IP *(Itinerário Principal)* roads. A road with an E *(Estrada Europeia)* number indicates that it is also a direct international route.

The Bragança-Oporto road is now the IP4, part highway (A4) and part dual carriageway.

IP 4

210

E 82

The road's original **EN number** *(Estrada Nacional)*

The **E82** is an international route, ending in Spain near Valladolid.

DIRECTORY

ARRIVING BY CAR

Brittany Ferries
0990-360 360.

P & O
0990-980 980.

CAR RENTAL

A.A. Castanheira, Lisbon
21-357 00 60.

Avis, Oporto
22-205 59 47.

Budget, Faro
289-81 88 88.

Budget, Lisbon
21-994 24 02.

Eurodollar, Faro
289-81 82 94.

Hertz, Lisbon
21-941 10 60.

Hertz, Oporto
22-205 23 87.

BREAKDOWN SERVICES

ACP South of Pombal
21-356 39 31.

ACP North of Pombal
22-834 00 01.

CYCLING

Instituto Português Cartografia e Cadastro
Rua Artilharia Um 107,
1070 Lisbon.
21-381 96 00.

Euro-Bike Tours
P.O. Box 990, De Kalb
IL 60115.
(800) 321-6060.
FAX (815) 758-8851.

Traveling by Bus

The logo of EVA, one of the country-wide bus companies

S INCE THE PRIVATIZATION of Portugal's bus network, the Rodoviária Nacional (RN), bus companies have multiplied, and some routes are now even operated by foreign companies. Regional operators compete with each other to offer better services to more destinations, and as a result, many bus journeys, such as Lisbon to the Algarve, are quicker and often more comfortable than the equivalent train journeys. Buses also cover the increasing number of defunct sections of railroad, such as Mirandela-Bragança and Beja-Moura.

A Rodonorte bus, which covers the far north of the country

GETTING TO PORTUGAL BY BUS

T RAVELING TO PORTUGAL by bus is cheap but very time-consuming. **Eurolines** runs a weekly summer service from Victoria Coach Station in London to Oporto, avoiding Paris. Passengers change in Valladolid in central Spain, and the journey takes 31 hours in total. The London to Lisbon service, which runs all year, takes even longer. Passengers change in Paris and spend two nights on the bus.

TRAVELING AROUND BY BUS

B US OPERATORS in Portugal include **Renex**, who link Faro, Lisbon, Oporto, and Braga, and **EVA**, which covers the whole country. **Rodoviária Estremadura** connects Lisbon with Estremadura. In Vila Real, **Rodonorte** covers the extreme north, and **Rede Expressos**, based in Oporto, covers the inland areas of Portugal.

There is no central bus station in either Lisbon or Oporto as companies are private and operate separately, but the main bus terminus in Lisbon is on Avenida Casal Ribeiro. In Oporto, the main departure and arrival points are at Rua das Carmelitas and Praça Dona Filipa de Lencastre. Information on routes and prices is available from tourist offices and travel agencies.

BUS TOURS

B US TOURS in and around Lisbon and Oporto are plentiful. **Cityrama** runs sight-seeing tours of Lisbon and its coast, and daytrips to sights such as Batalha, Sintra, and Mafra. It also offers a nighttime tour of the city, taking in the Jerónimos monastery and then dinner with a *fado* show. From Oporto, it runs tours of the Minho and Douro valleys, and a six-day trip to Lisbon. **Gray Line**, part of Cityrama, also offers daytrips running from Lisbon to Évora and Coimbra, a cruise on the Tagus, and a trip lasting three days to the Algarve. Pickup points are at the main hotels or central locations. It is also possible to arrange longer trips to areas of historical or scenic interest.

In the Algarve, there are frequent bus trips to places of interest such as Loulé, Silves and Monchique, the southwest and the Guadiana River, and farther afield to Évora and Lisbon. Tourist offices, hotels, and travel agencies can help with these, and pickup points are the main coastal hotels.

A Cityrama bus on an excursion along the Lisbon coast

Traveling Around the Islands

ON THE ROCKY, MOUNTAINOUS ISLANDS of Madeira and the Azores, the pace of transportation is slow, and some places are accessible only on foot. Driving needs care and patience, and you may find organized trips by bus or taxi are more relaxing and rewarding.

Inter-island aircraft on the runway on Pico

ISLAND HOPPING

TAP FLIES SEVERAL times a day between Funchal and Porto Santo in the Madeira group, and on the Azores, flights are operated by SATA *(see p441)*. Flights to Flores and Corvo are often disrupted by adverse weather conditions, so for extensive island hopping it is a good idea to insure against delays. SATA flights should be confirmed at least 72 hours before takeoff.

Logo of the Azorean airline

The most useful ferry connections are between the five central islands of the Azores, especially the Faial-Pico run.

AROUND MADEIRA

BUSES OPERATE throughout Madeira but cater mainly to islanders' needs. However, companies such as **Intervisa** and **Blandy** organize bus trips around the island. Taxis can be hired by the day or half-day, but car rental offers the most flexibility *(see p444)*. Book well ahead and allow plenty of time for trips: roads are steep, tortuous, and full of potholes. The new road along the south coast is due to be finished by 2000, but many places are still accessible only on foot.

AROUND THE AZORES

CARS CAN BE RENTED on all the Azores except Corvo, from firms such as **Avis**. Charges are high compared to the mainland and the roads are precipitous with hairpin turns, so it may be more restful, at least on the smaller islands, to take a tour by taxi. Many drivers speak English, and they often make memorable companions. Before setting off on a day trip, you should agree on a price, itinerary, and return time. You should also offer to pay for the driver's lunch. Check the weather beforehand: if the mountains and calderas are concealed by clouds, there is no point setting out. Buses are cheap but, as on Madeira, of little use to visitors. Tourist offices can supply information on bus trips by **Agência Açoriana de Viagens** and others, and also on boat trips along the coast. Bicycles can be rented, but the mountainous terrain makes cycling difficult. On the smaller islands you can usually hitch a ride with ease.

The best way to enjoy the Azores is on foot. Taxi drivers are willing to drop visitors off at the start of a route, give them directions and pick them up farther on. Detailed maps of the Azores are difficult to find, so try to get one prior to arrival. Some routes are described in the special guidebooks sold locally.

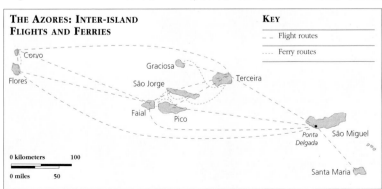

THE AZORES: INTER-ISLAND FLIGHTS AND FERRIES

KEY
— — Flight routes
···· Ferry routes

Corvo · Flores · Graciosa · São Jorge · Terceira · Faial · Pico · Ponta Delgada · São Miguel · Santa Maria

0 kilometers 100
0 miles 50

City Travel

Sign for Metro in Lisbon

MOST CITY CENTERS are small, so walking is the best way to explore them if you have both the time and inclination. Lisbon also offers a full range of transportation options including a Metro and funiculars, while the other cities are well served by buses, trolleybuses, and taxis. Lisbon's Metro is being expanded, due for completion by the year 2001, and its trolleys are slowly being upgraded with futuristic models. Transit of any kind should be avoided during rush hour (8–10am and 5:30–7:30pm).

Lisbon's Elevador da Glória ascending to the Bairro Alto

BUSES

BUSES ARE A PRACTICAL way to travel around and see the main cities, though in Lisbon they are more expensive than the Metro. When boarding the bus, enter at the front door and exit by the central door.

For a single trips you can buy your ticket from the driver, but it is cheaper to buy multiples of 10, or a one- or three-day ticket, or a two-trip ticket for the same price as a single. Tickets must be validated in the machine (*obliterador*) near the driver when you board, or you will be liable to a heavy, on-the-spot fine. Every bus (*autocarro*) displays its destination (*destino*) at the front, and each bus stop (*paragem*) has information about the route that the bus will take.

Orange and white Lisbon bus heading for Praça do Comércio

TROLLEYS AND FUNICULARS

FUN WAYS of exploring Lisbon are by trolley (*eléctrico*), funicular, or elevator (both *elevador*); Oporto has trolleys running down to the river and a route along the waterfront. In Lisbon, **Carris** runs a "hill tour" (*Linha das Colinas*)

by antique trolleycar. Its *Linha do Tejo* tours the sights from Belém to the bullring.

Funiculars go from river level up to the Bairro Alto: the Elevador da Bica starts near Cais do Sodré station; the Elevador da Glória goes from Praça dos Restauradores. The Santa Justa elevator (*see p86*) is also useful, running between the lower Baixa area and the Bairro Alto.

BUS TOURS

IN OPORTO, **Gray Line** runs city tours at least twice a week, and more often in summer. They include a visit to a port lodge with tasting (*see p247*). Tickets are sold at the Gray Line office and at the tourist office in Praça Dom João I, from which the buses depart. Cityrama runs a once-weekly tour of Coimbra. They have no office there, but the tourist office can take bookings and inquiries, and the bus departs from just outside.

LISBON METRO

LISBON'S METRO network is in the process of being extended. By 2001, it should have a total of four lines, giving improved coverage of the city center and suburbs, and in time for the millennium there should be a link to Santa Apolónia station.

Tickets are inexpensive and can be bought at a discount in books of ten, known as a *caderneta*. Tickets should be validated before going through the station barriers using the *obliterador* machine. The Metro operates between 6am and 1am, but rush hours should be avoided, as the Metro can get very crowded with commuters.

One of Lisbon's new set of longer, streamlined trolleys

Antique red trolley operating the Linha do Tejo tour in Lisbon

TICKETS IN LISBON

Buses, trolleys, funiculars, and the elevator all accept the same tickets. Discounted ones can be bought from the Carris kiosks at Praça da Figueira, Santa Justa elevator, or Sete Rios station. Metro tickets bought from machines at stations are cheaper, and multiple ticket purchases offer discounts.

One-day metro ticket

One-day travel ticket

Two-trip ticket

The LISBOA card gives the holder access to 26 of Lisbon's museums and travel on public transit for one, two or three days (see p427).

Lights showing which rate applies

"Taxi for hire" sign

New-style beige city taxi

TAXIS

TAXIS HAVE traditionally been black with a green roof, but these are being phased out in favor of a beige livery. They are relatively cheap and if you share the cost it sometimes works out cheaper than a bus or trolley. You can flag a taxi down in the street or call a firm such as **Autocoope**. The meter is switched off for trips outside the city, so agree on a price first. The cost of the journey is calculated according to the number of kilometers covered, and the starting rate is 250$00. A flat rate of 300$00 is charged for luggage, but only if it is placed in the trunk. Do not pay extra otherwise. Rides between 10pm and 6am and those on Saturdays, Sundays, and public holidays are at a higher rate. The two green lights on the roof indicate which rate is being charged: one light for the cheaper rate and two for the higher one. When the center light is on, the taxi is available.

Details about who to contact in case of a problem is on the rear left window of the cab.

DIRECTORY

BUS AND TROLLEY TOURS

Carris, Lisbon
Rua 1º de Maio 101–3,
2300 Lisbon.
(21-363 20 21.

Coimbra Tourist Office
Largo da Portagem,
3000 Coimbra.
(239-82 38 86.

Gray Line, Oporto
Rua Doutor Albino Montenegro
447, Valbom, 4420 Gondomar.
(21-352 25 94.

RADIO TAXIS

Autocoope (Lisbon)
(21-793 27 56.

Radio Taxis (Oporto)
(22-502 80 61.

LISBON'S METRO SYSTEM

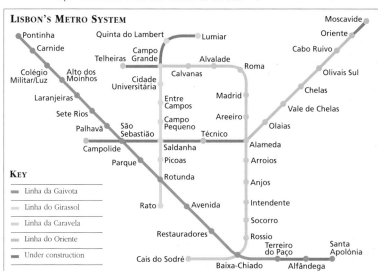

KEY

- Linha da Gaivota
- Linha do Girassol
- Linha da Caravela
- Linha do Oriente
- Under construction

General Index

Acknowledgments

DORLING KINDERSLEY would like to thank the following people whose contributions and assistance have made the preparation of this book possible.

CONSULTANT

MARTIN SYMINGTON was born and brought up in Portugal. A freelance travel writer, he is the author of *New Essential Portugal* (AA), and contributed to *Eyewitness Great Britain* and *Eyewitness Seville and Andalusia*. He writes extensively on Portugal and is a regular contributor to the *Daily Telegraph, Sunday Telegraph*, and other British national newspapers.

CONTRIBUTORS

SUSIE BOULTON studied history of art at Cambridge. She is a freelance travel writer and author of *Eyewitness Venice and the Veneto*.

CHRISTOPHER CATLING is a freelance travel writer and author of *Madeira* (AA) and *Eyewitness Florence & Tuscany*. He also contributed to *Eyewitness Italy* and *Eyewitness Great Britain*.

MARION KAPLAN has written for a wide range of magazines and newspapers. She has lived in Portugal and wrote *The Portuguese* (Viking/Penguin 1992). She also contributed to the *Berlitz Travellers Guide to Portugal*.

SARAH MCALISTER is a freelance editor and writer for *Time Out* guides and has spent much time in Lisbon and the surrounding area.

ALICE PEEBLES is a freelance editor and writer and has worked on several *Eyewitness Travel Guides*.

CAROL RANKIN was born in Portugal. As an art historian, she has lectured extensively on most aspects of Portuguese art and architecture and has acted as consultant for various cultural projects.

JOE STAINES is a freelance writer and co-author of *Exploring Rural Portugal* (Helm).

ROBERT STRAUSS is a travel writer and publisher. He worked for the Luso-British Institute in Oporto and has written several titles for Lonely Planet and Bradt Publications including the Portugal sections for *Western Europe* and *Mediterranean Europe* (Lonely Planet 1993).

NIGEL TISDALL is a freelance journalist who has written many articles on the Azores. He also contributed to *France, Spain*, and *California* in the Eyewitness Travel Guide series.

EDITE VIEIRA has written many books on Portuguese food including *The Taste of Portugal* (Grub Street). She is a member of the Guild of Food Writers and broadcasts regularly for the BBC World Service.

ADDITIONAL CONTRIBUTORS

Dr Giray Ablay, Gerry Stanbury, Paul Sterry, Paul Vernon.

ADDITIONAL ILLUSTRATIONS

Richard Bonson, Chris Forsey, Chris Orr, Mel Pickering, Nicola Rodway.

DESIGN AND EDITORIAL ASSISTANCE

Gillian Allan, Douglas Amrine, Gillian Andrews, Vivien Crump, Joy FitzSimmons, Paul Hines, Felicity Laughton, Helen Markham, Rebecca Mills, Robert Mitchell, Adam Moore, Helena Nogueira, David Noonan, Alice Peebles, Marianne Petrou, Andrew Ribeiro-Hargreave, Alison Stace, Amanda Tomeh, Fiona Wild.

INDEX

Hilary Bird.

ADDITIONAL PHOTOGRAPHY

Steve Gorton/DK Studio, John Heseltine, Dave King, Martin Norris, Roger Phillips, Clive Streeter, Matthew Ward.

PHOTOGRAPHIC AND ARTWORK REFERENCE

Steven Evans, Nigel Tisdall.

SPECIAL ASSISTANCE

Emília Tavares, Arquivo Nacional de Fotografia, Lisboa; Luísa Cardia, Biblioteca Nacional e do Livro, Lisboa; Marina Gonçalves and Aida Pereira, Câmara Municipal de Lisboa; Caminhos de Ferro Portugueses; Carris, Lisboa; Enatur, Lisboa; Karen Ollier-Spry, John E. Fells and Sons Ltd; Maria Fátima Moreira, Fundação Bissaya-Barreto, Coimbra; Maria Helena Soares da Costa, Fundação Calouste Gulbenkian, Lisboa; João Campilho, Fundação da Casa de Bragança, Lisboa; Pilar Serras and José Aragão, ICEP, London; Instituto do Vinho de Porto, Porto; Simoneta Afonso, IPM, Lisboa; Mário Abreu, Dulce Ferraz, IPPAR, Lisboa; Pedro Moura Bessa and Eduardo Corte-Real, Livraria Civilização Editora, Porto; Metropolitano de Lisboa; Raquel Florentino and Cristina Leite, Museu da Cidade, Lisboa; João Castel Branco G. Pereira, Museu Nacional do Azulejo, Lisboa; TURIHAB, Ponte de Lima; Ilídio Barbosa, Universidade de Coimbra, Coimbra; Teresa Chicau at the tourist office in Évora, Conceição Estudante at the tourist office in Funchal and the staff at all the other tourist offices and town halls in Portugal.

PHOTOGRAPHY PERMISSIONS

DORLING KINDERSLEY would like to thank
the following for their assistance and kind
permission to photograph at their establishments:
Instituto Português do Património Arquitectónico
e Arqueológico (IPPAR), Lisboa; Fundação da
Casa de Alorna, Lisboa; Instituto Português dos
Museus (IPM), Lisboa; Museu da Marinha,
Lisboa; Museu do Mar, Cascais; Igreja de Santa
Maria dos Olivais, Tomar and all the other
churches, museums, hotels, restaurants, shops,
galleries and sights too numerous to thank
individually.

PICTURE CREDITS

t = top; tl = top left; tlc = top left center;
tc = top center; tr = top right; cla = center
left above; ca = center above; cra = center right
above; cl = center left; c = center; cr = center
right; clb = center left below; cb = center below;
crb = center right below; bl = bottom left;
b = bottom; bc = bottom center; blc = bottom
left center; brc = bottom right center;
bra = bottom right above; bla = bottom left
above; br = bottom right; d = detail.

The work illustrated on page 120 tl, *Reclining
Figure, 1982*, is reproduced by kind permission
of the Henry Moore Foundation; the work
illustrated on page 121b, *Terreiro do Paço* by
Dirk Stoop, is reproduced by kind permission
of the Museu da Cidade, Lisboa.

The publisher would like to thank the following
individuals, companies and picture libraries for
permission to reproduce their photographs:

MAURÍCIO ABREU: 33t/cr, 145tr, 338bc/br, 358, 360t,
364b/c, 365b, 366ca, 367c, 368tr/ca/cb, 370t,
371t, 399b; AISA: 38tr, 39tc, 39br, 56br, 106b;
PUBLICAÇÕES ALFA: 186b. ALGARVE TOURIST OFFICE:
286tr; ALLSPORT: Mike Powell 57crb; ARQUIVO
NACIONAL DE FOTOGRAFIA-INSTITUTO PORTUGUÊS DE
MUSEUS, Lisboa: Museu Nacional de Arte
Antiga/Pedro Ferreira 98t, 99t; Francisco Matias
49tl; Carlos Monteiro 46cla; Luís Pavão 39tl,
52clb, 53c, 60t, 96bl/br, 97b, 99c; José Pessoa
20bl, 21tr, 45c, 49tr, 50tr, 51t/clb, 96tl/tr, 97t/cr,
98b, 99b; Museu Nacional do Azulejo: *Painel de
azulejos Composição Geométrica*, 1970, Raul
Lino-Fábrica Cerâmica Constância 23tr; Francisco
Matias 22b; José Pessoa 22cra/23cb/bl; Colecções
Arquivo Nacional de Fotografia/San Payo 39tr;
Igreja de São Vicente de Fora/Carlos Monteiro
39bl; Museu Nacional dos Coches/José Pessoa
39bc, 103bl, 144br, 145b; Henrique Ruas 104b;
Museu Nacional de Arqueologia/José Pessoa
40t, 41ca/cb, 105c; Museu Monográfico de
Conímbriga 41tl; Museu de Mértola/Paulo

Cintra 42cl; Igreja Matriz Santiago do
Cacém/José Rubio 43tl; Museu Nacional
Machado de Castro/Carlos Monteiro 44tl; José
Pessoa 45tl; Biblioteca da Ajuda/José Pessoa
44cla; Museu de São Roque/Abreu Nunes
47tl; Museu Grão Vasco/José Pessoa 48bl;
Universidade de Coimbra, Gabinete de
Física/José Pessoa 52tr; Museu de Cerâmica
das Caldas da Rainha/José Pessoa 54 cla;
Museu do Chiado 55tl; Col. Jorge de Brito/José
Pessoa 62/3tc; Col. António Chainho/José
Pessoa 66b; Arnaldo Soares 66tr, 67tl; Museu
Nacional do Teatro/Arnaldo Soares 66cl; Luisa
Oliveira 67tr; Museu de Évora/José Pessoa 303
cra; TONY ARRUZA: 282–3, 38c, 44bl, *Portrait of
Fernando Pessoa* by Almada Negreiros © DACS
1997: 56tr; 57br, 62/3c, 145ca.

JORGE BARROS S.P.A.: 226cr; INSTITUTO DA BIBLIOTECA
NACIONAL DO LIVRO, Lisboa: 37b, 46bca/b, 47crb,
50cb, 51br, 53br, 165bl, 183b; 283 (inset);
GABRIELE BOISELLE: 144bl; BOUTINOT PRINCE WINE
SHIPPERS, Stockport: 228br; THE BRIDGEMAN ART
LIBRARY, with kind permission from Michael Chase:
Landscape near Lagos, Algarve, Portugal by Sir
Cedric Morris (1889–1982), Bonhams, London:
8–9; By permission of THE BRITISH LIBRARY,
London: *João I of Portugal being entertained by
John of Gaunt* (d), from de Wavrin's *Chronicle
d'Angleterre* (Roy 14E IV 244v) 46/7c; © Trustees
of THE BRITISH MUSEUM, London: 43cla, 48br, 54bl.

CÂMARA MUNICIPAL DE LISBOA: 51crb, António Rafael
62cl; CÂMARA MUNICIPAL DE OEIRAS: 52clb; CENTRO
EUROPEU JEAN MONNET: 57tr; CEPHAS: Mick Rock
28crb, 29c; CERAMICARTE: 24bl; COCKBURN SMITHES
& CIA, S.A. (an Allied Domecq Company): 228crb.

D & F WINESHIPPERS, London: 29bc; DIÁRIO DE
NOTÍCIAS: 55cl; MICHAEL DIGGIN: 334t/b, 359t/b,
360b, 361t, 365t, 369t.

EMPICS: Steve Etherington 32c; ESPAÇO TALASSA:
Gerard Soury 368b; ET ARCHIVE: Naval Museum,
Genoa 357b; Wellington Museum 193b; GREG
EVANS INTERNATIONAL: Greg Balfour Evans 287br;
MARY EVANS PICTURE LIBRARY: 51bl, 63tr, 161b,
210b; EXPO '98: 57cra.

FOTOTECA INTERNACIONAL, Lisboa: Luís Elvas 33cl,
44tl/tr/cr; César Soares 27t, 38bl; LUÍZ O
FRANQUINHO/ANTÓNIO DA COSTA: 337bla; FUNDAÇÃO
DA CASA DE BRAGANÇA: 298t/c/b, 299bl; FUNDAÇÃO
CALOUSTE GULBENKIAN: 65t; FUNDAÇÃO DA CASA
DE MATEUS: Nicholas Sapieha 254b; FUNDAÇÃO
RICARDO DO ESPÍRITO SANTO SILVA, MUSEU-ESCOLA
DE ARTES DECORATIVAS PORTUGUESAS 72c.

JORGE GALVÃO: 57clb; GIRAUDON: 48c.

ROBERT HARDING PICTURE LIBRARY: 13b; KIT HOUGHTON: 32b; 145cb.

THE IMAGE BANK: Maurício Abreu 30bl; Moura Machado 19t, 361b, 371b; João Paulo 31cb, 227cl, 363t; IMAGES COLOUR LIBRARY: 226b.

MARION KAPLAN: 144cl, 227t/cr.

LUSA: António Cotrim 67c; André Kosters 93t; Manuel Moura 56bc, 357t; Luís Vasconcelos 92b.

JOSÉ MANUEL: 29br, 63br; ANTÓNIO MARQUES: 296c, 297b; ARXIU MAS: 50tl; METROPOLITANO DE LISBOA, Paulo Sintra: *Four Tiles from Lisbon Underground Station* (Cidade Universitária), Maria Helena Vieira da Silva © ADAGP, Paris and DACS, London 1997, 56tl; JOHN MILLER: 21b; MUSEU CERRALBO, Madrid: 42tl; MUSEU CALOUSTE GULBENKIAN, Lisboa: *Enamelled Silver Gilt Corsage Ornament, René Lalique* © ADAGP, Paris and DACS, London 1997, 116ca; 116t/ca/cb/b, 117t/ca/cb/b, 118c/b/t, 119b/t/c; MUSEU DA CIDADE, Lisboa: António Rafael 62tl/bl/br; 63c/bl; MUSEU DA MARINHA, Lisboa: 38br, 56cl, 108b.

NATIONAL MARITIME MUSEUM, London: 50ca; NATIONALMUSEET, Copenhagen: 48tr; NATURE PHOTOGRAPHERS: Brinsley Burbidge 336br, 337br; Andrew Cleave 336clb/bl, 337bl; Peter Craig-Cooper 329crb; Geoff du Feu 329b; Jean Hall 336bcr; Tony Schilling 336bcl; Paul Sterry 319c, 337bra/blc; NATURPRESS: Juan Hidalgo-Candy Lopesino 32tl, 33br; Jaime Villanueva 24t; NHPA: Michael Leach 369crb; Jean-Louis le Moigne 329cra.

ARCHIVO FOTOGRÁFICO ORONOZ: 38bc, 42/3c, 43b, 46lb, 179br.

Fotografia cedida y autorizada por el PATRIMONIO NACIONAL: 42cb; THE PIERPONT MORGAN LIBRARY/ART RESOURCE, New York: 37t; POPPERFOTO: 55b; POUSADAS DE PORTUGAL: 378t/cla.

QUINTA DO BOMFIM: 29cl, 229t/cla/cra; Cláudio Capone 229bc.

NORMAN RENOUF: 374b, 379b; RCL, PAREDE: Rui Cunha 30t, 31cl, 32tr, 64b, 332–3, 336cra, 337cra, 339tr, 365c, 366t/b, 377; REX FEATURES: Sipa Press, Michel Ginies 57bl; MANUEL RIBEIRO: 22t; RADIO TELEVISÃO PORTUGUESA (RTP): 54t, 55clb, 56cr.

HARRY SMITH HORTICULTURAL PHOTOGRAPHIC COLLECTION: 337cla; SOLAR DO VINHO DO PORTO: 252b; TONY STONE IMAGES: Tony Arruza 30ca; Shaun Egan 286b; Graham Finlayson 41crb; Simeone Huber 284b; John Lawrence 31b; Ulli Seer 317t; 426b; SYMINGTON PORT AND MADEIRA SHIPPERS: 28cla/cra.

NIGEL TISDALL: 339tl , 362, 363b, 364t, 370c/b, 447t; TOPHAM PICTURE SOURCE: 57ca; ARQUIVOS NACIONAIS/TORRE DO TOMBO: 36, 44bla, 267b; TURIHAB: Roger Day 376tl; 376b.

NIK WHEELER: 314; PETER WILSON: 30br, 31tr, 56bl, 93b, 226tl/r/cl; WOODFALL WILD IMAGES: Mike Lane 169b; WORLD PICTURES: 287tc/bl.

Cover: All special photography except THE IMAGE BANK: João Paulo FC cl.

Front Endpaper: All special photography except MAURÍCIO ABREU tl; NIK WHEELER br; PETER WILSON blc.

Phrase Book

In Emergency

Help!	Socorro!	soo-**koh**-roo
Stop!	Páre!	pahr'
Call a doctor!	Chame um médico!	**shahm'** ooñ **meh**-dee-koo
Call an ambulance!	Chame uma ambulância!	**shahm'** oo-muh añ-boo-**lañ**-see-uh
Call the police!	Chame a polícia!	**shahm'** uh poo-**lee**-see-uh
Call the fire department!	Chame os bombeiros!	**shahm'** oosh bom-**bay**-roosh
Where is the nearest telephone?	Há um telefone aqui perto?	ah ooñ te-le-**fon'** uh-**kee** pehr-too
Where is the nearest hospital?	Onde é o hospital mais próximo?	ond' eh oo ohsh-pee-**tahl'** mysh **pro**-see-moo

Communication Essentials

Yes	Sim	seeñ
No	Não	nowñ
Please	Por favor/ Faz favor	poor fuh-**vor** fash fuh-**vor**
Thank you	Obrigado/da	o-bree-**gah**-doo/duh
Excuse me	Desculpe	dish-**koolp'**
Hello	Olá	oh-**lah**
Goodbye	Adeus	a-**deh**-oosh
Good morning	Bom-dia	boñ **dee**-uh
Good afternoon	Boa-tarde	boh-uh **tard'**
Good night	Boa-noite	boh-uh **noyt'**
Yesterday	Ontem	oñ-**tayñ**
Today	Hoje	ohj'
Tomorrow	Amanhã	ah-mañ-**yañ**
Here	Aqui	uh-**kee**
There	Ali	uh-**lee**
What?	O quê?	oo keh
Which?	Qual?	kwahl'
When?	Quando?	**kwañ**-doo
Why?	Porquê?	poor-keh
Where?	Onde?	oñd'

Useful Phrases

How are you?	Como está?	**koh**-moo shtah
Very well, thank you.	Bem, obrigado/da.	bayñ o-bree-**gah**-doo/duh
Pleased to meet you.	Encantado/a.	eñ-kañ-**tah**-doo/duh
See you soon.	Até logo.	uh-**teh** loh-goo
That's fine.	Está bem.	shtah bayñ
Where is/are . . . ?	Onde está/estão . . . ?	oñd' shtah/ shtowñ
How far is it to . . . ?	A que distância fica . . . ?	uh kee dish-**tañ**-see-uh fee-kuh
Which way to . . . ?	Como se vai para . . . ?	**koh**-moo seh vy puh-ruh
Do you speak English?	Fala inglês?	**fah**-luh eeñ-**glehsh**
I don't understand.	Não compreendo.	nowñ kom-pree-**eñ**-doo
Could you speak more slowly please?	Pode falar mais devagar por favor?	pohd' fuh-**lar** mysh d'-va-**gar** poor fuh-**vor**
I'm sorry.	Desculpe.	dish-**koolp'**

Useful Words

big	grande	**grañd'**
small	pequeno	pe-**keh**-noo
hot	quente	**keñt'**
cold	frio	**free**-oo
good	bom	boñ
bad	mau	**mah**-oo
enough	bastante	bash-**tañt'**
well	bem	bayñ
open	aberto	a-**behr**-too
closed	fechado	fe-**shah**-doo
left	esquerda	**shkehr**-duh
right	direita	dee-**ray**-tuh
straight ahead	em frente	ayñ **freñt'**
near	perto	**pehr**-too
far	longe	loñj'
up	suba	**soo**-buh
down	desça	**deh**-shuh
early	cedo	**seh**-doo
late	tarde	tard'
entrance	entrada	eñ-**trah**-duh
exit	saída	sa-**ee**-duh
toilets	casa de banho	**kah**-zuh d' **bañ**-yoo
more	mais	mysh
less	menos	**meh**-noosh

Making a Telephone Call

I'd like to place an international call.	Queria fazer uma chamada internacional.	**kree**-uh fuh-**zehr** oo-muh sha-**mah**-duh in-ter-na-see-oo-**nahl'**
a local call.	uma chamada local.	oo-muh sha-**mah**-duh loo-**kahl'**
Can I leave a message?	Posso deixar uma mensagem?	**poh**-soo day-**shar** oo-muh meñ-**sah**--jayñ

Shopping

How much does this cost?	Quanto custa isto?	**kwañ**-too koosh-tuh **eesh**-too
I would like . . .	Queria . . .	**kree**-uh
I'm just looking.	Estou só a ver obrigado/a.	shtoh soh uh vehr o-bree-**gah**-doo/uh
Do you take credit cards?	Aceita cartões de crédito?	uh-**say**-tuh kar-**toinsh** de **kreh**-dee-too
What time do you open?	A que horas abre?	uh **kee** oh-rash **ah**-bre
What time do you close?	A que horas fecha?	uh **kee** oh-rash **fay**-shuh
This one	Este	ehst'
That one	Esse	ehss'
expensive	caro	**kah**-roo
cheap	barato	buh-**rah**-too
size (clothes/shoes)	número	**noom'**-roo
white	branco	**brañ**-koo
black	preto	**preh**-too
red	roxo	**roh**-shoo
yellow	amarelo	uh-muh-**reh**-loo
green	verde	**vehrd'**
blue	azul	uh-**zool'**

Types of Shop

antique shop	loja de antiguidades	**loh**-juh de añ-tee-gwee-**dahd'sh**
bakery	padaria	**pah**-duh-ree-uh
bank	banco	**bañ**-koo
bookstore	livraria	lee-vruh-**ree**-uh
butcher	talho	**tah**-lyoo
cake shop	pastelaria	pash-te-luh-**ree**-uh
fishmonger	peixaria	pay-shuh-**ree**-uh
hairdresser	cabeleireiro	kab'-lay-**ray**-roo
market	mercado	mehr-**kah**-doo
newsstand	kiosque	kee-**yohsk'**
pharmacy	farmácia	far-**mah**-see-uh
post office	correios	koo-**ray**-oosh
shoe shop	sapataria	suh-puh-tuh-**ree**-uh
supermarket	supermercado	soo-**pehr**-mer-**kah**-doo
tobacconist	tabacaria	tuh-buh-kuh-**ree**-uh
travel agency	agência de viagens	uh-jen-**see**-uh de vee-**ah**-jayñsh

Sightseeing

cathedral	sé	seh
church	igreja	ee-**gray**-juh
garden	jardim	jar-**deeñ**
library	biblioteca	bee-blee-oo-**teh**-kuh
museum	museu	moo-zeh-oo
tourist information office	posto de turismo	posh-**too** d' too-**reesh**-moo
closed for holidays	fechado para férias	fe-**sha**-doo puh-ruh **feh**-ree-ash
bus station	estação de autocarros	shta-**sowñ** d' oh-too-**kah**-roosh
train station	estação de comboios	shta-**sowñ** d' koñ-**boy**-oosh

Staying in a Hotel

Do you have a vacant room?	Tem um quarto livre?	tayñ ooñ **kwar**-too **leevr'**
room with a bath	um quarto com casa de banho	ooñ **kwar**-too koñ **kah**-zuh d' bañ-**yoo**
shower	duche	doosh
single room	quarto individual	**kwar**-too een-dee-vee-doo-**ahl'**
double room	quarto de casal	**kwar**-too d' kuh-**zahl'**
twin room	quarto com duas camas	**kwar**-too koñ doo-ash kah-mash
porter	porteiro	poor-**tay**-roo
key	chave	shahv'
I have a reservation.	Tenho um quarto reservado.	**tayñ**-yoo ooñ **kwar**-too-re-ser-**vah**-doo

EATING OUT

Have you got a table for . . . ?	Tem uma mesa para . . . ?	tayñ oo-muh meh-zuh puh-ruh
I want to reserve a table.	Quero reservar uma mesa.	keh-roo re-zehr-var oo-muh meh-zuh
The bill please.	A conta por favor/ faz favor.	uh kohn-tuh poor fuh-vor/ fash fuh-vor
I am a vegetarian.	Sou vegetariano/a.	Soh ve-je-tuh-ree-ah-noo/uh
Waiter!	Por favor!/ Faz favor!	poor fuh-vor fash fuh-vor
the menu	a lista	uh leesh-tuh
fixed-price menu	a ementa turística	uh ee-mehñ-tuh too-reesh-tee-kuh
wine list	a lista de vinhos	uh leesh-tuh de veeñ-yoosh
glass	um copo	ooñ koh-poo
bottle	uma garrafa	oo-muh guh-rah-fuh
half bottle	meia-garrafa	may-uh guh-rah-fuh
knife	uma faca	oo-muh fah-kuh
fork	um garfo	ooñ gar-foo
spoon	uma colher	oo-muh kool-yair
plate	um prato	ooñ prah-too
napkin	um guardanapo	ooñ goo-ar-duh-nah-poo
breakfast	pequeno-almoço	pe-keh-noo-ahl-moh-soo
lunch	almoço	ahl-moh-soo
dinner	jantar	jan-tar
cover	couvert	koo-vehr
appetizer	entrada	eñ-trah-duh
main course	prato principal	prah-too prin-see-pahl'
dish of the day	prato do dia	prah-too doo dee-uh
set dish	combinado	koñ-bee-nah-doo
half portion	meia-dose	may-uh doh-se
dessert	sobremesa	soh-bre-meh-zuh
rare	mal passado	mahl' puh-sah-doo
medium	médio	meh-dee-oo
well done	bem passado	bayñ puh-sah-doo

MENU DECODER

abacate	uh-buh-kaht'	avocado
açorda	uh-sor-duh	bread-based stew (often seafood)
açúcar	uh-soo-kar	sugar
água mineral	ah-gwuh mee-ne-rahl'	mineral water
(com gás)	koñ gas	sparkling
(sem gás)	sayñ gas	still
alho	ay-oo	garlic
alperce	ahl'-pehrce	apricot
amêijoas	uh-may-joo-ash	clams
ananás	uh-nuh-nahsh	pineapple
arroz	uh-rohsh	rice
assado	uh-sah-doo	baked
atum	uh-tooñ	tuna
aves	ah-vesh	poultry
azeite	uh-zayt'	olive oil
azeitonas	uh-zay-toh-nash	olives
bacalhau	buh-kuh-lyow	dried, salted cod
banana	buh-nah-nuh	banana
batatas	buh-tah-tash	potatoes
batatas fritas	buh-tah-tash free-tash	french fries
batido	buh-tee-doo	milk shake
bica	bee-kuh	espresso
bife	beef	steak
bolacha	boo-lah-shuh	cookie
bolo	boh-loo	cake
borrego	boo-reh-goo	lamb
caça	kah-ssuh	game
café	kuh-feh	coffee
camarões	kuh-muh-roysh	large shrimp
caracóis	kuh-ruh-koysh	snails
caranguejo	kuh-rañ-gay-joo	crab
carne	karn'	meat
cataplana	kuh-tuh-plah-nuh	sealed wok used to steam dishes
cebola	se-boh-luh	onion
cerveja	sehr-vay-juh	beer
chá	shah	tea
cherne	shern'	stone bass
chocolate	shoh-koh-laht'	chocolate
chocos	shoh-koosh	cuttlefish
choriço	shoh-ree-soo	red, spicy sausage
churrasco	shoo-rash-coo	on the spit
cogumelos	koo-goo-meh-loosh	mushrooms
cozido	koo-zee-doo	boiled
enguias	eñ-gee-ash	eels
fiambre	fee-añbr'	ham
fígado	fee-guh-doo	liver
frango	frañ-goo	chicken
frito	free-too	fried
fruta	froo-tuh	fruit

gambas	gañ-bash	shrimp
gelado	je-lah-doo	ice cream
gelo	jeh-loo	ice
goraz	goo-rash	bream
grelhado	grel-yah-doo	grilled
iscas	eesh-kash	marinated liver
lagosta	luh-gohsh-tuh	lobster
laranja	luh-rañ-juh	orange
leite	layt'	milk
limão	lee-mowñ	lemon
limonada	lee-moo-nah-duh	lemonade
linguado	leeñ-gwah-doo	sole
lulas	loo-lash	squid
maçã	muh-sañ	apple
manteiga	mañ-tay-guh	butter
mariscos	muh-reesh-koosh	seafood
meia-de-leite	may-uh-d' layt'	white coffee
ostras	osh-trash	oysters
ovos	oh-voosh	eggs
pão	powñ	bread
pastel	pash-tehl'	cake
pato	pah-too	duck
peixe	paysh'	fish
peixe-espada	paysh'-shpah-duh	scabbard fish
pimenta	pee-mehñ-tuh	pepper
polvo	pohl'-voo	octopus
porco	por-coo	pork
queijo	kay-joo	cheese
sal	sahl'	salt
salada	suh-lah-duh	salad
salsichas	sahl-see-shash	sausages
sandes	sañ-desh	sandwich
santola	sañ-toh-luh	large crab
sopa	soh-puh	soup
sumo	soo-moo	juice
tamboril	tañ-boo-ril'	monkfish
tarte	tart'	pie/cake
tomate	too-maht'	tomato
torrada	too-rah-duh	toast
tosta	tohsh-tuh	toasted sandwich
vinagre	vee-nah-gre	vinegar
vinho branco	veeñ-yoo brañ-koo	white wine
vinho tinto	veeñ-yoo teeñ-too	red wine
vitela	vee-teh-luh	veal

NUMBERS

0	zero	zeh-roo
1	um	ooñ
2	dois	doysh
3	três	tresh
4	quatro	kwa-troo
5	cinco	seeñ-koo
6	seis	saysh
7	sete	set'
8	oito	oy-too
9	nove	nov'
10	dez	desh
11	onze	oñz'
12	doze	doz'
13	treze	trez'
14	catorze	ka-torz'
15	quinze	keeñz'
16	dezasseis	de-zuh-saysh
17	dezassete	de-zuh-set'
18	dezoito	de-zoy-too
19	dezanove	de-zuh-nov'
20	vinte	veent'
21	vinte e um	veen-tee-ooñ
30	trinta	treeñ-tuh
40	quarenta	kwa-reñ-tuh
50	cinquenta	seen-kweñ-tuh
60	sessenta	se-señ-tuh
70	setenta	se-teñ-tuh
80	oitenta	oy-teñ-tuh
90	noventa	noo-veñ-tuh
100	cem	sayñ
101	cento e um	señ-too-ee-ooñ
102	cento e dois	señ-too ee doysh
200	duzentos	doo-zeñ-toosh
300	trezentos	tre-zeñ-toosh
400	quatrocentos	kwa-troo-señ-toosh
500	quinhentos	kee-nyeñ-toosh
700	setecentos	set'-señ-toosh
900	novecentos	nov'-señ-toosh
1,000	mil	meel'

TIME

one minute	um minuto	ooñ mee-noo-too
one hour	uma hora	oo-muh oh-ruh
half an hour	meia-hora	may-uh-oh-ruh
Monday	segunda-feira	se-goon-duh-fay-ruh
Tuesday	terça-feira	ter-suh-fay-ruh
Wednesday	quarta-feira	kwar-ta-fay-ruh
Thursday	quinta-feira	keen-ta-fay-ruh
Friday	sexta-feira	say-shta-fay-ruh
Saturday	sábado	sah-ba-doo
Sunday	domingo	doo-meen-goo

DORLING KINDERSLEY *TRAVEL GUIDES*

TITLES AVAILABLE

THE GUIDES THAT SHOW YOU WHAT OTHERS ONLY TELL YOU

COUNTRY GUIDES

AUSTRALIA • CANADA • FRANCE • GREAT BRITAIN
GREECE: ATHENS & THE MAINLAND • THE GREEK ISLANDS
IRELAND • ITALY • MEXICO • PORTUGAL • SCOTLAND
SOUTH AFRICA • SPAIN • THAILAND

REGIONAL GUIDES

BARCELONA & CATALONIA • CALIFORNIA
FLORENCE & TUSCANY • FLORIDA • HAWAII
JERUSALEM & THE HOLY LAND • LOIRE VALLEY
MILAN & THE LAKES • NAPLES WITH POMPEII & THE
AMALFI COAST • PROVENCE & THE COTE D'AZUR • SARDINIA
SEVILLE & ANDALUSIA • SICILY • VENICE & THE VENETO
GREAT PLACES TO STAY IN EUROPE

CITY GUIDES

AMSTERDAM • BERLIN • BUDAPEST • DUBLIN • ISTANBUL
LISBON • LONDON • MADRID • MOSCOW • NEW YORK
PARIS • PRAGUE • ROME • SAN FRANCISCO
ST PETERSBURG • SYDNEY • VIENNA • WARSAW

TRAVEL PLANNERS

AUSTRALIA • FRANCE • FLORIDA
GREAT BRITAIN & IRELAND • ITALY • SPAIN

DK TRAVEL GUIDES CITY MAPS

LONDON • NEW YORK • PARIS • ROME
SAN FRANCISCO • SYDNEY

DK TRAVEL GUIDES PHRASE BOOKS

CONTINUALLY UPDATED

Road Map of Mainland Portugal

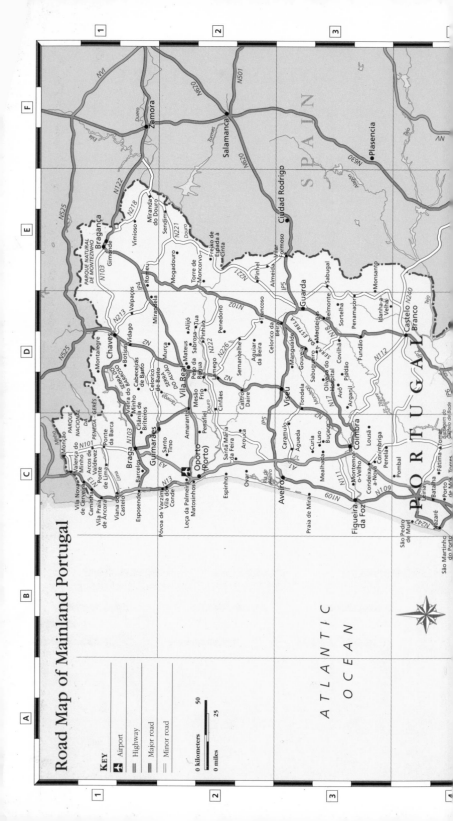

KEY

✈ Airport

━━━ Highway

━━━ Major road

─── Minor road

0 kilometers   50
0 miles   25